A HISTORY OF MOD

Ishita Banerjee-Dube

CAMBRIDGE
UNIVERSITY PRESS

CAMBRIDGE
UNIVERSITY PRESS

Cambridge House, 4381/4 Ansari Road, Daryaganj, Delhi 110002, India

Cambridge University Press is part of the University of Cambridge.

It furthers the University's mission by disseminating knowledge in the pursuit of education, learning and research at the highest international levels of excellence.

www.cambridge.org
Information on this title
For SAARC countries: www.cambridgeindia.org/9781107659728
Others: www.cambridge.org/9781107659728

First published 2015

Printed in India by Shree Maitrey Printech Pvt. Ltd., Noida

A catalogue record for this publication is available from the British Library

Library of Congress Cataloging-in-Publication Data
Banerjee-Dube, Ishita.
A history of modern India / Ishita Banerjee-Dube.
pages cm
Summary: "Takes up the subject of modern India, tracing developments that have occurred from the eighteenth century to independence"– Provided by publisher.
Includes bibliographical references and index.
ISBN 978-1-107-06547-5 (hardback) — ISBN 978-1-107-65972-8 (paperback)
1. India–History–British occupation, 1765-1947. I. Title.
DS463.B24 2014
954.03–dc23
2014010480

ISBN 978-1-107-65972-8 Paperback

For Saurabh

Captain Hodson arresting Bahadur Shah Zafar, 1857; a nineteenth century illustration by G. H. Thompson

Contents

Photographs, Maps, Posters and Figures

Publisher's note: Cambridge University Press would like to thank the following for granting us permission to reproduce photographs: Alamy (for photographs 1–7, 10–11, 14–16), Houghton Library, Harvard University (for photograph 9), Victoria Memorial Hall and Rabindra Bharati Society, Kolkata (for photograph 8), Joseph E. Schwartzberg, Distinguished International Emeritus Professor, University of Minnesota (for photograph 13 from *A Historical Atlas of South Asia*).

Maps

Publisher's note: Cambridge University Press would like to thank Joseph E. Schwartzberg, Distinguished International Emeritus Professor, University of Minnesota, for granting us permission to copy and adapt maps 1–2 and 4–13 from *A Historical Atlas of South Asia* for use in this book. A map depicting the 'Political Events of the Nationalist Period, 1879-1947' from the same atlas is available as an online resource. Map 3 is from *Imperial Gazetteer of India*, 1909. Maps have been made available to us by the Digital South Asia Library, http://dsal.uchicago.edu. We are grateful to them for their support.

Posters

2. Independence is our Birth Right, c. 1940. Chromolithograph printed by Bolton Litho Press Bombay, after a painting by an Indian artist with reference of different photographs.

3. Last Journey of Mahatma Gandhi (1869–1948). Chromolithograph halftone printed at Brij Basi Press, Mathura, after a painting by Narottam Narayan Sharma, Nathdwara.

Publisher's note: Cambridge University Press is extremely grateful to Anil Relia, Manan Relia and the Archer Art Gallery, for granting us permission to reproduce images from *The Indian Portrait III: A Historical Journey of Graphic Prints up to Independence* in this book. Anil Relia is one of India's most prominent art collectors, with a rare and valuable collection. Under his able guidance the Archer Art Gallery has published limited edition serigraphs of renowned artists like M. F. Husain, S. H. Raza, K. G. Subramanyan, Manjit Bawa, Jogen Chowdhury and many more.

Figures

Publisher's note: Cambridge University Press would like to thank Joseph E. Schwartzberg, Distinguished International Emeritus Professor, University of Minnesota, for granting us permission to copy and adapt all figures from *A Historical Atlas of South Asia* for use in this book.

About the Author

Ishita Banerjee-Dube is Professor of History at the Centre for Asian and African Studies, El Colegio de México, Mexico City, and a member of the National System of Researchers (SNI), Mexico, where she holds the highest rank. Her authored books include *Divine Affairs* (2001); *Religion, Law, and Power* (2007); and *Fronteras del Hinduismo* in Spanish (2007). Among her eight edited volumes are *Unbecoming Modern* (2005); *Caste in History* (2008); and *Ancient to Modern* (2009).

Acknowledgements

In the five years over which this book gestated, developed, and culminated, I have received support and solidarity from many, many people. It is impossible to thank them individually. My apologies, but I presume they know who they are.

At the same time, I would like to begin by thanking Debjani Mazumder, the person who conceptualized the project, invited me to write the book, and has sustained it since with care, enthusiasm, and professional skill. My editors Doel Bose and Qudsiya Ahmed at Cambridge University Press have kept me company through the long process, shared in and added to my excitement and passion. Their editorial expertise and research on photos, maps and other pedagogical elements for the book have enriched and improved the manuscript in significant ways. I wish to thank the several anonymous readers—of the book proposal, the initial chapters, and the final manuscript—for their incisive comments and constructive suggestions. My friend and fellow historian Shashank Sinha extended support and advice, while Shinjini Chatterjee, my cousin and a talented editor, went out of her way to offer critical advice at different stages.

Ajay Skaria's arrant enthusiasm and critical insights have enhanced the project in countless ways, and the advice of my teachers Sekhar Bandyopadhyay and Gautam Bhadra has steered me through the arduous process of writing and revision. I am grateful to Tanika and Sumit Sarkar, David Arnold, Mrinalini Sinha, Ajay Skaria, and Anshu Malhotra who have offered valuable encouragement by writing endorsements. Charu Gupta's practical help and Anupama Rao's infectious excitement concerning the book have bolstered my fledgling efforts at several moments.

Edgar Pacheco, Eduardo Acosta, and Luis Quiñones—at once students, research assistants and younger friends—have made this work possible through their zeal in digging up sources and materials as well as their meticulous care in checking references. Discussions with different cohorts of students at the Centre for Asian and African Studies, the Centre for International Relations, and the Centre for Historical Studies of El Colegio de México have stimulated me in distinct ways, as have the interest expressed by colleagues at the institution. Neha Chatterjee, Atig Ghosh, and Bodhisattva Kar have induced me to think and reflect more with their ideas and criticism. Rajat Sur has lent a hand by checking references at the National Library; Nivedita Mohanty has answered queries and provided references on Odisha at short notice; Amit Sanyal has helped to tie up loose ends on several occasions; and Sharmita Ray has searched for and supplied interesting pedagogical elements. My thanks go out to all of them.

My sister and nieces, extended family of cousins, aunts, and uncles, and my friends Sarvani

Gooptu, Gina Mathai, Sushweta Ghosh, Rupa Dutta, Susmita Mukherjee, Moushumi Mukherjee, Sayanti Mukherji, Kakoli Bandyopadhyay, and Anuradha Gupta have made the going easy by being there. Sarvani Gooptu, in particular, has answered numerous calls for help and shared her own insights on the history of modern India.

My historian mother, Gitasree Bandopadhyay, has searched for references and engaged me in discussions on meanings and understandings of India's pasts. To her, I owe my first lessons in history. The thought that my philosopher father—Sankari Prosad Banerjee—gone for over a decade now, would have been irrepressibly happy and proud, has kept me going through this long and intense process.

Saurabh Dube—fellow academic and life partner—has endured, with fortitude, especially in the midst of immense personal loss, the times and travails of a book that entirely consumed me. My sternest critic and staunchest ally, Saurabh has prodded me to read and reflect by setting an example—of immersion in thought and ideas, while inhabiting at once intellectual arenas and social worlds. This book is dedicated to him.

Prologue

The photograph that serves as the cover to this book depicts Gandhi as walking towards a distant horizon, leaning on the shoulders of a young man and a young woman. Under an overcast sky, does Gandhi appear tired? Or, is there determination in his posture and gait? Is Gandhi exhausted on account of shouldering the burden of freedom, worn down by the enormous cost of Indian independence? Or, is he confidently walking towards a new beginning, the birth of an independent nation?

There is purpose in beginning *A History of Modern India* with the uncertainty that marks the photo on the cover of the work. For, this book is aimed as an open-ended account that both unravels the making of modern India yet questions the intimate linkages between the writing of history and the narration of the nation. Here, I wish to engage students and scholars of history (as well as general readers) in a dialogue and debate concerning the nature of pasts and formations of the present. This is to say that, instead of a singular, seamless story, the chapters ahead offer a tapestry of diverse pasts and different perceptions that shaped modern India.

The open-ended account in itself has a past, formed and transformed over the last five years over which the book has taken shape. On the one hand, there is much owed here to hermeneutic traditions of history writing that emphasize interpretative understandings of the past and the present. On the other hand, it is equally the case that as I wound my way through numerous imaginative writings and immense historical materials, which of course provoked further reading and reflection, the chapters acquired lives of their own. Indeed, the writing of the book has been an enormous learning process, changing my understandings of Indian history and its formidable heterogeneity. The book seeks to convey a sense of such plurality of pasts. Here, coherence and sequence help in the telling of various tales—rather than just one story—that best portray the making of modern India; and tales told from distinct viewpoints offer divergent perspectives on the same processes and personalities.

The book reflects particular inclinations towards socio-cultural history, including the perspective of gender as crucial to understanding the past and the present. Thus, the text features the clash of sensibilities between distinct Indian aristocracies and European trading companies; the debates over ideology in the framing of land revenue (and governance) policies by the East India Company; the creation of the colonial archive and its implications for Indian society; formulations of Indian 'tradition' that draw upon orientalist scholarship; insights offered by the work of the Subaltern Studies collective; feminist readings of nationalist discourses; and key implications of environmental histories. Economy, politics and political-economy find due respect with detailed discussions of, for example, revenue settlements, famines, and the contentious debate on 'de-industrialization'. At the same time, the central focus is on the exploration and interpretation of social and cultural processes, which have often not found adequate reflection in histories of modern India.

The chronology of modern India offered in this book runs from the eighteenth to the twentieth centuries, a time when India is said to have become a modern nation. At the very outset, however, the work discusses the concept of the 'early modern' in order to raise questions about when and how the modern begins and what it stands for. The different connotations and implications of the notion of the 'modern' that run through the subsequent chapters consider processes set in motion by Britain's self-conscious projection of itself as a modern state that was superior to 'traditional' Indian society, which came to be widely diffused and reinterpreted on the subcontinent. In Britain as well as India, projections of the modern were now premised upon a rupture with the past and innately associated with Western science, reason and progress, carrying profound implications that continue into the present.

Indeed, in the work, chronological sequence is interwoven with thematic threads running through the chapters, which makes for interpretive overlaps and conceptual continuities. The first chapter presents invigorating worlds of the eighteenth century on the subcontinent. Here were to be found port cities on the Indian Ocean with thriving trade and cosmopolitan cultures; and provincial capitals where nawabs and European adventurers vied with each other as collectors of arts and antiquities. In these eighteenth-century worlds, the lines between politics, art and consumption were blurred; conscious national identities (of Europeans and Indians) were conspicuous by their absence; and the gradual dismantling of an immense central administration, that of the Mughal state, was accompanied by the rise of several smaller states, their dynamic economies and vibrant energies.

Chapters 2 through to 4 track the events and processes as well as the ideas and ideologies that shaped East India Company's forms of rule alongside the making of Indian society from, roughly, 1757 to 1900. The making of colonial cultures, their intersections with Indian ideas and practices, and, finally, Indian endeavours and responses find a place here. All of these together resulted in the changeover from Company to Crown Rule in 1858. The discussion begins with the distinct styles of governance across the second half of the eighteenth century of the first four important British governors: the dual government of Robert Clive; the Orientalist-cosmopolitanism of Warren Hastings; the Whig inheritance of Cornwallis; and, finally, the open imperialism of Wellesley that brought large parts of India under Company rule. The account analyses, for instance, the impact of Hastings' search for and codification of 'Gentoo laws'; Cornwallis' attempts to make the administration more British, while permanently settling the land revenues of the vast province of Bengal; and Wellesley's drive to train the Company's servants toward improved rule through better knowledge of Indian customs, measures reflected in the establishment of the Fort William College in Calcutta.

This sets the stage for exploring the intimate intersections between the colonial 'civilizing mission' *and* the educated Indians' enthusiasm for Western learning, science and reason. Such linkages generated ardent debates over social reform and the condition of women, resulting in diverse apprehensions and articulations of Indian 'tradition'. At the same time, at work during this period was the unequal impact of colonial cultures and British policies on distinct groups and different regions, including the cartographic demarcation of spaces and peoples into plains and hills and forests (as well as the spread of railway networks), on the subcontinent. All of this underlay the Revolt of 1857, and the book discusses the period, critically and extensively. The account then considers the divergent processes set in motion by the direct takeover of India by the British crown. These include the British policies of classifying, mapping and enumerating Indian society by means of census and other surveys; imperial institutional reforms designed to prepare Indians for eventual self-rule; and the contending consequences of these policies and reforms, especially claims toward greater political representation by different groups of Indians, including the assertions of lower-castes in these terrains.

Chapters 5 to 10 follow the fortunes of Indian nationalism, especially examining its contradictions and contestations. Highlighting a gendered analysis of the cultural discourse of Indian nationalism, these chapters point to the complex interplay between imperial initiatives and Indian endeavours. This dynamic underlay processes of insurgency and accommodation, resistance and resignation, collaboration and conflict, and (eventually) freedom and Partition. The narrative undertakes different tasks. It traces the discrete paths of nationalism, including engagements at once with colonial politics and subaltern peoples. It tracks the efforts to ground the sentiments of nationalism in an economic collective that was being 'drained' by colonial exploitation. It reflects on the cultural exuberance produced by the nationalist endeavours, inspired by the first partition of Bengal and the resultant Swadeshi movement alongside their contradictory economic and social impact. It brings into relief the material grounding of the discursive space of the nation in Gandhi's active enterprise of promoting *khadi*.

Exploring the many worlds of business, labour, peasants and groups that participated only tangentially in nationalist initiatives, these chapters attend also to the articulations of politics, high and popular, of leaders such as Gandhi, Ambedkar, Jinnah and Nehru. Taken together, the aim is to probe the different ways in which a nation is imagined and brought into being, asking also whether nation and nationalism mean the same thing to all people. The discussion also includes those groups and communities who could not relate to the notion of the nation. Unsurprisingly, along these tracks, the account does not project the Partition as inevitable, unravelling it instead as the result of contending agendas of peoples, those included within and excluded from the nation.

Beginning with the pain and suffering that accompanied independence and Partition, the final chapter explores the distinct visions and conflicting ideologies that shaped the Indian Constitution, a landmark document that simultaneously signalled a break with the colonial past and retained some of its important emphases. It focuses on the manifold ideals of justice and equality, development and modernity that went into the drafting and implementation of the constitution, and reflects on the experiments with positive discrimination and legal pluralism in India, which in turn have produced furious debates on the nature of secularism on the subcontinent. India today forms an instructive example of the problems and possibilities that underlie the working out of democratic ideals.

At the end, it bears mention that historical maps, old photographs, imaginative time-lines, and intimations of cutting-edge research complement the narratives at the core of *A History of Modern India*. These visual and textual aids and devices not only add to the textures of writing but they facilitate further understanding. In tune with the times it discusses, the book uses Calcutta, Bombay and Madras and not Kolkata, Mumbai and Chennai, and Simla and Orissa in place of Shimla and Odisha. If the book encourages its readers—scholars and students—to pose new questions about the past and the present, it would have served its purpose.

EXTENT OF THE MUGHAL EMPIRE, 1504–1556

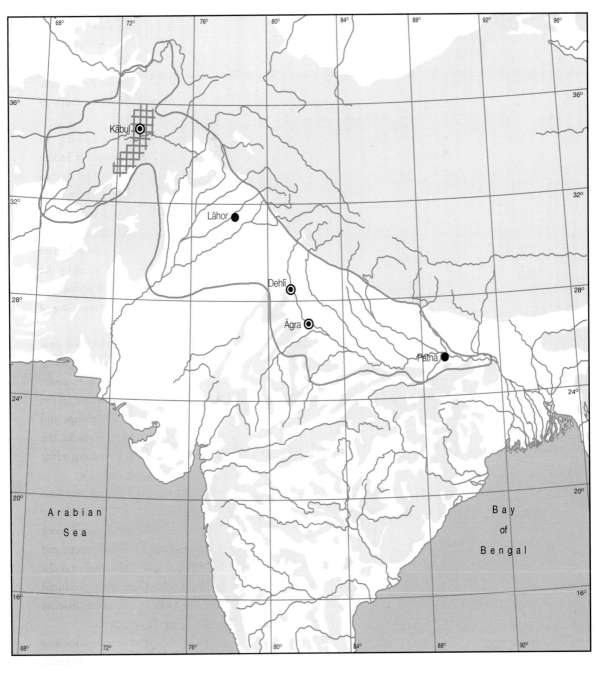

Maximum extent of area at some time controlled by Mughals

Note: Map not to scale

Core areas   ◉ Capitals   ● Other places of importance

Extent of the Mughal Empire, 1556–1857

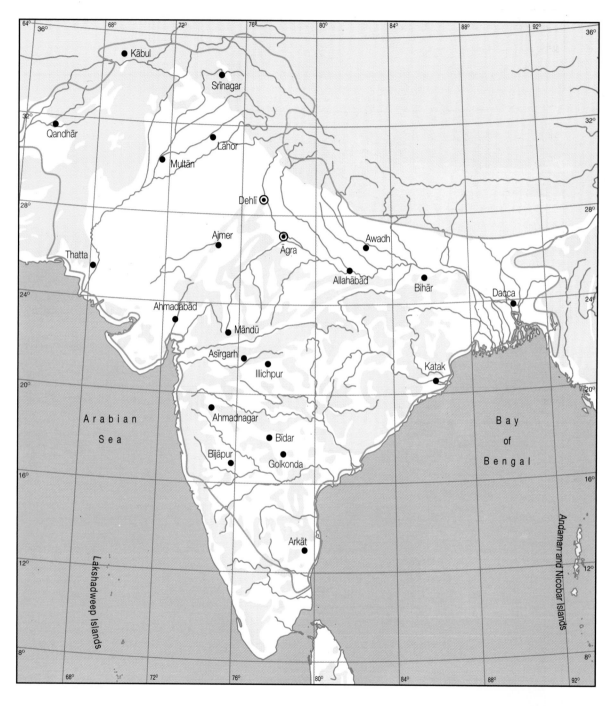

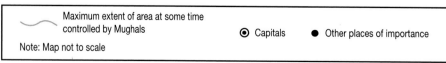

Maximum extent of area at some time controlled by Mughals

⊙ Capitals   ● Other places of importance

Note: Map not to scale

INDIA, 1765

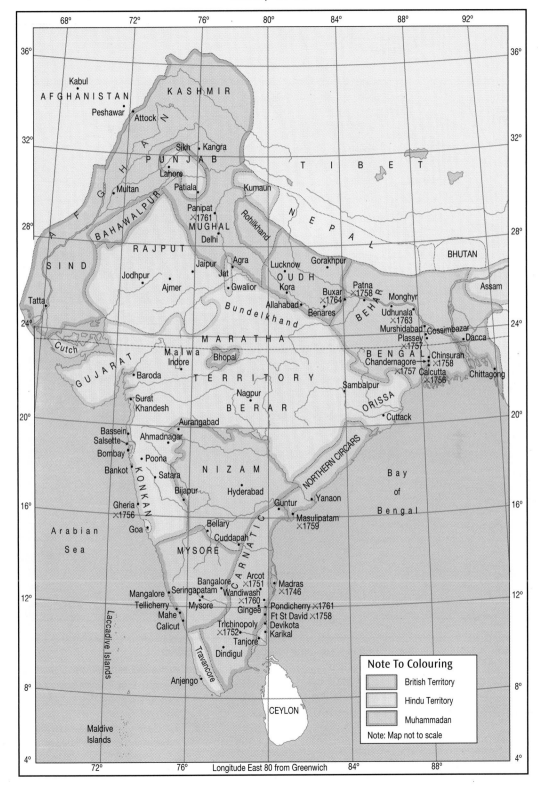

STAGES IN THE EXPANSION OF BRITISH POWER, 1819

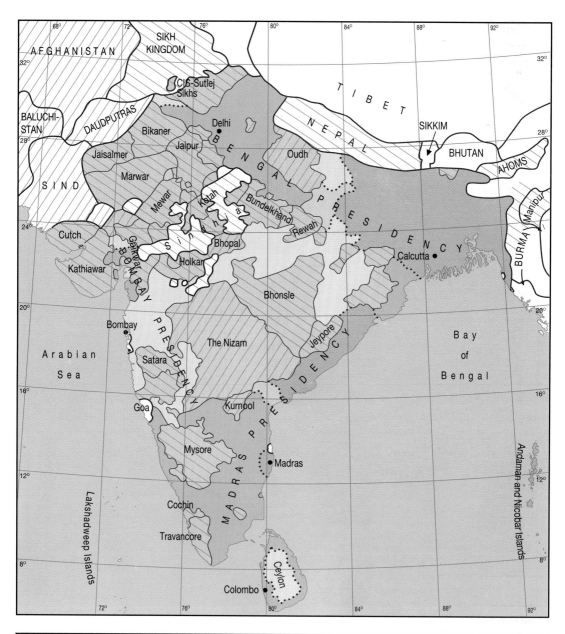

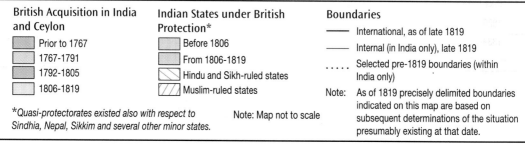

British Acquisition in India and Ceylon	Indian States under British Protection*	Boundaries
Prior to 1767	Before 1806	—— International, as of late 1819
1767-1791	From 1806-1819	——— Internal (in India only), late 1819
1792-1805	Hindu and Sikh-ruled states	····· Selected pre-1819 boundaries (within India only)
1806-1819	Muslim-ruled states	

*Quasi-protectorates existed also with respect to Sindhia, Nepal, Sikkim and several other minor states.

Note: Map not to scale

Note: As of 1819 precisely delimited boundaries indicated on this map are based on subsequent determinations of the situation presumably existing at that date.

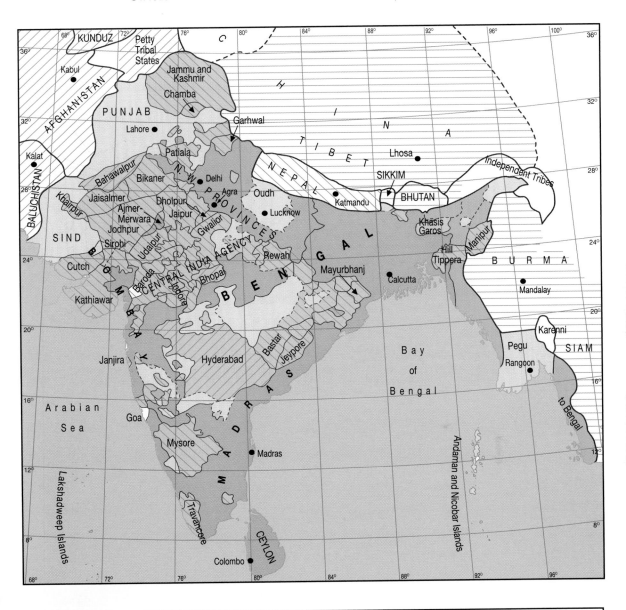

Stages in the Expansion of British Power, 1819–1857

British Acquisition in India and Ceylon
- Prior to 1820
- 1820-1838
- 1839-1857

Note: Map not to scale

Indian States under British Protection
- Before 1820
- 1820-1838

- Hindu and Sikh-ruled states
- Muslim-ruled states
- Buddhist-ruled states

THE INDIAN SUBCONTINENT, 1857

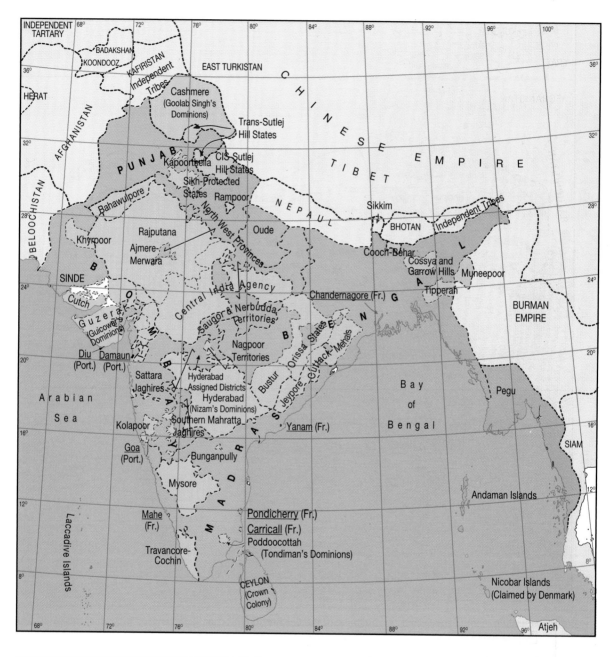

INDEPENDENT TARTARY
BADAKSHAN
KOONDOOZ
KAFIRISTAN
Independent Tribes
EAST TURKISTAN
HERAT
AFGHANISTAN
CHINESE EMPIRE
Cashmere (Goolab Singh's Dominions)
Trans-Sutlej Hill States
PUNJAB
Kapoorthella
CIS-Sutlej Hill States
Sikh-Protected States
Rampoor
TIBET
BELOOCHISTAN
Bahawulpore
North West Provinces
NEPAUL
Sikkim
BHOTAN
Independent Tribes
Khyrpoor
Rajputana
Ajmere-Merwara
Oude
Cooch-Behar
Cossya and Garrow Hills
Muneepoor
SINDE
Cutch
Guzerat (Guicowar's Dominions)
Central India Agency
Chandernagore (Fr.)
Tipperah
BURMAN EMPIRE
Diu (Port.)
Damaun (Port.)
Saugor & Nerbudda Territories
Nagpoor Territories
Bustur
Orissa States
Cuttack-Mehals
BENGAL
Arabian Sea
Sattara Jaghires
Hyderabad Assigned Districts
Hyderabad (Nizam's Dominions)
Jeypore
Yanam (Fr.)
Bay of Bengal
Pegu
Kolapoor
Southern Mahratta Jaghires
BOMBAY
Goa (Port.)
Bunganpully
SIAM
Mysore
MADRAS
Andaman Islands
Mahe (Fr.)
Pondicherry (Fr.)
Carricall (Fr.)
Poddoocottah (Tondiman's Dominions)
Travancore-Cochin
Laccadive Islands
CEYLON (Crown Colony)
Nicobar Islands (Claimed by Denmark)
Atjeh

British India and Ceylon   Native States   Non-British Colonial Possessions

- - - - - Presidencies and Provinces   - - - - - - States within State Agencies   Note: Map not to scale

THE REVOLT OF 1857–1859

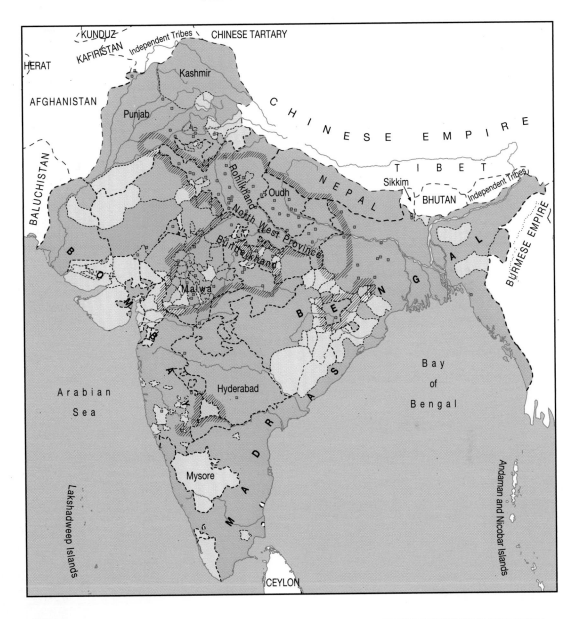

Territorial and Administrative Changes, 1857–1904

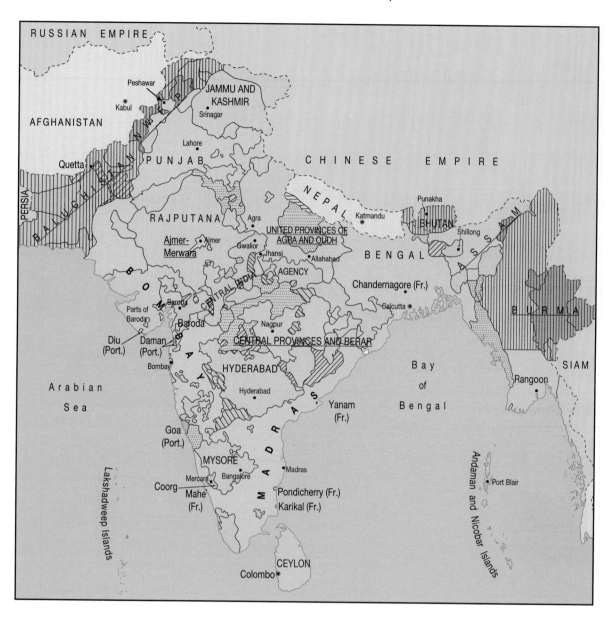

RUSSIAN EMPIRE

Peshawar
Kabul
JAMMU AND KASHMIR
Srinagar
AFGHANISTAN
Lahore
Quetta
PUNJAB
CHINESE EMPIRE
PERSIA
BALUCHISTAN
N.W.F.P.
NEPAL
Punakha
BHUTAN
Katmandu
Shillong
RAJPUTANA
Agra
UNITED PROVINCES OF AGRA AND OUDH
Ajmer-Merwara
Ajmer
Gwalior
Jhansi
Allahabad
BENGAL
ASSAM
BOMBAY
CENTRAL INDIA AGENCY
Baroda
Chandernagore (Fr.)
Calcutta
BURMA
Parts of Baroda
Baroda
Nagpur
CENTRAL PROVINCES AND BERAR
Diu (Port.)
Daman (Port.)
Bombay
HYDERABAD
SIAM
Arabian Sea
Hyderabad
Yanam (Fr.)
Rangoon
Bay of Bengal
Goa (Port.)
MADRAS
MYSORE
Mercara
Bangalore
Madras
Andaman and Nicobar Islands
Coorg
Mahe (Fr.)
Pondicherry (Fr.)
Karikal (Fr.)
Port Blair
Lakshadweep Islands
CEYLON
Colombo

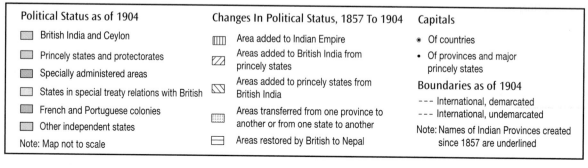

Political Status as of 1904
- British India and Ceylon
- Princely states and protectorates
- Specially administered areas
- States in special treaty relations with British
- French and Portuguese colonies
- Other independent states

Note: Map not to scale

Changes In Political Status, 1857 To 1904
- Area added to Indian Empire
- Areas added to British India from princely states
- Areas added to princely states from British India
- Areas transferred from one province to another or from one state to another
- Areas restored by British to Nepal

Capitals
- Of countries
- Of provinces and major princely states

Boundaries as of 1904
- --- International, demarcated
- --- International, undemarcated

Note: Names of Indian Provinces created since 1857 are underlined

The Bengal Partition and Related Territorial and Administrative Changes, 1905

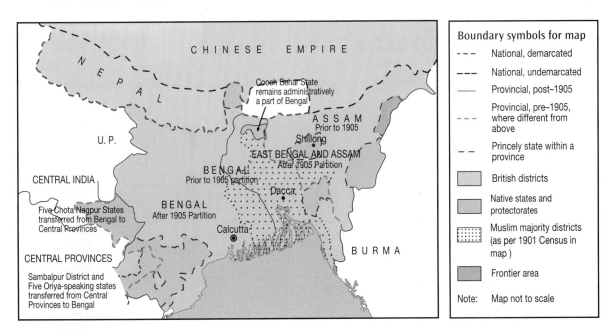

The Reunification of Bengal and Related Territorial and Administrative Changes, 1912

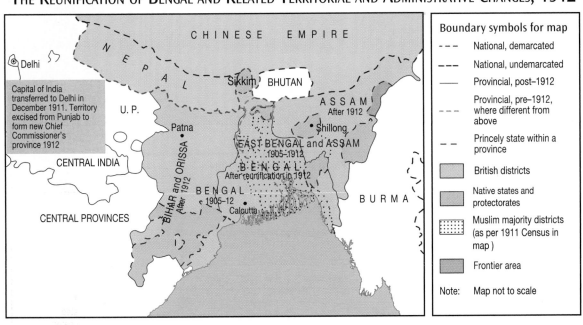

TERRITORIAL AND ADMINISTRATIVE CHANGES, 1913–1947

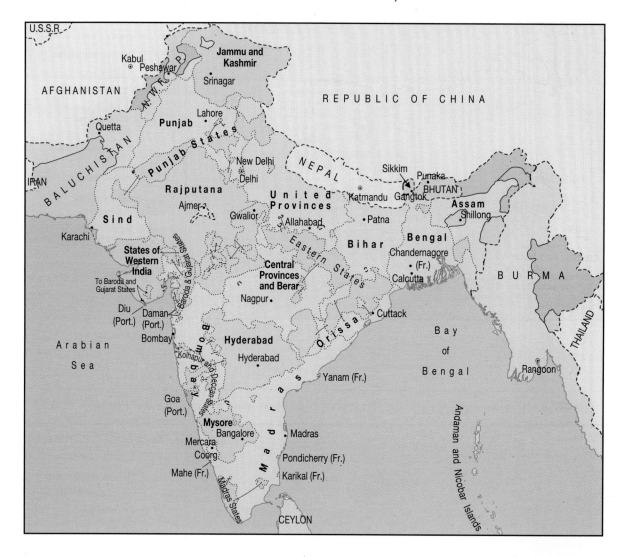

U.S.S.R.

Kabul
Peshawar
N.W.F.P.
Jammu and Kashmir
Srinagar

AFGHANISTAN

REPUBLIC OF CHINA

Quetta

Lahore

Punjab

Punjab States

IRAN

BALUCHISTAN

New Delhi
Delhi

N E P A L

Sikkim
Punaka
BHUTAN
Katmandu Gangtok

Rajputana

Ajmer

U n i t e d
P r o v i n c e s

Assam
Shillong

Sind

Gwalior
Allahabad
Patna

Bihar

Karachi

Eastern States

Bengal
Chandernagore
(Fr.)
Calcutta

States of Western India
To Baroda and Gujarat States

Baroda & Gujarat States

Central Provinces and Berar
Nagpur

B U R M A

THAILAND

Diu
(Port.)
Daman
(Port.)
Bombay

Bombay

Kolhapur and Deccan States

Hyderabad
Hyderabad

Orissa

Cuttack

B a y
of
B e n g a l

Rangoon

A r a b i a n
S e a

Yanam (Fr.)

Goa
(Port.)

M a d r a s

Mysore
Bangalore
Mercara
Coorg
Mahe (Fr.)

Madras
Pondicherry (Fr.)
Karikal (Fr.)

Madras States

Andaman and Nicobar Islands

CEYLON

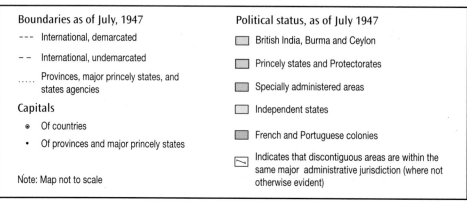

Boundaries as of July, 1947

\- - - International, demarcated

\- - International, undemarcated

..... Provinces, major princely states, and states agencies

Capitals

⊚ Of countries

• Of provinces and major princely states

Note: Map not to scale

Political status, as of July 1947

British India, Burma and Ceylon

Princely states and Protectorates

Specially administered areas

Independent states

French and Portuguese colonies

Indicates that discontiguous areas are within the same major administrative jurisdiction (where not otherwise evident)

The French in the Indian Subcontinent

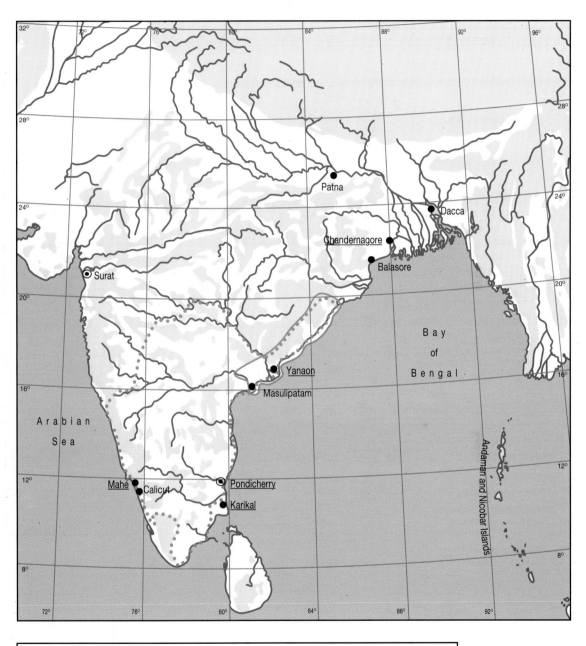

Legend:

- ····· Limit of states in which French at some time exercised a dominant political influence
- ⊙ Capitals
- Note: Places underlined remained under French control from 1816 to 1950-54
- ——— Lands assigned by the Nizam to the personal government of Charles Bussy
- ● Other places of importance
- Note: Map not to scale

Map labels: Patna, Dacca, Chandernagore, Balasore, Surat, Bay of Bengal, Yanaon, Masulipatam, Arabian Sea, Andaman and Nicobar Islands, Mahé, Calicut, Pondicherry, Karikal

MAJOR ADMINISTRATIVE DIVISIONS, 1947

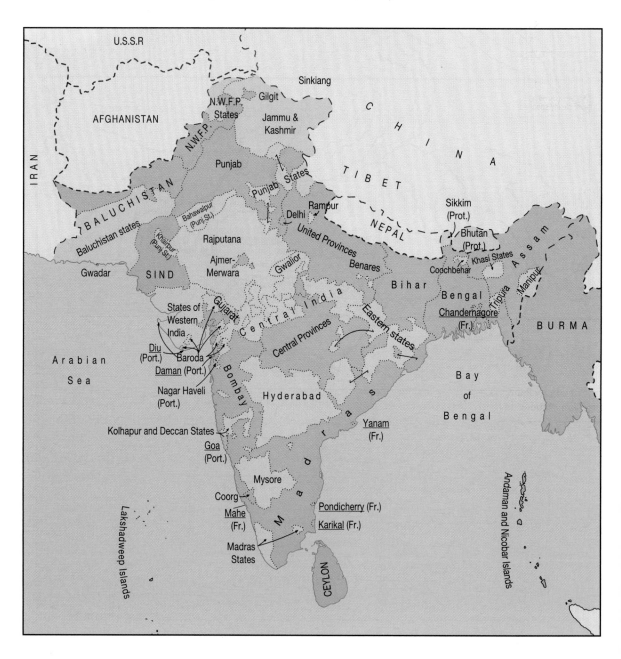

U.S.S.R

Sinkiang

AFGHANISTAN

N.W.F.P.
States

Gilgit

Jammu &
Kashmir

C
H
I
N
A

N.W.F.P.

Punjab

T I B E T

IRAN

B A L U C H I S T A N

Punjab States

Baluchistan states

Bahawalpur
(Punj. St.)

Khairpur
(Punj. St.)

Rampur

Delhi

Sikkim
(Prot.)

NEPAL

United Provinces

Bhutan
(Prot.)

Rajputana

Gwalior

Benares

Khasi States

A
s
s
a
m

Gwadar

SIND

Ajmer-
Merwara

Central India

Coochbehar

Bihar

B e n g a l

Tripura

Manipur

Arabian
Sea

States of
Western
India

Gujarat

Eastern states

Chandernagore
(Fr.)

BURMA

Diu
(Port.)

Baroda

Daman (Port.)

Central Provinces

Bombay

Hyderabad

B a y
of

B e n g a l

Nagar Haveli
(Port.)

Kolhapur and Deccan States

Goa
(Port.)

Yanam
(Fr.)

Mysore

M
a
d
r
a
s

Andaman and Nicobar Islands

Coorg

Mahe
(Fr.)

Pondicherry (Fr.)

Karikal (Fr.)

Lakshadweep Islands

Madras
States

CEYLON

British India, Burma and Ceylon

Indian States Agencies and Protectorates

Non-British Colonial Possessions
(Names are underlined in black)

Note: Map not to scale

Proposals for the Partition of India, 1930–1946

Sir Muhammad Iqbal's suggestion for a 'Northwest Indian Muslim State', 1930

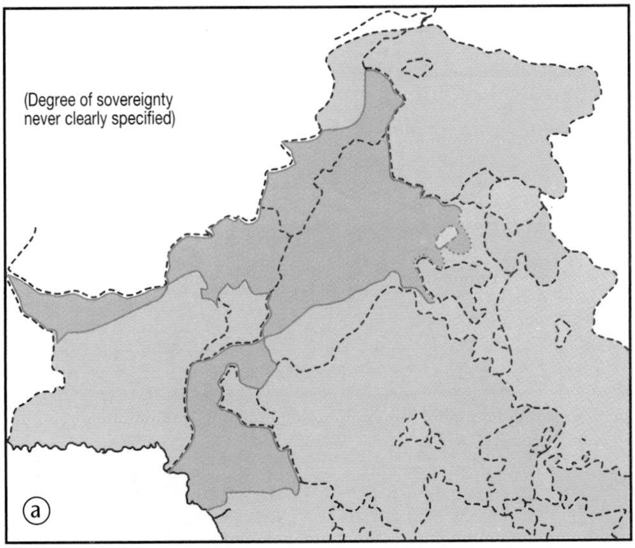

(Degree of sovereignty never clearly specified)
a

Legends for maps (a) (b) and (c)

- Internal boundaries as of date of proposal
- Proposed boundaries of new sovereign states
- Proposed internal territorial boundaries
- Conjectural boundaries of above two types

Names of proposed sovereign states are in red
Names of proposed internal territorial units are in black

- Princely states not specifically provided for in proposal
- Muslim majority areas as of 1941
- Hindu majority areas as of 1941
- As above with proposed Muslim control
- Foreign enclaves

Note: Map not to scale

Choudhary Rahmat Ali's scheme for three independent Muslim 'Nations' to be formed into a 'Triple Alliance', 1940

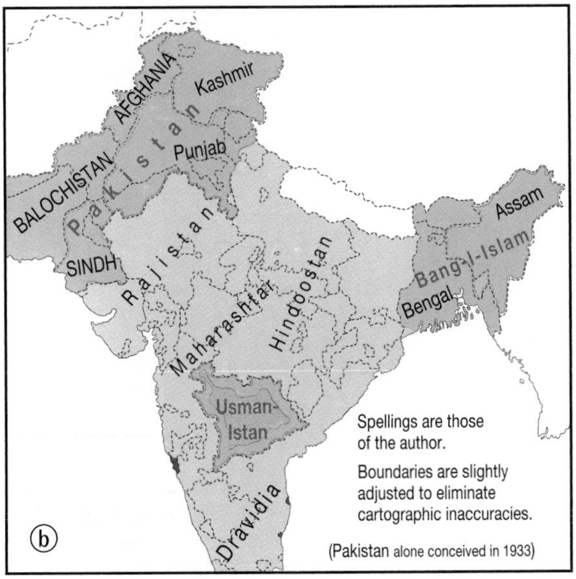

AFGHANIA
Kashmir
Pakistan
Punjab
BALOCHISTAN
SINDH
Rajistan
Maharashtar
Hindoostan
Assam
Bang-I-Islam
Bengal
Usman-Istan
Dravidia
Spellings are those of the author.
Boundaries are slightly adjusted to eliminate cartographic inaccuracies.
(Pakistan alone conceived in 1933)
b

Muslim League Demand for a Sovereign Muslim State Of Pakistan, 1946*

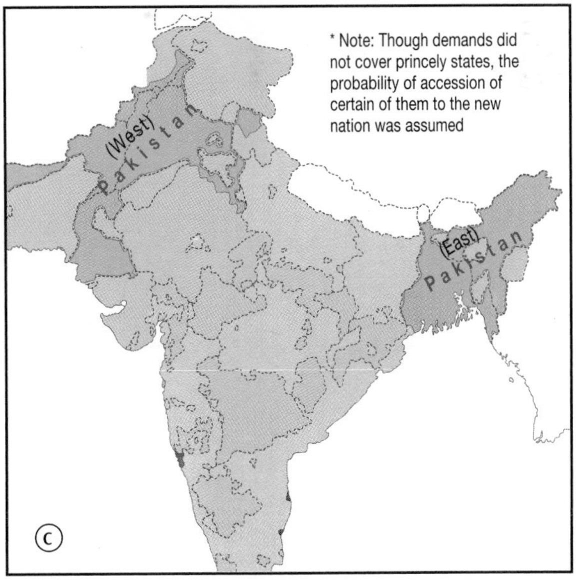

* Note: Though demands did not cover princely states, the probability of accession of certain of them to the new nation was assumed
(West) Pakistan
(East) Pakistan
c

'With the emergence of Indian-run chromolithograph presses in the late 1870s, mass-produced images came to occupy a significant position in India's public and domestic spaces. Mostly every house in India had a Ravi Varma print. These prints provided an entrée into the modern world – a world where icons such as nationalist heroes and leaders could be bought for a pittance. The trends set by the Poona Chitrashala and the Ravi Varma Press encouraged others to set up presses and cash in on the print-making movement. While the images were mostly of gods, goddesses, historical warriors and nationalist leaders, they extended to posters, labels and other advertisement prints.'

The Indian Portrait III: A Historical Journey of Graphic Prints up to Independence. 2014. Ahmedabad: Archer, p. 130.

Ruling Princes of India

'The return of Mahatma Gandhi to India in 1915 gave printers a new iconography in the form of leaders and national heroes. Gandhi's prints even went where he could not physically go. Prints in this phase were done using the half-tone technique and they tended to be small in size. This was mainly done to reduce costs and make the prints readily available. The rise of smaller printing presses all over India helped produce smaller inexpensive prints that could cater to the popular taste with locally relevant designs and language.'

The Indian Portrait III: A Historical Journey of Graphic Prints up to Independence. 2014. Ahmedabad: Archer, p. 140

Independence is our Birth Right, c. 1940.

Published by
S. S. BRIJ BASI & Sons,
Picture Publishers,
MATHURA (U.P.)

Copy Right Reserved by Publishers
Printed at
S. A. OFFSET WORKS
MATHURA

गांधीजी की स्वर्गयात्रा

Last Journey of Mahatma Gandhi (1869–1948)

A HISTORY OF MODERN INDIA

The Colourful World of the Eighteenth Century

1

Shah Alam reviewing the East India Company's troops; c. 1781 illustration, artist unknown

Chapter outline

Jab chod chale Lucknow nagari (As/when I leave the city of Lucknow)…, lamented the poet Nawab Wajid Ali Shah on the eve of his departure from Lucknow when the East India Company formally annexed Awadh in 1856. What was this *nagari* of Lucknow and how had it become so dear to the nawab? To understand this lament, we need to enter the Lucknow of late-eighteenth century, the buzzingly dynamic capital set-up by Asaf-ud-Daula in 1775. Asaf-ud-Daula succeeded his father, the courageous warrior-king Shuja-ud-Daula, who had joined forces with the Nawab of Bengal, Mir Qasim and the Mughal emperor, Shah Alam II, to fight the East India Company in the Battle of Buxar in 1764, and had zealously guarded Awadh's autonomy till his death.

Asaf-ud-Daula, the young nawab, 'fat and dissolute' and averse to politics, left the tiresome affairs of the state to his chief steward Murtaza Khan, packed up the court at Faizabad and moved to the small provincial town of Lucknow. This enabled him to evade the influence of his powerful mother and his father's retainers. The move turned Awadh's administration on its head and shattered the autonomy nurtured by Shuja. Yet, the lack of political prestige was compensated by the cultural prominence that Lucknow came to acquire. The simultaneously 'debauched, corrupt and extravagant' and 'refined, dynamic and generous' nawab founded a city that echoed his flamboyance; Lucknow was 'awash with extravagance and excess' and attracted pioneers, drifters and people on the make. Its ranks swelled with 'eighteenth century's most unlikely "imperialists" and most remarkable profiles in self-fashioning' (Jasanoff 2005: 51).

This picture of eighteenth-century India sharply contrasts the image evoked by the debates that surround it. For long, the eighteenth century in India was regarded as a period of decline and chaos; an inexorable interlude between the collapse of the Mughal empire and the rise of the British. At the same time, this understanding and the arbitrary separation of a century as an independent category of analysis fomented intensive work on it, which yielded richer understandings and revised earlier perceptions. The fact that the eighteenth century retains its importance as a theme of analysis finds reflection in the continued publication of anthologies on it (Alavi 2002; Marshall 2005, for instance). Interestingly, a study of the eighteenth century is considered relevant not only for India, but also for Asia. India's historiography conforms to the wider debate on eighteenth century as a period of Asian decline in maritime trade and the rise and intrusion of European commercial, mercantile and imperial interests in Asian countries on account of certain significant developments in Europe. This Eurocentric analysis, which focused on the eighteenth century only in terms of happenings in and their implications for Europe, was countered by a Dutch historian and administrator, Job Van Leur, in the 1930s.

In a pioneering review article of the fourth volume of *Geschiedenis van Nederlandsch Indië* (History of the Netherland Indies) written in 1940, Van Leur advocated an Asia-centric history by juxtaposing the vitality and strong continuity in Asian history with the abrupt and significant changes in Europe. The continuity was affirmed by the presence, in the eighteenth century, of dynamic polities in Asia uninterrupted by European encroachment, from Persia in the West to Japan in the Far East (Van Leur 1940: 544–67).

There are obvious problems with Van Leur's analysis. But his provocative thesis inspired a range of revisionist writings which vigorously debated the models of continuity and change in Asia. For Cambridge historian Christopher Bayly, a strong advocate of the continuity thesis, Van Leur's essay is more 'heuristic' than a substantive exercise in historical writing. According to Bayly, the question to ask of the eighteenth century, is not whether there was change or continuity or dissolution or resilience in Asian societies, but why in spite of the transformation of the world economy and the transplanting of the European state in Asia, many features of the earlier order persisted (Bayly 1998: 301). For us, the question is rather what the 'transplanting of the European state' did to the enduring features of Asian societies, and how this resilience affected the European state that was sought to be transplanted. Moreover, did this transportation happen only in the eighteenth century or did the presence of Europeans from the sixteenth and seventeenth centuries affect the nature of polities that were taking shape (Subrahmanyam 2001: 3–4)? Is it possible that a combination of changes underway and the occurrence of new happenings produced fascinating mix-ups and conferred on the eighteenth century a new vivacity?

THE END OF AN EMPIRE

In 1707, the year of Aurangzeb's death, the Mughal empire had reached its farthest physical limits. The conquest of the kingdoms of Bijapur and Golconda in the late 1680s had made the empire spread to the southern edge of the Deccan Peninsula and brought almost the entire subcontinent under Mughal sovereignty. Yet, the Mughal imperial structure collapsed within 40 years of Aurangzeb's death. By the middle of the century, the empire lay in ruins with its vast possessions reduced to a 'roughly rectangular wedge of territory about 250 miles from north to south and 100 miles broad' (Spear 1951: 5). How do we understand this apparent paradox?

To do so, we need to trace briefly the 'fault lines' of the Mughal administrative system (Metcalf and Metcalf 2003: 28). To begin with, the Mughal emperor was *Shah-en-Shah*, king of kings, one sovereign among many (Bayly 1988: 13), not the lone, 'despotic' sovereign. This meant that the empire was poised on negotiation and accommodation of competition—between different groups of nobles and aristocrats, military and revenue officers—among whom authority was distributed hierarchically. The emperor stood at the apex of this 'segmentary' structure (Stein 1980, 2010), with members of the aristocracy owing different degrees of personal loyalty to him. Effective functioning of the system depended on the judicious tweaking of conflicts and maintaining balance by the emperor.

Alongside, there was a centralized administrative apparatus developed by the genius of Emperor Akbar in the sixteenth century that intimately linked bureaucracy and military aristocracy. Power was distributed and delegated among the elite in a manner that strengthened the military basis of the 'war state' and retained the supremacy of the emperor. The *mansabdari* system conferred on each *mansabdar*, military officer, a dual numerical rank of *jat* and *sawar*, where *jat* signified personal rank and *sawar* denoted the number of horsemen that the *mansabdar* was required to maintain for the Mughal state. Payment for service and maintaining soldiers and horses was made, in most cases, with the assignment of the right to collect revenue from a *jagir* (landed estate). *Jagirs* were of two kinds—*tankha* (transferable) and *vatan* (non-transferable). Given the logic of the system, most *jagirs* were transferable. *Vatan jagirs* represented a compromise with powerful local princes and landlords, who agreed to offer allegiance to the emperor only on condition that their lands were recognized as *vatan*. While some princes and landlords were incorporated as Mughal officers by the acknowledgement of *vatan jagirs* in regions under direct imperial control, powerful princes on the fringes of the empire retained autonomy over internal affairs and only agreed to pay an annual tribute to the emperor in recognition of his overall suzerainty.

The *mansabdari* system, undoubtedly consolidated the emperor's position as *Shah-en-Shah*—ranks and *jagirs* were conferred, transferred or dismissed at his will; and power was shared on the basis of direct loyalty to him. The imperial government commanded the right to assemble and dispatch *mansabdars* with their contingents to any points at any time, if the need arose. This centralized apparatus allowed an absolute monarchy to hold its own and function for 150 years without any serious threat (Habib 1999: 364–65).

At the same time, the system produced intense competition among various ethnic and caste groups who comprised the Mughal nobility. It also pushed the Mughal state toward constant expansion of territories; it was the only way of increasing resources and assigning new *jagirs*.

Aurangzeb's wars in the Deccan were expensive; they stretched the treasury to its limits. Acquisition of new territories brought new players in the tussle for prestige and authority. In particular, the incorporation of what is known as the Deccani group in the aristocracy heightened tension and conflicts among the established nobility composed of rival Irani, Turani and Hindustani factions. These groups resented the favour Aurangzeb showed as a diplomatic gesture to the new *mansabdars* and commanders recruited from the defeated territories of the southern sultanates of Bijapur and Golconda (Stein 2010: 181). On the other hand, officials stationed in the Deccan complained that the slender revenue from their *jagirs* was insufficient for their expenses. Thus, the ties that bound the old and the new officials in the Deccan to the Mughal empire became less and less firm. In fact, *mansabdars*, affected by the gap in the demand and actual collection of revenue, reduced the number of soldiers and horses that they were supposed to maintain and tried to extract as much revenue as possible from landlords and peasants. This simultaneously weakened the military might of the empire and caused disaffection among landlords and peasants.

The years between 1689 and 1719 witnessed unrest in the heartland of the empire. The Jat chieftains and zamindars in Agra and Mathura came out in open revolt. They used their strategic position to intercept and plunder the 'bullock trains of treasure and trade passing into the Gangetic basin from the Deccan', causing that route to be abandoned (Stein 2010: 182). Aurangzeb's army, sent to subdue the Jats, was humiliated and his subsequent attempts to quell the revolt prompted some alienated Rajput houses—resolute in opposing the restoration of imperial control—to support the Jats. Aurangzeb died at this critical juncture and his death occasioned a struggle for power among his three surviving sons. The winner, Muazzam, ascended the throne with the title of Bahadur Shah. He was 63 at the time and was to die within the next five years.

There was little Bahadur Shah could do to stave the decline. The Jat revolt had encouraged other recalcitrant forces—the Sikhs in Punjab and Marathas in the Deccan—to challenge Mughal authority. The Sikhs, a loose and divergent group spread across northern India, particularly the urban centres of the vast Gangetic plain (Oberoi 1997: 42), were followers of Guru Nanak (1469–1539), an upper caste Hindu, who founded the Sikh community in central Punjab in the 1520s (Mann 2001: 3). Under the guidance of a line of gurus, the community evolved and expanded its base, and by the turn of the seventeenth century had come to be perceived as a threat to the Mughal administration at Lahore. The tensions between the Sikhs and Mughals resulted in the execution of the fifth guru Arjan (1563–1606) in Lahore, following which the Sikh centre was moved to Shivalik hills. The tenth guru, Govind Singh (born 1666, guru 1675–1708), dissolved the line of personal gurus and conferred its authority on the *Adi Granth* (the original book, the primary scripture that contains the sayings of Guru Nanak) and in the Sikh *panth* (path), that came to include the community (ibid.).

At the beginning of the eighteenth century the Sikhs were provided leadership by Banda Bahadur, a charismatic Muslim-born Sikh who gained political power after the assassination of the last guru, Govind Singh. Earlier, in the late-seventeenth century, the Marathas under Shivaji had also successfully demonstrated the vulnerability of the Mughal army. This did not, of course, signify that there was a new self-contained 'Maratha system' or a 'Shivaji's Maharashtra' from the seventeenth century. Rather, there was a 'gradual, many-sided process of centralization' that co-existed with several centrifugal institutions and identities well into the eighteenth century (Perlin 1985). In the late-nineteenth, twentieth and twenty-first centuries, however, Shivaji's resistance has come to be viewed as a 'Hindu' challenge to 'Muslim' aggression and Shivaji has been appreciated as a popular hero and, at times, as a national 'Hindu' hero. The Sikh challenge, similarly, has come to be seen as ideologically motivated. Such perceptions, linked to the 'ambience of the times' produce particular understandings of history (Alam 1986: 3) that are not at par with the contingent configurations of identities in the seventeenth and eighteenth centuries.

As we will see in the section on the mighty Marathas, Maratha speakers were divided by caste and class status and they owed different degrees of allegiance to the Mughals. Competition was rife among these groups—not only did they actively participate in Mughal factional rivalry and strike deals to gain access to contested territory (Metcalf and Metcalf 2003: 31), some of them also offered help to Aurangzeb against Shivaji's son Shambhuji. Finally, the Marathas came to the aid of the emperor during the Afghan invasions in the middle of the eighteenth century. Similarly, in Punjab, the authority of the Mughals was exercised on the basis of an accommodation of dominant regional interest groups by the emperor (Singh 1981). Indeed, for the Marathas, as for the Sikhs, alliances proceeded from expediency and not from religious or community identity, which are neither fixed nor permanent.

At the same time, the successful resistance of the Marathas and Sikhs encouraged many zamindars—landholders with local roots, power and prestige—to disavow the authority of the emperor once central power weakened. Mughal officers, such as *diwan*s (revenue collectors/administrators) and *subadar*s (governors), who did not have local roots but had authority as representatives of the sovereign, followed suit. In the 1720s, revenue officers and governors of the rich provinces of Bengal and Awadh set themselves up as independent rulers, appointed their own officials and nominated their own successors, severing virtually all ties with the Mughal state.

The trend was set by the imperial Prime Minister Nizamu'l Mulk Asaf Jah. He moved to Hyderabad in 1724, withdrew from imperial projects and started functioning as an autonomous ruler. The emperor granted dignity to this defiant move by recognizing the Nizam as the Viceroy of the southern part of the empire. But for all practical purposes, the Nizam and the nawabs of Bengal and Awadh had become independent. Soon, this was followed by autonomous local princes who stopped paying tribute to the emperor. Such local rulers and provincial magnates received support from Hindu and Jain moneylenders and merchants—vital players in the functioning of the Mughal taxation system and commodity production. This support enabled them to consolidate their authority. Paradoxically then, commercial growth, which had 'succoured the power of Delhi ultimately eroded it' (Bayly 1988: 4).

After Aurangzeb, the absence of an astute emperor capable of commanding loyalty and allegiance and handling the conflicts with care, as well as the incessant wars of succession hastened Mughal decline. To make matters worse, internal rebellions were accompanied by foreign invasions, often propelled by the decline of Islamic empires in West and Central Asia. The Persian invasion under Nadir Shah in 1738–39, which entailed loot and plunder of Delhi, including the famed Kohinoor diamond, dealt a severe blow to Mughal prestige. The repelling of the first Afghan raid in 1748 signified very limited and temporary success. The Afghans under Ahmad Shah Abdali returned in 1755–56; they conquered Punjab and ransacked Delhi. The Mughals and Marathas combined against the Afghans in the Battle of Panipat in 1761, but were defeated. To the relief of the Mughals, Abdali had to return hastily to Afghanistan. But the days of the Mughals were all but over.

Trouble was brewing all over the empire. Weakness of the central power encouraged not only local elites, but also ambitious figures of lowly origin to stake claims to power. Papadu, a member of the low toddy-tapping caste of Telengana, gathered an army of several thousand men from untouchable and low castes and carried out year-long assaults in several major towns in Telengana. Such resistance was not destined to succeed. Yet, it revealed the frustrations of the subordinate members of society, subject to the double authority of imperial-local and social hierarchies and their aspirations for a different social order.

CAUSES AND CONSEQUENCES

The intricate picture of the collapse of the Mughal empire, as described in the earlier paragraphs, underscores the diversity of processes and factors contributing to its decline. It also projects the various reasons that scholars have formulated to explain the decline. Early historians, such as Sir Jadunath Sarkar, placed the blame squarely on Aurangzeb's religious bigotry and the weakness of later Mughals and their nobles (Sarkar 1916, 1924, 1938). According to Sarkar, Aurangzeb's discriminatory religious policy generated a 'Hindu reaction' among Rathor, Bundela, Maratha and Sikh groups, which his weak successors could not set right. In a different manner, William Irvine also focused on the 'ruling elite' and ascribed Mughal decline to a deterioration of character of emperors and their nobles (1922).

Sarkar's view is no longer accepted by historians. It is evident that it was not only the Hindus, but also the Muslim nobility and members of religious orthodoxy who created problems for the Mughals. More significantly, contemporary sources identify the rebels and the 'disturbers' in terms of their class (zamindar, for instance), clan or region (such as Rajputan or Gujaran), and not as 'Hindu' (Alam 1986: 2). Finally, the eighteenth century did not lack able generals and politicians who formed a part of the Mughal coterie. The fact that they did not provide leadership at critical moments and got embroiled in personal aggrandisement highlights that the causes of decline were insipient in the very nature and structure of the Mughal administrative system.

Satish Chandra's *Parties and Politics at the Mughal Court, 1707–1740* (1959), drew attention to the 'jagirdari crisis' of the late-seventeenth and early-eighteenth century as the root cause of Mughal weakness. This represented the first serious effort at examining the structural weaknesses of the Mughal state. For the proper functioning of the key institutions—the *mansab* and *jagir*—it was necessary that the *mansabdars* and *jagirdars* collect the revenue efficiently. The inability of imperial officials to ensure the smooth collection of revenue from the late-seventeenth century produced a fiscal crisis. This was heightened by several other factors, such as an intense rivalry among *mansabdars* occasioned by the increase in their number during Aurangzeb's reign and the decline or stagnation of *jagirs* that could be assigned to them. Wars further affected revenue collection in the disturbed areas and widened the gap between demand (*jama*) and collection (*hasil*) of revenue, a gap present since the beginning.

In a later work, Chandra revised his own position somewhat and ruled out the general view that the Deccan was a deficit area and the crisis was on account of *be-jagiri*, that is, the absence of a *jagir* for a newly appointed *mansabdar*. The crisis in the system was intimately tied to its non-functionality, not necessarily to the increase in the number of aristocrats and the decline in *jagirs* (Chandra 1982). It is true, however, that the system of transfer of *jagirs* put the aristocracy under strain; this was compounded by a rise in the price of luxury goods (brought about by increased export to European markets). An added complication was created by the intricate power-plays between *jagirdars*, zamindars and *khudkasht* (resident) cultivators. All this made it evident that by the end of Aurangzeb's reign, the *mansabdari* system had become non-functional.

Territorial expansion itself put the Mughal state and treasury under strain, although, as mentioned earlier, acquisition of new territories was almost a compulsion. This double-bind was made worse, according to J. F. Richards, by Aurangzeb's wrong policies. In Richard's view, there was no real shortage of *jagirs* in the Deccan. While conquests brought newer areas under Mughal control, Aurangzeb decided not to distribute them as *jagirs*. He retained them as *khalisa* (royal lands) to fund further wars in the Deccan. This faulty policy was complicated further by the politics of the 'warrior aristocracies' that made problems of Mughal administration in the Deccan acute (Richards 1975). Undoubtedly, Richards' point that *be-jagiri* was not the main problem in the Deccan is significant. At the same time, collecting revenue in the Deccan had always been problematic. Hence, it is difficult to decide whether the distribution of lands of Bijapur and Golconda as *jagirs* would have resolved the 'crisis' in the system.

The most influential theory of Mughal decline was offered in the early 1960s by Irfan Habib, a notable Aligarh historian of the Marxist strain (Habib [1963] 1999), in a work he revised and republished in 1999. Through a detailed reading of Abul Fazl's *Ain-i Akbari* and a range of other available manuscripts and published accounts, Habib provided a coherent picture of the agrarian system of Mughal India, which encompassed land revenue administration, the agrarian economy and social structure in regions that had been 'under Mughal control the longest' (Habib 1999: x). His meticulous study of the different modes of assessing and fixing land revenue and its collection, led Habib to conclude that the agrarian crisis was the primary cause of Mughal decline in the eighteenth century (Habib [1963] 1999: 190–230). The crisis was caused by endemic state oppression, which generated resistance on the part of exploited peasants who had to choose between 'starvation or slavery and armed resistance' (Habib 1999: 378).

Such a situation arose owing to the high revenue demand set by imperial Mughals. The demand was kept high in order to allow the *mansabdars* to maintain their military contingents out of the revenues of their *jagirs*, even though caution was exercised so as not to deprive peasants of the bare minimum required for survival. In Habib's words, the revenue demand was designed 'ideally to approximate to the surplus produce' that left the peasant with 'just the barest minimum needed for subsistence' (Habib 1998: 219; 1999: 367). While this appropriation of the surplus produce generated great wealth for the Mughal ruling class, the common people were subjected to utter poverty (ibid.).

It is not easy, affirms Habib, to get a clear idea of the state's revenue demand; it varied from region to region and depended on the nature of crops. Systems of measuring and assessing were also distinct, and often, part of the revenue was paid in cash and part in kind. It is true, however, that in extensive areas where land surveys had been conducted and revenue assessment and collection systematized, the demand amounted to about a third of the produce. Some of it was sent directly to the imperial treasury; most of it was assigned to *jagirdars*.

The disturbed conditions of the late-seventeenth and early-eighteenth centuries coupled with the crisis in the *jagirdari* system prompted *jagirdars* to try and extract more from the peasants. This made the life of poorer peasants extremely difficult. The tendency to press hard upon the peasant, of course, was inherent in the system from the beginning. The imperial administration was aware of it and attempted to set a limit to the demand from time to time (Habib 1999: 367). There was, however, a contradiction in the interests of the Mughal state and individual *jagirdars*. A *jagirdar*, who had rights over the revenue of a land only for three or four years and whose assignment could be transferred any moment, did not have any interest in long-term agricultural development. His personal interests sanctioned 'any act of oppression that conferred an immediate benefit upon him' (ibid.: 368). The constant and unpredictable transfer of *jagirs* in the late-seventeenth century made *jagirdars* abandon the practice of helping peasants totally; it became even worse in the eighteenth century. Frequently, peasants were forced to sell their women, children and cattle to meet revenue demands (ibid.: 370). When even this did not suffice, peasants fled from their lands, adversely affecting cultivation (ibid.: 377).

The last resort for peasants, of course, was rebellion, after they had refused to pay the land revenue. What converted isolated acts of peasant resistance into an uprising was the help of richer peasants who possessed men and weapons, and ties both of caste and of faith—in particular, the large variety of monotheistic sects, current since the fifteenth–sixteenth centuries—that attracted common people. Of far greater significance, in Habib's opinion, was the intervention of zamindars—the hereditary local potentates—who had their own reasons for opposing the Mughal ruling class. The zamindars, it is true, had never liked the extraction of almost the entire revenue surplus from the villages by the Mughals, as it left them with only a marginal share (Alam 1986: 303).

These 'potentially seditious' zamindars made common cause with the peasants in their tussle with the imperial administration. Often these zamindars gave refuge to peasants who had fled their lands to evade the oppression of *jagirdars*. Such peasants added to the resources of the zamindars in two ways: by engaging in cultivation and by providing recruits for their armed bands. The increased strength of the zamindars was reflected in the fact that from the time of Aurangzeb's reign, their struggle against the Mughals ceased to be only defensive. They started making use of their large band, even armies in predatory warfare, to extend their areas of dominance (Habib 1999: 389).

A combination of two elements, therefore, transformed agrarian difficulties into an 'agrarian crisis' in the eighteenth century. They were the coming together of the peasant and the zamindar on the one hand, and the severing of ties between the zamindar and the *jagirdar*, on the other. Although the peasant-zamindar combine was neither uniform nor widespread, the fact remains that the leadership of the two major revolts against Mughal power, those of the Marathas and the Jats, was provided by zamindars or men who aspired to be so (Habib 1999: 389). Through an exploration of the 'agrarian aspects' of several revolts in northern and central India that shook the Mughal empire to its foundations (ibid.: 390–405), Habib affirms that peasant distress was the root cause of such rebellions, although, paradoxically, alleviation of such distress was not the proclaimed aim of the rebels. This analysis, advanced also by K. M. Ashraf (1960) and extended by Athar Ali (1975; 1978–79), made 'societal crisis' responsible for Mughal decline, in which economic failures coincided with and sometimes preceded political decline.

Although of great value, this argument overstates the link between the *jagirdari* crisis and the rebellion by zamindars and peasants. It is neither clear nor self-evident. Indeed, in his analysis of the effects of Mughal administration on the economy, Habib makes a clear distinction between the agrarian and commercial sectors and maintains that imperial policies stimulated urban and commercial growth, implicitly inferring that prosperous commerce could co-exist with stagnant agriculture (Chaudhuri 2008: 52), an inference that is inherently problematic. The influence of Habib's theory, however, has meant that explorations of Mughal decline have paid exaggerated attention to the Mughal state's fiscal structure and policy, and overlooked socio-cultural processes. Moreover, explaining the decline in terms of structural weakness closely resembles earlier works that held individual rulers responsible.

Both views accept the 'centre' as the principal point of analysis and concentrate on imperial policies and practices. They also hold the fact of 'decline' and its resultant anarchy and chaos as given and unquestionable, although 'decline' is only inferred from a general assumption of political disorder (ibid.: 51). In 1983, Tapan Raychaudhuri indicated that the assumption of 'decline' rested on very slender evidence. He argued that although political disarray and armed conflict undoubtedly affected economic life in many parts of the country, it did not imply 'a general decline in India as a whole. Even at the heart of the much ravaged empire, Agra under Jat and Maratha occupation, was a flourishing city until 1787 with many wealthy Delhi citizens finding refuge in its comparative security' (ibid.: 7). In a similar manner, the real decline in Bengal's economy was largely a post-Plassey and even a post-1813 phenomenon (ibid.).

Recent works have seriously revised this picture of unqualified decline by moving away from the centre and looking at regions of growth and vibrancy (Alam 1986; Barnett 1980; Bayly 1983; Grover 1966; Perlin 1983; Stein 1980; Subrahmanyam 1992; Washbrook 1988; Wink 1986). They proffer a 'disaggregated picture' of different regional trajectories instead of a 'monolithic one' (Subrahmanyam 2001: 8), and urge for an understanding of the eighteenth century 'in terms of its own structure' and not in terms of what preceded it and what came after—namely, Mughal decline and colonial rule (Alam 1986: 10). According to this literature, the eighteenth century, far from being a period of decay was one of slow population growth and rise in prices, urbanization, commercialization and the growth of new markets and of new economic and political forces. Muzaffar Alam's study of two important provinces—Punjab and Awadh—in the eighteenth century, shows that although the histories of the two regions varied in the four phases that he marks out (1707–1713; 1713–c.1722; c.1722–1739; 1739–1748), both showed signs of economic growth reflected in the rise in revenue figures and the emergence and affluence of a number of towns with links to long distance trade (ibid.: 14).

The inability of the weak central power to control these new flourishing regions of surplus production, accompanied by the erosion of the support of established landlord, trader and mercantile groups to the empire, contributed to its gradual substitution by 'successor states'. The prosperity of the regions benefitted the zamindars, who were in 'constant conflict' with the central administration, and merchants who dominated markets. This engendered not only a strong sense of regional identity, but also brought different regional elements in competition and conflict with each other, a fact that allowed Mughal nobles to exercise their hegemony for a time by playing off one element against the other.

There was, however, a significant shift in the relationship with the centre by the middle of the eighteenth century—zamindars, merchants and *madad-i-ma'ash* (rent free) holders who tried to make their lands hereditary were joined by imperial governors in asserting autonomy. The office of the governor in Awadh, Bengal and Hyderabad, for instance, became hereditary with the province being designated as the 'home province' of the governor. Mughal functionaries, such as *amildars*, tried to take advantage of this struggle between the centre and the provinces by carving out independent niches for themselves (Cohn 1960). While the persuasive influence of Mughal authority meant that these new *subadars* and military adventurers, such as the Marathas, continued to seek support and legitimacy from the Mughal court, it was 'in order to secure firmly *their positions in the regions*' and not to reinforce the centre (Alam 1986: 17). Provinces now made their claims on the centre, rather than the centre controlling the peripheries.

In other words, Mughal centralization, which rested on discreet balancing and sharing of rights among an elaborate group of central and regional elite, and a constant accommodation of 'shifting rivalries and alliances' (Wink 1986), left the way open for multiple and rival principles of organization of authority and management. What mattered more over time was Mughal 'concession' rather than Mughal centralization. Bernard Cohn's early essay on the Banaras region clearly marked out four levels in the political system of the eighteenth century: the imperial, the secondary, the regional and the local (1962). And, it was precisely because there were always 'many sharers in the dignity and power of kingship with overlapping rights and obligations' that 'empire' and 'state' represented 'limited political entities in India' (Bayly 1988: 13). More importantly, centralized political power never coincided completely with total control of economic forces (Perlin 1983), as Habib would have us believe. Athar Ali's later work tends to support this—it questions the linear relationship between economic growth and political consolidation by showing that local and regional economic expansion continued even while the central political edifice crumbled (Ali 1986–87; 1993).

On a similar note, Alam and Subrahmanyam argue that the first half of the eighteenth century was undoubtedly one of 'considerable political turmoil' in which regional states were formed with rapidity and there was a great deal of fluidity in the system, but this turmoil did not have a counterpart in terms of general social and economic dislocation (1998: 68). Viewed from Delhi, the eighteenth century was certainly a period of gloom, but it was hardly so for the inhabitants of other centres of India, although their experience of political decentralization and economic reorientation varied widely. It was only after the 1750s that warfare became more disruptive of social life, but that did not totally invert the earlier processes (ibid.: 69–70).

That strong political power did not translate into complete control of economic forces is pointed out, in a different way, by Karen Leonard ([1979] 1998). Her article highlights the significance of indigenous bankers and merchants, particularly the ones who pertained to 'great firms' in the sustenance, and later, the disruption of the Mughal empire. The Mughal state relied heavily on indigenous banking firms, which maintained an intricate network of revenue collection, banking and credit by validating and minting money, maintaining exchange ratios between different regional currencies and receiving and remitting land revenues through *hundi*s (indigenous bills of exchange) that made the transfer of land revenue easier and safer. Indigenous bankers also financed tax farmers and served as lenders of cash and credit (ibid.: 403). The shift in their loyalty from the imperial government to rising regional powers between 1650 and 1750 caused severe erosion of Mughal power and eventually caused its downfall. Revenue supply from the regions to the centre declined continually over the eighteenth century as the great banking firms got involved in collection at local levels and diverted their resources of credit and trade from the Mughal government to regional powers. The importance of such banking firms is reflected in the fact that the East India Company entered into the power politics of the regions by way of partnership with them, but dislodged them as soon as it achieved political dominance.

Ashin Dasgupta's (1979) work on maritime trade with focus on port cities, particularly Surat, indicates that transformations in trade and mercantile capital were crucial in the rise of the English East India Company. Tracking the changes in patterns of inland and export trade, Dasgupta argues that although inland trade increased, India's export trade suffered a reversal of fortunes on account of European competition. This affected Indian mercantile institutions that functioned at a supra-regional level to oversee transportation of goods and offer credit and insurance services (Alavi 2002: 7). The reversal found reflection in the gradual replacement of the port cities of Surat in Gujarat, Masulipatnam in Madras and Dacca in Bengal, by the emergent port cities set up by the East India Company—Bombay, Madras and Calcutta respectively.

To put it briefly, a surge and confidence of contending 'centrifugal forces' in an ambience of buoyancy of trade and agriculture caused the decline of the Mughals. A range of studies that have focused on the socio-economic, political and cultural effervescence of different regions have emphasized economic realignment and not chaos or crisis, as the primary factor that induced a dissociation of regions from imperial control. According to such studies, the decline of the Mughals resulted in a sense from 'the very success of their earlier expansion' (Bayly 1988: 3). In northern India, the local gentry of Hindus, Muslims and Jains who prospered under the loose regime of the Mughals, separated themselves off as much more stable landlords. The 'potentially hostile' zamindars turned into enemies and organized local resistance against the centre. What was remarkable was the speed with which they recovered from defeat and 're-engaged themselves against the Mughals' (Alam 1986: 303). The intensity of their resistance particularly in Awadh, followed upon economic growth and prosperity (ibid.).

The success of the zamindars too depended largely on their ability to secure the support of an energetic, militarized and belligerent peasantry. This peasantry, far from being docile, meek and exploited (Habib 1999), was ready to turn violent at any time in order to defend itself (Kolff 1989). J. F. Richards ascribes great significance to Kolff's insight. He affirms that the presence of a 'bristling, militarized rural society' in north India—of a 'martial ethos shared by peasant-cultivators and rural aristocrats'—infinitely compounded the problems of the centralizing Mughal state: it fared much worse than its counterparts in the rest of Eurasia (Richards 2004: 397).

Hence, it was the ambitious zamindars and assertive peasants, resurgent *jagirdars* and enterprising governors, and wealthy merchants and leading bankers, rather than indigent landlords and impoverished peasants, who occasioned local political turmoil and undermined Mughal rule. This revised picture does not, as Subrahmanyam reminds us, confront the 'thorny question' of the nature of social distribution of gains from economic growth (Subrahmanyam 2001: 9), a question that certainly requires greater attention.

The polarity of opinions rather than conclusively settling the debate, underlines how processes underway in the eighteenth century allow alternative interpretations (Chaudhuri 2008: 93). They also indicate the distinct interest of historians who participate in the debate. While scholars of Mughal India pay greater attention to the first half of the century, and either 'view change in the shadow of the Mughal political collapse' or concentrate on 'the transition from Mughal to regional political formations', scholars of modern Indian history 'focus on the more critical transition to colonial rule that characterized the second half of the century' (Alavi 2002: 37, 38). The eighteenth century is significant precisely because of the distinct ways in which old and new actors successfully asserted themselves, sometimes working in the name of the Mughal regime and sometimes directly challenging the edifice of the Mughals. Mughal culture held sway for long after the demise of the empire, even as new players and political elites concretized their visions of governance and culture in regions, provinces, cities and monumental buildings (Goetz 1938, for instance). It is to such tales that we now turn.

THE LAND OF KINGS: RAJASTHAN

The 'land of kings' offers an intriguing picture. The collapse of Mughal power and support enabled many Rajput rajas to turn their regions into 'nascent' regional kingdoms (Richards 2004: 397). At the same time, the lack of Mughal support occasioned 'intense stress and instability', particularly for the Rathor rajas of Jodhpur who had to negotiate with myriad forces to maintain their regime (Sahai 2007: 691). They had to carefully balance military might and coercive strength, the two principal elements of state power, with 'other more subtle ingredients', since cultural prescriptions of statecraft implied that protection of subjects entailed their economic well-being (ibid.: 689). The rulers had to court and incorporate powerful lineage chiefs, politically influential clansmen and confident and belligerent peasantry, as well as several groups engaged in manufacturing and commerce. Interestingly, the fact that different artisanal groups possessed specific skills for the manufacture of particular goods, lent them strength despite their ritually impure status. The contenders for authority, therefore, had to 'display a certain degree of piety and extend patronage' toward craftsmen in order to 'spatially fix within the territories of Jodhpur' a group of castes 'habituated to frequent and recurrent migrations' (ibid.: 696).

Rajasthan in this sense was representative of the political culture of India which revolved around the 'art of negotiating and shifting alliances', of keeping open a number of options, and 'around the maintenance of patronage networks' (Kolff 2004: 459).

THE MIGHTY MARATHAS

The Marathas, comprising dominant peasant clans in western India where the Marathi language was spoken, rose to prominence in the sixteenth century as soldiers in the armies of the sultans of Bijapur and Ahmadnagar. They were trained as light cavalry, which Shivaji perfected and used to great advantage against the Mughals in the seventeenth century. The sultans also employed Deshasta and Chitpavan Brahmans in their administration. These Brahmans augmented their high standing further by participating in the *bhakti* cults in Maharashtra. However, they carefully maintained their distance from peasant Marathas (Stein 2010: 186).

As the principal area where cotton was cultivated, spun and woven, Maharashtra played an important role in the economy of the region, supplying a valuable commodity to the trade from the port of Surat. There was also a thriving inter-regional trade between the plateau and the coast where coconut products, fish, salt, timber and fruits of the coast were exchanged for cotton, sugarcane, tobacco and pulses of the plateau.

Even though Maharashtra was well integrated with the wider Deccan region, its politics was controlled by rural chiefs, the *deshmukhs*. The *deshmukh*s held between 20 and 100 villages. Each village in turn had its *patil* (headman), who was assisted by a *kulkarni* (record-keeper). The *patil* was invariably from the peasant caste while the *kulkarni* was a Brahman. The head of the *deshmukh*s was a *sardeshmukh* and that of the *kulkarni*s a *deshkulkarni*. These people ran the administration with minimal interference from the Deccan sultans or the Mughals, who were content with an irregular share of the taxes collected from agriculture, in return for which they granted documents of investiture on *deshmukh*s, *patil*s and *kulkarni*s. Consequently, these people became the *dayada*s (co-sharers) of the kingdom. This vigorous localized socio-political system could easily be energized under an able leadership, a trend that began with Shivaji.

The Maratha 'state' that emerged under Shivaji was premised on a 'co-sharing' of power between the Martha king (and later the Peshwa) and the existing chiefs and lineages of the region, a relationship characterized by reciprocity and deep unease (Deshpande 2007: 40–41). In a similar manner, Maratha *Swarajya* (self-rule) did not stand for abstract and absolute sovereignty over specific territories, but claims to revenue that overlapped with Mughal *pararajya* (rule by others) (Wink 1986). Claims to revenue, termed *chauth* and *sardeshmukhi* respectively, represented a quarter and an additional exaction of one-tenth of the Mughal government's share of the revenue, in return for not plundering (Gordon 1994: 28).

Shivaji's son Shambhuji continued his defiance of Aurangzeb by giving shelter to the rebel prince Akbar, an act that Aurangzeb sought to punish by the use of force. Shambhuji faced the challenge astutely, although in the end he was captured and executed. Shambhuji's royal pretensions aroused the hostility of important *deshmukh* families, who offered Aurangzeb help on the condition that he confirmed that all the special rights that their families had accumulated would remain hereditary. They also got valuable *jagirs* from the emperor.

Shambhuji's successors had to contend with similar dithering loyalty from the *deshmukh*s. By the time Shambhuji's grandson Shahu, raised in the Mughal court, came to rule in 1708, Maratha fighting bands were operating autonomously, raiding and pillaging Mughal tracts along the northern frontier. The multiple alliances that the Mughals had forged in the course of territorial expansion had conferred different rights and privileges on *deshmukhs*, who had come to form zamindaris encompassed by the Mughal empire (Wink 1986).

Shahu tried to mediate between the Maratha bands and the emperor, but his claim to the throne was challenged by Tarabai, wife of Shambhuji's brother Rajaram, who tried to rule in Satara in the name of her son, Shivaji II. The *deshmukh*s were divided between the two camps, and as before, some of them continued to owe loyalty to the Mughals. What won the day for Shahu was the help and advice he got from his Chitpavan Brahman ministers, who on account of their charismatic leadership, ability to negotiate and capacity to consolidate, played a major role in the growth of Maratha power in the early eighteenth century (Gordon 1993).

Balaji Viswanath, appointed Peshwa (Prime Minister) and chief financial officer by Shahu in 1713, helped the Sayyid brothers (who headed the Hindustani faction of the Mughal aristocracy) install a puppet emperor on the throne of Delhi in 1719. He also negotiated a treaty with the Mughals, which virtually recognized Maratha control over the Mughal provinces in the Deccan. The Marathas were granted the right to *chauth* over the six Mughal provinces and Shahu also got an additional right to *sardeshmukhi* in the Deccan in recognition of his status as the head of *deshmukh*s. With this began a trend that would make the Brahman Peshwas the *de facto* rulers of the Maratha state based in Pune (Asher and Talbot 2006: 240).

The office of the Peshwa became hereditary and was held by Balaji's son Baji Rao from 1720 to 1740 and by his son Balaji Baji Rao till 1761. Under the able guidance of these astute politicians, royal power was consolidated by means of conferring prestige and privileges to old and new local chiefs who served Shahu and the Peshwa. Balaji Viswanath patronized other Chitpavan Brahmans who formed the core of 'a rapidly expanding literate elite' who served as tax collectors and administrators, and provided 'a surprising number of military leaders in the coming decades' (Gordon 1993: 113). This group was bound through ties of marriage and loyalty to the Peshwas. Balaji also enlisted the support of several Brahman banking families, whose credit was crucial for Shahu's bid to the throne. These families advanced money against future revenue receipts; within a decade, the arrangement acquired the elements of a sophisticated government finance system.

The territory under Maratha sway from which tribute was extracted increased steadily during Shahu's reign, particularly after the young Baji Rao took office. Baji Rao, in Gordon's characterization, was 'the most charismatic and dynamic leader in Maratha history' after Shivaji (ibid.: 114). Soon after assuming power, the 20-year-old Peshwa convinced Shahu and the inner circle about the importance of marching northward in order to launch an assault on the Mughals. In the following decade, Gujarat and Malwa were attacked on two and sometimes three fronts by Maratha bands during the campaigning season (October–April).

Baji Rao assumed the post of commander to fight in Shahu's name. He also continued the trend of appointing new men who owed personal loyalty to Shahu and to him. The established elite *deshmukh*s were bypassed and men were appointed from the Gaekwad, Holkar and Shinde families as commanders of military bands in the Peshwa's concerted move against the Mughals (Stein 2010: 188). Such men were given *jagirs* not only in the newly conquered territories but also in the *Swarajya*, or core Maratha territory. The loose state structure that resulted from this arrangement came to be called the Maratha

Confederacy, in which the kings at Satara nominally ruled over the powerful Peshwa and several groups of feudatory chiefs who administered their own territories (Fukuzawa 1982: 199).

Mughal rule over Malwa and Gujarat virtually ended in the late 1720s, when the joint forces of the Mughal commander and the Nizam of Hyderabad were defeated by Baji Rao. Subahdar Girdaur Bahadur, the Mughal head of Malwa was captured and killed towards the end of 1728, and Maratha military commanders started collecting tribute (Gordon 1994: 30). However, it has to be borne in mind that even though the local gentry and petty zamindars of these regions allowed the Marathas to divert resources away from the Mughal court, they did not allow the Marathas to 'appropriate the rituals and symbols of sovereignty' and take the place of the Mughal "state"' (Hasan 2004: 48).

Baji Rao also took on the Nizam—with whom he had been fighting off and on from 1725—outmaneouvered his troops in guerrilla warfare, trapped them in the dry hills of Palkhed, cut off their supplies and forced the Nizam to come to terms in March 1728. The Nizam had to recognize Shahu as the sole Maratha monarch who had the right of *chauth* and *sardeshmukhi* over the Deccan. Maratha revenue collectors, driven out by the internecine warfare and competition among various groups, were reinstated and the Nizam agreed to pay the outstanding *chauth* and *sardeshmukhi* arrears. The implications of the victory at Palkhed, therefore, were significant—by defeating 'the best-equipped Mughal army of the day under its best general' (Gordon 1993: 122), Baji Rao had succeeded in establishing Shahu's legitimate authority over the Deccan. The tactics of cutting off supplies and rapid movement had enabled him to outdo the Nizam's superior artillery.

The same tactic prevailed in Malwa, control over which allowed Baji Rao to reach Rajasthan in 1729. Baji Rao's successful tactics produced a change in the method of warfare; the heavy cavalry and large, slow-moving armies of the Mughals were outdone by the raiding warfare of Maratha bands. The bands generally ignored forts; they ransomed cities and drew Mughal armies into unfavourable areas of the plains, where they cut them off from reinforcements and supplies (ibid.: 129). Baji Rao's success was such that he dared to raid Delhi in 1737 and obliged the humiliated Mughal emperor to formally cede Malwa—the region between the Narmada and the Chambal rivers in 1739. This allowed Maratha rule to spread close to Agra.

By the time of Baji Rao's death in 1740, the frontiers of the Maratha state extended to Rajasthan, Delhi and the Punjab in the north; to Bihar, Bengal and Orissa (now Odisha) in the east; and to Karnataka and the Tamil and Telugu areas in the south. The Nawab of Bengal and the Nizam of Hyderabad, despite offering vigorous opposition, had to virtually give away Orissa and share Karnataka with the Marathas. Peshwa Baji Rao reigned as the de facto ruler of the Maratha polity, having survived and subdued factional resistance at court for more than two decades. Through incessant activity, he had transformed many areas of 'revenue-paying Mughal province' into a 'revenue-paying Maratha province' (ibid.: 127).

Military conquest went hand in hand with administrative centralization. A new elite of tax collectors, administrators and bankers rose to prominence. Conquest was followed by establishing civil rule; often the existing structure of administration and local magnates was kept in place, but Maratha tax collectors were appointed in the courts. Their ability as scribes opened new avenues to Brahmans; the Chitpavan kinsmen of the Peshwas got special honours and office as bureaucrats and military commanders. Enterprising peasant Marathas were employed as tax collectors and Brahmans and other traditional banking groups were drawn into state service. A sophisticated banking system fostered trade and made it possible for the army to be paid in cash, enhancing its size and strength. There was a new market for luxury goods in metal, ornamental ivory, wood and silver. Poets and musicians found patronage in the 'quasi-court life' of the elite (Stein 2010: 192) and gave tremendous boost to the local language and literature, a trend that had an important effect in the growth of regional consciousness.

The wealth of the elites also found reflection in architecture—a special kind of house called *wada* was developed for the rich. These houses were large, multi-storey wooden structures and built both for defence (spiked doors and secret passages) and for comfort (gardens and waterways, festival halls, multiple courtyards) where accessibility was governed by the rules of *purdah*. Forts, particularly hill forts, the 'key to the foundation, expansion and preservation of Maratha authority' (Asher and Talbot 2006: 243) were constructed, repaired and maintained. Fort-like square temples built inside the forts got transformed in the eighteenth century into tall, elegant structures that dotted Maratha territories, sustaining the notion of the Marathas as an ascendant Hindu community.

Success and territorial expansion, however, 'contained the seeds of grave economic consequences' similar to the ones faced by the Mughal state (Fukuzawa 1982: 199). When the third Peshwa, Balaji Baji Rao succeeded to office in 1740, the central exchequer had accumulated a debt of ₹ 1.45 million. The Peshwa ordered fresh expeditions to Rajasthan and the south to do away with the debt, but the expeditions caused further expenditure and the debt increased. Land revenue was maximized and the government vigorously encouraged the cultivation of state lands and wastelands by offering favourable terms to peasants. Peshwa rule also encouraged the construction of dams and canals and bore the cost of lime, stone, wood and the wage of skilled artisans, such as masons and carpenters, while the villages provided free unskilled labour (ibid.: 200).

The end of Shahu's long reign in 1749 caused confusion and conflict in the royal family. Balaji Baji Rao intervened to restore order on his terms. Pune, where Shahu had held court, replaced Satara as the capital and certain royal offices were abolished along with royal rights. Power and authority came to be concentrated in the person of the Peshwa, who also commanded an army of paid soldiers. The days of the peasant-soldiers were over. Paid, full-time soldiers now spent their time in forts far from home, receiving training as infantrymen and horsemen. On the other hand, since many peasant-soldiers took to full-time agriculture to avail of the special terms being offered by the central government, there was a 'denationalization' of the Maratha army and its gradual decline. Maratha soldiers were replaced by foreign mercenaries (ibid.: 199).

Peshwa and Maratha chiefs also got deeply embroiled in the complicated politics of the Mughal court and the Mughal–Maratha relationship remained fraught with overlapping revenue rights and simultaneous moves towards diplomacy and warfare (Deshpande 2007: 11). The Marathas were named protectors of the Mughal throne in 1752 and given *chauth* rights in Punjab; Maratha armies also went deep into the northwest. This was also the time that Peshwai (Peshwa rule) emerged as 'Brahman Raj' which increasingly patronized Brahmans and sought to enforce a Brahmanical hierarchy across Maratha lands (ibid.: 12).

Artillery remained the weak link in the Maratha army—large guns were fired by Europeans under the notional command of Maratha chiefs. Besides, it lagged far behind in sophistication. This was to prove fatal for the Marathas in the Third Battle of Panipat in 1761 when the light, mobile artillery of the Afghan king Ahmad Shah Abdali wiped out the Maratha infantry and cavalry, bringing an end to Maratha supremacy in the subcontinent.

Estimates about Maratha loss vary widely, but it is believed that 'as many as 50,000 combatants and non-combatants were killed' and Abdali's forces captured 'thousands of horses, pack animals, and whatever could be looted from the bazaar' (Gordon 1993: 153). The Maratha loss of money, credit, manpower and prestige was aggravated by a crisis of leadership at the centre. The Peshwa died within weeks of the battle and the Bhonsles of Nagpur, the Nimbalkars of Phaltan (Satara) and the Patwardhan family of southern Maharashtra, who had been incensed by Chitpavan dominance, joined forces with the Nizam's successor, who invaded the Maratha territory from the East.

Maratha reversal at Panipat also helped Haidar Ali consolidate his position, although Peshwa Madhav Rao led four attacks on Mysore between 1764 and 1771 (ibid.: 158). News of the defeat encouraged uprisings by local armed lineages and invasion and subversion by rival contenders in the regions under Maratha control. 'In the area around Delhi, between the Ganges and Jumna rivers and south as far as the Malwa plateau, local landed lineages and remaining Muslim powers fought incessantly through the decade after Panipat. There was, in fact, little the Marathas could do to retain any control' (ibid.: 157).

The Third Battle of Panipat, in effect, 'marked the beginning of a shift of power between the [Maratha] centre and the periphery', i.e. between the Raja/ Peshwa and the powerful Maratha chiefs—the Shinde (Scindia), Gaekwad, Holkar and Bhonsle families—and enabled the English to emerge as the main competitor on the subcontinent (ibid.: 156, 154).

NAWABS OF BENGAL

Aurangzeb had appointed Shia nobleman Kartalab Khan as the *diwan*, the collector of revenue in Bengal in 1701. Khan held this post till 1708 and was reappointed by Bahadur Shah in 1710, after a break of two years. Farukshiyar confirmed this position and also made him the Deputy Governor (*naib subadar*) of Bengal and the Governor (*nazim/subadar*) of Orissa. Later known as Murshid Quli Khan, Kartalab increasingly expressed a sense of independence. In 1703, he transferred the capital from Dacca to Maksusabad, which he renamed Murshidabad after him. His appointment as *subadar* of Bengal in 1717 strengthened his position immensely by giving him, for the first time in any province, the joint powers of the *diwan* and the *nazim*, two offices that the Mughal emperors had carefully kept apart. Undoubtedly, this did away with the Mughal system of checks and balances. At the same time, the arrangement suited both sides—Delhi regularly got its revenue and Murshid Quli enjoyed a remarkable degree of freedom to handle affairs within Bengal (Prakash 1998: 239).

Murshid Quli put the system of collecting revenue on a solid footing. He conducted surveys and introduced a rigorous system of collecting land revenue by means of powerful, intermediary zamindars. It was not that he increased the total revenue demand significantly, but his 'unremitting severity introduced regularity in revenue payment and put an end to disorder', considerably raising the amount of revenue collected and heralding 'a new and illustrious era of finance' (Sinha 1968: 3). Between 1700 and 1722, Bengal's revenue increased by over 20 per cent, from 11.72 to 14.11 million (Prakash 1998: 240–41). Sixteen very big zamindars were put in charge of the revenues of 615 *parganas* (fiscal units). About 1,045 more *parganas* were in the hands of smaller zamindars and *taluqdars* or intermediate rent receivers. More than three-fourths of the zamindars, big and small, and most of the *taluqdars* were Hindus. Dispossession was very rare. Murshid Quli also introduced the custom of employing Bengali Hindus on a large scale in the Mughal state service (Sinha 1965: 4).

The zamindari system of Bengal, argues N. K. Sinha, was 'strengthened rather than weakened by the severity of Murshid Quli' (Sinha 1968: 3). The stipulated amount charged was 'moderate' and the possessions of a zamindar were regarded as permanent and hereditary as long as he paid the amount regularly. In case of failure to pay, punishment was inflicted on the zamindar, but his property was not forfeited. Moreover, if the Mughal officer assessed that there was a real shortage of produce, the zamindar got an abatement of the demand. Similarly, *subadariabwab*, or a permanent pecuniary levy that Murshid Quli imposed on the zamindars in lieu of the earlier practice of taking *nazranas* or presents, was not 'burdensome' on account of the new resources created (ibid.: 5). That Murshid Quli regarded zamindari property as a secure investment was revealed in the fact that he bought a zamindari for his grandson Sarfaraz (ibid.: 4).

Philip Calkins extends Sinha's argument to assert that Murshid Quli's policies encouraged the rise of a small but powerful group of zamindars who were almost autonomous with regard to internal affairs, and led to the creation of a large and stratified base of big landholders (Calkins 1970). Alam and Subrahmanyam (1998), however, take strong issues with this position. In their view, Murshid Quli's principal concern was to tighten his control over the countryside and extend the *khalisa* or land under direct administration, in order to 'impose constraints in a more concentrated and organized manner on the *zamindars*' (Alam and Subrahmanyam 1998: 48). This was clearly reflected in his decision to transfer the *jagirs* of *mansabdars* of Bengal to Orissa, by means of which he extricated the finances of Bengal from the grasp of the *jagirdars* and the zamindars and increased the finances of the royal treasury (ibid.). The severity that Murshid Quli imposed in collecting revenue bears testimony to this.

Murshid Quli's successors, Shuja-ud-din and Alivardi Khan, introduced newer *abwabs* and maintained rigour in the collection of revenue. There were almost no remissions and balances, but there was also no 'corruption and chicane'. Revenue demand was based on the idea of an 'original rent' and *amils*, responsible for collecting revenue from zamindars, as well as *faujdars* or subordinate military commanders who collected revenue in frontier areas, were provided with accurate information on revenue collection over the past several years by the office of the *qanungo* (record-keeper). While it is true that both the rigour of revenue collection and the added demand of *abwabs* were passed unto the *ryots* (*raiyats*) by the zamindars who added their own *abwabs*, the intimate knowledge and information of the customary rent in each area possessed by the *qanungo*'s office made it inconvenient for zamindars to exploit the peasants (Sinha 1968: 6–7).

Murshid Quli also got rid of most of the Mughal noblemen who enjoyed sinecures in Bengal, and the flourishing banking business of the house of Jagat Seth partially stopped remittances of bullion from Bengal after 1728 (Sinha 1965: 13–14). The surplus income that came from their branches outside

Bengal was sufficient to pay for tribute to the Mughal emperor by *hundis*. Bengal's vigorous export trade in silk and cotton textile, sugar, oil and clarified butter through overland and sea-routes, and its efficient banking allowed merchants and bankers to join the important zamindars in the rank of elite. In addition, Bengal produced rice in such abundance that it was sent not only to its neighbours, but also transported by sea to Masulipatnam (now Machilipatnam in Andhra Pradesh) and other ports in the Coromandel coast (in south-eastern India), Ceylon (Sri Lanka) and the Maldives (ibid.: 109). The trade, though partly affected by the turmoil of the eighteenth century and the Maratha raids of the 1740s, got revitalized by the increasing investments and purchase of Bengal textiles by European companies, who pumped in bullion. Bengal played a prominent role in the intra-Asian trade carried on by the Dutch—it supplied raw silk for Japan trade and opium for the Indonesian market. This role as a critical intermediary enabled manufacturing production in Bengal to respond positively to the great increase in international demand for Bengal products (Prakash 1998: 242).

A variety of Hindu, Muslim and Armenian merchants participated in this buoyant trade with the biggest ones owning fleets of ships. Their wealth, coupled with their cordial relations with the state and bureaucracy, gave them a high standing in local society (Chaudhury 1995). As indicated earlier, bankers and merchants were also vital players in the collection of revenue and its faithful remittance to Delhi, since they ensured the safety of the entire process. Key supporters of the local ruler, they enjoyed great power and prestige. The career of the banking house of Jagat Seth, which was appointed as the treasurer of the provincial government in 1730, offers the best illustration.

Murshidabad developed as one of the most interesting new capitals in the eighteenth century. Reflecting Murshid Quli's blend of autonomy with loyalty, Murshidabad became a 'statement of Mughal affirmation within a Bengal context' (Asher and Talbot 2006: 250). The new capital had a Mughal-style palace and audience hall where Murshid Quli sat on a throne of polished black stone earlier used by Prince Shah Shuja. The city came to acquire a mint, wells and tanks and a Jami mosque, distinctive for its blend of Mughal and pre-Mughal regional traditions of Bengal. In the same pre-Mughal style, Murshid Quli arranged for his burial below the main entrance of the mosque, thereby asserting his regional rather than pan-Mughal affiliation and identity. Without formally severing his ties with Delhi, Murshid Quli functioned as an independent ruler and laid the foundation for a viable autonomous state. His successors followed the trend till the time Alivardi Khan, Sarfaraz Khan's army commander, ousted the *nazim* in 1740 and virtually cut off all ties with Delhi.

Alivardi Khan did not formally declare his independence from Delhi. But he acted on his own, making all important appointments without the sanction of the emperor and eventually stopping the remittance of revenue to Delhi. He continued the fiscal innovations set in motion by Murshid Quli, which made the Bengal revenue increase by 40 per cent between 1722 and 1756 (McLane 1993: 39).

Alivardi's authority, however, was challenged by the Marathas and Afghans. The severe damage to life and property caused by the constant raids of the Marathas, prompted Alivardi to stop sending the tribute to Delhi. The situation was complicated further by the takeover of Patna by rebel Afghan troops. Alivardi recovered Patna but was forced to come to a settlement with the Marathas in 1751. He ceded Orissa and agreed to pay *chauth*. By the time the settlement was reached, Bengal's overland trade had declined considerably. Sea-borne trade thrived, but only with increased investment and participation of European trading companies, particularly the English East India Company. When Alivardi died in 1756, his nominated successor, Siraj-ud-Daula, had to compete with two other contenders to the throne. The English East India Company took advantage of this flux to do away with Siraj-ud-Daula's rule in 1757, effecting thereby a radical change in the course of Bengal's history.

THE DECCAN AND THE NIZAM

Frustrated by the politics of the imperial court and the sway of the Indian Muslim faction led by the Sayyid brothers, Chin Qilich Khan, the leader of the Turani group, had moved away to the Deccan. We have seen that in 1724 he assumed the title of Nizamu'l Mulk Asaf Jah and set himself up as an independent ruler with his base in Hyderabad, which was the core region of the erstwhile Golconda Sultanate (Alam and Subrahmanyam 1998: 37). Asaf Jah tried to consolidate his hold over the six *suba*s in the region that were nominally subservient to the Mughals, although his real power was exercised in the coastal districts of Srikakulam, Masulipatnam and Nizampatnam, as well as the eastern regions of the *suba* of Hyderabad. In these areas, the offices of the *amin*, *shiqdar* and *faujdar* were concentrated in one person who was entrusted with collecting revenue. He was also permitted to maintain 'substantial crops of troops from the revenue that he collected' (ibid.: 38).

Until 1740, Asaf Jah notionally functioned as a Mughal administrator, and continued to coin money in the name of the emperor and mentioned him in the Friday prayers till his death in 1748. But in reality, Hyderabad emerged as a self-governing, significant political entity in the south, with a distinctive culture nurtured by a mixed elite composed of Hindus and Muslims. The Nizam led wars, signed treaties, granted *mansabs* and made other important appointments without consulting the Mughal emperor.

Asaf Jah and his successors, in a manner similar to the Marathas and the nawabs of Bengal, did not totally disrupt the existing power balance in the region. They brought in powerful local rulers and zamindars into a subsidiary relationship where they paid tribute and retained internal autonomy. Nonetheless, like in Bengal, new revenue farmers gained prominence as did traders, merchants and military aristocrats by virtue of their personal loyalty to the Nizam. *Jagirs* and *mansabs* became hereditary and people from lower ranks and status became a part of the new aristocracy.

The growing importance of Hyderabad in the mid-eighteenth century prompted the Marathas and the rulers of Mysore and the Carnatic to try to settle scores with it. This served to substantially reduce Hyderabad's power at a time when it was beset by wars of succession and other internal problems. The state's need to extend revenue collection had made it dependent on the efficiency and goodwill of those who held the combined posts of *amin*, *shiqdar* and *faujdar* (ibid.: 38). European trading companies, particularly the French, actively intervened in local politics after the 1740s and supported one rival faction against the other. This seriously affected revenue collection and substantially weakened the Asaf Jahi state. Hyderabad was representative of what was to happen to other states when European trading companies emulated the French example with greater success. Before we take up that story, let us turn to the region that had initially drawn European traders to India.

THE EDEN OF THE EAST: MALABAR

The Malabar coast, the northern part of present Kerala, had attracted merchants from across the globe since very early times. Its rich harvest of spices, particularly pepper—'black gold'—had created the 'myth of India' as Eden or 'God's garden'. Vasco da Gama's arrival there in 1498 transformed existing trade relations from an individual to an institutional level. The Portuguese, the Dutch, the French and the British all sought to gain trade monopolies and control over goods, production and the political set-up (Frenz 2003: 1). This opening up of a 'contact-zone' did much more than spike up the life of the region; it eventually led to the takeover of India by the English East India Company.

Malabar was important for its own well-integrated, socio-political and economic structure, held in place by the absence of any threat from outside for a long period. The Nayars, the largest group in the population, also ran the administrative units in the region. They worked in close association with the Nambutiri (Namboodiri) Brahmans, who held important functions in the temple, owned landed property and often leased them to the Nayars for farming. The Mappilas, Arab merchants who had settled in Malabar in the seventh century, had an important presence in the region although they did not hold political positions. The Nayars and those among their groups who headed local institutions and called themselves *samanta*s along with the Nambutiris, dominated local affairs.

Nayar families were distinguished by their matrilineal descent. In ruling families, the sons of the king's sister had claims on the throne in accordance with their seniority and not according to the branch they belonged to. The head of the family was the eldest male who held the position of the raja, while two other eldest members of two other branches helped him as vice-regents. Nayar family groups, the *taravatu*s, usually resided in a large house at the centre of their landed property. It was presided over by the eldest male member, while the landed property was owned jointly by all female members. The autonomy of *taravatu*s as self-sustaining 'house-and-land' economic units meant that ownership remained intact when the men went to war. When a *taravatu* split, the house-and-land-unit was divided equally among the newly created branches.

This pattern was replicated in the administrative units of the village and in the region. A group of *taravatu*s was run by an assembly of *taravatu* heads, the *tarakuttam*, which took all important local socio-economic and political decisions. The village elder, *desavali*, ran the affairs of the village, the *desam* and the *natuvali* that of the *natu*, composed of two or more villages. The *natuvali* collected the raja's share of profit in the harvest and commanded the *natu*'s army and was entitled to a portion of the raja's share. The *desavali* and *natuvali* held considerable power; yet they had to constantly seek the consent of their respective assemblies. The assembly of rajas, the *Malabarkuttam*, constituted the highest political unit. Given the fact that Kerala had not been ruled by a maharaja since the ninth century, the *Malabarkuttam* functioned under the chairmanship of one of the several rajas. Moreover, in the absence of external pressure for a long time, the *Malabarkuttam* met once every 12 years during the Mahamakham festival in Tirunavaya in southern Malabar.

In the latter half of the eighteenth century, Kottayam and its adjoining regions were under the command of Kerala Vamma Palassi Raja. In southern Malabar, Martand Varma had consolidated a large region centred on Travancore under his rule from the third decade of the eighteenth century. He had countered the growing importance of the Dutch and the English by imposing his own terms on the pepper trade and successfully rebutted an invasion from Mysore in 1766. Under his patronage, Travancore had developed as an important centre of art and scholarship. The scene changed drastically after Martand Varma's death at the close of the century. Earlier, tumult in Malabar had brought to an end the meeting of the rajas after 1743.

The turbulence was caused, to a large extent, by the entry of new contenders to the spice trade. The 'Age of Discovery' in Europe had brought the Portuguese to Malabar in 1498. Soon after their arrival, the Portuguese sought to monopolize trade in their sphere of influence by imposing the system of *cartaz*— licences for traders—from 1502. Although merchants tried to evade buying *cartazes* by trading through alternative land routes, the use of force and establishment of administrative units by the Portuguese to bolster their effort to gain monopoly of the spice trade gave them control over a significant portion of trade in the Indian Ocean (Frenz 2003: 68–69).

Portuguese predominance was rivalled by the Dutch and the British East India companies which began their activities in India at the onset of the seventeenth century. Their intent was also to command the Indian Ocean trade, but their trading system was structurally capitalist and was based on the notion of free trade. Their challenge led to a collapse of the institution of *cartaz* and a decline in Portuguese sway and economic prosperity. The change, of course, was not peaceful. The first major fight between the Dutch and the Portuguese occurred in the second half of the seventeenth century; the Dutch conquest of Kochi in 1663 ended the dominance of Portuguese merchants. The Dutch took control of Portuguese forts and trading routes and compelled local rulers to sign treaties that gave them economic advantages, even though the local rulers often managed to gain the upper hand in the constant tussles and negotiations.

Dutch authority, however, did not last long. Apart from the challenge from the British, the Dutch companies became less involved in trading and more in investing capital in the eighteenth century. Their trade stagnated and they gave up many of their bases in the Malabar Coast. The resultant success of the British was soon challenged by the French who captured Mayalí (renamed Mahé) in 1725. The efforts of the English and French companies to establish peace in the interest of keeping the price of pepper low was brought to a naught by British and French hostilities in Europe. The Seven Years' War in Europe occasioned battles in India in 1756; the French briefly occupied the British holding of Fort St. George in Madras and lost it again in 1759. Once more, the French turned to local politics and began establishing links with Haidar Ali of Mysore from 1766.

An incessant struggle for control over the Indian Ocean trade indicates the significance of the region. European traders were by no means the only participants; but they brought about far-reaching transformations by openly using force in order to gain control of the trade (Chaudhuri 1985; Subrahmanyam 1990). Mughal and local rulers had initially welcomed the presence of European companies. The bullion they brought bolstered the Indian economy by encouraging the twin trends of monetization and commercialization (Asher and Talbot 2006: 256). At the same time, it was precisely to keep a check on the amount of bullion they were importing from Europe that these companies tried to establish monopolies and demanded special privileges.

Dutch and British merchants outclassed their Indian counterparts in organization—they put their capital in joint-stock companies, which gave them long-term security over financial matters (Chaudhuri

1985: 87). They also tried to impose a system of national monopoly which, though partly implemented, gave the companies exclusive rights to trade in certain goods. Amsterdam and London not only became the leading trading cities of Europe in the eighteenth century; they were also the principal emporia of re-export (Frenz 2003: 71). Textiles and pepper got from India were sent to South East Asia to be exchanged for more spices or to the Middle East and Africa. Important regions of the Indian Ocean trade—India, China and South East Asia—were co-opted as dependent partners in the trade although their traders managed to retain internal autonomy.

MYSORE AND MEDDLING MERCHANTS

Maisur (present-day Mysore), located in the north of Malabar, emerged as a powerful state and a formidable opponent of the British in the wake of the Mughal decline in the eighteenth century. Technically a part of the Mughal *sarkar* of Sira, its ruler Chikka Deva Wodeyar had rendered allegiance to the Mughal Emperor Aurangzeb (1659–1707), when Mughal armies invaded southern India (Habib 1999: xix).

Haidar Ali, the architect of Mysore's power and prestige in the eighteenth century, was the son of Fat'h Muhammad, an employee of the Mughal *faujdar* (commandant) of Sira (ibid.: xix). Born in 1721 or 1722, Haidar entered the service of the Mysore state in the 1740s and became a cavalry officer around 1749. His involvement as a *faujdar* of Dindigul in the Second Carnatic War (1753)—in which the English and the French companies fought over control of southern India—made Haidar aware of the sophisticated European methods of fighting and brought him close to the French. Indeed, the realization had been brought home by the First Carnatic War (1747), when a small French force had overthrown the Mughal cavalry headed by Anwaruddin Khan, the *faujdar* of Arcot (later the Nawab of Carnatic). Mysore, nominally under Hyderabad, sided with the French in the three Carnatic wars in supporting the candidate backed by the French as a claimant to the viceroyalty of Hyderabad, left vacant by Nizamu'l Mulk Asaf Jah's death in 1748. From 1755–56, Haidar began seeking the help of Frenchmen to organize his artillery, arsenal and workshop (ibid.: xx).

Haidar's ascent after this was rapid. It was based both on his armed power and on his personal diplomatic skills. The army he raised combined mobile cavalry on the Mughal pattern with a well-disciplined musket-using infantry. The tangled situation in the south allowed him the opportunity to actively intervene in struggles in the region and gain prestige. Haidar Ali also participated in the internal struggle between the Mysore raja and his powerful minister and sided with the raja against his own patron, the minister. He had usurped power by 1760–61 but maintained the semblance of the raja's authority. At the same time, he sought to supersede the raja's authority by getting recognition as the *faujdar* of Sira from a claimant to the title of the Mughal Viceroy in the Deccan. He consolidated his position through the acquisition of Sira, conquests in the north and in Malabar, and came to rule over a territory much larger than what the raja had ever had under his control. Haidar took advantage of Maratha weakness following the Third Battle of Panipat (1761) and forced many local rajas—who had so long paid tribute to the Marathas—to pay tribute to him.

Haidar demonstrated his organizational skills in centralizing the administration, which combined existing institutions of the Mysore raj with elements drawn from Mughal rule. In an effort to augment the state's share in agrarian revenue, he imposed the land tax directly on peasants, taking the Mughal view that local hereditary potentates, like the *deshmukh*s and *palegar*s, were nothing more than zamindars with no inviolable rights to land (ibid.: xix). Francis Buchanan Hamilton, the famous British administrator sent by Governor-General Wellesley to Mysore in 1800–01 to gather information on the recently conquered territory, described how the harvest—the heap—was measured and divided equally between the government or renter, and the farmer, because Haidar had done away with intermediaries such as *deshmukh*s and zamindars, and commented that most of Haidar's operations in finance seemed 'judicious and reasonable'. Indeed, it was because of his 'justice, wisdom and moderation' that his memory 'is greatly respected by natives of all descriptions' (Buchanan Hamilton 1807, 1: 300). This recognition of the judiciousness of Haidar's (and Tipu's) measures would later find reflection in the introduction of the Ryotwari (Raiyatwari) Settlement of revenue in the region.

In a related move to centralize fiscal revenue, Haidar resumed *jagirs* and limited the *jagirdar's* responsibility of maintaining troops, turning instead to the raising of a central army to be paid directly by the state. This transformed the nature of the army; while earlier it was constituted of contingents that varied in size depending on the resources of an individual commander, it now came to be composed of *risalas*—divisions of a fixed number of soldiers with definite allotment of guns and transport—similar to European armies (Habib 1999: xxii). Haidar also looked to the Europeans for support in strengthening this army, and the French offered it willingly. An astute politician, Haidar realized that the Europeans drew their strength from the navy, and paid attention to the establishment of one (Kumar 1999: 171). This prompted him to conquer Malabar to gain control over the ship-building yards of the region. Portuguese reports suggest that by 1765, the Mysore navy possessed 30 vessels of war and a large number of transport ships commanded by an Englishman and some European officers (ibid.: 172).

Haidar invaded Malabar in the spring of 1766. He succeeded in capturing a part of Malabar, which he left in the charge of his newly appointed Governor, Ali Raja of Kannur, and moved eastwards. The Nayars of Kottayam, however, soon challenged his authority. They were joined by other princes who refused to recognize Mysore's hegemony over Malabar. Haidar crushed the rebellion ruthlessly and enacted edicts, which sought to curb the power and prestige of the Nayars. The rulers of Malabar appealed to the British in Talasseri for help and signed a treaty with them. Haidar had to relent. The Marathas in the north and the Nizam of Hyderabad in the northeast were posing threats to his advance; he did not want to encounter another enemy at the same time. He left the pepper harvest of Malabar to the British post in Talasseri. This did not put an end to hostilities. In March 1769, the Nayars and the British fought against Haidar Ali under British command but were unsuccessful. Haidar dictated the terms of a peace treaty in Madras that ended the First Anglo–Mysore war.

The second war erupted in 1778 when Haidar decided to use Anglo–French hostilities to his own advantage. The English and the French were at loggerheads in India over the issue of French recognition of the American War of Independence. Haidar, who had been in close alliance with the French for over a decade, sided with them against the British. In 1775, Haidar had entered into communication with the French at Pondicherry with a proposal of a joint alliance against the British, which had been readily accepted (Hasan 1999: 35). The rajas of Malabar, on the other hand, had remained loyal to the British.

As a result, when the French capitulated in 1779, the rajas were given back some lands that Haidar had captured from them earlier. Haidar, however, managed to regain his hold over southern Malabar in 1780. He entered into negotiations with the rulers that resulted in another short-term agreement. The British continued to fight Mysore. Haidar got no help from the French beyond a supply of military stores when he attacked the Carnatic in July 1780 (ibid.: 35). Haidar died in the middle of it in 1782, forcing his son Tipu to rush back to Mysore from Malabar. The Second Anglo–Mysore War finally ended in 1784 with a peace settlement that favoured Tipu Sultan. The rajas of Malabar, despite their continued loyalty to the British, came under Tipu's suzerainty. The raja of Travancore had to accept a British resident in his court by 1800.

The intersecting struggles over trade and political power between Indian rulers and European merchants made possible the gradual rise of the English East India Company as a significant political force in India. We now turn to this.

BEGINNINGS OF A NEW EMPIRE

On the last day of 1600, a charter of the British monarch permitted the foundation of the English East India Company, a joint-stock company of London merchants, to carry on trade in the East. As a rival to the Dutch Company, the English East India Company was allowed special privileges. It was given monopoly over all trade between England and Asia and permission to export bullion from England to finance this trade.

Formal trading began in 1613, when a *farman* of Emperor Jahangir allowed the Company to set up factories in India. By then, the English East India Company had become well informed about the essential facts related to the 'structure of commerce in the Indian Ocean and India's place in the interlocking network' (Chaudhuri 1982: 391). This knowledge prompted the governing body of the Company to embark on a policy of expansion, reflected not only in the rapid expansion of factories in inland areas of trade but also in the appointment of Sir Thomas Roe as the official ambassador of James I to the Mughal court. Relations with the Mughals were strengthened when Roe went as a resident British envoy to Jahangir's court in 1617. The first English factory was established in the western port of Surat after English merchants scored a victory over the Portuguese. At home, the Company was under the supervision of its own Court of Directors and the regulating hand of the British Parliament, while its power and prestige in India developed in concordance with a healthy relationship of reciprocity with the British Crown. The Company's celebration of the restoration of Stuart monarchy in 1660 and its offer of loan to the British Crown was favoured by the granting of charters with additional privileges by the king.

In 1668, Charles II handed over the island settlement of Bombay, received as dowry from the Portuguese crown for his marriage to Catherine of Braganza, to the East India Company for a minimal rent of 10 pounds a year. Bombay, which enjoyed greater autonomy than Surat and was safe from Maratha attacks, replaced Surat as the headquarters of the western presidency in 1678. Earlier, in 1640, the Company had purchased Madras on the Coromandel Coast from a local ruler for a small fee. Madras would soon be the headquarters of the southern presidency. Most of the textiles sent from India to Europe in the seventeenth century was produced in the south-eastern coast of Coromandel, particularly in its southern half. Here, competition for trade among several small kingdoms made it easy for the Company to obtain greater concessions, such as the complete remission of import and export duties in Madras from the Nawab of Arcot (Asher and Talbot 2006: 259).

Chronology of The East India Company

Period	Events
1600	East India Company established in London
1709	United East India Company emerges as union of the Old and New Companies
1757	Battle of Plassey
1765	Mughal emperor grants *Diwani* of Bengal, right to collect land revenue, to East India Company
1773	Warren Hastings appointed as first Governor of Bengal
1784	British Government Board of Control established in London
1813	End of East India Company's monopoly rights over trade with India
1833	End of East India Company's monopoly rights over trade with China
1857	Indian uprisings
1858	East India Company and Board of Control replaced by India Office and Council of India
1937	Separation of Burma from India. Establishment of Burma Office
1947	Partition of India and Pakistan. Independence granted to both countries. Abolition of India Office.
1948	Independence of Burma and abolition of Burma Office

Madras and the Coromandel trade proved vital to the rise of the English East India Company in the late seventeenth century when it came to match the strength of the Dutch Verenigde Oost–Indische Compagnie (VOC). A 'calico craze' swept England, making Indian textiles hugely fashionable and inducing a ten-fold increase in the Company's purchase and export of cotton piece-goods from India between the 1660s and the 1680s (Chaudhuri 1978). Textiles also overshadowed the spice trade, which had initially drawn Europeans to India. By the end of the century, the Company's Coromandel trade was 'well founded in two substantial Forts (St. George and St. David) and a number of residencies in important ports of outlet from Vizagapatnam in the north to Cuddalore in the south' (Arasaratnam 1979: 19). Investment and enterprise, accompanied by diplomacy and force, turned the Company's settlements into 'nodal-points' of Indo–British exchange and interaction (ibid.). Besides being the most important textile supplier to Europe, Madras was also an important centre of trade with South East Asia. East India Company's employees increasingly participated in this trade in their individual capacity as private traders, often amassing huge fortunes.

Re-export of Indian textiles to other markets in Europe and Asia was a vital component of East

India Company's trade. It allowed the Company to counter the argument of those who felt that large-scale increase of Indian textiles threatened the manufacturers of woollen products in England. Apart from being highly profitable, re-export encouraged shipping and ship-building, contributing thereby to England's naval strength and its lordship of all oceans (Bagchi 2010: xxiv). The Company's monopoly over East India trade was also deemed desirable—it was the only way the Company could maintain expensive factories and troops and ships to defend itself against competitors. Duties, however, were imposed on the import of Indian textiles to England from the 1660s, and in 1700 all import of Indian textiles, 'except for the purpose of re-export was banned' (ibid.). Re-export of Indian textiles constituted about 40 per cent of corresponding imports into England because of its demand in European markets.

The success of the Company's servants as private traders on the Madras coast was in contrast to the decline of Hindu ship-owners in central and southern Coromandel and trade with the Malayan archipelago, and the decay of the important port of Masulipatnam (Arasaratnam 1998: 266). Trade continued with the mainland ports of South East Asia from Madras, Palekat and other ports further south, and this changed the earlier orientation of export trade toward Western Asia, the Red Sea and the Persian Gulf, trade commanded by the indigenous merchant class (Dasgupta 1998: 46). This new orientation obliged Hindu overseas traders and ship-owners to enter into partnership with the European merchants, particularly servants of the English East India Company, the dominant European trading power in the eighteenth century.

The Company 'as a state' was uncommon in maritime Asia (ibid.: 276). Its combined use of privileges, monopoly and conquest was totally against custom; but the Company justified its use of 'regulation and restriction' to turn the terms of trade in its favour on grounds that it was necessary to cover the cost of conquest and security. As in the case of VOC, conquest was thought to be an imperative for the security of the goods and capital accumulated in trade, and conquest in turn spurred the need for further generation of revenue, making the twin processes fuel one another. And so it happened that by the late 1780s in Madras, the 'Company's military servants outnumbered their civil colleagues by four to one' (Furber 1970: 199).

IN REVIEW: THE COMPANY AS STATE?

It is in order here to reflect briefly on the nature of the Company 'state', a theme we will discuss in greater detail in the following chapter. Scholars who worked on the seventeenth and eighteenth century trade and the Indian Ocean (Chaudhuri; Dasgupta; Furber; Prakash; Arasaratnam; Pearson, for instance), focused primarily on the intricate commercial networks and trading patterns and operations, implying thereby that the period prior to the East India Company's conquest of Bengal in the mid-eighteenth century was dominated by trade, where issues of sovereignty and authority were largely absent. Philip J. Stern's *The Company State: Corporate Sovereignty 'and the' Early Foundations 'of the' British Empire 'in' India*, recently countered this view by shifting the focus from trade to territory. Locating the English East India Company within a fluid world of early-modern political formations where the 'state' had not yet become normalized, Stern argues that the Company, as a corporation, was a 'government over its own employees and corporators' from the beginning (Stern 2011: 3). In addition to claiming jurisdiction over English trade and traffic and, by extension, over English goods, ships and subjects in Asia, the Company also became a 'colonial proprietor' by the beginning of the seventeenth century, ruling over a small yet growing network of plantations in Asia and the South Atlantic and their variegated, multi-racial populations (ibid.). The Company, moreover, experimented with British municipal forms within its settlements, struck coins, indulged in pomp and ceremony and dealt with rebellions as well as with challenges to its authority, Indian and European. Colonial governors and councils of the Company as proprietors, therefore, were like 'manorial lords, who could alienate land, administer justice, exact fines, and control populations within the bounds of their estates' (ibid.: 24). Stern's book examines the Company as 'a body politic on its own terms', and offers a vision of an early-modern 'empire' constituted by 'a variety of competing and overlapping political and constitutional forms'. Such forms allied with and rivalled the national state and its claims to coherent and central power (ibid.: 6).

The fact that use of force by European companies was distinct from trading practices in India has been commented upon by all scholars, even though there was 'considerable disagreement' in 'Anglo–Indian historiography' on 'the role of force and fortifications' (Watson 1998: 26). K. N. Chaudhuri's important work (1978) asserted that force was an implicit part of European trade with Asia, and was 'profitable' when the sale of protection became an economic transaction and when revenues through customs and taxes could be extracted from territorial bases in the Company's control (Chaudhuri 1978: 111).

Free use of *sipahi*s (sepoys) and peons, who helped enforce the English East India Company's writ in the weaving districts, enabled the Company to deal first with merchants and later directly with weavers in the Madras region. 'Laboreres and labor market', argues Prasannan Parthasarathi, were not seen as 'legitimate sites for the exercise of the state's coercive power' in eighteenth-century India. The Nawab of Arcot, in response to the Company's request that he round up and force the weavers who had fled to his territories during the Cuddalore weavers' protest of 1778 to return to the Company's settlement, stated clearly in a letter to the Company that seizing the weavers and taking them by force from his country was 'contrary to custom' and had never been done before (cited in Parthasarathi 2001: 126).

In addition to the use of force, the Company substituted cash advances made by the nawab's *amil*s to the weavers by advances in raw material and kept a certain number of looms for its exclusive use. If this freed a weaver from the taxes and imposts imposed by the nawab's government, and supply of raw material improved the quality of his products, it made him, for all practical purposes, a wage labourer of the Company, with no power to decide on the price of his finished product. Company officials fixed the price on the basis of the cost of the raw material advanced and the labour invested in manufacture, a strict watch over which was kept by the Company's Indian servants in the weaving districts (Arasaratnam 1998: 277). The derogatory term 'coolie', used by the English to designate weavers who had been independent craftsmen, is representative of their change in status.

The huge financial crisis of the Company, the near bankruptcy of the Nawab of Arcot on account of the wars with Haidar Ali and Tipu Sultan and the revival of the French threat in the 1770s and 1780s, forced the Company to open up weaving villages under its command to competitive investments. This brought the Dutch, French and the Danes back into the game and occasioned a revival of the weaving industry and general commerce. In addition to the continued demand for Indian textiles in European markets, the revival also related to developments in Asian trade from the 1760s. A leap in demand for

Chinese tea in Europe occasioned a revival of the export of Coromandel textiles to South East Asia, the yields of which were used to purchase goods to be sold in China. English free merchants along with a few Armenian, Portuguese and Dutch free burghers were the chief players in this, but they faced healthy competition from Chulia (Tamil) Muslims. Virtually the only important Indian ship-owners in the coast, the Chulias had capital, middlemen contacts in weaving villages and excellent connections with the Islamic states of the Malay Peninsula and Sumatra at their disposal. The Europeans were indulgent to this challenge, since Coromandel and South East Asian trade constituted only a small part of their much wider trading cycle. Besides, the help of Chulia Muslims came in handy in establishing new trading posts such as the one in Penang in 1786 (ibid.: 279).

The third coastal region where textiles could be obtained was Bengal, where the Portuguese held sway in the early-seventeenth century. The Mughals, after getting proper hold over Bengal, drove away the Portuguese from the important port of Hughli in 1632 and invited other Europeans there. Hughli became a thriving Dutch settlement in the 1660s, with the English chafing under Mughal restrictions and Dutch competition. In order to press for better trading privileges from the watchful Mughal state, the English East India Company declared a virtual war on it in the 1680s, blockading Surat and seizing Indian ships off the west coast. The Mughals retaliated by attacking Bombay and forcing the English to flee from Hughli. In the Treaty of 1690, the Company had to pay heavy indemnity and stop issuing silver coins in the name of British monarchs in Bombay, which they had done as a mark of defiance. Their turn towards Calcutta was a direct result of their flight from Hughli.

Calcutta, surrounded by marshes and swamps, was not the healthiest place to live; yet its location closer to the Bay of Bengal than Hughli made it a convenient settlement. The East India Company soon became a landlord of the villages around Calcutta and built the fortified structure of Fort William. By 1700, the Company had established itself in Bombay, Madras and Calcutta, the chief Presidency towns and centres of British power in the colonial era.

Indeed, it was in Bengal that the Company made its 'most startling conquests' (Travers 2007: 3). The ground was provided by the young and inexperienced Nawab Siraj-ud-Daula in 1756. Angered by the arrogant behaviour of British traders in Calcutta, Siraj swept into the city and forced the British to flee. But soon, British naval and infantry forces, assembled in Madras to fight the French, were quickly diverted to Bengal. This army, under the command of Robert Clive, recaptured Calcutta. The enterprising Clive also struck deals with the big traders, merchants and political players of the Bengal government; this support led to the defeat of Siraj-ud-Daula's army against that of the Company in the Battle of Plassey in 1757. Clive appointed a new nawab securing from him the grant of tax revenues of new territories around Calcutta.

Bengal's takeover by the East India Company brought to an end the 'favourable configuration of circumstances, by which foreign trade served essentially as an instrument of growth in the economy' (Prakash 1998: 247–48). The structure of production retained its vitality and market responsiveness, but silver imports by European companies, particularly the British, stopped almost completely once the East India Company got the right to collect the revenue of Bengal in 1765. This came in the wake of the Company's victory over the joint armies of the Mughal emperor and the nawabs of Awadh and Bengal in the Battle of Buxar in 1764. The Company's exports from Bengal became 'unrequited', contributing to a drain of the region's resources. Further, it ended the long 'bullion for goods' tradition of Indo–European trade and radically altered relations between the Company, merchants, suppliers, artisans and peasants, processes we will examine in greater detail in the following chapter. Such dealings were no longer governed by market forces of demand and supply, but by the unequal terms imposed by the Company, which effectively robbed these groups of their legitimate share in the growing trade (ibid.: 249).

AN INDEPENDENT CENTURY?

It is time now to return to the story of Lucknow, the capital set up by Nawab Asaf-ud-Daula after his father's death in 1775. But before that, let us briefly pull together the different strands of the tale narrated so far in order to link them to the debates around the eighteenth century—of continuity and change, of decay and decline, and the almost 'unconscious' entry of the English East India Company into the power vacuum left by Mughal decline (Dodwell 1929).

The discussion so far demonstrates that the century was one of effervescence, animated by a blend of opposites—Mughal fragmentation and regional resurgence, and the rise of the English East India Company. The Mughal state, we have noted, never ruled over all of India and its degree of dominance varied from region to region. Hence, its collapse hit the economy and politics of different regions distinctly. The zones most adversely affected were the 'hubs of the diffuse, but closely intermeshed, imperial economy'—the Agra–Delhi corridor as well as the route between Agra and Surat, made unsafe by Jat insurrection, and Sikh and Maratha assertion (Asher and Talbot 2006: 276). Punjab and Gujarat also faced the brunt of the decline of trade with Central Asia and the Middle East. Parts of Rajasthan, on the other hand, prospered under the measures adopted by Sawai Jai Singh of Jaipur (1700–1743), as did the Deccan under the Peshwas. Similarly, Malabar, Mysore, Coromandel and Bengal developed their own trajectories, albeit through constant conflicts with other Indian states, ups and downs in trade and negotiations with European trading companies as well as Hindu and Jain merchants and bankers. Processes that contributed to the blurring of politics and economy enabled the emergence of new elite groups, laid the foundations of a new social order and stimulated cultural efflorescence of varying degrees. It was the same amalgamation of politics, economy and power that gave the East India Company the opportunity to establish its hold over India.

The eighteenth century, therefore, can hardly be characterized by decay. Nor can it be defined either by total rupture or by unbroken continuity. Undoubtedly, several features of the earlier polity and economy continued, including in the new regional kingdoms influenced by Mughal ideas and Mughal imaginings (Bengal, for instance), and there was a transformation, rather than decline of the Mughal elite through 'the ascent of inferior social groups to overt political power' (Bayly 1988: 9). And these 'local power-holders' persisted till the early nineteenth century as did the clan landholding structures in the north and segmentary state structures in the south (Cohn [1960] 1987; Stein 1985; Yang 1989).

At the same time, if Mughal ideas and systems continued, they were given new meaning and significance by the new political players. Moreover, the presence and power of the Europeans acquired such importance that their armies and military techniques became models for several rulers. If this encouraged their active participation in local politics, it gave them degrees of power they had not enjoyed before. The East India Company did not 'absent-mindedly' or reluctantly get sucked into the vacuum left by the Mughal state, it got involved with a clear sense of acquiring and defining 'sovereignty' as recent works (Stern 2011) have indicated. In a fluid situation where the creation of a new order of successor states was uneven and varied widely from region to region, the European companies had 'both incentives and opportunities for intervention' (Marshall 2005: 121). It is possible that there was a difference of purpose between the early and later governor-generals as we shall see in the following chapter (Marshall 1987); but the close ties between the Company and the British Crown and between Britain's commercial expansion and its empire are too obvious to be ignored.

It is useful, perhaps, to take note of Sanjay Subrahmanyam (1997, 2001) and other scholars' characterization of the period between the fifteenth and eighteenth centuries in India as 'early modern' in order to break out of the constraining dichotomy of continuity and change, and of tired discussions of how British rule transformed 'traditional' India into a modern one. In tune with historians such as Fernand Braudel, who characterize the history of the world between 1500 and 1800 as 'early modern' on grounds that human societies shared in and were affected by worldwide processes of change 'unprecedented in their character and intensity' (Braudel 1981–84), Subrahmanyam urges us to go beyond the constraints of time and scale. Arguing in favour of 'connected histories' of South Asia and the world, he defines the 'middle of the fourteenth to the middle of the eighteenth, with greater focus on the period after 1450' as 'early modern' (Subrahmanyam 1997: 736).

If a sense of 'rupture', a break, characterizes the idea of being modern, the 'early modern' period demonstrates such a break in the 'new sense of the limits of the inhabited world' created by extensive travel and of 'discovery' that produced 'radical geographical redefinition' (Subrahmanyam 2001: 262). This included European voyages of exploration as well as cultures of travel by overland routes and the development of travel literature. The early modern period also witnessed intensive, long-term structural conflict in relations between urban societies and those based on settled agriculture and the ones of nomadic groups; a conflict that raises important questions about agricultural innovation, the expansion of agricultural frontiers, patterns of settlement, demography and urbanization (ibid.). Once again, it was not just a conflict between modern, expanding Europe and non-European societies, but universal conflicts in modes of lifestyles and use of resources, which in turn were connected with global trade flows (ibid.: 162–63).

In addition, all these shifts were accompanied by 'complex changes in political theology' resulting in the sixteenth-century construct of the 'Universal Empire'. Constructs of Universal Empire were deployed in Central and West Asia, Iran, north India and China, and were present in pre-Columbian America and south and central Africa (ibid.: 263). The question that needs to be addressed, therefore, is that of the co-existence of such 'seemingly archaic forms of political articulation' with emerging modernity represented by the technological advance of the West. Finally, the early modern prompts one to reflect on why notions of humanism and universalism that emerge in distinct vocabularies do not bring about a unified world but end up intensifying hierarchy, domination and separation (ibid.: 264–65). Such questions and reflections will offer insights into the idea of the 'modern' that have been neglected so far.

John F. Richards also defines the sixteenth to the eighteenth centuries as 'early modern' since they encapsulate 'the reality of rapid, massive change in the way humans organized themselves and interacted with other human beings and with the natural world'(1997: 197). The early modern, distinct both from the 'Middle Ages that preceded it and from modern nineteenth and twentieth centuries', witnessed the rise of 'a true world economy' based on long-distance commerce, the growth of large, stable states and of population, the intensification of land use and the diffusion of new technologies (ibid.: 199–204). South Asia was marked by all these processes in some form or the other. Hence, it is important, almost imperative, to define South Asia between the fifteenth and eighteenth centuries as 'early modern' and not call it 'Mughal India', 'late medieval India' or 'late pre-colonial India' terms that view India's history as 'exotic' and detached from the rest of the world. The much needed contextualization, asserts Richards, would yield better understandings of the more specific unfolding of Indian history in the three centuries (ibid.: 198).

I have discussed the 'early modern' at length, even though it does not apply just to the eighteenth century, because it enables us to reflect differently both on the eighteenth century and on the idea of the 'modern'. If the eighteenth century forms part of a long period that is 'early modern', does it make sense then to study it separately as an 'independent' century? The study of it as an independent century, as mentioned at the beginning of this chapter, relates to a different, earlier debate that characterized the eighteenth century as one of decline. While new works have revised the picture of decay, Subrahmanyam's formulation of the 'early modern' and his plea to move away from an exaggerated focus on the 'modern' colonial period, has been taken over and applied to the eighteenth century in a manner that substantiates the 'continuity' thesis.

The most important contribution of the debate on the eighteenth century 'to the realm of colonial studies', asserts Seema Alavi, is that it provides a valuable corrective to the reified notions of 'tradition' and 'modernity' (2002: 39). By showing that colonial power was mediated through a continuous process of negotiations with pre-colonial structures and notions of governance, authority and normative codes—albeit through a process fraught with tension—eighteenth-century studies have helped to 'collapse' the essentialized categories of 'colonial'/modern and 'indigenous'/traditional (ibid.: 40).

Apart from the fact that such 'reified notions' have been questioned in 'the realm of colonial studies' (Ray 1975: 3 is an early example), the argument that the 'early modern' eighteenth century was a period of vigorous commercial and economic activity and political dynamism, often lends support to the view that Indian colonial rule did not occasion a serious rupture. Rather, Indian conditions are stated to have moulded and tempered colonial transformation, and many policies of the colonial state drew upon the earlier ones (Bayly 1983; Stein 1985, for instance). Prasannan Parthasarathi's work on south India refutes that there was economic continuity between the pre-colonial and colonial periods but affirms that colonialism had indigenous roots (2001: 6). The characterization of the eighteenth century as 'early modern' in this qualified sense does not, therefore, help us supersede the terms of the early debate on the nature of the eighteenth century. We are still stuck with the problem of whether it was distinguished by 'revolution' or 'evolution' (Marshall 2003). Arguably, the eighteenth century was a period of major transformation, and it would perhaps be useful to pay attention to works that have indicated that it was only in the eighteenth century that the 'full impact' of European trade was felt on the domestic economy

(Chaudhuri 1982; Dasgupta 1979) or that changing conditions of the eighteenth century were, to a large extent, the result of the 'increasingly belligerent role' played by Europeans in parts of the continent (Marshall 2005: 121).

Returning to the spirit of Subrahmanyam's argument, one could apply 'early modern' to underscore the most fascinating aspect of the eighteenth century, namely, its unlikely blends and the co-existence of contradictions. Such jumbles permitted the persistence of Mughal systems in regions that were asserting their autonomy and the working out of Anglo–French rivalry in battles fought amongst competing Indian rulers. Several decades ago, Bernard Cohn had urged us to move beyond the 'sordid record' of anarchy, confusion, selfishness and treachery and see how 'the political system of the period actually worked'—whether there were enduring structures of political relationships, whether parts of the social system involved were connected and whether there were common principles that guided the organization and utilization of power and authority in the society of the time (1962: 312). With due regard for the warning, one also needs to track the muddles of the time—muddles that produced charming cross-country and cross-community combinations. Indian Hindu and Muslim merchants and bankers allied with European traders, while European power-brokers of different countries made fortunes in the service of the East India Company and Indian princes and adopted the lifestyle of Indian Muslim rulers. This was a century in which complex changes in regional societies and the rise of the Company helped the crystallization of a 'caste order' (Bayly 1999: 4, 26). Lucknow, the emblematic capital of the eighteenth century, offers brilliant illustrations of cross-country and community combinations.

LUCKNOW, ONCE MORE

The young prince, Asaf-ud-Daula, was a laughing stock as a ruler. He buckled under the Company's pressure soon after becoming nawab and signed a 'devastating' treaty that forced him to cede territory and with it almost half of his revenue, for the upkeep of the Company's troops. This alienated his powerful mother and most of Awadh's nobility, already estranged by his move to Lucknow from Faizabad. The trends for Asaf's 22-year rule were set in the first few months. For the next two decades, Awadh would be split by strife between his mother's faction at Faizabad and the Lucknow court, and 'paralyzed by Company pressure on its borders, treasuries, and politics' (Jasanoff 2005: 53). This, however, did not deter Asaf from fulfilling his dream of turning Lucknow into the cultural capital of India.

Asaf's model was the great Emperor Akbar who had abandoned Delhi for Agra and Fatehpur Sikri, a place where Akbar had brought together the finest talents in arts, sciences, philosophy and letters. In the wake of Asaf's astounding programme of construction, patronage and court entertainment, Lucknow became dotted with monumental buildings such as the Bara Imambara, celebrated Shiite religious scholarship and festivals, encouraged the arts and letters of Mughal India, and 'welcomed a fat payroll of Europeans'—men who influenced everything from the food on the nawab's table to the design of his many palaces (ibid.: 55). The nawab earned for himself fame as a leading patron of Asian and European art, and for generosity, and notoriety for extravagance. Lucknow became a melting pot that defied categorization.

Lucknow was a city that beckoned. And so it was that Antoine Polier, the Swiss-born architect of Fort William (Calcutta), affected by the Company's newly imposed stringent measures against promoting non-English Europeans, crossed the western border of Company-controlled Bengal and entered Awadh in the early 1770s. Polier made Lucknow his home for 15 years, amassed a fortune and gathered a circle of distinguished Indian and European friends. 'Polier was one of many who discovered in Lucknow the means and chance to collect and cross borders' (ibid.: 47).

Polier lived richly and well. He built a huge mansion which he named Polierganj, gathered a spectacular collection of manuscripts and paintings of Hindu gods of whose history he 'informed himself' and spent his time in the company of European expatriates in the style of other Orientalists. At the same time, he married two Indian Muslim women, lived his life in Lucknow (spoke Persian), lounged at home in Mughal robes tending his hookah and enjoying the performance of Indian dancers and musicians. Emperor Shah Alam gave him a jagir near Aligarh and the name of *Arsalan-i-Jang* (Lion of Battle).

Polier's best friend was Claude Martin, a French-born officer who thought of himself as British, but did not get entry into the Company hierarchy. Martin arrived in Lucknow in 1776 to take up the post of superintendent of the nawab's arsenal. By dint of his 'natural talent for business, and relentless energy in exercising it' (ibid.: 73), he accumulated a phenomenal fortune during his 25-year stay in Lucknow.

By 1800, Martin was perhaps the richest European in India. His fortune was invested in land, houses and political influence, but like his friend Polier, he was also a passionate collector, not just of manuscripts, but of objects of all kinds. Through his Lucknow friends who had returned to Europe and through letters and constant traffic of objects across the seas, Martin joined an elite brotherhood of collectors from his base in Lucknow. Unlike his friend Polier, who went the way of a Mughal noble, Martin modelled himself on an English nobleman, but made India his home.

Asaf-ud-Daula matched Martin's passion for collection. He stuffed his armoury with elaborate weapons, packed his jewel house with dazzling stones and stacked his library with hordes of miniature paintings and illuminated manuscripts of Mughal times. Perhaps the nawab was in competition with Claude Martin, 'a king of his own minting' (ibid.: 79), or perhaps his display was meant to compensate for his lack of power. Together, Asaf-ud-Daula and Claude Martin represented what was corrupt and what was good about Lucknow. Lucknow's eccentric exterior guarded an amazing cosmopolitanism. Polier, Asaf and Martin, all displaced persons who remade themselves in an extravagant style, were not the typical representatives of their own culture. They were the best exemplars of a world where an Indian environment was infused with European influences and Europeans soaked up Indian ones; a time when empire and nation were being formed in the 'crucible of a global history that could not yet conceal its contradiction' (Dirks 2006: 336).

This was to change by the end of the century when Claude Martin breathed his last. His death in 1800 fell at a threshold. It marked the end of an era in which permeable socio-cultural and political boundaries between British, Europeans and Indians would give way to more clearly defined borders that would make it impossible for the likes of Polier and Martin to remain suspended in between. Martin's legacy lingers in the three secondary schools he endowed in his will—the La Martinières of Lucknow, Calcutta, and Lyon. Students of La Martinière in Lucknow and Calcutta were taught English and Persian and instructed by *mollah*s and Catholic priests and they raised a glass to Martin's memory on his death anniversary. The schools persist as reminders that all fusions did not fade in the nineteenth century, although the world of mixed inheritances was over.

REFERENCES

Alam, Muzaffar. 1986. *The Crisis of Empire in Mughal North: Awadh and Panjab, 1707–1748*. New Delhi: Oxford University Press.

Alam, Muzaffar and Sanjay Subrahmanyam, eds. 1998. Introduction to *The Mughal State 1526–1750*, 1–72. New Delhi: Oxford University Press.

Alavi, Seema, ed. 2002. Introduction to *The Eighteenth Century in India*, 1–56. New Delhi: Oxford University Press.

Ali, M. Athar. 1975. 'The Passing of Empire: The Mughal Case'. *Modern Asian Studies* 9 (13): 385–96.

———. 1978–79. 'The Eighteenth Century: An Interpretation'. *Indian Historical Review* 5 (1–2): 175–86.

———. 1986–87. 'Recent Theories of Eighteenth Century India'. *Indian Historical Review* 13 (1–2): 102–08.

———. 1993. 'The Mughal Polity: A Critique of Revisionist Approaches'. *Modern Asian Studies* 27 (4): 699–710.

Arasaratnam, S. 1979. 'Trade and Political Dominion in South India, 1750–1790: Changing British–Indian Relationships'. *Modern Asian Studies* 13 (1): 19–40.

———. 1998. 'Merchants and Commerce in Coromandel: Trends and Tendencies in the Eighteenth Century'. In *On the Eighteenth Century as a Category of Indian History: Van Leur in Retrospect*, edited by Leonard Blussé and Femme Gaastra, 261–88. Aldershot: Ashgate Publishing Ltd.

Asher, Catherine B. and Cynthia Talbot. 2006. *India Before Europe*. Cambridge: Cambridge University Press.

Ashraf, K. M. 1960. 'Presidential Address to the Medieval History Section'. *Proceedings of the Indian History Congress*, 143–52. Aligarh.

Bagchi, Amiya K. 2010. 'Introduction; Colonial Rule as Structural Adjustment: Expropriation, Agency, and Survival'. In *Colonialism and Indian Economy*, edited by Amiya K. Bagchi, xv–liii. New Delhi: Oxford University Press.

Barnett, Richard. 1980. *North India Between Empires: Awadh, the Mughals, and the British, 1720–1801*. Berkeley and Los Angeles: University of California Press.

Bayly, C. A. 1983. *Rulers, Townsmen and Bazaars: North Indian Society in the Age of British Expansion*. Cambridge: Cambridge University Press; Indian edition, Delhi 1992.

———. 1988. *Indian Society and the Making of the British Empire*. Cambridge: Cambridge University Press.

———. 1998. 'Van Leur and the Eighteenth Century'. In *On the Eighteenth Century as a Category of Indian History: Van Leur in Retrospect*, edited by Leonard Blussé and Femme Gaastra, 289–302. Aldershot: Ashgate Publishing Ltd.

Bayly, Susan. 1999. *Caste, Society and Politics in India: From the Beginning of the Eighteenth Century to the Modern Age*. Cambridge: Cambridge University Press.

Braudel, Fernand. 1981–1984. *Civilization and Capitalism, 15th–18th Century*. 3 vols. New York: Harper and Row.

Buchanan Hamilton, Francis. 1807. 'A Journey from Madras through the Countries of Mysore, Canara and Malabar. Part I'. In *Resistance and Modernization under Haidar Ali and Tipu Sultan*, edited by I. Habib, 165–68. New Delhi: Tulika.

Calkins, Philip B. 1970. 'The Formation of a Regionally-Oriented Ruling Group in Bengal, 1700–1740'. *The Journal of Asian Studies* 29 (4): 799–806.

Chandra, Satish. 1959. *Parties and Politics at the Mughal Court, 1707–1740*. Aligarh: Aligarh Muslim University.

———. 1982. 'Review of the Crisis of the Jagirdari System'. In *Medieval India: Society, the Jagirdari Crisis, and the Village*, edited by Satish Chandra, 61–75. New Delhi: Oxford University Press.

Chaudhuri, B. B. 2008. *Peasant History of Late Pre-colonial and Colonial India*. In *History of Science, Philosophy and Culture in Indian Civilization*, edited by D. P. Chattopadhyaya. Vol. 8, 2. New Delhi: Pearson Longman.

Chaudhuri, K. N. 1978. *The Trading World of Asia and the English East India Company, 1660–1760*. Cambridge: Cambridge University Press.

———. 1982. 'European Trade with India'. In *The Cambridge Economic History of India*, Vol. 1, edited by Tapan Raychaudhuri and Irfan Habib, 382–407. Cambridge: Cambridge University Press.

———. 1985. *Trade and Civilisation in the Indian Ocean: An Economic History from the Rise of Islam to 1750*. Cambridge: Cambridge University Press.

Chaudhury, Sushil. 1995. *From Prosperity to Decline: Eighteenth Century Bengal*. Delhi: Manohar.

Cohn, Bernard S. 1960. 'The Initial British Impact on India: A Case Study of the Banaras Region'. *The Journal of Asian Studies* 19 (4). Included in *An Anthropologist among the Historians and other Essays*. 1987, Bernard S. Cohn, 320–42. New Delhi: Oxford University Press.

———. 1962. 'Political Systems in Eighteenth Century India: The Banaras Region'. *Journal of the American Oriental Society* 83 (3): 312–20.

Dasgupta, Ashin. 1979. *Indian Merchants and the Decline of Surat: c.1700–1750*. Wiesbaden: Franz Steiner Verlag.

———. 1998. 'Trade and Politics in 18th Century India'. In *The East India Company 1600–1858*, Vol. IV. *Trade, Finance and Power*, edited by Patrick Tuck, 46–81. London and New York: Routledge.

Deshpande, Prachi. 2007. *Creative Pasts: Historical Memory and Identity in Western India, 1700–1960*. New York: Columbia University Press.

Dirks, Nicholas B. 2006. *The Scandal of Empire: India and the Creation of Imperial Britain*. Delhi: Permanent Black.

Dodwell, H. H. 1929. *British India, 1497-1858, The Cambridge History of India*, Vol. 5. Cambridge: Cambridge University Press.

Frenz, Margaret. 2003. *From Contact to Conquest: Transition to British Rule in Malabar, 1790–1805*. New Delhi: Oxford University Press.

Fukuzawa, H. 1982. 'Maharashtra and the Deccan: A Note'. In *The Cambridge Economic History of India*, vol 1, edited by Tapan Raychaudhuri and Irfan Habib, 193–203. Cambridge: Cambridge University Press,

Furber, Holden. 1970. *John Company at Work: A Study of European Expansion in India in the Late Eighteenth Century*. New York: Octagon Books.

Goetz, Hermann. 1938. *The Crisis of Indian Civilisation in the Eighteenth and Early Nineteenth Centuries: The Genesis of Indo–Muslim Civilisation*. Calcutta: University of Calcutta.

Gordon, Stewart. 1993. *The Marathas, 1600-1800, The New Cambridge History of India*, Vol. 2.4. Cambridge: Cambridge University Press.

———. 1994. 'The Slow Conquest: Administrative Integration of Malwa into the Maratha Empire, 1720–60'. In *Marathas, Marauders, and State Formation in Eighteenth-Century India*, Stewart Gordon, 23–63. New Delhi: Oxford University Press.

Grover, B. R. 1966. *An Integrated Pattern of Commercial Life in the Rural Society of North India During the 17th–18th Centuries*. Delhi: Indian Historical Records Commission.

Habib, Irfan. [1963] 1999. *The Agrarian System of Mughal India 1556–1707*. New Delhi: Oxford University Press.

———. 1998. 'The Eighteenth Century in Indian Economic History'. *Proceedings of the Indian History Congress,* 1995, 58th Session. In *On the Eighteenth Century as a Category of Indian History: Van Leur in Retrospect,* edited by Leonard Blussé and Femme Gaastra, 217–36. Aldershot: Ashgate Publishing Ltd.

———. 1999. Introduction to *Resistance and Modernization under Haidar Ali and Tipu Sultan,* edited by Irfan Habib, xvii–xlvii. New Delhi: Tulika.

Hasan, Farhat. 2004. *State and Authority in Mughal India: Power Relations in Western India, 1570–1730.* Cambridge: Cambridge University Press.

Hasan, Mohibbul. 1999. 'The French in the Second Anglo–Mysore War'. In *Confronting Colonialism: Resistance and Modernization Under Haidar Ali and Tipu Sultan,* edited by Irfan Habib, 35–48. New Delhi: Tulika.

Irvine, William. 1922. *Later Mughals.* Vol. 1 (1707–1720). Vol. 2 (1719–1739). Edited and augmented with J. Sarkar. Calcutta: Sarkar & Sons.

Jasanoff, Maya. 2005. *Edge of Empire.* New York: Alfred Knopf.

Kolff, Dirk. 1989. *Naukar, Rajput and Sepoy: The Ethnohistory of the Military Labour Market in Hindustan, 1450–1850.* Cambridge: Cambridge University Press.

———. 2004. 'Retrospection'. *Journal of the Economic and Social History of the Orient* 47: 458–62.

Kumar, Raj. 1999. 'The Mysore Navy under Haidar Ali and Tipu Sultan'. In *Confronting Colonialism: Resistance and Modernization Under Haidar Ali and Tipu Sultan,* edited by Irfan Habib, 171–73. New Delhi: Tulika.

Leonard, Karen. 1998. 'The "Great Firm" Theory of the Decline of the Mughal Empire'. In *The Mughal State, 1526–1750,* edited by M. Alam and S. Subrahmanyam, 398–420. New Delhi: Oxford University Press. Originally published in *Comparative Studies in Society and History* 21 (2): 161–77 (1979).

Leur, J. C. Van. 1940. 'Eenige aanteekeningen betreffende de mogelijkheid der 18e eeuw als categorie in de Indische geschiedschrijving' (*Tijdschrift voor Indische Taal, Landen Volkenkunde*) LXXX: 544–567. Review of Vol. IV of *Geschiedenis van Nederlandsch Indië,* ed. F.W. Stapel (Amsterdam, 1940), written by the late Dr. E. C. Godée Molsbergen. English translation, 'On the Eighteenth Century as a Category in the writing of Indonesian History' (*Indonesian Trade and Society. Essays in Asian Social and Economic History by J.C. Van Leur,* (1955), 268-89. The Hague.

Mann, Gurminder Singh. 2001. *The Making of Sikh Scripture.* New Delhi: Oxford University Press (paperback edition).

Marshall, P. J. 1987. *Bengal: The British Bridgehead, Eastern India, 1740–1828.* Cambridge: Cambridge University Press.

———, ed. 2003. *The Eighteenth Century in Indian History: Evolution or Revolution?* New Delhi: Oxford University Press.

———. 2005. *The Making and Unmaking of Empires: Britain, India, and America c.1750–1783.* Oxford: Oxford University Press.

McLane, John R. 1993. *Land and Local Kingship in Eighteenth Century Bengal.* Cambridge: Cambridge University Press.

Metcalf, Barbara D. and Thomas R Metcalf. 2003. *A Concise History of India.* Cambridge: Cambridge University Press.

Oberoi, Harjot. 1997. *The Construction of Religious Boundaries: Culture, Identity and Diversity in the Sikh Tradition.* New Delhi: Oxford University Press (paperback edition).

Parthasarathi, Prasannan. 2001. *The Transition to a Colonial Economy: Weavers, Merchants and Kings in South India, 1720–1800.* Cambridge: Cambridge University Press.

Perlin, Frank. 1983. 'Proto-Industrialization and Pre-colonial South Asia'. *Past and Present* 98: 30–95.

———. 1985. 'State Formation Reconsidered'. *Modern Asian Studies* 19 (3): 415–80.

Prakash, Om. 1998. 'Trade and Politics in Eighteenth-Century Bengal'. In *On the Eighteenth Century as a Category of Indian History: Van Leur in Retrospect*, edited by Leonard Blussé and Femme Gaastra, 237–60. Aldershot: Ashgate Publishing Ltd.

Ray, Rajat K. 1975. Introduction to *Rammohun Roy and the Process of Modernization in India*, edited by V. C. Joshi, 1–20. New Delhi: Vikas Publishing House.

Raychaudhuri, Tapan. 1983. 'The Mid-Eighteenth-Century Background'. In *The Cambridge Economic History of India. c. 1757–c. 1970*, Vol. 2, edited by Dharma Kumar, 3–35. Cambridge: Cambridge University Press.

Richards, John F. 1975. *Mughal Administration in Golconda*. Oxford: Oxford University Press.

———. 1997. 'Early Modern India and World History'. *Journal of World History* 8 (2): 197–209.

———. 2004. 'Warriors and the State in Early Modern India'. Sp. Issue *Between Flux and Facts of Indian History: Papers in Honour of Dirk Kolff, Journal of the Economic and Social History of the Orient*, 47 (3): 390–400.

Sahai, Nandita Prasad. 2007. 'Crafts and Statecraft in the Eighteenth Century Jodhpur'. *Modern Asian Studies* 41 (4): 683–722.

Sarkar, Jadunath. 1916. *History of Aurangzeb*. Vol. 3. Calcutta: University of Calcutta.

———. 1924. *History of Aurangzeb*. Vol. 4. Calcutta: University of Calcutta.

———. 1938. *Fall of the Mughal Empire*. Vol. 1. Calcutta: University of Calcutta.

Singh, Chetan. 1981. *Region and the Empire: Punjab in the Seventeenth Century*. New Delhi: Oxford University Press.

Sinha, N. K. 1965. *The Economic History of Bengal: From Plassey to the Permanent Settlement*. Vol. 1. Third edition. Calcutta: Firma K. L. Mukhopadhyay.

———. 1968. *The Economic History of Bengal: From Plassey to the Permanent Settlement*. Vol. 2. Calcutta: Firma K. L. Mukhopadhyay.

Spear, Percival. 1951. *Twilight of the Mughals*. Cambridge: Cambridge University Press.

Stein, Burton. 1980. *Peasant State and Society in Medieval South India*. New York: Oxford University Press.

———. 1985. 'State Formation and Economy Reconsidered'. *Modern Asian Studies* 19 (3): 387–88.

———. 2010. *A History of India*. Revised and edited by David Arnold. Sussex, UK: Wiley-Blackwell. (First published 1998. Oxford: Oxford University Press).

Stern, Philip J. 2011. *The Company-State: Corporate Sovereignty 'and the' Early Modern Foundations 'of the' British Empire 'in' India*. Oxford, New York: Oxford University Press.

Subrahmanyam, Sanjay. 1990. *The Political Economy of Commerce: Southern India, 1500–1650*. Cambridge: Cambridge University Press.

———. 1992. 'The Mughal State–Structure or Process? Reflections on Recent Western Historiography'. *The Indian Economic and Social History Review* 29 (3): 291–321.

———. 1997. 'Connected Histories: Notes Towards a Reconfiguration of Early Modern Eurasia'. *Modern Asian Studies* 31 (3): 735–62.

———. 2001. *Penumbral Visions: Making Polities in Early Modern South India*. New Delhi: Oxford University Press.

Travers, Robert. 2007. *Ideology and Empire in Eighteenth Century India: The British in Bengal*. New York: Cambridge University Press.

Washbrook, David. 1988. 'Progress and Problems: South Asian Economic and Social History'. *Modern Asian Studies* 22 (1): 57–96.

Watson, I. B. 1998. 'Fortifications and the "Idea" of Force in Early English East India Company Relations with India'. In *The East India Company 1600–1858*, Vol. IV. *Trade, Finance and Power*, edited by Patrick Tuck, 26–45. London and New York: Routledge.

Wink, André. 1986. *Land and Sovereignty in India: Agrarian Society and Politics under the Eighteenth Century Maratha Svarajya*. Cambridge: Cambridge University Press.

Yang, Anand A. 1989. *The Limited Raj: Agrarian Relations in Colonial India, Saran District, 1793–1920*. Berkeley and Los Angeles: University of California Press.

Emergence of the Company Raj 2

Surrender of the two sons of Tipu Sultan during the siege of Seringapatam in 1792; artist unknown

Chapter outline

Between 1757 and 1807, the 50 years that followed Plassey, Great Britain came to acquire a territorial empire in India run by a commercial organization, the English East India Company. The dramatic expansion of the Company and its engagement with the 'business of empire' created considerable uncertainties in Britain about its nature and the role it was to play in Britain and Asia (Bowen 2006: 7). The Company, as Stern's work suggests, made claims to sovereignty from the late-seventeenth century; however, it depended heavily on the home authorities for resources, manpower and legitimacy. As a maritime power, it also needed constant support of the British Admiralty to ensure the safety of sea-lanes to its factories in India and South East Asia (Stern 2011). If this made the early stages of the Company's 'empire building' in India appear to be a 'performance for home authorities' (Travers 2007: 32), the East India Company, through all this confusion and uncertainty, contributed to the 'epochal shift' in world power (Bayly 1988).

The shift was occasioned by the vigorous interventions caused by the militarization of European nation states in the agrarian empires of Asia that led to the foundation of colonial regimes (ibid.). The Company's close ties with the British Crown were too evident and its claims on autonomy brought it in competition with an ambitious British Parliament, after the Glorious Revolution of 1688. This chapter tracks the diverse, multiple and contradictory processes through which colonial rule gathered roots in India; the causes and consequences of the Battle of Plassey; and the policies pursued by three important governor-generals who placed the Company's rule on a solid footing.

THE FIRST 'REVOLUTION'

The 'revolution', we have noted in the last chapter, arrived early in Bengal (Travers 2007: 31). By 1756, Calcutta had become the most important Indian trading port of the Company, and a 'presidency town' with a Governor and Council and an extensive fort complex (Fort William). The Governor and Council derived powers both from the *farmans* granted by Mughal emperors and from a series of British royal charters. Such charters had authorized the Company to found civil and criminal courts of English law in its Indian settlements and establish a line of appeal to the English Privy Council. In addition, the Company's directors in Leadenhall Street regularly sent out detailed instructions to their agents in India, maintaining a highly developed system of bureaucratic record-keeping and accounting that gave cohesion to the far-flung operations of the Company. By 1761, the Company's Court of Directors was convinced that Bengal needed 'priority over all its other commitments in India' (Marshall 2005: 241), on account of the growing significance of Calcutta as the most important colonial city, and the slow establishment of an administrative structure centred on Calcutta.

The East India Company's purchases in India were called 'investment' (Sinha 1965: 6). The Company's investment or public trade referred to goods purchased with 'ready money' and procured by means of a contract made with *dadni* merchants (brokers). This system meant that the Indian weaving communities were often made to work for the Company under some degree of coercion (Marshall 2005: 243). The *dadni* system constituted a considerable amount of the Company's investment (Sinha 1965: 6–7) till 1753, after which it was abandoned. After 1753, *dadni* merchants were replaced by *gomastas*, paid Indian agents of the Company, who made their purchases under the direct supervision of the Company's European servants.

In 1717, a *farman* of Emperor Farukshiyar granted exemption to the Company's merchandise from customs duties in lieu of an annual sum of ₹ 3,000. With a *dastak* (a handwritten pass/permit), the Company's goods could pass without inspection through the toll station or *chowki* (ibid.: 75). The Company's servants quietly extended this privilege to their own private trade, a trade that grew considerably after the abandonment of the *dadni* system. It is worth mentioning here that the East India Company paid abominably low salaries to its servants in India and, as compensation, recognized their rights to private trade in goods that did not infringe on the Company's monopoly. Initially, the servants' private trade did not affect the East India Company; the 'chief sufferers' were the government of the nawabs who lost out on customs duties, and rival Indian traders who faced unequal competition (ibid.: 8). The emperor's *farman* and royal charters from England had made the important settlement in Calcutta almost independent of the nawab's jurisdiction.

Bengal as a source of the flourishing Asian trade was significant not only for the British, but also for the Dutch and the French. The rice-producing delta of lower Bengal yielded high revenue and provided rice for other parts of India, and the well-developed system of water transport throughout the province greatly aided trade in agricultural produce. By the mid-eighteenth century, Bengal had a commanding position in Indian textile production. Silk and cotton textiles were exported by sea to Europe and the Middle East and by overland route to Central Asia. Finally, Bengal also supplied most of the saltpetre required for the production of gunpowder in Europe (Marshall 2005: 148).

It is not surprising, therefore, that the British, the Dutch and the French all had settlements in Bengal: the British in Calcutta, the Dutch in Chinsurah and the French in Chandernagore, all along the Hooghly River, the most navigable arm of the Ganges delta. In an effort to gain access to textiles and other products, the Europeans had spread inland in a way they had not done in the south (the Carnatic), where they stayed to the coast. There were trading stations as far east as in Dacca (now in Bangladesh) and as far west as in Patna (in Bihar). European, particularly British, penetration of the Bengal economy was also on a much greater scale than in the south.

On the other hand, in contrast to the south which lacked a stable successor state, Bengal had a strong state with a centralized administration and a skilled bureaucracy; an established system of taxation and revenue collection; and wide networks of banking, credit and trading. While this made Bengal attractive to European traders, it also meant that the European techniques of trade and their attempts to extend privileges by means of coercion were not likely to be tolerated by the powerful nawabs. The Anglo–French wars in the Carnatic and the Coromandel Coast between 1744 and 1748 that followed British–French hostilities in Europe—the War of Austrian Succession—witnessed direct contravention of the Carnatic nawab's prohibition of hostilities within his territories when the French attacked the British settlement of Madras. In Bengal, however, both the French and the English thought it advisable to pay heed to the nawab's command and observe neutrality on the Ganges (ibid.:149).

Such conscious decisions did not root out tension completely. 'The Company's commercial practices led to war' because there was 'a growing incompatibility between the investment patterns of the Company servants' and the 'permissible bonds of commerce under the scrutiny of the Nawabs' (Sen 1998: 74).

Propelled by the logic and imperatives of the Industrial Revolution in Britain, the Company laid great stress on commerce and manufacture and encouraged consumption. This made markets the focal points of individual access to resources (Gadgil and Guha [1992] 1993: 116). Individual mercantilist logic of the Company's officers failed to grasp the subtle and intricate meanings of the exchange of gifts and patronage on which relationships stood poised during Mughal rule. The Company's officers misread such practices as bribe and abuse, to be complied with in order to carry on trade in India. The Company's attempts at fortification and use of arms for the defense of its territorial possessions, in turn, went patently against the norms and boundaries that distinguished the ruler from the merchant. This had caused Nawab Alivardi Khan great concern. Alivardi never attacked the English: he regarded them as 'a hive of bees' (Sinha 1965: 76) best left undisturbed; but he was worried about the wealth that was accumulating beyond his reach in Calcutta and the very large volume of trade being conducted outside his regulations and customs (Marshall 1987: 80). Alivardi is also believed to have asked the English, 'You are merchants, what need have you of a fortress?' (Sen 1998: 74).

Alivardi's predecessor, the astute Murshid Quli, had insisted that his officers examine whether the goods handled by English merchants were imports of the East India Company or goods to be exported by the Company's servants engaged in private trade (Sinha 1965: 75). This alertness had prevented an extension of the inland private trade of the Company's servants, but they extended it to maritime trade, which was a part of country trade. Country trade included inland trade, coastal trade and trade between Indian and other Asiatic ports. Murshid Quli's successor, Shuja-ud-din, had also been alarmed by the rapid expansion of Calcutta's maritime trade owing to the use and abuse of the exemptions enjoyed by the Company. The Company pacified him with occasional payments of large sums of money.

Matters went awry with Alivardi's grandson and nominated successor, Siraj-ud-daula. The Company did not attend his accession ceremony in 1756 and pay respect at his court to pledge their trade. The young nawab, for his part, appears to have taken no proper steps to consolidate his position, which he won after a battle with the strong contender Shaukat Jang, *faujdar* of the autonomous district of Purnea (Marshall 1987: 75). On assuming power, Siraj remodelled the civilian and military administration, replacing earlier office holders with men of his own choice. This caused serious discontent among the 'grandees and commanders—the chief officers of the army, the ministers of the old court, the secretaries and the writers of the Durbar' (Ghulam Husain Khan cited in Marshall 1987: 75). Mir Jafar, the distinguished general of Alivardi's army and Rai Durlabh, a leading Hindu administrator, were among those alienated. They were soon joined by important merchants and bankers, including the Jagat Seths and large zamindars of western Bengal. The English, who had become adept at interfering in local politics, made use of this disaffection to strike deals, particularly after the nawab stormed Calcutta in 1756.

The nawab's storming of Calcutta was a punitive measure; he wanted to demonstrate his sovereign power over a European company that had failed to show due respect to him. The attack took the English by surprise and demonstrated the vulnerability of their settlements. Although the Company's servants did not fully understand the nawab's act, they realized that his purpose was not just to demand money, which the Dutch and the French had given him on his accession and the English had not. And they were right: What the nawab wanted was obedience.

From the nawab's point of view, argues Sudipta Sen, the English were permitted to live under his rule as merchants, trade custom-free and protect and adjudicate over Indians who were their own servants; they had no right to interfere with the administration of the realm. For the Company's civil and military officers, on the other hand, the regulation and the duties imposed by the nawab hampered the free movement of commerce. For them, 'the Moor' (as the nawab was referred to) was mistaken in thinking that the Company will carry on trade by paying the customs duty he asked for. Consequently, the 'long *dastak* account' (relating to trade carried out by the Company and its servants as private traders without paying customs duties to the nawab) that Siraj had 'to settle with the English' constituted a crucial bone of contention (Sinha 1965: 9). In addition, the fortifications in Calcutta were a direct reminder to the nawab that the English Company was not ready to trade—like several other groups of merchants—in compliance with his jurisdiction.

The confrontation then was much more over ideology than over the right to trade in the 'merchandise of honor'—salt, betel nut and tobacco—'objects endowed with distinctive value and signs of the ruler's substantive authority' (Sen 1998: 82). Rather, it was the result of 'a prolonged contest over habits, terms and meanings of goods, markets and people that constituted a vital link between authority, patronage and material culture in premodern Bengal' (ibid.: 88). The right to trade in salt, betel nut and tobacco was reserved by the nawab, who followed the Mughal practice of granting this right to a favourite or to the highest bidder. Although the monopoly was undercut by smugglers, the nawab's exclusive right to grant such contracts was recognized. European companies, we have seen in the last chapter, had challenged the Indian norms of trade by establishing monopolies, building fortifications and using arms under the apparent cause of making their trade 'secure'. In Bengal, the English Company not only questioned and evaded paying the customs duties imposed by the nawab; its servants also questioned the nawab's monopoly over salt from the early eighteenth century.

Siraj-ud-daula's attack on Calcutta offered the English an opportunity to end their enforced 'neutrality' and enter into a direct trial of strength with the nawab. Admiral Watson and Robert Clive came to Hooghly from Madras at the head of the naval and infantry forces in 1756, and quickly recaptured Calcutta. The nawab had to sign a treaty that restored the Company's settlements and its privileges. Soon the British eliminated the French from Chandernagore, and Clive entered into clandestine negotiations with Siraj-ud-daula's 'enemies': important aristocrats, bankers, merchants, traders and military commanders in Bengal. Clive, in fact, outdid the French in their game of attrition, of local intrigues and of playing off one party against the other, in order to gain greater strength and prominence. In addition, British naval superiority and access to greater capital resources enabled them to beat off the French challenge and consolidate their hold, first on the Nawab of Arcot, and later on the nawabs of Bengal (Bayly 1988: 45).

Clive's negotiations with Siraj-ud-daula's rivals proved vital and valuable in the Battle of Plassey. The Company's forces easily overcame the nawab's army, which was substantially weakened by the withdrawal of a large force at a strategic moment by Mir Jafar. Siraj was killed in the battle and the victorious Company appointed Mir Jafar as the new Nawab of Bengal. Mir Jafar was obliged to 'pledge himself to make vast payments as indemnities and rewards to the victors' accounting to, as Clive put it, 'three million sterling' and to concede the territory around Calcutta to the Company (Marshall 2005: 150).

Merchants, Commerce and a Dual Government

The position of the Bengal nawabs was severely weakened after Plassey. Plassey offered the Company an opportunity to press for greater privileges in its treaties with them. It got entry into local rights, expanded territorial revenues and extended duty-free trade into the interior of Bengal. Inland trade became a part of the 'prize of Plassey' (Sinha 1965: 78). The Company also got control of 24 Parganas as payment of the 'debt' that Mir Jafar had accumulated, on account of the pledges he had made and the forced obligation of maintaining the Company's army. The Company thus began its first experiments in revenue collection.

Robert Clive, the Governor of the Company after Plassey, set about earning easy wealth by means of winning gifts rather than waiting for slow returns from commerce. He was soon followed by others. The peak period of giving gifts to Englishmen in power extended from 1757 to 1766, until it was prohibited by the Company's Court of Directors. Duty-free inland trade continued and caused more harm than the receipt of presents, since the Englishman's supremacy in trade deterred native traders as well as other European traders from coming to Bengal. The Company's servants, even in their individual capacity as private traders, began to trade freely in salt, betel nut and tobacco, which were hitherto prohibited to all Europeans (ibid.: 78). The 'massive invasion of the private trade of Bengal by private British enterprise' (Marshall 1987: 102), threw the division between the Company's public and private interests into confusion and unleashed what has been termed the 'post-Plassey plunder' (ibid.).

The Court of Directors ordered the Governor and Council in Bengal to draw up a 'proper and equitable plan for carrying on inland trade' (ibid.: 82). Clive and his Select Committee decided to establish an exclusive society comprising of senior servants of the Company with complete control and monopoly over the manufacture of salt, tobacco and betel nut (ibid.: 82). This society also reserved the right to grant contracts. Corruption became rampant, and the market was glutted. In 1772, the government abolished the exclusive society and assumed full control over the salt trade. 'Native' merchants were once again allowed to get contracts by paying a duty of 30 per cent.

The Company's servants, however, continued to build fortunes from lucrative, collusive contracts. Such contracts allowed them to make private gains at the expense of both the Company and the primary producer (peasant or weaver), with the *gomasta* intercepting a considerable portion. The directors became so exasperated that they filed a suit in the Chancery for fraudulent contracts against some of their servants who returned to England.

Mir Jafar, who headed 'a distracted and indolent administration' and 'attended very little to business' (Sinha 1968: 23–24), was replaced by Mir Kasim in 1760. Mir Kasim was forced to cede three rich districts—Burdwan, Midnapore and Chittagong—to the Company in return for the reward. Mir Kasim tried to win back some autonomy from the Company and defend Bengal's inland trade against the excesses of the Company's servants and their *gomastas* engaged in private trade. He stated in anger: 'In every pargana, every village and every factory they buy and sell salt, betel nut, ghee, rice, straw, bamboos, fish, gunnies, ginger, tobacco, opium and many other things'. Goods and commodities of the *ryots* (*raiyats*) and merchants are taken away forcibly for a fourth part of their value and *ryots* are obliged 'to give five rupees for goods which are worth but one rupee'. They 'expose my government to scorn and are the greatest detriment to me' (cited in Sinha 1965: 79).

Mir Kasim also complained against the Company establishing important market places without his permission and the Company's exercise of unprecedented influence on merchants loyal to him. The Company, unwilling to put up with such show of autonomy, expelled him in 1763 and reappointed Mir

Jafar. Mir Kasim made common cause with Shuja-ud-daula—the Nawab of Awadh and vizier of the Mughal empire—and Mughal Emperor Shah Alam II. But their joint forces were defeated by the newly strengthened Bengal Army in the Battle of Buxar in 1764; an event that heralded the 'second revolution'. The Second Revolution was the capture of Bengal by the East India Company that significantly altered the circumstances that had made foreign trade serve as an instrument of growth in the economy. The import of silver stopped almost completely after the grant of diwani by Emperor Shah Alam and the Company's exports from Bengal became 'unrequited', resulting in a serious drain of resources.

The Company became the dominant military power in eastern India, but the financial cost of winning the closely fought battle was very high for it. Military charges for 1764–65 far exceeded what the Company was getting from the newly acquired districts (Marshall 2005: 153). It needed to augment its resources to meet the additional expenses by acquiring further assignments in the revenue of the country and greater trading privileges. 'Further assignment' was secured in the following year when Clive negotiated a treaty with the captured Mughal emperor, who was under British protection in Allahabad. This was the Treaty of Allahabad, signed on 12 August 1765, by which the Mughal emperor appointed the East India Company as his *diwan* for the provinces of Bengal, Bihar and Orissa. The treaty transferred Bengal's remaining revenues to the Company (ibid.). The grant of *diwani* in 1765 made the Company the *diwan* of Bengal, 'the receiver-general of the Imperial revenues in the Province' (Dow 1772, 3: xlvi) in exchange for an annual tribute of ₹ 2,600,000. In addition, there was a steep rise in the sterling equivalent of the Company's Bengal exports from about 400,000 pounds per year to well over a million by the late 1770s (Marshall 2005: 242). The Nawab of Bengal retained the office of *nazim* with formal responsibility for defence, law and order and the administration of justice.

Mir Jafar died in 1765. He was succeeded by his eldest son Shuja-ud-daula, another 'puppet' nawab. The strength of Shuja-ud-daula's army was severely reduced and he was enjoined to pay a hefty tribute. The Company's Court of Directors granted Robert Clive extraordinary powers to expand the Company's armies and impose military and political control over the nawab. He was also allowed to work independently of the Council at Fort William with a Select Committee of handpicked supporters. Clive took charge of the revenue administration and delegated the task of actual administration to a *naib* (a deputy), Muhammad Reza Khan, who nominally functioned under the nawab but was actually appointed by the British.

On the surface then, Clive's 'dual-government' seemed like a return to the earlier Mughal practice of separating the *diwani* and the *nizamat* functions, a separation that Murshid Quli Khan had done away with. In reality, however, the nawabs after Plassey had become incapable of functioning autonomously. The independence of the *nizamat* was 'a fiction preserved by the company for its own convenience' (Marshall 1987: 93). Moreover, given the inexperience of the Company's servants, even in the sphere of land revenue administration, the Company had to depend on new Indian *diwans* in the districts who replaced the *qanungos*. Such *diwans* did not, of course, have adequate expertise and the *qanungos*, partially restored in 1774, lost their position and sense of responsibility. Thus, while Bengal's revenue administration became 'unhinged' (Sinha 1968: 45–46), the sovereignty of the Company remained 'masked' as Clive put it before the Bengal Council in 1765 (Stokes [1959] 1989: 1).

This dependence on Indian agency went well with the eighteenth-century ambience where a handful of Englishmen, without English wives and with no rigid moral or religious code, took to Indian ways of living (ibid.: 2), adopting the lifestyle of a nawab, if possible. The nawabs, on the other hand, were reduced to the status of retainers of the Company with a fixed allowance for court expenses and other duties they were notionally entrusted with (ibid.: 90).

The Company's virtual sovereignty did not put an end to the tension with the nawabs over the control of trade and commerce. As stated earlier, it was a conflict of ideology. Although the East India Company had the monopoly to trade in India, the Company's servants made use of the liberal ideology of 'free-trade' in their struggle to transform 'ideologies of conquest into languages of rule' (Travers 2007: 98). The use of 'free-trade' was, of course, paradoxical for a Company that enjoyed monopoly. What the Company wanted was a zone of trade 'free' from all earlier customs and duties collected by the nawabs and several of their functionaries. Through the force of arms and vigilant policing, the Company succeeded in making its department of customs the only legal one. A unified economic territory, under efficient European 'management' with standardized and exclusive duty on all goods and common ruling codes, emerged in place of what was referred to as the 'despotic' divergent and 'oppressive' policies of the nawabs (Sen 1998: 89–119).

The need to 'defend' and expand this territory led to expensive wars and constant conflicts, as well as an enormous increase in the number of Company personnel. All this cut into the revenues collected from Bengal. Clive's dual government came under close scrutiny. What were censured, however, were not the wars and the increase in the Company's functionaries, but the 'Asiatic manners' and 'corruption' of Indian deputy governors (Travers 2007: 76). This is because there was little realization that the gains accruing from the Company's assumption of the role of revenue collector were off-set by 'the multiplication in the number of Company employees, who had no interest in increasing the Company's profits at the expense of their own' (Furber 1970a: 18; 1970b: 416).

At the same time, unbound individual profiteering and complaints by British traders about the 'despotic' powers of the Company's governors caused concern among its directors. The British Parliament, which had become vigilant of the Company's increasing autonomy from the late-seventeenth century, took advantage of such complaints to exert greater control over Indian settlements. Indeed, from the late 1690s, a broad group of individuals and interests opposed to the Company had come to form a new Company sanctioned by an Act of Parliament; the two Companies merged in 1709.

The demands of the war effort against France in Europe (and India) from the 1750s had obliged the Company to share information with the British Parliament and with ministers who were directing the war effort. It had to present half-yearly financial statements and reports to various committees set up to examine the Company's affairs (Bowen 2006: 163–64). The Company's servants now got active help in their new role as revenue collectors.

The news of the grant of *diwani* generated a debate in Britain over whether the revenue from Bengal, believed to yield over 2 million pounds, belonged solely to the Company, or whether the 'British public' had a share in it (Marshall 2005: 208). In 1767, the Company had to agree to pay 400,000 pounds to the British state, in return for full control over its new territory and revenues (ibid.: 210). The Company's directors in London were fully aware of the great advantage of collecting local revenues from taxation: it relieved them of the huge burden of exporting silver to India.

Harry Verelst, who succeeded Clive as the Governor, drew up detailed instructions for the European supervisors of the revenue districts to do away with the 'intermediaries' between the peasant and the government. Zamindars—'greedy landlords'—became a crucial category of analysis and an object of reform, and peasant cultivators got attention as 'objects' oppressed by the mutual collusion of rapacious landlords and corrupt revenue collectors. Supervisors were asked to penetrate such collusive networks to gain 'authentic' knowledge of the 'real value' of land in their districts and draw up new rent rolls (Travers 2007: 76).

As Sinha puts it, 'during the years 1759–67 the East India Company as zamindar was distrustful of zamindars' (1968: 25). We will discuss the effect of such distrust on zamindars in a later section on Permanent Settlement. Company servants, as zamindars, first of the 24 Parganas and later of Burdwan, Midnapore and Chittagong, tried both direct administration and farming out of revenue without much success. In fact, such experiments and the Company's drive to collect greater revenue left many old substantial farmers in ruin (ibid.: 27). Despite this, mercantilism along with the enduring strand of British opinion that saw the government of the nawabs as a system of barely regulated plunder, justified increased intervention by supervisors and greater demand for land revenue.

Indeed, 'spectacularly after 1765', the Company's new role as a tax collector got priority over its role as a merchant and its trade came to be viewed as little more than the means of transferring revenue surpluses as 'tribute' to Britain (Marshall 2005: 243). The 'tribute' was extracted from Bengal's highly developed agriculture and manufacture by imposing taxes on the produce of the land and by levying duties on trade. The Company, by force of arms and a rigorous network of state-controlled checks and outposts, established and defended its regime of 'free-trade' and ensured smooth collection of revenue.

Alongside, however, officers of the Company were aware of the devastating effects of their regime on the economy of Bengal. The stoppage of bullion (silver) imports from England after Plassey and the directors' demand for rupees from Bengal to sponsor the Company's investment in China caused havoc. Drought and failure of crops in 1768 and 1769 produced acute distress; this was exacerbated by the negligence of the East India Company's administration to take measures on time to avoid tragedy. The Company and its servants continued in their policy of profit maximization through trade and revenue collection, and the Company did not stop the export of crops from Bengal to other parts of India. A catastrophic famine struck Bengal at the end of 1769 and the beginning of 1770; the self-confidence of local officials was replaced by a blaming of the 'improvident tax demands' and 'a nostalgic looking back at the imagined stability and prosperity of earlier eras' (Travers 2007: 98).

Bengal's domestic economy in the first half of the eighteenth century, centred mainly on textile manufacturing, was healthy and prosperous. The takeover of control by the Company and opening up of the economy to foreign trade exports produced a drastic reduction in local economic welfare. The Company's revenues, however, grew on a large scale. The famine, the first of its kind in a century and a half, was an 'appalling spectre on the threshold of British rule in Bengal' (Sinha 1968: 48). It prompted Company officials to turn back to the aura of Mughal legitimacy and to bestow coherence and stability on their chaotic territorial government.

The famine allowed the British Parliament to assert increased authority over the Company. Several enquiries into the Company's affairs were conducted during the premiership of Lord North and the

Regulating Act, an *Act for Establishing Certain Regulations for the Better Management of the Affairs of the East India Company*, in India and in Europe, was passed by the Parliament in 1773 (Horn and Ransome 1957: 811). The Company's Court of Directors was enjoined to submit all communication regarding the company's civil, military and revenue matters in India for scrutiny by the British government. A compromise measure, the Act asserted that the ultimate sovereignty over the territories in the East rested with the British Crown but allowed the Company to act as the sovereign power on behalf of the state, provided it was kept under a certain degree of 'regulation' (Marshall 2005: 197). The Act placed the executive and judicial administration of the Company and of India on a regular footing (Horn and Ransome 1957: 812).

STEPPING STONES

Warren Hastings became the Governor of Bengal in 1772, a time it was reeling under the effects of the famine. Lord North's Regulating Act of 1773 made him the Governor-General of India 'with ill-defined supervisory powers over the Company's other governors in Madras and Bombay' (Furber 1970a: 19). Hastings was entrusted with the task of bringing back order into the chaos caused by the Company's intervention in Bengal. With the other presidencies subordinated to the new capital of Calcutta, Hastings launched vigorous measures for crisis management and reform of the Bengal government, in order to mould 'a confused heap of materials' into a 'regular constitution' and infuse new life into the moribund polity of Bengal (Travers 2007: 104).

Hastings was plagued by uncertainty, resistance within his own council, restraining and contradictory orders from the directors in England and a crisis of legitimacy of the Company in Britain. Nevertheless, his measures laid the foundations of the British empire in India. His governorship represented 'an uneasy mix of economizing administrative accountancy, attempts to extend the coercive powers of the central state and grand gestures designed to legitimize the Company's government as a steward of an ancient constitution' (ibid.: 100–101). Interestingly, this urge to legitimize the Company's government in India as a successor to the Mughals was also premised on his belief that the sovereign powers that the Company's servants exercised in Bengal emanated from the 'British nation' and not from the Company in London (Hastings cited in Marshall 2005: 242). This double, perhaps opposing, belief critically shaped Hastings' administrative measures.

A veteran servant of the Company, Hastings had expertise in administration and had served in Bengal between 1750 and 1764. He was a close ally of Clive's major rival in the British Parliament. Upon his arrival in Bengal from Madras in 1772, Hastings devoted time and care to a close analysis of the numerous orders sent by the directors and the records produced by the Company's expanding bureaucracy. This served as the basis for the political reforms that he introduced between 1772 and 1774.

Faced with the dual, difficult tasks of reducing Company's expenses and enhancing revenue flows, Hastings extended direct control over the *diwani* territories and replaced the Indian deputy governor and his functionaries—the *amils* and *faujdars*—with European supervisors. The supervisors were now given the title of collectors. Controlling councils of revenue, set up in Murshidabad and Patna, assumed most of the authority of the nawab's ministers. The substitution of Indian officers was complemented by a second measure to improve revenue administration: the creation of long-term interests in the collection of revenue. The nawab's practice of making bargains with leading revenue payers annually at the *Punyah* ceremony held in Murshidabad was deemed to be 'deeply flawed' since annual renewals provided no incentive for long-term development (Marshall 1987: 119).

In 1772, Hastings introduced a system of granting farming contracts to 'farmers' for five years, in the hope that this would induce interest in improving the land and ensuring punctual payment of revenue to the Company. Apart from the fact that there was a lot of uncertainty relating to who should be 'farmers'—given British suspicion of zamindars who actually managed to make realistic offers—the scheme failed to serve both its purposes. Many of the 'farmers' could not pay the stipulated revenue on time and extorted cultivators in their attempts to collect revenue. News of the failure of this system was transmitted to the British Parliament and generated serious debates. Such debates eventually prompted the Company to grant full security of tenure to zamindars, as we shall soon see.

The issue of collecting land revenue continued to trouble Hastings. He was uncertain about the inexperienced supervisors who, he felt, were 'ill-suited' for their large responsibilities as collectors. The Company's senior officers also agreed that revenue collection kept up 'violently' to earlier standards 'even after the famine' was causing frequent clashes between the Company's army and armed groups of religious mendicants—*gosain*s, *faqir*s and *sanyasi*s—in the northern frontiers of Bengal (Travers 2007: 104). These were the groups, we need to remember, which combined mendicancy with mercenary soldiery and trading (Cohn 1964; Sen 1998; Lorenzen 1978).

Violent collection of revenue was not the only source of friction. The Company's constant efforts to erode the power of local potentates by disbanding their armies, its forced creation of a zone of 'free-trade' and rigorous control over land as well as water resources and markets, caused severe hardship to these groups. While the disbanding of armies of local chiefs closed an avenue of employment for them, the Company's strict control over market places and rigorous collection of dues on merchandise made them lose out as traders. In addition, the Company abandoned the earlier practice of collecting duty on the volume of goods for trade and introduced separate duties on each item of merchandise. All this transformed the mercenary mendicants into vagrants: from a tolerated group they became one of bandits, despised, marginalized and penalized (Ghosh 2009). Their first major outburst against the exploitative practices of the Company found expression in what has come to be known as the Rangpur rebellion (1793).

Hastings' sense of urgency for reform was tied to his anxiety relating to a 'merchant body' straying into unfamiliar Asiatic territories. He agreed with his predecessors that the constitution of the Company derived from charters framed for 'the jurisdiction of trading settlements' and not for the governance of a 'great kingdom' (Travers 2007: 104). Moreover, till the end of the eighteenth century, when the rule of English and Dutch companies over large populations had not become apparent, no one talked yet of the 'White man's burden' (Hutchins 1967; Nandy 1983). Rather, there was a fear that the Company's men were complicit in Asian despotism. The close supervision by the Parliament and several measures adopted by Hastings and Cornwallis were aimed at containing this complicity.

Hastings' scheme of reform demonstrated a desire both to overhaul the territorial administration and to control Company service. Hastings, who had served in Bengal during Alivardi Khan's rule and was a scholar of Persian, did not share the stereotype of the degenerate nawab. Indeed, he was among the few defenders of the nawab's independence. Besides, he also believed that the Mughal empire in its heyday had a centralized and regulated system of government. This accounts for his repeated allusions to the 'original constitution of the Mogul government' or 'the legal norms of the Mogul government', although his own idea of such a constitution and laws was extremely vague and confused (Travers 2007: 106–07).

Hastings was caught in the push and pull of conflicting concepts: an openness toward understanding all cultures was undercut by a lingering sense of Asian barbarism and oriental 'despotism' discussed eloquently in Alexander Dow's *History of Hindostan* published in 1770 (Metcalf 1995: 7–10). Hence, the idea of an organic, pre-existing constitution was accompanied by the need to expunge the most repugnant elements in 'Indian' custom. Hastings' invocation of the 'Mogul constitution' then was a way of attaching the Company's 'upstart sovereignty' to some idea of stability and longevity (Travers 2007: 107). Such contradictory visions inflected his reforms and measures with particular meanings and varied effects. It is perhaps not surprising that his measures occasioned severe criticism in the British Parliament and eventually led to Hastings' trial and impeachment after his return to England in 1785.

ORIENTALIST GOVERNANCE

The 'Regulations Proposed for the Government of Bengal' drawn up by Hastings (1772) declared the Company to be the 'civil magistrate' of Bengal, which was to run the administration from Calcutta under the direction of the President and Council. It also sought to confine all Europeans to Calcutta and entrust Indians with the administration of the districts. This would keep the Europeans under the jurisdiction of the English law court and protect the gentle Bengalee from the fierceness prevalent in European manners.

The Company, we need to remember, had been authorized to execute judicial powers in India a century before by the Charter of Charles II in 1662. The Charter of George I in 1726 had given it permission to establish Mayor's courts (courts of the King of England) in Calcutta, Bombay and Madras. This charter, however, had not mentioned anything about the Company's jurisdiction over natives. Warren Hastings' Judicial Plan, for the first time, brought the natives under the Company's jurisdiction through its provision for establishing civil and criminal courts in each district, that is, *mofussil* courts (Agnes 1999: 42).

The Regulating Act of 1773 converted the Mayor's court of Calcutta into the Supreme Court in 1774. In 1781, the Supreme Court was granted express jurisdiction over the natives. Although Hastings' declared purpose behind the separation of laws for Europeans and the natives was to protect the gentle Bengalee, for Justice William Jones, the primary object of the Supreme Court was to protect and govern British subjects resident in India (Sen 2010: 148). The natives of the provinces, he believed, 'indulged in their own prejudices, civil and religious, and suffered to enjoy their own customs unmolested'. This, moreover, was in concert with the regular collection of revenue (Jones cited in ibid.). Hastings' belief that the natives had a fixed body of laws and codes set down by 'lawgivers' got perpetrated as a norm because it allowed for the protection of the English in India, and enabled an uninterrupted and smooth collection of revenue. This double objective ended up defining the 'natives' as peoples who wanted to 'enjoy their customs unmolested' (Sen 2010).

Hastings' proposed regulations clearly stated that the 'Mahometan and the Gentoo [Hindu] inhabitants shall be subject only to their own laws', and that native inhabitants of Calcutta would be subject to English courts only in their dealings with the Europeans but not in their dealings with each other (Hastings cited in Travers 2007: 105). His Judicial Plan of 1772 clarified that 'in all suits regarding inheritance, marriage, caste and other religious usages, or institutions, the laws of the Koran with respect to the Mahometans and those of the *Shaster* with respect to Gentoos shall be invariably adhered to' (Acharya 1914: 153, quoted in Rocher 1994: 220). Let us try and unpack the implications of Hastings' statement.

The first decision of having Indians administered by Indian and not common laws was a basic principle of Orientalist government. Shored by a belief, both in a fundamental divide between the East and the West and in the existence of different codes for distinct groups, this ideal maintained that it was unfair to deprive the people of the protection of their 'own laws' and subject them to ones they were ignorant of.

The second decision, of much greater consequence, was to have 'native' laws apply to what were perceived as 'religious' usages and institutions. This corresponded to subjects that fell under the jurisdiction of ecclesiastical and Bishops' courts in Britain. It is interesting that inheritance and marriage were grouped together with 'caste and other religious usages or institutions' and left to the jurisdiction of the 'Gentoos' and the 'Mahometans' (Morley 1858). This was, it bears pointing out, the genesis of personal laws for religious communities, the far-reaching repercussions of which continue to be felt in India today. The decision of 'ceding jurisdiction in family and religious affairs to private authorities' was aimed at 'achieving native consent for foreign rule'. It was hoped that autonomy in the 'private' sphere would make up for the loss of governance in the public. That '[s]ecuring the affections of the natives' in order to ensure the 'stability of the acquisitions' of the Company certainly formed a part of Hastings' ideology was stated clearly in Halhead's Preface to *A Code of Gentoo Laws* (cited in Marshall 1970: 142).

The possibly well-meaning but extremely arbitrary assumption that multiple cultures and religious traditions in India were reducible to 'Hindu' and 'Muslim' and that Indians were defined by their adherence to Hindu or Muslim communities meant that myriad, fuzzy sectarian orders were categorized either as Hindus or as Muslims. Moreover, the Company's government set on the dangerous course of deciding not only what was Hindu and what was Muslim law, but also what was religious and what was lay.

The lumping together of different groups under the label 'Hindu' did not only cause confusion, the classification of most non-Muslims as Hindu made the Hindu majority appear 'even more overwhelming than it was, and they were precisely the people whom Hastings sought to enfranchise' (Rocher 1994: 222). Indeed, as Rosane Rocher points out, the most important yet unstated decision of the Judicial Plan was to 'discontinue the official monopoly Muslim law had enjoyed in civil courts under the regime the British were displacing' (ibid.). Thus, the declared simple purpose of the Judicial Plan of upholding local norms belied its much more radical impact.

It would be hasty, however, to deduce from Rocher's statement that Muslim law prevailed in civil matters prior to British rule. Civil law was not only administered in courts but also in non-official public fora, where norms of customary law and adaptations of *smriti* and Koranic injunctions were applied in accordance with the context. The limited knowledge of Company officers about local norms and customs made them depend heavily on Hindu *pundits* and Muslim *qazis*, resulting in the Brahmanization and Islamization of laws (Agnes 1999: 44).

The other consequence of the lack of local knowledge related directly to Hastings' view that the source of law was law books and not local customs. With this began the perpetual hunt for 'original' texts in order to return their own laws and customs to the natives that have been corrupted by later practice. If this occasioned a 'renaissance in *dharmasastra* literature', it also intensified dependence on Brahman *pundits*, upheld by the mistaken notion that all Brahmans were priests and that they commanded 'natural' authority for ecclesiastical law (Rocher 1994: 221). Further, the belief in 'original texts' as representative of an enduring Indian reality resulted in a devaluation of India's historical experience (Metcalf 1995: 13).

The absence of ready texts on law drove Hastings to the next step of having them codified. In 1776, he convened a panel of Sanskrit scholars (*pundits*) to compile a code of *Gentoo* laws. The process was long and laborious. The *pundits* had to identify legal decisions on various matters in different Sanskrit texts. They were then translated into Persian and from Persian into English by Nathaniel Brassey Halhed and published in 1773 under the title *A Code of Gentoo Laws*. The importance of the *Code* and the inherent belief in the Brahmans as the source of Hindu law found vivid articulation in Halhead's Preface to the *Code*. The compilation, he stated, 'was the only work of the kind, wherein the *genuine principles* of the Gentoo jurisprudence are made public, with the sanction of their *most respectable Pundits (or lawyers)*'. This book also offered 'a complete confutation of the belief too common in Europe that the Hindoos, have no written laws whatever...' (cited in Marshall 1970: 142, emphasis added).

Halhed's pen was only 'a passive instrument, by which the laws of this singular nation are ushered into the world from those Bramins themselves'. The 'professors of the ordinances', added Halhead, still spoke the original language in which the ordinances were composed, a language entirely unknown to the bulk of the people. 'The professors' not only had great endowments and benefactions 'in all parts of Hindostan', they also commanded personal respect from the people which was a 'little short of idolatry' (ibid.).

The problems that beset the arduous process through which the *Code* was produced, encouraged Orientalist scholars to learn Indian languages, particularly Sanskrit and Persian. Their crowning achievement was the founding of the Asiatic Society of Bengal under the leadership of William Jones in 1784. In tune with this, the Calcutta Madrassa was set up to encourage the study of Persian scriptures. By the 1790s, William Jones had gained enough command of Sanskrit to confidently retrieve Hindu laws from ancient Sanskrit texts on his own and not be ' ... at the mercy of our *pundits*, who deal out Hindu law as they please ...' (Mukherjee [1968] 1987: 118). Jones' *A Digest of Hindu Law on Contract and Succession*, translated into English and published after his death by Henry Thomas Colebrooke in 1796, would become, along with the *Code*, the two authoritative texts on Hindu law. The Company's government bore the entire cost of the compilation and publication of these texts. The genesis of these texts bears testimony to the ways the 'fathers of orientalism in India furthered colonial centralization by subordinating the Indian intelligentsia to English epistemological authority' (Ludden 1994: 253).

The 'Hindu Law' that the *Code* and the *Digest* brought into being was a construction based on appropriation of selective branches from the prescriptive, normative and moralistic tradition of the *Dharmasastras*, the *smritis* in particular. Apart from the fact that the meaning of the original text in

Sanskrit, *Vivadarnavasetu*, 'a bridge on the ocean of disputes' was totally transformed in the English rendering as *A Code of Gentoo Laws*, the use of terms such as Code, law, and Digest taken from English legal terminology conferred on the English texts meanings that were not associated with the original ones (Bhattacharya-Panda 2008).

At the same time, it is important to remember that Hastings' disregard of local customs was not common to all India. The Regulations of the Bombay Presidency, particularly the one drawn up under John Duncan in 1799, applied the English distinction between king's law and common law and gave due recognition to custom as an important source of law (Agnes 1999: 45). Monstuart Elphinstone, earlier as Commissioner of Deccan (1818–19) and later as Governor of the Bombay Presidency (1819–27), also believed that Hastings' belief in the Roman categorization of canon law and civil law was not applicable to India. Elphinstone presided over the reorganization of the legal and judicial administration, as well as the codification of the 'common law' of the natives, which resulted in the drafting of the Regulation Code of 1827. Despite the disjunction in views, the objective and the purpose of the two codes of Hastings and Elphinstone were the same: a desire to preserve for the natives their way of ruling, and an 'unwillingness to allow the natives to manage their own affairs' (ibid.: 45–46). Both were driven by the need to make the administration of justice certain and definite.

LAW AND ORDER

The search for laws to govern 'Hindus' and 'Muslims' went hand in hand with efforts at establishing colonial governance on a solid footing. Revenue collection, we have noted, was brought under the direct supervision of the Company's officers. Collectors were appointed for each district whose primary function was, as the designation suggests, the collection of taxes. The Judicial Plan made them supervisors of district civil courts. Each district, according to this plan, was to have a *diwani adalat* (civil court) and a *faujdari/nizamat adalat* (criminal court). European district collectors were to preside over the civil courts, to be assisted by Brahman *pundits* and *maulavis* for the interpretation of 'indigenous law'. The president (governor) and two members of his council were to look after the Court of Appeal—*Sadar Diwani Adalat*—in Calcutta.

Each district had a civil court, presided over by the European collector. The principal civil court, the Court of Appeal (*Sadar Diwani Adalat*), was in Calcutta under the jurisdiction of the governor and two members of his council. Administration of criminal justice was notionally left in the hands of Muhammad Reza Khan and the *Sadar Nizamat Adalat* was moved to Murshidabad. Each district had a criminal court, the *faujdari adalat*, where *qazis* and *muftis* dispensed justice. Reza Khan also supervised the police administration; *faujdars* and *kotwals* maintained law and order in rural districts and towns and zamindars took care of law and order in the villages by employing village watchmen.

When this system did not work and there was a huge increase in the number of crimes following the famine of Bengal in 1770, police administration and criminal justice were brought under the direct supervision of the Company's government. The *Sadar Nizamat Adalat* was moved from Murshidabad to Calcutta under the charge of the Governor and two members of his Council.

The Regulating Act of 1773, and efforts by the British Parliament to 'regulate' the excesses of the Company's servants in India, replaced the Appeal Court with the Supreme Court in Calcutta. This court administered English law independent of the Governor-General and Council. Although Jones' ideas were very similar to those of Hastings, the latter protested against the imposition of English laws, firmly holding on to his idea that 'the people of this country do not require our aid to furnish them with a rule for their conduct' (Gleig 1841, 1: 401). Soon, the Supreme Court was replaced by the *Sadar Diwani Adalat*, and Hastings and Sir Elijah Impey, the Chief Justice of the Calcutta High Court, set up six provincial and later 18 *mofussil* courts in place of the district courts (Morley 1858).

District collectors ceased to function as supervisors of the district and provincial courts as the increasing pressure of revenue administration took up most of their time. Also, there was partial deference to the Whig principle that executive and judicial functions needed to be kept separate. Covenanted officers of the Company, eventually called judges, were put in charge of civil courts. Elijah Impey took charge of the restructured *Sadar Diwani Adalat*. Law now became a specialized profession to be operated only by trained (European) lawyers. Adjudication of law was made consistent and systematic by recourse to the *Code of Gentoo Laws* and a Code of Muslim Laws complied by 1778. Judicial administration became centralized and was reduced to a system (Misra 1959 cited in Bandyopadhyay 2004: 99).

Interestingly, the *Code*, produced by a political definition of 'Hindu' and the belief that the *Dharmasastra*s were the only source of Hindu law, was used not only as a tool of law enforcement, but also as 'an advertisement for Indian culture' in Britain. In Britain, the targeted audience was neither the rulers nor the ruled in India, but the directors of the East India Company and the British public at large (Rocher 1994: 241). Books on India began to multiply from the 1760s, as the British public got more and more interested in India (Marshall 1970: 2). A study of London newspapers for 1772 concluded that 'India had become part of the daily newspaper diet of those with access to the press' (cited in Marshall 2005: 199). Civil administration was propped up by the force of arms, the mainstay of the Company's government. We have seen how the Company constructed fortifications at an early stage and used armed forces for maintaining, first trade monopoly, and later effective governance. The army was also used regularly for the rigorous collection of revenue, giving rise to what has been termed 'military fiscalism' (Peers 1995). Indeed, it has been argued that the Company's political dominance in north India rested on its superior military power. It was the army that provided social and political stability to the Company in the first 80 years of its rule, bringing the Company closer to Indian natives (Alavi [1995] 1998: 3).

The Company had become aware of the need for a permanent army in 1747, when it had to wait for the arrival of the British fleet with reinforcements during its wars with the French in the south. Soon after Plassey, Clive set about this by recruiting Indian soldiers—*sipahi*s (a Persian word corrupted into sepoys in English)—who were clothed in the manner of the British army and committed to the command of a British officer. Following the pattern of recruitment of the army in Britain, where a country soldier from Ireland or Scotland was rated highly, Company officials in India looked for soldiers from among the agricultural classes (ibid.: 35–37). But very early on, they also formed an opinion of 'martial' races, preferring the 'better built' people of the wheat-producing zones to that of the ones of 'short stature' who belonged to the rice-growing areas (ibid.: 37). We will track the far-reaching effect of this opinion in the construction of 'martial' races in Chapter 4. Significantly, the job of being a soldier now became a permanent one. The choice of employment that the militia had in the fluid military labour market where they could take to soldiery by pledging loyalty to the leader of a band and become farmers in the agricultural season, was done away with (Alavi 1993; Gommans and Kolff 2001). In the British army, *sipahi*s were put on payrolls; they had ranks which were fixed; and they were prohibited to take up or leave seasonal employment.

Hastings gave a further twist to this policy of recruitment. Distrustful of the soldiers who had served the nawab, and in accordance with his own notions about preserving Indian caste roles in military and civilian institutions, he looked for high-caste warriors and peasants outside the western frontiers of Bengal (Alavi [1995] 1998: 39). Hastings' policy was primarily welcomed by Rajput and Brahman zamindaris in Benares and peasant populations in Bihar and present Uttar Pradesh, particularly so because service in the army held out the prospect of regular pay and a pension. The Company's government, on the other hand, got political legitimacy from this 'high-caste overtones' of the army (ibid.: 45). Attentive to religious and caste sensibilities, the army celebrated 'religious' festivals and respected caste regulations in the cantonments. At the same time, the success of the company in recruiting Hindus by appealing to their religious sensibilities would soon have divergent socio-economic and political consequences.

The army gained in strength very rapidly. Initially, it needed to fight the French and outmanoeuvre the Bengal nawab. Soon, however, it was deployed to conquer new territories, defend Bengal against the attack of real or imaginary enemies, deal with peasant rebellions against exacting revenue demand, collect information about Indian society and economy and make alliances with the Indian elite. All this made the Indian army one of the largest European style standing armies in the world, and a major pillar of colonial rule in India. Numbering 100,000 in 1789, it expanded to 155,000 by the end of the century, with cavalry as well as infantry. As the Company's administration in Bombay and Madras intervened actively in local politics and sought to outdo opponents from the 1780s, Bengal provided both troops and money to these governments. Interestingly, Hastings made use of the opportunity to undo the Regulating Act of 1773 and enact a series of administrative reforms that centralized the administration.

In addition to safeguarding and expanding the Company's territories, the army performed the crucial function of gathering and generating knowledge on 'Indian customs and religious practices' as well as mastering India's geography. Originally tied to the need for recruitment, the knowledge so gathered became central to the Company's governance of north India. This nurtured and supplemented the scholarship produced by Hastings' great institutional creation—The Asiatic Society of Bengal—and the work of James Rennell, the Surveyor General of Bengal from 1764. By the time he left India in 1777, Rennell 'literally put India on the map' with his comprehensive *Map of Hindoostan* (Ludden 1994: 254). This entire body of knowledge produced in accordance with and yet not completely in conjunction with the needs of colonial rule, represented bold advances in the colonial scheme of classifying India in order to govern and laid the foundations for the vast colonial archive.

A 'Permanent' Settlement?

Scholars in general agree that there was a marked shift in the Company's administration between Hastings and Cornwallis. For Furber, the shift was one 'from unregulated to regulated imperialism' (Furber 1970a: 227). Furber argues that if in the last years of Hastings' governance, Europeans scrambled to get their wealth home in any way they could, in the last years of Cornwallis' government, the scramble was much more orderly. This is because Cornwallis' personal integrity and his vigorous and effective attacks on corruption in the Company services assured both the directors in England and all creditors of the Company that it would be able to continue with its government and meet the interest payments.

Lord Cornwallis, the first Governor-General appointed from outside the Company's service at a time when England was confronted by the pressures of American and French wars (1780–83), was sent to India in 1786 with clear instructions to 'reform the administration of Bengal and also to make British India's external boundaries safe' (Bayly 1988: 65). Cornwallis' appointment came in the wake of the passing of the East India Company Act of 1784 (known as the Pitt's India Act), by the British Parliament to address the shortcomings of the Regulating Act and to bring the Company's affairs under greater control of the Parliament. The act set up a Board of Control to 'superintend, direct and control' the government of Company's possessions. The governing body of the Board was to consist of six members, two of whom were members of the British Cabinet, and the rest members of the Privy Council. The President of the Board of Control also became the minister for the affairs of the Company, and came to supervise a joint government of the Company and the Crown where the British government held the ultimate authority (Keay 2010: 391–92).

Chronology of Governor Generals of India, 1774–1858

Sl. No.	Name	Term of Office
1.	Warren Hastings	20 October 1774–1 February 1785
2.	Sir John Macpherson	1 February 1785–12 September 1786
3.	The Earl of Cornwallis	12 September 1786–28 October 1793
4.	Sir John Shore	28 October 1793–March 1798
5.	Sir Alured Clarke	March 1798–18 May 1798
6.	The Earl of Mornington	18 May 1798–30 July 1805
7.	The Marquess Cornwallis	30 July 1805–5 October 1805
8.	Sir George Hilario Barlow	10 October 1805–31 July 1807
9.	The Lord Minto	31 July 1807–4 October 1813
10.	The Earl of Moira	4 October 1813–9 January 1823
11.	John Adam	9 January 1823–1 August 1823
12.	The Lord Amherst	1 August 1823–13 March 1828
13.	William Butterworth Bayly	13 March 1828–4 July 1828
14.	Lord William Bentinck	4 July 1828–20 March 1835
15.	Sir Charles Metcalfe	20 March 1835–4 March 1836
16.	The Lord Auckland	4 March 1836–28 February 1842
17.	The Lord Ellenborough	28 February 1842–June 1844
18.	William Wilberforce Bird	June 1844–23 July 1844
19.	Sir Henry Hardinge	23 July 1844–12 January 1848
20.	The Earl of Dalhousie	12 January 1848–28 February 1856
21.	The Viscount Canning	28 February 1856–1 November 1858

Cornwallis, a confirmed Whig politician, 'anglicized' the administration, urged on by the belief that the 'Orientalist' principles of government were fundamentally at fault (Stokes [1959] 1989: 4). The 'shift' then, was more in the ideology that governed colonial state-building: from one of restoration of an earlier Indian constitution to one of absorption into the British imperial state (Travers 2007: 207).

For its own trade, the Company had to depend on agency houses in Calcutta since the earning from revenue barely paid for the purchase of goods in India to be exported to Europe. As the debt structure of the Bengal government became increasingly complex with each passing year, the pressure on the Company's government to improve the management of resources through an efficient administration mounted. The Company was caught in a vicious circle. The need for greater revenue and resources to take care of its cost of trade and administration pushed it towards territorial expansion. Conquest in turn increased the expenditure on the army and a bureaucracy that expanded in line with the extension of the Company's territories. This required greater financial commitment, which the Company sought to meet by increasing its demand for land revenue, tribute from Indian rulers and increased internal revenue from customs and duties in trade.

The debate over revenue administration surfaced with great vigour under Cornwallis and the issue of the security of tenure of revenue farmers was discussed again. Philip Francis, a revenue Councillor (and member of the Calcutta Council) under Hastings, had argued that Bengal's zamindars not only possessed certain revenue rights that had become hereditary, but that they were also owners of the lands from which they collected revenue. This argument, which was valid to a certain extent (if we remember the trend set by Murshid Quli Khan), had not cut much ice with Hastings. Cornwallis, on the other hand, firmly believed that the key to the revival of Bengal's declining agriculture—that was putting Company's trade in danger—lay in creating a hereditary landed aristocracy and 'the security of property rights' (Marshall 1987: 122). This made him sympathetic towards the views of Philip Francis. Moreover, British public opinion was also favourably disposed towards the 'stark simplicity' of Francis' ideas (ibid.).

Edmund Burke—a renowned political thinker, a great critique of the Company's government under Hastings and a principal figure behind Hastings' trial and impeachment—had, in particular, given much publicity to such ideas in reports prepared by a House of Commons' Select Committee in 1782 and 1783. Consequently, the Pitt's India Act enjoined the Company 'to enquire into the alleged grievances of the landholders and if founded in truth to afford them redress and to establish permanent rules for the settlement and collection of revenue' (Sinha 1968: 147). It further stated that the administration of justice needed to be founded on ancient laws and indigenous traditions. In 1786, the Company's directors had also ordered their servants in Bengal to make a revenue settlement, to be considered 'permanent and unalterable' and made, 'in every practicable instance with the Zemindars' (Marshall 1987: 122). At a later stage, British administrators would try to deal directly with peasant-cultivators in other parts of India, but in the late-eighteenth century they lacked the expertise for such a move.

Cornwallis arrived in Bengal in September 1786. Revenue enquiries were made between 1787 and 1789 and Regulations for the Decennial Settlement of Bengal, Bihar and Orissa (Midnapore) were passed between September 1789 and February 1790 (Sinha 1968: 147). The Regulation stated that the ten-year settlement, if approved by the Court of Directors, would become permanent at the end of ten years. This generated controversy. John Shore, the leading revenue expert in the Company's service, felt that this part of the Regulation should be dropped. Cornwallis moved in at this stage to argue strongly in favour of the benefits of a permanent settlement, both for the zamindars and for the Company (ibid.: 148).

The Permanent Settlement of Bengal Revenues was enacted in 1793 and was to last, at least in name, until 1947. It was an open attempt to apply the English Whig philosophy of reducing the exercise of political power—believed to be essentially corrupting and inevitably abused—to a minimum by controlling the executive (Stokes [1959] 1989: 5). The Settlement was based on simple principles. The Company's revenue demand was fixed permanently and the zamindar was recognized as the absolute owner of the revenue-paying land. As long as he paid the stipulated amount of revenue punctually, he had the right to sell, mortgage or transfer the land and pass it on to his heirs. However, failure to pay was to result in its confiscation and sale by auction.

The Regulation of the Bengal Government left nothing ambiguous: 'A sale of the whole of the lands of the defaulter, or such as may be sufficient to make good the arrear, will positively and invariably take place' (Bengal Regulations 1793, 1: vii, cited in Islam 1979: 33). Penalizing the zamindar for failure to pay through the confiscation and sale of lands was an entirely new practice. Earlier, the Company had followed the Mughal practice of imprisoning the defaulting zamindar (Chaudhuri 1983: 93). This rigorous rule of collecting the revenue from the zamindar by the sunset of the exact date agreed upon gave rise to fearful stories around the 'sunset law'.

The Company's Court of Directors agreed with Cornwallis that a fixed revenue demand on the part of the government was '*the first step*' in the simplification and regulation of the demand of the landholders upon tenants (Sinha 1968: 151). The settlement of revenue in perpetuity, it was expected, would do away with 'native agency' and thereby with 'Asiatic tyranny' (Cornwallis' Minute cited in Bayly 1988: 66) and bring revenue collection under the supervision of a disciplined cadre of European collectors. In turn, this would divest the collectors and Boards of Revenue of all judicial and discretionary powers, confine their function to 'the mere collection of public dues' (as mentioned in the Despatch to the Court of Directors, 6 March 1793) and effectively draw a wedge between the executive and the judiciary. Freed of the need to constantly monitor and assess the revenue demand, the government could devote time to the reform of the constitution of internal government, good laws and their due enforcement (Sinha 1968: 149). Moreover, by welding the separate rights of collecting state revenue (and making profit), and of holding land as proprietor at the village level, the Settlement would successfully close the different avenues of income and exploitation open to revenue farmers and landholders.

THE IMPACT OF IDEOLOGY

The Permanent Settlement got the support of a whole range of Company officials and European observers of different personal and intellectual dispositions—Alexander Dow, Thomas Law, Henri Patullo and Philip Francis, for instance—because they all belonged to the shared ideological atmosphere of late-eighteenth century permeated by physiocratic and utilitarian strains of thinking (Guha [1963] 1982).

The physiocrats in France, deeply influenced by the transformation and success of English agriculture after the Enclosure (a process by which common land, over which poor people had mowing or grazing rights, was taken over, enclosed and given over to private owners), gave primacy to land as the source of all wealth. 'The social philosophy upon which this doctrine implicitly rested consisted in placing above all else private property, especially property in land' (ibid.: 97). This was tied to the notion of the gentleman-entrepreneur as the 'improving' landlord who, in Francis' view, was the key to England's prosperity.

This idea of private property in land as the source of wealth was taken a step further and given affective flourish by the utilitarians. Influenced by their founding figure, Jeremy Bentham, the utilitarians maintained that 'happiness and not liberty was the end of government, and happiness was promoted solely by the protection of the individual in his person and property' (Stokes [1959] 1989: 65). The physiocrats and the utilitarians both agreed that private property guaranteed personal security to the owner, and thereby fostered self-improvement leading in turn to an improvement of the social and economic standards of the empire as a whole. Moreover, landed property was a key element in the Whig conception of political society, 'an agency which affected the reconciliation of freedom with order' (ibid.: 5).

Cornwallis, in his debate with John Shore prior to the introduction of the Settlement, had pointed to the existence of vast tracts of 'jungle' in the Company's territory and stated that an advantageous tenure would induce industrious zamindars to clear waste lands and increase the value of landed property. This would make the government revenue secure against balances. As Sinha puts it, 'Cornwallis visualized Calcutta Banians with their business-like habits displacing the happy-go-lucky old type landlords' (1968: 148). Cornwallis' Minute was candid in this regard. 'It is for the interest of the State, that the landed property should fall into the hands of the most frugal and thrifty class of people, who will improve their lands ... and thereby promote the general prosperity of the country' (Governor-General's Minute 1789: 512). Cornwallis, it appears, acted on an 'implicit assumption of a declining trend in agriculture in Bengal in the recent past, and judged the permanent fixation of land revenue to be the best device toward its revitalization' (Chaudhuri 1983: 88). Revitalized agriculture, by ensuring the security of revenue, would also contribute to the prosperity of commerce, the vital need of the hour.

This ideological base of the Permanent Settlement did not, in any way, undermine its practical purpose of effective and optimal revenue farming. Indeed, in tune with the significance attached to land, the definition of a tenure called zamindari that would encourage effective proprietorship of land in return for payment of revenue, was given far greater attention than the rights of zamindars or landed proprietors (Marshall 1987: 123). Every bit of land in Bengal, Bihar and Orissa became a part of a zamindari and the revenue was fixed at 26,800,000 (approximately 3,000,000 pounds) of Company rupees, based on the standard of the year 1789–90, the highest revenue assessment made so far.

Philip Francis, the famed 'father' of the Settlement, argued that the revenue demand was too high and needed to be lowered (Travers 2007: 177). Francis believed that the government should strictly follow a policy of non-intervention with regard to the *ryots* and limit its revenue demand only to its needs, rather than look for a maximization of revenue. The Permanent Settlement that was implemented by Cornwallis differed in this important respect from the one proposed by Philip Francis (Sinha 1968: 152–53).

In addition, the Permanent Settlement did not mean a 'complete freezing of the land revenue, and the Company could secure an increase in it from time to time' (Chaudhuri 1983: 89). Estates of defaulting zamindars, which remained with the government for want of bidders, and portions of huge wastelands which were not included in zamindars' estates at the time of the settlement, returned large profits to the Company with the growth of cultivation and rise in prices. The Company's largest gain came from the resumption of 'rent-free lands' which earlier governments had exempted from the payment of revenue, so that the income from them could be spent on maintaining temples, mosques and educational institutions. In Patna, as Chaudhuri indicates citing the *Final Report on the Survey and Settlement of the District of Patna, 1907–12*, the increase in revenue through such resumption amounted to 48 per cent between 1790 and 1870.

Arguably, the high revenue demand and the extreme rigour in its collection hit the old zamindars badly. The zamindars, it is important to remember, had since Mughal times, owned land and looked after the maintenance of irrigation works and embankments, supervised water distribution, without however, engaging actively in organizing cultivation. A substantial landowner, who let out his land to share-croppers, had greater control over land and labour than the zamindar. The zamindar also did not have authority over the entire produce; some part of it was set apart to pay functionaries whose services were considered essential by the village community, before the zamindar could collect his due. The conditions under which different groups and castes of peasants held land were also often decided independently of the position of the zamindar in the village society (Chaudhuri 1984: 107–08). All this did not seriously affect the zamindar since his sources of power far exceeded those conferred by the right to collect tribute. They rested on the hereditary nature of the zamindari, the caste and kinship ties of the zamindar, his role in the local administration and maintaining of law and order. At the same time, exaction of a substantial part of the peasant surplus sustained the zamindar's power, and the exaction was premised on occasional increase of rent rates and various illegal or extra-legal cesses.

From the beginning, the land-revenue policy of the Company's government had been detrimental for zamindars. The government, 'keen on maximizing revenue, and convinced that old zamindars would seek to frustrate the aim' appointed strangers (ibid.: 109). The famine of 1769–70 caused serious damage to the resources of the zamindars, exacerbated by the perfidy of the Company's *amlahs*. In certain parts of Bengal such as Rangpur, Malda and Dinajpur, the zamindars faced direct competition from the Company's commercial establishments that looked after the production of cotton and silk; weavers and silk producers, as part-time agriculturists, were subject to the zamindar's authority. The presence of Commercial Residents provided the peasants with an alternative source of authority: weavers and silk producers sought the protection of the Commercial Resident against the zamindar's demand for an increase in rent and were readily afforded such protection.

The severity of the sale law introduced by the Permanent Settlement accounted for the sale of one-third to half of the entire landed property of Bengal (Sinha 1968: 177). The old zamindars in Bengal, particularly the big ones in Rajshahi, Dinajpur, Nadia, Bishnupur and Birbhum, suffered the most, both because they failed to keep up with the new rigidity and rhythm of revenue collection and because the government had full knowledge of their resources. Their lands were bought either by their own ruthless officials, particularly Brahmans and Kayasthas of the writer caste or by neighbouring zamindaris and Banias of the British, as Cornwallis had envisaged.

Some big zamindari houses, like the Burdwan Raj, survived by introducing a complicated process of sub-infeudation, which brought further complexity to the confused agrarian set-up (Chaudhuri 1975).

Indeed, a large number of under-tenures, that allowed old zamindars to retain a hold over property after it had been sold under the sale law, became a feature of the land system of Bengal after the Permanent Settlement (Sinha 1968: 178). The owners of 'backward and less known zamindaris' in East Bengal fared better because their resources were not accurately known (ibid.: 153). About 51.6 per cent of the old proprietors were eliminated in Orissa between 1804 and 1818, even though the system of fixing the revenue permanently was not the only one followed in the region (Chaudhuri 1983: 109). Bihar's zamindars suffered much less as a class, and big ones like the Darbhanga Raj and the Hutwa Raj in Saran and Champaran prospered, as did their counterparts in Burdwan.

On the whole, the zamindari system revived despite changes in the structure because the Company granted extraordinary powers to zamindars to improve agriculture. A land trade, so far non-existent in Bengal, came into being along with a new social class. The early works of Rajat and Ratnalekha Ray (Ray and Ray 1973, 1975) had argued that the *jotedar* (variously known as *abadkar, grantidar, hawaladar*), on whom the zamindars depended for the complicated work of land-reclamation and hence granted very liberal rent rates (Chaudhuri 1984: 118), benefitted greatly from the Permanent Settlement and emerged as a 'dominant village landholding class' by reclaiming and buying land and by efficiently collecting revenue. The *jotedars* distributed their broad acres to be cultivated by share-croppers and tenants-at-will; they also possessed the economic resources to control the labour force through money loans. The share-croppers had no other option but to cultivate 'for a half share with grain loans advanced by the *jotedars*' (Ray and Ray 1975).

Without directly challenging this argument, B. B. Chaudhuri has shown that the success of the *jotedars* varied greatly from region to region depending on the existing agrarian structure and land relations, the extent of the land available for reclamation, the extent of participation of *jotedars* as moneylenders that gave them greater control over peasants and their relation with the zamindar (Chaudhuri 1984: 118–19). The zamindars persistently asserted their 'right to redefine their relations with the jotedar' where 'they had not explicitly signed away their rights' (ibid.: 128). Chaudhuri argues that the *jotedars* gains had been exaggerated (ibid.). This view has been accepted by scholars who have examined later periods of Bengal's history but acknowledged the not-so-prominent or a negative position of the *jotedars* who arose from the Permanent Settlement (Bose 1986; Chatterjee 1984, for instance). Ratnalekha Ray's later work, published posthumously (1987), indicated that perhaps her earlier emphasis on the success of the *jotedar* was somewhat misplaced, which was substantiated by Rajat Ray in a review essay in *The Indian Economic and Social History Review* (1988).

Peasants (*ryots*) were the most serious victims of this new settlement. Zamindars who so far only had the right to collect revenue became landowners with enormous power; peasants became mere tenants and often lost their customary occupancy rights. This is because Cornwallis' ideas, as well as perhaps that of Dundas and his Board of Control were premised upon a misconception—that the property in the soil must vest 'in some class of inhabitants of Hindustan, sovereign or subject', as they did in European states (Sinha 1968: 150). Expediency prompted the government to acknowledge the zamindars as proprietors of the soil (Colebrook 1804: 44). It is true that the issue of whether the government should reserve any power to regulate relations between zamindars and their 'tenants' had caused debate even when the principles of the Settlement had been agreed upon. While John Shore had argued in favour of correcting errors and making revisions at the end of a ten-year span, Cornwallis had urged that anything less than 'unalterable permanence' would undermine confidence and defeat the central purpose of the Settlement, that is, improvement based on security (Marshall 1987: 124). Cornwallis' view had prevailed, although in recognition of the need to protect *ryots* a regulation had been enacted. It stated that the 'rents' paid by the *ryots* to the zamindars should be fixed and formally recorded in documents called *pattas*. This enabled a *ryot* to contest unauthorized demands. Once again, Cornwallis was wrong in assuming that zamindars would easily grant *pattas* to the *ryots* (Sinha 1968: 149).

Once the Permanent Settlement came into force, the *pattas* were ignored and the *ryots* were compelled to shoulder the burden of the high revenue demand. While earlier an official of the Mughal government could negotiate between the zamindar or the *taluqdar* and the peasant and lower the rent in times of distress, a point to which Reza Khan had referred, under the Permanent Settlement the zamindar as the 'master of the land' reserved the right to take away and re-let lands if peasants failed to pay. Although we do not have sufficient data on the existing rent rates on peasants prior to Company rule, contemporary reports from the late-eighteenth and early-nineteenth century definitely demonstrate that rent rates were excessive in Bengal and Bihar by 1793 and in Orissa by the 1810s, and the situation remained the same for a long time.

High rent rates also found mention in Rammohan Roy's *Exposition of the Judicial System of India*. In this exposition, the zamindar and social reformer stated that the amount of assessment fixed on the lands 'was as high as had ever been assessed and in many instances higher than had ever been realized by the exertions of any government, Mohammedan or British' (Roy cited in Sinha 1968: 153). Sinha aptly assesses the purpose and effects of the Settlement: it was shaped by a simplifying philosophy— physiocracy in practice, the rage for order and symmetry and the interests of the ruling power. However, the authors of the Settlement seemed to have been unaware that 'complex relationships are destroyed by simple solutions' (ibid.: 152).

A recent study has drawn attention to yet another important aspect of the Permanent Settlement, not analyzed seriously. We have noted the importance accorded by the Company to the reclamation of wastelands that were not parts of zamindari estates in order to increase revenue. Pointing to the recurrent discussion of 'waste' among the Company officials in relation to the Permanent Settlement, Vinay Gidwani has argued that what was under consideration was not the waste or wastelands but rather the people who lived there. The lands were lying waste, it was thought, because the 'natives' were indolent. The drive toward the 'recovery' of the waste, therefore, enabled colonial officials not only to ratchet up the amount of revenue obtainable by gaining and distributing wastelands but also, and more significantly, served to work out a hierarchical binary between the worthless, wasteful ruled and the suitable, civilized ruler. This provided the early underpinnings of the justification for colonial rule (Gidwani 1992: 39–46).

Other measures adopted by Cornwallis also demonstrated his unwavering faith in Whig theory that regarded the administration of justice to be the principal function of the government. Cornwallis reformed the Company's civil service in order to make it the principal player in administration. In an effort to ensure honesty in the civil service, he significantly increased the salaries of civil servants (Sinha 1968: 187–88). Indian participation was reduced to the level of 'petty agency'.

The Bengal Code of Regulations of 1793 sought to give concrete form to the English Rule of Law. Collection of revenue was put in charge of the Revenue Board in Calcutta and collectors in the districts. A European covenanted servant acted as judge and magistrate in each district. The lingering institution of the *nizamat* in Murshidabad was done away with, Muhammad Reza Khan pensioned off and the *Sadar Nizamat Adalat* was reconstituted and set up in Calcutta under the direct jurisdiction of the Governor-General and Council. 'Courts of circuits' were set up under British judges, who were to meet with and consult district magistrates in their travels through Bengal. *Qazis* and *muftis* now only had the job of offering legal opinion in writing, and criminal courts made systematic amendments to the existing pattern of Muslim criminal law (Travers 2007: 235). The provincial *diwans* and *amils* disappeared, as did the *sadar qanungos* and *naib qanungos* (Sinha 1968: 189). At the same time, litigation increased and the European judges' lack of knowledge of the local language made them depend on ill-paid native officers who had no responsibility in the administration of justice. Cases piled up and perjury became rampant (ibid.: 193).

With the lapsing of the *nizamat*, police became the responsibility of the Company, and the district magistrate became the superintendent of police. The districts were sub-divided into *thanas*, each with an Indian *darogah* and a troop of constables. Zamindars were divested of all policing duties and enjoined to disband their forces. Former institutions of local militia and village watchmen that had not been abolished came under the direct control of the Company's police (Marshall 1987: 130). Law and order became a total preserve of the Company. Once again, this did not put an end to corruption. Bengali literature, for instance, *Mrityunjay Darogar Ikrarnama* (Darogah Mrityunjoy's Contract) offered incisive, witty commentaries on the malpractices that prevailed in different branches of administration. Aware of the fact that the Permanent Settlement had made the Company's revenue 'inelastic', Cornwallis looked for compensation elsewhere. Zamindars were prohibited from collecting duties on goods passing through their territory and they were ordered to abandon the zamindari *chowkis*, located on the banks of rivers. Cornwallis tried to establish a regular system of taxation on the internal trade of the country and hoped that with the gradual increase of wealth and commerce, taxation on trade would add considerably to the government's income. His plan of making taxation on trade a total reserve of the government, however, was made effective only in 1801 (Sinha 1968: 194–95).

By the time he left India, Cornwallis had put in place the institutional structure of the Whig vision. The Company's servants were paid high fixed salaries and not allowed to engage in private trade; the district collector was entitled only to collect public dues and was made subject to trial for any undue exaction; and the district judge was endowed with magisterial authority and control of the police for the impartial administration of justice. The fear of British complicity in oriental despotism was brought to an end (Metcalf 1995: 23).

Conquest and Consolidation

The contours of the Company state, carved out of Hastings and Cornwallis' diverse measures, were given flourish and finesse by Richard Wellesley (Earl of Mornington 1798–1805). Driven by patriotism bolstered by events in Europe and the colonies—the world struggle for empire against Napoleonic

France and the simultaneous loss of America and the conquest of India—Wellesley deliberately set out to subject the entire Indian subcontinent to British power. This 'military despotism' of the Company in India was perfectly in tune with the new sense of 'Britishness' in Britain, which was now articulated *not* as an extended community shared with American colonists, but by means of an 'essential quality of difference' with the colonized (ibid.: 4). The new heroes of this 'Britishness' were no longer admirals but generals like Richard Wellesley, brother of Arthur Wellesley, the Duke of Wellington, who commanded a mercenary army composed of conquered subjects, and whose claim to fame lay in having defeated Napoleon in the Battle of Waterloo.

War also 'galvanized the whole taxation and political base of British society' and the reaction of the merchant and the gentry was 'distantly reflected in the governor-generalship of Lord Wellesley' when the Company went on a 'general offensive' against the oriental government in India (Bayly 1988: 5). There was a corresponding change in the nature of the Company. Originally set up to accumulate profits from oceanic trade, it turned to the conquest and acquisition of newer territories in order to draw sustenance from land revenue. The 'political safety' of Bengal, interpreted as the subjugation of powerful Indian rulers, became the priority of soldiers turned politicians in the Company's government.

Wellesley arrived in India determined to subdue Indian rulers—Tipu Sultan, Daulat Rao Scindia and the Nizam of Hyderabad—who had enlisted 'a noticeable number of Frenchmen in their service' (Sardesai 1948: 350–51). In order to attain his objectives, he abandoned the policy of non-intervention pursued by his predecessor John Shore, and gave new meaning and force to Clive's policy of Subsidiary Alliance. This afforded him 'the fullest scope for intervention in the concerns of Indian chiefs' (ibid.: 352). Under this alliance, a friendly Indian prince enjoyed British protection and got the support of British troops against his enemies, external and internal, if he agreed to provide 'subsidy' for the upkeep of the Company's troops, and accepted a British Resident at his court. He also lost the right to enter into diplomatic alliances with other powers without the knowledge of the Resident. The Company thus got the right both to use the Indian ruler's territory as a buffer against its own enemies and prevent a combination of Indian rulers against it. The nawabs of Awadh and Arcot and the ailing Nizam of Hyderabad were drawn into this alliance at an early stage; Wellesley increased the demand for subsidy from the Indian allies and subsequently forced the Maratha chiefs to enter the system.

Taming the 'Oriental Despot': Tipu Sultan

The Bengal army, which grew in strength from 115,000 to 155,000 under Wellesley, was employed first against Tipu Sultan of Mysore—a formidable enemy—stereotyped as an 'oriental despot' by the British. Let us make a brief detour here and take note of Tipu's achievements, a character who generated great interest among his contemporaries and continues to be evaluated differently by recent scholars (Habib 1999, for instance). Mysore's last independent ruler, Tipu has been hailed as an 'alternative element in late eighteenth-century South Asian political culture' (De 1999: 3). Plebian in his origins and 'more of a *ghazi* than the average feudal carpet-knight', Tipu is taken to be a 'throwback to the pre-Mughal Deccan Sultan' who sought acceptance of his imperial aspirations from West Asian and continental European peers, in order to effectively challenge British claim to supremacy in south India (ibid.).

In the last chapter, we discussed Haidar Ali's able measures to improve the army and the economy of Mysore. Tipu built upon and improved them. After bringing the Second Anglo–Mysore War to a successful stalemate in 1784 (Hasan 1999), he turned his attention to the army and took measures to build a navy. He, however, suffered a slight reversal at the hands of the Company's army in the Third Anglo–Mysore War in 1792, which convinced him even more of the necessity of a strong navy. In 1796, Tipu issued a *hukmnamah* (ordinance) that laid down the regulations for the naval programme (Husain 1999: 174).

The programme visualized a naval force of 40 ships to be built with great speed and put under the care of 11 *mir yam* or lords of admiralty, with headquarters at Seringapatnam. The ships were to be divided into three divisions or *kachehris*—the *kachehri* of Jamalabad or Mangalore, the *kachehri* of Wajidabad or Bascoraje and the *kachehri* of Majidabad or Sadasheogarh (ibid.: 174–75). Timber for the ships was to be procured from state forests and floated down rivers to the respective docks and seasoned properly before being put to use. The *hukmnamah* also contained detailed instruction on the kinds of ships to be built and the officers and employees who were to man the land establishment of the *kachehris*—a clear evidence of Tipu's efficiency as an administrator (ibid.: 175–76). Tipu's interest in ammunition in general was revealed in the musket he presented to the French authorities in Pondicherry in 1786. The musket, produced in the munitions industry in Nagar, was regarded as equal in quality to 'any produced in Europe' by the French Governor Cossingy (Sridharan 1999: 146). In a similar manner, French officers were duly impressed by the coins minted by Tipu.

As a ruler interested both in state power and its commercial capacity (De 1999: 3), Tipu attempted to revive commerce within his kingdom and forge commercial links with other parts of India and West Asia after the Third Mysore War in which he lost almost half his territories. In line with the European East India companies, Tipu endeavoured to build a 'public-sector company' with finance drawn from the state treasury (Khan 1999: 149). Here too, a *hukmnamah* laid down detailed instructions for the functioning of the Company where the Sultan was to wield personal control. He wished to encourage the export of merchandise and import of treasure and sought to back-up trade by investing in ship-building and creating a merchant navy (ibid.: 149). He sent personal letters to several important foreign merchants and invited them to come to Mysore. Diplomatically, Tipu sought friendly relations not only with the French, but also with the Nizam of Hyderabad and Maratha chief Mahadji Scindia.

In the sphere of agriculture and land administration, Tipu went far beyond his father. He drew upon his experience of managing *jagirs* for 15 years in Dharampuri to bring about serious modifications in land tenure and management after he assumed power (Sheik Ali 1999: 161). He laid down rules for the distribution of arable lands among the old and new *ryots* and gave preference to hereditary ownership of land tenures and fixed rent. Under hereditary ownership, a peasant and his heirs enjoyed the right of cultivation in return of regular payment of the customary rent of the district. The rent varied in accordance with the produce, but the state insisted that land should be cultivated continually and not left fallow. In the other system of fixed rent, a landlord owned the land and collected rent from his tenants in order to pay a fixed rent to the state. The right of succession of the landlord's son was recognized on condition that he continued to pay the fixed rent (ibid.: 162).

In the first system, where rents were fixed in accordance with the produce, lands were measured every year. Tipu abolished the system of farming out lands. The state assumed the responsibility of collecting rent directly from peasants. The rent, moreover, was now collected in cash. Rents were assessed on the category of land cultivated, namely wet or dry, as well as the fertility of the soil. Usually, a farmer cultivated both dry and wet lands and paid, on an average, about 40 per cent of his income to the state (ibid.: 163). The cultivation of dry crops—sown in June and reaped in January—was most extensive and most secure. Nearly 25 varieties of dry grains were harvested, including *ragi, jari, bajra*, pulses, horsegram, Bengal gram and green gram. The principal wet crops were rice and sugarcane, grown near river Kaveri or near reservoirs. Tipu discouraged the production of more than one crop on the same soil so that its fertility was not affected. Cash crops such as areca nut, pepper, cardamom, tobacco and sandalwood were grown as well, and they got good revenue for the state.

Tipu attended to the regular repair of tanks and encouraged cultivation in the wastelands by charging very low rents. Rents were 'fair and moderate' and state officers were 'strictly instructed not to harass the ryots' (ibid.). Together, Tipu's reforms made it almost impossible for tax collectors to exploit the peasants or rob the state of its rent, as was the custom in earlier times. This is perhaps the reason, comments Sheik Ali, why even his 'inveterate foes' were compelled to acknowledge that Tipu's country was the best cultivated and its population the most flourishing in India (ibid.: 164).

More significantly, Tipu's measures laid the basis for the Ryotwari (Raiyatwari) Settlement (settlement of revenue with *ryots*/peasants) to be introduced by the Company in the region. Captain Alexander Read initiated it in Baramahal districts surrendered by Tipu Sultan after his defeat in 1792 and extended it to Coimbatore, the Carnatic and the ceded districts (Mukherjee 1962). Tipu's revenue reforms made it easy for Read to introduce the Ryotwari Settlement in the areas the Company obliged Tipu to cede.

When Wellesley renewed hostilities against him in 1799, Tipu's territory was surrounded by Company territories, which comprised the more productive coastal areas. In addition, the Company's government, now armed with a cohesive system of intelligence, was better prepared to anticipate alliances and armed resistance by Indian rulers. Intelligence building had started from the time of Cornwallis, who had also tried to stop bilateral and multilateral channels of information between Indian powers (Bayly 1999: 58). Tipu also got no help from Revolutionary and Napoleonic France, although Wellesley's stated reason for marching against him was that as an ally of the French Tipu would encourage Napoleon to invade India. Tipu died gallantly in battle in the Fourth Mysore War at the gates of his capital Seringapatnam in 1799. His death occasioned great cheer in Britain. Tipu's death came before his orders for the construction of a navy had been put into practice. One is left to ponder what would have happened if he had managed to build his navy.

THE MARATHA CHIEFS

Wellesley's next move was against the Marathas, the four dominant families of Maratha chiefs—the Scindias (Shindes), Holkars, Gaekwads and Bhosles—with their respective strongholds in Gwalior, Indore, Baroda and Nagpur. These chiefs loosely functioned as a 'confederacy' managing taxation and revenue, but were also divided by mutual hostility, particularly between Daulat Rao Scindia and Yaswant

Rao Holkar (Sen 1928). The Peshwas, reduced considerably in influence after the death of the fourth Peshwa, Madhav Rao I, had ceased to be a rival of the British. Indeed, on the fifth day after taking office, Wellesley informed Peshwa Baji Rao II that he had assumed charge, and impressed upon him the necessity of continuing friendly relations with the British power, 'almost insinuating a threat against non-compliance' (Sardesai 1948: 352). The young Peshwa held out for a time, refusing to compromise his independence completely. Wellesley understood and waited, biding his time to overcome the Peshwa.

After the defeat of the combined armies of the Nawab of Bengal, the *vizier* of Awadh and the Mughal emperor at the hands of the East India Company in the Battle of Buxar (1764), in 1771, Daulat Rao's predecessor, Mahadji Scindia, reinstated Shah Alam II to his throne in Delhi, provoking Warren Hastings to send an army to capture Gwalior. This so-called First Anglo–Martha War had ended with the Treaty of Salbei in 1781, where Mahadji Scindia had been obliged to accept the terms set by the Company.

Wellesley's opportunity for intervention at the turn of the century was provided by Yaswant Rao Holkar's moves against his arch enemy Mahadji Scindia, which led him eventually into a war with the Peshwa, a friend of Scindia after the Peshwa failed to respect Holkar's repeated messages of negotiation. Scindia's army suffered heavy losses in the battle of 25 October 1802, and the Peshwa fled Poona and took refuge in the Maratha outpost of Vasai (Bassein) practically under British protection (Sardesai 1948: 379). He also wrote to Jonathan Duncan, the British Governor of Bombay, seeking his help. Finally, in December the Peshwa put himself completely in the care of the British. Wellesley used this opportunity to oblige him to sign the humiliating Treaty of Bassein on 31 December 1802.

Its main stipulations bound the Peshwa and the East India Company to respect each other's friends and enemies as such, which meant that the Peshwa could not enter into relations directly with the Nizam or Gaekwad without consulting the British. More significantly, Baji Rao had to cede districts yielding ₹ 26 lakh by way of subsidy for the Company's force stationed permanently in his territory. He had to agree to help the Company whenever it needed help; not employ any European hostile to the British; and not have any diplomatic relations with other Indian states without the knowledge of the Company (ibid.: 384).

The Treaty of Bassein has been regarded by some as the cause for the Second Anglo–Maratha War. The news of the treaty it is claimed, 'dismayed Holkar and other Maratha leaders, who organized a conference to deal with the British threat (ibid.: 384–85). At the same time, it is true that intrigues and mutual jealousy of the Maratha chiefs prevented them from forming a consolidated coalition, while some like Gaekwad were prevented from joining by the fact that they had already become subsidiary allies. On the other hand, Wellesley was determined to do away with Maratha power, particularly Scindia, and hence a clash was on the cards. Wellesley made full use of the opportunity—he and his brother Arthur Wellesley, along with Lord Lake, organized a vast, comprehensive set of coordinated campaigns, which put 60,000 trained men on widely different fronts (Gordon 1993: 175).

To begin with, Holkar, who was supporting a rival Peshwa in Poona, was neutralized and Baji Rao restored to his position. Wellesley's brother, Colonel Arthur Wellesley, marched at the head of a large army from the Deccan to subdue Holkar. This triggered the Third Anglo–Maratha War in which Wellesley's main target was Raghuji Bhosle of Nagpur, who had overrun the territories of the Nizam of Hyderabad, a subsidiary ally of the Company. Maratha armies were defeated at Assaye and Argaon and the forts of Ahmadnagar, Burhanpur and Gawilgarh were captured. Raghuji signed the Treaty of Deogaon and agreed to reduce his territories, transfer large parts of his land to the Company and not commit acts of aggression on the Company or its traders.

The Company consolidated its victory by sending another force from Bengal under Lord Lake, which defeated the combined armies of Scindia and Holkar and captured Delhi in 1803. The campaign against the Marathas was applauded as a great tactical achievement where rapid deployment of the army over a large distance and steadily maintaining its supply in terms of food and ammunition were seen as principal causes of success. The supply was kept up by means of bullocks and bullock carts provided by Indian merchants who also supplied money and food, and Indian foot soldiers fought under the command of British generals in the Company's army. The success then, though crucial for the extension of the Company's power in India, was actually a success of Indian merchants and mercenaries (Bates 2007: 39).

The Company's stringent demands threw the Indian rulers more and more into the arms of Indian bankers and merchants and induced occasional acts of defiance. One such act, by Nawab Wazir Ali of Awadh in 1798, led to greater intervention by the British and subsequently the annexation of half of Awadh by Wellesley as a substitute for the subsidy. The loss of fertile lands exacerbated the nawab's bankruptcy and made him dependant on *taluqdars*, who boldly consolidated their power in the countryside. This would eventually prompt the Awadh nawabs to withdraw from the affairs of the state and retreat into their courts as patrons of music, dance and the arts.

WELLESLEY'S ADMINISTRATION

Wellesley's open imperialism had made the Company the master of India by the time of his departure. At the same time, the enormous expansion of the military apparatus brought about significant changes in the policies of the Company's government. In the six years of Wellesley's administration (1798/99–1803/4), the army accounted for 42.5 per cent of the Company's total expenditure. As mentioned earlier, the army was entrusted with the collection and collation of information about Indian ruling families and the assessment of their commercial resources and military capabilities. The establishing of the Fort William College and a Persian secretariat under Wellesley made it clear that the Company's primary interest was no longer commercial.

Fort William College, founded against the opposition of the Court of Directors, was meant to foster the teaching of oriental languages and infuse public servants with new energy by training them to administer without depending on Indian intermediaries. As mentioned in the Minute in Council at Fort William, the college was also designed to 'extricate the young public servants from the "habitual indolence, dissipation and licentious indulgence", which were a "natural consequence" of living in close proximity to the "peculiar depravity of the people of India"' (cited in Bayly 1988: 83). The young servants were also distanced from the commercial character of the Company—the old designations of writers, factors and merchants were discarded and private trade was strictly forbidden. Gambling and drunkenness, as well as open concubinage with Indian women were censured.

The Persian secretariat, on the other hand, was designed to gain better knowledge of Indian affairs. Further, continuing with the trend of restricting administrative interference by separating the executive and the judiciary, Wellesley made the *Sadar Diwani* and *Nizamat Adalat* independent of the supervision of the Governor-General and Council. He also vigorously applied the regulations of the Company, codified by Cornwallis, in settling the newly annexed territories (ibid.). The 'anglicization' of the bureaucracy and the judiciary was complete.

It is important to remember that the British Parliament and the Company's Court of Directors were not always in agreement with Wellesley's imperialist measures. Indeed, the directors were worried about the escalating military expenditure and the damage to trade caused by constant warfare. However, given the fact that London lay at a distance of six months from Calcutta, communication between London and Calcutta took almost a year to complete. Wellesley, who had nothing but scorn for the 'narrow, counting-house mentality' of the Court of Directors (Stokes [1959] 1989: 10), acted quickly and made real his ventures before the restraining orders could reach him. And, he 'achieved much through patronage and reorganization in Calcutta' (Bayly 1988: 82).

New Measures

The Company's hold over the subcontinent was strengthened further by the introduction of new revenue settlements in the ceded and conquered districts. The revenue system adopted by Read and Thomas Munro in the territories seized from Tipu were simple adaptations of the revenue systems of the sultans, 'designed to provide money to pay for armies' (Bayly 1988: 86). In 1801, Company officers introduced a Permanent Settlement in the Madras districts and confirmed *poligars* (*paliagar*s) in possession of their land as zamindars (Ludden 1985: 104). When *poligars* were not found, several villages were aggregated into estates and sold to the highest bidder (Bandyopadhyay 2004: 87). As problems of the Permanent Settlement became evident, criticism of it gained prominence in British official circles. Indeed, the 'permanence' of the settlement had been modified, particularly in its application to Orissa and Assam. There the settlements had been made with landlords, but the Company reserved the right to review and raise the rent periodically.

In 1820, policy principles devised by Thomas Munro, who became the Governor of Madras Presidency that year, gained official supremacy. The change in official policy was a result, partly of the influence of the ideas of the Scottish Enlightenment—which gave primacy to agriculture and the yeoman farmer instead of the zamindar—on officials such as Munro and Monstuart Elphinstone, and partly of the new importance acquired by David Ricardo's theory of rent. According to this theory, the state had a legitimate share in the rent, which was the surplus obtained from land after deducting the cost of labour and production. A permanent settlement of revenue demand deprived the state of the surplus because unproductive intermediaries—zamindars—got the benefit of the surplus only because they owned the land. Munro wanted to reserve for the state the right to increase taxes in order to profit from the growth of agriculture and to tide over times of emergency (Stokes [1959] 1989: 83). The most important reason behind the need to change was, of course, the huge financial crisis of the Madras Presidency, exacerbated further by war. This prompted the Company to look for newer ways of extracting revenue.

The Ryotwari System that took shape in the Madras Presidency was governed by the same impulse that had dictated the Permanent Settlement—of clearly defining the rights between landlord and tenant, as well as public and private—so that the state could fix its revenue demand and grant legal 'rights' to subjects over their 'private' property, that is, the remaining produce of the soil. Since policies, argues Ludden, were formulated by Englishmen who defined meanings shared by them in London, Calcutta and Madras, 'the official lexicon for colonial discourse and the official language of Anglo–Indian governance that codified the policies' introduced two central concepts that were 'utterly foreign' to Tamil peasants—zamindar and *ryot* (1985: 104). The Ryotwari System defined the state itself as the supreme zamindar and vested a *ryot* with individual proprietary rights in land in return for annual cash payment or revenue assessments to the government (ibid.). The revenue to be paid by each village was fixed, as well as the rent or the revenue to be paid by each *ryot*. *Ryots* were given *pattas*, annual receipts that constituted a title to land. The state retained its claim over wastelands.

Munro advocated that rents be kept suitably low and be fixed for 30 years, a measure that would protect peasant-farmers from mounting and arbitrary exactions by 'intermediaries' who had caused much damage to peasant property rights. Meant to be attractive and equitable, this system could only function if the survey was fair and thorough, a survey that took into consideration the quality of soil, the area of the field and its average produce. This almost 'inquisitorial investigation' into the private concerns of the people conferred on the executive officials near exclusive power to decide what constituted public and private rights (Stokes [1959] 1989: 83–84).

Although to Munro the term *ryot* designated all peasants, it was virtually impossible for district officers to work effectively without recognizing distinctions among the peasantry, such as those between farmers of wet and dry zones, or greater and lesser families in the village community, or between different caste identities and 'customary relations of inequality' (Ludden 1985: 104–105). Zamindars too, remained little kings for their subjects; they retained the title of rajas and the customary ritual and caste authority in their domains. Caste privileges of the Brahmans, as well as the special rents of the *mirasidar*s (people with special shares in the dues in the former *mirasi* system prevalent in the region) were recognized. Consequently, the colonial state's drive for progressive centralization proceeded through mix-ups and through negotiations across cultural boundaries in which native officers were decisive. 'The men who translated the terms of Munro's Ryotwari policy into Tamil and interpreted rustic realities for English officers' were well equipped for the task (ibid.: 106–107). They were interested in the stability of the new regime and the advancement of their own power in it.

Indeed, the detailed survey and codification that the Ryotwari System entailed, allowed the *mirasidar*s of 'good agricultural castes' such as the Vellalas to acquire special prominence by virtue of their active collaboration in the process. They strengthened their position within the village hierarchy and monopolized jobs in subordinate positions of the revenue administration. Soon, they also handled police duties commanding thereby great power and influence at the local level. This system, therefore, did not do away with 'intermediaries'; rather it ended up granting great powers to them. This inevitably led to coercion and corruption.

In addition, the enormous land survey that was required for the system to work properly was often not carried out and the revenue demand and rents were fixed arbitrarily on the basis of village accounts. Such accounts often did not have the details of the quality of individual plots held by peasants. Peasants came to be saddled with very high demands which led to their gradual impoverishment. Despite such problems, the Ryotwari System was extended to Gujarat and a large part of the Bombay Presidency after the defeat of the Marathas in 1818 by Munro's disciple, Mountstuart Elphinstone. The same problems remained although attempts were made in the 1830s to reduce revenue demand to a level that could be met.

The introduction of revenue settlements was complemented by an almost unnoticed process that would become more pronounced in the nineteenth century and have significant consequences on the way India would get spatially mapped and managed. As zones of settled agriculture were increasingly brought under the purview of the Company state's revenue settlements, forests got demarcated first as areas that constituted an 'obstruction to agriculture' and were treated with disregard or destroyed, and later they acquired prominence as 'a distinct domain of management under the colonial government' (Sivaramakrishnan 1999: 76). We will explore this in the next chapter.

To sum up, by the end of the eighteenth century, the Company state had taken definite shape through contradictory yet confident measures adopted by its governor-generals and local functionaries. It had firmly cut the cord between Indian commerce and political power (Bose and Jalal 1998: 65), and effectively undermined the eighteenth century state system. Clear changes in the ideology of governance through the 1780s and 1790s meant that colonial state building decisively broke away from 'Asiatic tyranny', declaring that it was a 'purified agency of imperial virtue' (Travers 2007: 207).

The process, of course, was intricate and tortuous. It was shaped as much by transformations in Britain's political ideology and the fluctuating fortunes of the East India Company, as it was by the multiple and shifting modes through which colonial expansion proceeded in India. Moreover, state building was plagued by 'competing agendas for using power, competing strategies for maintaining control and doubts about the legitimacy of the venture' (Cooper and Stoler 1989: 609). Nevertheless, by the time Wellesley left India, a very large part of the subcontinent had come under the rule of the Company, the governments of the three presidencies had become consolidated and the main pillars of the colonial state—army, bureaucracy and judiciary—were in place. State making and knowledge production had come together to strengthen the construction of the 'colonial state'. With the final defeat of the Marathas in 1818, the East India Company would become the unchallenged ruler of India. The stage was set for a more vital intervention in Indian society, a story we will take up next.

In Review: The Dhangars

By the end of the eighteenth century, the East India Company faced a problem in the territories under its command: groups of people who had enjoyed virtual independence in the Mughal period now posed a serious threat to the revenue collecting system of the Company. These people, whose generic name was 'hill-people', comprised in fact a lot of different groups: Santals, Paharias and Bhumijs, to name a few. They generated fears and anxieties in the governance of the north and central states in India; their frequent raids in the plains threatened colonial calculations of revenue. It was clear that something had to be done, but the war effort against the 'hill-people' was not cheap and the Company state's success did not last more than a few weeks. The chiefs of the hill-people stopped paying tributes and continued their raids.

The 'pacification' of the hill-people was a process that lasted several years and was supported by two main institutions: a highly disciplined colonial army, capable of suppressing any revolt and rebellion in the hills; and an extended land tenure system that dispossessed many hill villagers, farmers and even chiefs. This produced a growing market in land and a thriving moneylending business that pushed many villagers into huge debts. Soon, many hill-people found themselves with no land and no jobs. On the brink of starvation, many of these people accepted any job in order to survive: 'the pacification that was thus brought about led to the creation of an enormous population that had to move out of the region in search of a livelihood' (Ghosh 1999: 13). Soon, the images of these people changed from savage and fierce raiders to 'hard-working' and docile people who worked in plantations in near slavery conditions.

As we will see in Chapter 4, the development of tea gardens (plantations) in Assam accompanied the creation of this new wage-labour. The 'coolies', as these people were to be called, fed the colonial imagination of an unrelenting flow of people whose major activity was working in plantations. All over the empire, the coolies were seen as a major option if there was shortage of labour force in the fields. By 1837, 'Dhangar' (coolies) had become a generic name in the colonial vocabulary. 'In Mauritius, in British Guiana, in Trinidad, in the agency-houses of London and even in Australia', writes Kaushik Ghosh, 'all the hysteria over the loss of profit' on account of slave-emancipation or over the scarcity of labour in comparison to the vastness of land, came to be treated with 'dreams of Dhangars arriving from India by ship in the thousands'. And 'these dreams moved fast' within the 'global plantocracy' (Ghosh 1999: 19).

The 'coolie' system was violent not only because it uprooted a large number of people from their lands; the recruiting system was quite similar to slavery. In the words of Ranajit Dasgupta, recruitment was made by a class of licensed contractors, many of whom were Europeans, with headquarters in Calcutta. Hundreds of professional recruiters (arkattis), villagers, men and women on the spot, worked under the contractors. The contractor and their men, concerned only with rounding up as many people as possible, resorted to all forms of deceit and trickery, intimidation, actual violence and even abduction of married women and children, to recruit coolies. The entire system of indentured labour, 'the coolie-catching, their transit to the tea gardens…, the selling of recruits at a market price, the hunt for run-away coolies' resembled 'the slave-running in Africa and the global slave trade' (Dasgupta 1981: 1784)

In the colonial imagination, the Dhangars were remarkable for their 'incredible suitability' for plantation labour. Plantation owners believed that the dhangars demanded little space to sleep and a very small quantity of food. Even during travel from the ports of India to several destinations in the British colonies, the coolies were crammed in a very small space, with scarcely any food and no medical supervision. The mortality rate was sometimes as high as 50 per cent (Ghosh 1999: 22).

Conditions were not any better in the plantations. Often the tea coolies, worked to exhaustion, minimally fed, badly housed and severely tortured, tried to flee the plantations. Local Assamese tribesmen, whose villages dotted the landscape outside the plantations, were paid by the planters to hunt down the deserters and bring them back for small cash rewards. The reward was deducted from the coolie's wages who was 'often severely flogged in addition' (Ghosh 1999: 44).

REFERENCES

Acharya, Bijay Kisor. 1914. *Codification in British India*. Calcutta: S.K. Banerji and Sons.

Agnes, Flavia. 1999. *Law and Gender Inequality: The Politics of Women's Rights in India*. New Delhi: Oxford University Press.

Alavi, Seema. 1993. 'The Makings of Company Power: James Skinner in the Ceded and Conquered Provinces, 1802–1840'. *The Indian Economic and Social History Review* 30 (4): 437–66.

———. [1995] 1998. *The Sepoys and the Company: Tradition and Transition in Northern India, 1770–1830*. New Delhi: Oxford University Press.

Bandyopadhyay, Sekhar. 2004. *From Plassey to Partition: A History of Modern India*. Hyderabad: Orient Longman.

Bates, Crispin. 2007. *Subalterns and the Raj: South Asia Since 1600*. London: Routledge.

Bayly, C. A. 1988. *Indian Society and the Making of the British Empire*. Cambridge: Cambridge University Press.

———. 1999. *Empire and Information: Intelligence Gathering and Social Communication in India, 1780–1870*. Cambridge: Cambridge University Press.

Bhattacharya-Panda, Nandini. 2008. *Appropriation and Invention of Tradition: The East India Company and Hindu Law in Early Colonial Bengal*. New Delhi: Oxford University Press.

Bose, Sugata. 1986. *Agrarian Bengal: Society, Economic Structure and Politics 1919–1947*. Cambridge: Cambridge University Press.

Bose, Sugata and Ayesha Jalal. 1998. *Modern South Asia: History, Culture, Political Economy*. Paperback edition, 2000. London: Routledge.

Bowen, H. V. 2006. *The Business of Empire: The East India Company and Imperial Britain, 1756–1833*. Cambridge: Cambridge University Press.

Chatterjee, Partha. 1984. *Bengal 1920–1947: The Land Question*. Calcutta: K. P. Bagchi and Co.

Chaudhuri, B. B. 1975. 'The Land Market in Eastern India, 1793–1940'. Pt. 1. *The Indian Economic and Social History Review* 12 (1): 1–41.

———. 1983. 'The Land and Its People: Eastern India'. In *The Cambridge Economic History of India, Vol. 2, c.1757–c.1970*, edited by Dharma Kumar, 86–177. Cambridge: Cambridge University Press.

———. 1984. 'Rural Power Structure and Agricultural Productivity in Eastern India, 1757–1967'. In *Agrarian Power and Agricultural Productivity in South Asia*, edited by Meghnad Desai, Susanne Hoeber Rudolph and Ashok Rudra, 100–170. New Delhi: Oxford University Press.

Cohn, Bernard S. 1964. 'The Role of Gosains in the Economy of Eighteenth and Nineteenth Century Upper India'. *The Indian Economic and Social History Review* 4 (1): 175–82.

Colebrook, Henry T. 1804. *Remarks on the Present State of Husbandry and Commerce of Bengal*. Calcutta: n.p.

Cooper, Frederick and Ann Laura Stoler. 1989. 'Introduction; Tensions of Empire: Colonial Control and Visions of Rule'. *American Ethnologist* Sp. Section 'Tensions of Empire' 16 (4): 609–21.

Dasgupta, Ranajit. 1981. 'Structure of the Labour Market in Colonial India'. *Economic and Political Weekly* 16, 44/46, Special Number (Nov.): 1781–1806.

De, Barun. 1999. 'The Ideological and Social Background of Haidar Ali and Tipu Sultan'. In *Confronting Colonialism: Resistance and Modernization under Haidar Ali and Tipu Sultan*, edited by I. Habib, 3–12. New Delhi: Tulika.

Dow, Alexander. 1772. *History of Hindostan, from the Death of Akbar, to the Complete Settlement of the Empire under Aurangzeb*. 3 volumes. London: T. Becket and P. A. de Hondt.

Furber, Holden. 1970a. *John Company at Work: A Study of European Expansion in India in the Late Eighteenth Century*. New York: Octagon Books.

———. 1970b. 'The History of East India Companies: General Problems'. In *Sociétes et Compagnies de Commerce en Orient et dans l'Océan Indien*, edited by Michel Mollat, 415–18. Paris: S.E.V.P.E.N.

Gadgil, Madhav and Ramchandra Guha. [1992] 1993. *This Fissured Land: An Ecological History of India*. New Delhi: Oxford University Press. Paperback 1993.

Ghosh, Atig. 2009. 'Colonial Making of the *Mofussil*: Political Economy and Culture in Nineteenth-Century Bengal'. PhD. Dissertation, Centre for Asian and African Studies, El Colegio de México.

Ghosh, Kaushik. 1999. 'A Market for Aboriginality: Primitivism and Race Classification in the Indentured Labour Market of Colonial India'. In *Subaltern Studies X: Writings on South Asian History and Society*, eds Gautam Bhadra, Gyan Prakash and Susie Tharu, 8–48. Delhi: Oxford University Press.

Gidwani, Vinay K. 1992. '"Waste" and the Permanent Settlement in Bengal'. *Economic and Political Weekly* 27 (4) (25 January): 39–46.

Gleig, G. R. 1841. *Memoirs of Warren Hastings*. 3 volumes. London: R. Bentley.

Gommans, J. L. and Dirk H. A. Kolff, eds. 2001. *Warfare and Weaponry in South Asia, 1000–1800*. New Delhi: Oxford University Press.

Gordon, S. 1993. *The Marathas, 1600–1818, The New Cambridge History of India*. Vol. 2.4. Cambridge: Cambridge University Press.

Governor General's Minute. 18 September 1789. *Fifth Report* Vol. 2: 512.

Guha, Ranajit. [1963] 1982. *A Rule of Property for Bengal: An Essay on the Idea of Permanent Settlement*. New Delhi: Orient Longman. Reprint 1982.

Habib, I., ed. 1999. *Confronting Colonialism: Resistance and Modernization under Haidar Ali and Tipu Sultan*. New Delhi: Tulika.

Halhed, Nathaniel B. 1970. 'The Translator's Preface to a Code of Gentoo Laws'. In *The British Discovery of Hinduism in the Eighteenth Century*, edited by P. J. Marshall. Cambridge: Cambridge University Press.

Hasan, Mohibbul. 1999. 'The French in the Second Anglo–Mysore War'. In *Confronting Colonialism: Resistance and Modernization under Haidar Ali and Tipu Sultan*, edited by I. Habib, 35–48. New Delhi: Tulika.

Horn, D. B. and Mary Ransome, eds. 1957. *English Historical Documents, 1714–1783*. London: Eyre and Spottiswoode.

Husain, Mahmud. 1999. 'Regulations of Tipu Sultan's Navy'. In *Confronting Colonialism: Resistance and Modernization under Haidar Ali and Tipu Sultan*, edited by I. Habib, 174–81. New Delhi: Tulika.

Hutchins, Francis G. 1967. *The Illusion of Permanence: British Imperialism in India*. Princeton, NJ: Princeton University Press.

Islam, S. 1979. *The Permanent Settlement in Bengal: A Study of its Operation 1790–1819*. Dacca: Bangla Academy.

Keay, John. 2010. *The Honourable Company*. UK: Harper Collins.

Khan, Iftikar A. 1999. 'The Regulations of Tipu Sultan for His State Trading Enterprise'. In *Confronting Colonialism: Resistance and Modernization under Haidar Ali and Tipu Sultan*, edited by I. Habib, 148–60. New Delhi: Tulika.

Lorenzen, David. 1978. 'Warrior Ascetics in Indian History'. *Journal of the American Oriental Society* 98 (1): 61–75.

Ludden, David. 1985. *Peasant History in South India*. Princeton, NJ: Princeton University Press.

———. 1994. 'Orientalist Empiricism: Transformations of Colonial Knowledge'. In *Orientalism and the Postcolonial Predicament*, coord. by Breckenridge and Van der Veer, 250–78. New Delhi: Oxford University Press.

Marshall, P. J. ed. 1970. *The British Discovery of Hinduism in the Eighteenth Century.* Cambridge: Cambridge University Press.

———. 1987. *Bengal: The British Bridgehead, Eastern India 1740–1828.* Cambridge: Cambridge University Press.

———. 2005. *The Making and Unmaking of Empires: Britain, India, and America c.1750–1783.* Oxford: Oxford University Press.

Metcalf, Thomas R. 1995. *Ideologies of the Raj.* New Delhi: Cambridge University Press.

Misra, B. B. 1959. *The Central Administration of the East India Company.* Manchester: Manchester University Press.

Morley, W. H. 1858. *The Administration of Justice in British India; Its Past History and Present State: Comprising an Account of the Laws Peculiar to India.* Reprint, 1976. London: Williams and Norgate.

Mukherjee, Nilmani. 1962. *The Ryotwari System in Madras.* Calcutta: Firma K. L. Mukhopadhyay.

Mukherjee, S. N. [1968] 1987. *Sir William Jones: A Study in Eighteenth-Century British Attitudes to India.* Hyderabad: Orient Longman.

Nandy, Ashis. 1983. *The Intimate Enemy: Loss and Recovery of Self Under Colonialism.* New Delhi: Oxford University Press.

Peers, Douglas M. 1995. *Between Mars and Mammon: Colonial Armies and the Garrison State in Early Nineteenth Century India.* London: Macmillan.

Ray, Rajat K. 1988. 'The Retreat of the Jotedar?' Review article. *The Indian Economic and Social History Review* 25 (2): 237–247.

Ray, Rajat and Ratna Ray. 1973. 'The Dynamics of Continuity in Rural Bengal under the British Imperium'. *The Indian Economic and Social History Review* 10 (2): 103–28.

———. 1975. 'Zamindars and Jotedars: A Study of Rural Politics in Bengal'. *Modern Asian Studies* 9 (1): 81–102.

Ray, Ratnalekha. 1987. 'The Changing Fortunes of the Bengali Gentry—The Palchaudhuri's of Maheshganj 1800–1950'. *Modern Asian Studies* 21 (3): 511–19.

Rocher, Rosane. 1994. 'British Orientalism in the Eighteenth Century: The Dialectics of Knowledge and Government'. In *Orientalism and the Postcolonial Predicament*, edited by Carol A. Breckenridge and Peter Van der Veer, 215–49. New Delhi: Oxford University Press.

Sardesai, G. S. 1948. *New History of the Marathas.* Vol. 3. Bombay: D. B. Dhawale for Phoenix Publications.

Sen, Sudipta. 1998. *Empire of Free Trade: The East India Company and the Making of the Colonial Marketplace.* Philadelphia: University of Pennsylvania Press.

———. 2010. 'Subordination, Governance, and the Legislative State in Early Colonial India'. In *Subaltern Citizens and their Histories: Investigations from India and the USA*, edited by Gyanendra Pandey, 145–60. Abingdon and New York: Routledge.

Sen, S. N. 1928. *The Military System of the Marathas.* Calcutta: The Book Company.

Sheik Ali, B. 1999. 'Developing Agriculture: Land Tenure Under Tipu Sultan'. In *Confronting Colonialism: Resistance and Modernization under Haidar Ali and Tipu Sultan*, edited by I. Habib, 161–164. New Delhi: Tulika.

Sinha, N. K. 1965. *The Economic History of Bengal.* Vol. I. Calcutta: Firma K. L. Mukhopadhyay.

———. 1968. *The Economic History of Bengal.* Vol. II. Calcutta: Firma K. L. Mukhopadhyay.

Sivaramakrishnan, K. 1999. *Modern Forests: Statemaking and Environmental Change in Colonial Eastern India.* Stanford: Stanford University Press.

Sridharan, M. P. 1999. 'Tipu's Drive toward Modernization: French Evidence from the 1780s'. In *Confronting Colonialism: Resistance and Modernization under Haidar Ali and Tipu Sultan*, edited by I. Habib, 143–47. New Delhi: Tulika.

Stern, Philip J. 2011. *The Company State: Corporate Sovereignty 'and the' Early Modern Foundations 'of the' British Empire 'in' India*. New York: Oxford University Press.

Stokes, Eric. [1959] 1989. *The English Utilitarians and India*. London: Oxford University Press.

Travers, Robert. 2007. *Ideology and Empire in Eighteenth-Century India: The British in Bengal*. Cambridge: Cambridge University Press.

An Inaugural Century 3

Mounted rebel sepoys charging through the streets of Delhi in May 1857; c.1895 engraving, artist unknown

Chapter outline

Wellesley was recalled from India in 1805. By the time he left, he had brought about a political revolution by acquiring for the Company territorial possessions as extensive and expensive as to 'stagger the imagination of his contemporaries' (Philips 1961: 103). The aristocrat had also occasioned a 'cultural revolution' by setting up the College of Fort William, the 'Oxford of the East' in 1800. The College wanted to transform 'inept, self-seeking servants of the East India Company into efficient, devoted servants of the British Empire in India' (Kopf 1969: 46–47). Between 1801 and 1805, the College evolved into an institution not only for training civil servants, but also for patronizing literary and linguistic research and Orientalist scholarship in general. Further, it gave the Asiatic Society—in disarray after the death of William Jones (in 1794)—a new breath of life by revitalizing its structure, promoting its scholarship and, most importantly, by producing a new generation of potential scholars among civil servants willing to carry on the work of the Society.

The College, moreover, interacted closely with the Serampore Mission. The Baptist missionaries were the only ones who had managed to evade the ban imposed by the Company on the entry of missionaries, by taking refuge in the Danish enclave at Serampore (Srirampur). Despite the Company administration's suspicion of missionary activities, the expertise of the missionaries as printers and publishers helped the College enormously (Hatcher 1996: 49). The collaboration of scholars, officials and missionaries, such as William Carey and Joshua Marshman, occasioned an extensive study of Indian languages, the production of dictionaries, translation of manuscripts and Indian classics, and significantly, close examinations of Hindu popular culture in Bengal.

Henry T. Colebrook, a renowned Orientalist scholar and William Jones' successor, who was appointed professor of Sanskrit at Fort William in 1800, undertook a serious study of the *Vedas*. Although he did not carry out the arduous task of translating them, his essay on the *Vedas* placed the texts chronologically prior to the *Puranas* and outlined the existence of a monotheistic tradition, 'the unity of the Godhead' in ancient India (Kopf 1969: 41). The essay, read in the Asiatic Society on 4 July 1804 and published in the eighth volume of *Asiatick Researches*, was considered to be 'the most important *desideratum* in Indian literature' by the *Edinburgh Review*, since it opened a whole new line of inquiry for students of Indology (Kejariwal 1988: 98). The essay also put an end to the controversy among western scholars about the existence and authenticity of the *Vedas* and their continued existence.

About 50 years later in 1859, the *Calcutta Review* lauded Colebrook's essay as 'a masterly analysis' and 'the most valuable contribution to Indian literature that has yet been made' (1859: 401). Apart from the impact the essay had among Indologists, the idea of a single godhead was also drawn upon by Indian intellectuals like Rammohan Roy, a point we will explore later in the chapter. For now, we need to remember that Colebrook and the College's other professors contributed to the emergence of a new generation of administrators-cum-scholars. Such men were to induce significant changes in Indian society by applying their 'knowledge' of India to administration and implementing it in their policies.

From the end of the eighteenth century then, India increasingly became an object of British knowledge, and the empire in India became more a 'blessing' than an 'embarrassment' for the British. As indicated in the last chapter, numerous books on India started being published in Britain from the 1760s and British newspapers came to carry regular reports on India. With the imperial nature of the Company's rule becoming apparent from the turn of the century, the need to make it legitimate became urgent. This was provided by the civilizing (civilizational) mission, made forceful by a combination of different players. To use Ashis Nandy's provocative words, 'Colonialism minus a civilizational mission is no colonialism at all' (1983: 11).

Before we turn to an analysis of this civilizing mission, an examination of the different trends in orientalism current at the time will proffer a better understanding of the impact of the distinct trends on Indian intellectuals (Hatcher 1996: 46); and guard against a simplistic use of orientalism as a monolith that constructed knowledge solely to seek power (Said 1978). The orientalism of Warren Hastings and William Jones stemmed from a cosmopolitanism that urged love and respect for other cultures. William Jones, in particular, wanted to find out more about man and nature, in what is 'performed by one' and 'produced by the other'; he regarded history, science and art to be the three main branches of learning (Jones 1807: 6). Jones was interested in languages insofar as they disclosed the connected nature of nations and races (Trautmann 2006: 15). 'The Sanscrit language', he affirmed in his inaugural speech at the Asiatic Society of Calcutta, had 'a wonderful structure that was more perfect than the Greek, more copious than the Latin, and more exquisitely refined than either'. At the same time, it bore such a strong affinity to Greek and Latin, in the roots of verbs and the forms of grammar that no philologer could examine the three of them 'without believing them to have sprung from some common source' (Jones 1807: 7).

It is a paradox, writes Thomas Trautmann, that someone 'so gifted in languages' regarded them as only one of many means to 'disentangle ethnological relationships'. Relations among languages, for Jones, indexed relations among nations (Trautmann 2006: 15). Representative of the tensions that European scholars faced at the end of the eighteenth century in their encounter with India, Jones tracked a chronology for India that fitted well with Mosiack history by tracing the foundation of the Indian empire about 3,800 years from his time, that is, safely within the confines of the Biblical account and within the parameters of the Great Flood, which Jones considered to have occurred in 2350 BCE (Bryant 2001: 15). Jones' compromise with the Biblical narrative made the new orientalism safe for Anglicans. He demonstrated that Sanskrit literature was 'not an enemy but an ally' of the Bible, which supplied 'independent corroboration of the Bible's version of history'(Trautmann 1997: 74). This laid the basis for the idea that the Aryans had come to India from outside, the far-reaching consequences of which we will examine in the following chapter.

The interest of evangelicals like William Carey in promoting vernacular languages was geared primarily towards making the Bible available to Indians, only after they had been morally prepared to receive it. Official orientalism of the early-nineteenth century and that of scholars like H. H. Wilson and Colebrook, on the other hand, showed respect only for the mysteries of the ancient civilization of the Hindus and scant regard for the later period: for them, 'improvement' was the need of the hour.

Colebrook and many others of his time had imbibed the sense of history advanced by Voltaire: history was not just a chronicle of political events but a record of the growth of civilizations. In tune with this, Asia, the cradle of ancient civilizations, appeared to be in a state of decline while the West was taking large strides forward (Kopf 1969: 38–39). Parallel to and in conjunction with the grand historical narrative in Europe—offered by Gibbon, for instance—of a classical civilization, a long age of barbarism and religion and a recent dawning of enlightenment occasioned by reason and commerce, British India constructed its own variant of the enlightenment historical narrative. Here, classical Hindu civilization, a dark age of 'barbarism and religion' under Muslim tyranny and a modern era of colonial enlightenment came to constitute the different periods of history.

Nationalism and a strain of Protestant evangelism also prompted the Company to make its administration more 'British': honest and reliable (Bayly 1988). The Company's directors set up the Haileybury College in Oxford, a rival of Fort William, to train the Company's servants to be worthy bureaucrats. This College was to ensure that the 'boys', the future servants of the Company, were indoctrinated 'well' by the Cambridge clergymen before they were sent off to India and placed under the influence of Orientalist scholars at Fort William (Kopf 1969: 135). We have seen in the last chapter that the old division of writers, factors and merchants was replaced by a well-defined and coherent hierarchy in the Company's administration; its servants were paid better and were totally prohibited from engaging in private trade and from adopting 'native practices'. Marriages with Indian women or taking Indian mistresses were also forbidden. In a move common to all colonial powers, policies of exclusion were put in place to mark identities and construct categories. Race and gender became crucial in the construction of contingent identities of the colonizers and the colonized (Ghosh 2006; Stoler 2002: 42–43). All this made the nineteenth century stand in stark contrast to the preceding one in terms of principles and beliefs (Bates 2007: 44).

FORCES OF CHANGE: FREE TRADERS, EVANGELICALS, UTILITARIANS

The Charter Act of 1813 marked a watershed in the history of the Indian economy. It abolished the East India Company's monopoly of India's trade that had governed the character of Indo–British commerce for 200 years, and allowed the entry of British private merchants, the free traders, into India (Majumdar [1963] 1970: 1077). The success of the Industrial Revolution drastically altered conditions in Britain: rather than buying finished products, Britain now needed to secure markets for its factory goods produced on a massive scale, and captive suppliers of raw materials for the production of these goods. Opposition to the Company's monopoly of trade with India had been mounting since the beginning of the nineteenth century. At pace with the altered conditions, Company rule in India now had to act as an accessory, an instrument to ensure 'the necessary conditions of law and order' to make the vast Indian market captive for British goods (Stokes [1959] 1989: xiii). As K. N. Chaudhuri points out, between 1814 and 1858 the value and volume of Indian exports and imports quadrupled, but the commodity composition and the direction of trade also changed radically (Chaudhuri 1971: 1).

All this affected India's domestic economy in significant ways. India's political connection with Britain made her a 'primary producing country with her economy controlled and directed from outside' (*Minutes of Evidence Taken Before the Select Committee of the House of Lords Appointed to Consider the Petition of the East India Company for Relief 1840*, Parliamentary Papers, 1840, cited in ibid.: 2). While India became swamped with British factory-made goods, high protective duties prevented the entry of Indian manufacturers into the British market (ibid.: 3). The age-old cotton industry in India all but disappeared because it could not face the full blast of the Industrial Revolution. India came to depend critically on the production of raw materials, and India's primary producers were subjected to the vagaries of international economic forces. The Company's commercial capitalism succumbed to the irrepressible force of industrial capitalism represented by Lancashire and Sheffield, and India's agrarian economy was 'geared to the industrial economy of Great Britain' (Majumdar [1963] 1970: 1077).

The Company, of course, did not lose its commercial interest in India despite its gradual transformation into a colonial ruler. The annual revenue of 3 million pounds that it got from the grant of *diwani* in 1765 soared to 22 million pounds by the time of the final defeat of the Marathas in 1818. But expensive wars and a growing bureaucracy forced the Company to make good its investment: its purchases in India. Indeed, expansion in India had forced the Company to run into debt. Since the Court of Directors barely sent any money for expansion, the governments in India incurred remittable debt, that is, they allowed their creditors to demand principal and interest in London. Napoleonic wars and general commercial stagnation made such remittances through proper trading channels increasingly difficult; the Company became dependent on agency houses to remit the debt by means of bills on debt account. From 1806, the Company's creditors deluged the Company's Court of Directors with such bills and forced them to petition the British Parliament for loans in order to keep up its credit. Therefore, by 1813 the Company had lost all its bargaining power to counter the pressure of agency houses, which demanded free movement of capital between England and India; British private merchants, who demanded the import of cheap raw materials and export of surplus produce; and out ports, like Liverpool, which wanted employment of shipping because the stoppage of the American and the continental trade had rendered them idle (ibid.: 1077).

After the loss of monopoly of trade in India, China became crucial in the sustenance of the Company's trade with India. Sale of raw cotton and, more significantly, opium, in China provided a reliable source of revenue for the Company's Indian government. It also paid for the procurement of Chinese tea, an important article of import from China to Britain. The procurement of Chinese tea became more and more popular in Britain. Here, it is important to remember that the idea of exporting opium to China had started with Warren Hastings and the first shipments were sent as early as the 1780s. Initially, there was hardly any demand for opium in China. The situation changed radically over the next ten years and within a period of 30 years there was an enormous expansion in opium trade. During this period, most of the opium was grown in the Bihar region of the Bengal Presidency, and later, with an increase in demand, western India, Malwa in particular, began growing opium on a massive scale. Also, from about the 1830s, indentured emigration of opium growers out of India acquired significant proportions (Ghosh 2008).

The Company tightly controlled the production of opium by means of the advances it paid to growers. It also sold opium at a high price to British traders who smuggled it into China. Profits from opium sale, which amounted to about 17–20 per cent of Indian revenues, balanced the Company's precarious finances and freed its directors of the responsibility of exporting bullion to China for purchasing tea and other goods. In a similar manner, the tightly controlled production of indigo in India also provided the Company with finances to meet its requirements of remittances. In both cases, opposition led to wars and reprisal. The late 1830s witnessed opium wars against China. Bonded indigo cultivators' refusal to grow indigo in the 1850s ended in their relative success because by then indigo planters had lost their political clout and Germany had invented a chemical dye which made indigo lose its importance as a commercial crop. The plight of indigo growers formed the core of early middle-class reflection on agrarian and legal thinking in Bengal, although such writings left the peasants entirely undefined (Sinha 1965: 13). We discuss the implications of 'middle-class' empathy for peasants in Chapter 5.

In Review: Time for Tea

The history of tea plantation in India goes back to the late-eighteenth century, when members of the East India Company in London debated the profitability of producing tea in India. The person who brought the subject to the Company's functionaries was Joseph Banks.

Sir Joseph Banks (1743–1820) came from a wealthy but untitled family in Lincolnshire. While attending the famous Eton College at Oxford, Banks rejected the classic model of education and pursued studies on natural history, especially botany. During his subsequent voyages abroad in the company of the famous adventurer James Cook, Banks discovered several new species of plants, which he carefully catalogued and described in his journal notebooks. Thanks to his research, many aspects of the natural history of the new territories in South and South East Asia became known to the scientific community in Europe. Banks' extensive travel and research also caused new commercial routes to emerge that changed the landscape of some colonized territories as imperial policies were implemented to make profits in the rich market of tea and spices.

The Calcutta Botanical Garden was founded in 1787 under the aegis of Banks: it conducted experiments in growing foreign plants on Indian soil. Banks was particularly interested in growing tea extensively in India in order to break the Chinese monopoly of that market. He urged the Company's functionaries to try and plant tea trees on Indian soil; eventually tea growing was made possible in the nineteenth century by another man, the Scottish botanist named Robert Fortune.

Introducing tea to India was not easy. For a long time, the Chinese government forbade the sale of tea plants to foreigners. Moreover, tea plantations were so far away from the ports that it was very unlikely that any plant could survive the journey. But the real challenge was not to acquire a tea plant; it was the know-how of processing the final product, which only Chinese tea makers had. Robert Fortune had to hire Chinese tea makers in order to obtain the recipes and the details of the process. He also brought Chinese workers to India. Fortune spent two years in South China trying to acquire all the secrets and the skills necessary to produce high quality tea; he even disguised himself as a local in order to gain entry to a Chinese tea plantation and factory.

While Fortune and some others were in China trying to learn the secrets of tea-making, there were rumours in India that a native variant of tea, that grew up to ten feet high, had been found in Assam. Major Robert Bruce went to explore the region and to register the local knowledge on tea. Bruce's research and the help of Chinese black tea makers made it possible for tea to be produced in India from the 1830s. By 1841, 54 tonnes of tea had been exported to London (Chatterjee 2001: 56).

The 'discovery' of the native variant of tea in Assam brought about a new quest for the origins of the tea plant. English botanists thought that tea was native to India and British production of tea in India was a way of bringing back what was originally Indian. 'Despite the evidence of thousands of years of Chinese production and trade', remarks Piya Chatterjee, English entrepreneurs were determined to prove that 'India was the original birthplace of tea'. English planters argued that stories of Chinese tea were 'cloudy legends and mythological narratives' of the Chinese imagination (ibid.: 56).

With this economic scenario in mind, let us turn to the other important changes introduced by the Charter Acts of 1813 (and later, that of 1833). Free traders, it is important to remember, did not only attack the Company's monopoly over trade, they were also against its entire system of government, which was premised on the principle of leaving Indian customs and institutions undisturbed (Stokes [1959] 1989: 40). 'Philosophic radicalism' of the nineteenth century, embodied in liberalism and utilitarianism, bolstered this challenge by offering an intellectual grounding for the aggressive need to 'improve' India. The mood of 'expansive optimism' (Metcalf and Metcalf 2003: 80) resulting from Napoleon's defeat and the success of the Industrial Revolution, boosted the confidence of middle-class liberals and utilitarians: represented by Adam Smith, Jeremy Bentham, James and John Stuart Mill, and Thomas Macaulay. They came to believe that the triumph of science and reason, of political economy and of law and government, that had made the West superior, would also help India to strip herself off the shackles of despotism, custom and tradition. Indians would prosper under able English rule, making Bentham's utilitarian idea of the 'greatest good for the greatest number' come true.

Evangelism provided this project of improvement with a missionary zeal. The two distinctive features of evangelism, 'intense individualism and exaltation of individual conscience', were rooted in the belief that 'human character could suddenly be transformed by a direct assault on the mind' (Stokes [1959] 1989: 30). Thus, while liberals and utilitarians attempted to effect change through introducing science and reason, evangelists sought to save souls through an educative process that entailed the spread of true faith and the eradication of ignorance and superstition. The Charter Act of 1813 is also significant because it allowed the entry of missions into India. Charles Grant and William Wilberforce won the battle for the evangelicals in the British Parliament.

Grant, a Company servant and a leading evangelical, strongly argued that British policy should be based on the 'principle of assimilation'. Assimilation would ensure the promotion of civilization and material prosperity in India, which in turn would benefit British commerce (ibid.: 34). This notion that worldly success should not be pursued for one's own gain, but for the sake of duty in order to make the world 'pour forth her abundance', brought together duty and self-interest in intricate ways to give England's commercial interest in India a moral grounding (ibid.: 33–34).

The success of the mission project was slow and halting; its modes and objectives were not homogeneous and they were severely circumscribed by Indian conditions. Alexander Duff, the fiery, Scottish Presbyterian missionary, was sorely disappointed because his confident hope of converting the entire city of Calcutta to evangelical Christianity remained unfulfilled. At the same time, the mission school (The Free Church School) that he established in Calcutta, inspired thinking and self-awareness eventually encouraging many of the young students to take to the true faith. The missionaries moreover, drew attention to what they considered to be the 'barbaric' customs of the Hindus, and to their religion in general as the basic cause of ignorance, complementing in important ways the liberals' urge to reform and 'civilize' India.

The blending of the distinct forces of free trade, liberalism, utilitarianism and evangelism was reflected in the publication of Grant's 1797 treatise titled *Observations on the State of Society Among the Asiatic Subjects of Great Britain, Particularly with Respect to Morals; and of the Means of Improving It* as a parliamentary paper in 1813 and 1832, and James Mill's *History of British India* ([1817] 1975), which ran into several editions. Grant and Mill were ruthless in their indictment of 'Hindu' and 'Muslim' civilizations, and both held despotism to be solely responsible for the primitive and barbaric state of society in India.

Mill was candid in his rebuttal of the Orientalist idea that India was formerly 'in a state of high civilization' from which it had fallen. The opening lines of his *History of India* displayed the contempt he had for such an idea, as also for India. 'Rude nations', he wrote, 'seem to derive a peculiar gratification from pretensions to a remote antiquity'. 'Oriental nations' distinguished by a 'boastful and turgid vanity' have carried 'their claims extravagantly high' (ibid.: 27). It is not surprising, therefore, that India remained 'visibly outside' the domain of John Stuart Mill's works on *Representative Government* and *On Liberty* (Mehta 1999: 65). Such systematic and sustained exclusion of various groups and types of people, in Uday Singh Mehta's forceful formulation, accounted for the exclusionary effect of liberal practice inspite of the inclusionary, universal claims of liberal theory (ibid.: 46). For our purposes, it is important to remember that the liberal-utilitarian policy-makers of the Company felt that reform and improvement were the need of the hour: reform, both of morals in public life as advocated by Edmund Burke and of public and social life in general that the evangelicals aimed at (Stokes [1959] 1989: 14). Together, these forces gave shape to the 'civilizing mission' which found expression in the 'Age of Reform'. This 'Age' was characterized by the 'passionate conviction that the ideals of altruism and the strongest claims of self-interest coincided' (ibid.: 46).

Eric Stokes writes that 1818 saw the emergence of liberalism as a force in England (ibid.: xvi). This in turn, marked a turning point in the history of India and Britain. The final defeat of the Marathas freed the Company of the severe burden of warfare; an effective, efficient and 'legitimate' administration of the vast territories under its possession became imperative. The year followed the publication of James Mill's *History of British India,* and saw the avowed conversion of Macaulay to adulthood and radicalism (ibid.: xvi). The mood of confidence and enthusiasm was aptly captured in Shelley's Preface to his *Prometheus Unbound*, which he started writing in 1818 and finished in 1819. The Preface passionately proclaimed the restoration of equilibrium between institutions and opinions with 'the cloud of mind discharging its collected lightning' (Shelley 1820: Preface). The stage was set.

'THE AGE OF REFORM'

The 'era of reform', writes Crispin Bates, has been 'much misunderstood' (2007: 43). It began as an overhaul of the bureaucratic structure of the East India Company and was later interpreted by British and imperial historians as a period of change for the benefit as much of Indians as of the British. Undoubtedly, there is some truth in this assertion. At the same time, from what has been said earlier, it is clear that efficient administration and the restructuring of the bureaucratic set-up included forming policies and implementing laws. All of it was governed by the firm belief that India was a 'despotic and chaotic land, inhabited by various despotic governments and roving bands of thugs and bandits' and characterized by 'a myriad of superstitions and contradictory religious practices' (Harlow and Carter 1999: 67).

The active participation of an important section of the Indian literati gave a critical edge to the Age of Reform. Placed between a rich culture that sustained them and the appeal of new 'western' ideas, most Indian men tried to strike a balance between reform and 'tradition'. They passionately complemented and countered the British urge to change. It is not a matter of surprise, therefore, that the Age of Reform coincided with the period of the 'Bengal Renaissance'. Indeed, in addition to the prevalence of and debate over a wide range of ideas, the work of Indian scholars associated with the Fort William College—Mrityunjay Vidyalankar, Ramjay Tarkalankar and Ram Ram Basu—helped Bengali prose gain maturity and contribute directly to the Renaissance (Sinha 1993: v).

The interface of colonial rule and Indian culture affected two vital areas of 'social development' (Bates 2007: 50). The first was the introduction of a western-style education. The next one, with extensive application and far-reaching consequences, was the implementation of legislation related to certain social practices. This ranged from attempts to prevent child marriages to the introduction of widow remarriages and a general move to stop 'human sacrifice', believed to be current among certain 'tribal' communities, and violent killings resulting from banditry of the elusive but villainous thugs.

The thugs or 'thugees', the notoriously ferocious bandits, fanned wild fantasies of the British populace; their vivid representations in stories, photographs and paintings justified maintaining an ever-expanding police force in the colony. It is very difficult to account for the appearance of the 'thugees'; colonial officials possibly designated different groups of dispossessed poor peasants, petty traders and mercenary soldiers who had taken to theft as the last resort, as 'thugs'. In Anglo–Indian parlance, states Radhika Singha, thugs were believed to constitute 'a hereditary criminal fraternity, organized around rites which upheld a profession of inveigling and strangling travellers' (1998: 169). Apart from the fact that the 'thugs' could barely be distinguished from an ordinary traveller, official accounts indicate that they came from among the Hindus and Muslims (ibid.: 202).

At the same time, the British administrators' belief in the existence of a fraternity led them to affirm the 'caste-like attachment' of 'thugees' to their 'hereditary profession characteristic of Indian society' (Sherwood 1820: 260). This conjured an image of thugs as an organized group of criminals who operated all over India and bolstered colonial efforts to control all wandering groups consistently. Judicial correspondence of the time, argues Singha, reveals 'a continuous flow of suggestions about the policing of "the Stroller, the vagrant, and … the fugitive"' (*Circular*, 19 June 1829, cited in Singha 1998: 199). With the establishing of a criminal department in the 1830s, such sporadic efforts to distinguish the thugs got concretized into definite knowledge. The passing of The Thuggee Act XXX of 1836 and the relentless pursuit not only of thugs but of all groups of religious mendicants by Sleeman, the superintendent of thugee operations, eventually 'purged India of this great pollution' (Kaye 1853: 376). Sleeman, who had 'discovered' the notorious thugs, wrote a long self-congratulatory account of his successful operation (Sleeman 1839 in Harlow and Carter 1999: 81–87). The provision of the 1836 Act of legally trying 'criminal communities' and the knowledge compiled by the criminal department would, after the Revolt of 1857, provide the basis for the demarcation of 'criminal castes' and 'criminal tribes' (Nigam 1990).

In a similar manner, the suppression of alleged human sacrifice, stated to be a practice prevalent among some *adivasi* groups, particularly the Khonds of Orissa, took a different direction and came to be focused on the practice of *sati* or the immolation of the wife on her husband's funeral pyre. Subsequent endeavours were also made to ban female infanticide. Although such practices were largely the product of British perceptions (Oldenburg 2002, for instance), they got defined in particular ways on account of the controversy that the efforts to stop them generated.

The Classical and the Modern

The Company did not take measures to introduce 'English education' for the Indian population till 1813. English schools, however, were set up in the eighteenth century through charities in Calcutta, Bombay and Madras for the education of English and Anglo–Indian children. Baptist missionaries, who took refuge in the Danish settlement of Madras and in Serampore, ran schools for Indian boys and girls although the number of enrolment was very small. The Charter Act of 1813, apart from allowing missionaries to enter India, allocated an annual sum of ₹100,000 for encouraging learned natives and the revival of literature, and for promoting knowledge of the sciences among the inhabitants of the country. Although the main purpose behind this provision was to inculcate a sense of commitment among the Company's servants by forcing them to train the 'natives', it was remarkable in the sense that public funding for education was not in vogue even in England at that time (Bandyopadhyay 2004: 140–41).

The Company had a group of 'learned natives' who assisted European professors of the Fort William College in compiling textbooks and in language teaching. This group, though heterogeneous in composition, was largely made up of three sub-castes of Brahmans—men who controlled the *tols* in Bengal and had little interest or knowledge of Persian and English. They had started coming to Calcutta from their ancestral villages and towns in rural Bengal in the 1790s. Their position became shaky when their patrons, the old zamindars, were almost wiped out owing to the Permanent Settlement. The other group consisted of Persianized Hindus, who also lost employment because of the Company's move to replace natives from responsible posts in the administration. At the same time, these people, on account of their long association with Islamic culture, were better suited to adjust themselves to the new conditions. The landlord families of Tagore and Rammohan Roy, for instance, had entered into profitable relations with the French in Chandernagore and the English in Calcutta, while some others had close connections with Baptist missionaries (Kopf 1969: 108–109).

Warren Hastings had tried to make Calcutta the centre of a new cultural life. Different groups of people flocked to the new capital city; not only the adventurers intent on rapid accumulation of riches, but also people who helped Charles Wilkins translate the *Bhagavad Gita* or William Jones acquire mastery of Sanskrit language and literature, and Halhead to compile his *Code* of *Gentoo Laws*. Such men refused to accept more than the bare minimum that was needed for their subsistence (Sinha 1968: 226). Hence, their salaries did not match the earnings of the upcoming class of Indian traders and businessmen but they fared much better than their counterparts who taught in Indian institutions. Further, service in the College turned a 'traditional' scholar into a professional: a teacher, prose stylist, philologist or linguist compositor, printer, publisher or librarian. Moreover, there were others who amassed wealth from the opportunities offered by the new colonial capital.

There was yet another group of literati represented by men like Radhakanta Deb who, wealthy by birth, avoided any professional or commercial contact with Englishmen. Increasingly, however, from the end of the eighteenth century educated high-caste Hindus in and around Calcutta took up jobs in British institutions. In addition to clerks in commercial firms, the expanding judicial system and mounting litigations produced a class of able pleaders. It was 'western education' in this sense, which 'reinforced the new pressure of urbanism' by attracting 'people to new professions and services' and helping in the formation of 'a middle class society' (Sinha 1965: 91).

The importance of Fort William College and of Jones' legacy meant that the Company's official policy on education in the first decades of the nineteenth century tilted towards the Orientalist view of patronizing and reviving classical and vernacular Indian literatures and sciences. This was also supported by Governor-General Minto (Earl of Minto, 1807–13) and then by Marques of Hastings. The General Committee of Public Instruction, set up after the Charter Act of 1813 and headed by H. H. Wilson, chalked out a plan that involved establishing a Sanskrit College in Calcutta, two oriental colleges in Agra and Delhi and sponsorship of the existing *tol*s and *madrassa*s.

Sanskrit College, founded for encouraging 'Hindu' literature among educated Indians, eventually developed a curriculum that included law, logic and music. The method of teaching, however, conformed entirely to that of an English institution with a clearly defined syllabus and working hours. Sanskrit College, therefore, contributed to the 'anglicization' of Sanskrit studies, best represented perhaps by Pandit Iswar Chandra Vidyasagar (Sinha 1993: vi). The popular imagery of Sanskrit *luchi*s (pancakes) fried in English *ghee* (clarified butter), used jokingly to refer to Vidyasagar's works, proffers a candid representation of this 'anglicization'. At the same time, Sanskrit College was better suited to the metropolitan atmosphere of Calcutta than the traditional *tol*s.

Despite its hybrid character, official policy patronizing Indian literature and sciences was countered by an increasing interest in English education among the Indian intelligentsia and the rapid establishment of English schools by missionaries and European individuals. This was reflected in the petition sent by Rammohan Roy to the Governor-General, opposing the decision of the Committee of Public Instruction to establish a Sanskrit College. Rammohan represented an influential group, which firmly believed that India could become modern only by means of English education and the knowledge of western sciences. Conviction in this belief found ample articulation in the founding of the Hindu College in Calcutta—the first English language institution of higher learning—in 1817, under Indian and private European initiative.

In the words of Baptist missionary Alexander Duff, 'English education was in a manner forced upon the British Government' by the 'advanced thinking members of the Hindu community' who 'started an institution for imparting English education' (Duff Parliamentary Papers, vol. XXXII, cited in Sinha 1968: 192). By the 1830s, Calcutta alone had several thousand Indians studying English; several printing and publishing establishments producing thousands of textbooks on western scientific knowledge in Indian languages; a free public library (set up in 1816); three colleges with science laboratories; a full curriculum of courses on science; and three Bengali newspapers that carried foreign and local news (Kopf 1979: 42).

With the growing importance of liberal and utilitarian ideas in Britain, many officials in the Company's service began to push for the introduction of English education. This was strengthened by the urgent need to cut down the expenses of the Company's administration—the Company needed to insert Indians in its administrative apparatus as useful servants of the empire (Viswanathan 1998: 5). The divergence in ideas between 'allowing' indigenous systems of learning, culture and religion to flourish without official intervention (Viswanathan 1989: 24–25) and the need to 'anglicize' Indians, occasioned what has come to be viewed as the debate between the 'Orientalists' and the 'Anglicists'.

The Orientalists, in their bid to promote indigenous learning, argued in favour of continuing the system of stipends granted to students of Arabic and Sanskrit and the continued publication of texts in these languages. The 'Anglicists', on the other hand, wanted to reduce the expenditure on stipends held by 'lazy and stupid schoolboys of thirty and thirty-five years of age' and cut down the huge sum spent on Sanskrit and Arabic printing (Majumdar [1965] 1981: 81). The victory, as is well known, was for the 'Anglicists' led by Thomas Babington Macaulay. In his oft-quoted 'Minute on Indian Education' as the President of the Committee of Public Instruction, written on 2 February 1835, Macaulay made the colonial rulers the 'agency' for promoting 'western education'. He ended the controversy by stating forcefully that since the committee was free to employ the funds as it chose, it ought to employ it in teaching English. He stated that English was 'better worth knowing than Sanskrit or Arabic'. Moreover, the natives really wanted to be taught English and not Sanskrit or Arabic, and they could be turned into 'thoroughly good English scholars' to which the efforts of the Company should be directed (Macaulay 1972: 249). This Minute was immediately endorsed, despite protest from the 'Orientalists' by Governor-General Bentinck.

The new education, it was believed, would propagate 'modern' western knowledge through modern institutions and pedagogic processes, and supplant indigenous knowledges which were variously condemned as 'superstitious', 'mythic', 'primitive' and 'untrue' (Seth 2007: 1). The objective then was to reproduce, replicate and disseminate knowledge produced in Britain among Indians (S. Bhattacharya 1998; Bandyopadhyay 2004: 142). The training of a small section of rich, learned men of business was vital for the downward filtration of western education to the elementary level. This confidence contributed to a neglect of vernacular and elementary education imparted through indigenous village schools.

Adam's Reports on Vernacular Education in Bengal and Behar (and Orissa), (submitted to the Government in 1835, 1836 and 1838), and drafted by William Adam, a Unitarian missionary in 1832 under instructions from Bentinck to enquire into the status of education in Bengal's villages in order to determine both the level of literacy and the source of funding of village schools, provided a detailed and meticulous account of the condition of elementary and secondary vernacular schools in the different districts of the province of Bengal. Adam advocated 'a theory of general rural education' based on the *pathshala* (the indigenous village school) and urged government support for vernacular education, which he felt was the most effective (though expensive) way for the Company to modernize education in Bengal (Sengupta 2011: 23). This report challenged the Calcutta-centred nature of the educational debate and insisted on the Company's responsibility of extending vernacular education to the cultivating classes in the villages; it also proposed measures to train indigenous teachers to impart education in the vernacular. The report was largely ignored. The Company's neglect resulted in a decline of the *pathshala* system, since declining revenue and loss of local control reduced the villages' ability to support their local schools (Sengupta 2011: 30). The missionaries, on the other hand, continued their effort of expanding their network of rural primary schools with no regulation from the government.

When the government finally adopted a system of grants-in-aid for education in 1854, in the wake of inquiries made by the Parliament in educational developments in India during the renewal of the Company's charter in 1853, its purpose was to encourage native Hindus and Muslims to open their own schools. The findings of the inquiry, published in 1854 as Wood's Educational Despatch, found faults with Macaulay's Anglicist position of 'downward filtration' and publicly acknowledged the Company's responsibility of educating all its subjects (ibid.: 31). The Despatch provided for the founding of a Department of Public Instruction (DPI) in all the five provinces, to be headed by a director of public instruction and assisted by a series of inspectors and assistants. It also asked for a certain amount to be spent on the opening of universities in urban centres and on schools to train teachers. The Despatch charted the establishing of a network of graded schools from the primary level to the university and a system of grants-in-aid to fund these schools. This resulted in the founding of the universities of Calcutta, Bombay and Madras in 1857. It appears then that from 1835 onwards, *The Education of the People of India* (Trevelyan 1838) became a task of the colonial government, a grand scheme that made 'western education' extremely significant. In reality, however, the money spent on it was 'miniscule' and the numbers affected constituted a very small portion of the total population (Seth 2007: 2).

Yet, 'western education' became a common term, naturalized and self-evident, a term that epitomized a particular cultural orientation and moral uprightness. The earlier discussion makes it clear that education, in its widest sense of various external influences forming the individual mind, was given utmost importance by evangelicals, liberals and utilitarians alike. Moreover, western education was enthusiastically accepted by a small but vocal section of the Indian population. There were, of course, significant differences between the role played by the colonial state behind the introduction of western education and its understanding and deployment by the Indian elite. All the different British advocates of western education thought of education as an important means for the 'improvement' of the 'moral character' of the Indians. Soon, however, they began to lament that western education, rather than encouraging 'improvement' had occasioned 'moral crisis' and 'moral decline' among educated Indians. This is because the Indians used western education instrumentally and focused exclusively on its 'intellectual' aspects and neglected its moral and religious elements (Seth 2007: 47–48).

It is not as if 'instrumentality' was absent in British policymaking. Indeed, the recurrently cited sentence of Macaulay's Minute was candid: Indians educated in European literature and sciences via the medium of English were to become important intermediaries between 'us' (the rulers) and the 'millions whom we govern': hybrid characters with Indian blood and colour but with 'British taste, opinions, morals and intellect' (Minute recorded by Macaulay, law member of the Governor-General's Council, 2 February 1835, reprinted in Zastoupil and Moir 1999). It is interesting that for Macaulay and many of his contemporaries, the snapping of political ties between Britain and India was nothing unexpected.

Therefore, it was even more important to have an educated and civilized India with which close commercial links could be maintained after India's independence (Stokes [1959] 1989: 44). To the dismay of Macaulay's generation, however, the delicate purpose of transforming Indians into 'deracinated replicas of Englishmen even while they remained affiliated to their own religious culture'

(Viswanathan 1998: 5) floundered because Indians failed to acquire British 'morals'. Indian perceptions and apprehensions about western education had a lot to do with this dissonance between intent and outcome. At the same time, the baggage of moral improvement made social reform a vital and a vibrant issue.

REFORMING MEN AND WOMEN

The Governor-Generalship of Lord William Cavendish Bentinck (1828–36) is generally taken to be the high point of liberal reform. Lord Bentinck, who succeeded Lord Amherst in July 1828, was the second son of the Duke of Portland. He had begun his career as a soldier, had taken part in the Napoleonic wars and had been appointed Governor of Madras in 1803. However, his conduct in relation to the Mutiny at Vellore in 1806 had angered the Court of Directors who recalled him in 1807 (Majumdar [1963] 1970: 2). By the time he returned to India as the Governor-General, Bentinck had become thoroughly influenced by utilitarian ideas. He was entrusted with the task of economizing and rationalizing the Company's administration and clearing the huge debt that had accumulated owing to expensive wars, particularly the First Burmese War (1824–26), carried out during Lord Amherst's administration. Although opinions vary widely on Bentinck's ability as an administrator, his regime is remembered for important educational and social reforms, particularly the suppression of the 'thugee', endorsing the abolition of *sati*, and the official adoption of English education. Bentinck's administration also saw the renewal of the Company's Charter in 1833, which resulted in important changes in the nature and method of the Company's administration (ibid.: 2–3).

The 'debate' on *sati*—a term that refers both to the practice of upper-caste Hindu wives burning themselves on the funeral pyres of their husbands and to the woman who commits the act (Yang 1989: 8)—had begun in the 1780s, much before Bentinck's arrival. It continued after the implementation of the abolition in 1829 (Mani 1998). 'Debate', or public debate, as Tanika and Sumit Sarkar remind us, was a very new historical development of the time and requires understanding of how and among whom it took place (Sarkar and Sarkar 2008: 2). The debate, in this case, took place among British officials and different strands of the Indian literati, where Indian 'reformers' engaged in sustained arguments and conversations with one another and with their orthodox opponents in the public domain. The practice of *sati*, it is important to remember, pertained to the domain of family or personal law as delineated by Hastings, a domain where the native 'Hindus' were supposed to be governed by their own laws. The debate arose precisely because the Company's administration sought to tread into an arena it had left to the 'natives'.

The sensational depiction of *sati* in British official discourse added to its significance. The ban on *sati* epitomized the 'noble' implications of the reformist drive of liberals and evangelicals; a success story in which western, Christian sensibility, horrified by a cruel practice imposed on and carried out by Indian 'women' put an end to it.

In the words of Lata Mani, the abolition of *sati* in 1829 has become a 'founding moment' in the history of women in modern India. The debate on *sati* is believed to have provided the context for a thorough re-evaluation of Indian 'tradition' along lines 'more consonant with the modern economy and society' much desired after India's incorporation into the world capitalist system (Mani 1989: 88). The debate, however, was driven by considerations that had very little to do with women.

Sati, it bears pointing out, was a heroic practice and hence 'exceptional' (Kumar 1993). Its socio-religious basis lay in the notion of the wife as the true 'half' of the husband, who followed him in life and death. The 'virtue' of the practice derived from a religious logic that deemed a widow inauspicious for having outlived her husband; an unnatural circumstance caused by her 'sinful nature in this, or a previous life' (Yang 1989: 13). It is difficult to trace the exact origin of the rite, although it is believed that *sati* may have been practised by upper-caste Hindus for almost 2,000 years (Nandy 1975: 171). The *Puranas* mentioned *sati* as an option for widows; they also prescribed a life of asceticism for them (Yang 1989: 13). Studies indicate that remarriage of widows was definitely sanctioned by ancient Hindu laws and that sacred texts were not well disposed towards the practice of *sati*. The rite gained some degree of legitimacy from the time of the *Puranas* and there is evidence that *sati* was prevalent among Rajputs in Rajasthan in Mughal times and among the upper castes in the kingdom of Vijayanagar in south India. By the seventeenth century, however, *sati* had become 'mainly voluntary' and, by the beginning of the eighteenth century, it was 'a rare occurrence'. A symbol of honour and privilege, the practice of *sati* suddenly gained prominence in and around Calcutta in the late-eighteenth and early-nineteenth centuries, acquiring the 'popularity of a legitimate orgy' (ibid.: 170).

This was the time when upwardly mobile members of middle and lower-ranking castes compelled their women to become *sati*s in order to consolidate their newly earned economic prosperity with social prestige. Some scholars argue that the *dayabahaga* system of Hindu personal law (codified in a Sanskrit legal text of the twelfth century), which gave the widow greater rights to inherit the deceased husband's property as well as her father's property, induced male members of the husband's family to force the widow to commit *sati* (Roche 2002). According to Nandy, Rammohan himself thought of economic reasons crucial for the practice (1975: 172). It needs to be pointed out, however, that *dayabahaga* as it prevailed in Bengal gave widows only usufruct rights on behalf of their minor sons (Sarkar 2001: 19).

Sati had drawn the attention of Christian missionaries and had been outlawed in Calcutta, which was under the jurisdiction of English law, by the Chief Justice of the Supreme Court as early as 1798 (Mani 1998: 16). At the same time, Brahman 'pundits' were constantly called upon to interpret scriptural law in civil cases, and their opinion on whether or not the practice of *sati* had a basis in 'scriptures' had become vital in the debate on *sati*. This is what had inspired Mritunjay Vidyalankar of the Fort William College to argue against the practice of *sati daha* (burning of wives of dead husbands) before the cause was taken up by Rammohan Roy.

Official knowledge on *sati* was constituted by means of putting specific questions to the *pundits*, whose responses, to begin with, were shaped by the questions and were later interpreted in specific ways. Since official concern over whether the practice could be safely prohibited by legislation was premised on a belief that *sati* was sanctioned by the scriptures, the debate turned entirely on whether the scriptures did indeed endorse *sati* or not (Mani 1989: 92). The debate over *sati*, therefore, rather than being a debate over women, was much more a modernist 'colonial' debate on what constituted tradition, with women providing the site on which 'tradition' came to be discussed, contested and formulated (Mani 1989, 1998).

Even when officials offered 'eyewitness' accounts of *sati*, women who committed *sati* were portrayed either as heroines who entered the raging blaze of the funeral pyre with grace and calm or as pathetic victims forcibly thrown into the flames against their volition. These poles precluded the possibility of female subjectivity that is 'shifting, contradictory, inconsistent' and turned women into passive objects to be saved, never as subjects who act (Mani 1993: 276). Mani challenges this formulation by analysing eyewitness accounts of incidents where the widow was saved or dissuaded from burning, or where she tried to escape from the pyre when the flames become unbearable. In such incidents, the *sati* was much more than someone to be acted upon; she was a subject whose action was the result of complex forces (ibid.).

The debate is important for us for two different reasons. One, it provided educated Indian males like Rammohan Roy—acclaimed to be 'the first modern man of India'—a cause to rally around, a cause that allowed them to draw upon, interpret and show their mastery over Indian scriptures understood now through the lens of English education. This reflection and apprehension of 'tradition' entailed an understanding of 'Hinduism' and Hindu society which had far-reaching consequences. Two, and equally important, the debate over *sati* introduced an enduring discussion on the 'condition' of Indian women, a discussion that would end up making Hindu and Muslim women 'moral exemplars' and repositories of 'normative tradition'—significant signifiers of the level of 'advancement' of Indian society—an idea that had little provenance in Hindu and Islamic thought till then (Metcalf 1994: 3).

Moreover, as Radhika Singha and Tanika Sarkar have argued with distinct emphases, even though the nineteenth century was not a time when individual rights as 'inalienable, public, and explicit' could be asserted by a woman (Sarkar 2000: 601) and although women were not allowed any participation in the debate, colonial officials' attempts to establish whether *sati* was performed voluntarily by the woman or whether she was forced to become *sati*, that is, whether the *sati* was 'good' or 'bad' had, unwarrantedly, allowed recognition of women's 'will' and, consequently, of women as individual subjects (Singha 1998: 106ff.) An argument for an unabridgeable right to the woman's life slowly made its appearance as a 'perceived necessity' in the free-ranging, self-reflexive debates within the public sphere (Sarkar 2000: 601–02). This, together with the emergent notion of the 'status of women' as 'a crucial signifier of the degree of the colonized people's civilizational backwardness' (Sunder Rajan 2003: 3), and of the effeminacy of its male members, would have important consequences for the nationalist discourse, a theme we explore in Chapter 5.

The debate ended with the victory of those who supported the abolition of *sati*. Regulation XVII of the Bengal code, approved by the Governor-General in Council on 4 December 1829, upheld the abolition. The Regulation stated that the practice was 'revolting to the feelings of human nature' and was 'nowhere enjoined by the religion of the Hindus as an imperative duty' (Kumar 1993). Although this legislation marked the success of Rammohan and his group, Rammohan's own position with regard to *sati* is intriguing. On the one hand, he believed that the practice embodied all that was wrong with the content of 'new Hinduism': an aberration of and deviation from the 'original' one. Such a practice could continue only because the 'advocates of idolatry and their misguided followers' believed that such 'crimes of the most heinous nature' formed a part of their religious system (Roy 1818, II: 23). On the other hand, he did not deny that *sati* was permitted in scriptures. He argued against *sati* because it involved a desire for *sakam karma* (the fruits of one's action), in this case, the promise of heaven. This desire made the practice of *sati* less virtuous than that of *brahmacharya* (austere abstinence), which the widow was expected to carry out in *niskama karma* (detached action) for the rest of her life. Widows, therefore, had to earn greater virtue by leading a desire-free life rather than aspire for easy access to heaven by committing *sati* (Rammohan cited in Sen 1977: 74).

This ambivalent stance prompts reflection, not only on the title of the 'Father of Modern India' that was conferred on Rammohan on the bi-centenary of his birth (1972), but also on the nature of the 'modern' that gained prominence in the nineteenth century in India. Rammohan's writings and activities, in Sumit Sarkar's analysis, 'do signify a kind of a break with the traditions inherited by his generation', but this break was 'deeply contradictory and limited' since it remained confined to an intellectual plane and did not bring about social transformation (1975: 46–47). Rather than just call this break limited, it is perhaps more useful to examine why the idea of the 'modern' lays such stress on 'break' and novelty, and what implications that has for the constant construal of 'tradition' by the modern. Such an exploration will make us aware that although modernity seeks to speak a universal language of reason, science and progress, it is deeply fissured and contradictory, which makes its constructions of 'tradition' widely divergent. Rammohan and the debate on *sati* offer lucid examples of how ideas of tradition get constructed and reinforced through the efforts of the modern. It was this debate which perpetrated the Orientalist idea that Hindu scriptures were the basis of Hinduism. Radhakanta Deb and his 'conservative' group had affirmed that practices were as important to Hinduism as textual precepts. However, since this group lost out, the very pertinent argument—that practices were an inherent part of Hinduism and not a later aberration—lost its significance.

Much more important than the legislative abolition of a practice, which was not widely prevalent and, in any case, did not stop with the legal abolition, was the understanding of 'Hinduism' that this debate reinforced. The 'rational' interpretation of 'tradition' on which Rammohan premised his arguments in favour of abolition, became a strong trend in Indian intellectual thought and found distinct articulations as the century progressed. Such interpretations displayed an internalization of the colonial critique that nineteenth century Hindu society was impoverished.

'Status of women' retained prominence in discussions on social reform in the first half of the nineteenth century. After the ban on *sati*, attention turned to the issue of remarriage of widows, as their 'plight' found prominent mention in the writings of missionaries and liberals. The problem of widows, and in particular of child widows, related to the higher castes among whom child marriage was practised and remarriage prohibited. The lower castes, the 'Sudras' and the 'Untouchables' who represented 80 per cent of the population, 'neither practised child marriage nor prohibited the remarriage of widows' (Carroll 1983: 364).

In Bengal the lead was taken by Iswar Chandra Vidyasagar, a scholar of great repute who had dedicated his life to promoting Bengali language and the printing of school textbooks designed to train young minds morally. Although Vidyasagar had been influenced by William Carey, his intent of training young minds morally had nothing to do with evangelism but with his own understanding of *dharma*. A scholar rooted in the indigenous tradition, Vidyasagar was inspired by the English sensibility of equating life with reason, which conferred on him an 'untiring will for social action'. He found the rational influence of western knowledge and humanism attractive but not the 'alien styles of living' (Sen 1977: Preface).

In a manner similar to Rammohan, Vidayasagar drew upon the *sastras* to argue that widow remarriage was sanctioned by the scriptures. But his use of *sastras* differed from that of Rammohan in that he deployed them to tap 'the root of popular support for social reforms' and to supplement it with the power of intellect and the 'renewal of common Hindu sensibility' (ibid.: 75). Vidyasagar's simultaneous and contradictory location in two different worlds—the Indian and the English—was never properly understood in Bengal; his cause, however, found support among reformers in Maharashtra, the Telugu-speaking parts of the Madras Presidency, Haryana, and other parts of India.

The Hindu Widow's Remarriage Act (Act XV of 1856), an act of statutory social reform that generated judicial controversies over its interpretation and application, and set in clear relief the three categories of Hindu Law, Customary Law, and Statutory Law utilized by the judicial branch of the Company's administration (Carroll 1983: 364), allowed widows to remarry. Its impact, however, was limited and contradictory. In Maharashtra, where the issue of widow remarriage had greater force, supporters for the cause were found to be at fault in a public debate in Poona in 1870 by the Shankaracharya of the Kabir Math and obliged to do penance. The number of widows who remarried remained extremely small; social acceptance of the act was difficult. Indeed, upwardly mobile middle and lower caste peasants, whose widows had the right to remarry, now tried to prevent their widows from doing so. More significantly, the conservative nature of the legislation, which disinherited the widow who remarried of her right to the property of her deceased husband, dissuaded her from remarrying. She was obliged to remain the 'chaste and prayerful widow' much as Rammohan had visualized her, in order to retain a minimum claim to subsistence (Carroll 1983: 379).

On the other hand, support for the cause of remarriage grew slowly after the passing of the act. In the Haryana–Punjab region, where *karewa* (levirate marriage), in which the widow was accepted as the bride by one of the brothers of the deceased husband, was a common practice among the overwhelming majority of the landowing castes, the act vested greater power on the deceased husband's family to oblige the widow to marry again (Chowdhury 2008: 153). *Karewa* emanated from the need to retain landed property within the patrilineal family. A throwback to the early *Rig Vedic* custom of *niyog* (levirate marriage), and associated with early Vedic Aryan settlements, *karewa* was advocated by the Arya Samajists from the 1880s even though Dayanand Saraswati, the founder of Arya Samaj, was not in favour of widow remarriage. By the beginning of the twentieth century, *karewa* had come to be followed not just by the Jats and other agricultural castes, but also by the Brahmans of the region (ibid.). A collusion between a patrilineal family structure, the colonial state and Arya Samaj reformers resulted in the imposition of increased control over the widow. She could not marry again without the consent of her late husband's family; they decided on who she could remarry. Besides, even though she could not be compelled to marry one of the brothers, she was often forced to yield to the wishes of her husband's family in a region where the dominant cultural ethos was to hold land and wife through the use of force (ibid.: 154–55).

In the Madras Presidency, which was slow to take up the cause of social reform, a Society for Social Reform was established by Veeresalingam Pantulu in 1878 to encourage widow remarriage. In spite of initial opposition, his venture won over many important residents of Rajahmundry who formed the Widow Remarriage Association in 1891 (Bandyopadhyay 2004: 149). The number of remarried widows, however, continued to remain very small. Vidyasagar persisted in his struggle turning first against polygamy and then the marriage of young girls. His efforts bore fruit in the Age of Consent Act of 1860, which fixed the age of consummation of marriage at ten for young brides. Attempts to raise this age to 12 in the early 1890s would generate fierce debates all over India.

Bombay, it bears pointing out, had taken the initiative in social reform prior to Bengal and this effort was not an offshoot of the movement for religious reform (Majumdar [1965] 1981: 265). This is because Maratha and Peshwa rule in Maharashtra had regulated social affairs, and encouraged inter-marriages, remarriage for girls married forcibly or fraudulently, prohibited the sale of girls and allowed the 'readmission into Hinduism of converts'. Following this trend, Gangadhar Shastri Jambhekar and Jagannath Shakershet had carried on a campaign in the 1830s to take back Christian converts into Hindu society. The Hindu Missionary Society of Gajananrao Vaidya was a direct consequence of this campaign. This Hindu missionary zeal found a different articulation in the 1840s. A secret association called the Paramhansa Sabha (1849), sought to erase social discrimination and restrictions on commensality. In its gatherings, the members partook of food cooked by people of a lower caste and also consumed food and drink forbidden for upper castes. These ventures did not last very long, but they initiated moves that would be taken up with greater enthusiasm later.

This discussion makes it clear that the effort to implement 'reform' through law had limited success and its impact was uneven across regions. Such efforts demonstrate not only the faith of the English-educated intelligentsia in the Company state, whose beneficiaries they were, but also their uncritical acceptance of the ideas of enlightenment—science and reason—as well as their 'absence' in India. Yet, the 'age of reform' and the so-called Bengal renaissance are significant for the processes they set in motion. The 'civilizing mission' of the Company state combined in intricate ways with the enthusiasm for English education and western knowledge in the thought of Indian intellectuals to take the dual notions of reason and justice to new heights, which constituted the supporting arch of a new structure of values (Ray 1995: 8). 'Rational assessment of current needs and received traditions', affirms Tapan Raychaudhuri, 'became the hallmark of Bengali thought in the nineteenth century' (1995: 48); a point he develops with greater finesse in his book that examines the nuances and ambiguities in the changing and shifting perceptions of and attitudes toward the West among three key Bengali intellectuals of the nineteenth century (Raychaudhuri 2002). Emphasis on reason went hand in hand with a belief in western science, and the two together came to embody a 'cure' for all problems and backwardness of the Indian feudal order. Promotion of science did not only underlie the 'language of reform' (Prakash 1999); vital efforts were set afoot to promote 'the cultivation of science' in Calcutta and several other towns such as Benares and Aligarh.

This new structure of values did not exclude the lower classes from its purview: 'slavery' and the slave trade came to be discussed. Indeed, after the abolition of slavery in Britain in 1820, attention turned to India, and the Charter Act of 1833 enjoined the Company's government to abolish slavery in India. Two legislations of 1849 also prohibited the branding of convicts and provided for the custody of lunatics. At the same time, since slavery as prevalent in Britain and as practised in India primarily in systems of bonded labour in agriculture were very different, the effect of this abolition was barely felt by the sections affected by it.

A critical examination of 'Indian society' and the condition of women by Orientalist scholars, liberal policymakers and evangelicals prompted Indian males to look at their own society and 'tradition' in ways they had not done before. The inevitable but imperceptible result of this was the objectification of 'Indian society' (Cohn 1996). On the other hand, the debates and reforms paved the way for a broadening social and political criticism, if not social change, and unleashed a diverse range of 'interanimating movements for rights' that included self-determination against colonialism, social justice for the low castes and human rights for the labouring poor (Sarkar and Sarkar 2008: 6).

Colonial critique produced a wide variety of responses. At one end, there was outright rejection and repudiation of certain Hindu practices and prohibition, including the adoption of an English way of life and of evangelical Christianity. Members of the 'Young Bengal' group—the very young students of Hindu College who were inspired by their Eurasian teacher Louis Henri Derozio—largely represented this trend. Derozio, who had joined Hindu College in 1826 or 1827, became the nucleus of a small group of young students who were enthused by the 'age of reform' pioneered by Rammohan, but who expressed their 'challenge to tradition' in a very different way.

Derozio was not bound by 'tradition' in the ways his students, primarily from upper-caste and middle-class families, were. In addition, the 'orthodox' forces represented by Radhakanta Deb's Dharma Sabha, founded in 1830, as a rival to Rammohan's Brahmo Samaj, were large and powerful (Sastri 1907: 83). The intensity of the 'conservative' reaction made Young Bengal an isolated force. This isolation 'created a unique cohesion among them and urged them into social extremism' (Sinha 1965: 95). Their attacks on Hinduism were directed against Brahmanical domination. They resented the continued influence of *pundits* and priests whose presence they felt, 'thwarted free thinking and encouraged superstition' (cited in Sastri 1907: 52). Their Academic Association was the main platform through which criticism of prevalent religious practices and superstitions was given expression. These young men were greatly attracted by David Hume's scepticism. They openly ate beef and drank whiskey. Notable among them were Derozio, the Eurasian teacher and Krishnamohan Banerjea, a Brahman who converted to Christianity.

The other extreme reaction found reflection in a valorization of Indian (Hindu) ideas and practices, which related also to the condition of women. It resented the 'wholesale and harsh condemnations of Indian and Hindu customs' (Seth 2007: 133), evoked a past when women in Hindu India were educated and had rights and pointed to the not so elevated status of European women in the recent past to argue for India's superiority. Although the extreme positions were mediated by attempts to strike a balance between the 'richly textured cultures' that sustained the intelligentsia and the excitement of new ideas (Metcalf and Metcalf 2003: 83), understandings of Indian 'tradition' were inflected by western norms of what constitutes a 'rational' tradition.

RETHINKING RELIGION

The Brahmo Samaj set up by Rammohan in 1828, as successor to his Atmiya Sabha of 1815, offers an illustrative example of how the idea of a unified, well-defined 'Hinduism' took shape. Rammohan, it bears pointing out, had mastery over Persian and Arabic and great familiarity with Hindu and Islamic trends of logic and reason (Sarkar 1975: 49). Consequently, he found it difficult to accept both the missionary claim of the superiority of Christianity and the liberal proclamation of the absence of rational thought in India. Vedantic monism and the ideas of the *Koran* had great appeal for him as did unitarianism, which he came in contact with after his move to Calcutta. Together, they confirmed his belief in the superiority of rational faith over prevailing popular religions, which impaired human beings' freedom by tying them to mechanical rituals, irrational myths and superstitions.

The unity of civilizations advocated by Orientalist scholars and the 'unity of Godhead' proclaimed in Colebrook's essay on the *Vedas* consolidated Rammohan's conviction that monotheism was the basis of Hinduism and that practices that differed from ancient textual prescriptions were all aberrations that had to be done away with. *Sati* was only one such practice. He also condemned polytheism, idol worship and priestcraft, and translated the *Upanishads* into Bengali to substantiate his claim that monotheism was the basis of Hindu thought. Perhaps unwittingly, Rammohan's innumerable tracts perpetrated the idea of an authentic Indian (Hindu) tradition and outlined the contours of a Hinduism that bore close resemblance to Christianity as a rational faith rooted in sacred texts.

Ideas similar to that propagated by the Brahmo Samaj were echoed in other presidencies. In Maharashtra, in particular, Atmaram Pandurang, enthused by the visit of the Brahmo leader Keshab Chandra Sen, took the initiative in establishing the Prarthana Samaj (Prayer Society) in Bombay in 1867. Following Keshab Sen's subsequent visit in 1868, M. G. Ranade and R. G. Bhandarkar joined the Prarthana Samaj and infused it with new vigour (Majumdar [1965] 1981: 106). The Samaj took a two-pronged stand—it proclaimed the unity of God and argued against the 'existing corruption of Hindu religion'. Individual members of the Samaj laid stress on social reform and sought to gain support for abandoning caste, introducing widow remarriage, abolishing *purdah* and child marriage, and encouraging female education. Ranade also attempted to give the Samaj a comprehensive philosophic basis through his essay, 'Theists Confession of Faith' (ibid.: 106–07). The Prarthana Samaj was preceded by organizations, such as the Manav Dharma Sabha and the Paramhansa Mandali (1844 and 1849, respectively), which also confronted issues of the caste system and widow remarriage. This agenda of social reform was complemented by the work of scholars like Bhandarkar and K. T. Telang, who drew inspiration from Orientalist scholars and undertook painstaking examinations and translations of Sanskrit texts in order to rediscover Indian civilization.

In the decade of the 1870s, the redefinition of Hinduism along the lines of a religion of the Book found vociferous articulation in the Arya Samaj movement of Swami Dayananda Saraswati, which became very popular in Punjab and the North-Western Provinces. Dayananda internalized the Orientalist privileging of texts as the basis of religion and affirmed that the *Vedas* were the most authentic religious texts of the Hindus. All post-Vedic developments, according to him, were accretions to be purged. Dayananda also rejected authoritative commentaries on the *Vedas* and upheld his own interpretation of these sacred texts. [T]he *Samhita* of the *RigVeda*, as interpreted by Dayananda in his books, 'formed the bed-rock on which stood the entire structure of the Arya Samaj' (ibid.: 113). He refused to recognize the hereditary basis of the caste system as an organic division of society, sought to create an 'open social system' where women and *shudras* received a measure of learning and made education and not birth the determinant of status (Jones 1989: 33). He denounced the worship of gods and goddesses and advocated the worship of the Supreme Being. Encouraging inter-caste marriages followed upon Dayananda's understanding that caste was not defined by heredity but by the character and achievements of each individual.

Anshu Malhotra reminds us that Dayananda's reformed society was equally 'an organically structured social body' where different castes performed functions suitable to their status determined by merit. Moreover, this efficient social organism was a 'robust Vedic counterpart' to the masculine West that had 'emasculated and enslaved the Aryavarta' (Arya nation) (Malhotra 2006: 121). Dayananda's notion of Aryavarta as espoused in his important work *Satyarth Prakash* was beset with ambiguities and contradictions. His attempt to order the chaos he found around him and 'shape the contours of a healthy and self-confident people holding their own in a comity of nations' entailed an integration of the masses. The 'open society' he tried to create, however, still remained a nation of castes that retained and at times sharpened existing hierarchies (ibid.: 122–23).

Concern with a healthy robust nation as a counterpart to the masculine West found reflection in the emphasis Dayananda laid on the work of *shuddhi* or the reconversion of the millions of Hindus, who had converted willingly or under duress to Islam, Christianity and Sikhism, but were ready to come back to the fold of Hinduism. Orthodox Hinduism did not allow for reconversion; we have noted that the Hindu Missionary Society in Maharashtra had made limited attempts, but Arya Samaj gave a new significance to *shuddhi*. It became a prime instrument in realizing its goal of attaining the religious, social and political unity of India. India, in Dayananda's vision, was essentially Hindu and it could be regenerated through a revival of Vedic rituals, including *shuddhi*. It is not surprising that *shuddhi* caused chronic friction between the 'Hindus' and the 'Muslims' in northern India in the latter half of the nineteenth century.

The constitution of the Arya Samaj drawn up in 1875 also provided for voluntary contributions, a hundredth part of the earnings of each member, to the Samaj's fund. The money thus collected was spent on social service like famine relief and, more importantly, on establishing and running educational institutions. The Dayananda Anglo–Vedic School set up in Lahore soon developed into a college and became a model for several such institutions, which imparted English education but on the principles of the 'Vedas'.

The simultaneous advance of 'the Raj and the church' in Punjab that propagated the 'glory of God and Queen' (Oberoi 1997: 218), generated reactions among all sections of 'natives'; the Sikhs too were alarmed by conversions to Christianity (ibid.: 222). They were disturbed by Maharaja Duleep Singh, the son of Ranjit Singh, renouncing his religion and accepting evangelical Christianity in 1853. The ruler of Kapurthala's nephew soon followed. Members of the Sikh community participated actively in the work of 'native' associations of different hues that emerged to combat Christian missions. A Brahmo Samaj was set up at Lahore in 1862–63 and an Anjuman-i-Punjab or the Society for the Diffusion of Useful Knowledge was founded in 1865 with the support of the Lieutenant-Governor of Punjab by Dr Gottlieb Wilhelm Leitner, a cosmopolitan man of Hungarian-Jewish background.

The lessons learnt through the work in these associations—of setting up voluntary bodies, holding regular meetings to discuss and broadcast a particular cause, of appointing office bearers, collecting funds, establishing schools—were soon 'to be applied in upholding Sikh interest' (Oberoi 1997: 235). The Sri Guru Singh Sabha was founded by leading Sikh public figures and traditional intellectuals at a meeting in 1872. The Singh Sabha movement spoke of reviving the teachings of the Sikh gurus and made a serious effort to repress heterogeneity within the Sikh community–the deviant paths taken by distinct groups according to them–and tried to establish strict norms and codes of conduct to be followed by the Sikhs. The Singh Sabha also tried to increase literacy and popularized religious literature written in the Gurumukhi script; literature that made available the teachings of the gurus to ordinary Sikhs. The activities of the Singh Sabha contributed to the crystallization of a unified, homogenized identity of Sikhs, the Sikhs as they think of themselves today (ibid.).

A form of neo-Vedantism, or the practical application of Vedanta philosophy, was propagated by the Ramakrishna Mission, founded under the leadership of Swami Vivekananda in 1887. Narendranath Dutta, who became famous as Vivekananda, was a disciple of Ramakrishna Paramhansa. Born in a poor Brahman family, Gadadhar Chattopadhyaya, Ramakrishna, earned fame on account of the 'strange fits of God-consciousness that often came upon him' (Majumdar [1965] 1981: 120). A simple, pious man, Ramakrishna realized God only when he was touched by a 'divine madness'; his earlier attempts to reach God through different paths had not borne fruit. Ramakrishna preached an eclectic religion that proclaimed the realization of God through knowledge and devotion to be the highest human ideal. In order to reach this ideal, one had to strive for a spiritual life that transcended the lure of material prosperity and the desire for gold and women, without, however, renouncing worldly life.

Swami Vivekananda extended Ramakrishna's ideal of the realization of divinity in humanity by making service to mankind the prime goal of the Ramakrishna Mission. After Ramakrishna's death, about a dozen of his close disciples and associates—most of them English-educated middle-class Bengali youth—set up a monastery in Baranagar, performed Vedic rites, adopted monastic names and ceremonially accepted the vows of monasticism under the leadership of Narendranath Dutta, now called Swami Vivekananda. Distressed by the poverty, squalor and loss of mental vigour and with the lack of hope for the future that he found everywhere during his tour of India, Vivekananda groped for a way to help India pull out of this morass, by means of 'the only hope' that India still retained—'her religion, the source of her life' (Gambhirananda 1955: 70). Vivekananda found an opportunity to implement his vague plan of seeking help from the West, 'not as a beggar, but in exchange for the spirituality which the West lacked and India alone could supply' by attending the Parliament of Religions held in Chicago in 1893 (Majumdar [1965] 1981: 126). His speech there made him famous overnight and won support and acclaim for the Mission. The idea of a spiritual India superior to the material West gained wide currency through this speech, an idea that got reinforced and replenished through recurrent deployments down to the present. India became almost synonymous with Hinduism, and both attained high levels of prestige and renown.

A very distinct and different offshoot of the 'profound upheaval' in religious values and confidence in existing social institutions caused by the assimilation of new ideas by educated Hindus (O'Hanlon 1985: 105) was a growth in radical lower-caste sentiments and movements. These movements based themselves squarely on the view that India as a society was 'materially and culturally impoverished' (ibid.:

118), and aimed at reforming traditional Hindu society through practical means. Jotirao Phule, born in a family of agriculturists in the service of Peshwa Baji Rao II and a member of the Mali caste, who went to a school run by the missionaries of the Free Church of Scotland in Poona in the 1840s, took the lead in this regard. Phule and his friends felt that lack of education was the single most important cause for the backwardness of untouchables and lower castes, and that education was the prime way of bringing about a change in social attitudes. In 1848, he set up a school for untouchables and lower-caste girls in Poona. In 1873, Phule and his friends set up the Satyashodhak Samaj (Truth-Seeking Society), which represented the first of the many attempts made by lower-caste politicians at setting up organizations and ideologues in the last three decades of the nineteenth century (ibid.: 220). We will take up these movements in greater detail in the following chapter. For the moment, it is important to stress the wide divergence in ideas and understandings of 'traditional Hindu society' and in efforts to reform it. In addition, all this rethinking reflected in the growth of a public sphere, urban and vernacular, aggravated Hindu–Muslim tensions in north India and Hindu and lower-caste tensions in western and southern India, even as they allowed the formation of new constituencies (Freitag 1989; Gooptu 2001; Gupta 2002; Naregal 2001; Omvedt 1976; Rao 2009).

In areas away from urban capitals, reforms acquired a very different hue. Barely influenced by western ideas, reform and resistance in many parts of the country were articulated through faith and devotion. In Orissa, for instance, the nineteenth century saw a surge of new religious preachers who spoke with great force about *kaliyuga*, the last and the worst of the four eras of classical Hindu time, ascribed the troubles of the times to the predominance of Kali, and offered ways out for subordinate peoples. Most of them advocated belief in one God, who was accessible to all through devotion. This challenged both the validity of the caste system and of ritual and social hierarchies; it also decried idol worship, rituals and the primacy of Brahman priests. Such preachers gained great acceptance among 'tribal', untouchable, and lower-caste peoples, who deified their preceptors as human incarnations of the divine (Banerjee-Dube 2007). These preachers' ideas found resonance in other trends of Vaishnava devotionalism, such as the Swami Narayan movement in Gujarat and that of Sankardev in Assam, which spoke of an equal and unified community of devotees. Similar ideas had also been propagated among the *chamar*s of Chhattisgarh by Guru Ghasidas in the 1820s, who had urged untouchable *chamar*s to ritually reconstitute themselves as a pure group, the *satnami*s, by means of believing in *santampurush*, the true God, and discarding certain impure practices (Dube 1998). The emergence of several other religious orders in different parts of India that drew their following from the poor, untouchable and lower-caste groups vividly reflected the force of religion as a mode of resistance as well as the massive transformations underway at all levels of Indian society in the nineteenth century.

Trends in Islam

Reform and revival within 'Islam' followed a different trajectory. Muslim aristocrats, in general, kept their distance from the English. They considered themselves to be superior in culture to the Company's merchants and were also resentful of the fact that they were slowly but steadily being dislodged from their position of prestige and authority. 'Movements' within Islam, in the first half of the nineteenth century, propelled by a concern for the decline of Islam and of Muslims in general, were informed by a need to find the cause of decline and a remedy for it. Wahabism, a trend named after its preacher Abdul Wahab of Nejd (1703–87), advocated a return to the simplicity of faith (and society) in the Prophet's Arabia and rejected 'all accretions to and declensions from pure Islam' (Isaac 1874: 46).

This trend became a powerful religio-political creed in the first half of the nineteenth century under the leadership of Saiyid Ahmad Barelvi (1786–1831) who had come under the influence of Shah Abdul Aziz, son of Shah Waliulllah, the famous saint of Delhi (1702–62). Abdul Aziz had translated the Koran into Urdu in order to bring its precepts closer to the people. Saiyid Ahmad fiercely advocated a 'return' to the principles of the *Koran* and the *hadith* (reports on the sayings and deeds of Prophet Muhammad), which entailed a discarding of the worship of saints and other accretions introduced by the Sufis although Waliullah had spoken of a comprehensive Islam which had room both for the Sufis and for the Shias along with the Sunnis. Large groups of aristocrats in northern India adopted Walliullah's message of regeneration to be acquired by means of countering internal decay and later abuses; Saiyid Ahmad also found a following among 'hard-pressed Muslim weavers and artisans' of the Gangetic plain (Metcalf and Metcalf 2003: 84). In 1829, Saiyid Ahmad organized a campaign against the Sikh state of Ranjit Singh in order to establish a state of his own. His small band of followers, however, could not face the might of Ranjit Singh, and Saiyid Ahmad died fighting in the Himalayan foothills. His memory served to inspire subsequent Islamic uprisings along the frontier, and to 'frighten the British with imagined "Wahabi" conspiracies' (ibid.).

Shariat Allah (1780–1840), who had spent two decades in Mecca, returned to Faridpur in Bengal in 1821 and spread the message of a purified Islam. Beginning with denouncing superstitions and corruptions that had crept into Islamic society, he moved on to declare the country under British occupation *dar-ul-harb* (enemy territory), where Friday and festive prayers were not held. Poor peasants and artisans of eastern Bengal understood the message of enemy territory in their own ways and refused to pay dues collected for Hindu temples and festivals. These people, who came to be known as the Faraizis, grouped under Shariat Allah's son Dudu Mian and boldly asserted their rights against Hindu zamindars, moneylenders and indigo planters. 'Purified' Islam, therefore, often encouraged subordinate peoples to radicalism, articulated in terms of agrarian protest.

In the 1860s, a significant venture for religious and social reform was initiated by Sir Sayyid Ahmad Khan, a Delhi-born aristocrat, whose family had been in the service both of the Mughal emperors and of the East India Company. Trained in two distinct systems of thought, Sayyid Ahmad, a judge in the subordinate judicial administration in the North-Western Provinces, sought to reform Islam along lines of reason that often appeared non-conformist to the orthodox section of the Muslim community. In a manner similar to his earlier contemporary, Rammohan Roy, Sayyid Ahmad emphasized the urgent need for western education. This was the only way out of the current 'backwardness' of the Muslims, he candidly stated in his speech at the Mohammedan Literary Society of Calcutta in 1863. The reason for the Mulisms' current backwardness, he affirmed, was their almost complete ignorance of the philosophy, science and arts of modern times, all of which were highly admired by the youth of the present age. For him, educated Muslims were 'learned in and benefited by philosophy, sciences, and arts of antiquity' but not those of modern times. He mentioned that many works had been composed in German, French and other languages, but since it was impossible to gain proficiency in all of them, and since most of these works were available in English, it was best to devote full attention to English. English, moreover, was the language of the people who governed Hindustan (Graham 1885: 77).

Sayyid Ahmad set-up two *madrassa*s in Moradabad and Ghazipur, and followed these up by establishing a school in Aligarh, which developed into the Muhammedan Anglo–Oriental College. But as we will see in the following chapter, a seven-month trip to England between1869–70 brought about a significant shift in Sayyid Ahmad's thought and vocabulary (Lelyveld 1978: 104). In England, he encountered both the self-confidence and sense of achievement of the British and the humiliation of Islam at the hands of Christianity in Europe. He now wanted to bring about a confluence of religion and education. This was reflected in Anglo–Oriental College's programme.

Sayyid Ahmad's ideas about reforming Islam, reflected in his article in *Tahzib al-Akhlaq*, a magazine he started in 1870 shortly after his return from England, aroused the ire of the *ulema* (Muslim scholars, jurists in particular, with specialized knowledge of the legal system). He turned his principal attention to education and social reform. Actively supported by a group of friends and scholars, the Anglo–Oriental College also got help from British authorities, whose attitude towards the Muslims had undergone a radical transformation after the Revolt of 1857. The college soon became a university, the famous Aligarh Muslim University, an institution that has produced 'some of the most eminent Muslim scholars of modern times' (Majumdar [1965] 1981: 144). Very much in tune with the idea of the modern, Sayyid Ahmad also established a Scientific Society and urged his fellowmen to read works of history produced by 'modern, civilized nations'. This is because works of history written by 'our own authors' do not 'contain that information which is necessary to improve the civilization and morality of men' (Sayyid Ahmad, compilation edited by Muhammad 1978: 14). He also advocated the translation of scientific texts and small works on 'natural philosophy' into Urdu.

Sir Sayyid, of course, could not find support from all Muslim aristocrats; apart from personal rivalries, many of them were troubled by the 'anglicization' of education and the 'Europeanization' of Muslim society. Their fear was reinforced by government support of 'modern' Muslim learning reflected in the founding of the Calcutta Madrassa and the Anglo–Arabic School (College) in Delhi. Although recent assessments acknowledge the immense debt of the Muslims of India to the Aligarh movement, Hindu nationalist constructions project Sayyid Ahmad as a fundamental British loyalist and an enemy of Indian nationalism. It is true that Sayyid Ahmad took a resolute stand against the Indian National Congress. His prime concern, however, was to dissuade 'his fellow Muslims' from 'the plague of religious bigotry' (Jalal 1998: 81). His Muslimness was 'rarely at odds with his Indianness' since Muslims in India, much like Hindus, thought of it as their homeland (ibid.). Unfortunately, Sir Sayyid strove for English education and social reform about four decades after his 'Hindu' contemporaries, who by then had faintly begun to question colonial rule.

Punjab in the second half of the nineteenth century saw the appearance of new schools of theology that regarded the *Koran* and the *hadiths* of the Prophet to be the final authority for interpreting Muslim rituals. Mirza Ghulam Ahmad, influenced by Sayyid Ahmad's 'rationalist' movement, attempted to reform Islam in a way as to make its tenets and beliefs logical and reasonable. His followers came to be called Ahmadis or Qadianis (Qadian being Ghulam Ahmad's place of birth). Ghulam Ahmad was driven by an urge to counter the onslaught on Islam being carried out by Scottish missionaries and members of the Arya Samaj. Ghulam Ahmad gained rapid popularity, but lost it when, in 1891, he declared himself to be a prophet, a claim that went against the widely held belief of Sunni Muslims that Muhammad is the last Prophet.

Different efforts at constructing a 'community' of Muslims undoubtedly generated a distinctive religious sensibility amongst various groups. But, as Ayesha Jalal reminds us forcefully, much of Muslim thought and ideas of the period was inflected by individual nuances, and not by a predetermined 'Muslim' community. Indian Muslims' approach to religion and politics, particularly in Punjab and northwest India in the nineteenth century, was marked by an individuality that divided Muslims along a range of issues and conferred on Muslim thought and politics far greater complexity than is generally acknowledged (Jalal 2001).

The wave of reforms touched other communities too, such as the Parsis. English-educated young men from the Parsi community based in Bombay, started the Rahnumai Mazdnedayasan Sabha or Religious Reform Association in 1851. It aimed at regenerating the social condition of the Parsis and restoring Zoroastrian religion to its pristine purity. K. R. Cama gave a great boost to the association on his return from Europe in 1859. While in Europe, he had read the *Avesta* in the original under the guidance of important scholars. He started teaching Parsi scriptures in Bombay in order to produce a new generation of educated and well-aware priests who would free the Parsi community from the thraldom of all those practices, rituals and creed which had no sanction in Zoroastrian scriptures. Reform of morals was complimented by efforts to raise the age of marriage, encourage female education and remove the system of *purdah*. Dadabhai Naoroji, a lead actor in this reform venture, would soon play a crucial role in the political 'regeneration' of India, a point we will discuss in Chapter 5.

The project of socio-religious reform had a late start in the Madras Presidency. English education took time to take roots here and the 'reform' societies retained a distinctly Brahman and upper-caste flavour for a long time. This perhaps explains the vitality of the non-Brahman movement in the south, which started in the last decades of the nineteenth century. Together, these distinct efforts and movements served to delineate the contours of separate communities, primarily religious, even though the contours were blurred and hazy. Unfortunately, such marking of frontiers got a great fillip through the measures and policies of Queen Victoria's Raj, a tale we track in Chapter 4. The British notion about 'traditional' India as being composed of religious communities took shape precisely on account of the interaction of different sections of Indians with the Company and colonial state and Protestant missionaries. This will have immense import for the story of nationalism that we will take up from Chapter 5.

Land and Revenue

As indicated in the last chapter, profound changes were set afoot by the imperatives of the Company in land and land revenue. The Permanent Settlement of Bengal and the Ryotwari (Raiyatwari) System in Madras and subsequently the Bombay Presidency tried to integrate elements of the existing agrarian structure. At the same time, the urge to make land revenue the basis for the primary accumulation of capital (Sarwar 2012: 16), and the dynamics of the Company's policy produced different results and hybrid forms (Dutt 1963: xiiv). The Permanent and Ryotwari Settlements had stemmed from the conviction that the existing practice in India, which was based on 'precarious' and unwritten customary rights of agricultural communities, needed to be changed because fluctuating and irregular modes of collection caused decay in agriculture and loss of valuable revenue for the state. Certainty and regularity had to be established through a clear demarcation of public and private rights that would enable the state to fix its revenue demand and allow the subjects legal 'rights' over the remaining produce of the soil, their 'private' property. Private property in land, it bears mention, did exist prior to the arrival of the British. Land grants were made to temples, ritual functionaries and people who offered services to kings and princes in different capacities. Land rights came with clear obligations—landholders had to pay land tax or supply material and manpower to the ruler. All these features continued under the British.

The drive of the British administration for order and clarity, however, drastically reduced different types of rights in land. Landholders were given definite rights that went with clear obligations which were legally specified. The land they owned was measured, surveyed and settled, and laws recorded and codified. Sub-proprietors and self-cultivating (*khudkashth*) peasants with resident rights were recognized but as different classes of 'tenants' who had to pay fixed rents. While the Permanent Settlement granted legal rights over land to the zamindars, Munro's Ryotwari System tried to make an individual *ryot* (*raiyat*) the proprietor of the land and responsible for the payment of state dues. A scholar has argued recently that the Ryotwari System was more pragmatic than doctrinal (Sarwar 2012: 18). Local chiefs in the regions where the system was introduced had been eliminated or reduced to insignificance and the state's direct dealing with an individual farmer meant that it had direct access to the area being cultivated and the income that accrued from it. Both helped the state assess and collect the revenue better (ibid.).

Arguably, the utilitarian philosophy of a political economy elaborated by Ricardo had a 'distaste for landlordism' which got reflected in the Ryotwari and the Mahalwari Settlements (Stokes [1959] 1989: 81). James Mill, responsible for drafting the revenue despatches to India between 1819 and 1830, played a 'master role' in instituting new revenue settlements in India in accordance with liberal utilitarian principles (Sarwar 2012: 18).

The Mahalwari Settlement was introduced in the North-Western Provinces, the territory stretching between the foothills of the Himalayas through the Ganga–Jamuna Doab to the central Indian plateau. It included a large part of Punjab, the United Provinces and most of the Central Provinces. This was a region dominated by the *taluqdars* ('intermediary' zamindars) who did not possess land but contracted with the state to realize the revenue of a particular territory (Hasan 1969: 24) and proprietary zamindars. At first, the Company tried to enter into short-term settlements with the *taluqdars*, which did not work properly.

In the Mahalwari Settlement, which was put in place according to Holt Mackenzie's instructions and by Regulation VII of 1822, *mahals* or estates' proprietary bodies, the 'village community' was recognized as the landowner. Land belonged jointly to the village community technically called the body of co-shares that was collectively responsible for paying revenue (Sarwar 2012: 18), although individual responsibility was not totally done away with. This 'community' included peasant proprietors, *taluqdars* and resident cultivating peasants whose rent was also sought to be ascertained and recorded (Bandyopadhyay 2004: 94). The head of the community, the *lambardar*, signed the agreement with the government as the person responsible for paying the revenue of the community.

This system, a mix of the Permanent and the Ryotwari, required even more detailed and complicated land surveys, which were impossible to implement. Once again, revenue demand was fixed arbitrarily and at a very high level. Revenue arrears mounted as buyers could not be found; the agricultural depression of 1828 made the situation worse. The government of William Bentinck reviewed the scheme of 1822 and concluded that it had caused widespread misery. Regulation IX of 1833 introduced a reformed and more flexible system under the supervision of R. M. Bird. The revenue of an entire *mahal* or fiscal unit now came to be assessed on the basis of the net value of the potential produce of each field, the value of land and the price of crops. The Settlement was made for 30 years in UP and for 20 years in Punjab and the Central Provinces and two-thirds of the net produce of the land was fixed as the share of the state. The revised settlement was led astray by corrupt settlement officers who did not pay heed to the carefully laid out rules in collecting revenue. Misery and discontent continued (R. C. Dutt's letters to Lord Curzon, 12 May 1900, cited in Sarwar 2012: 19).

The three settlements were based on different principles. At the same time, they were governed by certain key and common concerns. First and foremost, the Company state was driven by the need to maximize the revenue to be collected from land. This again was based on the belief that all lands belonged to the state, which recognized the 'private property rights' of different categories of landowners and tenants in return for the revenue or the rent that they paid to the state. The state's search for and fixing of proprietors of land, who were given definite rights, produced different groups with interests in land: the state, the zamindars and the cultivating holders in the permanently settled areas; the state and the farmers in regions under the Ryotwari Settlement; and the state, the landlord, the tenant holders and cultivating holders in Mahalwari areas. The introduction of ownership and of a judicial notion of agrarian relations based on contract, initially reinforced the dominant power structures within the village but gradually changed social relations (between owners and tenants) that turned on land. 'Customary' rights and practices were disregarded, and a series of informal arrangements with a host of poor people who depended on agriculture in different ways was done away with. It is not just that the revenue demand increased enormously or that land became a marketable commodity and landed property changed hands acutely affecting the local power structure; it is more that the occupancy and other 'customary' rights of the poor peasants, share-croppers and agricultural labourers were ignored. Women, who did not own land but had rights to the produce, were not taken into consideration at all in the new arrangements and they were wiped out completely from the codified laws and regulations, a point barely noted by scholars. This, of course, happened with the complicity of the local male elite, active players in the process of codification.

Debates on the impact of revenue settlements turn on whether and how far the earlier zamindars and village headmen were displaced (Chaudhuri 1967), the extent of peasant indebtedness (Kumar 1965, 1982), the increase in the number of moneylenders (Charlesworth 1972; Fukuzawa 1982; Guha 1992; Kumar 1968), and whether the revenue settlements caused complete rupture with earlier patterns of agrarian relations or whether there were continuities (Bayly 1988, 1989; Stein 1992). These themes are self-explanatory in that they indicate the important changes brought about by the new revenue settlements. That high revenue demand caused peasant distress and agrarian depression, particularly in the Bombay-Deccan-Madras region, that is, the areas under Ryotwari Settlement, was acknowledged by the Company's government. In the second round of settlements arrived at in the 1840s, the tax burden was reduced considerably (Sarwar 2012: 24). Unfortunately, this was neutralized by the excessive powers granted to revenue collectors. From 1816 on, the collectors were put in charge of police duties, and their subordinate officers used their powers to coerce subjects in the countryside (Arnold 1986: 20). Constant complaints about exploitation of peasants by zamindars in the Bengal Presidency prompted the colonial government to pass a series of tenancy acts between 1859 and 1928 after the Revolt of 1857 brought the East India Company's rule to an end.

Land tax remained the single most important source of the government's revenue (Charlesworth 1982). In 1851–52, the net revenue earned from land totalled 19,927.039 pounds with the gross revenues collected from the three presidencies of Bengal, Madras and Bombay amounting to 10000,000, 5000,000 and 4800,000, respectively (Sarwar 2012: 25). In 1858–59, land revenue constituted 50.3 per cent or more than half of the government's total revenue. High revenue demand and its rigorous collection together with the drive to extend cultivation through reclamation of waste and common lands stretched the eco-system of the villages to the limit, with the effect becoming evident during the several famines that occurred all over the nineteenth century. Agrarian depression also induced large-scale labour migration not only to capital cities and to the tea plantations but also overseas as indentured labour (Bates 2000), a story we will briefly touch upon in the following chapter. The urge to extend cultivation seriously affected forests and woods and transformed patterns of land use and the relation between the different topographical zones. It is time to explore this.

FORESTS AND FRONTIERS

In recent years, there has been a growing awareness about the ecological changes brought about by the specific needs of the British administration. Innovative works have paid attention to the production of spaces through the 'partitioning of landscapes and social spheres' as integral parts of the process of 'state-making' (Sivaramakrishnan 1999). This occasioned qualitative changes in the relationship between the people and the natural environment (Gadgil and Guha 1993; Guha 1999; Rangarajan 1996) and involved the classification of peoples who lived in those spaces in particular ways. The people in turn, imaginatively drew upon and appropriated such classification—as 'wild' for instance—to muddle or overturn the government's intent of trying to regulate them (Skaria 1999). As is evident from the themes addressed by these works, a connected history of agrarian and environmental issues is essential for a proper understanding of processes through which the colonial state and rural social relations evolved and shaped one another.

Scholars have argued that pre-colonial South Asia was shaped and reshaped by the close interaction between pastoral nomads, agriculturists and forest dwellers (Habib [1963] 1999; Kosambi 1965, for instance). The boundaries between the three zones—forests, grazing grounds and cultivated fields— were fluid and porous, with the fluidity extending to occupation as well. People in the three zones acquired different occupational skills and could move between one another depending on economic needs and conditions (Guha 1999).

The Company administration's basic drive to establish order, extend cultivation and collect revenue resulted in the marking of clear frontiers between plains and hills or jungles—stable areas of settled agriculture and 'zones of anomaly'(Sivaramakrishnan 1999), and serious efforts to restrict the movement of people of the different zones from one to the other.

Arguably, there was disagreement among administrators with regard to particular policies. At the same time, certain fundamental ideas and obligations gave a particular method and direction to the Company's policies. This, together with the fact that colonial intrusion in the production process of uncultivated lands was 'unprecedented in its level and scale' (Rangarajan 1996: 198), produced fundamental changes in peoples' relationship with their environment. An absolute notion of landed property among groups who lived on the fringes of settled, arable cultivation was sought to be introduced, and efforts were made to transform the forest into 'a managed landscape where land use would be under imperial supervision and control' (ibid.: 8). Moreover, the Company state's insistence on reclaiming 'wastelands' meant that grazing lands and common grounds disappeared almost completely, a fact that was to have serious consequences during droughts, famines and other natural calamities (Satya 2004). The introduction of punitive grazing taxes hit the pastoralists very badly and deprived the peasantry of customary grazing runs and common grounds (N. Bhattacharya, 1998). All this was accompanied by the state's incessant drive to preserve order, which underlay its distinctive perception of 'wildness'. Wildness and civilization were constructed as totally antagonistic categories and civilization was given complete preference over wildness (Skaria 1999: 155). This understanding crucially affected the demarcation and creation of particular spaces and the classification of inhabitants.

The process began early. As the Company struggled to strengthen its rule in the Jungle *Mahals* of Bengal in the late-eighteenth century, its administrators marked out 'tribal spaces' from those of settled agriculture. 'Tribal spaces' were also the 'zones of anomaly' in the sense that they were 'unredeemable from backward agriculture' and were inhabited by people prone to conducting raids on arable lands (Sivaramakrishnan 1999: 81). The Paharias in woodland Bengal were among the first to incur official opprobrium because they refused to change over to settled agriculture. They were forced to move further and further up to the hilltops and their raids into the plains were dealt with sternly (ibid.: 81–82). The Santals, on the other hand, were welcomed as enterprising cultivators familiar with techniques of wet farming and plough cultivation and very good at clearing wastelands.

Zamindars, we need to remember, had allowed Santals to reclaim and settle in deserted villages in their estates soon after the famine of 1769–70. The government allowed the Santals to settle in the *Damin-i-Koh*—the huge area of settled agriculture marked out in 1832 and brought under the government. The government had to create the *Damin-i-Koh* because clashes between the Paharias—the hill 'people'—and those of the plains over rights to grazing, forest products and boundaries of terrains, continued even after the Paharias were 'pacified' by administrator Cleveland in 1782. The Paharias, now classified as 'irremediable' because they belied the government's hope by refusing to change from *kurao* (shifting cultivation) to wet rice farming (Chaudhuri 2008: 712–13), were strictly forbidden to move beyond the territory marked out for them. No attempt, of course, was made to understand the grounds of Paharia 'conservatism'—their lack of resources in men and money for investing in ploughs and irrigation. On the other hand, Santals' were given 'every encouragement' to clear jungles from 1837. The number of Santal settlements went up from 51 villages in 1838 to 1,473 in 1851 (ibid.: 714).

Large parts of central India—the Sagar and Narbada territories—consisting of sparsely populated hills and plateau, were similarly categorized as 'backward' and the British, like earlier rulers, invited 'colonisers' to clear forests. The Marathas, who controlled the region prior to the British, had left the process of production in the 'tribal areas' intact and only collected an annual tribute from the chiefs of the 'hilltops'. They had also not intervened in the regular exchange of goods and services between the people of the plains and that of the hills and forests, or tried to control the mobile groups of traders and soldiers, such as the Pindaris (Rangarajan 1996: 35–44).

The British, on the other hand, were interested in consolidating their political hold over the region from the beginning and tried vigorously to check the mobile groups. The Pindaris were subdued militarily and then encouraged to settle as landholders (ibid.: 45). This was in harmony with the need to extend cultivation, but it brought about important changes in patterns of land use that affected the peoples of the hills and forests. Here too, the urge to civilize meant that the tribes, imbued with the developmental spirit, were induced to take up a sedentary life and mobility of the obdurate ones was curtailed by restricting them to a particular zone.

In Review: Famine and Land Reclamation

An important but tragic consequence of the forcible expansion of cultivation, the reclamation of grazing lands and 'wastelands', and the commercialization of agriculture was the increased incidence of famines, particularly in the second half of the nineteenth century. The expansion of the cultivation of cotton as a cash crop in the 1860s in the black soil area of Berar increased the already intense pressure on agriculture. Over three decades between 1869–70 and 1902–03, there was a dramatic increase in the cultivable acerage from 45.7 to 71.3 of the total acerage in the six districts of Berar after survey and settlement operations were conducted by the colonial state. The active encouragement given to the cultivation of cotton, a commercial crop linked to British networks of production, pushed out other food grains. Cotton cultivation extended to common lands, and prime grazing lands were forcibly put under the plough (Satya 2004). Extension of railway networks severely depleted the forest resources of the region. Deforestation resulted in decline of rainfall and water scarcity became a perennial problem as commercialization of agriculture undermined earlier communal forms of water management. Unsurprisingly but tragically, this region became a prey to droughts and famines with deaths reaching alarming proportions in the devastating famine of 1899–1900 (Satya 2004). The famines, argues Laxman D. Satya, were not the result of 'natural' causes, as the colonial state would want us to believe, but a consequence of ongoing, ecologically devastating policies of the colonial state (ibid.).

The clear separation of wild and civilized spaces took a distinctive form in western India, comprising parts of Gujarat, Maharashtra and the Deccan plateau. Here the *dang*—a term that referred to hilly tracts or regions with dense bamboo growth—was constructed as a wild zone that was in opposition to the plains. The Dangis, communities who lived in the *dang*s (the Bhils being the largest), came to represent the very embodiment of wildness. They were defined as *janglijati* and *kaliparaj* (Skaria 1999: 37–38). Their fluctuating kings, practice of shifting cultivation, habit of raiding the plains and of taking up different jobs in different seasons, were totally opposed to British notions of order and civilization. In particular, the raids which had been recognized by earlier chiefs of the plains like the Gaekwads as rival claims to authority and had often led to negotiations, were treated by British officers as 'acts of aggression on territory under their exclusive sovereignty' (ibid.: 157). Consequently, raids were suppressed ruthlessly as 'criminal acts', reparation was demanded and there was retaliation against those who had participated in the raids.

The transformation of raids from a mode of asserting co-shared sovereignty over loosely defined frontiers into 'criminal acts' occasioned a total lack of comprehension on the part of the 'wild' chiefs. Soon, however, Bhil chiefs would make imaginative use of their 'wildness' to evade complete submission, and chiefs of hills and plains would accept and implement their own notions of exclusive sovereignty perpetrating the demarcation of definite frontiers. This 'othering' of peoples who inhabited demarcated spaces thus allowed the spatial practice of a survey to decisively represent space (Sivaramakrishnan 1999: 80).

The urge to extend cultivation soon came into conflict with the need to 'conserve' forests as there was an increasing recognition of the commercial value of forests. Forests were denuded on a large scale in the initial phase to extend cultivation. The Company also razed forests to the ground to set the seal of triumph over powerful enemies. Teak plantations in Ratnagiri, carefully nurtured by the legendary Maratha admiral Kanhoji Angre, for instance, were destroyed after the defeat of the Marathas in the early-nineteenth century (Gadgil and Guha 2000: 118–19). The onslaught on forests continued till the late nineteenth century to meet the demand of the British Royal Navy for durable timber, particularly after forests in England had been devastated (ibid.: 119).

The setting up of the railway network in India in the middle of the nineteenth century produced contradictory consequences. The massive demand for timber needed for railway sleepers caused widespread felling of trees. Often felling operations were not supervised properly and more trees were cut than were necessary (Stebbing 1922: 298–99). The rapid pace of the extension of railway tracks— from 1,349 km in 1860 to 51,658 km in 1910—and the havoc it caused to forests forcefully brought home the fact that Indian forests were not inexhaustible (Gadgil and Guha 2000: 121). This occasioned an early environmental debate in the Company's administration and made 'conservation' necessary.

The imperial forest department was formed in 1864 with experts from Germany, the leader in 'forest management' among European countries. 'Scientific' knowledge generated by the work of surveying and new sciences, such as geology, was applied to the 'management' and conservation of forests, and European techniques applied to harvest and regenerate forests. This reinforced the delineation of tribal spaces and contributed to the classification of several groups as obdurate or criminal. The department made a clear separation between the use of timber by the government and the use made by private individuals. While the massive use for railways by the government was deemed 'insignificant', the number of trees cut by private traders or 'clandestine' destruction by individuals was stated to be 'fatal to the forest' (Rangarajan 1996: 55).

The entry both of private traders and of forest dwellers on government forests was restricted in the name of 'conservation' ending eventually in the marking off of huge forest areas as reserved ones. Total state control was introduced in the reserved forests while in the 'protected forests' also under the supervision of the state, certain rights were recorded but not settled (Gadgil and Guha 2000: 134). In the case of private or non-reserved forests, such as those of the Kalrayan hills in Salem and Baramahal in the Madras Presidency, the state employed different strategies to encroach in order to bring the forest resources under its sole control. Such strategies disregarded the customary rights of the tribals and were prompted by the state's urge to further its own commercial interests; they did not stem from a desire to protect the 'tribal' from private contractors or to conserve forest resources (Saravanam 2003). Commodification of forests resulted in strict regulations on hunting and the use of forest goods, as well as the exercise of grazing rights and collection of fuel-wood by the hills and forest peoples; 'transgression' was dealt with severely.

Conservation of forests brought in its toe two related issues: the need to prevent forest fires and to eradicate vermin. Once again, knowledge and techniques derived from scientific European forestry were projected as being far superior to older, 'primitive' techniques of conservation. As K. Sivaramakrishnan remarks, by the 1870s, 'when forest policy was framed and institutionalized in various parts of India, it certainly drew on such a language of improvement, casting the project of colonialism in terms of reclamation—of both colonial peoples and lands' (Sivaramakrishnan 1999: 211).

Paradoxically, the need to make tribal spaces 'secure' encouraged the hunting of wild animals by the British. Widely upheld in nineteenth century Britain as a sport that celebrated masculinity, hunting was encouraged not just by the evolution theory and Darwinian notions of competition and hierarchy that countered the anti-hunting idea of Romanticism; it became an imperial ritual which symbolized the paternalism of the colonial administrator. Landscape ordering went hand in hand with the redrawing of wild land boundaries in the name of eradicating vermin.

The killing of a tiger enhanced the prestige of an administrator amongst his colleagues and earned him acceptance among the local populace. Tigers were the prime target in eradicating vermin, but elephants, bear, wild buffaloes, bison, boar and even deer counted among vermin throughout the nineteenth century. Their eradication along with that of poisonous snakes made tribal spaces 'secure', helped in extending cultivation and the hold of colonial governance. Former groups of indigenous hunters dislodged by the colonial officer and also disarmed after the Revolt of 1857, were armed again in the 'border' villages in the late-nineteenth century to fight the tiger menace (ibid.: 98). Eradicating vermin, of course, was contradictory to the ideology of forest conservation and efforts to prevent forest fires. Indeed, after the widespread felling of trees, particularly timber, the government undertook a scheme of selective plantation, which reordered the landscape further. In addition, the effort to make the landscape secure also included rigorous drives to suppress inhuman practices of primitive peoples, and, as discussed earlier, the subjugation of itinerant groups.

The process of 'state-making' in colonial India, through its contingencies and contradictions, produced 'several dispossessions'. Such dispossessions reshaped local landscapes and the social identities of their inhabitants (ibid.: 123, 277). The triple objectives of community construction, establishing regimes of control and compiling bodies of standard expertise provided material that made possible the transition of forests from wild space to managed forests, which could be incorporated into regimens of production (ibid.: 279). Wildness was effectively tamed and notions of private property introduced to an extent that by the 1860s most conflicts in the forests came to turn on property rights. At the same time, the 'wild' chiefs took recourse to their notorious ignorance to upset British policy. This ignorance was as much a ploy to evade impositions as the result of real incomprehension of the British ways of thinking and the fear of deception and coercion (Skaria 1999: 185ff). In a manner similar to the way hybrid categories were produced through the mixed interaction of the state and society, ploy and incomprehension jumbled the tidy categories of resistance and collaboration.

Unrest and Uprising

It is true that there was no 'pure' resistance to colonial policies of land and forest management in the way it was perceived in the early works on the subject (Guha1999). At the same time, there is no doubt that colonial intervention produced qualitative changes in patterns of land and forest use. In addition to the introduction of absolute property rights and severe regulations on the use of forests, 'commodification' brought about serious transformation in forest ecology. It is interesting to note that the trees preferred by commercial foresters (such as teak, pine and deodar) 'were invariably of little use to rural populations' whereas the trees they replaced (such as oak and terminalia) were 'intensively used for fuel, fodder, leaf manure and small timber' (Gadgil and Guha 2000: 147).

Hence, evasion and complicity, resistance and negotiation accompanied the extension of colonial control over woods and forests. If the Chenchus of Kurnool were forced to turn to banditry, the Baigas of central India stubbornly stuck to their hunting skills and continued with the practice of *jhum* cultivation (slash and burn method of cultivation; a form of subsistence and shifting agriculture) in forbidden areas, although government regulations and repression reduced their numbers drastically (ibid.: 148–53). Enforcing control on 'wild' peoples finds brilliant articulation in the *goth*s (stories) of the Dangis explored by Skaria. Here, the past is framed in terms of the overlapping epochs of the *moglai* and *mandini*—roughly corresponding to the time of freedom and of the end of that freedom. *Moglai* represents 'freedom to move in the forests, to raid, to collect a due called *gira*s from the plains, and to have a distinctive pattern of political authority'. *Mandini*, on the other hand, embodies both an epoch and an event that signals the end of *moglai* when British dominance undermined Dangi political authority (Skaria 1999: 15). *Mandini* stories also evoke the creation of reserved forests in 1901–02 and the violent exclusion of Dangis from rights to cultivate there.

The *goth*s, of course, also portray *dhum* or rebellion against the *sarkar* as an almost natural occurrence. This is a direct consequence of the reimagining of the forest communities in the nineteenth century that reaffirmed their insurgent attitude in the early twentieth century. While early Bhil insurrections of 1819 and 1831, both of which were crushed by the British, do not figure as prominently in the *goth*s, the three rebellions between 1907 and 1914, find proud mention. Resistance was also offered by Bhils' rivals, the Kolis of Ahmadnagar district in 1829, which was suppressed rapidly, and again in 1844 when a local Koli ruler successfully held out against the British for two years.

The most sustained resistance perhaps was offered by the Koya, Konda and Dora tribesmen of present day Gudem and Rampa hill tracts in Andhra Pradesh (Arnold 1982). Primarily *jhum* cultivators, these groups were severely affected by a variety of restrictions imposed by British regulations and persistently challenged them. First, the demarcation of frontiers and government opposition to *jhum* not only caused havoc to the practice, it also meant the loss of control of tribal groups over lands.

Government leases brought in 'outsiders'—men of the plains who got leases from the government for the commercial use of the forest.

The *fituri* (revolt) of 1879, for instance, was occasioned by the government's ban on the brewing of local liquor, an important source of nourishment, and the granting of leases to traders of the plains to brew palm liquor. Already reduced to a position of dependence and subordination, the tribesmen of Rampa hills felt that since they could not live anyway, 'they might as well kill the constables and die' (Gadgil and Guha 2000: 155). Consistent attacks on police stations, a visible symbol of state authority in all *fituri*s well illustrate Ranajit Guha's analysis of these insurgencies as conscious political acts, and the consciousness of the rebel as 'negative', that is, defined against the other, the dominant oppressor. Tammam Dora, the leader of the 1879 uprising, was shot by the police in June 1880, but insurgency spread to the Golconda Hills in Visakhapatnam and the Rekepalle country in Bhadrachalam, which had been recently transferred to the Madras Presidency from the Central Provinces and had been subject to increased restrictions on *jhum*.

The Santal *hool* (rebellion of the Santal peoples in present day Jharkhand) of 1855–56, offers another instance of an uprising against the oppression of local police and European officers and the penetration of 'outsiders' that is well documented (Chaudhuri 2008). The Santals, we need to remember, had earlier dislodged the Paharias from woodland Bengal in reclaiming wasteland and bringing it under the plough. However, in the course of the nineteenth century, government leases and a series of forest regulations, as well as the setting up of railway networks brought severe pressure on the Santals who lived scattered in the districts of Cuttack, Manbhum, Balabhum, Chota Nagpur, Palamau, Bankura and the area around Rajmahal hills, the *Damin-i-Koh*. Their skills as cultivators and rights as 'original' settlers came under severe strain on account of the British leasing lands to zamindars and moneylenders, and their existence was made even more difficult by the demands of the police and European officers.

The *diku*s or leaders of the Santals, finally made a desperate attempt to restore their lost lands by throwing out the outsiders. They rose in open rebellion against the three prime oppressors—zamindars, *mahajans* and the government. The rapid spread of the insurrection to a wide region between Rajmahal and Bhagalpur and the active support that the rebels got from low-caste peasants caused panic in government circles. Drastic measures were adopted to crush the rising. Santal villages were burnt and the people killed recklessly. This produced large-scale migration of Santal, Oraon and Munda tribal labourers into north Bengal, where they helped clear the jungle. They also moved to tea plantations in Darjeeling and Jalpaiguri and later overseas as indentured labourers (Bates 2000: 6). All this finally put an end to the uprising but it retained its hold in popular imagination. To this day, *Chitrakar*s (artists/painters) in Bengal sing songs of the *hool* as they give vivid articulation to the event in their *pata chitra*s (paintings on the bark of a tree).

In official records, on the other hand, such uprisings got inscribed as the 'antithesis of colonialism': insurgency that upset the very vital 'law and order' established by the colonial regime (Guha 1983: 2–3). Administrators compared and contrasted one peasant revolt with another in their reports in order to make sense of what had occasioned such an event. The purpose, of course, was to implement measures that would prevent the recurrence of such happenings. Consequently, in its analysis of the Deccan Riots of 1875, the Deccan Riots Commission stressed the importance of the Santal *hool* as a 'precedent'. In the case of these 'riots' the insurgent Kunbi cultivators of Poona and Ahmadnagar districts, like their Santal counterparts, attacked outsiders, in this case the Marwari and Gujar moneylenders (Kumar 1968). Colonial records show a remarkable lack of concern for the real distress that drove people to take such extreme steps; they only looked for causes and precedence in order to legitimize counter-insurgency (Guha 1983: 2–3).

1857: Different Visions

The fear and outrage produced by the open racial superiority and arrogance of British rule found expression in a historic event—the Revolt of 1857. Officially declared to be the 'First War of Indian Independence' on the occasion of its 150th anniversary in 2007, the Revolt continues to generate fresh interpretations and lively controversies (Bandyopadhyay 2008; Bhattacharya 2007; Nayar 2007; Roy 2008, for instance). This is because it is a 'peculiarly difficult phenomenon to define' conceptually (Ray 2007: 357). In Rajat Ray's elegant formulation, the 'Mutiny' was a 'war of the races that was not a race war'. This is because the subject race thought of it as a war of religion. At the same time, it was not really a religious war since it challenged the political subjection imposed by the British, and not their religion (ibid.). It was rather 'a patriotic war of the Hindu–Muslim brotherhood' or the inchoate social nationality of Hindustan, 'but not a national war either' (ibid.).

Let us try and understand the different issues addressed by Ray's formulation. First, the term 'Mutiny' was used in British official historiography to highlight that it was essentially a rebellion of the *sepoys* (*sipahis*) of the British Indian army. It spread only because an unruly mob joined the *sepoys* and caused a total breakdown of law and order in large parts of northern India. Formal histories published in the 1880s and 1890s took it upon themselves to explain why the *sepoys* rebelled and why they were joined by the unruly mob. Richard Holmes' widely read *A First History of the Indian Mutiny and of the Disturbances Which Accompanied It Among the Civil Population* (1882) admitted that the Indian soldiers could be treated better. The conditions of service offered to them left a lot to be desired. In particular, *sepoys* chafed under the obligation to serve overseas because it went directly against their caste prejudice of not crossing *kalapani* (black water). For Holmes then, the 'Mutiny' could have been prevented if the Indian soldiers had been treated somewhat better, were kept under stricter discipline and were numerically matched by British soldiers within the army. Holmes, however, lashed out against the dispossessed landholders, Gujars, and the 'budmashes' of India who took advantage of the first sign of weakness of British power demonstrated by the 'Mutiny'. In a manner similar to the 'thieves and rogues of England' these 'budmashes' took advantage of the mutiny to gratify their self-interest.

H. G. Keene, a member of the Indian Civil Service between 1847 and 1882, blamed the mutiny and the Revolt on the 'over-ambitious changes' introduced by Dalhousie. In his *History of India* (1893) written for college students, Keene stated that Dalhousie's policies alarmed the 'two main classes of the Natives' who, being in an earlier stage of human development, found the 'ideas and practices of Christendom unintelligible' (Robb 2007: 60). Hindus were incensed by attempts to curb the polygamy of 'certain classes of Brahmans' and the effect English education had among sections of the youth. Muslims for their part were alarmed by the deposition of the Nawab of Awadh and threats to Delhi as well as lack of employment (ibid.). Dalhousie's fault, therefore, was marginal—he was 'over-ambitious' and misjudged the level of backwardness and conservatism of the subjects he ruled over.

Let us pause here and examine the 'over-ambitious changes' introduced by Governor-General Dalhousie in order to understand why the 'natives' reacted the way they did. Dalhousie's policy of 'Doctrine of Lapse' culminated the process begun by Wellesley and his Subsidiary Alliance. Dalhousie classified the Indian states into three different groups. The first group was composed of states which he regarded to be the creation of the British government. 'Tributary and subordinate' states formed the second group, while the third group consisted of 'independent' states (Majumdar [1963] 1970: 62). The 'Doctrine of Lapse' was applied most vigorously to the first group of states. Here, the right of an adopted heir to the throne was disregarded completely and the state automatically 'lapsed' into British dominion if the ruler died without any natural, biological heir. Rulers of tributary states were allowed to adopt heirs only with the prior consent of the Company. Rulers of independent states were left free to make their own decisions.

Understandably, the Doctrine of Lapse caused great fear among Indian princes, a fear made tangible by the annexation of Satara (1848), Punjab (1849), Sambalpur (1850) and Jhansi and Nagpur (1854). Although the Governor-General acted with the consent of the authorities at home, in most of these cases his strong views in favour of annexation made him overrule the wishes and entreaties of the dying rulers who wanted the Company's consent for adoption. Dalhousie's highhandedness also got reflected in the deposition of Nawab Wajid Ali Shah of Awadh on charges of misgovernment in 1856. Awadh, we have seen, had become a subsidiary ally at the turn of the century and the nawabs had remained loyal to the Company even though its increasing demands had forced them to cede parts of their kingdom. Consequently, Awadh's annexation caused anger and outrage.

In a similar manner, Dalhousie rejected the claim of Dhundu Pant (Nana Sahib), the adopted son of ex-Peshwa Baji Rao II, to the annual pension of ₹ 8 lakh in 1851, on grounds that the pension granted to the Peshwa was personal and that Nana Sahib had enough property at his disposal to maintain himself. The Governor-General also refused to recognize the succession of the uncle of the deceased Nawab of Carnatic in 1855. He argued that Wellesley's treaty with Nawab Azimuddaula of Carnatic in 1801 was personal and that the Company had shown special favour in allowing the Nawab's successors to continue with the title. It was time that nawabhood was abolished in the Carnatic.

What Dalhousie embodied was the arrogance, confidence and contempt for the 'natives' that Company rule had acquired by the middle of the century. The 'Doctrine of Lapse' was one part of Dalhousie's programme of bringing a unified India under strict control by doing away with alternative sovereignties held by Indian rulers and princes; direct conquest was the other part. Here, an early opportunity was provided by the Second Anglo–Sikh War, 1848–49, which enabled the Company to occupy the rich and strategically important province of Punjab. Punjab was placed in the charge of two brothers, John and Henry Lawrence, who echoed Dalhousie's vision and sentiment, and assumed discretionary powers not easily paralleled by administrators elsewhere in India. Although not his own plan, the Governor-General also conducted a successful campaign against Burma to protect the commercial interests of the Company. Lower Burma was annexed in 1852.

Annexation was complemented by measures which were adopted to integrate India legally and administratively. While individuals' rights were fixed as far as possible in consonance with English law, new technologies that were transforming the West—railways, telegraph and the postal system—were eagerly embraced.

Railway construction began under Dalhousie's supervision with two starting lines from Howrah near Calcutta and Bombay. The construction was funded entirely by British capital and all investors were guaranteed, both by the Company and later by the Crown, a 5 per cent return, which made their investments risk-free. The railways' profits went back to England without helping India's industrial development at all. On the whole, the railways in India served Britain extremely well—port cities were connected with the hinterland, big cities were linked with each other and the well-incorporated Indian dominion was brought under closer supervision of the home country. British manufactured goods now had very easy access to Indian markets and British industries could exploit the hinterland for raw materials. Moreover, the movement of the British Indian army became fast and easy, making British control more efficient. Hence, Dalhousie's idea that railways would 'immensely increase the striking power of military forces in every corner of the Indian Empire' and 'bring British capital and enterprise into India' was fully realized (Dalhousie cited in Majumdar [1963] 1970: 384). For India, on the other hand, the extension of the railway network caused havoc to forest reserves and transformed her economy into a 'classic' colonial one, where market crops like cotton, tea and jute were exported in return for British cloth and other manufactured goods (Metcalf and Metcalf 2003: 96).

The introduction of railways was accompanied by the construction of roads on a massive scale, particularly in the newly annexed territories, and the establishing of a Public Works Department in each province under the direct control of the central government to look after the maintenance of roads. The innovation of steamships with faster and safer iron-hull and high-pressure engines from 1848 and the postal system set up in 1854, established rapid communication between England and India. If a letter took almost six months to travel from India to England in the 1830s, by the 1870s after the opening of the Suez Canal, the same letter could reach Bombay in a month from London (Metcalf and Metcalf 2003: 97). Arguably, the postal service brought benefits for the Indian population, especially the 'penny post' which enabled people to send letters at a very low cost to any destination within the country. The postal system, however, also strengthened the infrastructure of a centrally controlled state that Dalhousie aimed at. Annexation and innovation made the strong state impinge on the lives of the subjects in ways it had not done before.

Soldiers of the Bengal army did not escape the pressure of the invasive state—the General Services Enlistment Act of 1856 obliged the *sepoys* to accept any posting, including in Burma, which forced them to cross *kalapani*. This was a consequence of the reforms undertaken within the army from the 1820s that had done away with many of the privileges granted by Warren Hastings primarily to the upper-caste Brahman, Rajput and Bhumihar soldiers of the Bengal army, such as respect for their dietary and travel restrictions. The erasure of such privileges, however, had not brought parity with English army officers. Indians and Englishmen lived in two different worlds within the cantonments and English officers often showed distrust of and hatred for Indian soldiers. Indian soldiers were paid lower salaries and were given very few opportunities of promotion.

Discrimination within the army coupled with widespread disruption occasioned by the Company's rule, open assault on native beliefs and practices by evangelical missionaries and the liberal project of social reform generated fear and anxiety that the alien rulers were out to destroy the faith of the people. When the new Lee Enfield rifle, whose cartridge had to be bitten off, was introduced, rumours spread that the cartridge was smeared with cow and pig fat, polluting for Hindus and Muslims, respectively. Mangal Pandey of the 34th regiment at Barrackpore, Bengal—celebrated as the first martyr of the mutiny and recently glorified on the big screen—refused to use the cartridge on 29 March 1857 and fired at his European officers. Although this is taken to be the official beginning of the mutiny, Mangal Pandey's resistance did not directly relate to the events that unfolded in northern India from May. The *sepoys* of Meerut gave vent to pent-up grievances and transformed the 'limited defiance' of the 'accidental hero' (Mukherjee 2005) into a collective challenge to British rule (Roy 2008: 135).

Chronology of Revolt of 1857

Date	Name of Revolt
March 29	Barrackpore: Mangal Pande, a sepoy from Oudh, mutinies. Said to be initial action of Revolt.
May 10	Meerut: Initial mutiny of Indian troops. Troops march to Delhi.
May 11	Delhi: Mutiny. City seized by rebels.
May 13	Ferozepore: Mutiny. 45th Regiment joins rebels at Delhi.
May 14	Simla (Shimla): Commander-in-Chief Anson leaves for Delhi. (Dies May 27 at Karnal.)
May 30	Hindan River: First battle of Revolt.
May 30	Lucknow: Mutiny.
June 2	Peshawar: Forty surviving mutineers from Hoti Mardan blown from guns as example of retribution.
June 4	Benares: Mutiny of troops during disarmament.
June 4	Cawnpore: Mutiny.
June 6	Rebels' siege of city begins.
June 7	Fyzabad: Mutiny. Maulavi Ahmad Shah becomes a major rebel leader.
June 8	Delhi Ridge: Arrival of British troops.
June 9	Benares: Gen. Neill begins punitive measures.
June 18	Fatehgarh: Mutiny.
June 26	Cawnpore: City falls to rebels.
June 27	Massacre of British evacuees.
July 1	Lucknow: Rebels set siege to British Residency.
July 16	Cawnpore: Bibigarh massacre.
July 17	City retaken by British.
Aug. 12	Jagdispur: First battle at stronghold of rebel leader, Kunwar Singh, who then moves into Central India.

Date	Name of Revolt
Aug. 16	Bithur: Capture of place of exile of Maratha rebel leader, Nana Sahib.
Aug. 17	Poonamallee: 8th Madras Native Regiment, en route to Madras, refuses to go north and is disbanded. (Other Madras Regiments were used in quelling rebellions in Central India and Chota Nagpur.)
Sept. 20	Delhi: Retaken by British.
Sept. 25	Lucknow: British reinforced.
Nov. 22	2nd relief and evacuation except for Alambagh defended under Gen. Outram.
Nov. 23	Mandasor: British take stronghold of rebel leader from Delhi, Firoz Shah.
Nov. 28–Dec. 6	Cawnpore: Occupied by rebel Gwalior contingent.
Jan. 3, 1858	Fatehgarh: Occupied by British.
March 2–22	Lucknow: Retaken by British after siege. Securing of Oudh assured this victory.
March 19–April 3	Jhansi: Siege and capture by British under Maj-Gen. Rose of rebel leader, the Rani of Jhansi.
April 22	Kalpi:(Gathering place of rebels under the Rani and Tantia Tope.) Captured by British.
May 5–6	Bareilly: Sir Colin Campbell takes capital of Rohilkhand leader, Khan Bahadur Khan.
June 16–21	Gwalior: British take city and defeat fleeing rebels at nearby Jaura–Alipur ending effective Central India rebellion. Rani of Jhansi killed. Tantia Tope leads British on 1,000-mile, ten-month chase.
Aug. 31	Multan: Disarmed troops revolt. 1,300 Indian rebels killed.
Nov. 1, 1858	Proclamation of Queen Victoria, taking on Government of Indian Territories, offering clemency to all rebels not convicted of murder of British subjects.
April 7, 1859	Paron Jungles: Tantia Tope betrayed and captured.
May 21, 1859	Sirwa Pass Battle; remnants of rebels flee into Nepal.

Unfolding Processes

On 24 April, three months after Mangal Pandey's defiant act, which occasioned the disbandment of the 34th regiment of the Bengal army, 85 soldiers of the 3rd cavalry regiment at Meerut refused to use the greased cartridges. They were publicly disgraced on 9 May. On 10 May the entire regiment at Meerut, including the infantry, revolted. The *sipahis* killed English officers, released prisoners and marched to and captured Delhi on 12 May and obliged the Mughal Emperor Bahadur Shah Zafar to give leadership: the Revolt had become open and formal. The rebel *sepoys* were soon joined by those at Firozpur and Muzaffarnagar. On 20 May, the 55th Infantry Regiment rebelled near Peshawar and joined the mutineers who had marched to Delhi. Within a few months, the Revolt spread to the entire territory between Delhi and Bihar and caused a near collapse of Company rule in large parts of northern and central India. The mutinies generally followed the pattern set by Meerut. The *sepoys* killed British officers and other

Europeans, released prisoners from jail, burnt government offices, looted the treasury and then 'either set out for Delhi or joined some local chiefs, or roamed at large ...' (Majumdar [1963] 1970: 477).

Awadh witnessed an intense civilian revolt that accompanied the revolt of the *sipahi*s. In addition to the fact that the deposition of the Nawab and the confiscation of villages of *taluqdar*s during the land settlement of 1856 had caused outrage, Awadh was the region that supplied large numbers of soldiers to the British army. After the Company exiled Wajid Ali Shah and made John Lawrence the Commissioner of Awadh, Begun Hazrat Mahal crowned her 14-year-old son as the ruler and rallied a large number of people, particularly in Lucknow. The revolt took the form of a popular movement in Awadh with the participation, as Mukherjee (1984) has shown, not only of *taluqdar*s who had been dispossessed, but also of peasants who had got titles to land in 1856. These people fought in the name of their deposed Nawab and their *sipahi* kinsmen. Lawrence and other Europeans were compelled to take shelter within the fortified compound of the Residency in Lucknow, which was attacked and Lawrence was killed. Lucknow was recaptured in 1858 when Colin Campbell came at the head of a large army and killed and captured the rebels.

The mutiny at Kanpur has achieved remarkable notoriety on account of the part supposedly played by Nana Sahib. Nana Sahib, it bears mention, was loyal to the British in the early stages of the Mutiny. It was only after *sepoy*s of the 2nd Cavalry and 1st and 56th Native Infantry rebelled on 4 and 5 June and plundered the treasury, released prisoners, took possession of the magazine and marched towards Delhi that Nana came into the limelight. In a dramatic turn of events, the rebellious *sepoy*s returned to Kanpur on 6 June under the leadership of Nana Sahib. Nana's astute civilian Brahman commander Tantia Tope (Ramchandra Pandurang) also joined the rebellious *sepoy*s and together they put Kanpur under a long siege. When the British officers finally decided to leave, charged emotions and confusion occasioned the massacre of Bibi Ghar, making Kanpur one of the bloodiest sites of the Revolt (Mukherjee 1990). British reaction on the recapture of Kanpur was equally, if not more, harsh and ruthless. The Company's generals made the punishment of rebels exemplary in order to intimidate and ward off any future ideas of rebellion. Nana Sahib, however, managed to disappear.

Rani Lakshmibai of Jhansi also put together a large rebel army under her command and challenged the Company's rule in her territory. When Jhansi was captured by British troops in June 1858, Lakshmibai fled to Kalpi, joined forces with Tantia Tope, and captured Gwalior fort by defeating the army of the Raja of Gwalior. The Rani, however, was killed in battle and Tantia Tope went into hiding before he was finally caught and hanged in 1859. This signalled the end of the Revolt.

In Review: A Rebel Rani?

The figure of Rani Lakshmibai, a warrior woman in a predominantly patrilineal milieu, has lent itself to diverse perceptions and representations. Portrayed in Victorian novels as the widowed and barren wife who sought revenge by disrupting English homes but was eventually subdued by English males, Rani Lakshmibai has featured in poems, novels and films, as well as in historical accounts of twentieth century India as a heroic and pioneering figure of the movement toward independence. The profusion and diversity of her representations have prompted scholars to delve into the 'myth' and 'reality' of the Rani (Mukherjee 1995), and inspired others to explore the distinct dimensions of the representations of Lakshmibai in the different genres (Singh forthcoming). Lakshmibai, in Rudrangshu Mukherjee's terms, was a 'reluctant rebel'. For long, the lines of loyalty and rebellion were not clearly drawn for her, and she took recourse to rebellion only when she was forsaken by the British and was 'threatened by an insurgent population that wanted her to assume leadership' (Mukherjee 1995: 10).

For Harleen Singh, Lakshmibai serves as a symbol of the dual role of Indian women as valued members of the nation and of India's 'tenacious allegiance to tradition' (Singh: 128). In Subhadra Kumari Chauhan's famous poem *Jhansi ki Rani* (1930), the Rani is at once an *avatar* (incarnation) of the goddess of war and a brave daughter of the Marathas, even though her ultimate dishonour prompt men to take up arms. In the weaving of regional and religious iconography, affirms Singh, the Rani is chosen as the 'the harbinger and catalyst of India's freedom in a modern mobilization of the state within traditional sources of power' (Singh: 146–47). Her transformation from queen into goddess culminates in her final incarnation as the embodiment of independence, *swatantrata*, which simultaneously enacts 'a restaging of the feudal, the queen, to the mythic, the goddess, and finally to the modern, independence' (ibid.: 147). Chauhan's poem, by reimagining the Rani of Jhansi as *swatantrata*, shakes up the gendered discourse of nationalism by simultaneously placing rescue and resistance in the hands of the mother (ibid.: 149).

Vrindavan Lal Varma's historical novel, *Jhansi ki Rani Lakshmi Bai* (1946), on the other hand, applies Gandhi's notion of *swaraj* as disciplinary self-rule to identify the Rani unequivocally as an anti-colonial rebel dedicated, from the onset of her political consciousness, to independence for Jhansi, and inevitably for India. Jhansi, in the novel, embodies a microcosmic India with varied religious, ethnic, and caste alliances that unifies as one political entity against the East India Company where the Rani epitomizes the nationalist archetype (ibid.: 151–52). On a different plane, the figure of the Rani, an undisputed heroine of India, and a monarch under whom both Muslim and Hindu subjects united in the past, serves as a particularly potent symbol of 'secularism' in Hindi literature, apparently resolving Hindi and Urdu contestations of the historical and literary past (ibid.: 139). In Sohrab Modi's fim *Jhansi ki Rani* (1953), the male figure of Rajguru, the monarch's advisor, commands crucial powers to mould a headstrong girl into a queen, and then to persuade her to live for the nation and not commit *jauhar* (ibid.: 168). The film gives gendered discourse another twist by means of a complicated obeisance to traditional notions of Indian womanhood: a particularly 'elastic rendering that allows for a compromise between the progressive and regressive mode of representation' (ibid.: 173).

A Peoples' War?

Evidently, fear about 'officially induced impurity and the consequent loss of faith' was not confined only to the military classes. Kaye and Malleson's official *History of the Mutiny* (1864) mentioned that a disturbing rumour was circulating and it took many 'portentous shapes'. All the rumours proclaimed that the English designed to defile both Hindus and Muslims by polluting their daily food with unclean matter (Kaye and Malleson 1897, vol. 1: 416). For the authors of the *History* and for other British officials, the 'single theme of defilement addressed to all sections of indigenous population was a shrewd unifying stratagem' (Guha 1983: 263). It explained for them why the mutiny was joined by huge masses. Given the discussion here, it is not difficult for us to see why there was collective anxiety about the ways of the British: fear got expressed in such rumours which circulated wildly.

It is perhaps telling that rumours about polluting food were accompanied by widespread circulation of *chapatis*, unleavened bread made of wheat, maize or barley flour, in the North-Western Provinces in the winter of 1856–57 (ibid.: 239). We do not know exactly what this circulation meant. At the same time, its rapid spread through villages of north India demonstrates that peasant villagers identified it as a signal of something about to happen. This is borne out by the fact that there were huge gatherings of local populations that preceded the outbreak of violence. It is almost as if the peasants, 'shaken out of their habitual docility and subservience', were responding to some 'invisible, unspoken and yet universally understood signal to meet their enemy in an armed struggle' (ibid.: 118).

In Ranajit Guha's classic analysis of peasant consciousness, all these processes were indications of the unease of an agrarian society 'poised on the brink of a violent upheaval' (ibid.: 239). The British, of course, noticed the signs but failed to understand their meaning: they mistook the signs as the index of a great conspiracy that resulted in the Mutiny. There was no such conspiracy, but a vague yet pervasive recognition of the vile and distant ways of alien rulers—the common enemy—on the part of subject peoples, a recognition produced by the arrogance and proclaimed racial superiority of the English and the physical force on which their rule was based. It is in this sense that the Revolt was a 'war of the races' although Indians did not think of it in terms of race.

The civilian revolt that followed the mutiny was disparate and diverse and the motives behind it were wide ranging. Dispossessed rulers and princes, disgruntled zamindars and *taluqdar*s, pious men of some local standing and ordinary poor peasants all gave leadership to the numerous outbreaks that occurred in 1857 and 1858 in different towns, provinces and districts in northern India (Bhadra 1985; Ray 1993). If Awadh's 'masses' stood behind their ruler, the tightly knit cultivating Jat and Rajput communities led the uprising in the neighbouring North-Western Provinces in protest against the heavy differential revenue assessment imposed on them.

Reports of insurgency drawn up by local administrators are full of references to the unknown leaders of 'jaqueries'. The term 'jaquerie' originated in late medieval Europe. It was used to refer to peasant insurgency in France during the Hundred Years' War. British colonial officials called most peasant revolts of nineteenth century India 'jaqueries'. Such 'jaqueries' demonstrated that for peasants and poorer peoples, the British were not the only enemy. Moneylenders and zamindars were as much their targets of attack as the police *thana* and other symbols of British power. Moreover, princes and landlords were often coerced, like the reluctant Mughal emperor, to join the *sepoys* and peasants and become leaders. Understandably, this 'chaos' cemented the British idea of the 'unruly mob'. At the same time, the 'unruly mob' acted on the basis of an acute recognition—the mutiny of the *sipahis* had generated a reversal in relations of power. The world had turned upside down and it was time for them 'to exercise force on those who had coerced them so far' (Ray 2007: 254). This accounts for the extreme violence exercised by *sepoys* and civilians, a cataclysmic release of all the pent-up emotions they were labouring under.

The Revolt then, eludes categorization. This has contributed to its very distinct classification in imperial and nationalist histories. Unrest among the dependable *sepoys*—founding pillars of the British–Indian army—caused shock, disbelief and dismay among the British. The reaction to this unnerving event was fierce and the measures adopted to suppress it were severe. In imperial histories, the 'sepoy war' embodied the irremediably backward nature of the Indian people, and proved the necessity of British rule in India (Kaye 1864). This impression was substantiated by tales of horror and excess, such as the massacre of Bibighar (Mukherjee 1998), committed both by the *sepoys* and the 'budmashes', which justified the ruthless suppression of the Revolt. The story of the Revolt thus became the story of its suppression in which valour and courage of the English race and the glory of the Empire got reflected (Bandyopadhyay 2008: 2).

The forced presence of the Mughal emperor among the rebels and the declared aim of the *sepoys* to restore Mughal authority induced some imperial historians to condemn the uprising as a Muslim conspiracy. This was passionately countered by Sayyid Ahmad Khan in an essay written in Urdu in 1858. In this essay, which was later translated into English, Sayyid Ahmad, a loyal employee of the Company, argued forcefully that the Revolt was not just a mutiny of 'disgruntled sepoys' but a general outbreak resulting from multiple grievances. The cultural policy of the British, the severity of revenue assessments and the degradation of the landed and princely elite had caused such grievances (Metcalf and Metcalf 2003: 99).

Sayyid Ahmad did not make any reference to the hold of the Mughal ethos in popular imagination. As Ray observes, till 1857 the East India Company notionally ruled in the name of the Mughal Emperor, and in government orders announced to the public by the town criers, the sovereignty of the Mughal *badshah* was underscored (Ray 2007: 419–20). What the rebellious *sepoys* sought to reinstate was a world and an order with which they were familiar. The march of the mutinous troops to Delhi made it clear: they had to take control of Delhi if their rebellion was to succeed. Moreover, Bahadur Shah, for them, was the only 'legitimate ruler of Hindustan' (Dalrymple 2007: 13). This sentiment was shared by other rebels. The decision to 'restore' Mughal reign was taken by the people, and not by the rulers.

Thus, even though religion constituted a key element in the Revolt and feudal lords frequently provided leadership and the rebels wanted to bring back an earlier order, the terms and meaning of this 'restoration' had changed. This makes the categorization of the Revolt as 'backward looking'—as has been done by many historians, particularly of the Marxist strain (Sarkar 1979) problematic. Early leaders of the Congress and members of the British Indian Association had also denounced the Mutiny on similar grounds. Even Jawaharlal Nehru could not help calling it a 'feudal outburst', although he recognized 'popular sentiment' in the support given to the feudal chiefs (Nehru 1946: 268–69). A recent essay, on the other hand, has gone so far as to say that what the *sepoys* wanted was to repudiate not just the rule of the Company but also the indigenous power structure and 'carve out an autonomous space for themselves' (Dasgupta 2008).

Eric Stokes' sensitive study of the Revolt has sought to counter the separation made between the mutiny and the civil rebellion by defining the Revolt as the revolt of a 'peasant army breaking loose from its foreign master' (1986: 14). It is interesting that Stokes had earlier argued that there were several movements and not one rebellion, and that the presence of landlords gave an 'elitist' character to the rural revolt (1980). He had also pointed to the differential effect of high revenue demands in different parts of Awadh and the North-Western Provinces, and ruled out an easy commonness of purpose between peasants and landlords, as had been argued by Chaudhuri (1957). The intensity of the Revolt, argued Stokes, did not have a necessary connection with the severity of economic grievances. Ties of community and kinship, caste and religion among Jats, Rajputs, Gujars and Sayids—the key players in the Revolt—had played a very important role. This was perfectly in tune with the 'non-modern' world-view of the peasant.

Soldiers, we are aware, were predominantly drawn from cultivators. At the same time, once he joined the army, a *sipahi* did not simply remain a 'peasant in uniform' (Mukherjee 1984). Apart from the duties and responsibilities of the post, he gained a perspective that was much wider than that of the peasant villager. Significant still was the fact that the 'uniform' conferred on him special privileges and a sense of power, which in turn aroused aspirations of forming a part of the elite (Dasgupta 2008: 161–62). He ceased to be just a peasant. At the same time, the interchange of news and ideas between the soldier and the peasant, and the collective hatred of British rule allowed the Revolt to assume the proportions it did. Faith played a major role in the accumulation of this hatred, but the fear of losing faith was propelled by varied and severe dislocations caused by Company rule. This is why although Hindus and Muslims fought against the British in the name of faith, what they challenged was British political domination and not evangelical Christianity.

The magnitude of the Revolt, and the joint participation of 'Hindus' and 'Muslims' that it commanded, has allowed a powerful trend of nationalist historiography to call the Revolt a 'War of Indian Independence'. This definition has resulted in the incorporation of 1857 into the 'prehistory' of nationalism, and reinforced the notion that the story of Indian nationalism is a linear one of success and progress, which led to independence (Guha 1982–1989). It was Veer Savarkar who described the Revolt thus in 1908, although a recent essay has shown that the word 'first' in the title of Savarkar's book is a later interpolation (Sharma 2008: 123), which has gained wide currency. A little after the time Savarkar called it the war of Indian independence, Jawaharlal Nehru displayed qualms about the 'feudal character' of the Revolt, highlighting once again the disparity in visions. Moreover, nationalism in the mid-nineteenth century was a barely recognized concept and the story of nationalism does not have a single uncontested history.

Besides, it is well known that all of south India, Bengal and Punjab remained unaffected by the Revolt, which swept through the North-Western Provinces and the Ganga-Jamuna Doab. This is because people of these parts, particularly the Sikhs, the Gurkhas, the Trans-Indus Pathans and the Bengalis made 'strategic' alliances with the British during 1857, on grounds that they stood to gain more 'in a resurrected British *Raj* than in the Hindustani sepoy-sawar *Raj*' (Roy 2008: 1). The soldiers of the recently conquered Punjab, we need to understand, could not possibly have much sympathy for the *sipahi*s of the Bengal army who had defeated them. Neither did the Bombay or the Madras armies rebel, and there was no civilian revolt anywhere in southern India. The English-educated Bengali middle-class and the Permanent Settlement landlords owed their prestige and prosperity to the Company, as did many other rulers and landlords in different parts of India. Therefore, it would be a mistake, a 'teleological trap', to look for 'a united nationalist pan-Indian movement in the mid-nineteenth century or to portray 1857 as an all-India anti-colonial struggle' (Roy 2008: 1).

At the same time, this 'teleological trap' and the polarized projections of 1857 by British imperialist and Indian nationalist historiography have produced perceptions of groups that joined the Revolt as 'patriotic' and the ones who did not as 'loyalists'. The Revolt undoubtedly was the result of 'patriotic feelings', but the motivations of the various participants were so different that it is impossible to reduce the analysis to a simple cause and effect or to portray it as a 'war of independence' (Roy 2008: 1). When the Revolt occurred, there was no clear sense of India as a united nation, nor a vision of independence. Moreover, the history of nationalism itself, as we will see later, was fractured and fragmented. It cannot be reconstructed as a single story. It is more useful, perhaps, to give the rebels their due as conscious political actors, and not just take them as clogs in the wheel of the nationalist struggle. If nationalism and independence were in vogue in 1857, leaders of the British Indian Association, and later of the Indian National Congress, would not have condemned the Revolt. Independence, moreover, was not the result of a series of 'wars'. The term 'First War', therefore, prompts us to reflect on when and why it was important to configure such a belligerent history of nationalism.

Following Dalrymple, it would probably make sense to understand the Revolt as 'a human event of extraordinary, tragic, and often capricious outcomes' (Dalrymple 2007: 15), and pay attention to the significant transformations it brought about and the ramifications it had on British imaginings and popular perceptions in India. Barun De affirms that 1857 provides a significant milestone because people from all classes of society within the 'nation in the making' found 'some elements, and not necessarily the same ones, to empathize with' (2007). It is to the repercussions of the Revolt that we now turn.

References

Arnold, David. 1982. 'Rebellious Hillmen: The Gudem Rampa Rebellions (1829–1914)'. In *Subaltern Studies I: Writings on South Asian History and Society*, edited by Ranajit Guha, 88–142. New Delhi: Oxford University Press.

———. 1986. *Police Power and Colonial Rule in Madras, 1859–1947*. New Delhi: Oxford University Press.

Bandyopadhyay, Sekhar. 2004. *From Plassey to Partition: A History of Modern India*. Hyderabad: Orient Longman.

———. 2008. 'Eighteen Fifty Seven and its Many Histories'. In *1857: Essays from Economic and Political Weekly*, edited by S. Bandyopadhyay, 1–22. Hyderabad: Orient Longman.

Banerjee-Dube, Ishita. 2007. *Religion, Law, and Power: Tales of Time in Eastern India, 1860–2000*. London: Anthem Press.

Bates, Crispin. 2000. 'Coerced and Migrant Labourers in India: The Colonial Experience'. *Edinburgh Papers in South Asian Studies* 13: 1–33.

———. 2007. *Subalterns and the Raj: South Asia Since 1600*. London: Routledge.

Bayly, C. A. 1988. *Indian Society and the Making of the British Empire*. Cambridge: Cambridge University Press.

———. 1989. *Imperial Meridian: The British Empire and the World*. London: Longman.

Bhadra, Gautam. 1985. 'Four Rebels of Eighteen-Fifty Seven'. In *Subaltern Studies IV: Writings on South Asian History and Society*, edited by R. Guha, 229–275. New Delhi: Oxford University Press.

Bhattacharya, N. 1998. 'Pastoralists in a Colonial World'. In *Nature, Culture, Imperialism: Essays on the Environmental History of South Asia*, edited by D. Arnold and R. Guha, 49–85. New Delhi: Oxford University Press.

Bhattacharya, Sabyasachi. 1998. *The Contested Terrain: Perspectives on Education in India*. Hyderabad: Orient Longman.

———, ed. 2007. *Rethinking 1857*. New Delhi: Orient Longman.

'Brief account of the life of Joseph Banks'. 2009. Retrieved July 2013 from http://www.ntu.ac.uk/hum/document_uploads/75559.pdf

Bryant, Edwin F. 2001. *The Quest for the Origins of Vedic Culture: The Indo–Aryan Migration Debate*. Oxford: Oxford University Press.

The Calcutta Review. 1859. Vol. XXXIII, no. 64 (July–December), 396–439. Calcutta: University of Calcutta.

Carroll, Lucy. 1983. 'Law, Custom and Statutory Social Reform: The Hindu Widow's Remarriage Act of 1856'. *The Indian Economic and Social History Review* 20 (4): 363–88.

Charlesworth, Neil. 1972. 'The Myth of the Deccan Riots'. *Modern Asian Studies* 6 (4): 401–21.

———. 1982. *British Rule and the Indian Economy 1800–1914*. London: The Macmillan Press.

Chatterjee, Piya. 2001. *A Time for Tea: Women, Labor, and Post/Colonial Politics on an Indian Plantation*. Durham, NC: Duke University Press.

Chaudhuri, B. B. 1967. 'Agrarian Economy and Agrarian Relations in Bengal (1859–1885)'. In *The History of Bengal*, edited by N. K. Sinha, 237–336. Calcutta: University of Calcutta.

———. 2008. *Peasant History of Late Pre-Colonial and Colonial India*. New Delhi: Pearson Longman.

Chaudhuri, K. N. 1971. *The Economic Development of India Under the East India Company, 1814–1858. A Selection of Contemporary Writings*. Cambridge: Cambridge University Press.

Chaudhuri, S. B. 1957. *Civil Rebellion in the Indian Mutinies*. Calcutta: The World Press.

Chowdhury, Prem. 2008. 'Customs in a Peasant Economy: Women in Colonial Haryana'. In *Women and Social Reform in Modern India,* edited by Tanika Sarkar and Sumit Sarkar, 146–68. Delhi: Permanent Black.

Cohn, Bernard S. 1996. *Colonialism and Its Forms of Knowledge*. Princeton, NJ: Princeton University Press.

Dalrymple, William. 2007. *The Last Mughal. The Fall of a Dynasty: Delhi, 1857*. New York: Alfred A. Knopf.

Dasgupta, Sabyasachi. 2008. 'The Rebel Army in 1857: At the Vanguard of the War of Independence or the Tyranny of Arms?' In *1857: Essays from Economic and Political Weekly*, edited by S. Bandyopadhyay, 161–74. Hyderabad: Orient Longman.

De, Barun. 2007. 'The Call of 1857'. *Frontline* 24 (June 16–29): 12.

Dube, Saurabh. 1998. *Untouchable Pasts: Religion, Identity, and Power among a Central Indian Community, 1780–1950*. Albany, N.Y.: State University of New York Press.

Dutt, Romesh C. 1963. *The Economic History of India: In the Victorian Age*. Vol. II. New Delhi: Ministry of Information and Broadcasting, Government of India.

Freitag, Sandria B. 1989. *Collective Action and Community: Public Arenas and the Emergence of Communalism in North India*. New Delhi: Oxford University Press.

Fukuzawa, H. 1982. 'Agrarian Relations. Western India'. In *The Cambridge Economic History of India*, Vol. 2, edited by Dharma Kumar, 177–206. Cambridge: Cambridge University Press.

Gadgil, Madhav and Ramachandra Guha. 1993. *This Fissured Land: An Ecological History of India*. New Delhi: Oxford University Press.

———. 2000. *The Use and Abuse of Nature: Incorporating 'This Fissured Land, an Ecological History of India'*. New Delhi: Oxford University Press.

Gambhirananda, Swami. 1955. *The Life of Swami Vivekananda*. Calcutta: Advaita Ashrama.

Ghosh, Amitav. 2008. 'Opium Financed British Rule in India'. BBC Interview (23 June).

Ghosh, Durba. 2006. *Sex and the Family in Colonial India: The Making of Empire*. Cambridge: Cambridge University Press.

Gooptu, Nandini. 2001. *The Politics of the Urban Poor in Early Twentieth-Century India*. Cambridge: Cambridge University Press.

Graham, G. F. I. 1885. *The Life and Work of Syed Ahmed Khan*. Edinburgh: William Blackwood and Sons.

Guha, Ramachandra. 1999. *The Unquiet Woods: Ecological Change and Peasant Resistance in the Himalaya*. New Delhi: Oxford University Press.

Guha, Ranajit. 1983. *Elementary Aspects of Peasant Insurgency in Colonial India*. New Delhi: Oxford University Press.

———, ed. 1982–1989. *Subaltern Studies: Writings on South Asian History and Society*. Vols. 1–6. New Delhi: Oxford University Press.

Guha, Sumit. 1992. 'Society and Economy in the Deccan, 1818–1850'. In *The Making of Agrarian Policy in British India 1770–1900*, edited by B. Stein, 187–214. New Delhi: Oxford University Press.

———. 1999. *Environment and Ethnicity in India, 1200–1991*. Cambridge: Cambridge University Press.

Gupta, Charu. 2002. *Sexuality, Obscenity, Community: Women, Muslims, and the Hindu Public in Colonial India*. Delhi: Permanent Black.

Habib, Irfan. [1963] 1999. *The Agrarian System of Mughal India 1556–1707*. New Delhi: Oxford University Press.

Harlow, Barbara and Mia Carter, eds. 1999. *Imperialism & Orientalism: A Documentary Sourcebook*. Malden, MA: Blackwell Publishers.

Hasan, S. N. 1969. 'Zamindars Under the Mughals'. In *Land Control and Social Structure in Indian Society*, edited by R. E. Frykenberg, 17–31. Madison, WC: University of Wisconsin Press.

Hatcher, Brian A. 1996. *Idioms of Improvement: Vidyasagar and Cultural Encounter in Bengal*. New Delhi: Oxford University Press.

Holmes, Richard. 1882. *A First History of the Indian Mutiny and of the Disturbances Which Accompanied it Among the Civil Population*. London: W. H. Allen.

Isaac, Allen. 1874. 'Revival of Islam'. *Calcutta Review* LVIII: 1–46.

Jalal, Ayesha. 1998. 'Exploding Communalism: The Politics of Muslim Identity in South Asia'. In *Nationalism, Democracy and Development: State and Politics in India*, edited by Sugata Bose and Ayesha Jalal, 76–103. New Delhi: Oxford University Press.

———. 2001. *Self and Sovereignty: Individual and Community in South Asian Islam since 1850*. New Delhi: Oxford University Press.

Jones, Kenneth W. 1989. *Arya Dharm: Hindu Consciousness in 19th Century Punjab*. New Delhi: Manohar. First published 1976.

Jones, Sir William. 1807. *The Works of Sir William Jones*. Vol. 3, London: n.p.

Kaye, J. W. 1853. *The Administration of the East India Company: A History of Indian Progress*. London: R. Bentley.

———. 1864. *A History of the Sepoy War in India*. Vol. 1. London: W. H. Allen and Co.

Kaye, John W. and G. B. Malleson. 1864. *History of the Indian Mutiny of 1857–8*. Vol. 1. London: W. H. Allen and Co.

———. 1897. *History of the Indian Mutiny of 1857–8*. 6 volumes. London: Longman, Greenwood Press.

Keene, H. G. 1893. *History of India*. Vol. II. London: Allen.

Kejariwal, O. P. 1988. *The Asiatic Society of Bengal and the Discovery of India's Past*. New Delhi: Oxford University Press.

Kopf, David. 1969. *British Orientalism and the Bengal Renaissance*. Berkeley and Los Angeles: University of California Press.

———. 1979. *The Brahmo Samaj and the Shaping of the Modern Indian Mind*. Princeton, NJ: Princeton University Press.

Kosambi, D. D. 1965. *Ancient India: A History of its Culture and Civilization*. New York: Pantheon Books.

Kumar, Dharma. 1965. *Land and Caste in South India: Agricultural Labour in the Madras Presidency in the Nineteenth Century*. Cambridge: Cambridge University Press.

———. 1982. 'Agrarian Relations in South India'. In *The Cambridge Economic History of India*, Vol. II, edited by Dharma Kumar, 207–41. Cambridge: Cambridge University Press.

Kumar, Radha. 1993. *The History of Doing: An Illustrated Account of Movements for Women's Rights and Feminism in India, 1800–1990*. New Delhi: Kali for Women.

Kumar, Ravinder. 1968. *Western India in the Nineteenth Century*. London: Routledge and Kegan Paul.

Lelyveld, David. 1978. *Aligarh's First Generation: Muslim Solidarity in British India*. Princeton, NJ: Princeton University Press.

Macaulay, Thomas Babington. 1972. 'Minute on Indian Education'. In *Selected Writings, T. B. Macaulay*, edited and with an introduction by John Clive and Thomas Pinney, 237–51. Chicago: The University of Chicago Press.

Majumdar, Ramesh Chandra, ed. [1963] 1970. *British Paramountcy and Indian Renaissance.* Part 1. Bombay: Bharatiya Vidya Bhavan.

———. [1965] 1981. *British Paramountcy and Indian Renaissance.* Part 2. Bombay: Bharatiya Vidya Bhavan.

Malhotra, Anshu. 2006. 'The Body as a Metaphor for the Nation: Caste, Masculinity, and Femininity in the *Satyarth Prakash* of Swami Dayananda Saraswati'. In *Rhetoric and Reality: Gender and the Colonial Experience in South Asia,* edited by Avril A. Powell and Siobhan Lambert-Hurley, 121–53. New Delhi: Oxford University Press.

Mani, Lata. 1989. 'Contentious Traditions: The Debate on Sati in Colonial India'. In *Recasting Women: Essays in Colonial History,* edited by Kumkum Sangari and Sudesh Vaid, 88–126. New Brunswick: Rutgers University Press.

———. 1993. 'The Female Subject, the Colonial Gaze: Reading Eyewitness Accounts of Widow Burning'. In *Interrogating Modernity: Culture and Colonialism in India,* edited by Tejashwini Niranjana, P. Sudhir and Vivek Dhareshwar, 273–290. Calcutta: Seagull Books.

———. 1998. *Contentious Traditions: The Debate on Sati in Colonial India 1780–1833.* Berkeley and Los Angeles: University of California Press.

Mehta, Uday Singh. 1999. *Liberalism and Empire: A Study in Nineteenth-Century British Liberal Thought.* Chicago and London: The University of Chicago Press.

Metcalf, Barbara D. 1994. 'Reading and Writing About Muslim Women in British India'. In *Forging Identities: Gender, Communities and the State,* edited by Zoya Hasan, 1–21. New Delhi: Kali for Women.

Metcalf, Barbara D. and Thomas R. Metcalf. 2003. *A Concise History of India.* Cambridge: Cambridge University Press.

Mill, James. 1817. *The History of British India.* London: Baldwin, Cradock, and Joy. Available at http://babel. hathitrust.org/cgi/pt?id=nyp.33433081558532.

———. [1817] 1975. *The History of British India.* Chicago: The University of Chicago Press.

Muhammad, Shan, comp. 1978. *The Aligarh Movement. Basic Documents: 1864–1898.* Vols. 1–4. New Delhi: Meenakshi Prakashan.

Mukherjee, Rudrangshu. 1984. *Awadh in Revolt, 1857–1858: A Study of Popular Resistance.* New Delhi: Oxford University Press.

———. 1990. 'Satan Let Loose upon Earth: The Kanpur Massacres in India in the Revolt of 1857'. *Past & Present* 128: 92–116.

———. 1995. 'The Reluctant Rebel: Rani Lakshmibai of Jhansi'. *Manushi,* issue 87 (March–April): 6–10.

———. 1998. *Spectre of Violence: The 1857 Kanpur Massacres.* New Delhi: Viking.

———. 2005. *Mangal Pandey: Brave Martyr or Accidental Hero?* New Delhi and New York: Penguin Books.

Nandy, Ashis. 1975. 'Sati: A Nineteenth Century Tale of Women, Violence and Protest'. In *Rammohun Roy and the Process of Modernisation in India,* edited by V. C. Joshi, 168–94. Delhi: Vikas Publishing House.

———. 1983. *The Intimate Enemy: Loss and Recovery of Self Under Colonialism.* New Delhi: Oxford University Press.

Naregal, Veena. 2001. *Language Politics, Elites, and the Public Sphere.* Delhi: Permanent Black.

Nayar, Pramod K. 2007. *The Great Uprising: India, 1857.* New Delhi: Penguin India.

Nehru, Jawaharlal. 1946. *The Discovery of India.* New York: The John Day Co.

Nigam, Sanjay. 1990. 'Disciplining and Policing the "Criminals by Birth" Part 1: The Development of the Disciplinary System, 1871–1900'. *The Indian Economic and Social History Review* 27 (2): 131–62; and 'The Making of a Colonial Stereotype Part 2: The Criminal Tribes and Castes of Northern India'. *The Indian Economic and Social History Review* 27 (3): 257–87.

O'Hanlon, Rosalind. 1985. *Caste, Conflict and Ideology: Mahatma Jotirao Phule and Low Caste Protest in Nineteenth-Century Western India.* Cambridge: Cambridge University Press.

Oberoi, Harjot. 1997. *The Construction of Religious Boundaries: Culture, Identity, and Diversity among the Sikhs.* New Delhi: Oxford University Press.

Oldenburg, Veena Talwar. 2002. *Dowry Murder: The Imperial Origins of a Cultural Crime.* New York: Oxford University Press.

Omvedt, G. 1976. *Cultural Revolt in a Colonial Society: The Non-Brahman Movement in Western India.* Poona: Scientific Socialist Education Trust.

Philips, C. H. 1961. *The East India Company, 1784–1834.* Bombay: Oxford University Press. Reprint.

Prakash, Gyan. 1999. *Another Reason: Science and the Imagination of Modern India.* Princeton, NJ: Princeton University Press.

Rangarajan, Mahesh. 1996. *Fencing the Forest: Conservation and Ecological Change in India's Central Provinces 1860–1914.* New Delhi: Oxford University Press.

Rao, Anupama. 2009. *The Caste Question: Dalits and the Politics of Modern India.* Berkeley and Los Angeles: University of California Press.

Ray, Rajat K. 1993. 'Race, Religion and Realm. The Political Theory of the "Reigning India Crusade", 1857'. In *India's Colonial Encounter: Essays in Memory of Eric Stokes,* edited by N. Gupta and M. Hasan, 133–82. New Delhi: Manohar.

———. 1995. Introduction to *Mind, Body and Society: Life and Mentality in Colonial Bengal,* edited by R. K. Ray, 1–44. New Delhi: Oxford University Press.

———. 2007. *The Felt Community: Commonality and Mentality Before the Emergence of Indian Nationalism.* New Delhi: Oxford University Press.

Raychaudhuri, Tapan. 1995. 'The Pursuit of Reason in Nineteenth-Century Bengal'. In *Mind, Body and Society: Life and Mentality in Colonial Bengal,* edited by R. K. Ray, 1–44. New Delhi: Oxford University Press.

———. 2002. *Europe Reconsidered: Changing Perceptions of the West in Nineteenth Century Bengal.* Oxford: Oxford University Press.

Robb, Peter. 2007. 'On the Rebellion of 1857. A Brief History of an Idea'. *Economic and Political Weekly* 42(19): 1696–1702. Reprinted in *1857: Essays from Economic and Political Weekly.* 2008, edited by S. Bandyopadhyay.

Roche, Ludo (trans.). 2002. *Jimutavahana's Dayabhaga: The Hindu Law of Inheritance in Bengal.* London: Oxford University Press.

Rose, Sarah. 'The Great British Tea Heist'. Available at: http://www.smithsonianmag.com/history-archaeology/The-Great-British-Tea-Heist.html?c=y&story=fullstory

Roy, Kaushik. 2008. *1857 Uprising: A Tale of an Indian Warrior.* Translation of Durgadas Bandopadhyay's *Amar Jivancharit.* Kolkata: CSCW.

Roy, Rammohan. 1818. 'Translation of a Conference Between an Advocate for, and an Opponent of, the Practice of Burning Widows Alive; from the Original Bungla'. In *The English Works of Raja Rammohun Roy* (1901), edited by Jogendra Chunder Ghose. Vol. 2. Calcutta: S. K. Lahiri & Co.

Said, Edward. 1978. *Orientalism.* New York: Pantheon Books.

Saravanam, Velayuthan. 2003. 'Colonial Commercial Forest Policy and Tribal Private Forests in Madras Presidency, 1792–1881'. *The Indian Economic and Social History Review* 40 (4): 403–23.

Sarkar, Sumit. 1975. 'Rammohun Roy and the Break with the Past'. In *Rammohun Roy and the Process of Modernisation in India*, edited by V. C. Joshi, 46–68. New Delhi: Vikas Publishing House.

Sarkar, Susobhan. 1979. *On the Bengal Renaissance*. Calcutta: University of Calcutta.

Sarkar, Tanika. 2000. 'A Pre-History of Rights? The Age of Consent Debate in Colonial Bengal'. *Feminist Studies* 26: 601–22.

———. 2001. *Hindu Wife, Hindu Nation: Community, Religion, and Cultural Nationalism*. Bloomington, IA: Indiana University Press.

Sarkar Tanika and Sumit Sarkar. 2008. Introduction to *Women and Social Reform in Modern India,* edited by Tanika Sarkar and Sumit Sarkar, 1–12. Delhi: Permanent Black.

Sarwar, Firoj High. 2012. 'A Comparative Study of *Zamindari, Raiyatwari* and *Mahalwari* Land Revenue Settlements: The Colonial Mechanisms of Surplus Extraction in 19th Century British India'. *IOSR Journal of Humanities and Social Sciences* 2 (4): 16–26.

Sastri, Sibnath. 1907. *Ramtanu Lahiri, Brahman and Reformer: A History of the Renaissance in Bengal.* London: Swan Sonnenschein.

Satya, Laxman D. 2004. *Ecology, Colonialism and Cattle: Central India in the Nineteenth Century*. New Delhi: Oxford University Press.

———. 2007. 'The British Empire, Ecology and Famines in Late 19th Century Central India'. *ICFAI Journal of History and Culture* 1(2): 35–46. Pdf version accessed on 26–27 June 2013.

Sen, Asoke. 1977. *Iswar Chandra Vidyasagar and his Elusive Milestones*. Calcutta: Riddhi.

Sengupta, Parna. 2011. *Pedagogy for Religion: Missionary Education and the Fashioning of Hindus and Muslims in Bengal*. Berkeley and Los Angeles: University of California Press.

Seth, Sanjay. 2007. *Subject Lessons: The Western Education of Colonial India*. Durham and London: Duke University Press.

Sharma, J. 2008. 'History as Revenge and Retaliation: Rereading Savarkar's *The War of Independence of 1857*'. In *1857: Essays from Economic and Political Weekly*, edited by S. Bandyopadhyay, 123–32. Hyderabad: Orient Longman.

Shelley, Percy Bysshe. 1820. *Prometheus Unbound: A Lyrical Drama*. London: C. and J. Ollier.

Sherwood, R. 1820. 'Of the Murderers Called P'hansigars'. *Asiatick Researches* XII (13): 250–81.

Singh, Harleen. Forthcoming. *The Public Life of Lakshmibai, Rani of Jhansi: Gender, History and Fable in India*. New Delhi: Cambridge University Press.

Singha, Radhika. 1998. *A Despotism of Law. Crime and Justice in Early Colonial India*. New Delhi: Oxford University Press.

Sinha, N. K. 1968. *Economic History of Bengal*. Vol. 2. Calcutta: Firma K. L. Mukhopadhyay.

Sinha, Pradip. 1965. *Nineteenth Century Bengal: Aspects of Social History*. Calcutta: Firma K. L. Mukhopadhyay.

Sinha, Samita. 1993. *Pandits in a Changing Environment: Centres of Sanskrit Learning in Nineteenth Century Bengal*. Calcutta: Sarat Book House.

Sivaramakrishnan, K. 1999. *Modern Forests: Statemaking and Enviromental Change in Colonial Eastern India*. Stanford, CA: Stanford University Press.

Skaria, Ajay. 1999. *Hybrid Histories: Forests, Frontiers and Wildness in Western India*. New Delhi: Oxford University Press.

Sleeman, William Henry. 1839. *Rambles and Recollections of an Indian Official/Sleeman, William*. Serampore: Serampore Mission Press.

Stebbing, E. P. 1922. *The Forests of India*. London: J. Lane.

Stein, Burton. 1992. Introduction to *The Making of Agrarian Policy in British India 1770–1900*, edited by B. Stein, 1–32. New Delhi: Oxford University Press.

Stokes, Eric. 1980. *Peasant and the Raj*. Cambridge: Cambridge University Press.

———. 1986. *The Peasant Armed: The Indian Revolt of 1857*. Oxford: Clarendon Press.

———. [1959] 1989. *The English Utilitarians and India*. New Delhi: Oxford University Press.

Stoler, Ann Laura. 2002. *Carnal Knowledge and Imperial Power: Race and the Intimate in Colonial Rule*. Berkeley and Los Angeles: University of California Press.

Sunder Rajan, Rajeswari. 2003. *The Scandal of the State: Women, Law, and Citizenship in Postcolonial India*. Durham, NC: Duke University Press.

Trautmann, Thomas R. 1997. *Aryans and British India*. Berkeley and Los Angeles: University of California Press.

———. 2006. *Languages and Nations: The Dravidian Proof in Colonial Madras*. Berkeley and Los Angeles: University of California Press

Trevelyan, Charles E. 1838. *On the Education of the People of India*. London: Longman, Orme, Brown, Green and Longmans.

Viswanathan, Gauri. 1989. *Masks of Conquest: Literary Study and British Rule in India*. New York: Columbia University Press.

———. 1998. *Outside the Fold: Conversion, Modernity, Belief*. Princeton, NJ: Princeton University Press.

Yang, Anand A. 1989. 'Whose Sati? Widow Burning in Early Nineteenth-Century Bengal'. *Journal of Women's History* 1 (2): 8–33. Reprinted in *Women and Social Reform in Modern India*, 2008, edited by Tanika Sarkar and Sumit Sarkar, 15–37. Delhi: Permanent Black.

Zastoupil, Lynn and Martin Moir, eds. 1999. *The Great Indian Education Debate: Documents Relating to the Orientalist–Anglicist Controversy, 1781–1843*. Richmond: Curzon Press.

Creating Anew 4

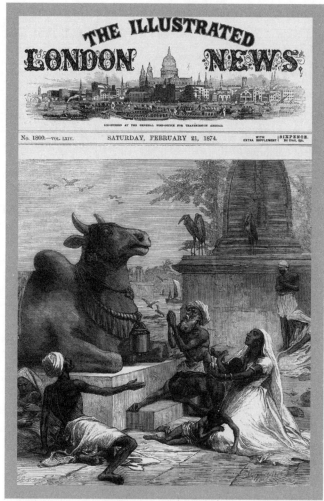

The Illustrated London News showing people praying to Nandi for relief during the famine in Bengal, February 1874

Chapter outline

Maharani Victoria
Ei bhaja khae roj kinia
Bhaja kheye bojhena se
Keba Raja keba praja
(The great queen Victoria snacks on this savoury every day,
It makes her forget who is the king and who the subject)

Thus ran a song in a popular Bengali film of the late 1970s, a poignant reminder of Queen Victoria's hold over the Indian middle classes, and possibly, the 'people' in general. In this chapter, we track the various processes spread across the late-nineteenth and the early-twentieth century that made Queen Victoria the imposing icon she continues to be.

Queen Victoria became the ruler of India after the Revolt of 1857, although she formally assumed the position in 1877. The recapture of Delhi by British troops on 20 September 1857, and the imprisonment and later deportation of Bahadur Shah signalled a reversal of fortune for the rebels, even though they put up strong resistance till early 1859. Governor-General Lord Canning gathered British forces in Calcutta and sent them first to Delhi and then to Benares, Allahabad, Kanpur and the rest of Awadh. By the beginning of 1859, Gwalior, Doab, Rohilkand, Lucknow and central India had been recaptured, owing to the unlimited men and resources that the British commanded and their ruthlessness in killing the rebels. The *sipahi*s and other rebels, on the other hand, suffered from a chronic shortage of cash; moreover, they did not have the sophisticated weapons of the British army.

The immediate impact of the Revolt was the British Parliament's decision to terminate the 'mismanagement' of Indian affairs by the English East India Company. The Government of India Act, passed by Parliament on 2 August 1858, transferred all Company's powers to the Crown; declared Queen Victoria to be the sovereign of British India; and provided for the appointment of a Secretary of State. Nominal subservience to the Mughal emperor was severed totally and violently as—what the British regarded to be—a corrective to the huge cost to British lives and revenues that the Revolt had occasioned. Indeed, widely publicized stories of the cruelty and atrocities of the *sepoys* led to an uproar for punishment and retribution among the British in England and in India. Not for once were the rebels taken to be honourable opponents—they were regarded as 'disloyal' and ignominious subjects, who had to be punished with the greatest severity. The fear occasioned by the Revolt heightened British racism, a fact that will get reflected in the demarcation of spaces (Metcalf and Metcalf 2003: 107–08). The act of suppression and punishment cost the Company a huge sum—it accumulated a debt of about 50 million pounds. The Company owed most of it to the British Crown for deploying troops needed to 'restore order'. This 'debt' of course was to be extracted from India. Moreover, as the East India Company was wound up, compensation to its shareholders also became a part of the 'debt' to be paid by Indian taxpayers (Bates 2007: 80).

In an ironic turn of events, Bahadur Shah, notionally the emperor of India till 1857, was charged with treason in a military court. His defence did not fail to point out that since he was the legitimate ruler, the British in fact were the rebels. This did not have any impact. Bahadur Shah was found guilty and deported in chains to Rangoon, where he died four years later. The emperor's trial, in the words of Bernard Cohn, 'formally announced a transformation of rule'. The ones who brought him to trial believed that it was an act of justice and explicitly denied the King's claim to rule (Cohn 1992: 178). It severed the past from the present, established new political principles and marked the triumph of a new kind of government. British rule now became a rule by 'insiders' with the assumption of the responsibility to govern by the Crown (ibid.: 165). It was no longer an indirect rule of 'outsiders', the East India Company. India became a colony that would play a pivotal role in the economic and strategic sustenance of Britain's hegemony in the world capitalist economy.

Proclamations and Promises: The New Imperial Rule

On 1 November 1858, the day the Act of the Parliament was to come into effect, the Queen issued a proclamation. It appraised the 'Princes, Chiefs and People of India' of the changes. The Viceroy of the Queen replaced the Governor-General of the Company as the supreme authority in India. The Viceroy retained the title of the Governor-General, but he was made directly responsible to the British Cabinet. As the Viceroy, he represented the Queen to the princes and people of India. The Government of India was placed in the care of a new government department in London, the India Office, to be headed by the Secretary of State, who was a member of the British Cabinet. The Secretary of State was to be advised by a new Council of India located in London. Consequently, the existing Council in India (the Governor-General's Council) was renamed the Council of the Governor-General of India by the Act. The position of the Secretary of State roughly corresponded to that of the President of the Board of Control, set up in 1784 to bring the affairs of the Company under greater supervision of the British Parliament (Chapter 2). Indian affairs came under close and regular scrutiny of the British Parliament, in contrast to the earlier pattern of 20-year reviews during the renewal of the Company's charter. Increased involvement of the Cabinet introduced an element of party politics in the appointment of the Governor-General/Viceroy, but the Viceroy, once appointed, served his full term even if his party resigned from power in Britain.

As a corollary, the British government completed the construction of a new imperial seat, Whitehall, located on King Charles Street. The imposing bulk of the administrative complex consisting of the foreign office and the yet to be built home and colonial offices made of polished granite, marble and Portland stone, adequately reflected the expanding administrative activity of the British empire (Lelyveld 1978: 3).

The Councils Act of 1861 changed the composition of the existing Council of the Governor-General, which had had a long career beginning in 1773. Elected by the Court of Directors of the East India Company, the Council, initially called the Council of Four, had important powers to run the administration. All four members of the Council had voting rights along with the Governor-General, who had an additional casting vote. The first Council, it is important to remember, had tried to impeach Warren Hastings. The Act of 1784 had reduced the number of Council members to three, and in 1786 the Council's decision had ceased to be binding on the Governor-General. The Charter Act of 1833 had made a distinction between the executive and legislative duties of the Governor-General and provided for the election of a fourth member who could participate only when legislation was being decided.

The Act of 1858 took away the power of the Company's Court of Directors to elect the members of the Council. The one member to participate in legislation was to be elected by the British sovereign and the three other regular members by the Secretary of State. The Commander-in-Chief of the army was its extraordinary member. The law member was a barrister and the other three were covenanted servants of the Company. In 1869, the Crown assumed the power of electing all members of the Council. The Viceroy was given the power to nominate a President who was to preside over the meetings of the Council during his absence. The Viceroy was also given the authority to enact rules and regulations for the proper conduct of the business of the Council. Moreover, he was allowed to increase the strength of the Council by appointing not less than six and not more than twelve members. Half of these members were to be 'non-official'.

Lord Canning, who assumed the title of the Viceroy after the Queen's proclamation, introduced important changes in the mode of functioning of the Council in 1859, when he appointed a Finance Minister. By making an individual member responsible for a particular department, Canning replaced the earlier practice of the Council deliberating each matter collectively through the exchange of minutes. The new system of granting portfolios facilitated the work of the Council and allowed the Government of India to cope with the steadily growing volume of work (Majumdar [1963] 1970: 733). Increased communication between the Viceroy and the Secretary of State, particularly after the establishment of telegraphic communication between Britain and India in 1870, reduced the importance of the Council of the Governor-General and constrained the Governor-General's freedom to take quick action in emergencies without consulting the Home authority.

The power granted to the Viceroy by the Councils Act of 1861 of increasing the strength of the Council altered its composition significantly, since half of the new members were to be non-official. The government was wary of the Revolt of 1857 and other uprisings, such as the Santal rebellion and the Indigo riots; the Secretary of State, Sir Charles Wood, in particular, sought to redress the grievances that had occasioned such widespread unrest. There was, of course, a general awareness that land and revenue settlements had impoverished the peasantry in Bengal, Madras and other parts of India. However, Wood also paid serious attention to Sayyid Ahmad's Urdu text, *Asbab-e-baghawat-e-Hind*, translated into English as *Essay on the Causes of the Indian Revolt*, which pointed to the non-admission of Indians into the Legislative Council of India as a prime cause of antagonism. Wood and Canning made use of the clause of the Act of 1861 by appointing non-official Indian members to the Council. This part of the Council, with legislative powers, came to be called the Imperial Legislative Council (Sharan 1961). The Act of 1861 gave Indians a share in the administration of their own country for the first time.

Chronology of Viceroys of India, 1858–1947

Sl. No.	Name	Term of Office
1.	The Viscount Canning	1 November 1858–21 March 1862
2.	The Earl of Elgin	21 March 1862–20 November 1863
3.	Sir Robert Napier	21 November 1863–2 December 1863
4.	Sir William Denison	2 December 1863–12 January 1864
5.	Sir John Lawrence	12 January 1864–12 January 1869
6.	The Earl of Mayo	12 January 1869–8 February 1872

Sl. No.	Name	Term of Office
7.	Sir John Strachey	9 February 1872–23 February 1872
8.	The Lord Napier	24 February 1872–3 May 1872
9.	The Lord Northbrook	3 May 1872–12 April 1876
10.	The Lord Lytton	12 April 1876–8 June 1880
11.	The Marquess of Ripon	8 June 1880–13 December 1884
12.	The Earl of Dufferin	13 December 1884–10 December 1888
13.	The Marquess of Lansdowne	10 December 1888–11 October 1894
14.	The Earl of Elgin	11 October 1894–6 January 1899
15.	The Lord Curzon of Kedleston	6 January 1899–18 November 1905
16.	The Earl of Minto	18 November 1905–23 November 1910
17.	The Lord Hardinge of Penshurst	23 November 1910–4 April 1916
18.	The Lord Chelmsford	4 April 1916–2 April 1921
19.	The Earl of Reading	2 April 1921–3 April 1926
20.	The Lord Irwin	3 April 1926–18 April 1931
21.	The Earl of Willingdon	18 April 1931–18 April 1936
22.	The Marquess of Linlithgow	18 April 1936–1 October 1943
23.	The Viscount Wavell	1 October 1943–21 February 1947
24.	The Viscount Mountbatten of Burma	21 February 1947–15 August 1947

Arguably, there were severe limitations. The function of the Council was strictly confined to legislation and it was not allowed to interfere in the work of the executive. Moreover, legislation on certain specified matters could only be introduced with the prior consent of the Viceroy and no act passed by the Council was valid till it was ratified by him. At the same time, the provision for the mixture of official and non-official members in the Viceroy's Council set the terms for institutional reforms and political demands, and set in motion an entwined process that would involve efforts and energies of colonial administrators and the Indian elite. The number of non-official members in the Council was to be raised to between ten and 16 in 1892 and to 60 in the 1909 reforms (Keith 1936).

Other supposed causes of the Revolt were also addressed by Queen Victoria's proclamation. In a direct reversal of Dalhousie's policy, the proclamation guaranteed the princes their 'rights, dignity and honour' as well as their control over territorial possessions. The right of adopted heirs was also acknowledged. A similar move was made to protect the 'ancient rights, usages and customs of India' in the arbitration of law and justice, and a promise made that British rule will not attempt to impose its convictions upon its subjects. The Queen sought to embody a benevolent and neutral administration, since she 'was bound to the natives of Our Indian territories by the same obligations of duty which bind us to all our other subjects' (Cohn 1992: 165). This benign rule was to ensure internal peace and good government and thus stimulate 'social advancement', 'improvement' and the general well-being of India.

All this perhaps was a response to Sayyid Ahmad's call for warm personal relations between Englishmen and Indians as the 'emotional basis of political stability' (Lelyveld 1978: 74).

The underlying assumption of the proclamation, of course, was the necessity of British rule for India. It reiterated the earlier assumption of the Company's administrators that there was a diversity of culture, society and religion in India, and that it was the duty of the British to protect the integrity inherent in this diversity through an equitable government. The proclamation contained opposing theories of rule. On the one hand, it sought to allow Indian participation in liberal politics and administration and, on the other, it made Indian princes an important element of the new Raj. The autonomy granted to Indian rulers over their territories was aimed at protecting a feudal order—almost a third of India's population remained under indirect rule till 1947. Alongside, the introduction of institutional reforms sought to bring about changes by means of a representational mode of government that would steadily undermine the feudal order (Cohn 1992: 166).

Proponents of the two different forms of governance agreed on the inability of Indians for self-rule and devoted themselves to the construction and consolidation of the 'authority' of British rule in India. This entailed creating a usable past for this authority and adopting practical measures to prevent occurrences such as the Revolt. First and foremost, the new order required allies. The recognition of the rights and titles of princes and landlords, the conservative aristocrats, was a prime move to secure their loyalty. It was complemented by establishing a Court of Wards, which had the right to take over the estate of a prince, landlord or aristocrat in case of bankruptcy, put it under the care of a manager, and return the estate to the original owner, once the arrears had been cleared and the property had become solvent (Bates 2007: 81; Metcalf 1995).

In an effort both to demonstrate that British rule had effectively replaced Mughal rule and to vest colonial rule with an aura of legitimacy and continuity, Lord Canning toured large parts of north India and held Mughal-style durbars with Indian princes, notables and Indian and British officials. In such durbars, Indians who had demonstrated their loyalty to the British during the uprising of 1857–58 were honoured with titles, such as Raja, Nawab, Rai Sahib, Rai Bahadur and Khan Bahadur, presented with special clothes and emblems, granted special privileges and exemptions, as well as given pensions or land grants (Cohn 1992: 167–68). This was supplemented by establishing a new royal order of Indian knights, such as the Star of India (1861, enlarged subsequently with the addition of lower ranks), and regular visits to India by members of the royal family.

The most spectacular durbar was the one organized in 1877 through the joint efforts of newly appointed Governor-General Lytton, Secretary of State Salisbury and British Prime Minister Disraeli. The occasion was the passing of the Royal Titles Act by the British Parliament that declared Queen Victoria to be the 'Empress of India'. An imperial assemblage in the style of a grand durbar in Delhi was planned to mark the assumption of the title by the Queen, an event that would signal the final rupture with Mughal rule and yet install Queen's rule as its true successor. The assemblage was also designed to 'make an impact upon the British at home as well as upon Indians' (ibid.: 185).

The durbar, as Cohn demonstrates brilliantly, reinstated a 'Victorian feudal'. This is because from the beginning the British misunderstood and misconstrued the significance of the relationship of the princes and aristocrats with the Mughal emperor, concretely manifest in the closeness of the person to the emperor in durbars and in ritual incorporations represented by the exchange of *nazar* (gold coins) and *peshkash* (precious possessions) in return for *khelat* (robes of honour). The exchange of gifts, a symbol of incorporation, was misread as bribe and done away with. In a vivid demonstration of the neutrality of British rule, the 63 important ruling princes were placed at the centre in the durbar of 1877 with equal distance from Governor-General Lord Lytton, and were presented with a silk banner that made them legal subjects of the Queen (ibid.: 191). The best reflection of the warped British understanding of Mughal India was reflected in the title *Kaiser-i-Hind*, phrased in two different languages and assumed by Queen Victoria. Not surprisingly, the title and the durbar evoked critical response from the press in India and in Britain and the assemblage was derided as being a *tamasha* (a folly). At the same time, this durbar retained its significance as a marker, as a before and after event that crucially moulded Indian political practices, and contributed considerably to the iconization of Maharani Victoria.

Pacification of aristocrats was accompanied by measures to offer respite to cultivators. A series of tenancy acts that gave occupancy rights to ordinary cultivators started being introduced in Bengal and Awadh from 1859, and were extended to other provinces. As problems with revenue settlements and high revenue demand became clear, the Crown government avoided increasing land revenues for a long time, resorting instead to elevating excise and income taxes to secure extra income. There was no significant hike in land revenues till the time of World War I (Bates 2007: 81), which, nevertheless continued to remain the most important source of the government's income, as we have seen in the last chapter. By 1870, the imperial government had established a centralized financial administration with a definite budget assigned to each province that did not necessarily correspond with the revenue generated in the respective provinces. As a further step to ensure peace in the countryside, an Arms Act was passed that prohibited people from carrying weapons without a license.

With the kings and landlords won over and cultivators appeased, Queen's rule turned its attention towards the army, its vital pillar. In an effort to prevent future insurgency by Indian *sepoys*, the British–Indian army was reorganized in a way that tilted the ratio in favour of Europeans. Till the outbreak of the First World War, this ratio never fell short of 2:1, for European and Indian soldiers respectively. Moreover, the artillery was left only in the care of British officers. In addition, the British also took recourse to the 'insidious counterpoise of natives against natives' (Bose and Jalal 1998: 98). Recruitment was now made from among social groups that had remained loyal during the Revolt—the Sikhs, Gurkhas, Punjabi Muslims and Pathans—and they were cleverly mixed in the regiments so that 'a Sikh might fire into Hindu, Gurkha into either' in case of need (ibid.: 98; Roy 2009).

The reorganized army not only maintained 'peace' within India, it also played a critical role in the defence of Britain's worldwide empire, from North Africa to East Asia. The British–Indian army was deployed to suppress the Mahdi uprisings in 1885–86 and 1889 in Sudan, the Boxer rebellion in China (1900) and the Boer War of 1899–1902 in South Africa (Bose and Jalal 1998: 98). Indian troops enabled the British to conquer Burma in the 1880s, and impose their dominance over Tibet at the beginning of the twentieth century. Moreover, the intervention of the Indian army in Egypt in 1882 eventually led to the partition of Africa. The cost of such expeditions, needless to say, was borne primarily by Indian tax payers.

The reorganization of the army, it bears pointing out, was shored up by anthropological classifications of races and castes as 'martial' and 'effeminate', 'criminal' and 'noble', classifications that would form the bedrock of the huge colonial archive and set in motion policies and processes that would crucially shape 'modern' India (Nigam 1990; Sharan 2003; Pandey 1992). The Punjab region gained critical prominence after the Revolt as it came to be regarded as the key that will hold the empire. The 'martial races' of Punjab found disproportionately high representation in the newly revamped Indian army (Oldenburg 2002: 46). This would have serious implications for developments in the region.

IMPERIAL KNOWLEDGE AND IMPERIAL GOVERNANCE

Before we examine the strategies and politics of Victoria's India, let us take note of the lively debate that has emerged on the nature of 'colonial knowledge' and how it enabled European colonizers to achieve domination across the globe. The debate was inaugurated, to a large extent, by the publication of Edward Said's path-breaking work *Orientalism* (1978). Its central claim was that the West has 'produced and managed' by means of a long history of literary production, academic writing, ethnography and stereotyping, an image of the non-western world as 'degenerate, exotic, despotic, essentially religious, effeminate, and weak'; an exact 'Other of the West' (Dodson 2010: 2). This discursive construction was a key element in Europe's domination of the world. Cohn's work, it is worth mentioning, had presaged some of this argument, but Said's bold assertion that all knowledge is contingent and historically constructed and needs to be understood with reference to politics and power, made the 'power knowledge' debate acquire a new significance.

From the late 1970s, scholars have reflected critically on the potential implications of Said's analysis. All of them agree that colonial conquest was made possible not just by the force of superior arms, military organization, political power or economic wealth but also by 'cultural technologies of rule' (Dirks 1996: ix). At the same time, they disagree over the role of the colonized subject in producing knowledge that sustained this 'cultural technology'. At one end are those who minimize or dismiss the significance of native intellectuals. They are treated as near passive informants who provided raw material to the European colonizers. The terms and modes of knowing were set by the colonizers who asked for, understood and appropriated information offered by native informants in distinct ways to generate new knowledge (for instance, Cohn 1968, 1987, 1996; Dirks 1987, 1992, 2001; Inden 1986, 1990). At the other end are the proponents of the 'dialogic' theory of the production of colonial knowledge (Subrahmanyam 2001: 5). Such scholars affirm that colonial knowledge was the result of an intricate process of collaboration between the colonizers and the colonized, in which indigenous intellectuals participated actively and the knowledge produced involved a constant adjustment between European and indigenous knowledge systems (Bayly 1995; Eaton 2000; Irschick 1994; Lorenzen [1999] 2006; Peabody 2001; Trautmann 1999; Wagoner 2003).

While both positions are partly valid, we need to watch out against a clear separation between the 'colonizer' and the 'colonized'. The two categories were in constant flux and were mutually shaped through their interaction. Moreover, it is important to keep in mind that the colonial state was not a monolith incessantly driven by a thrust for knowledge in order to quench its thirst for power. As we have seen in earlier chapters, it was not until the end of the eighteenth and the beginning of the nineteenth century that the production of 'new' knowledge about India became closely tied to political patronage (Ludden 1994; Rocher 1994). Moreover, the situation of the East India Company's government in India was complex as it struggled to lay the foundations of a colonial administration keeping in mind the needs and expectations of the home administration of the Company, the Parliament and the Crown. Besides, a large section of the British population took an interest in Indian affairs.

Arguably, the British Crown did not have to worry about the Parliament or British public opinion; the colonial state after 1858 took long and fast strides to 'know' India in order to govern her better. 'In the new rhetorical economy of colonial rule' argues Dirks, 'political loyalty replaced landed status'; and 'knowledge of peoples and cultures' was given primacy in understanding issues of loyalty (2001: 43). 'Officializing' procedures that allowed power to become more extensive and more visible now came to complement the dramatic display of power that the European states had relied on from the eighteenth century. India was drawn into the vortex of this transformation, since the process of state building in Britain was closely linked to its emergence as an imperial power. 'India' was Britain's 'largest and most important colony' (Cohn 1996: 3). Often, the 'officializing' procedures of documentation, legitimation, classification, bounding and the institutions connected to them, reflected theories and experiences that were initially worked out in India and then applied to Britain. The reverse was also true (ibid.: 2–3). In addition, since the 'facts' of India's epistemological space did not exactly correspond with the facts of the invaders, the British tried to establish correspondence by means of 'translation'. This kind of 'translation' was to make the unknown and the strange knowable. This imperative of classifying and categorizing India's social world in ways that would make it 'knowable' crucially shaped the 'investigative modalities' devised to collect facts (ibid.: 4–5).

The increasing interest of the post-1857 colonial state in the customs of the land was governed by its need to face 'more prudently the vexed question of social reform'. It also wanted precise knowledge of the internal divisions in Indian society in order to mark out the ally from the enemy, and develop an administrative system 'capable of exerting greater social control' (Bandyopadhyay 1985: 57, 7). All these requirements slowly transformed the colonial state into an 'ethnographic state' in which anthropology replaced history as the principal mode of knowing (Dirks 2004: 70–88).

Bold measures were set afoot to gather material about castes and tribes, often separated in terms of the zones they inhabited into plains people and forest people (Chapter 3) and their customs. Descriptions of particular customs, ritual forms and kinship behaviour—considered to be appropriate and necessary—became formalized and canonic (Dirks 2001: 44–45). Despite being bewildered by its complexities, British administrators-cum-ethnographers persisted in their efforts at mapping the world of the colonized. Beginning with a systematic survey of land tenures and rights in land, they went on to classify the population in terms of number and composition taking religious communities to be the basis for such enumeration. And, here the works of both Orientalist scholars and missionaries came in handy.

Orientalist scholars, British administrators and missionaries differed widely in their approaches to caste and in their evaluation of the effects of caste on Hindu society. At the same time, they believed that caste differentiated 'traditional' India from the 'modern' West. From the late-eighteenth and early-nineteenth centuries, their efforts and their works had slowly marked out caste and religion as 'natural' categories, so that by the second half of the nineteenth century they embodied the 'sociological keys to the understanding of Indian people' (Cohn 1987: 242; abbreviated version reprinted in Banerjee-Dube 2008). This 'discourse of differentiation' (Cohn 1986: 284) came to be strengthened and perpetrated in the ethnographic surveys carried out on a massive scale by Victoria's regime, albeit with different motivations and unto distinct ends and purposes. And since all this knowledge was produced 'under the Enlightenment rubric of objective science', Orientalism as a body of knowledge became objectified 'as a set of factualized statements about a reality that existed and could be known independent of any subjective, colonizing will' (Ludden 1994: 252).

This does not, of course, imply that Orientalism was a 'static *modus operandi*'. A recent work has argued that Orientalism is best understood 'as a shifting set of policy positions and localized practices' that were constantly adapted to the changing circumstances in the colony and to the evolution of British thought in the metropolis (Dodson 2010: 4). It is important to examine colonial policies in the context of diverse applications of Orientalism.

In the fresh moves to know India, caste replaced the village community as the primary object of social classification and understanding. Moreover, the underlying assumption that Indian society was 'traditional' and hence composed of communities, meant that attempts to 'know' it were geared towards an exploration of the primordial 'religious' identities of communities. Consequently, the needs, policies and politics of the 'ethnographic' colonial state fomented and stabilized identities around new orientations. Caste, certainly, was not an 'invention' of British rule, even in the special sense that Dirks (1989) and Inden (1990) have used it, but it did come to acquire special meaning and significance in the colonial period.

Undoubtedly, census operations and other measures of British administration often 'built upon' indigenous initiatives (Peabody 2001), 're-accentuating' and 'renewing' existing identities rather than creating them (Datta 1993). Moreover, as Conlon puts it succinctly, even if caste were 'invented,' 'did it follow that which was "invented" could also be "not real"?' (2009: 293). The assumption, on the part of some scholars, of an 'over-imagined agency and power of colonial rulers' (Pennington 2005: 167) can mislead us into treating invocations of 'tradition' by Indians as measures just of self-interest and not of resistance (Conlon 2009: 293). With due deference to all these important insights, it needs to be acknowledged that caste underwent an important transformation as it came to function as the meeting ground between Indian reality and colonial knowledge and strategy (Washbrook and Baker 1975).

The best illustration, both of the colonial will to know in order to classify and govern, as also of its effects on understandings of caste, is provided by the much discussed census operations, undertaken on a wide scale from 1871 (Bandyopadhyay 1985, 1992; Barrier 1981; Bates 1995; Bayly 1997; Cohn 1987; Pant 1987, for instance). By 1881, the British government had worked out a set of practices that would allow it to list not just the names of 'every person in India' but also to gather information about age, sex, occupation, caste, religion, literacy, place of birth and current residence (Cohn 1996: 8). Ostensibly, all the data collecting by the British was to understand Indian society as it was, not to change it (Lelyveld 1978: 8). Moreover, the initial idea behind the census, it has been pointed out, was nothing more than a 'statistical survey' (Samarendra 2008).

At the same time, queries about people's caste were made from the outset with the purpose of differentiating 'authentic' Hindus from those who had subsequently come within the fold of the religion on account of the 'Brahmanising' influence (Bandyopadhyay 1992: 26–36). The published census reports did not only summarize the statistical information compiled; they also included 'extensive narratives about the caste system, the religions of India, fertility and morbidity, domestic organization, and the economic structure of India' (Cohn 1996: 8). Of greater significance is the fact that census takers were given 'special keys' for converting unsuitable responses into officially formulated census categories (Plowden 1873, I: xix–xx). This is because Indian informants often failed to align themselves comfortably in the column under caste or religion, which demonstrates for us the blurred nature of the 'categories' or the relative insignificance of them in the everyday lives of people till then. For the British administrators, on the other hand, this 'failure' on the part of Indians was representative of their ignorance, of their incapability of identifying themselves for administrative purposes.

The census, for Cohn, is the best illustration of the Victorian encyclopaedic quest for total knowledge (1996: 8). The 'enumerative modality' of the censuses, also described as 'the single master exercise of tabulation of colonial society' (Bayly 1997: 244), fed into and supplemented other modes of knowing. Cohn distinguished the modalities based on historiography, survey, travel, museology and surveillance—together they produced sociological categories by means of which India was mapped for administrative purposes (Cohn 1996: 5–11).

It is not surprising, therefore, that problems resulting from a lack of uniformity in the classificatory categories of caste prompted the government to sponsor detailed ethnographic surveys about the institution of caste (Risley 1908; Gait 1914). This resulted in the Survey of India project, which began in 1878. The all-India census, in turn, had been preceded by photographic surveys, which provided 'exact' images of the physiognomy, dress and manners of the peoples of India (Metcalf and Metcalf 2003: 111). Indeed, in 1868, the first big compilation of photographs of different castes and 'tribes' called *The Peoples of India*, was published by the Government of India. By the end of the century, an enormous amount of information on castes, tribes and races as well as their customs and usages enabled the colonial state to assign Indian people prescribed roles in the 'colonial sociological theatre' (Cohn 1996: 10).

This was done by means of an intricate process. The detailed information collected and codified in gazetteers and census reports 'untethered' the huge diversity of castes, sects, tribes and other groupings from the agrarian landscape and rendered them into a vast 'categorical' landscape. Colonial sociology tried to map 'qualities of the subject population that were most germane to the business of administration'. This not only included a group's productive capacity, traditional occupation, its competence or the lack of it, but also its 'criminality, military prowess, truthfulness, litigious tendencies, and so on' (Pandey 1992: 68). Hence, the notional 'Indian individual' was stripped of his place in the 'village community' and clothed in 'caste' (Smith 1985: 173).

Indeed, as Richard Smith points out, the nature of the early, regional censuses changed dramatically from the mid-1850s, once they were taken out of the hands of settlement agencies (Smith 1996). The Settlement of Ludhiana in 1853, to cite an example, included an enumeration of households in the village and information about the number and measurement of agricultural fields they controlled. Similarly, the household census registers in Jullundur district were bound into the back of the settlement records (Kessinger 1974: 6). In the 1855 Census of Punjab, 'the first synchronous census throughout the province', figures of caste were abstracted from those compiled during the settlement of individual districts (Smith 1996, cited in Banerjee-Dube 2008: 68). Thereafter, the enumeration of castes became a central part of censuses in India and resulted in the construction of 'a morphological view of caste' (ibid.: 67).

Colonial policies were framed on the basis of such categorization. It is not only that caste was taken to be a measurable phenomenon, classifiable in accordance with some definite criteria; it is also that certain groups and categories of people were deemed to be 'threatening' to the prescribed sociological order. It is not surprising therefore, that census reports recorded minorities that were recalcitrant towards British law and order, such as Ramoshis, Thugs and other 'criminal tribes' (Pant 1987: 147).

The last chapter traced British moves to control and subdue the wandering population of *sanyasis*, *fakirs*, *sadhus*, dacoits, thugs, *goondas*, pastoralists and entertainers. Victoria's rule carried out intense investigation on groups defined as being beyond civil bounds. The Thagi and Dacoity Department, set up in 1835, had produced an archive on criminal ethnography; Victoria's state drew upon and extended this archive to designate an ever increasing number of people as members of criminal castes and tribes. 'The ghost of the "thugee"', argues Nigam, 'far from coming to rest with the end of thug gangs, kept haunting others'—the Buddhuks of Awadh, the Dhatura poisoners of the North-Western Provinces and the Meenas of Punjab, for instance—'till it was contained in an even larger organism: the Criminal Tribes Act of 1871' (Nigam 1990: 134).

Officials who tried to root out female infanticide—believed to be practiced widely in northern and western India— were the first to use the category of caste to order and interpret demographic data (Banerjee-Dube 2008: xxxviii; Oldenburg 2002). While it is true that female infanticide was prevalent among many communities in colonial Punjab, it was practiced among different groups at different times and for different reasons. The colonial state, by 'picking on social elites' and by publicizing and recognizing their customs, imparted on them 'a fixity that may not have been present earlier' (Malhotra 2010: 85). More importantly, the state's endeavours to stop female infanticide was more rhetorical than real. The Jats, in particular Jat Sikhs, the 'mainstay of the government's source of revenue' and the 'pride of its martial army', also practiced infanticide along with the elites. The colonial state, however, left the Jats alone with only 'desultory measures' that left infanticide unchecked (ibid.).

The use of caste to classify the population in accordance with occupation and social structure was soon applied to all of India (Bates 1995: 10). Assumptions of 'inborn criminality' also related to the more obdurate and recalcitrant 'tribes' and a large number of coercive measures were introduced from the beginning to tame them. All such measures, of different chronologies and dispersed locations, overlapped and drew upon each other to eventually aid the formulation of the Criminal Tribes Act—a general method of surveillance and control (Nigam 1990: 136).

This meant that individuals and groups were being classified in both descriptive and classificatory terms. Photography, which provided a clue to the physiognomy, now became inadequate; the new anthropometric system—developed by American physician Samuel Morton, French surgeon turned anthropologist Paul Broca and his disciple Topinard, and put in practice by the French prefect of police, Alphonse Bertillon—acquired great significance as a method that had the capacity to describe and classify accurately. In India, this system was put to effective use by Herbert Hope Risley. Risley had begun his career as the Assistant Director of Statistics in W. W. Hunter's Survey of India project in the

1870s; he rose rapidly in the profession to become Director of the Ethnographic Survey of Bengal in 1885, the Census Commissioner in 1899, and finally, the Director of Ethnography for India in 1901 (Banerjee-Dube 2008: xxxix). Convinced of the benefits of anthropometry, Risley proudly proclaimed that the 'first attempt to apply to Indian ethnography methods of systematic research sanctioned by the authority of European scientists' was being made in the ethnography in progress in Bengal under his guidance. The 'science' of anthropometry enabled Risley to assert that the classification of castes on the *varna* model was firmly rooted in facts.

Risley's affirmation needs elaboration. The completely unwieldy and bewildering data that queries about caste had generated, prompted the census commissioners to fall back on the classification of castes in accordance with the classical four-fold division of *varna* in the early censuses of 1865, 1871 and 1881, although the *varna* model neither corresponded to the existing relationships between castes, nor served any useful administrative purpose. Denzil Ibbetson, an acute local administrator of Punjab and the North-West Provinces, who headed the census of 1891, decided to return to occupation as the basis for classification. Ibbetson, in turn, was inspired by Nesfield's materialist evolutionary idea of castes as social guilds that descended from tribes, where 'function' provided the main criterion of classification (Bates 1995: 11–12; Dirks 2001: 211–12).

In direct opposition to Nesfield, Risley not only affirmed the validity of the *varna* model, but also stated boldly that the caste-based population of India could be classified in terms of race into Aryan and aboriginal (Risley 1908: 20–21). Risley made use of anthropometry to take cranial measurements of very few tribes and castes, but since he was clear as to what the results would indicate, he confidently fitted the results of few observations into a complex typology of racial types (Banerjee-Dube 2008: xxxix; Bates 1995: 21). This 'pseudo-scientific' method enabled Risley to prove something that Orientalist scholar William Jones had suggested in the early 1830s but had failed to establish—that there was a racial difference between northern and southern Indians and between high castes and low castes (Bates 1995: 14). Jones, we have noted in the last chapter, had laid the foundation of the race theory for India by speaking of the common origin of Sanskrit, Latin and Greek, and of the common origin of nations and races, which supported his belief that Sanskrit speakers had come to India from outside. Risley placed the notion of race on a 'scientific' footing.

This is not surprising. Scholars have argued that for leading ethnographers of the late-nineteenth–early-twentieth century British–India—Risley, Hunter Ibbetson—men who 'sought to make their mark in a wider learned world which had come to be dominated by ethnological debate', race and not caste was the prime theme of investigation and debate (Bayly 1995: 167). Consequently, in their effort 'to place themselves in the vanguard of contemporary scientific thought' (ibid.) these scholar-officials were not necessarily trying to make India a special or singular case, a self-contained and ethnographically separate 'other'. Rather, India was a ground that provided material for wider theorizing.

According to Ajay Skaria, the understanding of caste in terms of race derived from anachronistic thought that was closely linked to 'evolutionist beliefs and theory' (Skaria 1997: 728). This belief, current among colonial officials, that there was an Aryan invasion into India from Central Asia in the remote past, prompted ethnographers to rank castes in accordance with the degree of Aryan and Dravidian blood, with those believed to have more Aryan blood regarded as superior (ibid.; Bates 1995). The term *arya* (pure) used in Vedic texts for the first three *varnas* that were also qualified to be twice-born castes, now came to stand for race, and a racial distinction was made between native-born Indians and a 'European-related group of invaders' (Zelliot 2010). Modern scholarship, it bears pointing out, regards Arya as an Indo–European language group that has no connection to race. Castes, however, were 'really races' for Risley, and the distinction between castes was actually a distinction between peoples 'with supposedly superior and inferior racial endowment' (Bayly 1997: 168).

As indicated earlier, this wide difference of opinion among British administrators discredits the idea of a uniform colonial discourse. At the same time, it also reveals the prevalence of certain common needs to classify Indians. Whether or not caste was taken to be race, the detailed schema of colonial classification ceased to remain 'mere academic speculations'—it had 'important economic and political repercussions' (Carroll 1978). Categorization of castes as 'low' often excluded them from employment in the army. Caste, religion and place of origin were deciding elements for recruitment in the administrative services, the army and in the plantations. Indeed, information about each caste and its supposedly distinctive characteristics, collected and codified in scores of official manuals and handbooks, gave shape to communities of 'martial races' and of 'criminal castes and criminal tribes' (Nigam 1990). It also helped define the contours of the 'depressed/scheduled' castes as distinct both from the upper castes and the 'criminal castes' (Sharan 2003). Hence, although census operations and other measures of British administration 'built upon' indigenous initiatives, the motives and criteria behind the operations were clearly different (Peabody 2001: 819–50).

To give just one example, census in Britain was territorial and occupational and was confined to investigations of the social margins—the poor, the sexually profligate and the 'criminals' (Appadurai 1994: 317–18). In India, on the other hand, census was ethnic or racial and covered the entire subject population. This, apart from revealing British assumptions about the 'subject population', validates Appadurai's point that quantification is never totally 'innocent' (ibid.). As indicated earlier, the descriptive-normative classification of castes governed colonial policies. As such, Indian response to the categories was much more than 'idle striving for social symbols' (Carroll 1978).

Risley's faith in the 'immutability of caste ideology' and his confidence in his own knowledge about the subject population found eloquent expression in his decision to rank castes in the social hierarchy along with their enumeration in the Census of 1901 (Banerjee-Dube 2008: xxxix). This generated hectic activity on the part of the colonized, who saw this as a move to freeze a changing hierarchy. State-led and private scientific categorizations 'helped define new ways of perceiving and expressing identities' (Robb 2002: 220). Chapter 3 briefly discussed the efforts of low caste and untouchable groups, such as the Satnamis of Chhattisgarh or the Mahima Dharmis of Orissa to counter social-ritual discrimination by means of a new faith. Such moves were unconnected to state initiatives. The following section tracks some important movements of lower castes and the growth of caste associations in general in order to grasp the implications of the new ways of perceiving and expressing identities produced by colonial rule.

CASTE AND CASTE IDENTITY

Scholars do not agree over the exact impact of colonialism on caste; they do accept, however, that colonial rule created conditions and set processes in motion for the growth of a non-Brahman ideology and emergence of lower caste movements. This was because, on the one hand, there was a direct attack on the institution of caste by Protestant missionaries and, on the other, classification of castes according to numbers in the censuses made visible the discrepancy between numerical strength and social privileges of various castes.

'Caste' for the Christian missionaries was 'an unmitigated evil', a sign of the inferiority of the Hindu religion in relation to Christianity. In the words of John Wilson, missionary scholar and educator, the Hindus had brought imaginations of natural and positive distinctions among humanity found all over the world 'to the most fearful and pernicious development ever exhibited on the face of the globe'. Caste was 'the condensation of all the pride, jealousy and tyranny of an ancient people' with regard to tribes they had brought under their control and over whom they ruled 'without the sympathies of a recognized common humanity' (Wilson 1877: 9–11). Even if in missionary tracts and polemic caste mattered less than issues of the nature of truth, the manifestations of divinity and critiques of Puranic Hinduism (Conlon 2009: 302), their critique of caste and, in particular, of Brahman arrogance and inhumanity, was soon to find strong resonance among some Indian intellectuals.

Gopalrao Hari Deshmukh, a government servant, reformer and essayist of the Bombay Presidency, who wrote under the name 'Lokahitavadi' (spokesman of the well-being of the people), agreed that caste was indeed contributing to the weakness and decline of Indian society by hindering national unity (ibid.: 302). Jotirao Phule, radical lower caste intellectual and reformer, who undertook early efforts to spread education among members of untouchables and lower castes and among women, as we have noted in Chapter 3, zealously took up the missionary critique of caste and Brahmans. He made it the prime instrument in his polemic against Brahmans and his efforts to forge an identity of the Sudras and Atisudras (Chandals). It is important to remember in this context that the modern school, according to a recent work, was a powerful metaphor for community (and nation), and pedagogy was intimately tied to the formation of subjects, an idea drawn from evangelical missionaries but refashioned by Indian lower-caste and untouchable leaders, as well as by Muslim and Hindu intelligentsia (Sengupta 2011). We will see the implications of this argument in succeeding chapters.

Before we analyse Phule's movement and some other lower caste and anti-Brahman movements, it is important to keep in mind the impetus offered by ethnographic surveys and census operations, and the promise of institutional reforms held out by Victoria's regime. While most studies of caste movements affirm that they were products of colonial political modernity, they often do not pay adequate attention to the time of emergence of such movements, namely, the 70s and 80s of the nineteenth century, when surveys and censuses were enumerating and classifying the population on an all-India basis on new terms. The newness related to the fact that the census, the cadastral and several other surveys not only categorized Indian bodies, they also gave them quantitative values (Bayly [1988] 1995: 88–89).

Two points need to be considered here. First, the caste-wise inventory drawn up by the census underscored the inconsistency between number and privilege as it made different groups aware of their numerical strength in the population. This prompted them to claim a certain degree of equality in public employment—the limited opportunities open to Indians in the administrative service, in medical and legal professions and in the army. Soon, there would be demands for representation in local legislative councils, which started to include 'native' members from the 1880s, just as the Imperial Legislative

Council had started including non-official members from 1861. In consonance with the founding of the Indian National Congress and its demand for political participation, which we will discuss in detail in the following chapters, the 'non-official' element in the Imperial Council and the local councils rose slowly but steadily. This, unfortunately, sharpened regional, caste and community rivalries for scarce resources in education, jobs and political spoils in a situation of colonial underdevelopment (Sarkar [1983] 1995: 20), and at a time when ethnographic surveys were definitely fixing caste groups and communities in terms of numbers.

Second, Risley's decision to grade the castes according to their position in the social hierarchy in the Census of 1901, induced members of several upwardly mobile castes to come together in order to press for a higher placement in the hierarchy. 'Voluntary caste associations', states Sekhar Bandyopadhyay, 'emerged as a new phenomenon in Indian public life', associations that engaged in census-based caste movements, and made petitions to census commissioners in support of their claims for higher ritual ranks in the official classification scheme (2004: 344). Position in the social hierarchy, we are aware, was not just about social prestige; colonial recruitment in several services derived from such a classification (Carroll 1978). Institutional reforms introduced periodically by Victoria's reign from the 1860s to eventually prepare Indians for self-rule also drew upon caste in a distinct manner. From the early-twentieth century, it wanted to protect members of minority communities and untouchable castes and 'backward' classes by granting them special privileges.

Before the reservation of seats for Muslims in the provincial legislative assemblies was granted by the Morley–Minto Reforms of 1909, rulers of certain princely states, such as those of Mysore and Kolhapur, had introduced caste-based reservation in public employment for members of the 'depressed classes', a vague category that emerged out of the census (Banerjee-Dube 2008: xli; Sharan 2003). The rulers had been prompted by the huge gap in numerical strength and access to privileges that the census brought to the fore. Understandably, southern and western India witnessed the growth of non-Brahman movements relatively early. It was not just that in these parts the numerical proportion of Brahmans fell far short of their predominance and privilege. It was also that Maharashtra under the Brahman Peshwas in the eighteenth century (as we have noted in Chapter 1), and the southern kingdoms under Hindu kings had regulated social affairs in accordance with the *varna* classification and all that it entailed. This got reflected in the statistics obtained by the census.

If one were to use the figures cited by Anil Seal in *The Emergence of Indian Nationalism*, it would appear that of the 338 Hindus employed in the executive and judicial branches of the Uncovenanted Service of the Bombay Presidency in 1886–87, 211 were Brahmans, 26 were Kshatriyas, 27 were Prabhus, 38 Vaishyas or Banias, 1 Sudra and 15 others. The Hindus, moreover, accounted for 328 of the 384 Indians employed (Seal 1968: 118). Seal undoubtedly confuses the *varna* and the *jati* groupings; at the same time, the figures clearly reveal the predominance of Brahmans and the under-representation of Sudras in public employment in the Bombay Presidency.

By the time Jotirao Phule set up his Satyashodhak Samaj (Truth Seeking Society) in 1873, he had become convinced that Brahman monopoly was solely responsible for the predicament of Sudra and Atisudra castes. Phule attempted to bring together the huge conglomerate of non-Brahman peasant castes (*kunbis*) and the untouchables within a single fold by means of an ingenious inversion of the

Orientalist theory of Aryanization (Keer and Mashle 1969 cited in O'Hanlon 1985: 142–51; Banerjee-Dube 2008: 172–80). The Brahmans, in Phule's depiction, were the descendants of Aryan invaders who had conquered the indigenous peoples of India and forcibly imposed their religion as an instrument of social control. This religion allowed the Brahmans not only to deprive the original inhabitants of their power and property but also to perpetuate their domination.

Phule reclaimed a non-Aryan Kshatriya past for the lower caste groups of Maharashtra by imaginatively linking the word Kshatriya to the Sanskrit *kshetra* (field), and combining agricultural and military service, which gave the humble peasant-cultivator a resplendent past of military prowess. He also accorded the untouchable castes of Mahars and Mangs, the original inhabitants of Maharashtra, a glorious past in which they had offered the strongest resistance to Aryan invaders. Mahar, for Phule, derived from *Maha-ari* (the great enemy), the Dravidian Kshatriyas. It was no wonder therefore that with the ascendancy of the Aryans the Mahars were banished from society, condemned to poverty, made to feed on dead carcass and wear a black thread as a symbol of servitude (Phule cited in Rao 2009: 45). These central polemical arguments allowed Phule to 'deny the legitimacy of Brahmanic religious authority, to assert the hidden Kshatriya identity of all lower castes' and to look at Hindu popular stories and symbols afresh from a radical viewpoint (O'Hanlon 1985: 141).

Gopal Baba Valangkar (1840–1900), a close associate of Phule and a Mahar ex-army man, complemented Phule's work by trying to make members of the Mahar and Chambhar castes conscious of their oppression and exclusion imposed by Hindu scriptures and society. Influenced by Christian missionary writings on *bhakti*, Valangkar 'reformulated and radicalized' compositions of fourteenth-fifteenth century saints Tukaram and Chokhamela and laid the basis for a radical Dalit identity (Constable 1997: 326). He also made an ingenious use of the idea of Aryan invasion by asserting that the untouchables were almost the only original inhabitants of India, with the Brahmans and upper castes of the South and the West being descendants of 'Australian-Semitic-Non-Aryans' and African negroes, 'Barbary Jews,' and the Turks respectively (Zelliot 2010).

Phule's writings and activism succeeded in establishing a 'historical identity' for Dalits (a term that a radical group of untouchables started using only from around the 1930s) and non-Brahman communities by the late-nineteenth century. A 'distinctive stigmatized existence' united the two communities (Rao 2009: 40). At the same time, Dalit discourse underscored the instability of this collective identity as it confronted efforts of the non-Brahman Marathas to align themselves with Kshatriyas in the pan-Indian schema of *varna*. Nurtured by print journalism, a specific Dalit identity constituted itself between the late-nineteenth and early-twentieth centuries by focusing centrally on the disabilities of caste. It boldly countered upper caste perceptions of untouchability as ritual and transcendental by harping on the contingency and unfairness of the practice. It further launched a socio-political critique of caste-relations and held the religio-ritual stigmatization of Dalits to be the root cause for Dalit illiteracy, poverty and social backwardness (ibid.).

The emergence of this assertive Dalit identity, argues Anupama Rao, would lead to a parting of ways between the Dalits and the non-Brahmans in the twentieth century. The non-Brahman movement persisted, although it got divided into parallel conservative and radical tendencies. The 'conservative' group, composed of wealthy non-Brahmans, looked to the institutional reforms of the colonial government as a way for their advance. After the Montagu–Chelmsford reforms of 1919, which held out the promise of reserved seats for the 'depressed classes' in the legislative councils, this group formed the loyalist Non-Brahman Association. The radical strain represented by the Satyasodhak Samaj was opposed to the Congress, a party dominated by Brahmans in the early stages. However, it eventually merged with Gandhian nationalism by the 1930s (Omvedt 1976).

In the south, particularly in the Madras Presidency, a distinct Dravidian identity was sought to be forged as a counterpoint to Brahmanic dominance. The lead here was taken by members of the Vellala caste. Prior to the movement of the Vellalas, however, the caste of Shanans had gradually transformed themselves—between the 1820s and the 1880s—from being 'unclean toddy-tappers' to 'Kshatriya' Nadars (Hardgrave 1969; Robb 2002: 229). The occasion for this transformation was a controversy over the wearing of breast cloths by the women of this caste in the 1820s. Radical Shanans countered their unclean status by adopting the sacred thread, giving a twist to this symbol of prestige. They participated in the temple entry movement in the 1890s, and began to express their political ambition soon after. This allowed Kamraj Nadar to become the chief minister of Madras and the President of the Indian National Congress in the early twentieth century.

In a situation very similar to that of the Bombay Presidency, the Brahmans in the Madras Presidency monopolized 42 per cent of available government jobs in the late-nineteenth century, while they constituted only 3 per cent of the total population. Proud of their education, particularly their command over English, these Brahmans identified with Sanskrit as a classical language with a glorious past, and scoffed at Tamil, the language of the uneducated masses. This gave a particular twist to the anti-Brahman movement in the south; the Tamil language here became an object of devotion, an element that evoked intense passion and identification. In addition to forging a Tamil-centred, anti-Brahman identity, love for the language paralleled and countered love for the nation that the incipient nationalist struggle was trying to construct (Ramaswamy 1997). We will see the ramifications of this in the next chapter.

In addition to valourizing Tamil, the non-Brahman Tamil elite drew upon missionary and Orientalist theories of the Aryan invasion to argue that the caste system was not indigenous to the south, that it was an imposition by the Brahmans from the north who tried to colonize Tamil–Dravidian culture. The anti-Brahman movement found its political forum in the Justice Party that came into being in 1916 (Irschick 1969). Consciously constituted as a party of non-Brahmans, the Justice Party published a Non-Brahman Manifesto and opposed the Congress and its political programme. The party showed its full loyalty to the colonial administration and vied for privileges offered by government-sponsored reforms. Indeed, it demanded separate representation for non-Brahmans in legislative councils, as had been granted to the Muslims in the Morley–Minto reforms of 1909. Following the allocation of reserved seats to non-Brahmans in the Montagu–Chelmsford reforms in 1919, and particularly its introduction of dual rule with important powers granted to the legislative councils in the provinces (Baker 1976: 1), the Justice Party contested the elections to the Madras Legislative Council, in open opposition to the Congress programme of non-cooperation, and performed well. However, it soon came into clashes with a more militant group of non-Brahmans, who had developed non-Brahmanism as a political theory and ideology, drawing upon the writings, in Telugu and Tamil, of S. Raghavayya Chowdary and E. V. Ramaswamy Naicker respectively (ibid.: 83).

Naicker put great stress on 'Self Respect' in the Dravidian identity he was trying to construct. From 1925, he and his followers started publishing a weekly titled *Kudi Arasu* (People's Government). The circulation of this weekly increased considerably by the end of the decade; it became the main vehicle for propagating the political programme of the 'Self-Respect' movement. The programme was detailed and well-laid out. It urged social and political action to condemn the 'theory of superiority-inferiority' (ibid.: 83), abolishing untouchability and granting of the right of access to temples and wells to all communities; the proscription of holy books that promulgated Brahman mythologies; the channelling of temple funds for secular use; the conduct of marriages and other rituals without the presence of priests; abandoning the use of caste suffixes in personal names; and improving the condition of women (ibid.: 83). This was more radical than the criticism of the Brahman contained in the 1916 Anti-Brahman manifesto of the Justice Party, which rebuffed Brahmans for their 'skills to pass exams'. Although leaders of the Justice Party patronized the 'Self-Respect' movement, Naicker soon got frustrated with the lip-service they paid to the causes of his movement. He broke away from the Justice Party as it started associating itself with the Brahmans from the 1930s. By then, the 'non-Brahman idea which had begun as an appeal to the government' had acquired a life and momentum of its own (ibid.: 84).

Kerala offers an interesting example. Here, the differential effects of land reforms in Malabar—the area under direct Company and Crown rule—and in the princely states of Travancore and Cochin, had affected peasants, agricultural labourers and the caste and class structures differently. The Company's move to push the Indian rulers to grant greater rights to tenants in Travancore and Cochin, zones of cash crop production, produced a class of upwardly mobile peasants. They used caste ties to bring about solidarity among peasants and agricultural labourers; caste and class combined to augment peasant radicalism (Bouton 1985). The lower-caste movements that emerged in these states in the late-nineteenth and early-twentieth centuries were led by Ezhava peasants who had benefitted from the land reforms and commercial opportunities in the princely states. They rallied for a higher status in caste hierarchy and the removal of policies of segregation that denied them access to wells, temples and public roads, and, more significantly, schools and administrative positions.

Interestingly, members of the upper castes in Cochin and Travancore shared this enthusiasm for change to a certain extent—they wanted to get rid of certain 'antiquated cultural practices in view of the new educational and administrative opportunities opened by British rule' (Desai 2001: 44). This perhaps accounts for the introduction of 'reservation' in these states at an early stage, a point we have mentioned earlier. Lower-caste radicalism was boosted by the presence of a large group of plantation workers and labourers in coir factories. By the 1930s, the Ezhavas had started speaking in favour of the Russian model of socialism in their meetings (Jeffrey 1974), an indication of the hold of the Left ideology in the region.

In contrast, British-ruled Malabar did not see the growth of agrarian radicalism till the 1930s. Here, big landowners were Brahmans or hailed from other higher castes, and 'caste relations structured the patrimonial relations of domination and extraction between landlords and tenants' (Desai 2001: 44). The deep caste hierarchy, the daily rituals of subservience demanded by the upper-caste landlords and the 'sheer degradation of lower castes in everyday practices' made collective action on the part of tenants extremely difficult (ibid.). The 'natural basis of respect' for landlords that the caste hierarchy reinforced, seriously impeded the growth of strong peasant-agricultural labourer movement in the area (Moore 1966; Zagoria 1971).

The history of these different movements reveals an important feature analysed by Bandyopadhyay. In his study of the Namasudras of Bengal (1997), Bandyopadhyay argues that caste was neither undifferentiated nor monolithic; members of a caste shared their ritual rank but were clearly differentiated by economic and social status. This differentiation over time created fissures in a caste movement, after the initial impulse of a shared goal or experience that forged a united community lost some of its momentum (Bandyopadhyay 1997: 3–4). Caste movements, therefore, did not originate only from prosperity or deprivation of its members, nor were they 'exclusive expressions of either ambition or protest' (ibid.: 4); they represented a convergence of distinct ideas and aspirations at a particular historical juncture. The convergence was often brought about by the commonality of a low ritual status, which enabled the formation of a collective self. At a different juncture, however, this commonality gave way to a conflict or divergence of interests that made the contingent community pull in different ways. As with the movements in western and southern India, the Namasudras of Bengal came together as a community in the late-nineteenth century by means of a protest movement only to disintegrate and merge with different political trends in the twentieth century.

The validity of Bandyopadhyay's argument becomes evident if one probes the terms in which the radical non-Brahman and Dalit discourse were posed. While both severely interrogated caste-related ritual discrimination and harped on the injustice of the practice, they drew heavily on the *varna* model to forge a community. If, as Bandyopadhyay shows, this contingent community fell apart after a point of time, the strong symbolism of the *varna* also allowed the shaping of newer communities. And it was this complicated process that made caste identity, which was not an 'immutable given' of Indian society in the eighteenth century (Bayly 1995: 11), gain singular salience in the twentieth century. Both non-Brahman and Dalit identities have survived because they have changed, adapted and reconfigured; the significance of such identities in contemporary India does not require elaboration.

The *varna* schema, therefore, has divided and held together the ever-elusive institution of caste. Important works that have focused on specific caste groups in particular regions have repeatedly pointed to the innately changing nature of caste (Conlon 1977; Hardgrave 1969; Jeffrey 1976; Templeman 1996). They have also demonstrated how social boundaries and the continuity of family and kin groups among caste lineages are determined much more by 'economic resources and occupation strategies' than by considerations of purity and pollution (Leonard 1978: 3). Caste has always been about power and privilege, that is, it is political; but the perception of caste as rooted in *varna*, which is taken to be religious and ritual with a basis in Hindu 'scriptures' that got perpetrated during the colonial period continues to govern activities around caste.

Active participation of various groups of Indians have definitely fashioned caste identities; but the several understandings and appropriations of caste have not questioned the terms set down by colonial rule. It is significant that the term Dalit was a direct translation of the colonial categorization of the untouchables as 'depressed' (Zelliot 2010); it shows the impress of colonial categories even if it is true that Dalits have taken over and transformed the meaning of the term considerably. Debates and struggles have ranged around access to education and public employment and a parity of numbers and political representation, exactly in tune with the promises of institutional reforms offered by the colonial state. To this day, appeals to and criticism of the State continue precisely on grounds of whether or not it has successfully implemented the provisions of positive discrimination, or whether it has been partial and indifferent in dealing with backwardness, while different groups scramble over access to the scarce resources of education and employment.

THE MUSLIM MINORITY

'Majority' and 'minority' are states of mind—they are not just about numbers (Chatterjee 1997). To illustrate this perceptive point, Partha Chatterjee indicates how at the time of the inception of Company rule, different sections of Muslim aristocrats, particularly in the United Provinces, felt confident and complacent about their privileges and entitlement, elements associated with the 'majority'. Disdainful of the lack of culture of the employees of the East India Company, the Muslim aristocrats stayed away from them. And yet, within a few decades, important members of these groups had begun reflecting on why the 'Muslims' had fallen behind, why and how their Hindu counterparts had managed to overcome them. Chapter 3 briefly examined the efforts and arguments of Sir Sayyid Ahmad Khan, an English-educated Muslim aristocrat, to spread English education and science among his community as a way to offset their 'backwardness'. Here, we explore why 'backwardness' had become associated with Muslims, the erstwhile rulers, by the second half of the nineteenth century.

W. W. Hunter, a pioneering administrator-ethnographer who launched the Survey of India project in the 1860s, published an influential work, *Indian Musalmans: Are They Bound in Conscience to Rebel Against the Queen?* in 1871. Commissioned by Viceroy Mayo who wanted to assess the loyalty and status of Muslims in British India, this work traced the contours of a homogeneous community of Muslims and set the tone for official discussions of them as 'backward'. The colonial state, in Hunter's opinion, had sadly neglected its responsibility of educating the Muslim subjects, creating thereby a whole class of 'backward' and potentially seditious Muslim peasantry (Sengupta 2011: 2). Secular schooling, he argued, was suited to very few nations, and they did not include either Catholic Ireland or the 'illiterate and fanatical peasantry of Muhammedan Bengal' (Hunter 1871:179). In order to earn the loyalty of Muslims, the colonial state had to provide them greater access to education, in particular religious education. This bonding of religious belonging and imperial order, as we shall see in later chapters, would be taken over by Indians in their projects of nation-building (Sengupta 2011: 3).

In 1888, Viceroy Dufferin referred to the 'Muslims' as 'a nation of fifty millions' supposedly uniform in religious and social customs and sharing 'a remembrance of the days when, enthroned at Delhi, they reigned supreme from the Himalayas to Cape Comorin' (Dufferin to Cross, 11 November 1888, cited in Sarkar [1983] 1995: 20). Dufferin here is speaking only of the Muslim aristocrats who 'remembered the days when they reigned supreme' though evidently not from the Himalayas to Cape Comorin. What strikes us is the supreme confidence with which he refers to the 'Muslims' as a 'nation of fifty millions'. Not only had census operations mapped them numerically with exactitude, Hunter's surveys had also defined them as belonging to a nation with uniform religious and social customs. Is this very different from the appeal a beleaguered Jinnah would make in the 1940s, to 'all Muslims' who belonged to a single 'nation'?

The census operations of 1872 and 1881, in fact, revealed a wide divergence both in the composition and in the regional distribution of Muslims. In the United Provinces, the Muslims constituted a minority, amounting to just a little over 13 per cent of the population. But a large section of Muslims belonged to the aristocracy. In Punjab, on the other hand, Muslims accounted for more than 51 per cent of the population, although they did not command the privilege of the United Provinces' aristocrats. Surprisingly for the Bengali middle-class, the Census of 1872 showed that Muslims represented almost half of the population, nearly 49 per cent, with a very small *ashraf* (elite) group and a vast community of *ajlaf* (poor peasants and agricultural labourers) in eastern Bengal (Bandyopadhyay 2004: 262–64). In addition, these people spoke the regional language, Bengali, as distinct from the aristocrats of the United Provinces who spoke Urdu and Persian. There were significant Muslim populations in different parts of India, particularly in the several princely states, who similarly differed in terms of class, economic wealth and social prestige. There were also sectarian differences, such as that between the Shias and Sunnis, and of language and culture. Together, this diverse 'Muslim' community composed 19.7 per cent of the total population in 1881.

What had then given Hunter and Dufferin the confidence to speak of Muslims in India—an extremely heterogeneous community—as a 'nation' with shared religious and social customs and a common memory? Was it the fear and anger generated by the experience of the Revolt? Was it the imperial drive to know India in order to make her governable, the belief in superior 'western' modes of knowing based on 'rational' and 'scientific' thought, the need to find allies, or a combination of all these? What is significant for us is the impact of this classification on Muslims and on colonial policies.

We have noted in Chapter 3 that the idea of 'decline' had become prominent in Islam in different countries in the first half of the nineteenth century; we also discussed the diverse ways in which different trends tried to counter this 'decline'. Indeed, it was only after 1857 that Sayyid Ahmad got 'caught up in defining his own response to the reality of British rule' (Lelyveld 1978: 73), and became active in seeking accommodation with this rule in northern India (ibid.: 104). This is because it was clear after 1857 that the only way to participate in political decisions about the allocation and control of social resources was to make some accommodation with the ruling power. His efforts in the 1860s—schools in Moradabad and Ghazipur, translations of English scientific works into Urdu by the Scientific Society, local school committees, the *Aligarh Institute Gazette* and the petition for a vernacular university—all demonstrated his will to win a place for Indians within the British political system by drawing on British ideas and techniques, as well as the mission paradigm of religious education.

Sayyid Ahmad's efforts at gathering a following, moreover, were limited to men of his own milieu—government servants and legal practitioners—and in his speeches he metaphorically extended his idea of *qaum* and *biradari*, the birth-defined categories of Mughal society, to regional and linguistic designations, such as Hindustanis and Bengalis, to include both Hindus and Muslims (ibid.:74). His attempts to reform Islam along lines of science and reason, we have seen, incensed a particular group of Muslim aristocrats who were uneasy about the 'Europeanization' of Muslim society.

A trip to England at the end of 1869 had a great impact on Sayyid Ahmad. Overwhelmed by the accomplishments of British technology, the general level of literacy and the self-confident sense of achievement that he encountered, and conscious of the humiliation of Islam at the hands of Christian

Europe, he started believing that there was a correlation between worldly success and cultural superiority (Lelyveld 1978: 104–09). The older generation of Muslims in India were, in his view, better educated and hence, able to occupy positions of power. Now, the equivalent education was confined to Englishmen in England. That education had to spread in India, but in a way as to bring about a confluence of religion and education. Sayyid Ahmad incorporated this idea in his programme of public action upon his return to India, particularly in the programme of the Muhammadan Anglo–Oriental College. Consequently, Sayyid Ahmad's objective behind importing western education to upper-class Muslims has come to be viewed as an effort to foster among aristocratic Muslims a sense of corporate unity as Muslims (Sarkar [1983] 1995: 77).

Sayyid Ahmad's notion fitted in brilliantly with colonial policy, articulated in Hunter's *Indian Mussalmans*, which wanted to train 'a rising generation of Muhammedans' with 'the sober and genial knowledge of the West' who would, at the same time, have sufficient acquaintance with their own religious code so as to command the respect of their community (ibid.: 77). It is not surprising, therefore, that Sayyid Ahmad's endeavour to spread English education among Muslim aristocrats found adequate support from the British. The Aligarh College got a personal donation of Rs 10,000 from Viceroy Lord Northbrooke and Sayyid Ahmad became a champion and an advocate of his community although his unorthodox ideas about Islam had initially aroused consternation (Robinson [1974] 2007: 131).

Arguably, Sayyid Ahmad did want to construct an idea of Muslim solidarity and encourage the mentality of a *qaum* (nation, community) among the students of Aligarh. His Mohammedan Educational Conference (Congress till 1890), which met annually from 1886, was another means of forging Muslim solidarity. The Mohammedan Educational Conference, it is not difficult to see, was a direct rival of the Indian National Congress, which started convening annually from 1885. What is important is the success and significance conferred on these ventures by colonial patronage.

A different and a rival model of generating unity in Islam was promoted by Muhammad Qasim Nanautawi (1833–77) and Rashid Ahmad Gangohi (1829–1905) in the second half of the nineteenth century. Veterans of the Revolt, Muhammad Qasim and Rashid Ahmad attempted to train students in Islamic learning, but along the lines of western education, leading to the emergence of a 'Protestant Islam' (Robb 2002: 232). The seminary they set up at Deoband took its curriculum from an earlier one in the *farangi mahal* (foreign quarters) of Lucknow (Robinson [1974] 2007). This seminary did not function as a part of a mosque where learning was an adjunct to the students' religious observances.

The students of Deoband attended a formal residential college with a permanent staff, run by public funding and not by endowment. Their learning was continually assessed on the basis of examinations. Students got lessons in the *shari'a* and in *tariqah* (path of religious experience) from the *ulema*. Although it was modelled entirely on western educational institutions, the Deoband Seminary actually played a significant role in developing a unified and orthodox Islam in India. Its students were relatively poor, belonging to families that could not afford to send them to English schools. The seminary produced *madrassa* teachers and became prominent at a later stage, for the number of *fatwas* it issued. The Deoband group also retained a 'muted anti-British temper' and provided 'fairly consistent support to Congress nationalism' in the twentieth century (Sarkar [1983] 1995: 78). It was critical, both of Sayyid Ahmad's theological innovations and of his loyalism.

The working out of intricate political conversation in the educational arena found another articulation in Bengal, where the small group of *ashraf* Muslims stressed the need for separate funding and developing schools to preserve the distinctiveness of their religious and linguistic community. This was necessary, they argued from the late-nineteenth century, since the village level and Anglo-vernacular schools in Bengal were permeated by caste and religious bias of the Bengali Hindu *bhadralok* (a 'cultured' community of upper and middle caste and classes); and educational material, such as primers produced by Vidyasagar and other Hindu educators, used a Sanskritized Bengali that was different from the language spoken by the Muslims of Bengal.

The recommendations made by Muslim leaders of Bengal to transform Muslim elementary schools—the Koran schools (*madrassas*) and *makhtabs*—sought to standardize religious education along the lines of mission schools in terms of pedagogic methods and goals. They had very little in common with the earlier forms of Islamic education. On the whole, all efforts at generating and preserving religious sensibility through formal education served to homogenize sectarian schooling in the model of mission schools (Sengupta 2011: 5). The distinct systems of education that sought to foster and retain the religious and cultural identity of different groups did not, however, correspond to a demand for separate nations. Rather, the efforts reflected a 'pragmatic and hopeful effort by educators and reformers' to imagine the future of India as 'a pluralistic and integrated society' (ibid.: 6).

At the same time, it is important to place these efforts against the backdrop of the census construction of the Muslims as a 'minority' and of the Hindus as a majority, as well as reform and 'revival' within Hinduism and Sikhism. The strident efforts of the Arya Samaj in Punjab and north-western India, and the Singh Sabha movement in Punjab, as we have seen in Chapter 3, had brought the division between the 'communities' into sharp relief (Oberoi 1997). Added to it was the 'threat' faced by Muslim aristocrats of United Provinces—the landlords and traditional service families—from Hindu traders, merchants and moneylenders who were buying up land, capturing municipalities and obtaining jobs at their expense. Rivalry and 'separatism' therefore, emerged not from 'backwardness' but from this sense of threat. Indeed, the success of Arya Samaj in Punjab has been linked to the 'Muslim challenge' faced in business and professions by Khatri, Arora and Badia groups (Jones 1968).

In a way similar to the development of lower-caste movements, a section of Muslim aristocrats came to rely on the 'privileges' being offered by the colonial state, particularly after the special provision for Muslims in the Morley–Minto reforms, adding further complexity to the nationalist struggle. Sayyid Ahmad's efforts, it is worth mentioning, had limited success. Apart from the rival Deoband group and the animosity of the *ulema*, there was a section of Muslim elite that got attracted to the Congress—Badaruddin Tyabji of Bombay became the President of the Indian National Congress in 1887 (Bandyopadhyay 2004: 272). There was restlessness among the younger generation of Aligarh after Sayyid Ahmad's death. Significantly, a section of them patched up earlier tensions with the *ulema* and moved closer to their ideology in the early-twentieth century. We will discuss this in Chapter 6.

The emergence of a community identity was not limited only to the elite and their scramble over jobs and political favours, although they were not unconnected. Chapter 3 briefly discussed various movements for reform and purification among the poorer Muslim groups, which sometimes resulted in agrarian radicalism, as in eastern Bengal, or in attempts to return to a pure Islam, as in Punjab. The movement for reforms was complemented by activities of *anjumans* (local associations) and itinerant religious preachers and religious discussions in local gatherings, as we will see in Chapter 6.

Adverse socio-economic conditions faced by different groups of subordinate peoples inflected the reform ventures with particular significance at particular times. The 'Julahas'—Muslim weavers of the Benares region—came to figure prominently in colonial sociology by the mid-nineteenth century for their active involvement in sectarian strife. The stereotypical 'bigoted' Muslim of colonial historiography, the Julahas were mentioned from 1837 on as taking prominent part in Hindu–Muslim conflicts during festivals like Ramanaumi and Muharram in eastern Uttar Pradesh (United Provinces) and western Bihar, and their propensity to violence was directly linked to the spread of the 'tenets of Syed Uhmud' among them (Thomason 1837, cited in Pandey 1992: 70).

Apart from the fact that such reporting was extremely one-sided, these reports completely ignored the vulnerability of the weavers to the play of market forces and their dependence on moneylenders and middlemen, factors that were aggravated by the 'unpredictable shifts' in the general social, economic and political condition of the people of northern India (Pandey 1992: 71). The Julahas, moreover, comprised the largest group among the numerically small Muslim community of that region and 'they were concentrated in towns where the possibilities of serious and violent conflict was always greater' (ibid.: 70). Moreover, as Chris Bayly has shown, it was not just the weavers but also the 'mercantile newcomers' to the towns with little connection with the earlier Muslims rulers, who refused 'to acquiesce in a continued ceremonial inferiority' and took an active part in the conflict in 1837 (Bayly [1983] 1992: 337).

Several works have laid bare the severe economic and social dislocation occasioned in Bihar and Uttar Pradesh and in other regions with the onset of colonialism (Amin 1984; Bayly [1983] 1992; Metcalf 1979; Siddiqui 1973; Whitcombe 1971; for instance). Weavers and spinners in particular, faced violent fluctuations in the conditions of their trade in the immediate pre-colonial and colonial period. The quality of the cloth industry was directly affected by competition from mill-made goods, and the manufacture of coarser varieties of cloth also became subject to powerful new pressures (Pandey 1992: 72). It is not surprising therefore, that this vulnerable group became receptive to the ideas that sought to forge religious identities for the community. This, together with similar efforts underway among the Hindus, resulted in the outbreak of 'communal' riots in the 1880s, particularly in Punjab and in the eastern United Provinces and Bihar. By then, activities of the Arya Samaj and other organizations had made 'cow protection' a major issue in the north-west and Hindi belt.

Consequently, clashes occurred over issues apparently far removed from economic grievances (Sarkar [1983] 1995: 60). The one that caused the largest number of riots in the 1880s and 1890s was that of cow-slaughter; the rapid emergence of cow protection societies all over northern and western India had a direct bearing on this. In addition, Tilak's reorganization of the Ganapati festival on a community (*sarvajanik*) basis in Maharashtra and the festival's direct appeal to Hindus to boycott 'Muslim' ceremonies, such as Muharram, heightened 'communal' tensions. The emerging industrial labour force of the cities always remained volatile for reasons we will discuss in Chapter 8. The first riots in the industrial suburbs of Calcutta occurred during the Bakr-id festival of 1891, another indication of the swift dissemination of ideas of 'religious' community among different sections of society.

Unfortunately, these ambiguous and intricate processes of community formation complemented dominant colonial representations of the Indian past—of Indian history as a series of confrontations between Hindus and Muslims, and as a past filled with sectarian strife—in which the religious bigotry of the peoples was a distinctive feature (Pandey 1992: 24). This history, which became important from the end of the nineteenth century, set the pattern for the understanding of Indian history and society. And the rivalry and competition among different groups which largely followed the lines set down by colonial policies, reinforced the notion of sectarian strife. 'Communalism', thus, came to acquire a special connotation in South Asia, standing for a subcontinental version of nationalism in colonial historiography and later as an obdurate alternative to 'nationalism' in nationalist historiography (ibid.:1).

According to Sandria Freitag, communalism—a politicized community identity often marked by a 'consciously-shared' religious heritage that becomes the dominant form of identity—expressed itself through coherent, symbolic behaviour in public arenas, particularly in northern India from the late-nineteenth century (Freitag 1990: 6–7). It was linked directly to the rapid urbanization of the United Provinces over the course of the nineteenth century, particularly between 1850 and 1880, the emergence of distinct urban styles and increasing urban specialization, as well as a rapid rise in urban property values and widespread refurbishing of towns and zamindari palaces (ibid.:100–02). Such transformations produced new groupings and a new balance of power between old and new elites, who also had distinct followings among the urban poor. While members of the old order looked for a compromise till the middle of the century, the newcomers to the city, Hindu merchants and Brahmans in towns such as Bareilly, pushed for expanded recognition. By the late-nineteenth century, the new elite of the 'New City', the Hindu merchants and Indo–Persian service gentry, had outdone their earlier counterparts who were now confined to the 'Old Town'—a physical layout that itself reflected the changing configuration of power in the city (ibid.: 108–11). In the case of 'Hindus', competing claims to leadership were best expressed by means of sponsorship of additional religious festivals, particularly Ramanaumi processions; this drew support from the lower classes. In a similar manner, among the heterogeneous Muslims, *ashraf* and *ajlaf* activities came to overlap over issues of 'religion' in the last three decades of the nineteenth century (ibid.: 112–17). Together, they made 'riots' a regular feature of social life.

The picture is not so tidy or clear-cut. As indicated earlier, attempts to foster distinct religious education did not necessarily mean a demand for clear separation; they indicated attempts to accept and accommodate religious differences. If we follow Ayesha Jalal, the same is true of Muslim poets of Punjab and north-west India of the late-nineteenth and early-twentieth century (Jalal 2000). Representatives of Muslim individuality and a self not predetermined by community, these poets worked towards an Indian politics that would make room for religious differences even while they held on to their religious sensibility. As such, it is incorrect to think of a uniform 'Muslim' approach to politics that can be understood through the fixed lens of 'communalism' (ibid.). Neither the lower castes and Dalits nor the Muslims, nor, for that matter, the 'Hindus' ever managed to form a homogeneous block. They remained divided by economic deprivation and socio-political discrimination and the consequent conflict of interests; but 'caste' and 'religion' offered crucial elements for the construction of identity, perpetrating thereby the notion of Victoria's administrators that caste and religion were indeed the keys to the understanding of Indian society.

Issues of Economy

In the end, let us once again turn to the question of the effect of colonization on Indian economy. Chapters 2 and 3 discussed the impact of the three different revenue settlements and briefly examined the wide-ranging consequences of the colonial urge to maximize revenue and forcibly extend cultivation, reclaim 'waste' and grazing lands, and demarcate forests and plains on the economy and lives of the people, including the regular recurrence of famines in nineteenth century India. Here, we will try and offer a situated account that will relate the fortunes of industries and artisanal production to the commercialization of agriculture that entailed production of cash crops and plantations. We will also take a quick look at the changes that commercialization brought in the lives of plantation workers, a vast majority of whom were 'tribals'.

There is a general agreement among scholars that India's economic contact with industrializing Europe (Britain) had both constructive and destructive effects; opinions vary, however, on whether it was more destructive than constructive. The dominant view has tended to emphasize the destructive impact on Indian industries, particularly cotton-textile (Bagchi 1972, 1976, 2010). It has argued that both the history of capitalism and its effect on industrializing Europe differ totally from that of its colonies and semi-colonies in the third world in relation to 'industrial employment, investment in productive assets, and distribution of income' (Bagchi 1976: 124). The result is deindustrialization in the colonies, where there is a move of labour out of manufacture and into agriculture, measured either in terms of actual numbers or in terms of the total share of employment. Advocates of the deindustrialization thesis have highlighted the injurious effect of British factory-made goods on Indian cotton textiles industry in the nineteenth century and a decline in the number of people employed in industries between 1891 and 1931, to conclude that one can trace a direct link between England's industrialization and India's deindustrialization. Given the fact that 'handloom weaving and hand-spinning constituted the largest traditional industry and the numbers involved in it were enormous', the destructive effects on this sector had a 'generally depressive effect on the rest of the economy' (ibid.: 137).

Amiya Kumar Bagchi consulted and compared the data collected by Buchanan Hamilton in the early-nineteenth century with the records of gazetteers and census on the late-nineteenth and early-twentieth century to show that with the influx of British factory products there was a definite decline both in the number of people engaged in secondary industries, as well as in the condition of weavers and producers of cotton and silk goods in Gangetic Bihar (ibid.: 139–41). As cheap British yarn and cloth invaded the Indian market, weavers were forced to change over to the manufacture of very coarse varieties of cloth to cater to the needs of the poor. The proportion of the population engaged in industry declined from 18.6 in 1809–13 to 8.5 in 1901 (Bagchi 2010: xli). He also affirmed that given the absence of modern industries except in regions around Calcutta and Bombay, the picture of central Bihar applied to all of India.

A strong Indian business community survived only in the western region on account of the fact that the Peshwa's territories came under Company rule only in 1818, after the East India Company had lost its monopoly of trade (ibid.: xliv). British occupation of a province or region almost always brought about a decline in the number of people engaged in industries—not only were restrictions on the entry of foreign goods removed, but also demand for products of the secondary industry declined in the region on account of depression caused by colonial exploitation (ibid.: xliii). Moreover, this decline affected the income of women of all classes very badly since spinning was the most important source of earning for many women, particularly the ones who did not and could not work outside their homes (ibid.: xliii).

A process of deindustrialization, therefore, was a common feature of most of India over the nineteenth century and this process was not particular to India but pertained to most Asian countries. This was not only because of the 'backwash' effect of industrialization of developed countries (Myrdal 1968), but more on account of the intimate connection between the industrialized countries of Europe, particularly Britain, and their colonies and semi-colonies in Asia (Bagchi 1976: 146–50). A lot of the adjustments to technical changes in European countries took place overseas, and these processes together with other market and non-market forces led to the transfer of investible surplus from the third world countries to Europe, bringing about a marked asymmetry between the growth in capitalist countries and the process of change in underdeveloped countries (ibid.: 153–54).

There is no doubt that improved British productivity reduced the price of textiles and made India's cottage-based manufacture uneconomic (Roy 2002). In addition, a revolution in transportation and a decline in sea-freight rates fostered international trade and specialization making it possible for Britain to win over India's exports, and subsequently, the domestic market (Clingingsmith and Williamson 2004: 1). This view, as we will see in the following chapter, was the principal armoury in Indian nationalists' economic critique of colonial rule.

The picture, several scholars have pointed out, is much more complex and conflicting (Chandavarkar 1985; Ludden 1999). As we have mentioned earlier, in relation to the Julahas, India had been exposed to the international market and its fluctuations for a long time, even before the beginning of British colonization. Industrial Revolution and British imperialism undoubtedly accelerated the scale of such exposure and induced serious structural changes, but there were several other variables that tempered British initiative, particularly because India's conditions were very different from that of Britain from the beginning.

The important revisionist view offered by Tirthankar Roy has stressed that the histories of Britain and her colonies are similar in certain core respects and that changes and growth in long-distance trade, particularly between the opening of the Suez Canal (1869) and the Great Depression (1929), had a positive effect on Indian artisan production (Roy 1999, 2002). Focusing on five Indian industries that employed intensive artisan labour—handloom weaving, gold thread (*jari*), leather, brassware and carpets—Roy has argued that artisanal products responded and adapted to long-distance trade and increase in demand in distinct ways, including through increased productivity. In his view, only segments of cotton textiles were adversely affected by competition from British factories; hand-woven textiles faced no such competition, nor did the other crafts he examines. Indeed, they adapted successfully and aided export. The increase in demand brought about major institutional changes as well as changes in product composition, but there was a definite rise in productivity. Besides, many of the workers who moved from industry into agriculture were only part-time workers; and the fall in employment in the textile industry was compensated for by increased employment in indigo, opium and saltpetre. The fact that increased productivity did not generate prosperity or 'development' in South Asia, has to do more with the 'quality of the South Asian soil, where industrialization was born but did not attain maturity' rather than the regressive effect of trade, markets and colonialism (Roy 1999: 10).

It is interesting that Roy's emphasis on examining the different segments of cotton textiles separately to understand the effect of British competition had been articulated by Morris D. Morris decades before (1963, 1983). Morris had also questioned the notion of 'de-industrialization' by pointing to the early introduction and the brisk pace of extension of steam-powered technology within specific sectors of South Asia. In a long chapter in *The Cambridge Economic History of India* (vol. 2), Morris tracked the growth of jute manufacturing, cotton textile, iron and steel, handicrafts and small-scale industries and argued that the Indian economy in the nineteenth and twentieth centuries was largely a private-enterprise economy. Hence, neither the policy of the British government nor Indian values and social structure could be held responsible for 'diminished entrepreneurial drives' (Morris 1983: 54).

With regard to the effect of the Industrial Revolution on Indian cotton textiles in particular, Morris has stated that since technology did not develop simultaneously in the cotton spinning and weaving sectors in Britain, only Indian hand spinners felt British price competition prior to 1830–35. There was no competition for Indian handloom weavers since Britain still followed handloom manufacture. Indian weavers' suffering was the result, more of weather instability and crop failure, as well as decline in agricultural incomes and local demand for cloth, rather than British competition (ibid.: 668–69).

India would have faced strong competition in the period between 1835 and 1870, when Britain changed over to power loom and factory production, but, 'oddly' Indian weavers' condition did not receive public attention during these years. This was possibly because a dramatic decline in cloth prices increased the demand for cloth and 'cushioned' Indian producers from the full impact of British factory-made goods (ibid.: 669). And finally, Indian factory textile industry began its growth in the early 1870s. In fact, local hand spinners faced real competition from Indian mills that produced coarse-count yarns, since the cost structure and cheap labour had made it impossible for the British to penetrate the cheap-yarn market. Therefore, it was native rather than foreign industrial competition, 'which ultimately gave the death blow to the hand-spinning sector' although the effect was a delayed one (ibid.: 669).

This thesis about growth in Indian industries from the late-nineteenth century was given greater flourish in other works. They emphasized that around 1914 India boasted 'the world's largest jute-manufacturing industry' and possessed the fourth and fifth cotton-textile industry (Tomlinson 1979: 31), without making any distinction between widely divergent societies that were being compared.

In an essay that takes into account the different positions on Britain's economic impact on India, Harvard economists Clingingsmith and Williamson agree that there was long-term deindustrialization in India. They, however, do not ascribe it only to the 'globalization price-shocks caused by the increase in European productivity manufacturing (and the induced demand for industrial intermediaries such as cotton and indigo)' but also to 'the negative productivity shocks to Indian agriculture' occasioned by the earlier Mughal decline (2004: 11). They take 1750–1860 to be the period of India's deindustrialization, and divide it into two phases.

Deindustrialization in the first phase, between 1750 and 1810, was an 'indirect result of the dissolution of the Mughal empire' (ibid.: 24). Revenue farming expanded with the decline of the central authority, which in turn increased the revenue burden on peasants. Warfare and the decline of inter-regional trade decreased agricultural productivity and increased the prices of food grains. This pushed up the wages of the workers and adversely affected India's textile manufacturers by compromising their competitiveness with Britain at a time when England was still using the cottage system of production. In addition, 'the intersectoral terms of trade moved against textiles' and encouraged a shift to agricultural commodity production (ibid.: 24).

In the second phase, 1810–60, the changeover to the factory system in England pushed down the price of textiles and further reinforced the trend for agricultural commodity production in India. Falling prices of agricultural products between 1821 and 1854 intensified deindustrialization. Foreign and domestic causes, therefore, rather than competing, worked together and buttressed each other although their impact was felt differently in distinct periods. By the 1860s, deindustrialization was over and India was on the path of 'slow re-industrialization' (ibid.: 25). This view, in a way, returned to the one advanced by Daniel Thorner years ago: that deindustrialization occurred in India prior to 1881; and on a very modest scale between 1881 and 1901, after which it was over (Thorner 1962). Amiya Bagchi's figures refer primarily to the decline in spinning, a large part of which was done by women at home using very simple technology, and cannot be taken to account for large-scale deindustrialization. There is evidence though to suggest that decline in the production of yarn used for handloom happened all over India and not just in Gangetic Bihar and that decline in spinning was followed by decline in weaving and the decline in the two was complete by 1870 (Clingingsmith and Williamson 2004: 14).

Bagchi refutes the view that deindustrialization was over by the end of the nineteenth century. Employment in large-scale production units for jute and cotton and mining that developed from the 1850s did little to compensate the slow growth in cottage and small-scale units, even in the late colonial period (Bagchi 2010: xliii).

Whether or not we accept that deindustrialization was over by the late-nineteenth century, it is important to pay attention to the point made by Clingingsmith and Williamson—deindustrialization is intimately connected with the commercialization of agriculture. Important early works have shown that the commercialization of agriculture, especially in the Bengal region after the famine of 1770, had been brought about by the requirements of international trade (Chaudhuri 1964).

The introduction of opium cultivation on a system tightly controlled by European planters had followed the need of balancing trade with China (Chapter 3). The importance of opium in maintaining a healthy balance of trade for Britain eventually led to massive migration of opium growers as indentured labourers from India (particularly Bihar) to other British colonies from the 1830s after the abolition of slavery in most parts of the British empire. Indigo, grown in India on a large scale since the sixteenth century, began to be produced as a commercial crop in plantations from 1777 in the Bengal Presidency, with the greatest concentration in the Champaran region of current Bihar. There was great demand for Indian indigo in Britain. It was used to dye military uniforms and also used as a dye in textiles in general. European planters had almost total control over indigo growers; from 1837, when they were allowed to own land, the planters became even more exploitative.

Chapter 3 examined how, over the course of the nineteenth century, India changed from being an exporter of finished products to a major supplier of raw material for British factories, and a captive market for goods manufactured in England, particularly cotton textiles. The most important raw material it supplied was cotton for the mills in Lancashire, particularly after the American Civil War in 1861 cut-off supplies from southern USA. Evidently, cotton was not the only crop grown commercially. There were several others: tea, coffee, opium, sugar, raw silk, wheat, jute, oilseeds and indigo.

In Review: 'Junglee' Coolies and Civilized Assamese

The growth of tea plantations in Assam and Darjeeling accounted for the emergence of a significant immigrant, indentured labour population. Tea plantations transformed the landscape in Assam, allowing the Company state an opportunity to bring a jungle-laden region under profitable cultivation (Sharma 2011). From the mid-nineteenth century, almost from the time of their inception, the tea gardens of Assam relied on migrant labourers contracted through labour contractors and sardars (Verma 2009: 307). The 'opium addict' Assamese people were stated to be indolent, and their laziness justified the hiring of indentured labourers by planters. The coolies from the tribal regions of Chotanagpur and Central Provinces, called junglees (literally people of the jungle but used to designate wild people or savages), assumed a particular importance and preference among the employers of the Assam tea gardens. They were thought to be hardworking and hardy enough to withstand the 'wet and malarious' climate of the province. They commanded a 'high price' in the labour market and constituted a substantial portion of the labour force in Assam (ibid.)

Work in the plantation entailed long hours of labour intensive work; the living conditions were also far from satisfactory. Initially, the planters rewarded the coolies for extra work or a job well-done by offering them alcohol, a bottle of rum or brandy. Alcohol was seen as a stimulant to work in harsh and adverse conditions. From the 1880s, however, after Assam became a separate province (1874), and the colonial state imposed new excise duties, 'drunkenness' among the coolies became a major cause for concern and complaint by the planters (Verma 2009).

We have briefly indicated the turmoil the immigrant labourers went through in Assam in Chapter 2. It is important to relate their change over to indentured labourers from 'forest dwellers' or 'hills people' to the revenue and forest policies of the colonial state. The last chapter has indicated that a large number of Santals had to flee to the tea gardens of Darjeeling and then overseas to evade state repression after the Santal hool of 1855–56. David Baker's work on the Central Provinces documents the steady decline of different groups of 'tribals' between 1861–1920, i.e., from the time of the formation of Central Provinces, on account of the measures adopted by the colonial state (Baker 1991). The state sought to regulate or stop shifting and slash-and-burn cultivation practised by different groups of tribal peoples and tried to encourage them to change over from subsistence cultivation to a capitalist system of landownership and trade. It meted out severe punishment to obstinate and unruly, wild and drunken savages, without enquiring into the reasons for their resistance. In addition, protective forest policies and game protection in jungle clearings, including the prohibition of the use of bow and arrow, reduced the tribal groups to utter poverty and destitution. Their move in large numbers to the tea gardens and other factories was consequent upon their steady decline under colonial administration.

The recent work of Jayeeta Sharma has underscored the significance of the presence of large numbers of 'junglees in Assam' in the construction of an 'imagined Indo–Aryan community' by the Assamese elite. The indentured labourers of the nineteenth century were joined by several others in the twentieth century, who came voluntarily to look for livelihood. Together, they pushed up the immigrant population of Assam to over a million. The racialized construction of the tea garden labourer as 'primitive', argues Sharma, enabled the Assamese gentry to claim modernity for themselves and a modern political space for their imagined homeland in the nation that was being constructed, a story we take up in the following chapters.

Together, it is argued, all these crops 'commodified' agriculture. The debate, of course, is whether this had any beneficial effects for Indian peasants. A clear answer is difficult to offer, since commercialization, like industrialization, entailed several variables. Moreover, not all regions were commercialized in the same way and the effect was very diverse.

The cotton-growing regions of western India—Gujarat and Berar—prospered on account of commercialization, affirms Tirthankar Roy (Roy 2002). The opening of the Suez Canal in 1869 allowed for easier export of cotton and wheat from central India to the European markets. Labour itself, argues Roy, became more mobile with improvements in transportation and increased mobility offered to cultivators—share-croppers and agricultural labourers—that gave them more options and greater manoeuvring power. At the same time, the slow devaluation of the Indian silver rupee against the gold-based European currencies made raw materials cheaper for Europeans; it did not necessarily help Indian growers. If the easy availability of labour benefited the producers somewhat, it also meant an additional burden on agriculture.

The intense and increased burden on agriculture, in turn, led to depeasantization in large parts of India over the course of the nineteenth century. Commercialization of agriculture forced petty farmers and share-croppers to become landless labourers. The trend became acute after the Great Depression of 1929, particularly in central and western Bengal and the Malabar region of Kerala where share-cropping was predominant (Chaudhuri 1975; Dhanagare 1983; Menon 1994). And, even if peasants in Bengal were not evicted outright as they were in Malabar, they had to cultivate under worse conditions of inferior rights and superior rents (Chatterjee 1984). Consequently, India's increasing export surplus in raw materials and cash crops did not bring benefits for India; it only helped to cover the rising array of home charges and aided the 'drain of wealth' from India to England.

Scholars who have explored the effects of the spread of capitalism in 'traditional' societies by means of the 'capitalization' of world agriculture—Immanuel Wallerstein, Michel Beaud and Irfan Habib for instance—have paid serious attention to commercialization of agriculture and deindustrialization. They agree that commercialization or 'capitalization' occasioned dramatic changes in the social structure of traditional societies, particularly in Asia, and often led to the ruin of existing industries, the most important being the cotton textile industry in India (Wallerstein 1979: 57). The economic aspect of colonization, writes Beaud, became stronger and more intense after India became a Crown colony. There were increasing purchases of cash crops such as indigo, jute and cotton and a simultaneous flooding of the Indian market with English cotton fabrics. Together, they ruined local artisans (1983: 101). This same emphasis was extended by Gadgil and Guha who argued that commercialization occasioned sharp disjuncture in 'traditional' India (Gadgil and Guha 1993).

Sanjay Subrahmanyam, Christopher Bayly, K. N. Chaudhuri and David Ludden have tried to add greater complexity to the picture by pointing out that trade and commerce had been important in India for centuries prior to British rule and that commercialization in India had expanded rapidly after 1500. It is erroneous therefore to imagine that British capital invaded an India where commerce played a marginal role (Bayly [1983] 1992; Chaudhuri 1978, 1985; Ludden 1999; Subrahmanyam 1997). Rather, British imperialism emerged within and fed on the wider circulation of commodities in commercialized regions, and then acquired enough power to control commercialization to serve its own interests.

Our discussion in the earlier chapters demonstrates the validity of this argument. India had a dynamic network of trade and commerce, and the change of loyalty of important Indian merchants and bankers from the Mughal emperor and local rulers to the East India Company was an important element in the Company's success. At the same time, it is equally true that British imperial needs changed the pace of commercialization and engendered significant changes in commodity production, which seriously affected India's domestic economy.

As in the case of deindustrialization, more recent work on the commercialization of agriculture has tried to introduce nuance and intricacy to the debate. Peter Robb, for instance, has argued that economic changes induced by British rule did not comprise 'a one-way traffic to a single destination' (1992: 97). Focusing on nineteenth-century Bihar, an important region for the production of commercial crops, Robb has shown that several factors muted the process of commercialization, and that subsistent peasants did not automatically turn into capitalist farmers or landless agricultural labourers as a result of commercialization.

The nineteenth century did not occasion a major break in cultivation and trade in crops, be they food grains or cash crops. Robb in fact makes use of Rajat Datta's work (1986), which shows that there was vigorous local trade marked by the import and export of rice, barley and other grains in early nineteenth-century Bihar, to argue against Benoy Chaudhuri's premise that agricultural commerce during the post-famine recession in the Bengal region was related entirely to international demand (Robb 1992: 101). At the same time, Robb cautions us against Datta's assumption that the existence of local trade implied a well-integrated monetized economy at all levels of society. The rental and produce distribution system in the villages were 'highly interventionist' and this severely circumscribed 'peasant choices' of cropping and work (ibid.: 103).

The 'forced' cultivation of cash crops in the nineteenth century, particularly of opium and indigo planters, that had drawn the attention of the Bengali intelligentsia (Chapter 3), affected the peasants very differently. This is not only because different crops required different degrees of care and were grown on different kinds of land. It is also because their demand and price varied widely as did the percentage of profit reaped by the planters. Even in the cultivation of opium, which exhausted the 'soil and the cultivator' and 'deepened the subjection of the cultivators', the degree of subjection was neither absolute nor common to the same group of cultivators. In the latter part of the nineteenth century, many opium growers shifted to the cultivation of indigo, potato or tobacco, either on their own initiative or on that of local magnates (ibid.: 105–06). It was not subjection to planters but rather to local hierarchies of control, the presence of intermediaries, the intricacies of land use and agriculture and the differentiation in society, which made it impossible for a peasant to break out of his subordination impeding thereby 'commercialization from the inside' (ibid.: 108–09). From a different angle, Manali Desai's analysis of agrarian relations in Kerala, as discussed earlier, comes to a similar conclusion.

Robb, it appears, agrees with the view advanced in a different way by Christopher Bayly and Tirthankar Roy, that the combined forces of indigenous culture and imperialist exploitation prevented the replication of western capitalism in India. Other scholars make the point differently. For them, commercialization was a hybrid process, which combined local and imperial energies. It did transform Indian society in important ways and occasioned violence, conflict and radical socio-cultural and economic changes, but it did not amount to a drastic historical disjuncture, wrecking 'traditional' Indian society and forcibly producing a 'modern' one (Bayly [1983] 1992; Chaudhuri 1964, 1985; Roy 1999; Subrahmanyam 1997). Finally, in tune with the argument that modernity was not one, scholars contend that historically capitalism inhabits different spaces where the force of local conditions and peoples generates capitalisms that are diverse temporally, spatially and culturally (Ludden 2004). Hence, there are differing concepts both of capitalism and of globalization (Bose 1990).

What is perhaps more important for us to ponder are the assumptions on which many of the arguments are based. The crucial one, of course, is the inevitability of the spread of capitalism all over the world and the consequent acceptance of industrialization as a technologically determined process beyond the realm of social choice—an idea prevalent even in relatively nuanced accounts of industrialization in India (Ray 1979, for instance). In a finely textured essay written over a quarter century ago, Chandavarkar underscored how models of industrialization and social change, whether Marxist or functionalist, were largely derived from the historical experience of Western Europe, of Britain in particular (Chandavarkar 1985: 623). And since the experience of industrialization in other parts of the world was measured against such a 'universal' model, one came up with a 'litter of special cases' of arrested development or 'frustrated bourgeois revolutions' (ibid.: 624).

The validity of Chandavarkar's argument with regard to the uncritical acceptance of a region-specific model as universal is reflected in Roy's comment about the 'particularity' of Asian soil, where industrialization began but did not mature (Roy 2002), or the early anxious search of Habib for the 'potentialities of capitalist development' in South Asia (Habib 1969a). It is interesting that in the same year Habib had offered a sensitive critique of 'evolutionary Marxism' of the 1930s which argued that every state or geographical entity had to pass through the rigid stages of development—slavery, feudalism, capitalism, socialism—by stating that such evolutionary history was faulty (Habib 1969b.).

The problems with analyses that take the fact and force of industrialization as a 'given' do not only lie in their formalist nature. Apart from the fact that they take the 'traditional' order to be entirely static and passive on which industrialism can work ceaselessly and successfully, they also reveal a belief in an evolutionist, linear notion of history, a history in stages, where Europe's past can and does become the present of traditional societies, if proper steps are followed. In order to reach that stage, societies have to achieve 'an advanced level of technology' and large-scale enterprise, and arrive at a 'consensus on values governed by goals unknown in "traditional society"' (Chandavarkar 1985: 625). This near exclusive linking of industrialization with large-scale industries has meant that the level of industrial 'advancement' or 'backwardness' of a society has been determined by their presence or absence (ibid.: 623–24).

The pervasive influence of this notion of industrialization as an inevitable and stagist process finds reflection in the way economic and social histories are written. The economic history of India often begins in the mid-nineteenth century when historians discern the first signs of industrialization (ibid.). Prior to that, discussions focus almost entirely on the effects of revenue settlements. In social histories too, a simple and direct relation between levels of industrialization and patterns of social response are often assumed. In such histories, modern industrialism is given the credit for inducing a quickened pace of social change resulting in 'modernization' or 'anglicization' (Jeffrey 1976, for instance). Interestingly, industrialization, taken to be an autonomous process free from the influence of social forces, is credited with heralding social change.

It is time now to pay attention both to Chandavarkar's warning and to the argument advanced by historians of subaltern studies that India's history should not be read in the light of the history of world capitalism. Industrialization is not a neutral, technologically determined process that transcends social choice and shapes society in a particular way. Its choice is political and value loaded. In India's case, the political presence of the colonial state and the agency of social classes exerted considerable influence. Hence, if India did not 'industrialize' the way England did, it is not because 'conditions' of traditional India were different from that of England or because the 'nature of Asian soil' retarded industrialization. Rather, it is because conditions of colonial rule and structures of social hierarchies channelled the options of peasants and labourers in particular ways. Peasants and artisans, moreover, muddled the story of India's industrialization by attempting to chart a new course altogether, defying both the dictates of Victoria's rule and the decisions of Indian landlords and industrialists.

More on Famines

It is pertinent to link the debate on deindustrialization and the commercialization of agriculture with the incidence of famines in the nineteenth century, whose frequency made the century stand out in Indian history. We have seen the harmful effect of the expansion of cotton cultivation in the Berar region, where the reclamation of grazing lands and common grounds and the reduction in the production of food grains resulted in severe food scarcity and famines. Almost always, as we have noted in Chapter 3, famines followed drought and/or failure of crops.

The effect of famine, it has been argued, was far more extensive than the immediate reduction of food availability in the region. A famine disrupted the rural economy by bringing agricultural activity to a standstill and making it impossible for landless labourers to find work at a time when adversity had enormously increased the supply of casual labour (Dreze 1995: 72). Food prices increased simultaneously as the 'less vulnerable' groups tried to retain their normal levels of consumption by selling their assets and the grains they had stored in earlier years; and trade was normally slow to move food grains to the affected areas from other regions. All this together with the fact that wages lagged far behind the increase in food prices caused acute distress and starvation, most often leading to death for the most vulnerable groups. Localized but severe famines resulted even when grain production and supply over the whole of India were 'far from wanting' (ibid.: 73). The Famine Commission Report of 1880, the most detailed so far, noted that agricultural labourers and rural artisans were the worst victims of famines, even though very severe famines claimed the lives of cultivators as well.

Opinions differ on what occasioned famines. We have seen in the last chapter that scholars attribute them to the Company's faulty policies, a fact also accepted by the Report of the Famine Commission that spoke more of the Company's 'half-hearted' effort to provide relief than its faulty policy. Prevention of famines, it appears, became a major concern for the British Raj, although the reasons adduced for such a change of heart are 'extremely speculative and fragmentary' (ibid.: 76). Absence of contingency planning and weak motivation along with delays in transport and poor administration continued to plague the colonial state, just as they had accompanied the Company state. The colonial government, of course, never failed to point out the hugely beneficial effect of the railways in improving communications and in speeding up famine relief as also in extending the area from which food supplies could be drawn from 100 miles to 2,000 miles.

Needless to say, the expansion of the railway network promoted private trade and increased the dynamism of trade in grains; its benefit for different sections of the Indian population, however, has been a matter of debate among scholars. Based on empirical research carried out in western India, Michelle McAlpin argued that the expansion of railways contributed to reducing poverty and famines, and that by the beginning of the twentieth century movement of grains to regions with harvest shortfalls had become a common occurrence (McAlpin 1983). Several scholars, including Jean Dreze, have challenged this and pointed out that the uniformity of prices of food grains in India that resulted from improvements in communications did not necessarily help famine relief. The absence of international trade regulations and the government's policy of non-interference in private trade kept up the flow of food grains towards higher price regions across the national border. The flow was even greater when it came to England on account of the price difference between India and England. More importantly, the moderation of price increase or the reduction in the disparity of prices does not necessarily mean a reduction in the severity of a famine. The two famines that occurred towards the end of the nineteenth century were amongst the most severe in terms of the devastation that they caused. A situation of scarcity, writes Jean Dreze, can help vulnerable groups only if there is a corresponding increase in their purchasing power, which unfortunately was not the case (Dreze 1995: 80–81). The expansion of railways possibly contributed to the alleviation of distress to a certain extent; it was not, however, the sole factor in reducing the incidence of famines in the twentieth century (ibid.: 81). Political forces were to acquire predominance in India's history in the early-twentieth century, and it is to such processes that we now turn.

REFERENCES

Amin, Shahid. 1984. *Sugarcane and Sugar in Gorakhpur: An Inquiry into Peasant Production for Capitalist Enterprise in Colonial India*. New Delhi: Oxford University Press.

Appadurai, Arjun. 1994. 'Number in the Colonial Imagination'. In *Orientalism and the Postcolonial Predicament*, edited by Carol A. Breckenridge and Peter Van der Veer, 314–340. New Delhi: Oxford University Press.

Bagchi, A. K. 1972. *Private Investment in India, 1900–1939*. Cambridge: Cambridge University Press.

———. 1976. 'Deindustrialization in the Nineteenth Century: Some Theoretical Implications'. *Journal of Development Studies* 12 (2): 135–64.

———. 2010. *Colonialism and Indian Economy*. New Delhi: Oxford University Press.

Baker, Christopher John. 1976. *The Politics of South India 1920–1937*. Cambridge: Cambridge University Press.

Baker, David. 1991. 'State Policy, The Market Economy, and Tribal Decline: The Central Provinces, 1861–1929'. *The Indian Economic and Social History Review* 28 (4): 341–70.

Bandyopadhyay, Sekhar. 1985. 'Caste in the Perception of the Raj: A Note on the Evolution of Colonial Sociology of Bengal'. *Bengal Past and Present CIV*, Parts I and II (198-199): 56-80.

———. 1992. 'Construction of Social Categories: The Role of Colonial Census'. In *Ethnicity, Caste and People*, edited by K. S. Singh. Delhi: Manohar.

———. 1997. *Caste, Protest and Identity in Colonial India: The Namasudras of Bengal, 1872–1947*. Surrey: Curzon Press.

———. 2004. *From Plassey to Partition: A History of Modern India*. Hyderabad: Orient Longman.

Banerjee-Dube, Ishita. 2008. *Caste in History*. New Delhi: Oxford University Press.

Barrier, Gerald. 1981. *Census in British India: New Perspectives*. Delhi: Manohar.

Bates, Crispin. 1995. 'Race, Caste and Tribe in Central India: The Early Origins of Indian Anthropometry'. *Edinburgh Papers in South Asia Studies 3*. Edinburgh: University of Edinburgh, School of Social and Political Studies.

———. 2007. *Subalterns and the Raj: South Asia since 1600*. London and New York: Routledge.

Bayly, C. A. [1983] 1992. *Rulers, Townsmen and Bazaars: North Indian Society in the Age of British Expansion 1770–1870*. New Delhi: Oxford University Press (First published 1983, Cambridge University Press).

———. [1988] 1995. *Indian Society and the Making of the British Empire*. Cambridge: Cambridge University Press.

Bayly, Susan. 1995. 'Caste and "Race" in the Colonial Ethnography of India'. In *The Concept of Race in South Asia*, edited by Peter Robb, 165–218. New Delhi: Oxford University Press.

———. 1997. *Caste, Society and Politics in India: From the Eighteenth Century to the Modern Age*. Cambridge: Cambridge University Press.

Beaud, Michel. 1983. *A History of Capitalism 1500–1980* (Translated by Tom Dickman and Anny Lefebvre). New York: Monthly Review Press.

Bose, Sugata. 1990. *South Asia and World Capitalism*. New Delhi and New York: Oxford University Press.

Bose, Sugata and Ayesha Jalal. 1998. *Modern South Asia: History, Culture, Political Economy*. Paperback edition, 2000. London: Routledge.

Bouton, Marshall. 1985. *Agrarian Radicalism in South India*. Princeton, NJ: Princeton University Press.

Carroll, Lucy. 1978. 'Colonial Perceptions of Indian Society and the Emergence of Caste(s) Associations'. *The Journal of Asian Studies* 37 (2): 233–50.

Chandavarkar, Rajnarayan. 1985. 'Industrialization in India Before 1947: Conventional Approaches and Alternative Perspectives'. *Modern Asian Studies* 19 (3): 623–68.

Chatterjee, Partha. 1984. *Bengal: The Land Question*. Calcutta: K. P. Bagchi and Co.

———. 1997. *The Present History of West Bengal: Essays in Political Criticism*. New Delhi: Oxford University Press.

Chaudhuri, Benoy Bhushan. 1964. *Growth of Commercial Agriculture in Bengal, 1757–1900*. Calcutta: Quality Printers.

———. 1975. 'The Process of Depeasantization in Bihar and Bengal, 1885–1947'. *Indian Historical Review* 2(1): 105–65.

Chaudhuri, K. N. 1978. *The Trading World of Asia and the English East India Company, 1660–1760*. Cambridge: Cambridge University Press.

———. 1985. *Trade and Civilization in the Indian Ocean: An Economic History from the Rise of Islam to 1750*. Cambridge: Cambridge University Press.

Clingingsmith, David and Jeffrey Williamson. 2004. 'India's De-industrialization Under British Rule: New Ideas, New Evidence'. Cambridge: National Bureau of Economic Research.

Cohn, Bernard S. 1968. 'Notes on the History of the Study of Indian Culture and Society'. In *Structure and Change in Indian Society*, edited by M. Singer and B. S. Cohn, 3–28. Chicago: Aldine.

———. 1986. 'The Command of Language and the Language of Command'. In *Subaltern Studies III: Writings on South Asian History and Society*, edited by R. Guha, 276–329. New Delhi: Oxford University Press.

———. 1987. 'The Census, Social Structure, and Objectification in South Asia'. In *An Anthropologist Among the Historians and Other Essays*, B. Cohn, 224–252. Oxford: Oxford University Press. (An abbreviated version reprinted in *Caste in History*. 2008, edited by I. Banerjee-Dube, 28–40. New Delhi: Oxford University Press)

———. 1992. 'Representing Authority in Victorian India'. In *The Invention of Tradition*, edited by Eric Hobsbawm and Terence Ranger. Cambridge University Press (First published 1983 by Cambridge University Press. Cambridge: Canto edition).

———. 1996. *Colonialism and Its Forms of Knowledge: The British in India*. Princeton, NJ: Princeton University Press.

Conlon, Frank F. 1977. *A Caste in a Changing World: The Chitrapur Saraswat Brahmans 1700–1935*. Berkeley and Los Angeles: University of California Press.

———. 2009. 'Speaking of Caste? Colonial and Indigenous Interpretations of Caste and Community in Nineteenth-century Bombay'. In *Ancient to Modern: Religion, Power and Community in India*, edited by Ishita Banerjee-Dube and Saurabh Dube. New Delhi: Oxford University Press.

Constable, Philip. 1997. 'Early Dalit Literature and Culture in Late-Nineteenth and Early-Twentieth Century Western India'. *Modern Asian Studies* 31 (2): 317–38.

Datta, P. K. 1993. '"Dying Hindus": Production of Hindu Communal Common Sense in Early Twentieth Century Bengal'. *Economic and Political Weekly* Vol. 28 (25) (19 June): 1305–1319.

Datta, Rajat. 1986. 'Merchants and Peasants: A Study of the Structure of Local Trade in Late Eighteenth Century Bengal'. *The Indian Economic and Social History Review* 23(4): 379–402.

Desai, Manali. 2001. 'Party Formation, Political Power, and the Capacity for Reform: Comparing Left Parties in Kerala and West Bengal, India'. *Social Forces* 80 (1): 37–60.

Dhanagare, D. N. 1983. *Peasant Movements in India, 1920–1950*. New Delhi: Oxford University Press.

Dirks, Nicholas B. 1987. *The Hollow Crown: Ethnohistory of an Indian Kingdom*. Cambridge: Cambridge University Press.

———. 1989. 'The Invention of Caste: Civil Society in Colonial India'. *Social Analysis* 25: 42–52.

———. 1992. 'Castes of Mind'. *Representations* (Winter): 56–78.

———. 1996. Foreword to *Colonialism and Its Forms of Knowledge: The British in India*, Bernard S. Cohn, IX–XVII. Princeton, NJ: Princeton University Press.

———. 2001. *Castes of Mind: Colonialism and the Making of Modern India*. Princeton, NJ: Princeton University Press.

———. 2004. 'The Ethnographic State'. In *Postcolonial Passages*, edited by S. Dube, 70–88. New Delhi: Oxford University Press.

Dodson, Michael S. 2010. *Orientalism, Empire, and National Culture: India, 1770–1880*. New Delhi: Cambridge University Press India.

Dreze, Jean. 1995. 'Famine Prevention in India'. In *The Political Economy of Hunger: Selected Essays*, edited by Jean Dreze, Amartya Sen and Athar Hussain, 72–81. New York: Oxford University Press.

Eaton, Richard M. 2000. '(Re)imag(in)ing Otherness: A Postmortem for the Postmodern in India'. In *Essays on Islam and Indian History*, R. M. Eaton, 133–156. New Delhi: Oxford University Press.

Freitag, Sandria B. 1990. *Collective Action and Community: Public Arenas and the Emergence of Communalism in North India*. New Delhi: Oxford University Press.

Gadgil, M. and Ramchandra Guha. 1993. *This Fissured Land: An Ecological History of India*. New Delhi: Oxford University Press.

Gait, E. A. 1914. *General Report of the Census of India*. London: H. M. Stationery Office.

Habib, Irfan. 1969a. 'Potentialities of Capitalistic Development in the Economy of Mughal India'. *The Journal of Economic History* 29 (1): 32–78 and in *Enquiry* (n.s.) 3 (3): 1–56.

———. 1969b. 'Problems of Marxist Historical Analysis in India'. *Enquiry* (n.s.) 3 (2): 52–67.

Hardgrave, Robert L. 1969. *The Nadars of Tamilnadu: The Political Culture of a Community in Change*. Berkeley and Los Angeles: University of California Press.

Hunter, W. W. 1871. *The Indian Musalmans: Are They Bound in Conscience to Rebel Against the Queen?* London: Trübner and Company.

Inden, Ronald B. 1986. 'Orientalist Constructions of India'. *Modern Asian Studies* 20 (1): 1–46.

———. 1990. *Imagining India*. Oxford: Basil Blackwell.

Irschick, Eugene F. 1969. *Politics and Social Conflict in South India: The Non-Brahman Movement and Tamil Separatism*. Berkeley and Los Angeles: University of California Press.

———. 1994. *Dialogue and History: Constructing South India, 1795–1895*. Berkeley and Los Angeles: University of California Press.

Jalal, Ayesha. 2000. *Self and Sovereignty: Individual and Community in South Asian Islam since 1850*. London and New York: Routledge.

Jeffrey, Robin. 1974. 'The Social Origins of a Caste Association, 1875–1905: The Founding of the S.N.D.P. Yogam'. *South Asia* 4: 39–59.

———. 1976. *The Decline of Nayar Dominance: Society and Politics in Travancore, 1847–1908*. New York: Holmes & Meiers Publishers.

Jones, Kenneth W. 1968. 'Communalism in the Punjab: The Arya Samaj Contribution'. *The Journal of Asian Studies* 28 (1): 39–54.

Keer, D. and S. G. Mashle, eds. 1969. *The Collected Works of Mahatma Phule*. Bombay: Maharashtra State Society for Literature and Culture.

Keith, A. B. 1936. *A Constitutional History of India, 1600–1935*. London: Methuen and Co.

Kessinger, Tom G. 1974. *Vilayatpur, 1848–1968: Social and Economic Change in a North India Village*. Berkeley and Los Angeles: University of California Press.

Lelyveld, David. 1978. *Aligarh's First Generation: Muslim Solidarity in British India*. Princeton, NJ: Princeton University Press.

Leonard, Karen I. 1978. *The Social History of an Indian Caste: The Kayasths of Hyderabad*. Berkeley and Los Angeles: University of California Press.

Lorenzen, David N. [1999] 2006. 'Who Invented Hinduism'. *Comparative Studies in Society and History* 41: 630–59. Also included in 'Who Invented Hinduism', David N. Lorenzen. New Delhi: Yoda Press.

Ludden, David. 1994. 'Orientalist Empiricism: Transformations of Colonial Knowledge'. In *Orientalism and the Postcolonial Predicament*, edited by Carol A. Breckenridge and Peter van der Veer, 250–78. New Delhi: Oxford University Press.

———. 1999. *An Agrarian History of South Asia: The New Cambridge History of India*. Vol. 4.4. Cambridge: Cambridge University Press.

———. 2004. *Capitalism in Asia: Perspectives on Asia. Sixty Years of The Journal of Asian Studies*. Michigan: Association for Asian Studies.

Majumdar, Ramesh Chandra, ed. [1963] 1970. *British Paramountcy and Indian Renaissance*. Part 1. Bombay: Bharatiya Vidya Bhavan.

Malhotra, Anshu. 2010. 'Shameful Continuities: The Practice of Female Infanticide in Colonial Punjab'. In *Sikhism and Women: History, Texts and Experience*, edited by Doris Jakobsh, 83–114. New Delhi: Oxford University Press.

McAlpin, Michelle B. 1983. 'Famines, Epidemics, and Population Growth: The Case of India'. *The Journal of Interdisciplinary History* XIV (2): 351–66.

Menon, Dilip. 1994. *Caste, Nationalism and Communism in South India*. Cambridge: Cambridge University Press.

Metcalf, Barbara D. and Thomas R. Metcalf. 2003. *A Concise History of India*. Cambridge: Cambridge University Press.

Metcalf, Thomas R. 1979. *Land, Landlords and the British Raj: Northern India in the Nineteenth Century*. Berkeley and Los Angeles: University of California Press.

———. 1995. *Ideologies of the Raj*. New Delhi: Cambridge University Press.

Moore, Barrington. 1966. *Social Origins of Dictatorship and Democracy*. New York: Beacon Press.

Morris, Morris D. 1963. 'Towards a Reinterpretation of Nineteenth-Century Indian Economic History'. *The Journal of Economic History* 23 (4): 606–18.

———. 1983. 'The Growth of Large-Scale Industry to 1947'. In *The Cambridge Economic History of India*, vol 2, edited by Dharma Kumar, 551–676. Cambridge: Cambridge University Press.

Myrdal, Gunnar. 1968. *Asian Drama: An Inquiry into the Poverty of Nations*. New York: Twentieth Century Fund.

Nigam, Sanjay. 1990. 'Disciplining and Policing the "Criminals by Birth" Part 1: The Development of the Disciplinary System, 1871–1900'. *The Indian Economic and Social History Review* 27 (2): 131–62.

O'Hanlon, Rosalind. 1985. *Caste, Conflict, and Ideology: Mahatma Jotirao Phule and Low Caste Protest in Nineteenth Century Western India*. Cambridge: Cambridge University Press.

Oberoi, Harjot. 1997. *The Construction of Religious Boundaries: Culture, Identity, and Diversity among the Sikhs*. New Delhi: Oxford University Press (paperback edition).

Oldenburg, Veena Talwar. 2002. *Dowry Murder: The Imperial Origins of a Cultural Crime*. New York: Oxford University Press.

Omvedt, G. 1976. *Cultural Revolt in a Colonial Society: The Non-Brahmin Movement in Western India*. Poona: Scientific Socialist Education Trust.

Pandey, Gyanendra. 1992. *The Construction of Communalism in Colonial North India*. New Delhi: Oxford University Press.

Pant, Rashmi. 1987. 'The Cognitive Status of Caste in Colonial Ethnography: A Review of Some Literature on the North West Provinces and Oudh'. *The Indian Economic and Social History Review* 24 (2): 145–62.

Peabody, Norbert. 2001. 'Cents, Sense, Census: Human Inventories in Late Precolonial and Early Colonial India'. *Comparative Studies in Society and History* 45 (4): 819–50.

Pennington, Brian K. 2005. *Was Hinduism Invented? Britons, Indians, and the Colonial Construction of Religion*. Oxford: Oxford University Press.

Plowden, William C. 1873. *Census of the North-Western Provinces 1872, General Report*. Vol. 1. Allahabad, n. p.

Ramaswamy, Sumathi. 1997. *Passions of the Tongue: Language Devotion in Tamil India, 1891–1970*. Berkeley and Los Angeles: University of California Press.

Rao, Anupama. 2009. *The Caste Question: Dalits and the Politics of Modern India*. Berkeley and Los Angeles: University of California Press.

Ray, Rajat Kanta. 1979. *Industrialization in India: Growth and Conflict in the Private Corporate Sector, 1914–1947*. New Delhi: Oxford University Press.

Risley, H. H. 1908. *The Peoples of India*. London: W. Thacker and Co.

Robb, Peter. 1992. 'Peasants' Choices? Indian Agriculture and the Limits of Commercialization in Nineteenth-Century Bihar'. *The Economic History Review* (n.s.) 45 (1): 97–119.

———. 2002. *A History of India*. Hampshire and New York: Palgrave.

Robinson, Francis. [1974] 2007. *Separatism Among Indian Muslims: The Politics of the United Provinces' Muslims, 1860–1923*. Cambridge: Cambridge University Press.

Rocher, Rosane. 1994. 'British Orientalism in the Eighteenth Century: The Dialectics of Knowledge and Government'. In *Orientalism and the Postcolonial Predicament*, edited by Carol A. Breckenridge and Peter van der Veer, 215–49. New Delhi: Oxford University Press.

Roy, Kaushik. 2009. 'The Logistics of Victory: Punjab and Supplying the British–India Army During the 1857–59 Uprising'. In *Uprising of 1857: Perspectives and Peripheries*, edited by Suhas Ranjan Chakraborty, 262–93. Kolkata: Asiatic Society.

Roy, Tirthankar. 1999. *Traditional Industry in the Economy of Colonial India*. Cambridge: Cambridge University Press.

———. 2002. 'Deindustrialization'. In *Land, Labour, and Rights: Ten Daniel Thorner Memorial Lectures*, edited by Alice Thorner, 232–249. London: Anthem Press.

Said, Edward W. 1978. *Orientalism: Western Conceptions of the Orient*. London: Routledge and Kegan Paul.

Samarendra, Padmanabh. 2008. 'Between Number and Knowledge: Career of Caste in Colonial Census'. In *Caste in History*, edited by Ishita Banerjee-Dube, 46–66. New Delhi: Oxford University Press.

Sarkar, Sumit. [1983] 1995. *Modern India: 1885–1947*. Madras: Macmillan India.

Seal, A. 1968. *The Emergence of Indian Nationalism: Competition and Collaboration in the Later Nineteenth Century*. Cambridge: Cambridge University Press.

Sengupta, Parna. 2011. *Pedagogy for Religion: Missionary Education and the Fashioning of Hindus and Muslims in Bengal*. Berkeley and Los Angeles: University of California Press.

Sharan, Awadhendra. 2003. 'From Caste to Category: Colonial Knowledge Practices and the Depressed/Scheduled Castes of Bihar'. *The Indian Economic and Social History Review* 40 (3): 279–310.

Sharan, Paramatma. 1961. *The Imperial Legislative Council of India from 1861–1920: A Study of the Interaction of Constitutional Reform and Nationalist Movement with Special Reference to the Growth of Indian Legislature up to 1920*. Delhi: S. Chand.

Sharma, Jayeeta. 2011. *Empire's Garden: Assam and the Making of India*. Durham, NC: Duke University Press.

Siddiqui, Asiya. 1973. *Agrarian Change in a Northern Indian State, U.P. 1819–33*. Oxford: Oxford University Press.

Skaria, Ajay. 1997. 'Shades of Wildness: Tribe, Caste, and Gender in Western India'. *The Journal of Asian Studies* 56 (3): 726–45.

Smith, R. S. 1985. 'Rule-by-Records and Rule-by-Reports: Complimentary Aspects of the British Imperial Rule of Law'. *Contributions to Indian Sociology* (n.s.) 19 (1): 153–76.

———. 1996. *Rule by Records: Land Registration and Village Custom in Early British Panjab*. New Delhi: Oxford University Press. 'From Village to Community'. Reproduced in *Caste in History* 2008, edited by I. Banerjee-Dube, 67–69. New Delhi: Oxford University Press.

Subrahmanyam, Sanjay. 1997. 'Connected Histories: Notes Towards a Reconfiguration of Early Modern Eurasia'. *Modern Asian Studies* 31 (3): 735–62.

———. 2001. *Penumbral Visions: Making Polities in Early Modern South India*. Michigan, MI: University of Michigan Press.

Templeman, Dennis. 1996. *The Northern Nadars of Tamil Nadu: An Indian Caste in the Process of Change*. New York: Oxford University Press.

Thomason, J. 1837. *Report of the Collector of Azimgurh on the Settlement of the Ceded Portion of the District Commonly Called Chuklah Azimgurh*. Agra: Government Press (34 pages).

Thorner, Daniel. 1962. *Land and Labour in India*. London: Asia Publishing House.

Tomlison, B. R. 1979. *The Political Economy of the Raj, 1914–1947: The Economics of Decolonization in India*. London and Basingstoke: Macmillan.

Trautmann, Thomas R. 1999. 'Constructing the Racial Theory of Indian Civilization'. In *Aryan and Non-Aryan in South Asia: Evidence, Interpretation and Ideology*, edited by Johannes Bronkhorst and Madhav M. Deshpande. Cambridge, MA: Harvard University Press, Department of Sanskrit and Indian Studies: 277–293

Verma, Nitin. 2009. 'For the Drink of the Nation; Drink, Labour and Plantation Capitalism in the Colonial Tea Gardens of Assam in the Late Nineteenth and Early Twentieth Century'. In *Labour Matters: Towards Global Histories. Studies in Honour of Sabyasachi Bhattacharya*, edited by Marcel van der Linden, Prabhu N. Mohapatra, 295–354. New Delhi: Tulika.

Wagoner, Philip A. 2003. 'Precolonial Intellectuals and the Production of Colonial Knowledge'. *Comparative Studies in Society and History* 47 (3): 783–814.

Wallerstein, Immanuel. 1979. 'The Present State of the Debate on World Inequality'. *In The Capitalist World Economy. Essays by Immanuel Wallerstein.* Cambridge: Cambridge University Press.

Washbrook, D. A. and C. J. Baker, eds. 1975. *South India: Political Institutions and Political Change.* New Delhi: Oxford University Press.

Whitcombe, Elizabeth. 1971. *Agrarian Relations in Northern India*, Vol. 1: *U.P. Under British Rule, 1860–1900.* Berkeley and Los Angeles: University of California Press.

Wilson, John. 1877. *Indian Castes.* Vol. I. Bombay: Times of India Press.

Zagoria, Donald S. 1971. 'The Ecology of Peasant Communism in India'. *American Political Science Review* 65 (1): 144–60.

Zelliot, Eleanor. 2010. 'India's Dalits: Racism and Contemporary Change'. *Global Dialogue* 12 (2) (Summer/Autumn).

Imagining India

Abanindranath Tagore's epic painting 'Bharat Mata', 1905

Chapter outline

In his celebrated work, published a quarter of a century ago, Benedict Anderson had argued that nations are 'imagined communities' given concrete shape by institutions, such as print capitalism (Anderson 1991). Since then, writings on nationalism have tried to examine the distinct ways in which nations have been brought into being in different parts of the world, and these writings have tried to define what a nation is. If this underscores that scholars accept the 'modernity' of nations, the idea that the 'naturalness' of a national identity precedes history still has great prevalence in everyday worlds. In Anderson's words, there is a 'paradox' between the 'objective modernity' of nations to the 'historian's eye' and their 'subjective antiquity' in the 'eyes of nationalists' (ibid.: 5). This tension—of creating the nation while positing its long, unbroken existence—that lies at the heart of nationalism, makes the study of both nations and nationalisms fascinating, yet difficult.

A second tension underlies the historiography of nationalism. While it defines nationalism as a 'discourse' constituted at the level of ideas and consciousness, it seeks to make the nation concrete by locating it within institutions, social forms and practices. Stories of nationalism, therefore, ask 'why' the sentiment or idea, that is, nationalism emerged, and frequently and retrospectively, provide a social explanation for it by linking it to the rise of the middle-class, lending circularity to the story of nationalism (Seth 1999: 96). As a result, even though nations are no longer treated as the inevitable result of sociological factors, such as religion or history or a common language (Anderson 1991; Winichakul 1994), the need to look for concrete elements that help in the configuration of the 'imagined community' persists.

This need, it has been argued, is valid since social processes do play a key role in the constitution of 'a spatially bounded, self-enclosed national whole' (Goswami 1998: 610). It is important, therefore, to pay equal attention to the discursive formation and the social grounding through which a nation takes shape at different levels in order not to neglect 'the national social content of territoriality', and seriously address the question of why nationalist movements 'routinely claim a correspondence between people, economy, and culture' (ibid.).

Moreover, we have been told that nationalisms do not work everywhere in the same way. Indeed, if nations are 'imagined' and they claim their separate identity on the basis of difference, nationalism has to work differently in different nations (Balibar 1989: 19). Hence, even if we accept that the discourse on nationalism in India is a 'derived' version of the normative European form (Chatterjee 1986), it is true that it produces its own 'difference, slippage and excess' in order to be the same and yet not quite (Bhabha 1994). This further means that nationalism is not the sole identity that subsumes or organizes other identifications. Rather, it exists in conflict or in harmony with several others (Duara cited in Ramaswamy 1997: 5).

The idea of nationalism itself has links with two distinct, even opposing, intellectual trends. On the one hand, it draws upon the heritage of liberalism and secularism and intends to establish a polity based on self-determination, with no distinction of class, creed or colour. On the other hand, nationalism is intimately tied to 'a system of political meanings' associated with symbols of the 'community' (Stein 2010: 274). Such symbols can be of religion, caste, region or language; but the common idiom of community implies a perceived 'commonality', a commonality with the potential of transforming a disparate people into a collective body (ibid.: 274). This means that nationalism has to juggle constantly with distinct modes of creating 'commonality' as well as with other identifications that can produce a 'community' outside the fold of nationalism.

Our exploration of Indian nationalism will draw upon all these insights in order to understand its discursive and concrete configuration. It will pay attention to the tensions within nationalism and its tensions with alternate modes and sentiments of identification, such as that with language. These modes, argues Sumathi Ramaswamy, should not be read only within the rubric of nationalism—as its different and deviant versions—such as linguistic nationalism (Ramaswamy 1997: 5). In addition, and perhaps more importantly, we will place nationalism within the context and the discursive framework of a colonialism that 'colonizes minds in addition to bodies' and 'releases forces within the colonized societies to alter their cultural priorities once and for all' (Nandy 1983: vii). Nationalism, therefore, will not be seen as a single, unbroken narrative with a continuous history. Its articulation, similarly, is diverse—it is resistance both to colonialism and to colonization.

Imperceptible Beginnings

Till the decade of the 1980s, it was relatively easy for historians to locate the first stirrings of nationalism in the late-nineteenth century, with a direct link to the foundation of the Indian National Congress in 1885. The idea that a nation is imagined into existence has ruled out this easy identification. Imagination entails emotion, experience, passion—all of which add nuance and subtlety to the understanding of nationalism and make it impossible to trace its trajectory as a strictly political phenomenon. Experience underscores that nationalism is a process, and not a full-blown phenomenon that suddenly erupts at a particular point in time and that different groups might experience it differently. Historiography of nationalism reflects this change in understanding. From an earlier focus on factors that led to the growth of nationalism and the activities of the Indian National Congress (Desai [1946] 1959; Masselos 1985; McCully 1940; Mehrotra 1971; Rothermund 1979), it has moved to analyses of the discursive and material configuration of nationalism (Chakrabarty 1994; Chatterjee 1986, 1993; Goswami 1998; Guha 1988; Trivedi 2003, for instance).

Speaking of nationalism as a process, we also need to seriously consider an important and challenging reminder that Indian nationalism should not be thought of only as a direct result of colonialism. It 'solidified' under colonial rule no doubt, but nationalism drew upon earlier patterns of social relations, sentiments of attachment to land, loyalties and 'old patriotisms' which it recast in the course of getting constituted (Bayly 1998). At the same time, these earlier sentiments often engendered passions for the region and the language, sometimes strengthening and sometimes detracting from the nationalist struggle. Defined as regional nationalisms by the master narrative of nationalism, such passions demonstrated the constant negotiations that nationalism has to undertake in order to establish itself as the dominant form of identity.

Finally, the categories of the colonizer and the colonized, far from being fixed and self-evident, were historically constructed and got redefined in accordance with the imperatives of colonial rule. Any attempt at understanding nationalism, therefore, requires an exploration of the variegated experiences and processes that shaped the interaction of the colonizer and the colonized in particular ways and contributed to the growth of nationalistic sentiments.

Clearly, it is impossible to trace the experiences and endeavours of all sections of the population of a country as vast and varied as India. We will begin with the historic 'middle class' widely held to be the vanguard of nationalism. In India too, this class thought of itself as 'belonging to a nation and voiced nationalist demands' (Seth 1999: 96). It was composed of groups that came in early contact with colonial rule and members who consciously regarded themselves as the leaders of society—the (western) educated groups of Calcutta, Bombay and Madras, cities that boomed on opportunities offered by Company rule. We take them as representatives of the middle-classes that emerged all over India, albeit with different composition and character. Some historians of modern India hold the factors which contributed to the growth of the middle-class—such as English education and a uniform system of law—to be crucial in the growth of nationalism as well (Griffiths [1957] 1962: 67; McCully 1940). Rothermund goes so far as to say that nationalist consciousness in India emerged out of the vision of a steadily growing English-educated elite who 'learned to look at India with the intellectual armoury of her conquerors' (Rothermund 1979: 13).

The spread of western education, we are aware, was unequal and uneven. The presidencies of Calcutta, Bombay and Madras reaped the greatest benefit from higher education after the opening of universities in 1857. The number of students in these regions, particularly in the cities, exceeded those in the huge localities of North, North-West and Central India, grouped into North-Western Provinces and Awadh, Punjab and the Central Provinces. Even in the presidencies, certain groups took greater advantage of English and higher education than others. In Bengal, this group was composed mainly of people from the three higher castes of Brahmans, Baidyas and Kayasthas. They were not numerically insignificant because 'Kayasthas' included a very wide and diverse group. The Chitpavan Brahmans and the Parsis monopolized education in the Bombay Presidency, while in Madras, the Tamil Brahmans—the Iyers and the Iyengers—took the lead.

Muslim aristocrats kept their distance from the British till the mid-nineteenth century, with the result that they felt overtaken by their Hindu counterparts (Chapter 4). The uneven spread of English education was manifest in the way Bengalis dominated public affairs in the Bengal Presidency to the exclusion of Biharis, Assamese and Oriyas; the Marathi-speaking regions of the Bombay Presidency gained greater prominence over the Gujarati-speaking regions; and Tamil dictated affairs in the south at the cost of Telugu and Malayalam. In addition, members of lower castes were almost completely left out. This disparity generated distinct reactions and marked the nationalist struggle in significant ways.

The middle class in Calcutta, not bound by ties of caste but rather by that of common economic interests, lifestyle and status, and composed of merchants, absentee landlords and professionals in the lower rungs of the Company administration, and later in independent professions, such as law and medicine, was heterogeneous but it constituted itself as a recognizable group, the *bhadralok*, over the course of the nineteenth century by virtue of its activities with relation to the state and society. The first decades of the nineteenth century were alive with cross-currents of ideas and ideology that engendered hectic, enthusiastic endeavours among the elite in Bengal. An interest in western science and logic went hand in hand with an increasing interest in English language and literature and the beginnings of Indian writing in English. Tradition got redefined along rational lines on account of fierce debates on Hindu customs and practices and attempts at social reform. None of this, of course, was nationalistic; it did not confront the Company Raj as an adversary. Rather, this wide-ranging, fervent activity was, at a deeper level, informed by a sense of inferiority which reflects the penetration of western racial theories. In Ashis Nandy's terms, this exemplified the 'cultural cooptation' of the reformist men into colonial rule resulting from their 'identification with the aggressor' (Nandy 1983: 7).

The reformist zeal was driven, to a large extent, by an uncritical acceptance of the colonial definition of Hindu society as degraded and 'inferior'. The civilizing discourse of imperial power produced among Indian intellectuals an active desire to participate in the 'world-community of countries' where 'peoples and nations' were graded hierarchically. They fervently wanted to 'improve' India's condition in order to place her at a higher level (Chakrabarty 1994: 54). Consequently, a critical reflection on their own culture was dictated by colonial categorizations (Nandy 1983), and this reflection ended up objectifying culture as a self-evident entity, which could be 'cited, compared and referred to' (Bandyopadhyay 2004: 209).

Civil society and a public sphere evolved in the early-nineteenth century out of debates on education, social reform and social improvement. These issues occasioned the formation of numerous semi-official bodies, such as school-book societies and voluntary associations. They also led to a proliferation of presses that printed and circulated material related to matters of 'public interest' (Chakrabarty 1994: 69). These associations assumed the character of formal bodies—they were conducted on the basis of meetings with elections, votes, resolutions, and the recording of minutes, in brief, 'all rituals of public life built into them' (ibid.: 69). This collective activity resulted in the growth of a sense of identity and community which needed unity and improvement. It was in the first half of the nineteenth century that the words 'peoples' and 'nations' used interchangeably, figured prominently in books and texts written in Bengali, and regions and nations came to be identified in terms of language. Therefore, the civilizing mission of colonial rule, by creating the urge to work for the benefit of the community and the country among Indian intellectuals, indirectly fomented the growth of nationalist sentiments.

Bombay, the other metropolis that thrived on trade and commerce, paralleled Calcutta in organized public activity. Here the *shetia*s (successful merchants), who had come together as partners in trading ventures, increasingly identified with one another as a distinct group despite competition and rivalry. They were joined by the educated and wealthy Parsi traders and professionals. Like the Bengali elite, these men considered themselves to be natural leaders, and sought to consolidate this position by gaining access to posts within the administrative system, and more importantly by being accepted as members of the Grand Jury and Justices of Peace in the city. Over time, they came to be viewed as representatives of public opinion by the East India Company, and the Company's government turned to them for service in a range of official and semi-official public bodies. Consequently, their view of their own importance got reinforced by acts of the colonial government.

This group also emulated their Bengali counterpart in forming a number of voluntary associations, although the concerns and purposes of such associations were different. Both Bombay merchants and Bengali intellectuals were members of native school-book societies, and served on governing boards of schools and colleges. But 'reform associations' such as Atmiya Sabha and Dharma Sabha were unique to Calcutta. Bombay's first major association was the Bombay Chamber of Commerce, set up in 1836 as a joint enterprise of English merchants, European traders and Indian brokers to protect mercantile interests. It is not only that there was divergence of purpose; it was also that many of these associations had a very short life. And yet, these tentative experiments in public work fostered a sense of identity within a social group 'whose limits were defined by economic interests and awareness of a common status' (Masselos 1985: 46).

In contrast to Bombay, Madras' distance from the headquarters of the East India Company and later the Government of India in Calcutta, turned it partly into an 'administrative backwater' with the result that the elite of Madras learned to depend on their own resources (Irschick 1969: Intro). This limited their political and administrative horizons somewhat. At the same time, the city of Madras saw the rise of a wealthy group of traders who bought property in land and gained influence and prestige. Different in composition from the groups in Calcutta and Bombay, they did not come together to protect their 'feudal' rights. What brought them together was opposition to Christian missionary activity and legislation, such as the Lex Loci laws of 1850, which protected a Christian convert's right to property. The Madras Native Association came into being to counter this 'offence' to religion.

Public activities which started in big cities soon spread to several other towns and provinces all over India. To give just one example, chiefs, smaller princes, former nobles and landowners in Poona joined hands in the 1840s to protect their interests—a venture formalized in the formation of a short-lived public body. Indeed, often old towns with rich cultural traditions rivalled and countered the effort of societies in big cities, a fascinating history which still remains largely unexplored. The commitment to work for the benefit of a loosely defined and variedly understood 'community' would contribute to the establishment of more formal semi-political and political associations in the 1860s and 1870s. But before we turn to such associations, we need to take a look at another important development that resulted from and gave substance to nationalism and nationalist feelings—experiments in and the flowering of vernacular languages and literature and the associated need of grounding them in the territory of a region or the country by means of history.

LANGUAGE, NATION, HISTORY

The passionate public debates over social reform and education not only contributed to the creation of a public sphere, they contributed to the growth of vernacular literature that included historical novels, and related efforts to write the history of India by Indians. It is important to remember that the first decades of the nineteenth century were crucial for developing prose styles in several vernaculars, and these were closely connected to the enterprise of European and Indian teachers of the Fort William College and the evangelical missionaries (King 1994: 26–27). In Bengal, Rammohan Roy's polemical tracts and treaties, written in support of the abolition of sati, produced a kind of prose Bengali that had not existed in the same form earlier. The person directly involved in creating a new form of prose Bengali was educator and social reformer Iswar Chandra Vidyasagar. His mid-century readers and schoolbooks, particularly the primer *Barnaparichay*, not only became the template for all other primers; it was the most widely used primer even in missionary schools (Sengupta 2011: 41).

By the 1870s, the writing and publication of Bengali-language educational material had 'outstripped those of any other language, including English' (ibid.: 47). The market was dominated by a host of pamphlets—almanacs and religious manuals, Puranic and Persian stories—printed inexpensively by Battala publishers (Ghosh 2006). The language of these pamphlets was 'simple' and closer to the spoken language: very different from Vidyasagar's prose, a possible indication of the distance of the lower classes from the *bhadralok*. We need not go into the details here but what is important for our purposes is the patriotic and historical turn of vernacular literature produced by the literati of the period.

Bankim Chandra Chatterjee, a towering figure of Bengali literature in the late-nineteenth century, whose novel *Anandamath* has become a matter of considerable controversy on account of its Hindu nationalist overtones (Heimsath 1964, for instance), gave the call for the writing of Indian histories by Indians as the only way to set the records straight. This call for history, argues Prathama Banerjee, emerged out of a direct, bilateral engagement with colonial discursive practices, and not out of the interaction of the middle-classes with the everyday (Banerjee 2006: 42)

For Marathi intellectuals, history along with other sciences—logic, mathematics, grammar—was essential for the advancement of mankind. The first half of the nineteenth century had seen attempts to introduce these sciences in teaching, and new terms in Marathi were coined for them. Soon, history and history-writing caught the imagination of the intellectuals and great attention was paid to developing a 'native' historical tradition, which was sadly seen to be lacking in India. These intellectuals drew inspiration from the English tradition of history-writing and translated the *History of Saxons* into Marathi to imbue young students with knowledge of history. Studying history, they argued, was crucial to face and overcome the 'shame and embarrassment' that the Indians felt when asked about their country's past kings and events (Deshpande 2007: 95–96).

In Review: Critical History

Under the influence of Orientalist scholars, such as Franz Kielhorn of the Deccan College in Poona, Marathi scholars started paying serious attention to critical analysis of Sanskrit manuscripts. Kielhorn's firm belief in the existence of an 'original manuscript' as the source of all authority got transported to his disciples. A search for 'critical accuracy' came to inform the programme of Marathi historians trained under the ideology of antiquity, marking thereby a break with the Marathi Sanskrit tradition. Ramkrishna Gopal Bhandarkar, in an effort to apply 'critical accuracy', divided texts in two main categories. Texts that contained chronologies and dates and offered information to readers were treated as historical. The second category comprised texts that offered pleasure and recreation for readers, but lacked historical information. Puranas, epics, poems and *charitas* (biographies) came to be treated as non-historical, even though Bhandarkar felt that they were useful because they could reveal the 'thoughts and feelings, the aims and aspirations, and the manners and customs of the people' and the 'life and civilization of the period' (Bhandarkar cited in Deshpande 2007: 99).

This sharp separation of history and literature and, by extension, of 'politics' and 'culture' in the search for legitimate sources of early Indian history, affirms Prachi Deshpande, led Bhandarkar to reiterate the colonialist argument that 'India unfortunately [had] no written history' except for 'some chronicles written by Jains' and 'genealogies of certain dynasties'. It was possible to extract some information on ancient India from the available texts by means of impartiality and the use of 'critical power', but that only allowed a 'peep' into or a 'short sketch' of ancient Indian history. Bhandarkar's historical surveys have been instrumental in identifying—for generations of later historians and students—hierarchically graded sources for the study of ancient India: gold, silver and copper coins of early rulers; rock and metal inscriptions; and the accounts of foreign travellers. This hierarchy and the framing of the Sanskrit material in 'cultural' terms, together with the conceptualization of political history 'in narrow terms of battles, kings, and chronology' underlay Bhandarkar's perception of ancient Indian history as 'foggy' (Deshpande 2007: 100).

Vishnushastri Chiplunkar, another Marathi intellectual, agreed that history writing was not developed in ancient India and that the western intellectual tradition needed to be thanked for its introduction in India. At the same time, he firmly believed that India's history could only be written by Indians since an expression of affinity and closeness with a culture can be properly expressed by a nation's own people. More concerned about the emotive and expressive power of history than in its method, Chiplunkar tried to overcome the sense of powerlessness and shame through an affirmation of pride that could be found in history. For Maharashtra, the pride in history lay in its 'glorious' past, not of literary or artistic achievements, but of strong political and military power under Shivaji.

In order to inculcate this pride in the people, Chiplunkar underlined the need for a 'complete history' of Maharashtra that would reveal the 'special qualities' of the Maratha people that had enabled them to reach 'glorious heights' under Shivaji. In a programmatic essay delineating the contours of this complete history, he offered an account of political, administrative, social and religious developments within a broad framework of the rise and fall of rulers, but his insistence on the crucial ingredient— pride— led him to emphasize the rise of Maratha political and military power as the key element of new Marathi historiography. In addition, he advocated the use of a new prose in Marathi based on Sanskrit roots that would allow intellectuals to absorb English and its concepts without being suffocated by them.

Some recent scholars consider Chiplunkar to be the father of Hindu revivalism in Maharashtra. Deshpande disagrees. Chiplunkar's position on Sanskrit vis-à-vis English, she writes, was not revivalist: it clearly rejected traditional Sanskritic learning but sought to use its linguistic heritage to anchor Marathi expression as it adopted English genres. On several occasions Chiplunkar spoke of Sanskrit, Persian and Arabic as 'the three foundations of Marathi and of the importance of continuing all three in colonial education'. This position was clearly different from that of Hindutva, which insists on the need of purging Indian languages of the influence of Arabic and Persian (Deshpande 2007: 101–02).

The history-writing developed by Chiplunkar was significant for its new style of prose, which showed much more confidence in its anti-colonial claims. Writings of the famous nationalist leader Balgangadhar Tilak would bear the imprint of Chiplunkar's prose and its tone would be even more aggressive (Deshpande 2007: 103). Bhandarkar's empirical method in turn, enabled Indian historians and philologists to highlight the connections between classical languages, such as Greek and Sanskrit, and claim parity with western civilization. They contested European Indologists' remarks about Indian civilization by arguing that it was modern and rational (ibid.: 100). Bhandarkar's exploration of Sanskrit texts, moreover, was partly dictated by his involvement in debates on social and religious reform: he wanted to find out what Sanskrit texts had to say about widow remarriage. His findings led him to conclude that rather than representing a defilement of 'tradition', widow remarriage actually signified a return to the pristine past.

In Punjab, where the colonial administration encouraged Urdu at the cost of Punjabi, the *qissa*, a mix of epic and romance in the tradition of Arabic and Persian storytelling current in the region from the seventeenth century, developed into an important genre of Punjabi literature in the nineteenth century (Mir 2010: 4–5). Numerous *qisse* were composed and printed, and a continuous regional literary tradition and a literary community were sought to be forged. The Hir–Ranjha story, the earliest and the most well-known *qissa* (composed in 1605), became the most distinctive feature of Punjabi literary culture, and contributed to the shaping of Punjabi identity and political consciousness. The romance and tragedy inherent in the story of intense but unfulfilled love of Dhido (Ranjha) and Hir created affective ties between the inhabitants of Punjab and their language and literature (ibid.: 185). This would become evident in the twentieth century when the revolutionary Udham Singh, being tried in court for the murder of general O'Dwyer after the Jallianwala Bagh massacre (chapter 7), would take oath on a rendition of the Hir–Ranjha story.

Orissa offers an interesting example of the jumbled articulations of patriotism, language, history and territory. Administratively fragmented with large parts pertaining to the Bengal Presidency and sections to the Madras Presidency and the Central Provinces, middle-class Oriyas, humbled by the poor opinion that colonial officials had of them and overwhelmed by a sense of being overtaken by domineering neighbours in the north and the south, were moved to action in the late 1860s. This was a direct consequence of the attempt of a section of Bengalis to replace Oriya with Bengali in government offices and schools in coastal districts. These Bengalis argued that Oriya was not a separate language but a corrupt form of Bengali (Das Mohapatra 2007: 6–7). The controversy arose at a time when Oriya intellectuals from Cuttack and Balasore had initiated serious efforts to give a boost to Oriya. *Utkal Dipika*, the first Oriya newspaper, had made its appearance in 1866 and printing presses had been set up for publishing journals and periodicals as well as textbooks in Oriya (Mohanty 2005: 55). Experiments were underway in literary expressions and geography and the history of Orissa found prominent place in literature. The term *matru bhasha* (mother tongue) came in vogue to link space and language through the emotive evocation of the mother.

Consequently, the Oriya–Bengali dispute got transformed into a struggle to 'save' Oriya from annihilation and 'liberate' it from Bengali—a language-centred agitation that gave impetus to a strong movement for the unification of Oriya-speaking areas, and eventually led to the formation of present Orissa. Of course, in the context of emergent Indian nationalism, this move for political identity came to be classified as 'sub nationalistic' (ibid.: 45); for many Bengalis it was anti-nationalist.

Love for language reached remarkable proportions in the case of Tamil, where the vernacular came to be venerated as a goddess, devotion to which brought into being an imagined community of Tamil speakers in the late-nineteenth century (Ramaswamy 1997: 11). The people-centred ideology of modernity, writes Sumathi Ramaswamy, generates 'a *patrimonial* imagination' in which language becomes a personal, material possession of its speakers who form a community, the life of which in turn is predicated on the possession of the language (ibid.). This acute identification with and devotion for the language was distinct from nationalism; it rivalled the community of the nation by providing a supreme element of identification.

The efforts of Telugu writers to bring theatre to the people vitalized the vernacular. From the second half of the nineteenth century, writers no longer followed Sanskrit models of literature: Telugu was now a 'modern' vernacular and writers and playwrights used new styles to make their plays socially relevant. There was a noticeable change in content toward the end of the nineteenth century, when the cause of social reform was actively promoted by plays such as Veerasalingam's *Prahasanas* and Chilakamarti and Gurjada Apparao's *Kanyasulkam* (Ramakrishna 1993: 72).

Interest in western learning and literature and Indian classical tradition coupled with an awareness about the colonial critique of Hindu customs and practices produced yet another intriguing consequence. The Derozians, members of the Young Bengal group, reckless in their revolt against orthodoxy and disregard for Indian tradition, and ecstatic about the splendours of English language and culture (Chapter 3), were among the first to reflect on the problems of the colonial critique of India.

Let us take one example. Kasiprasad Ghosh, a young student of Hindu College, wrote an essay titled 'Critical remarks on the first four chapters of Mr Mill's *History of British India*' in 1828, 11 years before H. H. Wilson tried to correct some of Mill's 'misrepresentations'. As a piece that drew heavily upon Orientalist scholarship, Kasiprasad's critique received encouragement from H. H. Wilson. Following Orientalist scholars, Kasiprasad made a clear separation between India's 'Hindu' and 'Muslim' past and sought to defend 'a secular concept of a golden age among the Hindus' (Chaudhuri 2002: 65). A perfect example of 'cultural cooptation', Kasiprasad's essay tried to demonstrate the 'rational' and 'scientific' basis of Hindu chronology, law, institutions and practices, and harped on the need to bring back ancient glory. At the same time, it challenged Mill's sweeping dismissal of Hindu laws and institutions.

Kasiprasad for us is significant as a representative of a kind of consciousness where Hindu identity got enmeshed with emergent nationalism, and national identity found articulation through the unlikely medium of English. Kasiprasad, and even more his Young Bengal poet friends and companions, were unconsciously complicit in a process that eventually underscored the separation of Hindu and Muslim tradition and culture. The literatures and literary modes they engaged and experimented with were that of English and Sanskrit. English was the language being actively encouraged by the liberals and the 'Anglicists' and was vigorously supported by the Indian elite, while Sanskrit was being kept alive through government patronage and Orientalist pressure.

Persian, a classical language and the official language in Bengal till 1837, fell prey to these contending strains and slowly lost its importance, a fact barely noticed and rarely recorded. The decade of the 1830s saw Persian being replaced as the official language in different provinces, a time when language and education saw raging debates among colonial administrators and missionaries, as well as among Indian intellectuals (King 1994: 54–55). Rammohan Roy, we know, was well versed in Persian and Kasiprasad acquired a basic knowledge of it. But with the progress of the century, interest in Persian dwindled along with the number of people who knew it; Sanskrit tradition became almost synonymous with the 'classical' tradition. Later in the century, this identification of classical and Sanskrit was deployed by some to present an unbroken Indian/Hindu tradition through Sanskrit texts, which were put to newer use in contemporary contexts (Dalmia 1997: 15).

Bharatendu Harishchandra, almost universally recognized as the 'first great writer of Khari Boli Hindi' who used both Sanskritized and Persianized Hindi in his compositions, vigorously championed the cause of Hindi and the Nagari script, which he consolidated by the sheer quantity of his literary output. He also started several periodicals and strongly encouraged younger Hindi authors (King 1994: 32–33). All this produced important changes; in particular an immediate change in the preference for texts among the reading public. The by-passing of Islamic traditions and the long stretch of Muslim rule and the identification of Hindi with Hindu and Urdu with Muslim, would make the common identity being forged both exclusive and inclusive, and render nationalism as problematic and contested.

It would be hasty, however, to consider the likes of Chiplunkar or Kasiprasad to be inherently 'communal'. What responses like that of Kasiprasad reveal is the deep impress of British criticism of 'Hindu' customs (which, for them, upheld their civilizing mission and provided legitimacy to their rule), and the confusing and contradictory ways this criticism came to inform the thinking of Indian intellectuals.

The Bengali literary epic, *Megnadbad Kavya* (1861), written by another Derozian, Michael Madhusudan Dutta, proffers an illustrative example. This epic retold the story of the *Ramayana* in a way that turned Rama and Lakshmana, the traditional heroes, into 'weak-kneed, passive-aggressive, feminine villains, and the demons Ravana and his son Megnad into majestic, masculine, modern heroes' (Nandy 1983: 19). Although he maintained the gender divide of weak-feminine and majestic-masculine, Madhusudan drew upon existing south Indian and Jain traditions of the *Ramayana* to articulate dissent, both to Rammohan's redefinition of religion as organized, and monotheistic with a patriarchal godhead, and to western notions of hyper-aggressive masculinity by making them seem 'natural' in Indian tradition (ibid.: 19–20).

Madhusudan's effort, made at a time when British imperialism had not become an all-embracing and dominant force, is significant. As the century wore on and colonialism got consolidated, the additional charge of effeminacy labelled against the Bengali *babu* in combination with 'the homology between sexual and political dominance which western colonialism invariably used' (ibid.: 4), complicated matters further by adding a gendered dimension to nationalism. It is time to explore how gender featured in the nationalist discourse.

DOMESTIC DIFFERENCE

The status and condition of 'women' figured prominently in liberal and Protestant characterization of India as 'inferior' and 'rude'. This searing critique made middle-class Indian men, particularly in Bengal, get into a flurry of activity. They also engaged in a 'convoluted critical exercise' of interrogating power relationships and gender norms within indigenous customs and traditions (Sarkar 2001: 23). If this underscored the 'internalization of colonial role definitions' by such men and their acceptance of the 'homology between sexual and patriarchal stratarchies' (Nandy 1994: 6), it also produced responses that were wide-ranging and divergent. Together, they contributed to the clear etching of the contours of the private and the slow transformation of women into moral exemplars and repositories of normative tradition.

The reactions generated by the critique of the position of women were very similar to those produced by the linked issue of social reform. They ranged from a disregard of 'tradition' to a valorization of it, with reminders that the lot of women in Europe was not that exalted either. This critical streak would, through an intricate process, lead to a questioning of the colonial claim to rule on grounds of superiority. But, in the immediate context of early and mid-nineteenth century, it set men reflecting on family and conjugal relations at a time when the 'domestic' or the family was itself in a process of transition.

Partha Chatterjee's insightful and influential analysis of the nationalist discourse has demonstrated how the debates and controversy over social reform and the condition of women enabled Indian men to slowly mark out the inner domain—the interior frontier—of national life from the outer, the private from the public, the 'spiritual' from the 'material', re-articulating them in novel ways. And it was only after this domain was put in place and the position and role of women in it well-defined, that nationalism, indiscernible and tentative so far, gained enough confidence to stake its claim in the open, to come out and challenge the colonial state's power to legislate over the inner life of the nation (Chatterjee 1990, 1993).

Ranajit Guha has made a similar argument in a different way. For him, the nation as a historical imaginary emerged in the early-nineteenth century, the period of social reform, prior to the emergence of nationalism as politics (Guha 1988). Significantly, Chatterjee's argument about how nationalism was constituted at the discursive level was elaborated through a study of the reconfiguration of the ideal Indian woman. The intricate process through which Indian nationalism 'resolved' the women's question by undertaking projects of social reform and asserting, toward the end of the nineteenth century, that Indian women were educated yet different from their western counterparts, made it gain maturity and gave it confidence to enter the formal realm of institutional politics. By means of a rearticulation of Indian womanhood, the elite nationalist discourse overcame its 'constitutive contradiction' in the formation of an Indian identity (Chatterjee 1990); a contradiction constituted by efforts to modernize the nation along western lines while retaining an essential 'national identity' on which to base the political claim to nationhood (Sinha 1994: 249).

Critiques by women and feminist scholars have rightly pointed to the formalist nature of Chatterjee's argument that abstracts the 'women's question' from real life in order to offer a final resolution. Questions of internal power arrangements, they argue, were never completely resolved since they entailed distinct understandings and varied engagements on the part of both men and women. The women's question, therefore, constituted 'the internal limits' of the nationalist discourse (Sarkar 2001: 52).

Of greater significance is the danger, being pointed out only now by young scholars, in taking the 'hegemonic nationalist discourse' as possessing certain definite qualities, that is, in making it truly hegemonic. Greater sensitivity toward the author's uncertainty and tentativeness, not only with regard to issues such as 'tradition', but also of what he is trying to suggest, is likely to offer distinct understandings of the text (Chatterjee 2011). This opens up the possibility of reading the nationalist discourse as open-ended and polyvalent, and as oscillating between contesting evaluations and contradictory suggestions.

The analysis of Partha Chatterjee and its critiques agree on the centrality of the Hindu home and family as the vital inner core of the nation, and the critical place of women within the home and family. Such analyses, however, do not adequately explore why the home and family became so crucial at this stage, and why the upsurge of literature on family, in mid and late-nineteenth century, converged with efforts to constitute this new 'family'.

For a variety of reasons, home and family became the inner retreat of educated men around the time they wrote on it. By the 1860s, the confidence produced by new ideas, new education and new wealth reflected in public activity, was gradually overtaken by a sense of depression. The extremely limited nature of options in professions open to English-educated males became evident as rising prices and cost of living produced a severe financial crunch; jobs in the lower rungs of colonial administration or as clerks in foreign commercial establishments yielded relatively low and static salaries (Borthwick 1984; Malhotra 2002; Oldenburg 2002; Sarkar 1998: 285). The rigid time schedule of office jobs disrupted the earlier rhythm of everyday life. Moreover, a passive and subordinate lifestyle produced a deep sense of emasculation. Economic crisis put the structure of the joint family under strain, which was further heightened by educated sons moving to cities in connection with their education or jobs.

All this, together with the actual experience of subjection and the charge of inferiority, produced contradictory responses among middle-class men. Some, influenced by the ideas of Sri Ramakrishna, came to despise the subordination and humiliation (*dasatya*) in the world of employment, the routine life within the household (*sansara*)—complicated by the irresistible call of lust personified in the young wife (*kamini*)—and felt that renunciation of this mundane world of everyday-frets would alone permit the attainment of something spiritually higher and richer (Sarkar 1998: 289). Most, however, invested energies and passion in the reconstitution of the home, a passion that was rivalled and bolstered by interest in the world of theatre.

One important factor possibly aided their efforts. The formal inclusion of India in the British empire in 1858 signalled the culmination of a process that had begun with Warren Hastings' demarcation of personal laws—the separation of the family from the State. This allowed the emergence of the familial space as distinct from the political and administrative space of the State (Majumdar 2009: 4). For educated middle-class males, family came to provide the concrete basis of the 'community' for whose improvement they were striving. And accomplished women, educated in the 'true' sense of the term, women who devoted their skills to the well-being of the family, would not only help counter the charge of inferiority, they would allow these men, clamouring to be modern, the ground to show that their modernity was 'different' and better. Women's education and the redefinition of their role and purpose within the family gave these men the cause to fight for. And, as some feminist scholars argue, it also gave them a sense of power in a sphere that they thought was their own. Thus, personal, possibly unconscious, search for succour got entwined with the impulse to improve the condition of women, who would be the mistresses of reformed families, the foundation of the nation.

The models for such women were drawn from opposing sources—the Hindu goddess, particularly Lakshmi, the goddess of bounty, fortune, and well-being, and the *pativrata*, the devoted wife, as well as the Victorian wife as the ideal companion. Needless to say, the perceptions produced were many and conflicting, and the projects based on them multifarious. At the same time, they all sought to redefine the new woman along lines that were particular to India. The new mistress of the family was accomplished and educated but unlike a western woman who was lazy, self-indulgent and vain, she was diligent and totally dedicated to the family. The new mistress also stood in stark contrast to the coarse, garrulous woman of the lower class and caste who was uneducated and neglected family duties, and the prostitute devoted to obscenity and pleasure (Banerjee 1990; Gupta 2001; Kumar 1997).

This critical position assigned to the new woman in the positing of a different modernity accounts for the anxiety of men of middle and upper class and caste to exercise rigid control over women, a fact documented in academic works that relate to different parts of India (Chakravarty 2003; Gupta 2001; Malhotra 2002). Paradoxically, for all the talk on women's education, the actual number of women enrolled in formal institutions remained remarkably low. This is partly because the government's educational policy made no provision for the education of women and partly because elite families were reluctant to send their daughters to missionary institutions.

There was, however, an increase in the number of schools for girls from the middle of the century, opened on the initiative of individuals or voluntary associations. The Prarthana Samaj, the Deccan Educational Society, the association of Paris in Bombay, the Bramho Samaj in Calcutta and the Arya Samaj in Punjab came forward to set up schools for girls. In Madras and Agra, schools were started on private initiative, and the Gujarat Vernacular Society opened one in Ahmedabad in 1849. All men concerned with 'educating' women agreed that women needed a different kind of education—one that would groom them in the art of running a home efficiently. 'Home-science', hygiene and cooking featured in the curricula for girls' schools all over India, while debates and disagreements raged over other matters. Health, hygiene, nutrition and discipline typified the virtues of women's education—a clean, well-run, disciplined and orderly family, sustained by appetizing and nutritious food, was to lay the solid foundation for a healthy nation.

Muslim reformers of different dispositions almost echoed the Hindu men in their idea of women's education. Late-nineteenth century elite Muslim North India, states Faisal Devji, witnessed the emergence of 'a powerful new movement concerned with the reform of women's conditions' (Devji 1991: 141). The effort concentrated on women's education (literacy, home economics and 'orthodox' practices), as a means to improve the lot of women and the community in general (ibid.). Reformers were united by an interest in 'shaping women's character and knowledge, not merely in defining external controls' (Metcalf 1994: 5). The *ulema* sought to reform the 'enemy within'—the uneducated woman ignorant of Islamic doctrine and caught up in lavish, corrupt ceremonies to the neglect of the responsibilities of everyday life. Models of the European or the Hindu woman were irrelevant to his goal of restoring the moral values of the woman. Reading and understanding of religious texts was vital to this training (ibid.: 6–7).

Sir Sayyid Ahmad did not see any need for girls to go to school. At home, they were given lessons in the Koran in Arabic along with their male siblings, and were later exposed to some basic Persian books, which gave them elementary training in verb conjugation and in virtuous moral conduct. For the rest, girls helped their mothers to cook, sew and look after younger children, or supervise servants entrusted with these tasks. This way they gained practical training for their future roles as wives and mothers. They were also taught to keep household accounts, but writing was considered dangerous for women (Minault 1998).

Sayyid Ahmad's younger and more 'modern' contemporaries, such as Nazir Ahmad (1833–1912) and Khwaja Altaf Husayn Hali (1837–1914), were in favour of formal schooling for girls, and they wanted women to learn to write and also gave them credit for 'intelligence, understanding and memory' (ibid.: 36). Nazir Ahmad published a novel, *Mirat al-arus*, promoting women's education in 1869, and in 1874 Husayn Hali produced a didactic text on the benefits of female education (Devji 1991: 141).

In the decade between 1896 when a women's section was opened at the Muhammedan Educational Conference founded by Sir Sayyid and 1906 when the Aligarh Zenana Madrassa was opened, opposition to women's education was stilled and energies got concentrated on degrees and the kind of 'education' (*talim*) that women were to get (Devji 1991: 141–42).

The main purpose behind urging women's education was to tutor them into becoming 'real managers of the household', the focus of family life. A long-winded process turned the educated woman from the source of *fitna* (social chaos) into the guardian of orthodoxy and moral values, whose duty it was to 'save' men from the wickedness of the public, the impure outside world (Devji 1994: 30–33). In addition to books and stories for the instruction of women, Nazir Ahmad and Hali wrote novels in Urdu that dealt with the pressures and tensions of the family with empathy.

Urdu literature was not alone in its invocation of the family. The rapid transition in family and society was reflected in vernacular literature in general. Novels in different languages pondered on questions of family, class tensions, socialization of girls and relationship of husband and wife with incisive and indulgent concern. They portrayed tensions within the family generated by different values of different generations, the pressures of new professions, and gave elegant articulation to the problems and pleasures of young couples trying to be ideal companions within the norms and strict code of conduct of a joint family. Novels did not offer resolutions for difficulties. Rather, they made such problems palpable and real by exploring their nuances and complexities.

Women, of course, were not passive objects of the reform venture. Indeed, women's energy and will made the project of education fraught with tension. To begin with, women in joint families exerted considerable power and influence in the 'private' domain. The task of making them fall in line with the aspirations of an upwardly mobile emergent middle class was delicate and required a judicious mix of persuasion and coercion (Malhotra 2002: 118). For men acting on behalf of women, the moral vulnerability of women was almost a self-evident proposition, and this made them ever anxious to secure women's high moral conduct.

Male anxieties were heightened by the fact that the effect of education on women could neither be gauged completely nor monitored properly. This became evident once the women started writing and publishing. Their accounts and tales, instead of rendering the family as the domain of bliss, often underscored their pain of separation from their natal homes and yearning for their carefree maiden days.

More significantly, as the work of Padma Anagol on the women of Maharashtra demonstrates, women not only appreciated the new opportunities opened for them by education and public activity centred on social reform; they deployed notions of gender equality which they took to be 'western' to reflect critically on their own marital relations. They were also quick to make use of the rights granted to them by law, a point we will discuss in greater detail in a later section (Anagol 2005, 2010). Anagol's work offers an important corrective to the male-centred analysis of most scholars, including feminist scholars (Bannerji 1998; Sinha 1995, for instance), who focus almost exclusively on the connections between gender relations and structures of colonial power as well as the male nationalist discourse to highlight the constraints imposed on women. This results in a sad neglect of the vital aspect of women's endeavours and achievements (Anagol 2005: 182).

The women who gathered for the Saturday meetings of the Prarathana Sabha in the 1870s did not only hear prominent male reformers, they also learnt the art of oratory and took the initiative in founding the *Striyancha Sabha* (Women's Society) in the 1880s. In the weekly meetings of the Sabha, educated women read out essays and gave instructions to other women on various issues; they also underlined the necessity of combating popular prejudices against women's education (Anagol 2010: 284–85). The impact of this awareness and organization would soon find expression in the Maharashtrian women's active participation in the 'Age of Consent' debate.

At the same time, it is true that women from elite families often participated in the male project of creating the new woman, even if they made innovative uses of the connotations of Lakshmi and took over the role of educators themselves, a fascinating story we will not be able to enter into in detail. Women's inputs in the enterprise of creating the new mistress of a decorous household further contributed to an idealization of the home and family (Devi 1900, for instance). Through such joint energies, the woman and the home she embodied became, in the second half of the nineteenth century, the most important sites where the 'essential marks of cultural identity' were located and reproduced (Seth 2007: 135). This marked a space that was claimed to be out of bounds for the colonial state.

RIGHTS, REFORM, RETRIBUTION

Let us return to the domain of the public and the political from this foray into the inner and emotional life of the nation. In this sphere, the presence of the colonial state was conspicuous, since its policies and reforms had a direct impact on the activities of educated Indians. Equally, policies of the state were shaped by Indian understandings of rights and Indian demands for rights and representation in the government. The colonial state, moreover, had its own imperatives, just as the educated Indians were forced to take notice of the perceptions of different sections of society in order to be true representatives. This entangled process of interaction changed the contours of the colonizer and the colonized and gave distinct nuances to the engagement.

For a variety of reasons, some discussed in Chapter 4, the mid-nineteenth century occasioned a shift in the activities of public associations that had come into being to work for the well-being of the community, and middle-class efforts acquired a certain degree of urgency. Associations, such as the Landholder's Society, founded in Calcutta in 1838, with a mix of Indian and European members and dominated by the landed gentry, gave way to newer ones with different concerns. The membership and purposes of the Landholder's Society had been extremely limited and even though it had a few branches in the hinterland, it had become defunct by 1840. Nevertheless, it offered a lesson in constitutional agitation within the British system, which later organizations would learn from.

The issue of the renewal of the Company's charter in the early 1850s provided fresh impetus for elite mobilization. The British Indian Association set up in Calcutta in 1851 distinguished itself by its composition and efforts—it was entirely Indian, and attempted to coordinate the work of the three presidencies in petitions to the British Parliament to effectively voice the demands of Indian subjects. To this end, branches of the Association were set up in Bombay and Madras. The Associations of Calcutta and Bombay, aware of the importance of British public opinion and the Parliament in the shaping of Indian policies, made attempts to influence public opinion in Britain. Increasingly, organizations such as these came to see themselves as mediators between the British rulers and the Indian 'masses', confident that they were best suited to bring the grievances of the people to the notice of the government. Interestingly, this was accepted by the colonial government and members of the Associations were given entry into formal institutions. But rivalry among the Indian elite soon led to parallel organizations being established in Bombay and Madras, a reflection of regional tensions that would also mark the nationalist struggle at a later stage.

The Indian Councils Act of 1861 signalled the beginning of institutional reforms. Legislative councils were established at the centre and in provinces and this gave British India extended power to make laws (Chapter 4). The Councils Act strengthened the Viceroy's authority over his own executive council, but it provided for the inclusion of very few non-official Indian members with limited powers in the imperial and local legislative councils. Similarly, the municipal reforms of the 1870s allowed a minimum entry of educated Indians on the basis of elections to municipal boards. The municipal boards were presided over by district collectors and dominated by local administrators of the colonial government, but they did include a few 'non-official' members. British liberals believed that Indian members on boards and councils would, in addition to voicing 'public opinion', gain political education that would eventually make them ready for self-rule. At the same time, these non-official members were chosen for their expressed loyalty to the British government. This makes Anil Seal's claim that systems of nomination, representation and election were means of 'enlisting Indians to work for imperial aims' largely true (Seal 1968). It also demonstrates the contradictory expectations on the part of both the British and the Indians. Unsurprisingly, they resulted in unexpected consequences.

While reforms opened up partial but new opportunities of political campaign for educated Indians, several measures adopted by the colonial government gave them occasion to believe that their rights were being trampled. The very people who were selected to act as intermediaries and who felt that such a role was meant for them, increasingly became conscious of their lack of 'rights' and began to rally for them.

The government's attempts to impose an income tax in 1860, at a time of famine and scarcity in India, occasioned indignation and protest from middle-class Indians. Income and property taxes were imposed to meet the cost of 'developmental' activities of municipal boards. They were meant to help the government cope better with financial difficulties by shifting charges for local requirements on to new local taxes (Sarkar [1983] 1995: 19). Widespread protests caused this tax to be withdrawn in 1865, only to be reintroduced under the guise of 'certificate tax' of one per cent on all trades and professions in 1867 and reconverted to income tax the following year.

A different measure aroused the ire of the elite, particularly in Bengal. Responding to the propaganda of the Anglo–Indian press that higher education in English was only contributing to disaffection and discontent among the Indians, in 1870 the government resolved to cut back funding for English education in Bengal and spend the money ostensibly on mass education through the vernacular. Educated Indians, affronted by limited opportunities in government service and other professions and harassed by the income tax, were incensed by yet another measure that went straight against them. The reason offered by the government—that more needed to be spent on vernacular education—found very little favour with the intelligentsia. Apart from an indifference toward the education of the *hoi polloi*, they were aware of the excessive amounts being spent on the army, on extensive 'home charges'—

payments by the Indian state to Britain on various counts— and so-called 'public works' geared to serve imperial needs.

The final blow came in 1876 with the government's decision to lower the age for taking the Indian Civil Service Examination from 21 to 19 years. It was difficult enough for young Indians to travel to London to take the exam. They had been asking for simultaneous exams in London and India. This demand went completely unheeded and the age for taking the exam was lowered, which made the prospects of Indians entering the civil service bleaker. There was agitation and discontent with the demand for greater rights becoming more and more vocal. Surendranath Banerjea's Indian Association devoted itself with full vigour to this cause.

The sense of siege was heightened under the administration of Conservative Viceroy Lytton, who came to India in 1876 with clear ideas of how to deal with the growing critical attitude among educated Indians. The Indian press, which had grown steadily along with the expansion of the public sphere, was the first to face the brunt. The Vernacular Press Act of 1878 put vernacular newspapers under strict censure, prohibiting them to write anything critical of the government under the threat that the deposit that they made to the government and their machinery would be confiscated if they did so.

It is worth exploring why Lytton introduced this act against the counsel of his own law members. The first Indian-owned presses were set up in Calcutta in the early decades of the nineteenth century with other large cities following suit. Our Hindu College student Kasiprasad was the first to show the way— he ran an English press and published a weekly paper called the *Hindu Intelligencer*, which won great repute. An Indian press established in Bombay in 1861 utilized the advanced technology of telegraph and the Reuters news service in London to get news of Britain and the rest of the world. Madras was the first to launch an evening newspaper, the *Madras Mail*, in 1868 (which was, however, dominated by white Englishmen). Balasore began publishing an Oriya newspaper from 1866, and dailies appeared in Allahabad in the 1860s and in Lahore in the 1870s.

The Indian press was 'journalistically sophisticated' (Stein 2010: 259) and gave a lot of importance to administrative news, with detailed discussions of debates carried on in town and district assemblies created by the Indian Councils Act of 1861. It also tried to counter missionary propaganda. This is particularly true of Tamil journals and newspapers. Over time, the Indian press became more and more 'political and nationalistic' (ibid.). Apart from suggesting that it was unnatural for a conquered people to have admiration for British culture and institutions, it openly criticized unilateral government policies that did not take Indians into consideration. As early as 1858, the periodical *Hindoo Patriot*, a suggestive title indicative of the role of patriotism, had questioned the proposal for the transfer of the government to the British Crown. 'Can a revolution in the Indian Government', queried the editor of the *Hindoo Patriot*, Harishchandra Mukherjee, 'be authorized by Parliament without consulting the wishes of the vast millions of men for whose benefit it is proposed to be made?'. The answer, he affirmed, was a definite no. The time, he stated, 'is nearly come when all Indian questions must be solved by Indians' (*Hindoo Patriot* 1858, cited in Stein 2010).

A further testimony to the nationalistic spirit of the *Hindoo Patriot* was its manifest solidarity with the indigo peasants rebelling against the planters in 1859–60, a case we will take up shortly. Support was extended to the peasants through the genre of the novel—Dinabandhu Mitra's *Nil Darpan* poignantly portrayed the plight of the peasants. This became a widespread trend. The Indian intelligentsia and their associations and periodicals keenly followed and supported peasant causes, which became evident when Justice Ranade and the Poona Sarvajanik Sabha, as well as Marathi newspapers, upheld the cause of insurgent peasants against moneylenders during the Deccan riots of 1875. Newspapers provided an all-India forum for educated Indians to discuss and debate critical issues and often arrive at a consensus. This contributed considerably to the breaking of regional barriers. By 1875, there were about 400 Indian-owned newspapers in English and regional languages with a readership of 150,000. Viewed in the context of numerous associations and efforts to 'reform' or 'uplift' the community—religious, lower-caste, Dalit, regional, or even national—all these ventures, albeit with limitations and contradictions, point towards the intersection of the elite and subordinate groups, and a common awareness of working together against alien masters.

Chronology of Events Relating to Newspapers and Media, 1780–1969

Year	Events
1780	James Augustus Hicky establishes first newspaper in India, *Bengal Gazette,* 1780–82, Calcutta.
1785	First newspaper established in Madras, *Courier,* with government support.
1789	Bombay gets its first paper, *Bombay Herald.*
1799	Regulation order of Bengal Government prohibits publication of news without censor's approval.
1818	James Silk Buckingham establishes *Calcutta Journal;* deported in 1823 for editorial criticism of governor general.
	First vernacular papers established, *Samachar Durpan* at Serampore Mission, *Bengal Gazette* by Gangadhar Bhattacharya, Calcutta.
1822	First Persian newspapers established, *Jami-i-Jehan Numa* (with some pages in Urdu) and Ram Mohan Roy's *Mirat-ul-Akhbar,* Calcutta. Roy also takes over *Sambad Kaumudi,* Bengali weekly.
	Bombay Samachar (Gujarati) established by Fardoonjee Marzban in Bombay, now oldest surviving vernacular newspaper.
1823	Adams Regulation of Press law requires license for printing.
1832	Bal Shastri Jambhekar establishes first Marathi paper in Bombay.
	Englishman established by J. H. Stocquelor on ruins of John Bull in the East, Calcutta; becomes voice of Europeans in India.
1834	First independent paper established in Ceylon, now *Ceylon Observer.*
1835	Registration of Press Act (Metcalfe Act) repeals many of Adams Act restrictions. Basic law obtains today.
1836	First significant all-Urdu newspaper, *Urdu Akhbar,* Delhi.
1838	*Bombay Times* established by businessmen, becomes city's leading paper.
1840	*Sambad Prabhakar,* begun by Bengali poet, Iswar Chandra Gupta, Calcutta, becomes first significant vernacular daily.
1853	*Hindoo Patriot* established in Calcutta, first nationalist paper; serves as vehicle for indigo grievances 1859–61.

Year	Events
1861	Robert Knight merges *Bombay Times, Standard* and *Telegraph* to form *Times of India* in Bombay.
1865	*Pioneer* established in Allahabad; Kipling employed 1887–89, becomes Indian-owned in 1931; moved to Lucknow in 1933.
1868	*Madras Mail* established Charles Lawson editor; becomes voice of non-official Europeans in South.
1870	First Indian-owned English language daily, *Indian Mirror*, established as weekly in 1861, Calcutta.
1872	*Civil and Military Gazette* established in Simla, moved to Lahore in 1876; Kipling employed 1882–87; closed in 1963.
1875	Robert Knight establishes *Statesman* in Calcutta, incorporates *Friend of India* (1817) in 1883; Delhi edition begun in 1931.
1877	Birdwood survey shows 64 vernacular newspapers in Bombay Province, 60 in north and central India, 28 in Bengal, 19 in Madras Province. No circulation over 3,000.
1878	Lytton Act penalizing 'seditious' writing in 'Oriental' languages; repealed 1881. *Hindu* begun by G. Subramanya Iyer et al. in Madras.
1881	Tilak et al. establish *Kesari* in Marathi, *Mahratta* in English, Poona; sentenced for sedition in *Kesari* editorials in 1897.
1882	G. Subramanya Iyer establishes *Swadesamitram* (Tamil).
1888	*Malayalam Manorama* established in Kottayam by Kerala Christians.
1896	Lumiere Bros, put on first cinema show in Bombay.
1906	*Bande Mataram* established as voice of Bengal anti-partition movement; Aurobindo Ghose, chief editor.
1908	In response to terrorism, Newspaper (Incitement to Offences) Act passed; bolstered by 1910 Press Act; repealed 1921.
1911	Mahmud Tarzi begins first paper in Afghanistan, *Seraj ul-Akh-bar*.
1912	Abul Kalam Azad's nationalist *Al Hilal* (Urdu) established in Calcutta, gains 26,000 circulation before 1915 closure.
1913	D. G. Phalke produces first Indian movie, *Raja Harischander*, Bombay.
	Bombay Chronicle established by Pherozeshah Mehta; supports Congress under Benjamin Guy Horniman's editorship; dies 1959.
1918	Gandhi establishes *Young India* in English, *Navajivan* in Gujarati.
1919	Arya Samajists in Lahore establish *Pratap* as Urdu daily.
1923	*Hindustan Times* established by Akali Sikhs in New Delhi; taken over by G. D. Birla in 1927; becomes highly influential. *Mathrubhumi*, nationalist Malayam daily, established in Calicut.
1924	Madras Presidency Radio Club established, folds 1927.
1927	Broadcasting transmission stations established in Bombay and Calcutta; under government control after failure in 1930. Nationalist press service established by Swaminath Sadanand, soon folds but Bombay outlet, *Free Press Journal*, lives.
1931	A. M. Irani makes first Indian talkie, *Alam Ara*, Bombay.

Year	Events
1932	Motion Picture Society of India formed.
	Indian Express begun in Madras on *Daily Express* base; taken over by Ramnath Goenka, 1936; later published from six centres.
1933	Gandhi begins *Harijan* in English, later Hindi *Harijan*.
1937	*Sant Tukaram*, Marathi film, wins award at Venice.
1941	*Blitz*, popular leftist weekly, established by R. K. Karanjia.
1942	*Dawn*, voice of Muslim League, established in New Delhi.
1947	S. R. Dalmia takes over *Times of India* group from British. First Sinhala film made in Ceylon.
1948	Government Film Unit established in Ceylon; films win recognition.
1954	Report of Indian Press Commission results in closer governmental surveillance through Registrar and Press Council.
1956	Satyajit Ray's film *Pather Panchali* wins Cannes award.
1959	Inaugural of experimental television at Delhi.
1961	Government film Institute established at Prabhat Studios, Poona.
1963	Purchase of *Statesman* by consortium of Indian industrialists completes Indianization of daily press.
1964	Pakistan begins experimental television at Lahore.
1964	National Press Trust of Pakistan established; 12 papers jointly owned.
1965	Commencement of television broadcasting in India.
1965	Establishment of Indian Press Council.
1966	Multi-lingual news agency, *Samachar Bharati*, established in India.
1969	Indo–US, agreement to bring TV to 5,000 villages via communications satellite.

It is not difficult to understand why the Indian press aroused the ire of hard-headed British administrators. It was difficult to censor the English language press as it included Anglo-Indian and government publications. But it had become necessary to clip the wings of the vernacular press. Lytton's measure, interestingly, did not only cause consternation; the Bengali newspaper *Amrita Bazar Patrika* became English overnight to evade the act and its attendant censure. This is just one illustration of the political astuteness that the Indian middle classes had come to acquire. The Vernacular Press Act of 1878 became a major rallying point for the Indian elite and their associations all over India and occasioned intense agitation. Help also came from an unexpected quarter—Gladstone, the Liberal leader of the Opposition, created commotion in the British Parliament over the issue.

Lytton followed up on the Vernacular Press Act with the Arms Act of 1878, which made it obligatory for Indians to get a license for possessing arms, a provision not applied to Europeans and Eurasians. This act occasioned further indignation and intensified the ongoing agitation. In this situation of turmoil, news of the victory of the Liberal Party in Britain in 1880 brought joy and relief. Lytton resigned to be succeeded by liberal Lord Ripon. Paradoxically, a controversy during Ripon's viceroyalty widened the rift between the British and Indians, and hardened Indian demands for rights and citizenship, heralding the beginning of nationalism in the political sphere.

MASCULINITY, EFFEMINACY, CONSENT

On 9 February 1883, C. P. Ilbert, the Law Member of the Government of India, introduced a bill in the Imperial Legislative Council to amend the Code of Criminal Procedure of the Indian Penal Code. The bill proposed to grant limited criminal jurisdiction to native officials of the administrative service over British subjects in the *mofussil*, country towns of India. This was in keeping with the liberal promise of racial equality, proffered in the Queen's proclamation. The proposed bill, known as the Ilbert Bill, generated a 'white mutiny' and brought to the fore the deep-seated racism of England's European subjects in India. Anglo-Indian officials and non-officials alike united in vehement opposition to the bill, forcing Viceroy Ripon to come to an agreement with them. A modified bill, which preserved the special legal status of European subjects while granting native officers criminal jurisdiction over them, was passed in January 1884. This modified bill undermined the original principle of racial equality by allowing European and British subjects the right to demand trial by a special jury, composed at least partly of Europeans and Americans, under an Indian judge.

The Ilbert Bill and the controversy it generated are significant for various reasons. One, they evinced a total polarization of Anglo–Indian and Indian opinion and underscored the extremely limited nature and reach of liberal promises. Indeed, this controversy undercut Ripon's early measures, such as the repeal of the Vernacular Press Act and modification to the Arms Act, which had restored the 'faith' of educated Indians in the British liberal tradition. More importantly, flagrant racism now posited its claim of superiority on its powerful masculinity as opposed to the 'effeminacy' of the stereotypical Bengali *babu* and by extension the educated Indian middle-class man. This gave a gendered twist to the notions of decline and degeneration among Indians held by Europeans, and overlapped in important ways with concerns of the Indian elite, making their political project more anomalous.

It is vital to remember, as Mrinalini Sinha points out, that 'colonial race relations were constantly rearticulated in response to material conditions' (Sinha 1995: 14). Both the notions of the 'manly Englishman' and the 'effeminate babu' were adapted and redefined in accordance with political and economic shifts in the course of the nineteenth century, and this triggered off discrete reactions at different moments.

In Sinha's view, the *babu*, an old Bengali word of Persian origin, did not carry any pejorative connotation in British usage till the mid-nineteenth century. It was used as a title of respect for men like the English Mr. Indeed, the early negative connotations of the *babu* were to be found in Bengali satires, which commented on and ridiculed the *nouveau riche* culture of Calcutta which had imitated and adopted Persianized and later Anglicized lifestyles to climb up the social and economic ladder. This usage went into British satires as well, but did not influence colonial understandings significantly. While it is true that 'broad generalizations about the mild-mannered and effete nature of inhabitants of certain regions' or of adherents of some religions in India were 'long part of the stock of ideas held by Europeans' (ibid.: 15), and both the evangelical Charles Grant and the utilitarian James Mill had commented on the passive and soft character of Bengali Hindus, the charge of effeminacy did not acquire vigour before the middle of the nineteenth century.

Thomas Babington Macaulay was the first to clearly relate the 'feebleness' of Bengalis to their loss of independence and to their dubious moral character (Macaulay 1900). James Mill was equally eloquent. Comparing the Hindus to the 'half-civilized' ancestors of the British, he commented that the 'manliness and courage of our ancestors' was certainly superior to 'the slavish and dastardly spirit of the Hindus'. The ancestors, however, were 'inferior' to 'that effeminate people' in gentleness, a gentleness, he hastened to add, that was not sincere since 'under the general glossing of the exterior of the Hindu, lies a general disposition to deceit and perfidy' (Mill [1817] 1975: 247).

By the late-nineteenth century, this characterization became dominant and came to be applied to Indian middle-class males in general by the British. The prominent presence of the middle-classes in the public sphere and their increasing demands for rights and representation had made them particularly odious. Further, colonial scorn was aimed at the grandiose pretensions but economic 'impotence' of these 'potentially disloyal' English-educated Indians. Here, of course, gradations were made between the Bengali, who had 'failed' as an entrepreneur, and the Parsi, who had retained a share in the modern economic sector. At the same time, their lack of manliness and their ambiguous loyalty disqualified them from getting the rights that they were demanding. The politics of colonial masculinity thus 'gave a new lease of life to the racial exclusivity of the Anglo–Indians in India' and set in motion political, economic and ideological realignments in imperial social formation (Sinha 1995: 63).

Middle-class Indian men, for their part, took this charge of effeminacy very seriously since a combination of factors made it real for them. Limited economic opportunities and curtailed 'rights' circumscribed their attempts at leadership. Their general sense of frustration and disillusionment now got linked to the idea of physical decline as the main factor behind degeneration. Once again, the Indian middle-classes accepted and internalized the charge of effeminacy because it helped explain much of their frustration. In this sense, they were complicit in constructions of masculinity and effeminacy.

Responses to the charge of effeminacy varied in different parts of India according to the hierarchy of 'effeminacy' created by the colonizers. In the last chapter, we discussed how the censuses marked out the 'martial races' and gave them special opportunities in the British–Indian army. This affected developments in the Punjab region which were totally different from that in Bengal. The Bengalis, the most prominent in politics, were considered among the most effeminate, indeed the epitome of effeminacy. This spurred a range of reactions and efforts to counter physical weakness. Climate and eating habits were held responsible for physical weakness, and health, hygiene and diet came to hold the pride of place in discussions about family and the duties of the housewife. The mistress of the house was urged to pay rigorous attention to the health of the family by lovingly undertaking the task of preparing delicious and nutritious meals. Widespread efforts to define the home and coerce the women to be bound to it were in themselves moves to cope with the sense of emasculation and the charge of effeminacy.

The other way to cope with the lack of physical prowess was by developing it, a method advocated strongly by various reform associations of the late-nineteenth century. In Bengal, there were attempts to revive *akhara*s or gymnasiums in order to bolster physical training and instil a sense of pride.

Swami Vivekananda ardently advocated a way to God through physical activity, rather than reading and understanding the *Bhagavad Gita*. A firm believer in the 'spirituality and purity of the Hindu race', Vivekananda was envious of western vitality, skill in coordination, self-confidence and strength (Gordon 1974: 78). He exhorted his disciples to utilize the powers within themselves to build their country instead of just 'repeating things parrot-like but not doing them'; holding physical weakness to be responsible for such lack of action. 'First of all, our young men must be strong. Religion will come afterwards' (Vivekananda 1964: 156–57).

Novelist Bankimchandra Chatterjee, whom we have referred to earlier, mocked the Bengali *babu* as he explored the causes behind his lack of physical prowess. Bankim held the gentleness of Gaudiya Vaishnavism, advocated by the medieval reformer Sri Chaitanya, responsible for the meekness of Bengalis and sought to replace the love-worn Krishna of Vaishava *bhakti* (devotion) with the strong Krishna of the *Mahabharata* as the real deity of Vaishnavism (Kaviraj 1995). The novelist wanted to forge a community of Bengalis by linking the western-educated few and the Bengali-educated many by means of a common language; a deployment of historical knowledge and tradition was an effective mode of forging this community.

In his reconstructed historical novels, Rajput and Bengali Hindus matched Muslim and British heroes in strength and courage (Gordon 1974: 80). It has to be borne in mind, however, that Bankim never made a fetish of the past, and if he did not hesitate to make Sri Krishna the core of his religion, he did it with the full awareness that it was *deshachar* (custom) and not *shastra* that ruled the religious life in India (Tripathi 1967: 6–9). It is perhaps more important to understand the message Bankim sought to convey, rather than go into a discussion on whether he was 'communal'. His message was that the shortcomings of the Bengalis, their feebleness and cowardice, were more than overcome by their past physical and intellectual vitality, which urgently needed to be revived and strengthened.

As indicated earlier, the Rajput as the ideal Kshatriya and the Maratha as the great warrior was invoked in historical novels in different languages and they evoked nostalgia about a radiant Hindu past. This was particularly true of the Maharashtrian Brahmans and the Marathas. On the whole, white racism posed in gendered terms inspired trends of physical culture and militancy among the Indian youth, some of which was to later take a strident cultural nationalistic turn. It also left a tenuous but enduring imprint on the cultural constructions of a 'strong' nation current till today.

Not surprisingly, Indian backlash to the charge of effeminacy found eloquent articulation over an issue related to women. In January 1891, the Law Member of India introduced a bill in the Imperial Legislative Council raising 'the age of consent' for sexual intercourse with married and unmarried Indian girls from ten to 12 years. The bill came in the wake of the death of a child-wife, Phulmonee, after her husband subjected her to violent sexual intercourse. The bill also proposed to term intercourse with girls below the age of ten as rape, punishable by ten years of imprisonment. The bill became an act on 19 March 1891 with Viceroy Lansdowne's ratification. The Indian Penal Code and the Code of Criminal Procedure were amended to raise the age of sexual intercourse with girls from ten to 12 and to make its violation punishable by ten years' imprisonment or transportation for life. This act, according to a reformer and historian of nineteenth century India, was the last act as a measure of reform effected by influencing British public opinion and the first act where politics and reaction were successfully linked in India (Natarajan cited in Anagol 2010: 182). The Age of Consent Bill (and the Act) let loose a massive controversy and produced severe opposition. Bengal, where the problem of premature consummation of child-marriage was taken to be serious, took the lead in opposing the act. The zealous disapproval of Bengali men induced the Viceroy, with prompting from the Lieutenant Governor of Bengal, to work out a compromise. It became virtually impossible to bring cases of premature consummation of child-marriages for trial under the act.

The extant historiography of the Age of Consent controversy has tended to locate the significance of the controversy in its impact on the nationalist struggle. For Charles Heimsath (1964), this controversy marked the triumph of Hindu orthodoxy to gain popular support. Partha Chatterjee, on the other hand, sees in the 'conservative reaction' to the Age of Consent debate and the 'disappearance' of the women's question from the agenda of Indian nationalism after this, the coming of age of the nationalist discourse. The discourse had successfully demarcated the interior frontier of the nation and placed the home and the woman within it. While the discourse was ready to accept the superiority of the colonial state in the outer, material sphere (Chatterjee 1993: 121–22), it was no longer willing to accept the colonial state's authority to legislate on the inner cultural domain. The 'resolution of the women's question', therefore, was a bold declaration of the maturity of nationalism (Chatterjee 1990: 233–53).

In reality, the nationalist discourse with regard to women, even in Bengal, was never as univocal or unanimous and the 'resolution' was never complete. The Brahmo Samaj in Calcutta was split twice on the issue of consent, an illustration of the divergence of opinion only within one small group. Women in Bengal and in other parts of country, as well as men in different parts of India, supported the act on grounds of health and safety of child brides.

Feminist scholars such as Tanika Sarkar have seen in the conservative reaction a vigorous attempt by the men of a beleaguered middle class, to defend 'indigenism' and tradition, in order to hang on to their authority over home and women (2001). Mrinalini Sinha points to the direct appeal made by these men to the logic of colonial masculinity. Moving away from the issue of the abuse of the child-wife, Bengali men and their empathizers underscored the curtailment of the right of the husband. The defence of orthodox Hindu patriarchal norms was posed in the universal patriarchal language of the 'natural' right of all husbands (Sinha 1995: 140).

The 'beleaguered' men sought to make common cause with the 'crisis' in British masculinity arising from the women's movement for suffrage and other rights in England in the 1880s. While British feminists invoked the 'glories of the empire' to seek a place in its global power and universal social mission, particularly the redress of the condition of 'hapless' and helpless Indian women (Burton 1994: 7), Indian men appealed to male prestige and honour in order to protect their natural rights over women and family. This ingenious male bonding, posed on the innate connection of the empire and the colony, in conjunction with British uncertainty regarding interference with Hindu practices, gave the opponents a slight edge over those nationalists who were supporting the Consent Bill.

For the British administrators and the Anglo–Indian press, support of the bill was another evidence of effeminacy, of men succumbing to the wishes of women. This criticism came in handy for the Indian opponents of the bill. Balwant Gangadhar Tilak, the nationalist leader from Maharashtra, agreed completely with A. O. Hume's characterization of Indian men supporting the bill as incompetent 'masters of their own houses'. Their incompetence and 'unmanliness' was such that they could not even control affairs of their own household and had to appeal to the government for help (Tilak, *Mahratta*, 12 April 1891, cited in Sinha 1995: 159).

The victory of the nationalist opponents of the bill, in the sense that even though it became an act, the powers of its implementation were restricted, therefore, was not a great triumph of Indian nationalism. Quite apart from the fact that women's expressed views went unheeded, the success 'claimed on behalf of revitalized Indian masculinity' was hardly so since it had very close affinities with the colonial agenda. Nationalism got reinvigorated no doubt, but its claim of 'difference' was compromised (Sinha 1995: 160).

If we follow Anagol and move away from a focus on the links between imperialism and nationalism and the manipulation of the 'woman' in a cultural contest between the colonizer and the colonized over legitimation (Anagol 2010: 283), we get a different picture. Women of Maharashtra, argues Anagol, showed remarkable resourcefulness in 'casting themselves' before they were 'recast' by men (Anagol 2005: 182). Their political capacities found expression in the establishment of the first independent women's organization—the Arya Mahila Samaj—in the early 1880s. Founded by Pandita Ramabai, the Mahila Samaj received enthusiastic support from Kashibai Kanitkar and Ramabai Ranade who went from door to door persuading Hindu women to join the meetings of the Samaj (Anagol 2010: 285).

Marathi journals, printed by the 'Women's Press', expanded the notion of *bhaginivarg* (sisterhood) among a large women's collective (ibid.) and women's self-authorization programmes spilled over in the public sphere. Women started making use of law courts and state procedures of 'petition' in claiming their rights to property, livelihood, remarriage, mobility and custody of children. This was reflected in the large number of cases filed for the restitution of conjugal rights—an idea unknown in pre-colonial India, which was a direct importation from English ecclesiastical law—by Hindu (and Muslim) women including mothers of child brides, and dissolution of marriage by Christian women. Between 1880 and 1885, a total of 2,784 wives brought cases against their husbands in criminal courts demanding payment for ill-treatment (Anagol 2010: 290).

The debates around the Age of Consent gave women the opportunity to bring their concerns over domestic lives into the public sphere and gave vent to the tensions generated by their new-found aspirations for education, individuality, and desire for a change in conjugal relations and the unchanging balance of power within home, family, and society. A few years before the Age of Consent Bill was proposed, Behramji Malabari, a Parsi reformer from Bombay, had published his 'Notes on Infant Marriage and Enforced Widowhood' (1884), and urged the government to reform Indian domestic practices. Although Malabari had not directly asked for legal intervention by the state, and had rallied against child marriage on grounds that it produced over-population and poverty, and incapacitated adults and sickly children, the opinion on his Notes had been very mixed, exhibiting the overlap of disjunctive processes and sentiments. After the Revolt, colonial authorities had allegedly reverted to 'non-interference' in social and religious affairs and Indian social reformers had become ambivalent with regard to legal intervention of the state in the domestic sphere. And when reformers such as M. G. Ranade did ask for limited intervention, it was only to check the reproduction of a weak race that was to occasion the economic ruin of India.

Journals run by Maharashtrian women 'angrily noted' the indifference of Indian males to the suffering of the female sex (Anagol 2010: 298). Rakhmabai, who became famous for a 'social drama' that resulted from a case filed in 1884 in the High Court of Bombay for the restitution of conjugal rights by her husband Dadaji Bhikhaji (Chandra 1998: 1), constructed a gendered critique of child marriage in a series of letters in the *Times of India* published under the pseudonym of 'The Hindu Lady'. Hindu, Muslim, Christian and Jewish women showed great solidarity to the recalcitrant Rakhmabai, who, married at age eleven, had consistently refused to live with her husband on attaining puberty, and refused to do so even after the court ruled that she would be imprisoned if she did not return to her husband. Wedded at an age at which she was 'incapable of giving intelligent consent', Rakhmabai insisted that she was not bound to go back to that man (ibid.).

The Rakhmabai case was intricately interwoven with the Age of Consent debates, since the issue of restitution of conjugal rights was closely tied to that of the consummation of marriage (Anagol 2010: 293). Rakhmabai's defiance and the increasing assertiveness of the women of Maharashtra produced a clash of fears and hopes, of 'contending conceptions of the desired social order' (Chandra 1998: 2). While women held child marriage and arranged marriage responsible for the unhappiness of Indian wives, male discourse evaded acknowledging the existence of 'unhappiness' in child marriages. Indeed, for Tilak and large sections of orthodox men, Rakhmabai's defiance demonstrated the evil consequences of English education (Anagol 2010: 293), and needed to be countered by persuading women to abide by time-honoured tradition. The male backlash to the Age of Consent Bill arose from the 'real threat' posed by actions of women: actions that made Hindu patriarchy feel 'under siege' (ibid.: 306). It did not spring from charges of effeminacy, or a tussle between native and European masculinity. Male anxiety was a product not of the colonial state's entry into the private sphere, but of the increasing recourse taken by women to colonial structures, especially the law, to renegotiate conjugal relations (Anagol 2005: 182). The tidy 'resolution' of the women's question by nationalist discourse (Chatterjee 1990, 1993), was made messy by assertive women who moved forth into the public with their own agenda.

THE FIRST NATIONAL ORGANIZATION

Processes in the 1870s and early 1880s, we have seen, had conferred a new dynamism on the emerging nationalist consciousness among the educated middle classes. Centralizing policies of the colonial state and infrastructural technology made possible 'emergent territorially grounded conceptions of a national economy, culture, and identity' (Goswami 1998: 614). This was reflected in the change in the nature of associations in the presidencies, the organization of all-India agitations, including an attempt to raise a 'National Fund' to sponsor such agitations and the growth of political associations in towns all over India.

The Indian National Congress was formed at a national convention held in Bombay in December 1885. The circular sent out in March 1885 to inform political workers of the coming Congress session affirmed that the Congress intended 'to enable all the most earnest labourers in the cause of national progress to become personally known to each other' (Chandra et al. [1988] 2000: 77). W. C. Bonnerji, the first President of the Congress, declared the Congress's goal to be the 'eradication, by direct friendly personal intercourse, of all possible race, creed, or provincial prejudices amongst all lovers of our country' (ibid.), and to strive for the consolidation of a sense of national unity. Towards that end, the annual sessions of the Congress were held in different parts of the country each year with the president coming from a region distinct from where the session was being held. The Congress (which took its name from the US Congress), was organized in the form of a Parliament. Its sessions were conducted democratically on the basis of discussions and votes on important issues.

Despite such professed aims, the Congress suffered from a number of limitations, the major one related to its composition. Early Congress was primarily composed of urban elites, professionals and some landed gentry, who were high-caste Hindus. The membership of the Congress mirrored the shifts in organized political life: Bombay superseded Calcutta in leadership, and professionals replaced landed aristocrats. Of the 72 non-official Indian representatives who attended the first Congress session, 38 came from Bombay, 21 from Madras, and only four from Bengal. Leaders from Bengal were apprised of the Congress session at the very last moment, and the Indian Association had organized its own annual convention around the same time. The three towns of Punjab sent a representative each, and the four principal towns of the North-Western Provinces and Awadh sent seven members. The disparity in representation and social composition had serious repercussions on the programme and performance of the Congress. Needless to say, freedom from colonial rule was nowhere on the agenda.

The important role played by A. O. Hume, a retired British civil servant in the formation of the Congress, had for a long time caused confusion and disagreement among historians regarding its nature and purpose. It was believed that the Congress had been set up by Hume in consultation with Viceroy Lord Dufferin, in order to control the restive lower classes that were planning to overthrow British rule by force. The Congress, an organization of educated Indians, was to act as a safety-valve by being the mediator between the rulers and the ruled. This theory originated from Hume's biography written by William Wedderburn. The biography spoke of seven volumes of secret reports read by Hume in Simla in the summer of 1878 which bore testimony to the 'seething discontent' of the lower classes. An alarmed Hume spoke to Viceroy Lord Dufferin and together they decided on setting up an organization of educated Indians.

This theory has now been discarded. The seven volumes of secret reports have not been traced and the opening-up of Dufferin's private papers in the 1950s have shown his strong suspicion of the Congress. Indeed, Dufferin gave orders to the Governor of Bombay to keep a watchful eye on the first session of the Congress, worried that it might lead to the formation of something akin to the Irish Home Rule Movement. Further, he openly criticized the Congress soon after its formation, giving complete lie to the 'safety-valve' theory. However, early nationalists and Marxist historians believed in the theory, and criticized the modes and methods of early Congress. Imperialist historians, of course, used it to discredit the efforts of the Congress. Although the theory has been disproved, the fact of Hume's active involvement in the formation of the Congress still holds true. But Hume's participation was more as a political liberal who wanted an all-India body to voice Indian opinion and act as an opposition. From what we have discussed earlier, it is clear that educated Indians were getting ready to form such an organization.

'Moderate' Nationalism

The enthusiasm to establish an all-India association did not mean that it was radical in its aims and programme. This is not surprising in view of the composition of the Congress. In the words of W. C. Bonnerji, the Congress was an association of 'loyalist and consistent well-wishers of the British government' (Bandyopadhyay 2004: 223). Consequently, there was no open criticism of British rule, much less the idea of seeking freedom from it. Thus, it can hardly be called nationalist in our common understanding of the term. Early Congress, however, is treated as representing the early, the 'moderate' phase of nationalism by nationalist historiography where 'moderate' stands for an immature beginning which is gradually transcended by the growth of a full-fledged, mature and complete nationalism, making the history of nationalism one of linear and continuous progress towards independence. Marxist historiography, on the other hand, takes into account peasants and workers' efforts and admits of ruptures and regressions in nationalism, and yet accepts this phase as 'moderate', offering a sociological explanation for its 'moderate' character (Desai [1946] 1959: 99). What is uncritically accepted, thereby, is the intimate link of nationalism with independence.

The very recent work of Mrinalini Sinha suggests that till the early decades of the twentieth century, middle-class Indian ideas of rights and belonging were informed by the notion of British subjecthood. This sense of belonging to the empire, of being an imperial citizen—a direct extension of the promises of the Queen's Proclamation—would make 'freedom' from British rule seem incongruous (Sinha 2011). Moderate nationalism acquires new significance in the light of this insight.

Undoubtedly, the early career of the Congress was 'moderate' because of the demands it raised and the means it adopted to voice such demands. It wanted to secure greater representation of Indians in administration through an expansion of the powers of the provincial and central councils and an increase in the number of elected members in them. Election, however, was to be limited to a very small group—the classes and members of the community 'capable of exercising it wisely and independently'. The civil service needed to be Indianized, which could be done only if the civil service examination was held both in England and in India. The Congress also pressed for separating the functions of the executive and judiciary along with an extension of trial by jury. Such demands were concordant with the idea of British liberals of preparing Indians for eventual self-government.

The limited demands were posed in a language that was gentle and cautious. As Sanjay Seth puts it, Congress resolutions aimed at opposing government action or inaction or urging some new course of action would always 'regret' rather than 'condemn' and 'suggest' rather than 'demand'. Such modesty would later be regarded by 'extremist' leaders of the Congress as symbolic of a lack of self-respect and ridiculed as 'mendicancy'. The demands, however, were made in the name of the 'people of India' and were aimed at widening the basis of the government in order to give the people 'their proper and legitimate share in it'. In reality, this meant nothing more than an insistence that 'an appreciable portion of the advisers in the government should be their [the people's] elected representatives' (Banerjea quoted in Moin and Zaidi 1976: 1, 249).

At the same time, the repeated statements of loyalty and 'faith' in British rule were both real and tactical. If, following Sinha, we accept that 'moderate' leaders thought of themselves as subjects of the British Crown, it is not difficult to understand their trust in it. It is this trust that prompted them to exhort the government to fulfil its 'glorious mission' (Burton 1994) and to live up to its own promise. This implied that the disturbing features of its rule in India which made it 'un-British' needed to be done away with. This curious combination provided the ground for and set the limit to 'moderate' criticism.

The speeches made at the second session of the Congress held in Calcutta between 27 and 30 December 1886 are representative of this critique, which was launched from various angles. While for Raja Rampal Singh, the damage the British government had done was to degrade the nature of Indians by 'systematically cutting out of us all martial spirit' thereby 'converting a race of soldiers and heroes into a timid flock of quill-driving sheep' (*Report of the Second Indian National Congress*, Calcutta, 1887; also included in McLane 1970: 40), for Surendranath Banerjea, the colonial state was guilty of not allowing Indians to govern themselves. Indians, he stated, 'were passing through a period of probation and a period of trial under the auspices of *one of the most freedom-loving nations of the world*' and were emerging into 'the dawn of mature manhood' (ibid.: 42, emphasis added). They could, therefore, be 'partially entrusted with the management of [their] own affairs' (ibid.). Banerjea's speech offers a brilliant illustration of the faith of early leaders in British rule as well as their disappointment with it for not offering Indians the chance of self-rule it had promised.

The 'most important contribution' of moderate nationalism, in the words of leftist nationalist historians like Bipan Chandra, was the economic critique of colonialism which put the 'national movement' on a solid basis (Chandra et al. [1988] 2000: 91). Since the early leaders had no 'ready-made anti-colonial understanding or ideology' available to them, they developed their own through 'a thorough examination of the nature and interests of British rule in India' (ibid.: 78). In view of what we have seen so far, it becomes difficult, even problematic, to equate the history of the Congress with that of nationalism or for that matter write nationalism as an unbroken story of relentless advance towards independence. It is more fruitful perhaps, to understand the grounds of unease of those who had trust in British rule and were its beneficiaries.

Failure of the British was most prominently manifest in India's underdevelopment. As a consequence, poverty featured centrally in Congress discussions and resolutions. Leaders like Dadabhai Naoroji (1825–1917), devoted their lives to the examination of poverty and its causes and attacked the 'un-British' nature of British rule that had caused it, urging for a truly 'British' rule which would greatly benefit India. Apart from Naoroji's magnum opus, *Poverty and Un-British Rule in India*, several other works critically discussed the economic impact of imperialism in India. Prafulla Chandra Ray's *The Poverty Problem in India* (1895), Mahadev Govind Ranade's *Essays on Indian Economics* (1896), Romesh Chunder Dutt's two-volume *Economic History of India* (1902) and Subrahmanya Iyer's *Some Economic Aspects of British Rule in India* (1903), among several others, held colonial rule guilty of India's growing poverty caused by a prolonged and constant 'drain of wealth' from India to England. With distinct emphases and interpretation, all these leaders focussed on India's accelerated impoverishment, its integration within a global world system dominated by British capital, and they wanted to 'specify analytically and historicize the production of a "dependent colonial economy"' (Ranade cited in Goswami 1998: 615). They railed against the economic 'drain' of the nation, as well as policies of 'ruralization' and 'de-industrialization', and interrogated the abstraction and ahistoricism of classical economic theory by harping on the specific and distinct conditions of India as a colonial economy. They also looked for 'a conceptual framework that was at once historicist and nationalist' (ibid.: 616).

The stimulus was provided by the policies of the colonial state. The unprecedented expansion of the colonial state in the last third of the century and its myriad policies effected a social, economic and territorial closure (ibid.: 612). The constitution and regulation of a centralized monetary system, uniform and standardized taxation, a massive infrastructure of railways and telegraph and other communication technologies, the mapping of the geographical space into administrative divisions and the social space through census and several other surveys, production of 'built environment and architectural forms' that made visible the presence of the colonial state, and an intricate bureaucracy and legal machinery directed toward the collection of revenue and administration of justice, produced India 'as a bounded economic, juridical and political space' (ibid.). At the same time, this territorial whole was inserted within 'the deterritorializing dynamic of the world market', allowing 'globalization and nationalist particularization' to proceed in tandem (ibid.: 613).

Nationalists made use of the analytical and normative categories of a specifically national developmentalist model to ground their critique of colonial rule and classical political economy (ibid.: 616). Dadabhai Naoroji 'denaturalized' the territorial division of labour by directing attention to the production of a colonial economy, and all of them saw the persistently mercantilist policies of the metropole as a firm refutation of laissez faire and free-trade ideologies (ibid.: 615–16). In sum, moderate nationalists participated in the conceptual discovery of a spatially bounded national economy, which was a nineteenth century phenomenon but was given great force in the nationalist critique of the colonial economy.

The colonial regime was quick to recognize the politically radical implications of the drain theory and chided the nationalists for employing frameworks inadequate to what they considered to be the particularistic specificity of India (ibid.: 617). The significance of the works of these nationalists found reflection in the way their ideas were taken over and elaborated by Marxist scholars. In his seminal work, *India Today* (1949), R. P. Dutt chalked out three successive phases of British exploitation of India. The first one, between 1757 and 1813, was one of direct plunder by the East India Company; the second one, of free-trader industrial capitalist exploitation (1813–58), converted India into a source of raw materials and a market for Manchester textiles; and the third phase was that of finance imperialism from 1858 onwards, where the Indian economy came to be controlled by export capital and a chain of British-controlled banks, export-import firms and managing agency houses (Sarkar [1983] 1995: 24). Although the periodization is arbitrary and schematic and does not admit of overlaps, Dutt's theory holds largely true, even to this day.

Leaders of early Congress were greatly concerned with the magnitude of poverty in India and offered several suggestions for its alleviation. Reduction in home charges, particularly those arising out of expensive military ventures, extension of the Permanent Settlement, Indianization of the civil service, reform of income tax and the police, repeal of forest laws and opposition to an increase in the salt tax, were some of the measures they suggested. If implemented, such measures would encourage industrial development, reduce the drain of wealth, generate more jobs and thus result in an improvement in the situation.

It is interesting, however, that the 'obsessive invocation of Indian poverty' was not complemented by a concern for the poor (Seth 1999: 104). The Congress only expressed sympathy for peasant protests against the increase in revenue. On the whole, however, it either remained silent or was alarmed by surveys and laws that sought to give tenants and workers greater security. Does this mean, as Seth argues, that for these leaders poverty symbolized 'backwardness' and lack, which under colonial conditions meant powerlessness and humiliation? (ibid.: 105).

It is true that the solution offered—economic and industrial modernization—did not directly address the issue of the amelioration of the condition of the poor. Rather, it displayed the leaders' anxiety to become modern and strong, along the lines of Europe, particularly Britain. What caused indignation was the fact that even after a century of rule by Britain, India was poor and weak. This was a clear indication that Britain was not following the same policies in India and hence the reproach that Britain, its metropolitan bourgeoisie in particular, had failed to modernize and transform India. For Seth, if this lent a cutting edge to the poverty debate, it also served to give nationalism its 'specifically moderate character' by revealing its faith in Britain as 'the font from which modernity must radiate outward' (ibid.: 106).

At the same time, this critique was 'nationalist' since the goals the 'Moderate' leaders sought were sought in the name of India and the Indian people. Indeed, the nationalist claim of a spatially defined culture, history and economy was 'a self-conscious challenge to the colonial thesis of the "impossibility of India"', which argued that 'the heterogeneity of indigenous society was non-transcendable and could not be translated into a unified nation' (Goswami 1998: 622). John Strachey, the Financial Secretary in the 1880s, was a good representative of this theory. In his terms, there was never an India or even a country possessing, according to European ideas, any sort of unity, physical, political, social, or religious. Early sessions of the Indian National Congress debated and came up with a counter-response to this argument by construing an India co-extensive with its spatial boundaries.

SUBALTERN NATIONALISM

So far we have explored the worlds of the Indian elite, the beneficiaries of colonial rule, traditionally associated with the growth of nationalist consciousness. We will now enter the worlds of peasants and 'tribals' and other members of rural society, affected differently but adversely by colonialism. These peoples' responses vary widely from those of the middle classes—they are not framed by notions of civilization and progress. At the same time, they reflect clear efforts to cope with the disruption caused by British intervention. Such efforts were often propelled by imaginings of just rule and fair order and faith in a new religious leader who was to bring an end to *kalyug* (*kaliyuga*), the era of evil.

The key role of religion in tribal and peasant movements has meant that for a long time they were dismissed as non-political, millenarian upsurge with no conscious objective or programme. Ranajit Guha's work in the early 1980s offered an important corrective to this by arguing in favour of a wider notion of the political. Tracking over a hundred insurgencies between the late-eighteenth and the end of the nineteenth centuries, Guha showed how all of them were conscious projects of peasants. For Guha, the very condition of the existence of peasants, that is, of domination, made their act of rebellion a conscious, political one (1983: 6).

With capitalist development in agriculture remaining incipient and weak throughout this period, the most substantial income from property in land was provided by rent. The relationship between landlords and a variety of agricultural producers, such as tenant-cultivators, share-croppers and agricultural labourers, was defined by the extraction of the peasant's surplus by modes that were often extra-economic, such as the landlord's standing in the local society and in the colonial polity. The revenue settlements of the British fostered landlordism and encouraged the transfer of lands from a bankrupt and less effective aristocracy to a new, vigorous set of landlords. Often, this resulted in more intensive and systematic exploitation of peasants. There was a remarkable growth in peasant indebtedness, with moneylenders, *mahajan*s, *bania*s and *sahukar*s coming to play an ever-active role. The absence of rent laws and ceiling on interest rates and the lack of correspondence between the agricultural and fiscal calendars made the peasant totally vulnerable to the collective power of the *sarkar*, *sahukar* and the zamindar. In such a situation, the peasant could not but be aware of the power and coercion intrinsic to his dealings with his superiors. His efforts to redress a particular grievance, therefore, necessarily entailed an assault on the existing relationship of power. And such an act was inherently political.

The work of the subaltern studies collective extended this incisive analysis to systematically recover the '*politics of the people*' and highlight the presence of an autonomous domain of politics, a domain 'that neither originated from elite politics' nor depended on it for its existence (Guha [1983] 1994: 2). What characterized this domain was a notion of resistance to elite domination. The 'subalternity' common to all the diverse components of this sphere—'the mass of the labouring population and the intermediate strata in town and country' (ibid.: 4)—and the conditions of exploitation they were subjected to, meant that their resistance often exceeded the 'nationalist' sense of resistance to colonial rule and included other oppressors, the landlords and moneylenders, members of the middle classes who, we have noted, were assuming the role of 'natural' leaders of the Indian people. This contradiction of class, compounded by those of caste and community, and reflected in the resistance offered, occasioned severe tensions within the nationalist discourse and effort. This resistance to 'colonization' and not just to colonialism (Nandy 1983) went far beyond the 'resistance' offered by middle-class 'nationalists'; as a matter of fact, middle-class leaders often tried to contain, co-opt or repress these efforts.

With this discussion in view, we now examine some representative instances of peasant and tribal insurgency. We have analysed some in the earlier chapters, but here we will discuss a few more in order to appreciate their politics and trace their implications for nationalism.

The so-called 'Deccan Riots' of 1875 provide a brilliant illustration of peasant antagonism towards moneylenders. The introduction of the Ryotwari (Raiyatwari) System and its attendant recognition of private property in land in Maharashtra changed the long-standing relationship between *sahukar*s and *Kunbi* cultivators (Kumar 1968). The creation of property in land got the moneylenders interested in grabbing the land of defaulting peasants. They increased the interest rate on credit given to peasants and acquired their mortgaged lands through a court decree, if the cultivator failed to pay back (Catanach 1970). Those lands were then leased out to dispossessed peasants since caste injunction prohibited the *sahukar*s from touching the plough.

Peasant defiance of such pressure took the form of direct assaults on Gujarati and Marwari *sahukar*s over large areas of the Deccan. There was, however, very little physical violence on the moneylenders—

they were forced to hand over the debt bonds, which were then destroyed by *Kunbi* cultivators. Contrary to the idea of spontaneous, unconscious, aimless violence associated with rioting, the peasants demonstrated definite purpose and intent in destroying the debt bonds, the symbol and instrument of the moneylenders' power over them.

Processes that preceded the Deccan Riots showed that the peasants had a clear grasp of the impact of British land revenue policies. The decision of the Bombay government to increase land revenue demand in 1867, at a time when the peasants were in great distress, had met with stiff opposition. It came at a time when the artificial cotton boom in the Deccan caused by the American Civil War had just crashed. *Kunbi* appeals for revision of the rate of land revenue were bolstered by support from members of the Poona Sarvajanik Sabha, middle-class intellectuals abreast of 'modern' methods of politics. The concession granted by the Bombay government—that annexation of peasants' land by moneylenders would only happen if the 'movable' properties of the peasant were not enough to cover the amount loaned—further worsened relations between *Kunbis* and *sahukar*s. Consequently, the outbreak of the 1875 riots took the shape of an attack on moneylenders, but the factors that produced it were more intricate—crash of an artificial 'boom', increase in tax, mediation of elites and longstanding tension between peasants and moneylenders.

A revolt of a different order, which had also earned middle-class empathy and support, was the Indigo Revolt of 1859–60 in Bengal. The importance of indigo, developed as a cash crop by British planters with encouragement from the Company's government from the end of the eighteenth century, was on the decline by the 1850s. Indigo plantations, we have seen, had functioned on a system of *dadan*, advance given by planters to peasants to buy and sow seeds on their lands, a constant source of friction. Time and again, in different parts of Bengal, indigo planters had been the targets of attack of peasant followers of new religious movements within Islam like that of Titu Mir or Dudu Mian (Bhadra 1994). With indigo losing its economic importance, the planters became desperate and their coercion of peasants increased.

In the autumn of 1859, peasants in the districts of Nadia, Murshidabad, and Pabna, soon joined by those of Jessore, refused to take advance from the planters. This became a widespread phenomenon. The initiative was taken up by substantial cultivators, but they were aided by poorer peasants and patronized by local zamindars jealous of the importance of European planters in rural areas. The planters' Indian agents were subjected to social boycott. The planters' success in getting a resolution passed in 1860 that compelled the peasants to sow indigo, was offset by a series of suits filed by peasants in the local law courts and a militant no-rent campaign. Peasants made use of the Rent Act X of 1859 to claim rights as occupancy tenants to counter the planters' attempt to evict them, demonstrating thereby their familiarity with law as a way out of distress.

Dinabandhu Mitra's *Nil Darpan* (Indigo Mirror), published in 1860, lucidly portrayed the havoc caused by indigo planters on the lives of indigo cultivators. The novel was translated into English by Michael Madhusudan Dutt and published by Rev. James Long of the Church Missionary Society. The trial, by the Supreme Court, of James Long on grounds of libel and the fine of ₹ 1,000 imposed on him, caused indignation among intellectuals. Newspapers, such as the *Hindoo Patriot* and the *Somprakash*, and organizations, such as the Indian Association, came to the support of James Long. Although they appealed to the British sense of justice for the redress of the situation, their involvement brought peasant problems into the realm of institutional politics and to the notice of political circles in India and England. The planters had to relent, and indigo cultivation died a natural death.

The risings of the Moplahs (Mapillas) of Malabar in the 1880s and 1890s provide an instructive instance of the fused articulation of the religious and the political. The Moplahs, descendants of Arab settlers, who had married local Nair and Tiyar women, and had taken to agriculture as tenant cultivators or landless labourers, had been hit hard by the introduction of the Ryotwari System in Malabar at the end of the eighteenth century. This system recognized the *jenmi* (holder of *janmam* tenure) as the absolute owner of land and disregarded the cultivators' claim to the produce. This, together with over-assessment, illegal cesses and a pro-landlord attitude of the judiciary and the police reduced the Moplahs to conditions of extreme penury. Under the British, *janmam* tenure became the equivalent of Roman plenum dominium or the sum total of all rights on land. The proprietor had absolute right to his property, including alienating it and vacating occupants and tenants who did not have a lease from the proprietor (Dreze and Sen 1997: 282; Narayanan 2003: 91).

The curious combination of Hindu landlords and Christian officials gave a strong religious fervour to Moplah dissent. Their efforts to destabilize the existing relations of power acquired anti-Hindu and anti-White sentiment. If, in verbal exchanges, the Moplahs reversed the customary way of addressing the landlords, deferentially underscoring their will to challenge *jenmi* overlordship (Guha 1983: 51), in their numerous risings between 1882 and 1885 and 1896 they attacked *jenmi* property and Hindu temples, symbols of the landlords' economic and moral power. Moreover, the belief that martyrdom for a just cause would take them to heaven made the Moplahs fearless—they boldly faced police bullets. Such fearlessness gave great potency to the small bands of Moplahs and caused panic amongst high-caste Hindu landowners and moneylenders. The absence of such a divine mission made the Hindu peasants of the area turn to banditry as the only recourse.

Religion also aided the resistance of Muslim peasants of eastern Bengal. The Faraizi movement conferred on them dignity and self-confidence. The first Agrarian League was set up in 1873; it tried to counteract continuously rising rent rates and landlords' attempts to destroy occupancy rights of peasants through recourse to British courts. Spearheaded by substantial peasants, this venture had the support of the poorer peasantry. Agrarian leagues came up in different districts in eastern Bengal. The unfortunate and curious fact of the numerical preponderance of Hindu landlords and Muslim tenants led to a polarization of agrarian relations along religious lines. It also caused great ambivalence among the educated middle-classes of Calcutta—most of whom were Hindus with property in land—with regard to peasant questions. This became manifest in their uncertainty about the Bengal Tenancy Act of 1885 which, in any case, was limited in nature. The act only gave greater occupancy rights and offered no benefits to the poorer peasants.

PROMISING FUTURES

The most brutal, direct and disruptive forms of colonial violence were perhaps unleashed in the 'tribal' areas. We have noted the colonial marking of frontiers between the plains and the forest people that forced the 'forest people' to stick to a defined terrain and occupation. This is how the category of the 'tribal' got defined, while earlier it often symbolized people not governed by the rules of caste. Demarcation of territory and occupation, bolstered by efforts to 'civilize' the 'wild tribes' and settle the forests (Skaria 1999: 199), played havoc with the lives of the forest people.

The establishment of a forest department in 1864 followed by the passing of the Forests Act in 1865, severely curtailed the customary rights of tribal peasants and opened up the forests for commercial use. The great need for oak and timber for the Royal Navy and for railway sleepers prompted the government to take measures for the 'conservation' of forests, leading to the marking of some forest land as 'reserved'. *Jhum* or shifting cultivation, an essential means of subsistence for tribal peasants, was banned or restricted in the 'reserved' forests from 1867. Rights to the use of timber and grazing facilities were curbed and subsistence hunting prohibited. The jurisdiction of the government over forest lands was continuously extended with 20 per cent of India's land area coming under forest administration by 1900. The opening of roads and the commercial use of forest wood and other products encouraged the penetration of moneylenders, traders, contractors and land-grabbers—who successfully deployed British sense of private property in land and the colonial government's insistence on 'written records'— to dispossess the 'tribals' of joint ownership of land.

Efforts to cope with this massive disruption consisted in small acts of resistance and subversion and violent outbursts, which together made the woods 'unquiet' (Guha 1991). Religion, once again, provided impetus to political acts of insurgency, offering tribal peasants a mode of recovering self-respect through belief in a better future to be achieved through their own efforts.

The best illustration, perhaps, is provided by the well-known and well-researched *ulgulan* (great tumult) of Birsa Munda in the Chota Nagpur region in 1899–90, the classic work on which is Kumar Suresh Singh's *The Dust Storm and the Hanging Mist* (1966). Through the nineteenth century, the Mundas were slowly being dispossessed of their joint holdings by *jagirdars* and *thikadars* coming from the northern plains, and recruited as indentured labour by contractors. The appeal of Munda *sardars* (chiefs/leaders) for relief to the government and to missionaries had not borne fruit. Now, hope was provided by the appearance of a saviour in the form of Birsa.

The son of a share-cropper, Birsa had received some education from the missionaries and had subsequently come under Vaishnava influence. During 1894–95, he participated in a movement to stop the acquisition of village wastelands by the forest department. In 1895, Birsa had a 'vision' which turned him into a prophet with miraculous healing powers. His confinement by the British for two years increased his militancy and his fame. In a series of night meetings held in 1899, when Birsa took his Munda followers on a pilgrimage to holy places, he spoke with passion about *kalyug (kaliyuga)*, the era of evil, in which the Mundas had come under the rule of Queen Mandodari, the wife of demon king Ravana, and their lands had been taken over by outsiders. For the golden era of truth, *satyug (satyayuga)* to return, foreigners and outsiders had to be driven out of Munda territory and the unjust rule of the queen substituted by the just rule and faith of Birsa. Ingenious apprehension of the rule of the British Queen as symbolic of evil rule in the era of Kali, and belief in a bright future to be achieved by following the faith and path of Birsa, inspired the Mundas to rise up in open rebellion on Christmas day in 1899. Churches, temples, policemen, *thikadars* and *jagirdars*, rajas and *hakims*—all symbols of unjust power— became targets of direct assaults.

The uprising was brutally suppressed by government forces and Birsa and several others were caught and jailed. The revolt, however, caused the colonial government to enquire into the causes, and this eventually gave the Mundas a degree of legal protection with regard to their land rights. Significantly, the memory of Birsa lived on in popular imagination, encouraging recurrent acts of resistance that sought to undo existing, asymmetric power relations.

Chapter 3 briefly discussed the tiny acts of subterfuge carried out by the Dangis (Bhils) of the hills of Gujarat to negotiate with the force of the British administration. Apparently tamed by the British by the 1840s into not conducting raids on the surrounding plains to demonstrate their shared sovereignty, the Dangis often became deliberately 'wild' or consciously 'ignorant' when they raided the plains or pleaded lack of knowledge of 'written' regulations to account for their direct defiance of them (Skaria 1999). Their understanding of the past in terms of the epochs of *moglai* (time of freedom) and *mandini* (period of submission to *gora-raj*, White rule/governance), poignantly portray their understanding of the change in power relations (Skaria 1999).

Such 'hidden transcripts' (Scott 1990) of dissent were articulated in an intensification of 'forest crimes' in Travancore, and a refusal by peasants—who lived on terraced cultivation at the fringes of forests—to cooperate with officials of the forest department. The inhabitants of Tehri Garhwal in Uttar Pradesh appealed to their local raja for protection against the unjust conservancy laws and the peasants of Kumaun took recourse to the theft of timber and setting on fire the reserved forests to defy stringent laws. The Santals of the Jungle Mahals of the Bengal Presidency vented their anger and frustration by raiding village markets and fisheries, while the Baigas of Central India and the Reddis of Hyderabad defied forest laws and continued to hunt. The Saoras of Ganjam courted arrest for defying forest laws and clearing forests for *jhum* cultivation; and the Koya and Konda Dora tribes of the Gudem and Rampa hill tracts in Andhra Pradesh joined the *muttadars*, traditional estate holders, to rise up in *fituri*, a violent revolt, against the combined oppression of *mansabdars*, *sahukars*, trader-contractors from the plains and the British police.

This should not, however, lead us to think that the 'tribes' remained in constant opposition to the colonial regime. These communities often creatively participated in, made different sense of, and eventually reconfigured the world of colonial modernity in a variety of ways. The joint stock companies that ran vast paralegal trade circuits in rubber, ivory and timber along the entire north-eastern frontier of India, for instance, needed the consent and help of local 'tribal chieftains' to work this ill-mapped area, who in turn often demanded and received 'rent' from these companies (Kar 2007). If this underlines the limits of colonial domination over 'tribal' worlds, it also brings into relief 'tribal' perceptions and negotiations of colonial power.

We have tried to read colonialism and colonization together with nationalism in order to appreciate their interface and the crucial ways in which they shaped each other. The impact of colonialism on Indian society, undoubtedly profound, varied widely in a country that was 'culturally fragmented and politically heterogeneous' (Nandy 1983: 31). Consequently, the cultural impact of colonialism and imperialism remained confined largely to urban centres—among westernized and semi-westernized upper and middle classes and sections of traditional elite, who internalized imperial critiques of India. In Britain, on the other hand, the experience of colonizing produced a false sense of cultural homogeneity and channelled social mobility in aggrandizing wars of colonial expansion, which became the vehicle of nationalism (ibid.: 32–33).

In India, nationalism remained a contested terrain both in its imagination and in its articulation. If middle-class imaginings went beyond modular forms of nationalism derived from the west illustrating the force of imagination (Chatterjee 1993), subaltern insurgency exceeded and destabilized the elite nationalist discourse. The logic and politics of peasant and subaltern insurgency, as argued by the subaltern studies collective and demonstrated in the earlier discussion, often existed parallel to and autonomous of the formal domain of nationalist politics, even though they impinged upon formal politics in important ways. Not only did such militancy ignore the modern separation of religion and politics, it often challenged middle-class claims to dominance by identifying them as aggressors. Hence, although elite politics had to depend on the support of these subordinate peoples, it failed to appreciate or incorporate their demands or struggles. Consequently, contestation and multiple configurations, accommodation and exclusion, marked the history of the nationalist struggle; they continue in the India of today.

References

Anagol, Padma. 2005. *The Emergence of Feminism in India, 1850–1920.* Aldershot, Hampshire: Ashgate Publishing.

———. 2010. 'Rebellious Wives and Dysfunctional Marriages: Indian Women's Discourses and Participation in the Debates over Restitution of Conjugal Rights and the Child Marriage Controversy in the 1880s and 1890s'. In *Women and Social Reform in Modern India,* edited by Tanika Sarkar and Sumit Sarkar, Vol. 1, 282–312. Bloomington, IA: Indiana University Press.

Anderson, Benedict. 1991. *Imagined Communities.* London: Verso.

Balibar, Etienne. 1989. 'Racism as Universalism'. *New Political Science* 16/17: 9–22.

Bandyopadhyay, Sekhar. 2004. *From Plassey to Partition: A History of Modern India.* Hyderabad: Orient Longman.

Banerjee, Prathama. 2006. *Politics of Time: 'Primitives' and History-Writing in a Colonial Society.* New Delhi: Oxford University Press.

Banerjee, Sumanta. 1990. 'Marginalization of Women's Popular Culture in Nineteenth Century Bengal'. In *Recasting Women: Essays in Indian Colonial History,* edited by Kumkum Sangari and Suresh Vaid, 127–79. New Brunswick: Rutgers University Press.

Bannerji, Himani. 1998. 'Age of Consent and Hegemonic Social Reform'. In *Gender and Imperialism,* edited by Clare Midgley, 21–44. Manchester: Manchester University Press.

Bayly, C. A. 1998. *Origins of Nationality in South Asia: Patriotism and Ethical Government in the Making of Modern India.* New Delhi: Oxford University Press.

Bhabha, Homi. 1994. *The Location of Culture.* London: Routledge.

Bhadra, Gautam. 1994. *Iman o Nishan* (Honour and the Flag). Calcutta: Subarnarekha.

Borthwick, Meredith. 1984. *The Changing Role of Women in Bengal: 1849–1905.* Princeton, NJ: Princeton University Press.

Burton, Antoinette. 1994. *Burdens of History: British Feminists, Indian Women, and Imperial Culture.* Chapel Hill, NC: University of North Carolina Press.

Catanach, I. J. 1970. *Rural Credit in Western India, 1875–1930.* Berkeley and Los Angeles: University of California Press.

Chakrabarty, Dipesh. 1994. 'The Difference-Deferral of Colonial Modernity: Public Debates on Domesticity in Colonial India'. In *Subaltern Studies VIII: Essays in Honour of Ranajit Guha,* edited by David Arnold and David Hardiman, 50–88. New Delhi: Oxford University Press.

Chakravarty, Uma. 2003. *Gendering Caste: Through a Feminist Lens.* Calcutta: Stree.

Chandra, Bipan, Mridula Mukherjee, Aditya Mukherjee, K. N. Panikkar and Sucheta Mahajan. [1988] 2000. *India's Struggle for Independence, 1857–1947.* Calcutta: Penguin Books.

Chandra, Sudhir. 1998. *Enslaved Daughters: Colonialism, Law, Women's Rights.* New Delhi: Oxford University Press.

Chatterjee, Neha. 2011. 'Tantra, Sadhana and Public Culture in High Colonial Bengal'. New Delhi: Jawaharlal Nehru University, M.Phil dissertation.

Chatterjee, Partha. 1986. *Nationalist Thought and the Colonial World: A Derivative Discourse?* London: Zed Books.

———. 1990. 'The Nationalist Resolution of the Women's Question'. In *Recasting Women: Essays in Indian Colonial History,* edited by Kumkum Sangari and Sudesh Vaid, 233–253. New Brunswick: Rutgers University Press.

———. 1993. *The Nation and Its Fragments: Colonial and Postcolonial Histories.* Princeton, NJ: Princeton University Press.

Chaudhuri, Roshinka. 2002. *Gentlemen Poets of Colonial Bengal*. Calcutta: Seagull Books.

Dalmia, Vasudha. 1997. *The Nationalization of Hindu Traditions: Bharatendu Harishchandra and Nineteenth Century Banaras*. New Delhi: Oxford University Press.

Das Mohapatra, Lalatendu. 2007. *John Beames and Orissa*. Rourkela: Pragati Utkal Sangha.

Desai, A. R. [1946] 1959. *Social Background of Indian Nationalism* (Third edition). Bombay: Popular Book Depot.

Deshpande, Prachi. 2007. *Creative Pasts: Historical Memory and Identity in Western India, 1700–1960*. New York: Columbia University Press.

Devi, Prajñasundari. 1900. 'Bhumika' (Introduction). In *Amish o Niramish Ahar* (Non-vegetarian and Vegetarian Food), Prajñasundari Devi, Vol 1: 23–55. Kolkata: Kshirodh Chandra Raichaudhuri. Revised edition, Calcutta: Ananda Publishers 1995.

Devji, Faisal. 1991. 'Gender and the Politics of Space: The Movement for Women's Reform in Muslim India, 1857–1900'. *South Asia* 14 (1): 141–53.

———. 1994. 'Gender and the Politics of Space: The Movement for Women's Reform, 1857–1990'. In *Forging Identities: Gender, Communities, and the State*, edited by Zoya Hasan, 22–37. Delhi: Kali for Women.

Dreze, Jean and Amartya Sen. 1997. *Indian Development: Selected Regional Perspectives*. Oxford: Clarendon Press.

Dutt, Rajni Palme. 1949. *India Today*. Bombay: People's Publishing House.

Dutt, Romesh Chunder. 1902. *The Economic History of India*. London: K. Paul, Trench, Trübner and Co. (Reprint 1970. New Delhi: Publications Division, Ministry of Information and Broadcasting, Government of India).

Ghosh, Anindita. 2006. *Power in Print: Popular Publishing and the Politics of Language and Culture in a Colonial Society*. New Delhi: Oxford University Press.

Gordon, Leonard A. 1974. *Bengal: The Nationalist Movement 1876–1940*. New York: Columbia University Press.

Goswami, Manu. 1998. 'From *Swadeshi* to *Swaraj*: Nation, Economy, Territory in Colonial South Asia, 1870 to 1907'. *Comparative Studies in Society and History* 40 (4): 609–36.

Griffiths, Percival Joseph. [1957] 1962. *Modern India*. London: E. Benn.

Guha, Ramachandra. 1991. *The Unquiet Woods: Ecological Change and Peasant Resistance in the Himalaya*. New Delhi: Oxford University Press.

Guha, Ranajit. 1983. *Elementary Aspects of Peasant Insurgency in Colonial India*. New Delhi: Oxford University Press.

———. 1988. *An Indian Historiography of India: Nineteenth Century Agenda and Its Implications*. Calcutta: Centre for Studies in Social Sciences.

———, ed [1983] 1994. *Subaltern Studies I: Writings on South Asian History and Society*, edited by Ranajit Guha. New York: Oxford University Press.

Gupta, Charu. 2001. *Sexuality, Obscenity, Community: Women, Muslims and the Hindu Public in Colonial India*. Delhi: Permanent Black.

Heimsath, Charles. 1964. *Indian Nationalism and Hindu Social Reform*. Princeton, NJ: Princeton University Press.

Irschick, Eugene. 1969. *Politics and Social Conflict in South India: The Non-Brahman Movement and Tamil Separatism, 1916–1929*. Berkeley and Los Angeles: University of California Press.

Iyer, Subrahmanya. 1903. *Some Economic Aspects of British Rule in India*. Madras: The Swadesamitram Press.

Kar, Bodhisattwa. 2007. 'Framing Assam: Plantation Capital, Metropolitan Knowledge, and a Regime of Identities, 1790s - 1930s'. New Delhi: Jawaharlal Nehru University. Ph.D. dissertation.

Kaviraj, Sudipta. 1995. *The Unhappy Consciousness: Bankimchandra Chattopadhyay and the Formation of Nationalist Discourse in India*. New Delhi: Oxford University Press.

King, Christopher R. 1994. *One Language Two Scripts: The Hindi Movement in Nineteenth Century North India*. New Delhi: Oxford University Press.

Kumar, Radha. 1997. *The History of Doing: An Illustrated Account of Movements for Women's Rights and Feminism in India, 1800–1990*. London: Verso.

Kumar, Ravinder. 1968. *Western India in the Nineteenth Century*. London: Routledge and Kegan Paul.

Macaulay, Thomas Babington. 1900. 'Warren Hastings'. In *Critical and Historical Essays*, 602–667. Boston: Houghton, Mifflin and Company.

Majumdar, Rochona. 2009. *Marriage and Modernity: Family Values in Colonial Bengal*. New Delhi: Oxford University Press.

Malhotra, Anshu. 2002. *Gender, Caste, and Religious Identities: Restructuring Class in Colonial Panjab*. New Delhi: Oxford University Press.

Masselos, Jim. 1985. *Indian Nationalism: An History*. New Delhi: Sterling Publishers Private Limited.

McCully, Bruce Tiebout. 1940. *English Education and the Origins of Indian Nationalism*. New York: Columbia University Press.

McLane, John R., ed. 1970. *The Political Awakening in India*. Englewood Cliffs, NJ: Prentice Hall.

Mehrotra, S. R. 1971. *The Emergence of the Indian National Congress*. Delhi: Vikas Publishing House.

Metcalf, Barbara D. 1994. 'Reading and Writing about Muslim Women in British India'. In *Forging Identities: Gender, Communities and the State,* ed. Zoya Hasan, 1–21. Delhi: Kali for Women.

Mill, James. [1817] 1975. *The History of British India* (Abridged edition). Chicago: University of Chicago.

Minault, Gail. 1998. *Secluded Scholars: Women's Education and Muslim Social Reform in Colonial India*. New Delhi: Oxford University Press.

Mir, Farina. 2010. *The Social Space of Language: Vernacular Literature in British Colonial Punjab*. Berkeley and Los Angeles: University of California Press and Delhi: Permanent Black.

Mohanty, Nivedita. 2005. *Oriya Nationalism: Quest for a United Orissa, 1866–1936*. Jagasinghpur: Prafulla.

Moin, A. and Shaheeda Zaidi, eds. 1976. *Encyclopaedia of the Indian National Congress*. Vol. 1. New Delhi: S. Chand.

Nandy, Ashis. 1983. *The Intimate Enemy: Loss and Recovery of Self Under Colonialism*. New Delhi: Oxford University Press.

———. 1994. *The Savage Freud and Other Essays in Possible Retrievable Selves*. New Delhi: Oxford University Press.

Narayanan, M. T. 2003. *Agrarian Relations in Late-medieval Malabar*. New Delhi: National Book Centre.

Natarajan, S. 1959. *A Century of Social Reform in India*. Bombay: Asia Publishing House.

Oldenburg, Veena T. 2002. *Dowry Murder: The Imperial Origins of a Cultural Crime*. New York: Oxford University Press.

Ramakrishna,V. 1993. 'Literary and Theatre Movements in Colonial Andhra: Struggle for Left Ideological Legitimacy'. *Social Scientist* 21: 69–85.

Ramaswamy, Sumathi. 1997. *Passions of the Tongue: Language Devotion in Tamil India, 1891–1970*. Berkeley and Los Angeles: University of California Press.

Ranade, Mahadev Govind. 1896. *Essays on Indian Economics*. Bombay: Thacker and Co.

Ray, P. C. 1895. *The Poverty Problem in India*. Calcutta: Thacker, Spink and Co.

Rothermund, Dietmar. 1979. *The Phases of Indian Nationalism and Other Essays*. Bombay: Nachiketa Publications.

Sarkar, Sumit. [1983] 1995. *Modern India, 1885–1947*. Madras: Macmillan India.

———. 1998. 'Kaliyuga, Chakri and Bhakti: Ramakrishna and His Times'. In *Writing Social History*, S. Sarkar, 282–357. New Delhi: Oxford University Press.

Sarkar, Tanika. 2001. *Hindu Wife, Hindu Nation: Community, Religion, and Cultural Nationalism*. Bloomington, IA: Indiana University Press.

Scott, James C. 1990. *Domination and the Art of Resistance: Hidden Transcripts*. New Haven, NJ: Yale University Press.

Seal, Anil. 1968. *The Emergence of Indian Nationalism: Competition and Collaboration in the Later Nineteenth Century*. Cambridge: Cambridge University Press.

Sengupta, Parna. 2011. *Pedagogy for Religion: Missionary Education and the Fashioning of Hindus and Muslims in Bengal*. Berkeley and Los Angeles: University of California Press.

Seth, Sanjay. 1999. 'Rewriting Histories of Nationalism: The Politics of "Moderate Nationalism" in India, 1870–1905'. *The American Historical Review* 104 (1): 95–116.

———. 2007. *Subject Lessons: The Western Education of Colonial India*. Durham, NC: Duke University Press.

Singh, K. S. 1966. *The Dust Storm and the Hanging Mist: A Study of Birsa Munda and His Movement in Chhotanagpur, 1874–1901*. Calcutta: Firma K. L. Mukhopadhyay.

Sinha, Mrinalini. 1994. 'Gender in the Critiques of Colonialism and Nationalism: Locating the "Indian Woman"'. In *Feminists Revision History*, edited by A. L. Shapiro, 246–75. New Brunswick, NJ: Rutgers University Press.

———. 1995. *Colonial Masculinity: The 'Manly Englishman' and the 'Effeminate Bengali' in the Late Nineteenth Century*. Manchester: Manchester University Press.

———. 2011. 'The Strange Death of an Imperial Ideal: The Case of *Civic Britannicus*'. In *Modern Makeovers: Oxford Handbook of Modernity in South Asia*, edited by S. Dube, 29–42. New Delhi: Oxford University Press.

Skaria, Ajay. 1999. *Hybrid Histories: Forests, Frontiers and Wildness in Western India*. New Delhi: Oxford University Press.

Stein, Burton. 2010. *A History of India*. Revised and edited by David Arnold. Sussex, UK: Wiley-Blackwell. (First published 1998. Oxford: Oxford University Press).

Tripathi, Amales. 1967. *The Extremist Challenge: India Between 1890 and 1910*. New Delhi: Orient Longman.

Trivedi, Lisa N. 2003. 'Visually Mapping the "Nation": Swadeshi Politics in Nationalist India, 1920–1930'. *The Journal of Asian Studies* 62 (1): 11–41.

Vivekananda, Swami. 1964. 'Lectures from Colombo to Almora'. *The Complete Works of Swami Vivekananda*. Vol. III. Calcutta: Advaita Ashrama.

Winichakul, Thongchai. 1994. *Siam Mapped: A History of the Geo-Body of a Nation*. Honolulu: The University of Hawaii Press.

Challenge and Rupture

6

> Where the mind is without fear and the
> head is held high; where knowledge is free;
> where the world has not been frittered into fragments
> by narrow domestic walls; where
> words come out from the depth of truth;
> where sleepless striving stretches its strenuous
> arms towards perfection; where the clear
> stream of reason has not lost its way into
> the dreary desert sand of dead habit, and where
> the mind is led forward by thee into
> ever widening thought and action
> – there waken up my country into that
> heaven of freedom, my father!

'Where the mind is without fear ...' from Rabindranath Tagore's *Gitanjali* published in 1912.

Chapter outline

THE FIRST PARTITION OF BENGAL	RADICAL TRENDS
BOYCOTT AND SWADESHI	MUSLIM POLITICS
THE SURAT SPLIT	REFORMS AND AFTER

Bidhir bandhan katbe tumi eman shaktiman tumiki emni shaktiman?
Amader bhanga gada tomar hate eman abhiman tomader emni abhiman?

(You will cut the bond decreed by Providence you are that powerful, are you?
Your arrogance is such that you think you can destroy and build us at your will, do you?)

A humanist poet-philosopher, Rabindranath Tagore, put an angry rhetorical question to the government of Lord Curzon, which had decided to partition the province of Bengal in 1905. The sensitive song articulated anger as well as determination—the colonized were ready to challenge and unsettle the 'settled' decisions made by the overbearing colonial government drunk on its own sense of power. This chapter explores the evolution of the nationalist struggle in the early decades of the twentieth century, keeping in view its entangled interaction with colonial policies, as well as its configuration on discursive and material planes. It also pays attention to the criss-crossing and contrasting identities, sentiments and passion that the struggle generated, leading to unwarranted and unfortunate consequences. Ironically, by the middle of the century, the colonized themselves authorized the colonial state to construct and divide India, and turned the poet's insightful allegory into a tragic reality.

Let us, once again, reiterate the contradictions of nationalism referred to in Chapter 5. It is not only that nationalism claims a long unbroken history for the nation while, at the same time, trying to envisage it; it is also that nationalism encapsulates opposing trends—of liberalism and secularism that refuses to admit distinction of class or creed—and 'a system of political meanings' associated with symbols of the 'community' (Stein 2010: 274). This tension becomes evident in the distinction that the historiography of Indian nationalism makes between 'nationalism' and 'communalism'—the first, an applauded ideal and the second, a pejorative sentiment that relates to peoples who are 'backward' and parochial, who hold their 'community' above anything else.

Political history of the nationalist struggle often tends to view these distinct trends within nationalism as belonging to different phases. Thus, while late nineteenth-century 'moderate nationalism' of the Congress is taken to represent 'secular' nationalism based on institutional politics, 'extremist' nationalism of the twentieth century is said to embody 'communal' feelings and sentiments of hatred (ibid.: 275). Our analysis will eschew such clear categorizations and see the trends as parallel and co-existent, often shading into one another.

THE FIRST PARTITION OF BENGAL

As indicated earlier, the first occasion for a nationalist upsurge in the twentieth century was provided by the high-handed policy of Viceroy Lord Curzon (1899–1905) and his decision to partition Bengal. Curzon was a thoroughbred aristocrat who had but contempt for the nationalist aspirations of Indians. An imperialist through and through, Curzon repeatedly expressed his desire to establish a British sphere of interest over the Persian Gulf and Seistan, and persuaded the Crown to allow him to lead a 'flag-waving-mission to the region' (Sarkar [1983] 1995: 101–02). His open dislike for Russia caused embarrassment to Britain at a time when it was taking hesitant steps towards an entente with France and Russia.

Within India, the Viceroy was lucky to face a situation of surplus budgets on account of the adoption of the gold standard by the British government in the 1890s in place of the constantly depreciating silver rupee. This freed the colonial state of the excessive burden of home charges and enabled Curzon to allow remissions of land revenue after the famine of 1899–1900, reduce the salt tax and raise the limit of income-tax exemption. His government also established a Railway Board, opened 6,100 miles of railway construction, the highest ever under any Viceroy, and paid attention to irrigation, all intended to centralize the government and make it more effective.

Understandably, Curzon had no sympathy for the Congress and its demands. In 1900, he had written to the Secretary of State that the Congress was 'tottering to its fall', a fall over which he was determined to preside (Curzon to Secretary of State Hamilton, 18 November 1900, cited in Masselos [1985] 1996: 110). The Viceroy had been encouraged by a certain lull in Congress activity; he had, however, failed to realize that 'moderate Congress' had come to represent only 'a small segment of nationalist sentiment' (McLane 1977). British unpopularity, argues Sarkar, was growing on account of famines and plagues, and the potential base for political activity was expanding ([1983] 1995: 96). This was reflected in the great increase in the circulation of vernacular newspapers, which rose from 299,000 in 1885 to 817,000 in 1895. Many of the prominent ones among these—the *Kesari* and *Kal* of Poona and the *Bangabasi* of Bengal—for instance, were actually critical of Moderate Congress.

Famine, in particular the devastating famine of Orissa in 1866, had made British administrators aware of the unwieldy size of the Bengal Presidency, which, by then, had come to include the whole of Bihar, Orissa and Assam, in addition to Bengal proper. Following the suggestion of Sir Strafford Northcote, the Commissioner of Assam, to reduce the size of the Presidency, Assam along with Sylhet, a predominantly Bengali-speaking region, had been separated from Bengal in 1874 and made into a Chief Commissioner's province. In 1892, some officials in the foreign department had suggested that the entire Chittagong division (Chittagong, Chittagong Hill Tracts, Noakhali and Tipperah) should be transferred to Assam along with Lushai Hills.

In course of the ongoing discussion on the matter, William Ward, the Chief Commissioner of Assam, proposed the transfer of Dacca and Mymensingh to Assam in 1896–97. The addition of these divisions had the advantage of making Assam large enough to stand on its own with a separate administrative cadre. The plan did not meet with the approval of Sir Henry Cotton, Ward's successor, and found little favour with the Lieutenant Governor of Bengal. Consequently, the Government of India decided to transfer only Lushai Hills in 1897 (Sarkar 1973: 10–11).

The question of Bengal's boundaries came up again at the turn of the century, this time in relation to Orissa. Sir Andrew Fraser, the Chief Commissioner of the Central Provinces, proposed an adjustment of the boundaries of Bengal and the Central Provinces, in order to solve the problem of Sambalpur, an Oriya-speaking region within the Hindi-speaking Central Provinces. The last chapter has mentioned that a *bhasha andolan*, a language-centred movement, had begun in Orissa's coastal districts in the 1860s following the attempt of Bengali officials to replace Oriya with Bengali in government offices and schools. The movement had taken up the issue of the unification of Oriya speaking tracts under one administration (Dash 1978: 360–61; Das Mohapatra 2007). Orissa as a separate province came into being much later (1936); but Oriya was not replaced by Bengali in the coastal tracts of Orissa division of the Bengal Presidency. The move to replace Oriya with Hindi in the Sambalpur division of the Central

Provinces in 1895 occasioned another round of passionate protests and propaganda for the unification of Oriya speaking tracts. The people of the Sambalpur region drew encouragement from the success of Oriya speakers in the coastal districts; they made a very strong case for their solidarity with other speakers of Oriya and their basic identity as Oriyas (Dash 2007). They did not succeed, but their struggle made colonial administrators aware of the 'problem' of Sambalpur, an Oriya speaking region in a Hindi-speaking province.

By the time Andrew Fraser's proposal reached Viceroy Curzon after 14 months, the incorporation of Berar, acquired from the Nizam of Hyderabad in British India, had become an important issue. All this convinced the Viceroy that the 'readjustment of boundaries all around' was the need of the hour. Fraser's note to Curzon suggested the transfer of both Chittagong division and Dacca and Mymensingh to Assam and underscored the political benefits of the project. The Viceroy's Minute on Territorial Redistribution of India (*Curzon Collection* 19 May/1 June 1903) sanctioned this scheme. Risley edited and made the Minute ready for 'public consumption' in accordance with the wishes of the Viceroy; his letter of December 1903 strongly advocated the transfer of Chittagong, Dacca and Mymensingh to Assam (ibid.).

IN REVIEW: MAPPING THE NORTHEAST

It is worthwhile in this context to engage with 'geographical history' or historical geography to chart the construction of 'British Assam' and its transformation into the 'Northeast' by means of mapping. Maps, argue David Zou and Satish Kumar, are not mirrors that passively reflect the world. They have always been 'ways of seeing' or a 'mental image' to make sense of the world (Zou and Kumar 2011: 143). Taking a long-term view of the distinct ways colonial power surveyed, mapped, and demarcated India's northeast borderland as the ever-shifting 'turbulent frontier' that required order and stability, Zou and Kumar highlight how geographical discourses and cartographic cultures impinged upon the construction of a 'geo-ethnic' regional identity with inner and outer frontiers (ibid.: 144). Surveyors and mapmakers objectified and 'enacted' the geo-body of 'British Assam', pictured by European maps that reduced India's Northeast borderlands to thin boundary lines (ibid.).

Colonial boundary making and fixing of previously fluid realms, argues Sanghamitra Misra, entailed a 'confrontation between indigenous and colonial notions of political space' (Misra 2005: 222). While tribal chiefs of the north-east ruled over people bounded by patrimonial loyalties and not over a designated amount of land, which was a free gift of nature (Zou and Kumar 2011: 150), British authority was established over territory, a shift that enabled British officials to have firmer grasp on taxes, commerce and demographic movements. The demarcation of land and frontiers created an essentialist distinction between 'Hill' and 'Valley', and prevented the 'hill people' from crossing the 'inner line' to access lowland markets, a frontier that was not only crossed constantly in the past but that also moved in accordance with the shifting status of tribes (ibid.: 159).

The Anglo–Burmese war of 1824–26 brought the Northeast to the attention of the colonial authorities. The spectre of an aggressive Burma on the northeast frontier of British Bengal was made doubly complicated by the discovery that there was hardly any reliable information—anthropological and geographical—on that region. An 'information panic' made acquisition of quick maps of the region for military operation the highest priority (ibid.: 151). Even after the war was won, the distressful lack of information on Burma and the Northeast continued to inspire British surveyors to try and chart the region. The Tsangpo–Brahmaputra river controversy, that emerged during the first Anglo–Burmese war, spurred a long debate among imperial policy-makers and scholars on the source of the Brahmaputra river, a story that was also picked up by the press (ibid.: 154–55). Geographical discourses about the identity of a river invested British Assam with a new territoriality, and British cartography and ethnography 'objectified the regional personality' of the Northeast borderland.

In addition, European maps overturned the culture of map-making in pre-colonial India, where maps were drawn, not to the scale of distance and mensuration but to the scale of importance. Significant towns and villages often occupied greater map space and natural features attained fabulous shapes and sizes in cosmological maps; distances were expressed in terms of the time it took the traveller to cover them (ibid.: 145). Indigenous maps had a different way of seeing the world: 'they were remarkably tolerant of overlapping sovereignties', particularly in the indeterminate border zones (ibid.: 165). This was completely discarded by European cartography. In addition, missionary efforts to spread map-literacy among the hill tribes induced changes in their rich oral cosmography and often downgraded their pride. An American Baptist missionary noted in the early-twentieth century that on seeing the modern map from Boston hung up in front of him, the head of the Ao Nagas dropped his head and muttered almost under his breath as to how great he thought the Ao Nagas were: a much bigger part of the creation than what the modern map indicated (ibid.:149).

Colonial surveyors and mapmakers objectified the 'geo-body' of British Assam in a 'spatial fix' and visualized it as Northeast-on-the-map. The Indian nation-state, as an inheritor of imperial boundaries as well as its territorial techniques of rule, created the Northeast as an isolated zone along lines shaped by colonial concerns (ibid.: 165).

Risley's letter signalled the beginning of vigorous activity in official circles. An initial scheme for the transfer of certain districts got transformed into a full-fledged plan for the partition of Bengal (Sarkar 1973: 11). The public got to hear little of this expanding scheme, except for a vague hint given by Curzon during his tour of East Bengal in 1904 that a larger readjustment for the east of Bengal was being thought of. Indeed, the general impression was that the plan had been dropped. In reality, however, officials were merrily engaged in a 'game of switching other people's lands' (ibid.: 11). The list of transferable districts went on increasing and the final scheme that Curzon sent off to the Secretary of State for his approval in February 1905 demarcated the contours of a separate province—'Eastern Bengal and Assam'—comprising Chittagong, Dacca and Rajshahi divisions, Hill Tipperah, Malda and Assam. The consent of the Secretary of State came in June 1905; the Government of India announced its decision to set up the separate province on 19 July. The formal proclamation came on 1 September and Bengal was partitioned on 16 October 1905.

The partition scheme has been a bone of endless contention between British official discourse and Indian nationalists, whose position was later upheld by Indian historians. Risley and other administrators maintained that administrative considerations had urged the government to decide on the partition. The undivided province of Bengal was huge and unmanageable both in terms of area and in terms of population—it straddled 189,000 square miles and had a population of 78.5 million in 1901. There is considerable truth in the claim that the excessive burden on Bengal had to be reduced. Nor can it be denied that till 1903, administrative concerns dominated the minds of officials.

On the other hand, it is equally true that Risley, the official turned ethnographer, who had successfully aided the demarcation of a Hindu majority and a Muslim minority in the censuses and had taken the lead in classifying castes 'scientifically' by means of anthropometry, paid great attention to a British officer's mention of political privilege deriving from the division of Bengal. In 1896, W. B. Oldham, the Commissioner of Chittagong division, had pointed to the possible political benefits of a new province that would 'unite the most important part of the Mohammedan population of Eastern India' and, thereby, reduce the political threat posed by the 'Hindu minority' in undivided Bengal (ibid.: 14).

Eight years later, Risley found Oldham's Minute 'very instructive' and, from then on, political considerations came to feature prominently in discussions relating to the redrawing of provincial boundaries (H. H. Risley's note of 2 March 1904, Home Public Proceedings A, February 1905, n.155, cited in Sarkar 1973: 14). In 1902, Andrew Fraser opposed Ibbetson's proposal of attaching Berar to Bombay as a 'politically unwise' move that was likely to add to the 'influence of the Poona Brahmans' (Fraser to Curzon, 15 December 1902, *Curzon Collection*, cited in ibid.: 15). On explicitly political grounds, another local administrator objected to the transfer of the Ganjam area from Madras to Bengal—the union of all Oriyas under a common administration, he felt, could prove 'dangerous' in the future (ibid.).

In addition, alternative proposals of nationalist leaders and some British officials—that suggested the separation of Bihar and Orissa from Bengal—were brushed aside. In view of this, it is difficult to accept earlier views that political considerations remained insignificant in government schemes of redrawing provincial boundaries (McLane 1965; Masselos [1985] 1996). Undoubtedly, Risley and other British administrators, who headed the census and several other ethnographic surveys, were clearly aware of the concentration of a Muslim population in the northern and eastern districts of Bengal and the wide discrepancy in the percentage and representation of Muslims in educational institutions and government service and professions. Francis Buchanan's sociological and statistical surveys of the nineteenth century had pointed to this demographic distribution; Adam's report on vernacular education had substantiated it. The first Census of Bengal in 1872 had revealed that almost half the population of Bengal—49.2 per cent—was constituted of Muslims, who predominantly populated the eastern side of river Bhagirathi, and belonged to agricultural and low service groups (Bandyopadhyay 2004: 254).

This perhaps accounted for their poor representation in education and profession. According to a different estimate, 32.2 per cent Muslims constituted Bengal's population in 1871, and only 14.4 per cent were enrolled in schools and 4 per cent in colleges (Huque 1917: 54). Sumit Sarkar's detailed and sensitive study of the Swadeshi movement convincingly concluded that political considerations became significant in the final scheme for the partition. Curzon's Minute of 1 June 1903 acknowledged the Viceroy's debt to Andrew Fraser's argument that the separation of the eastern districts of Bengal—the 'hotbed of purely Bengali movement, unfriendly if not seditious in character'—would draw a wedge in Bengal's political aspirations (Minute by His Excellency the Viceroy on Territorial Redistribution in India, 1 June 1903).

Home Secretary Risley picked up this cue with alacrity. His notes of February and December 1904 stated: 'Bengal united is a power; Bengal divided will pull different ways' (Risley cited in Sarkar 1973:

17). Fraser and Risley were the two principal figures who drafted the final scheme for the partition. Finally, Lord Curzon's successor Lord Minto, who had little sympathy for Curzon's views, admitted in a Memorandum in February 1906 that although the partition had been 'carried through with an unfortunate disregard for local sentiment and public opinion' it had to be maintained, since 'the diminution of the power of Bengali political agitation will assist to remove a serious cause for anxiety…' (ibid.: 20).

Indeed, the partition of Bengal can be viewed as the culmination of a series of measures taken by Curzon to curb the political aspirations of the Congress and its educated Indian members. A firm believer in British righteousness and perhaps the last champion of self-confident despotic imperialism advocated by Fitzjames Stephen and Lytonn Strachey (Bandyopadhyay 2004: 249), Curzon was incensed by the increasing demands of educated Indians and decided to take action against them. He reduced the number of elected representatives in the Calcutta Corporation by passing the Calcutta Municipal Amendment Act in 1899. The Indian Universities Act of 1904 brought Calcutta University under complete government supervision, and the freedom of the press was curbed further by the Indian Official Secrets Amendment Act of 1904. In his convocation address at Calcutta University, the Viceroy, while offering to state truths plainly but not unkindly, insisted that the highest ideal of truth was to a large extent a western concept, and further slighted the pride of educated Indians.

The Calcutta Municipal Bill, which sought to reduce the number of elected representatives was, according to the Congress leader Surendranath Banerjea, a local measure with an all-India reach. The bill affected the principle of local self-government. Once the bill became an act, Moderate leaders, who had protested against the Bill, came to doubt the power of public opinion and their own influence. More importantly, their belief that the colonial government was taking progressive steps towards implementing local self-government came in for a rude shock (Gordon 1974: 82). Consequently, the decision to divide the Bengali-speaking areas of Bengal into two—Bengal (with Bihar and Orissa) and Eastern Bengal and Assam—caused great uproar and protests began almost immediately after news of the plan 'slipped out' in 1904. After the announcement of the final decision on 20 July 1905, protest meetings were held in more than 300 cities, towns and villages all over Bengal, in which Mymensingh, Midnapore and Khulna—towns and villages closer to Calcutta and Dacca—played a more active role than other areas (ibid.).

Boycott and Swadeshi

Curzon's scheme to partition Bengal, instead of weakening Bengali nationalists who, he believed, controlled the Congress, revitalized it in unexpected ways. To begin with, the government's highhandedness, and its disregard for the petitions sent by Congress leaders, eroded respect for governmental authority, even as it discredited the methods of Moderate leaders. The famines and epidemics of the 1890s had shaken the faith of the elite in British administration, and rising prices on account of bad harvests in the first years of the twentieth century had made life difficult for the professional middle classes (Bandyopadhyay 2004: 255). Political disappointment, it is true, directly affected only a limited circle, as British administrators never failed to point out, and conscious anti-British sentiment was mainly confined to the educated, primarily Hindu *bhadralok* (Sarkar 1973: 29).

At the same time, what colonial officials did not take into account was the cumulative effect on Indians of racial discrimination and arrogance, strengthened by the constant focus and publicity given to incidents of racial discrimination by Indian newspapers. In addition, Bengal had a strong sense of regional identity that stemmed from a history with long periods of regional independence. This identity was bolstered by the cultural developments of the nineteenth century—a rejuvenated language and literature, a swath of vernacular journals and newspapers that discussed issues of public importance, and several associations that worked for the benefit of the community. In sum, there was a sense of a community that cut across class, caste and other barriers. This, together with a general economic distress that affected all sections, served to unite the 'proudest zamindar' or *bhadralok* with the 'meanest of plebians' (ibid.: 24), at least for a limited period of time.

The mood of confidence was complemented by international events, such as British reverses in the Anglo–Boer Wars (1880–81 and 1899–1902) against the *boer*s (literally farmers in Dutch and Afrikaans but used to denote the descendants of Dutch colonial settlers) in the Transvaal region of South Africa, which 'tarnished the image of British strength'. And, the unexpected Japanese victory over Russia in 1904–05, 'blew up the myth of European superiority and sent a thrill of pride through the whole of Asia' (ibid.: 28; [1983] 1995: 108–09). Such events were hailed and widely publicized by the Bengali press. The news of Chinese boycott of American goods in protest against immigration laws was lauded as 'worthy of emulation' by the newspapers *Sanjibani* and *Hitavarta* on 22 and 25 June 1905 respectively, just a little before the beginning of the Boycott movement in Bengal.

At the turn of the century, therefore, 'British political prototypes' came to be called into question, and a 'search for new patterns in indigenous, Asian and continental European sources' began (Gordon 1974: 77). In this situation, the government's move to go ahead with the partition, despite petitions, meetings, conferences and demonstrations against it, confirmed the inefficacy of Moderate methods and made evident the need for alternative ones. Once the partition was announced in mid-July, a boycott of British goods and institutions was accepted as a mode of struggle against the partition by Congress leaders. The formal resolution of boycott was passed at a mass meeting in Calcutta's Town Hall on 7 August and the Swadeshi movement was launched.

On the appeal made by Rabindranath Tagore and Ramendrasundar Trivedi, secretary of the Bangiya Sahitya Parishad (Literary Council of Bengal, founded in 1894 and headed by Trivedi between 1904 and 1911), on 16 October 1905, the day when the partition came into effect, *rakhi* (*rakhsha*)-*bandhan* was observed—wristlets of coloured thread were exchanged as a symbol of brotherhood and unity—'unity of the two fragments of Bengal forced apart by alien rulers, unity of Bengal as a whole and the rest of India—in short the unity of the nation against the raj...' (Guha 1997: 108). The poet led a huge procession through the streets of Calcutta, singing a song written for the occasion. People fasted and the hearth was kept unlit as a symbol of mourning.

Students, mostly Hindus from both parts of Bengal and some Muslims of western Bengal, took the lead in spreading the boycott, which was fairly effective for some months. Bonfires of imported cotton textiles and boycott of British educational institutions and law courts became common occurrences. The Indian National Congress took up the cause, and boycott spread to other parts of India, particularly Punjab, Maharashtra and the Telugu-speaking areas of the Madras Presidency, in solidarity with Bengal.

Gopalkrishna Gokhale, a sophisticated Moderate leader from Maharashtra, paid tribute to Bengali leaders in his statement—'What Bengal thinks today, India thinks tomorrow'. Between August 1905 and September 1906, there was a 22 per cent fall in the quantity of imported cotton piece goods, 44 per cent in cotton twist and yarn, 11 per cent in salt, 55 per cent in cigarettes and 68 per cent in boots and shoes (Sarkar [1983] 1995: 116).

It is in order here to pause briefly and consider the significance attached to cloth as a commodity. Important analyses have shown that cloth and clothing articulated colonial power and authority in the nineteenth century (Cohn 1989) and that is precisely why nationalists tried to overturn the meaning of cloth in their challenge to colonial domination (Bayly 1986). Indeed, for Christopher Bayly, cloth and clothes had played an important role in Indian society from pre-colonial times—in 'symbolizing social and political statues' as well as in 'transmuting holiness, purity and pollution'—meanings which were transformed in the colonial period (ibid.: 285). Boycott of British textiles was the driving force of the Boycott movement, and the broad 'socio-aesthetic complex' of boycott and swadeshi entailed 'the reconstitution of social taste from Manchester cloth to coarse cotton' (Goswami 1998: 624). Boycott bolstered the efforts, underway since the late-nineteenth century to historically produce 'a national space and economy' that based itself on 'colonial spatial practices' (ibid.: 609, 611). Cloth was the prime element through which a 'language of commodity resistance' was forged (Appadurai 1986: 30), a language that was taken over and given great significance by Gandhi in his conception of khadi (Bean 1989; Trivedi 2003). We will discuss this in Chapter 7. The Boycott movement, therefore, was much more than a 'nativistic upsurge' that rejected European products (Bayly 1986: 309).

British crackdown on students and the government's threat to withdraw grants, affiliation and scholarships from nationalist dominated institutions gave force to the movement for the boycott of British educational institutions and the founding of national schools. This effort was bolstered by the handsome contribution of ₹ 100,000 by Raja Subodh Mullick. A National Council of Education was set up in 1906, and the Bengal National College and Bengal Technical Institute were established. Rabindranath had already begun his experiments at Santiniketan in 1901, where nature and culture were to be linked by the bond of human labour within 'the living tradition of creative practice' (Kapoor 2000: 106). The alternative model of education and training in arts, and the development of human personality in communion with nature, much in the style of earlier *tapovana*s, would result in the establishment of Visva-Bharati, a comprehensive educational institution where the world, *visva*, was to come together.

Even more important was the founding of a dozen national schools in Bengal and Bihar along with many more in the districts of eastern Bengal. Establishing of primary schools in Mymensingh, Faridpur and Bakharganj, which 'occasionally had large numbers of Muslim and lower-caste Namasudra pupils', alarmed the British authorities for a time; they were aware of the danger of nationalist ideals spreading to the children and youth by means of primary education (Sarkar [1983] 1995: 117). Unfortunately, the National Council of Education did not pay much attention to these village schools and they languished over time. The ones that survived functioned primarily as recruiting centres for revolutionaries (ibid.: 118).

The experiment with national education expanded to encapsulate a full-blown notion of swadeshi (literally of one's own country, often translated as 'indigenous manufacture'), and endeavours were set afoot to encourage large-scale production and use of goods made in India. The Tagore family took a leading role—it provided the movement with its emotional and cultural symbols, took the initiative in establishing national industries and encouraged village improvement work. The idea of patronizing Indian products had been gathering momentum since the 1890s; members of the Tagore family and other leaders had been organizing *melas* (fairs) and setting up stores in order to promote the production and sale of Indian handicrafts. Rabindranath's *Swadeshi Bhandar* (1897), Jogeshchandra Chaudhuri's *Indian Stores* (1901) and Sarala Debi's *Lakshmir Bhandar* (1903) are cases in point. Prafullachandra Ray had founded the Bengal Chemicals factory in 1893, and attempts had been made to manufacture porcelain in 1901 (Sarkar 1973: 55).

The swadeshi mood gave a tremendous boost to such efforts. Intellectuals like Satishchandra Mukherjee drew upon Engels to underscore the horrors of the Industrial Revolution and valorized handicrafts as the Indian alternative to large-scale industry. His newspaper *Dawn*, which had been in circulation since 1897, and his Dawn Society, set up in 1902, had been spreading the message of self-help in industry and education, and Mukherjee had pioneered the national education movement by founding the *Bhagabat Chatuspathi* in 1895. Through this alternative path of growth in artisanal products and national education, he stated, India as a nation would achieve a 'modernized but ethical life' (Satish Mukherjee 1901, cited in Goswami 1998: 623). In the educational institution established during the swadeshi era, Mukherjee sought to combine 'the traditional and the modern in a scheme for "higher culture" for a selected youth' (Sarkar [1983] 1995: 117).

'The first days of the Swadeshi agitation', writes Leonard Gordon (1974: 83), 'were an exhilarating time'. A time when the veteran Congress leader Surendranath Banerjea, as expressed in his *Speeches and Writings* (n.d.: 295–99), felt that the movement will bring 'classes and masses upon the same platform'. Apolitical men were swept into politics and students participated in large numbers. The final announcement of the partition in the middle of 1905 made self-reliance or self-help 'the creed of the whole of Bengal for a time' (Sarkar 1973: 56). Calcutta leaders and their supporters in East Bengal united in a political 'coalition' that amounted to a 'revolution in the political structure of the Bengali society' (Ray 1984: 150). The Swadeshi movement represented the 'first systematic campaign in colonial India to enlist the masses within the elite structure and organization of institutional nationalism' (Goswami 1998: 623). Moreover, swadeshi practices graphically represented how the conception of a common economic collective was popularized and fused with the vision of a social body (ibid.: 624).

This was the time when 'Moderate' leaders were pushed to the background, and 'constructive Swadeshi' characterized by *atmashakti* (self-reliance) came to propel the movement. If we follow Sarkar's discerning analysis, there were four identifiable trends in the movement for boycott and swadeshi, trends that competed, co-existed and overlapped, gaining different degrees of importance at different moments (1973; [1983] 1995)—the Moderate method of constitutional agitation; the social strand of self-strengthening which advocated self-reliance prior to a collision with the colonial state; the more radical strand of self-help that wanted to develop 'a relentless boycott of British goods and institutions' as a mode of passive resistance and was ready to use violence against state repression; and finally, a small group of angry and impatient men and women who believed in revolutionary terror as the only way to deal with the British (Bose and Jalal 1998: 119). We will look closely at the radical trends in the following sections. Here, we focus briefly on *atmashakti* and make an overall assessment of the movement and its implications for later developments.

Rabindranath, a key proponent of *atmashakti*, played a very active role in the struggle between 1905 and early 1907. From the 1890s, the poet had become increasingly aware of the 'inhumanity' of the bureaucracy and the deterioration in relations between the rulers and the ruled, and had vented a mild protest against the Moderate policy of 'mendicancy' in several essays published in the journal *Sadhana* in 1893–94 (Tagore 1941). Similar feelings, not just of the inhumanity of the bureaucracy but also of the highly circumscribed role and participation allowed to educated Indians in public service, had been expressed in the literary works of Akbar Illahabadi, a sub-judge of Allahabad and Bankimchandra Chatterjee, a deputy magistrate of Bengal. Illahabadi's biting Urdu couplets and Bankim's acerbic satire, *Kamalakanter Daptar*, had mocked sycophantic loyalism of the Aligarh group and of Moderate Congress leaders (Metcalf and Metcalf 2003: 135–36). The poet, for his part, had taken initial steps to promote indigenous goods, which found greater elaboration in *atmashakti*.

Atmashakti espoused a move away from conventional old-style politics in favour of constructive economic and educational work in order to foster self-reliance. It also addressed the need to build a bridge between the educated classes and the masses through the use of the vernacular language as a medium of instruction in schools and political meetings, promoting folk institutions such as the *mela* and in the work of village reconstruction (Sarkar 1973: 52). The ideal was laid out as a programme by Rabindranath in his 'Swadeshi Samaj' address in 1904. Interestingly, the poet insisted on the need for society uniting under one leader—'a concrete functionary and a symbol of the whole' (Gordon 1974: 87). He stated that if the community was to take care of itself, it would have to consolidate its united strength. The most effective way to do this would be 'to invest a strong personality with leadership, and rally around him as our representative…' (Tagore 1961: 59).

Aswini Kumar Dutta, 'a quiet school teacher' in Barisal, vigorously implemented Rabindranath's programme of village reconstruction: by means of dedicated and patient social work in his district, he built up a mass following 'unequalled by any other leader of Bengal' (Sarkar 1973: 51). He organized the students in his school into several volunteer bands in his Swadeshbandhav Samiti (Association of the Friends of Swadesh), which carried out work in the interior of the district. Village disputes were settled by means of arbitration and annual reports were drawn up on the projects being carried out in the villages. In many ways, constructive swadeshi anticipated Gandhi's programme of national schools and village improvement (Sarkar [1983] 1995: 113). Two official industrial surveys of 1908 revealed that the 'swadeshi mood' had brought about a revival in handloom, silk-weaving and some other artisan crafts.

Another novel and significant development of the period was a marked 'industrial unrest', where 'professional agitators' played important roles (*The Administration of Bengal under Sir Andrew Fraser 1903–1908*). This was a direct result of the cumulative effect of white racism and focus on incidents of racial discrimination by Indian newspapers, noted earlier. Strikes in white-controlled enterprises sparked off by rising prices and racial insults now drew the attention and support of the nationalist press and professionals—some barristers came forward in organizing the labourers and on occasions helped to set up trade unions. A walk-out of 247 Bengali clerks in the Burn Company in Howrah in protest against a derogatory work regulation in September 1905 was followed by strikes in some jute mills, railway workshops and government presses. It was in the midst of a bitter strike in government presses that the first proper labour union, the Printers Union, came into being in October 1905.

In a similar manner, a strike by clerks of East India Railway in 1906 resulted in the formation of a Railwaymen's Union (Sarkar [1983] 1995: 118). The barristers, Aswinicoomar Banerji, Prabhatkusum Roychaudhuri, Athanasius Apurbakumar Ghosh and Premtosh Bose (the proprietor of a small press in north Calcutta) played a pioneering role. Their success in working together with labourers was reflected in the concern voiced by the Anglo–Indian journal *Pioneer* in August 1906. This effort, however, remained limited to clerks and jute-mill workers in and around Calcutta; the huge group of plantation and mine workers remained largely unaffected (Sarkar 1984: 279). Moreover, nationalist interest in labour 'slumped suddenly and totally after the summer of 1908, and it would not be renewed before 1919–22' (Sarkar [1983] 1995: 119).

Self-help of a different order was propounded in the activities of the *samiti*s, or a national volunteer movement that made a powerful appearance during this period. Although historians widely link *samiti*s to the growth of terrorist societies, till the summer of 1908 they were open bodies engaged in a variety of activities—physical and moral training of members; social work during famines, epidemics or religious festivals; and an encouragement of the swadeshi ideal by organizing crafts, schools and work in villages. Apart from the *samiti*s in Calcutta, the majority of the others were in East Bengal with different approaches and programmes of work. The ones led by Aswini Kumar Dutta's Swadeshbandhav Samiti, as we have seen, succeeded in acquiring a base among the peasants of Barisal. The Dacca Anushilan Samiti, on the other hand, focused on secret physical and moral training of cadres through idioms steeped in Hinduism and paid little attention to mass contact. In general, however, *samiti*s concentrated on spreading the message of swadeshi to the people by means of festivals, songs and speeches and *jatras* (folk theatre), in addition to the publication of innumerable pamphlets and journals.

The Bengali patriotism of the swadeshi days, writes Sumit Sarkar, 'brought forth an extremely impressive cultural outcrop' (Sarkar 1973: 496). The impact was visible not only in the field of literature and theatre, even music and art got revitalized in novel ways. The Indian *Sangita Samaj* (Music Society) founded by Jyotirindranath Tagore and the Maharaja of Natore in 1897 to promote classical Indian music had acquired some political notoriety by 1905. In the field of art, Abanindranath Tagore and his pupils resisted the 'traps and temptations of Western education' and rejuvenated Mughal painting (Guha-Thakurta 1992: 242), and made a break with 'imitations of Victorian naturalist taste' of the late-nineteenth century, reflected in the works of Raja Ravi Varma (Kapoor 2000; Sarkar 1973: 499).

Abanindranath and several other students of the Calcutta School of Art were inspired by the Orientalist enthusiasm of Kakuzo Okakura, the Japanese art critic and historian, Sister Nivedita, Vivekananda's disciple, and E. B. Havell, the principal of the Art School, and enthused by active interaction with visiting Japanese artists. This group experimented with earlier Indian traditions, such as Ajanta, Rajput and Mughal paintings and with the wash technique of Japan. The particular context of the Swadeshi movement and Abanindranath's involvement in it placed him 'in the full throes of the new artistic mission' (Guha-Thakurta 1992: 242). His personal endeavours expanded into a public role and generated a movement around himself. He and his pupils produced art that invoked both a golden past and a kind of oriental naturalism (Kapoor 2000: 166, 207). Parallels between the works of Abanindranath and Japanese artists highlight the role of 'mutual participation' in creating a new art language. Here, the individual markings of Indian and Japanese artists were blurred and recast into a composite unit of a modern 'Oriental' style (Guha-Thakurta 1992: 253).

The harmonized combination of subtle and mellow colours with firm lines produced Abanindranath's most important painting in the 'wash technique'—the *Bharatmata* (c.1904–05), which, more than any other, 'firmly fixed the epithet nationalist to his recreation of an "Indian style"' on him (ibid.: 255). The image was originally conceived as *Bangamata* (mother Bengal), and then dedicated to the entire nation. Sister Nivedita hailed this work as the 'supreme example of the metamorphosis of the abstract ideal of nationalism into art form … both human and divine' (Nivedita 1907: 221; Guha-Thakurta 1992: 255). Mother India was '[v]isualized as a serene, saffron-clad ascetic woman' and 'carried the boons of food, clothing, learning and spiritual salvation in her four hands' (Bose 1997: 53; image Chapter 5).

This conscious creation of an artistic 'icon' of the nation offers valuable insight into how the nation was evoked discursively. In the case of India, argues Trivedi, where nationalism arose without the benefit of a common written language and rising literacy (Anderson 1991), the visual and the printed languages complemented each other in the discursive configuration of the nation (Trivedi 2003: 12–13).

The configuration of the nation as mother had found articulation in Bankim's *Bande Mataram* (Hymn to the Mother) written and printed in 1875, as a filler for a blank page in his journal *Bangadarshan* (Bose and Jalal 1998: 120). It was included in Bankim's controversial novel *Anandamath* in 1882, a novel which portrayed Hindu ascetics vigorously challenging Muslim domination. The verse was set to tune and sung publicly by Rabindranath at the Calcutta session of the Congress in 1896 (Bose 1997: 52), and taken up with great vigour by swadeshi activists. Indeed, very soon the nation imagined as the mother became an 'ubiquitous figurative presence' in songs, novels, political writings, visual and iconic representations, a 'cultural artifact' which also bore testimony to the increasing 'Hinduization and feminization of the body politic' (Goswami 1998: 25; Sarkar 1987: 2011, 2001).

In the thoughts of people like Bipin Pal, the nation as mother was not 'a mere idea or fancy' but a 'distinct personality' (Bose 1997: 54–55), a point we will take up soon. Suffice it to say, that while the conception of the mother in chains lent a special quality to the profoundly self-sacrificing love of her sons who fought for her freedom (ibid.: 55), the idea of 'a common economic collective' (Goswami 1998) generated through the boycott of British goods, particularly cloth, gave material force to the notion of motherland. The woman, reconfigured in the nationalist discourse as the mistress of the home and family, was now entrusted with the procreation of valiant sons to fight for the mother.

Pride in *Bharatmata* was enhanced by achievements in the field of science. Physicist Jagadishchandra Bose's pioneering idea of *Plant Response*, hailed by the journal *Prabasi* as the greatest swadeshi event of 1906, and the experiments of Prafullachandra Ray in chemistry, gave the Bengali intelligentsia the happy consciousness that a combination of science and patriotism were helping to put Bengal and India on the map of world culture (Sarkar 1973: 498). The 'social collective of *Bharat*' came to acquire great force and provided the template on which 'popular swadeshi repertoires were forged' (Goswami 1998: 624).

As in the case of boycott, Punjab, where the Arya Samajists had been promoting self-help since the 1890s, and Maharashtra, where similar efforts had been under way, joined Bengal in taking up swadeshi. Indeed, in Punjab, business groups that had started establishing banks, insurance companies and schools toward the end of the nineteenth century, participated actively in promoting swadeshi, along with members of the Arya Samaj. Swadeshi sentiment in fact, was boosted by the existing tension among Muslims, Hindus and Sikhs, as well as anger against the British for their construction of canal-irrigated colonies on the rivers in Punjab that increased water rates and imposed newer controls. This 'boiling discontent' provided radicals, particularly Lajpat Rai, with a large following and a rare opportunity 'to discomfit both Panjabi political opponents and the British by demonstrations in 1907' (Stein 2010: 282). Lajpat Rai was exiled from Punjab and all meetings were banned. Water rates, however, were reduced and regimentation in the canal colonies relaxed.

The Telugu-speaking regions of the Madras Presidency actively supported the cause of boycott and swadeshi—meetings were held in Rajamundhry, Kakinada and Masulipatnam from 1906 to express sympathy with Bengal, and students participated in what has come to be known as the Bande Mataram movement. Bipin Pal visited the region in April 1907. His meetings gathered huge crowds where the students wore Bande Mataram badges. State repression against students resulted in attempts to set up national schools in current Andhra Pradesh. There was also a new interest in Telugu language, literature and history (Sarkar [1983] 1995: 130). The region was party to 'terrorist' acts as well, including an attack on the European club in Kakinada and the murder of a British magistrate (Sarkar [1983] 1995; Stein 2010: 283).

In Maharashtra, Sakharam Ganesh Deuskar (1869–1912) popularized the ideas of Naoroji and Ranade and promoted swadeshi in a popular idiom. His text, titled *Desher Katha* (Story of the Nation/Country), written in 1904, warned against the colonial state's 'hypnotic conquest of the mind' (Deuskar cited in Goswami 1998: 624). By the time *Desher Katha* was banned by the colonial state in 1910, it had sold over 15,000 copies, inspired swadeshi street plays and folk songs, and had become a mandatory text for an entire generation of swadeshi activists (ibid.: 624).

It is remarkable that in spite of this general growth of 'national' and regional awakening and 'national' consciousness, there was no word in Bengali for 'nation', a fact noted by Rabindranath. 'When we borrow this word from other people, it never fits us', commented Tagore (Prabhu and Kelkar 1961: 19, cited in Gordon 1974: 11). A decade later, Tagore would become an outspoken critique of nationalism, arguing that 'India had never had a real sense of nationalism' and it would do India 'no good to compete with Western civilization in its own field' (Tagore 1917: 64). Earlier, he had described nationalism as a *bhougalik apadevata*, a geographical demon, towards the exorcism of which he had dedicated his *Visva-Bharati* (Nandy 1994: 7).

It is highly probable that Rabindranath's scepticism resulted from his own experience of the Swadeshi movement. The term swadeshi—of one's own *desh*—offered the best illustration of the use of *desh*, which originally meant place of origin; place in a geographic, social, linguistic and cultural sense, to refer to the nation. Such use had featured in the writings of Rabindranath and other urban Bengalis from the late-nineteenth century. It must also have been prevalent in Marathi. Deuskar used *desh* to mean nation in the text we have just discussed. The overlap of place of origin and nation, as well as *jati* (literally birth, family or caste) and nationality inflected understandings of the nation/country in distinct ways. Moreover, the constant overlap and conflation of Bengal and India, and Bengalis and Indians in the use of *desh* and *jati*, added further twists to notions of nationalism. These mix-ups apart, the Swadeshi movement failed to contain the differences among leaders and breach the socio-cultural and economic gap between the elite and the masses.

On the one hand, there was a turn to extremism and terrorism or militant nationalism, which occasioned a break with Moderate leaders, and, on the other hand, the increased use of religious symbolism, coercion and social sanction alienated the masses, both Hindus and Muslims, of rural Bengal. From 1908–09, when the state carried out the first round of repression, the open *samitis* disappeared and 'terroristic secret societies took their place' (Sarkar [1983] 1995: 120). The movement, as we have noted, was constrained by a totally bourgeois base and aspirations; it never managed to incorporate a radical economic programme that could appeal to peasants and labourers. Even Aswini Kumar Dutta's Swadeshbandhav Samiti had a very minor peasant representation; Bengali elite dominated the affairs of village societies. Rabindranath's Swadeshi Samaj address contained the same strain of offering socio-political solutions from the top to filter downwards. Consequently, despite repeated statements about the need for mass awakening, 'the Swadeshi movement of 1905–08 seldom got beyond the confines of Hindu upper caste *bhadralok* groups ... '. (Sarkar 1984: 278).

It is in order here to indicate that the *bhadralok* caste and class composition was much more intricate than it is often assumed to be and there are debates among scholars with regard to who formed part of the *bhadralok* and who did not (Bhattacharya 2005; Broomfield 1968; Sartori 2008, for instance). And yet, there was a distinction that the *bhadralok* made consciously between them and the *chotolok*, the lower groups, classes or castes. The idea of refinement and culture played a major role in this demarcation.

Coercion, argues Ranajit Guha, had established itself as a means of mobilization for swadeshi quite early in the campaign. This coercion was of two kinds—physical coercion aimed at the destruction of British goods and the intimidation of those who bought, sold or patronized such imports, or cooperated with the administration; and social coercion, implemented by means of caste sanction, withdrawal of ritual services, refusal of inter-dining and boycott of wedding receptions and funeral ceremonies of those 'considered guilty of deviating from Swadeshi norms' (Guha 1997: 110). Such coercion and mobilization based on violence, according to Guha, could never have popular consent.

In addition, in eastern Bengal, the landlords mostly came from among the Hindu *bhadralok*, while Muslims and low-caste Hindus were tenants and sharecroppers. Unfortunately, therefore, at the height of the movement, there were several instances of disputes between Hindu landlords and Muslim vendors, with landlords closing village markets to implement boycott, and social boycott taking the form of upper-caste landlords putting pressure on lower caste and untouchable tenants. There were also instances of *naibs* (deputies) of Hindu zamindars seeking vengeance on recalcitrant Muslim tenants by forcing boycott on them (Tripathi 1967: 141).

On the other hand, rumours about a conflict between the government and the patriotic gentry—a time when the *babus* seemed to have incurred official displeasure—encouraged peasants to take action in order to settle their grievances against rents and cesses. The discontent of the predominantly Muslim tenantry of East Bengal found articulation in assaults on Hindu gentry, traders and moneylenders (Sarkar 1984: 280–81). Lack of convergence and conflict between elite and 'subaltern' concerns and interests produced contradictory consequences. A movement that started by insisting on the unity and brotherhood of Hindus and Muslims, ended up worsening relations between the two communities.

We need to place coercion and conflict of interests among Hindu landlords and Muslim peasants and agricultural labourers alongside the efforts of the Muslim *ashraf* leaders, from the late-nineteenth century, of expanding basic education for the Muslim masses to 'more clearly delineate a Muslim subjectivity and Muslim community' (Sengupta 2011: 125). Muslim educators and the Director of Public Instruction felt that the rural Muslim peasantry, referred to as *atrap*, were 'religiously backward'; they designed a new curriculum that emphasized religious knowledge and practice. It is difficult to gauge the extent of the effect of these endeavours; they had, however, allowed the *ashraf* to 'intervene in the religious practices of rural Muslims' (ibid.).

The Bengali intelligentsia had also failed to gain the support of Marwari traders of Calcutta and the Saha merchants of the districts from the beginning. It is true that there was a sharp decline in sales of Manchester cloth in late 1905, but that owed more to the quarrel over trade terms between British manufacturers and Calcutta Marwari dealers. Once the dispute was settled, the Marwaris went back to selling Manchester cloth, and the Saha merchants in the districts aroused the ire of swadeshi volunteers by refusing to pay heed to the call for boycott. Bombay mill-owners took full advantage of the decline in the import of British cloth and hiked up the prices of their own goods, despite appeals from Bengal. The limited impact of boycott can, therefore, be ascribed to the fact that it was not taken up in other parts of India with equal zeal (Tripathi 1967: 140).

The movement for boycott and swadeshi was not only constrained by its bourgeois component, it also lacked real bourgeois support (Sarkar [1983] 1995: 115). The movement was led by an intelligentsia that came from landholding and professional classes, not traders and merchants. Hence, their experiments with industries, labour unions and mass contact methods eventually bore limited success or led to unintended but damaging consequences.

Rabindranath, once again provides the best example of the problems and tensions generated by the movement. Extremely active in the initial phase, he withdrew from it in the middle of 1907, when Hindu–Muslim relations got severely strained. His address in 1904, which spoke of the necessity of uniting under one leader, indicated the poet's dislike for infighting. When this got worse, he withdrew from politics and aroused the ire of many. He moved back to his literary pursuit, coming up with acute analyses of the tensions and ambiguities of the age. *Gora*, a brilliant novel published in 1909, ended on a note of optimism; *Ghare Baire* (the Home and the World), published in 1914, offered a much darker vision of the swadeshi era.

Ghare Baire demonstrates the poet's analysis of the problems—of social sanction and physical coercion—that increasingly came to form a part of the movement. The novel casts an enlightened zamindar, a patriot, an idealist and a firm believer in constructive swadeshi for long before the actual onset of the movement, as the hero in contrast to his friend, a scheming swadeshi militant, who not only tries to seduce the landlord's beautiful young wife, but also turns his estate into a base for swadeshi campaign. The volunteers, let loose all over the place, promote swadeshi by means of blackmail, assault and even robbery. They harass the poorer Hindu peasants and incense the Muslims by a 'blatant display of Hindu chauvinism' (Guha 1997: 109). This results in an anti-Hindu jacquerie, instigated by *moulavis* among the Muslim tenants, a disturbance that seriously wounds the landlord who goes out unarmed to pacify his tenants. The novel ends with the landlord's repentant wife anxiously overhearing a conversation between the doctor and the estate manager about a body with a battered head.

For Guha, the 'head wound was a metaphor for the author's own battered reputation of 1908' (ibid.: 109). Apart from the fact that the poet was criticized for withdrawing from the movement, the 'battered reputation' represents, in Guha's terms, a lack of individual freedom to chart one's own way of serving the cause of social and political emancipation. The lack of individual liberty coupled with the pressure introduced on subordinate groups was to make the national cause 'altogether self-defeating' (ibid.: 110). We do not need to draw our analysis to this extreme, but we have to take into serious account the constraining and harmful effects of the use of fear and coercion.

The Swadeshi movement of 1903–08, concludes Sarkar, leaves the observer with two contradictory but equally valid impressions—one is 'a sense of richness and promise', an outpouring of 'national energies bursting out in diverse streams of political activity, intellectual debate and cultural efflorescence'. And the second, 'a feeling of disappointment, even anticlimax, at the blighting of so many hopes' (1973: 493). Amales Tripathi calls it a movement that began 'with a bang and ended with a whimper' (1967: 139). The partition, it is true, was revoked in 1911, but by then it had become a minor issue in the face of several other processes that the initial partition and the Swadashi movement had let loose. There was a clear cleavage in the Congress leadership, a worsening of Hindu–Muslim relations and a turn towards Muslim separatism actively fanned by British policies and Muslim concerns, and sustained by terroristic and Hindu nationalist activities.

The Swadeshi movement, to a large extent, offers insights into the contradictions of nationalism—contradictions that pertained to the blending of a developmentalist, modernist, liberal vision inherited from the Moderate leaders of the late-nineteenth century, with the specifically Hindu iconography of nationalist imaginings that concretized the ideal of a community-based collective. These tensions continue to haunt the India of the present.

THE SURAT SPLIT

The fervent activity of the early boycott and swadeshi days did not lead to the emergence of a central leadership with systematic plans for political action. Differences among leaders could not be contained for long and cleavages became evident by 1906. The Congress leadership, it bears pointing out, was strife-ridden by the time. There were regional rivalries and personality clashes. Among the miniscule group of the Madras elite, for instance, there were two factions, one dominated by Brahmans who lived in the Mylapore neighbourhood of Madras city, and the second composed of Brahmans who had alliances that extended to subordinate political centres in the Telugu-speaking regions of the north and to the far south (Stein 2010: 278; Washbrook 1976). The Mylapore faction dominated the affairs of the Congress in the first decades of its existence; members of the rival group aligned themselves with the Extremists and supported the anti-partition agitation, thereby gaining an edge over their Moderate counterparts.

Till 1905, the Congress was not much more than an annual forum whose deliberations perhaps have been given an 'exaggerated significance' (Sarkar [1983] 1995: 135). The Calcutta Congress in 1906 decided to form district associations for sustained political work and several district conferences were organized in a number of provinces in the following years, primarily though not entirely on the initiative of the younger and more radical group (Sarkar [1983] 1995: 135). The Moderate leaders tried to cope with the mood of the time. They started holding industrial conferences along with Congress sessions from December 1905, in order to give a boost to non-militant swadeshi. Gokhale started his Servants of India Society in 1905, whose members were to carry on full-time national work and practice self-reliance and moral purity.

All this, however, did not convince the excited youth of Bengal and those of other parts of the country. They were impatient for rapid and striking results, which could be obtained through political extremism; the prospect of slow and 'unostentatious development' through *atmashakti* failed to satisfy them (Gordon 1974: 77). The Extremists, led by Aurobindo Ghose of Bengal, and the Lal-Bal-Pal trio—Lala Lajpat Rai of Punjab, Balwantrao Gangadhar Tilak of Maharashtra and Bipin Chandra Pal of Bengal—considered themselves to be representatives of 'a higher stage in Indian nationalism' (ibid.: 77). They wanted to challenge the very basis of British authority in India and set up parallel institutions outside the purview of the Raj. Real regeneration, they argued, was not possible without freedom (Bandyopadhyay 2004: 256).

What came to pass in the early-twentieth century, therefore, was not 'temporary lines of division but fundamental conflicts of generation, of views about the ends and means of nationalist action, and of political power' (Gordon 1974: 89). The cause of difference again was not just generational; criticism of the politics, values, cultural positions, and even the personal behaviour of veteran leaders came from younger men as well as from people who 'already controlled the Congress but who were without access to the process of decision-making' (Masselos [1985] 1996: 93). At the same time, what brought the 'new group' together was not a search for power and influence but a similarity of objectives and ideas held together by a sense of opposition to British rule (ibid.).

Bipin Chandra Pal offered a stringent critique of the 'old patriotism' in his *New India* on 8 April 1905. This patriotism, he claimed, 'panted for the realities of Europe and America only under an Indian name: not for the realities of India'. Nor did it pant for its colour, tone, expression, ideas and associations. The 'one good' which the radical social and religious reactions of the past 20 years had done was to 'cure us, to a very large extent, of this old, this unreal, this imaginary and abstract patriotism' (Pal 1905, also included in McLane 1970: 57–59).

Bipin Pal's critique has been taken seriously by scholars who say that the Moderate leaders were 'denationalized' (Argov 1967, for instance). Some others, however, feel that while Moderates admired the 'Westminster system of government' and 'sought guidance on constitutional method and tactic that might promote unity and common cause', Extremists who had 'lost patience with gentlemanly persuasion, were not averse to consulting revolutionary histories for a more vigorous, self-reliant strategy of resistance' (Brasted 1980: 41).

The Extremists played a major role in the Calcutta Congress of 1906—their pressure led to the adoption of the resolutions on boycott, swadeshi, national education and self-government—although Dadabhai Naoroji, the President of the session, defined self-government in ambiguous terms. Bipin Pal's attempt to extend boycott to other provinces was shot down by Madan Mohan Malaviya and Gokhale, and different leaders offered different interpretations of the four resolutions. For the Extremists, boycott was only the first step towards the attainment of *swaraj* (freedom). Bipin Pal had stated unequivocally in *New India* that the Boycott movement was not just an economic movement; it was a protest against British rule that aimed at the foundation of 'ultimate civic autonomy' in India (Mukherjee and Mukherjee 1958a: 31). For leaders like Surendranath Banerjea, on the other hand, boycott was the last desperate resort to revoke the partition by 'pulling at the purse strings of Manchester' (Sarkar [1983] 1995: 112). This fundamental difference in perspective brought about the well-known split among the Moderates and Extremists for control of the Congress in the following session in Surat in 1907.

The session was originally to be held in Poona, an 'extremists' stronghold'. The Moderates managed to move it to Surat. In this session, Moderate leaders put up Rashbehari Ghosh, a wealthy Bengali barrister, as their candidate for president in opposition to Lajpat Rai, the Extremist candidate. Lajpat Rai, the most moderate among the Extremists, declined his nomination in order to avoid a split in the Congress. The fight, therefore, came to centre around 'the retention or rejection of the four resolutions passed in the Calcutta Congress' (Bandyopadhyay 2004: 258). Pherozeshah Mehta conspired to keep the resolutions outside the agenda; and the Extremists led by Tilak and Aurobindo decided to challenge the selection of Ghosh as the president. They were supported by delegates from Bengal, Maharashtra, Punjab and the Central Provinces. Congress proceedings were disrupted on the first day; the next day a verbal challenge turned into hurtling of *chappals* (sandals) and shoes, and was followed by the entry of hired club-wielders. This resulted in pandemonium; the break could not be averted.

It is difficult to ascribe responsibility for the clash to a particular group. It is, however, true that Moderate leaders remained unmoved by the attempts of the Extremists for a reunion. Tilak, in fact, was willing to reunite the Congress by purging it of Extremist elements, but Mehta remained inflexible. The Moderate 'convention' in Allahabad in April 1908 made the split final; the constitution drafted at this convention made Congress methods 'strictly constitutional', aimed at bringing about 'steady reform in the existing system of administration' (Gordon 1974: 91; Sarkar 1973: 137). It also reiterated its loyalty to the Raj, and rejected the Bengal model of politics (Ray 1984: 171). Moderates and Extremists started meeting separately. The Moderate convention continued to meet till 1914 with declining membership and enthusiasm, in what was called a 'rump Congress' by one of its members.

The jubilant Extremists were subdued by the arrest of many of its leaders, and discouraged by the departure of some others from the political field. Aurobindo Ghose and Tilak were imprisoned, and Bipin Pal, dismayed by the violence and hatred produced by the Swadeshi movement and disturbed by his differences with colleagues who ran *Bande Mataram*, left for England. Tilak remained in confinement till 1914 and Aurobindo decided to leave politics in 1909. This led to further desperation and a small group turned to individual violence, political murders and robberies, actions that cut them off from many of those involved in the Swadeshi movement. They also alienated the Muslim population in general, a majority of whom had remained somewhat aloof from the anti-partition agitation from the beginning.

RADICAL TRENDS

There is a certain degree of truth in the assertion that the Extremists had intimate links with cultural and religious developments of late-nineteenth century that sought to reinvigorate both Hinduism and its adherents, particularly male members, who were charged with varied degrees of effeminacy. Chapter 4 briefly mentioned the different efforts undertaken to this effect—the work of the Arya Samaj and the Singh Sabha in Punjab, the reconfiguration of the teachings of Ramakrishna Paramhansha by Vivekananda, the reforms in Maharashtra; Chapter 5 discussed the flowering of vernacular literature, including the emergence of historical novels that sought to recover past heroes and lost glories, and the attempts made by the elite to write their 'own' histories. Extremism undoubtedly was indebted to Dayananda, Vivekananda and Bankimchandra for its ideology 'but not for its political heredity' (Tripathi 1967: 46).

The activities of the Arya Samaj and other groups, it needs to be remembered, had made 'cow protection' a major issue in the Gangetic region from the late 1880s, and had occasioned serious rioting between Hindus and Muslims around Patna in 1893. Such trends ran parallel to Congress attempts to foment an all-India consciousness by staying away from social issues that could cause tension and fissure. Hence, to use Burton Stein's words, both 'peaceful' and 'violent' methods as well as 'secular' and 'communal' nationalisms occupied the same historical moment, and functioned both as alternative trajectories or as combined ones for different groups at distinct points of time (Stein 2010: 276).

'Extremism in Indian politics', argues Amales Tripathi, was 'a response to the challenge of haphazard and superficial westernization of Indian life, thought and politics' (1967: 1). He succinctly summarizes the ideological base of Extremism, 'a movement of resistance along three planes': spiritual, cultural and political. Spiritually, it sought to counter the threat posed by Evangelism, Utilitarianism and Brahmoism to 'traditional' Hinduism; culturally, it tried to resist an individualistic civilization which seemed to be 'distorting indigenous tissues of growth' and politically, it challenged 'the slow merger of Indian national identity in the vast inchoate British empire, which boasted of the white man's burden, but put it squarely on the brown man's back'. A rebound from 'the mimesis of the West, it oscillated to another extreme— the mimesis of ancient India' (ibid.).

There are problems in the way Tripathi uses 'Indian national identity' as a self-evident category for a time when varied efforts were being made to forge such an identity; but his analysis of Extremism as a 'mimesis of ancient India' carries great force. This is doubly true if we remember that for many leaders and ordinary subjects of the Empire, the idea of being an imperial subject was significant in a way where the Queen was the embodiment of natural authority (Sinha 2011). In addition, as we have seen in Chapter 5, engagement with the West and modernity were central concerns of the elite nationalist discourse, which sought to resolve its constitutive contradiction of modernizing the nation along western lines, while insisting on an essential Indianness by reconfiguring the Indian woman.

Let us try and trace the antecedents of 'Extremism' by moving to Maharashtra, western India, where 'revolutionary terrorism and revolutionary nationalism—politics aiming at national independence— were both foreshadowed' even if they took 'definite shape in Bengal' (Heehs [1998] 2006: 2). Peter Heehs begins the story with Wasudeb Balwant Phadke, a Chitpavan Brahman, who was a clerk at the commissariat department in Poona. Phadke and other 'native' clerks were treated with 'undisguised contempt' by their British superiors, generating in Phadke an acute dislike for the English (Heehs [1993] 2004: 7).

At the time of the famine of 1876–77, which 'struck Maharashtra with particular severity', Phadke became obsessed with ideas of ruining the British. He failed to gain converts to his cause among the educated Maharashtrians; but the famine conditions enabled him to find a following among the Ramoshis and other subordinate peoples. Phadke provided his followers with weapons to conduct raids and robberies on moneylenders and other rich Indians. This was intended to procure funds for a 'full-scale rebellion' and inducing 'fear in the English'. He also had plans of disrupting communications and freeing prisoners, who were to join his cause. His followers, however, showed greater interest in 'gathering bootys than in taking part in a disciplined campaign' (ibid.: 7). Pursued by the British, Phadke fled to Hyderabad where he made another effort to raise an army. He was captured in 1879, sentenced to life imprisonment and transported to Aden where he died in 1883.

In the following decade, Congress leader Balwant Gangadhar Tilak, who had studied at Elphinstone College (Bombay) and then trained as a lawyer, started the Ganapati and Shivaji festivals in open defiance of the Congress' stance to stay away from religion, in order to attract a larger number of people to the nationalist movement. Tilak, we need to remember, had sharply disagreed with the reformers, who were in favour of the Age of Consent Bill, ridiculing such men as effeminate who could not keep their families and women under control (Chapter 5). The debate over the bill hinged on the interpretation of Hindu tradition. Tilak differed from the 'reformers' over the interpretation of this tradition; he also did not want 'unwarranted' British interference in Hindu customs (Masselos [1985] 1996: 98). Further, he opposed the Congress move to hold a session of the National Social Conference headed by reformers such as Ranade, in the wake of its own session in Poona in 1895, on the ground that the issue of social reform, particularly the 'Western-style reform' promoted by the conference, was creating a division within the Congress (Heehs [1993] 2004: 8).

On the other hand, Tilak felt that 'Hinduism must develop a congregational character' in order to be 'politically useful' (Tripathi 1967: 67). The Ganapati festival was started to that effect—it turned the domestic worship of Ganapati into a public event (Masselos [1985] 1996: 100). This appeal to religion was followed by an appeal to history and the Shivaji festival was started. It valorized Shivaji as a great Hindu hero who had successfully fought the Mughals. In the words of Tripathi, Shivaji, whose life was 'high drama', relieved the 'dull monotony of middle-class life' and 'compensated for the emptiness and impotence felt by a brave people who had once held the emperor of Delhi to ransom' (1967: 73). Shivaji, according to Bipin Pal, was not just the sign and symbol of a political revolution, but 'the symbol of a grand idea, the memory of a noble sentiment', 'the idea of a *Hindu Rashtra*, which would unite under one political bond' (Pal 1954: 81).

Tilak found moral justification for Shivaji's treacherous killing of the Mughal general Afzal Khan in the teachings of the *Bhagavad Gita*. In the *Gita*, Lord Krishna tells a despondent Arjuna prior to the *Mahabharata* war that killing is permissible in war as long as it is not for selfish ends (Heehs [1993] 2004: 11; McLane 1970: 53), and that Arjuna was only the instrument of what had been divinely ordained. The Shivaji festival made use of priests and prayers, which were supplemented by historical and religious discussions.

According to an article in the *Kesari* on the festival in 1897, Professor Jinsiwale stated in the course of a discussion that 'Shivaji Maharaja should be considered superior to Cesar and Napoleon' since the 'great men of Europe were attracted by ambition alone', whereas 'the uncommon attributes displayed by our Maharaja were not the blaze of the fire of ambition or discontent'; rather, they were the result of 'the terrible irritation at the ruin of the country and religion by foreigners' (*Kesari* 15 June 1897). The Hindu nationalist tone in the construction of Shivaji as the defender of the country and faith against 'foreigners' is evident; at the same time, as McLane notes, these festivals appealed to people who were ill at ease with the Anglicized gatherings of the Congress (McLane 1970: 53).

As a corollary to the festivals, cultures of physical training were sought to be revived in the 1890s in youth clubs set up in different parts of Maharashtra and elsewhere. Such culture had received a jolt with the passage of the Arms Act of 1878, which had made possession of firearms by 'natives' illegal. In addition, the colonial state encouraged the youth to engage in the game of cricket in place of wrestling and other martial arts practiced in the *akhara*s. Over time, the youth clubs of the 1890s developed into centres of 'pro-Hindu and anti-British feeling' (Heehs [1993] 2004: 8).

Damodar and Balkrishna Chapekar, two brothers of a Chitpavan Brahman family of Poona, followed Phadke's ideals of doing away with the British in India. Inspired by a belief that they were divinely ordained to defend their faith, these brothers gathered a bunch of about 30 boys into a club whose tutelary deity was Maruti (Hanuman). The lads were given physical training, taught traditional Indian games and were encouraged to break up cricket matches. Soon, they began to harass Indian Christians and reformers. The brothers, however, failed to inspire sufficient loyalty among the members of the club and decided to continue on their own. In 1895, they 'tarred a statue of Queen Victoria and garlanded it with shoes' (ibid.: 9). They also made public appearance in the Ganapati and Shivaji festivals where they used the form of *katha*, story-telling, to urge people to stop the English from killing cows and take active part in a struggle to free the country of the British.

When the bubonic plague broke out in Bombay and Poona in 1897, the brothers became incensed by reports that the plague commission was taking drastic and atrocious measures to stop its spread. The 'devitalized' peasants of Bombay and the Deccan, who had been struggling against landlords and moneylenders since the 1870s fell easy prey to the epidemic, which came in the wake of famines in 1896. The plague spread rapidly in the slums of Bombay; bad sanitation, poverty and starvation made it ideal for the disease to thrive. In a desperate effort to stop the spread of the fatal disease 'somehow', the Government of India gave extensive powers to the Bombay government to tackle the situation (Tripathi 1967: 69). Walter Charles Rand, the chairman of the plague commission, rode roughshod over orthodox sentiments in an 'overzealous haste' to control the plague; stringent and drastic measures of segregation and destruction of infected things were undertaken (ibid.: 70).

Tilak described Rand as 'suspicious, sullen and tyrannical' in the *Kesari*; the Chapekar brothers vowed to kill him. They invoked the blessings of Goddess Bhawani, shot and fatally wounded Rand, killed Lieutenant Ayers who had witnessed the attack and managed to escape. It was only when Damodar sought publicity by writing to a newspaper editor that the police managed to track them down. Both were tried and sentenced to death in 1898 and 1899. In a manner similar to Phadke, the Chapekar brothers' hatred of the British stemmed more from a concern with their faith than from the urge for political freedom. '[T]he British were seen as odious more on account of their religion than their administration' (Heehs [1993] 2004: 10).

Phadke and the Chapekars' maverick efforts were given a different direction and planning by

Extremist leaders, who, as we have just seen with Tilak, had a more definite political programme. These men had greater zeal in promoting Indian culture, and were openly critical of the 'Anglicized' values and way of life of leaders such as Pherozeshah Mehta and Surendranath Banerjea.

Aurobindo Ghose provides another good example. He did not share the hatred for the British that drove Phadke and the Chapekar brothers, both from families that had little access to English education. Born in 1872 in a professional middle-class Bengali family, Ghose was educated in England and trained to take the Indian Civil Services examination. He failed to qualify on account of poor horsemanship, returned to India and was employed by the Gaekwad of Baroda in the state's land-revenue department in 1893. The work was 'unspeakably boring' for young Aurobindo, a versatile man with command over English, French, Greek and Latin, and conversant with German, Italian and Spanish, who had read masterpieces of European literature in the original. During his stay in England, Aurobindo had joined Indian Majlis, an organization of Indian students in Cambridge, and had made 'nationalist speeches' (Gordon 1974: 105). He had also written on Home Rule, a dominant political issue in England in the 1880s, where he had made his Irish sympathies clear. In all likelihood, therefore, he was ambivalent about joining the Civil Services and not particularly disappointed by his failure.

Soon after his return to India in 1892, Aurobindo devoted himself to his literary and political passions by writing a series of articles on the Indian National Congress. Titled 'New Lamps for Old' and published in the Bombay weekly *Indu Prakash* between 1893 and 1894, the series offered a systematic critique of the Congress from a nationalist perspective. These articles criticized the elitism and moderation of Congress leaders and threw an open challenge to them. Thoroughly inspired by French and Irish revolutionaries, who had been purified by 'blood and fire', Ghose found the likes of Mehta and Banerjea to be 'less than men' (Mukherjee and Mukherjee 1958b: 77). He displayed an antipathy for British institutions and was incensed by the legalistic constraints on Indian political activity, which he attributed to the predominance of lawyers in politics (Gordon 1974: 108).

Aurobindo was not allowed to continue in this vein for long; Ranade, a former editor of the weekly, warned him that he would be charged with sedition. The articles, however, won him a following among other younger western-educated men—Lajpat Rai, Tilak and Bipin Pal being among them. Moreover, Extremism became the dominant creed in Maharashtra; Extremists 'captured' Ranade's Poona Sarvajanik Sabha in 1896 and founded the Deccan Sabha in the same year (Tripathi 1967: 59). When the plan for the partition of Bengal became public, Tilak, Lajpat Rai and Pal (a Moderate till the end of the nineteenth century), joined Aurobindo in advocating the founding of secret societies to oppose the partition.

In the 1890s, Aurobindo had started writing articles on Bankimchandra Chattopadhyay, the controversial doyen of Bengal Renaissance, in which he displayed his admiration for Bankim (Heehs [1993] 2004: 16). The influence of Bankim's *Anandamath*, which is said to 'drip with anti-Muslim prejudice' (Bose and Jalal 1998: 121), as well as of *shaktism* and tantrism, was clear in Aurobindo's *Bhawani Mandir* (Temple of Goddess Bhawani), a short pamphlet written in the 1890s, and published and circulated secretly.

The pamphlet provided an assessment of the Indian situation and a plan for revival by means of religious ideals. A perfect example of the combined articulation of the religious and the political, *Bhawani Mandir* asked the political *sanyasins* (ascetics) to build a temple of the Mother as Shakti (power/energy), put aside personal gratification, dedicate themselves to the regeneration of India and strive to give her a position in the world. The British, interestingly, are absent in this pamphlet, and India's degeneration is ascribed to her abandonment of Shakti. The work displays a much greater faith in the worship of Shakti than Bankimchandra; at the same time, it draws upon Bankim's idea that Indians (Bengalis) were responsible for their own downfall (effeminacy), an idea also shared by Tilak.

Following upon his belief in Shakti, Aurobindo was soon to declare that the 'Motherland is no other than Divinity itself' and 'the Motherland in all her beauty and splendour represents the Goddess Durga of our worship' (Aurobindo cited in Tripathi 1967: 68). Indeed, scholars have noted that the public worship of Goddess Durga on a grand scale became popular in Calcutta and elsewhere in Bengal from the early-twentieth century (Nandy 1994; Guha-Thakurta 1992), which was definitely tied to the nationalist trend of configuring the nation as mother and mother-goddess.

Sugata Bose argues that for Bipin Pal there was a clear correspondence between the real mother, the woman who bore and nursed her children and raised them with her own life and substance, and the land that 'bore and reared, and gave food and shelter' to its inhabitants (1997: 55). The basis of this idea lay in the nature philosophy of the Hindus which conceived of the earth as *prakriti*, nature/mother (Pal 1958: 108). Not surprisingly therefore, Pal chose to call his newspaper, *Bande Mataram* (Hail Mother), the 'all-India daily organ of Indian nationalism' (Mukherjee and Mukherjee 1958a: 44). In addition, Aurobindo, Tilak and Pal, as well as others formulated clear ideas of the 'inward character' of the nation that was taking shape. This is because they thought of *swaraj* not only as a necessary step to India's self-liberation, but also for the 'salvation' of humanity (Mukherjee and Mukherjee 1958b: 108). The nation was, like in ancient times, to be based on dharma where the caste system would provide the frame-work of 'a communal self-determined freedom', 'a training ground for the education of the human mind and soul and its development through the natural to the spiritual existence' (Aurobindo 1907 cited in Tripathi 1967: 75).

The Swadeshi movement was, for Aurobindo, a blessing in disguise; it 'awakened many Bengalis to political life who had previously been ignorant or uninterested' (Gordon 1974: 114–15). The movement also offered Aurobindo a brilliant opportunity to put his ideas into practice. During his stay in Baroda, Aurobindo had established contact with political workers in Maharashtra and revolutionary workers of the Bombay Presidency and had sent his brother Barindrakumar to Bengal to 'organize a revolutionary movement' (*Sedition Committee: 1918, Report*, Calcutta, 1919: 17). In 'New Lamps for Old', he had spoken emotionally of the widening gap between the rich and the poor and of the imminence of a revolution from below. At the same time, he had also 'participated in séances, searched for a guru, and beg[u]n to practice yoga' (Gordon 1974: 110).

Politics came to take priority during the Swadeshi movement and Aurobindo joined hands with the Extremist leaders to push for boycott. He collaborated with Bipin Pal in publishing *Bande Mataram* in 1906, which attacked the 'mendicancy' of Congress leaders and discarded the idea of 'peaceful ashramas and swadeshism and self-help' as inadequate. Aurobindo chalked out an alternative programme—that of passive resistance—which entailed 'organized and relentless boycott' of British goods, educational, administrative and judicial institutions to be backed up by the establishment of national institutions, law courts and industries, a civil-disobedience of unjust laws, and social boycott of loyalists (Ghose 1907).

Bengal Extremism, states Sarkar, 'wasted a lot of energies in purely verbal or literary violence and in-fighting over the Congress organization'. It did, however, contribute to 'building up an impressive chain of district organizations or *samitis* and in providing some novel political leadership to labour unrest' (Sarkar [1983] 1995: 114), a point we have discussed earlier. Centres of revolutionary work are said to have been set up in Khulna, Rangpur, Dacca and Midnapur by 1904–05, centres that had contact with their counterparts in Maharashtra (Mitra 1954: 58). The different *samitis*, such as the Anushilan Samiti of Calcutta (of which Barindrakumar was a member) and Dacca, and the one set up by Jnanendranath Bose in Midnapore took active part in political activity. Their newspapers—*Jugantar* (End of the Era), published from April 1906 by members of the inner circle of the Anushilan Samiti, and the evening daily *Sandhya*, of Brahmobandhav Upadhyay, as well as the *Bande Mataram*—began to write about the need for political independence, without which national unity and economic and social progress could not be achieved (Heehs [1998] 2006: 3). In late 1906, members of the Anushilan Samiti made an abortive attempt to kill the unpopular Lieutenant Governor of East Bengal.

After the attempt failed, Hemchandra Qanungo, 'the most remarkable figure among the first revolutionary generation' (Sarkar [1983] 1995: 123), went abroad to get military and political training. On his return in January 1908, a bomb factory and a religious school were set up in a garden house in the Maniktala suburb of Calcutta. Before that, there were plots, according to the Report of the Sedition Committee, to blow up the Lieutenant Governor's train on 6 December 1907 and on 23 December Mr Allen, a former District Magistrate of Dacca, was shot in the back. The committee also reported a burglary in the house of a wealthy man in Sibpur, Howrah, on 3 April 1908, in which the owner was forced to surrender 'money and ornaments of the value of ₹ 400' (*Sedition Committee: 1918, Report*, Calcutta 1919: 32).

On 11 April 1908, a bomb exploded in the house of the mayor of Chandernagore without injuring anyone. On the 30th of the same month, Kshudiram Bose and Prafulla Chaki threw a bomb into a carriage in Muzaffarpur in Bihar in an attempt to kill the Presidency Magistrate Kingsford. The bomb, however, killed two English ladies, Mrs and Miss Kennedy. This misdirected attempt led to the capture, not only of Kshudiram (Prafulla Chaki committed suicide before being caught), but also of the entire group associated with the bomb factory, including Aurobindo and his brother.

Chittaranjan Das, still a 'briefless barrister' who would later become an acclaimed leader of the nationalist struggle, offered a brilliant defence for Aurobindo at the Maniktala Conspiracy Case trial. He declared that the accused was guilty only if the preaching of the principle of freedom was a crime (Bandyopadhyay 2004: 261). Aurobindo was acquitted, but his brother and several others were sentenced to death, a penalty changed into life imprisonment on subsequent appeal. This gave a serious jolt to the society, which never really managed to resume its activities. The society is remarkable, in Heeh's view, for declaring complete independence to be its final goal, almost 20 years before the Indian National Congress (Heehs [1998] 2006: 14–15).

The Dacca Anushilan Samiti, which was more tightly organized, carried out revolutionary activities that included robberies in the houses of wealthy Saha merchants who had refused to pay heed to the boycott, and in trains as a measure to collect funds. This group, however, concentrated on training revolutionaries through the use of Hindu religious idiom. They barely had any programme of mass contact. The young revolutionary 'terrorists' captured the imagination of many Bengalis; the hanging of Kshudiram Bose was immortalized in folk songs and, in general, the spirit of selfless patriotism and sacrifice for the motherland of these young men were valorized and romanticized in literature and songs. Most of these young men, states McLane, belonged to Brahman and Kayastha castes and were students, and even though their impact was limited, terrorist activities in Bengal between 1906 and 1917 had killed 82 persons and wounded 121 (McLane 1970: 61).

In Maharashtra, Tilak fared better in getting the support and attention of different sections of the populace. His journal *Kesari*, which vigorously supported the cause both of swadeshi and *swaraj* by means of relentless passive resistance, had reached a circulation of 20,000 by 1907 (Sarkar [1983] 1995: 132). Swadeshi, we have noted, received very little support from the Gujarati and Parsi mill-owners of Bombay although swadeshi enthusiasm for indigenous cloth contributed to 'the super profits made by Bombay and Ahmedabad' mills during 1905–06 (ibid.). Tilak and his associates participated in mass picketing of liquor shops and made attempts to develop contacts with the predominantly Marathi working class in Bombay. The picketing of liquor shops, later to be an important part of Gandhi's programme, reduced the government's excise revenue; it also appealed to reformist trends among lower-caste groups.

Tilak and his men also succeeded in winning the factory workers of Bombay, almost half of whom came from Tilak's home district of Ratnagiri, to the cause of boycott and swadeshi. In the speeches he gave during 1907–08, Tilak, who had earlier opposed a Factory Law passed in 1881 by a British owner, stressed the need for boycotting foreign goods and liquor, and taking to the use of India-made goods since that would 'increase the work in the mills and benefit the employees' (Sarkar [1983] 1995: 133).

A measure of Tilak's success in drawing the attention of the workers was the 'outburst of proletarian anger' at his imprisonment on the charge of sedition for certain articles published in the *Kesari* in 1908 (ibid.:134). The beginning of Tilak's trial was marked by clashes with the police, stone-throwing and sporadic strikes, and when Tilak was convicted, cloth shop employees of the Mujli Jetha market gave the call for a six-day *hartal* (work stoppage), with the six days signifying the six years of imprisonment that Tilak had been awarded. The call was accepted by a majority of the factory workers; 76 out of the 85 mills in Bombay were affected by a six-day walk-out, despite firing by the police and the army. There was also a riot in the pilgrim town of Pandharparpur organized primarily by lower-caste people.

This popular outrage at Tilak's imprisonment fits in uneasily with the widely accepted belief that extremism in Maharashtra was largely a Chitpavan Brahman affair. Extremist efforts at bringing in the 'masses' did succeed, although temporarily. Moreover, as Heehs argues, it is too easy to draw a direct connection between the religious idioms used by Extremists and revolutionary terrorists and a deterioration of relations with Muslims. Not all Extremists adopted a particularly Hindu stance; some made serious efforts to address and include Muslims. Indeed, Muslim participation in the Swadeshi movement in 1905–06 was not negligible; leaders such as Abdul Rasul and Liakat Hussain 'joined heart and soul' with Surendranath Banerjea, Bipin Chandra Pal and Aswini Kumar Dutta 'in their crusade to unsettle' what Secretary of State Morley called the 'settled fact' of partition (Tripathi 1967:157–58). Besides, 'terrorism' was neither produced by the scheme of the partition, nor did it come to an end with its annulment.

After 1908, the centre of activities moved to Punjab and the United Provinces, and revolutionary 'terrorism' remained a constant strain of the nationalist struggle. Immigrant Punjabis founded a *Ghadr* (revolution) Party in North America in 1913; some of its members returned to India and joined hands with Bengali and Marathi revolutionaries. A series of dacoities were carried out in north India and in 1912 an unsuccessful attempt was made on the life of Viceroy Lord Hardinge. Severe government repression curtailed but could not contain revolutionary violence; the 'heroic' acts of the revolutionaries became legend. These revolutionaries challenged the dominant notion that the Indian nationalist struggle did not take recourse to violent methods. The prevalence of this notion owes its origin to the success of Gandhi and his non-violence (Heehs [1998] 2006: 1).

Hindu–Muslim relations worsened for a variety of complex factors—the demographic peculiarity of eastern Bengal where Hindus were landlords and Muslims tenants and labourers, and the colonial state's active propaganda that the partition would be beneficial for the Muslims, influenced ideas and ways of 'belonging' in distinct ways. We will take up the related story of the 'Muslims' to complete the intricate picture of diverse processes set in motion by the partition.

Chronology of Pre-Congress and Pre-Muslim League Organizations

Place/Year	Organizations
BENGAL	
1837	Zamindary Association of Calcutta. Re-named Landholders' Society in 1838. Established by Radhakant Deb and Prasanna Coomar Tagore.
1843	Bengal British India Society. Established by George Thompson and Peary Chand Mitra, Calcutta.
1851	British India Association (joined by above two.) Established by Radhakant Deb and Debendranath Tagore, Calcutta.
1856	Mohammedan Association. Established in Calcutta.
1863	Mohammedan Literary Society. Established by Abdul Latif, Calcutta.
1875	India League. Established by Shishir Kumar Ghose. Calcutta.
1876	Indian Association. Established by Surendranath Banerjea. Calcutta.
1877	National Mohammedan Association. Established by Sayyid Ameer Ali.
1883	All India National Conference, called by Indian Association.
1885	Second All India National Conference, called by Indian Association, National Mohammedan Association and British Indian Association.
BOMBAY	
1852	Bombay Association. Established by Jagannath Shankarshet. Revived in 1867 by Naoroji Furdoonji.
1867	Poona Association, became Sarvajanik Sabha in 1870. Established by Ganesh Wasudeo Joshi.
1885	Bombay Presidency Association. Established by Pherozeshah Mehta, K. T. Telang, Badruddin Tyabji. Host to first Indian National Congress session.

Chronology of Pre-Congress and Pre-Muslim League Organizations

Place/Year	Organizations
MADRAS	
1852	Madras Native Association. Established by G. Lakshminarasu Chetty. Revived in 1881 by C. V. Rangananda Sastri and Salem Ramaswamy Mudaliar.
1884	Madras Mahajana Sabha. Founded to coordinate 100 local associations in southern towns and cities. P. Rangiah Naidu, first president.
NORTHERN INDIA	
1861	British Indian Association of Oudh. Established by Man Singh and Dakhinaranjan Mukerji. Lucknow.
1866	British Indian Association, Aligarh. Established by Raja Jaikishandas and Sayyid Ahmad Khan.
1886	Mohammedan Educational Congress, became Conference in 1890. Established by Sayyid Ahmad Khan, Aligarh.
1887	United Indian Patriotic Association. Established by Sayyid Ahmad Khan, Aligarh.
1893	Anglo-Mohammedan Defence Association of Upper India. Established by Sayyid Ahmad Khan and Theodore Beck, Aligarh.
1900	Urdu Defence Association. Established by Nawab Muhsim-ul-Mulk. Lucknow.
1901	Conference of Muslims at Lucknow. Called by Nawab Viqar-ul-Mulk.

MUSLIM POLITICS

The 'Muslims', who constituted 19.7 per cent of India's total population including the princely states in 1881, were, by no means, a homogeneous community. As we have seen in Chapter 4, they were divided in terms of economic status and social prestige, language and region, as well as by different sectarian affiliations. Chapter 4 also noted the impact of the colonial categorization of the Muslims as 'backward', particularly Hunter's work *Indian Musalmans* spurring different efforts for reforms among the Muslim elite.

The 'backwardness' of the Muslims was paired with earlier European representations of Islam as 'static' and 'dogmatic' and their adherents as 'conservative, haughtily conservative of things "modern", and too much under the influence of an obsolete system of education' (Low 1907: 281). Such representations did not correspond to reality; they were also contested by foreign visitors to India. At the same time, the repeated and recurrent evocation of the presence and influence of pan-Islamism by colonial officers led some sections of Muslims to see themselves as being 'unified, cohesive, and segregated from the Hindus', a trend that became pronounced after the Morley–Minto Reforms of 1909 (Hasan 1996: 193).

On the other hand, it has been argued that even though 'regional' rather than 'religious' categories were more important for Muslims till the intervention of 'reformist orthodoxy and political communalism' in the late-nineteenth and twentieth centuries, these interventions occurred in the context of a 'long-standing sense of community among the Muslims' (Ghosh 2008: 1). The sense of community had been fostered by traditions of free movement among service elite and religious teachers, as well as by intellectual, economic and political communication (Robb 1993: 147). This did not, however, mean that 'Muslim identity' centred solely on Islam—such an assumption presupposes the existence of an absolute Islamic consciousness (Hasan 1995: 2995). The reform ventures of the nineteenth century deployed the diffuse sense of 'community' in distinct ways in their efforts to give cohesion to a Muslim collective. Here, we focus primarily on Bengal in order to gauge how different groups understood and appropriated the partition of 1905.

Bengali Muslims, it has been shown, were a highly fragmented group united by a vague allegiance to the essentials of Islam (Bandyopadhyay 2004: 264; Ahmed 1996). Even among the elite, the *ashrafs*, there were divisions between the urban Urdu-speaking Muslims and the rural/*mofussil* Bengali-speaking landlords, in addition to the clear separation from the poor Muslim peasants, tenants, agricultural labourers and artisans, all of whom spoke Bengali.

If we follow Richard Eaton, the predominance of Muslim peasants in eastern Bengal is explained by the expansion of cultivation in remote areas between the sixteenth and eighteenth centuries—the distance of East Bengal from the core of 'Brahmanic civilization' allowed Islam to spread as the 'religion of the plough'. This was a slow and gradual process through which inhabitants of the region, barely touched by Hinduism, came within the fold of Islam (Eaton 1993: 306–11). This meant that till the nineteenth century there was little interaction between the urban elite and the rural poor. Moreover, unlike the Hindus, the Muslims did not have an intermediary group of professionals who could bring the elite and the subordinate people together in the newly created public space (Bandyopadhyay 2004: 265).

Lack of formal education among the poorer groups was an important factor behind the extremely low representation of Muslims in education and government service, a fact noted earlier in this chapter. The lot of poorer peasants in general was indifferent to formal education and even when they sent their children to school they preferred the less expensive indigenous institutions such as the *maktab*s and *madrassa*s. The Muslim elite, also, were slow to take to English education. In comparison to the 93.4 per cent Hindus who attended college in 1875, Muslims numbered only 5.4 per cent, and only 1.50 per cent of them knew English. The notion of backwardness, therefore, found easy acceptance among some sections of the elite who started taking measures to deal with it. Sayyid Ahmad Khan and the *ashraf* of Bengal offer cases in point.

Movements for reforms among subordinate groups, discussed in chapters 3 and 4, were complemented by the activities of local associations (*anjuman*s), itinerant preachers (*mullah*s), and discussions in religious meetings (*baha*s). All such moves strove to return Islam to its pristine state by purging it of later deviations and syncretism introduced by the Sufis. These measures to 'Islamize' and 'Arabicize' Muslim culture made the lower groups socially mobile and nurtured the growth of an Islamic sentiment. These were complemented by Muslim educators' efforts to 'inculcate new forms of religiosity' along the lines of Christian mission day schools, among the 'backward' and 'nominal' Muslim peasants (Sengupta 2011: 125). Therefore, despite the socio-cultural distance, the poorer groups came to feel a sense of solidarity with the upper-class *sharif* Muslims (Bandyopadhyay 2004: 267) and it became easy for them to make use of this sentiment in their efforts to organize the 'Muslims' as a separate political group.

The *Anjuman-i-Islami* (Mohammedan Association), the first Muslim organization in Bengal founded in 1855, strove to bring together Muslims as a community and display its loyalty to the British in order to get 'a fair field' (Maitra 1984: 79) to compete with the Hindus on equal terms. It anticipated much of Sayyid Ahmad's programme. Abdul Latif Khan's Mohammedan Literary Society (1863) tried to adapt western education to the parameters of the Islamic educational system. Pained by the lack of 'political consciousness' among the members of his community, Syed Amir Ali, an England trained barrister of the Calcutta High Court, and a scholar of Muslim law, founded the Mohammedan Association in 1877 (Lahiri 1991: 62). Ali wanted to organize the Muslims politically so that they could articulate their views to the colonial masters like the Hindus. The association became the Central National Mohammedan Association with 34 branches all over India.

There was no necessary convergence between all these efforts; indeed, the apparent success of the Mohammedan Association made Amir Ali aware of the differences among Muslim leaders. While Abdul Latif dismissed him as a westernized man ignorant of the religious language of Islam and out of sync with true religious reform, Ali found himself disagreeing with Sir Sayyid Ahmad's exclusive stress on educational work. From the 1880s through to the 1920s, Ali, like Sayyid Ahmad, systematically opposed the 'Congress Muslims'. By the 1880s, Congress had many 'Muslim' sympathizers in north India and its 1887 Madras session was presided by Badaruddin Tyabji of Bombay, a lawyer and a leader of the Sunni Bohras. Amir Ali was driven by a growing antipathy towards the 'mental pliability' of the Brahmanical Hindus in the Congress (Gordon 1974: 67). Ali incurred the wrath of Congress leaders, including Surendranath Banerjea, who felt that by dissuading Muslims from joining the Congress, Ali and his sympathizers were dividing the Indian political front in its approach to the monolithic façade of colonial rule.

Sayyid Ahmad's views, we have seen, were not accepted by all. Apart from his rivals in the United Provinces, Urdu newspapers in Punjab asserted in the 1890s that the Aligarh school did not represent Indian Muslims (Bandyopadhyay 2004: 272; Jalal 2000: 68). Such frictions notwithstanding, there were common concerns that united the 'Muslims'. For reasons indicated earlier, Muslims all over India were becoming increasingly conscious of a sense of deprivation in relation to the Hindus in the second half of the nineteenth century. This fuzzy sense of identity on religious lines was strengthened by popular cultural activities sponsored by *anjuman*s and neighbourhood *akhara*s, festival committees and several other local bodies in north India.

A flourishing literature in Urdu sustained by an effervescent regional press further fomented the 'religiously informed cultural identity' in the United Provinces and in Punjab (Jalal 2000: 44–45). The redrawing of cultural boundaries along religious lines got reflected in contestation over sacred public space and ceremonies (Freitag 1990)—the issue of music in Hindu processions in the vicinity of mosques generated riots in Bareilly and Agra in the 1870s and 1880s, and religio-communal tensions were heightened by conflicts over cow protection in the 1890s and the Hindi–Urdu controversy at the turn of the century (Ahmad 1964; Metcalf and Metcalf 2003; Robinson [1974] 2007).

The 'Nagri decision' of the government taken on 18 April 1900 that made Hindi and the Nagri script equal with Urdu and Persian as the language of lower courts, stunned the Muslim elite of the United Provinces. Men like Bharatendu Harishchandra of Benares had been promoting a Sanskritized Hindi written in the Nagri script as different from Urdu; they had also been demanding official recognition of Hindi (Dalmia 1997). Their success and the support given by Congress leaders like Madan Mohan Malaviya to Harishchandra made the Congress unpopular among sections of Muslims in the United Provinces, who tried to work together for Muslim solidarity.

Colonial policy directly contributed to the coagulation of a Muslim political identity. Hunter's *Indian Mussalmans* not only defined the Muslims as 'backward', but also suggested special government favours to Muslims in matters of education and employment. The suggestion was accepted by the Government of India—Viceroy Mayo's note of 26 June 1871 indicated this change in imperial policy towards Muslim education (Hardy 1972: 90). The Government of India's resolution of 7 August 1871 increased state assistance to Muslim educational institutions.

Lord Northbrooke (1872–76), who succeeded Mayo as the Viceroy, was directed by the colonial office to remove 'any just cause of complaint' on the part of the Muslims, since the 'Mohametans of Central Asia, Afghanistan and Russia' were to be the allies of the British 'in the event of any action against Russia' (Indian Office Library and Records, 1874 cited in Hasan 1996: 193). Northbrooke was commended by the India office for directing his attention to the 'long and grievously neglected subject of Mussalman education' (ibid.). The Viceroy decided to make special provisions for Muslim institutions, a policy reaffirmed by the Education Commission in 1875.

In tune with this, the 'Muslim' stance also changed. Beginning with a plea for 'fair play' to compete with the Hindus equally, it inclined towards special privileges to make up for 'backwardness'. Several memoranda of the Central Mohammedan Association in the 1880s started demanding 'special favour' in matters of employment in government services. The colonial government was quick to recognize the advantage of winning 'Muslim' support in the face of the growing nationalist struggle. A resolution of July 1885 decided to provide special protection to the Muslims to ensure their proper representation in government services. A government circular of 1897 directed the Bengal government to fill up two-third vacancies in subordinate civil services by means of nomination in order to secure a balance of representation of the two communities. All this culminated in the partition of Bengal, which created a new province with a Muslim majority to ensure a greater share of power for Muslims (Bandyopadhyay 2004: 268; Maitra 1984).

In 1904, Lord Curzon had toured eastern Bengal explaining to Muslim leaders the possible benefits of his partition plan. He succeeded in convincing some, the Nawab of Dhaka, Khwaja Salimullah, among them. At the same time, 'Muslim' reaction to the partition of Bengal was not uniform. We have seen that the Swadeshi movement enjoyed considerable 'Muslim' participation in its initial phase. Even the students of Aligarh had passed a resolution in 1906 advocating Hindu–Muslim political cooperation for the swadeshi cause and condemned the 'slavish loyalty of their leaders to a regime that offered nothing to the Muslims' (Stein 2010: 285). Indeed, in Tripathi's view, it was Hindu–Muslim unity which prompted the British government to take further action. Viceroy Minto, who succeeded Curzon, was warned of the dangers of a 'Hindu–Muslim accord' by diehard bureaucrats like Lawrence (private secretary to Curzon), and 'shrewd journalists' Valentine Chirol and Sidney Low; he was also advised by 'knowledgeable people' to win over 'vacillating Muslims by some particular favour' (Tripathi 1967: 158).

Minto acted with alacrity. He took advantage of the 'fear' generated among some Muslims on account of the resignation of Lieutenant Governor Bamfylde Fuller, known for his pro-partition and pro-Muslim sympathies, to publicly declare the 'great hopes' he placed in the 'Mohammedan population' and his unflinching commitment to safeguarding their interests (Minto 1934: 5–6). The coercion imposed by swadeshi agitators on Muslim tenants and vendors, and their use of religious idiom played directly into the government policy of playing off Hindus and Muslims against each other. Secretary of State Morley made use of this opportune moment to hint at the possibility of forthcoming constitutional reforms during his budget speech in 1906. It produced the desired effect. Muslim leaders from Bengal and the United Provinces—afraid that Muslims would be overwhelmed by the Hindu majority organized under the Congress in the new self-governing bodies—came together to ask for a meeting with the Viceroy. Minto agreed without delay.

The Simla Deputation to Minto in October 1906 did not have any Bengali Muslim representative; the petition it submitted was drafted by old Aligarh leaders like Mohsin-ul-Mulk. It marked a shift in Aligarh politics—Sayyid Ahmad's emphasis on *qaum*, community based on common descent, was superseded by the notion of the *ummah* or community based on allegiance to common faith (Lelyveld 1978). The petition to the Viceroy projected Muslims as a separate community with distinct political interests and asked for 'minority rights' to proportional representation in public employment and in the organs of representative government. The deputation got a patient hearing. The Viceroy also assured that the rights of East Bengali Muslims would be safeguarded.

Following upon this successful deputation, which energized Muslim politics in a significant way, the All India Muslim League—a separate political party for the Muslims—was established in December 1906 in Dacca, the capital of the new province of eastern Bengal and Assam. The occasion was the annual meeting of the Educational Conference. Nawab Salimullah of Dacca, who had been won over by Curzon's line of reasoning, took the initiative in launching the Muslim League, which was to signify the 'next stage of political life' for the Muslims (ibid.). The party intended to safeguard the interests and political rights of the Muslims, preach loyalty to British rule and work towards inter-communal amity.

In its initial years, the League functioned as an adjunct of the Mohammedan Educational Conference till its separation in 1910. At the same time, provincial Muslim Leagues were formed in all major provinces between 1907 and 1909, with autonomy to draft their own constitutions and programmes. Amir Ali and Aga Khan founded a London branch of the League in 1908 and Ali, in his memoirs, took the credit for shaping the constitutional reforms of 1909, the Morley–Minto Reforms. Amir Ali was baffled by the hostility of Congress leaders towards him—he had, he believed, always had cordial relations with the 'Hindus' (Gordon 1974: 67).

This lack of understanding was emblematic of the impending and unbridgeable fissures that would remain a part of the nationalist struggle and eventually end up in the second partition—the Congress' failure to comprehend distinct understandings and deployment of notions of collective and political community, as well as of 'freedom', and a corresponding inability on the part of the others, who did not feel that the Congress represented them to understand the Congress' insistence on a united front. This lack of understanding was fomented, nurtured and exacerbated by colonial policy. In spite of imagining the nation in a variety of ways, Indian nationalism could never break out of the terms imposed by colonial rule. Recourse to a 'religious' community to form a political collective became increasingly important as this community was given political recognition by institutional reforms. It is time to turn our attention to the constitutional reforms introduced in 1909, short-lived reforms that had somewhat far-reaching consequences.

REFORMS AND AFTER

The Indian Councils Act of 1909, better known as the Morley–Minto Reforms (after the Secretary of State Lord Morley and the Viceroy, the Earl of Minto), came as a concession after the intense repression leashed on swadeshi activists—extremists and revolutionary terrorists. It was intended to assuage the feelings of all those still loyal to the British—Moderate Congress leaders who believed in reaching self-governance by constitutional means, Muslim leaders who wanted special privileges from the colonial government and wanted it to stay and rulers of the princely states. The Councils Act reflected the change in official policy induced by the 'intensity' of the nationalist struggle. Lord Morley, in particular, was a liberal scholar who impressed upon the Viceroy the need to balance the unpopular partition with reforms, to allow Indians a greater share in the administration of their country (Bandyopadhyay 2004: 280).

The Councils Act of 1909 provided for limited self-government by increasing the number of Indians, initially allowed by the Councils Act of 1861, who could be elected to the lower legislative councils. Indian members of councils at all levels were given some power to discuss budgets, move resolutions and make amendments to government-sponsored resolutions, but 'hobbled by the way elective seats were apportioned' (Sarkar [1983] 1995: 141; Stein 2010: 285). Although each province was given the power to work out the number of allocated seats, the principle of separate electorate prevented possible combinations of Indians in the lower councils that could be 'damaging' to the British. In addition to separate electorate for Muslims, there were provisions for the representation of professional classes, landholders and members of the European and Indian business communities and even British officials.

More significantly, British officials retained their majority in the Imperial Legislative Council. Out of a total of 60 members in the Imperial Legislative Council, 27 were to be elected members, eight seats were reserved for Muslims. The seats reserved for Muslims in the imperial and provincial legislatures exceeded their numerical proportion in the population; they were assigned in keeping with their political importance. Provincial legislatures were to have a 'non-official' majority, but many of the 'non-official' members were to be nominated, not elected. Elections, moreover, were constrained by several qualifications, income being an important one. Muslims with a certain income were entitled to vote while Hindus with the same income were deemed too poor to qualify. Finally, the Government of India reserved the power to disqualify any candidate from contesting the elections, if he was considered politically dangerous.

GOVERNMENTAL ORGANIZATION OF BRITISH INDIA, INDIAN COUNCILS ACT 1909, REVISED IN 1913

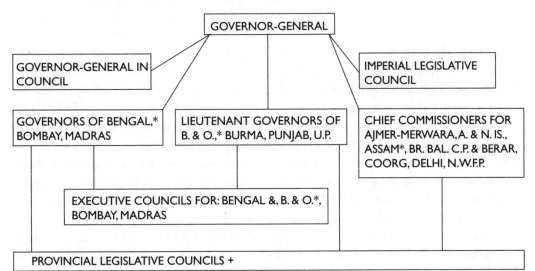

* Prior to 1911, in place of Bengal, Bihar and Orissa, and Assam, there were the two provinces of West Bengal and East Bengal and Assam. Both were then governed by Lt. Governors without the aid of Executive Councils.

\+ Assam and C.P. Legislative Councils date from 1913. Other Chief Commissionerships did not have Legislative Councils.

The reforms, it is evident, were extremely limited in nature; they did not satisfy any group of Indians. Nationalist leaders did, however, take advantage of the limited opportunities offered by the state. Gokhale, the 'humane and articulate professor of English literature, mathematics and political economy', served in the Poona Municipal Council, the Bombay Legislative Council and, finally, in the Imperial Legislative Council between 1902 and 1915 (Metcalf and Metcalf 2003: 135). He spoke critically and creatively in the interest of a good government and insisted on the need for universal primary education, greater Indian representation in government and greater opportunities of employment. He took the government to task for its repressive policies, drew public attention to the plight of indentured labourers and of Indians in South Africa (Sarkar [1983] 1995: 143). Leaders like Madan Mohan Malaviya of UP, on the other hand, severely criticized the Act of 1909 for the concessions it gave to Muslims.

The Morley–Minto Reforms testified to the success of the Muslim League in gaining official recognition for the status of Muslims as an important minority. The government had actively encouraged the forging of such a status. Clamour for greater rights on the part of Indians and pressures of World War I would prompt the government to announce a fresh set of reforms within ten years; the legacy of the Reforms of 1909 would continue in the principle of separate electorate, to be awarded to members of lower castes in the Reforms of 1919. Efforts to unite on the part of Indians, constricted by several factors, were dented even further by a colonial state that acted on the assumption that India had an 'unchanging' social order composed of a mosaic of diverse communities, whose 'natural' leaders spoke for them (Metcalf and Metcalf 2003: 133).

The 'fickleness' (Stein 2010: 286) of the British position on India's Muslims found expression in the government's decision to annul the first partition and reunite Bengal in 1911. As a retaliatory move against the militant people of Bengal, the capital was moved from Calcutta to Delhi. Calcutta remained the capital of a united Bengal but lost its pride of place as the capital of British India. The decision was announced by the newly-crowned King-Emperor George V, who was present with the Queen at the imperial durbar organized by Viceroy Lord Hardinge, the only visit paid to India by a ruling monarch during the Raj (Metcalf and Metcalf 2003: 159). Delhi was considered to be more centrally located and was much nearer to the summer capital at Simla.

A new capital, worthy of the majesty of the Raj, was constructed under the guidance of well-known architects Sir Edwin Lutyens and Sir Herbert Baker in the south of Delhi and named New Delhi. Through the move, the British sought to associate themselves and their loyal subjects with old Mughal glory. This, however, only served to demonstrate their insensitivity to Indian sentiments; it was not Mughal glory that the subjects recalled but the more recent humiliating memory of the trial and indictment of the last Mughal emperor after the Revolt of 1857 (Stein 2010: 286).

It was not surprising, therefore, that the pomp and grandeur of the durbar, which 'posed a dramatic counterpoint to the Indian cries for increased self-rule' was met by a 'terrorist' attack on Hardinge in 1912. 'Terrorist' activities, we have noted earlier, did not end with the Swadeshi movement. Rather, revolutionary organizations came up among the diaspora in London and North America. An India Office official was murdered in London in 1909, and members of the Punjabi *Ghadr* Party, on board the ship under siege *Komagata Maru*, clashed with the army near Calcutta in 1914 (Bandyopadhyay 2004: 261).

The annulment of the partition, on the other hand, brought the Moderates back into prominence and baffled the Muslim League. Muslims opposed to the League, and the new members of the League—Dr Ansari, Saifuddin Kichlu and Mohammad Ali Jinnah among them—disenchanted with British policies, sought to find ways of working together with the Congress in order to put pressure on the Raj. At a more popular level too, Muslims were upset with Britain's growing distance from Turkey and its rapport with Russia, Turkey's arch enemy. The situation was complicated further by the emergence of a national movement in Egypt, the Young Turks revolt in Turkey, the outbreak of war between Italy and Turkey in 1911 over Tripoli, and Britain's neutrality. All these events, publicized by an energetic Urdu press, generated a spirit of pan-Islamism and weakened loyalty to the British.

The new group led by Jinnah dominated the League session in Lucknow in 1912; a resolution demanding self-rule was passed in the session. British profanation of a mosque in Kanpur in 1913 resulted in a riot. Relations with the rulers deteriorated, while the loyalists and the radical younger members of the League came closer.

When Britain declared war on Germany in August 1914 for herself and the entire Empire, all political parties in India extended their support. India made extraordinary sacrifices for the war effort. In return, Indians expected that India would win self-determination that the allies were fighting for. New alliances were formed, between moderates and radicals, and the Congress and the League to achieve this end (Metcalf and Metcalf 2003: 161).

In 1915, Tilak returned from imprisonment in Mandalay jail and rejoined the Congress. He became interested in the Home Rule League, headed by an Englishwoman, Annie Besant (1847–1933).

Besant had come to India as a convert to theosophy, preached by Madame Blavatsky, a Russian woman. Theosophy advocated a mix of social reform, a cultivation of occult practices and a celebration of ancient Hindu wisdom. Besant became the head of the Theosophical Society based in Adyar, Madras, and used this core group as the base to popularize the militant ideas of the Irish Home Rule League, particularly in Madras and Bombay, and in parts of the United Provinces. This enabled her to get people hitherto uninvolved in politics interested in ideas of Home Rule. She also caught Tilak's attention. Tilak founded his own Home Rule League, which was to collaborate with that of Besant's.

Besant joined the Congress where she proposed the launching of an agitation in order to compel the British to concede Home Rule, and allow the Extremists to come back within the fold of the Congress (Masselos [1985] 1996: 144). Pherozeshah Mehta and Gokhale refused to accept Tilak, but both died in 1915. Tilak returned to the Congress and he and Annie Besant started playing important roles. The Home Rule Leagues did not directly oppose the government; they sought to impress upon the British the necessity of granting Home Rule to entire India.

The Congress and the Muslim League met in Bombay in 1915 and in Lucknow in 1916. In Lucknow, the two decided to demand elected majorities in all councils, an expansion of the franchise and a separate electorate for Muslims with provision for representation corresponding to weightage in minority provinces. This essentially meant that Muslims in the United Provinces got an edge over the Muslims in Bengal and Punjab, Muslim majority provinces. Mohammad Ali Jinnah played a major role in these negotiations, and was instrumental, along with Tilak, in pulling off the 'Lucknow Pact'. This joint front of Indians in a situation of war forced the government to announce fresh reforms.

On the other hand, incensed by the attempts of revolutionaries to take the help of the enemies of the British in procuring arms and organizing revolts in the Indian army, the Sedition Committee drafted stringent laws, laws against which Gandhi launched his *satyagarha* in 1919, a move that inaugurated a new phase in the fight for independence.

References

The Administration of Bengal under Sir Andrew Fraser, 1903–08. Calcutta, 1908 IOR/V/27/242/8 1908.

Ahmad, Aziz. 1964. *Studies in Islamic Culture in the Indian Environment.* Oxford: Clarendon Press.

Ahmed, Rafiuddin. 1996. *The Bengal Muslims, 1871–1906: A Quest for Identity.* New Delhi: Oxford University Press.

Anderson, Benedict. 1991. *Imagined Communities: Reflections on the Origin and Spread of Nationalism.* New York: Verso.

Appadurai, Arjun. 1986. 'Introduction: Commodities and the Politics of Value'. In *The Social Life of Things: Commodities in Cultural Perspective*, edited by Arjun Appadurai, 3–63. Cambridge: Cambridge University Press.

Argov, D. 1967. *Moderates and Extremists in the Indian Nationalist Movement, 1883–1920.* Bombay: Asia Publishing House.

Bandyopadhyay, Sekhar. 2004. *From Plassey to Partition: A History of Modern India.* Hyderabad: Orient Longman.

Banerjea, Surendranath. (n.d.). *Speeches and Writings of Hon. Surendranath Banerjea.* Madras: G. A. Natesan and Company.

Bayly, C. A. 1986. 'The Origins of Swadeshi (Home Industry): Cloth and Indian Society'. In *The Social Life of Things: Commodities in Cultural Perspective*, edited by Arjun Appadurai, 285–321. Cambridge: Cambridge University Press.

Bean, Susan. 1989. 'Gandhi and Khadi, the Fabric of Indian Independence'. In *Cloth and Human Experience*, edited by Annette B. Weiner and Jane Schneider, 355–76. Washington DC, London: Smithsonian Institute Press.

Bhattacharya, Tithi. 2005. *The Sentinels of Culture.* New Delhi: Oxford University Press.

Bose, Sugata. 1997. 'Nation as Mother: Representations and Contestations of "India" in Bengali Literature and Culture'. In *Nationalism, Democracy and Development: State and Politics in India*, edited by Sugata Bose and Ayesha Jalal, 50–75. New Delhi: Oxford University Press.

Bose, Sugata and Ayesha Jalal. 1998. *Modern South Asia: History, Culture, Political Economy.* Paperback edition, 2000. London: Routledge

Brasted, Howard. 1980. 'Indian Nationalist Development and the Influence of Irish Home Rule, 1870–1886'. *Modern Asian Studies* 14 (1): 37–63.

Broomfield, J. H. 1968. *Elite Consciousness in a Plural Society: Twentieth-Century Bengal.* Berkeley and Los Angeles: University of California Press.

Cohn, Bernard S. 1989. 'Cloth, Clothes and Colonialism: India in the Nineteenth Century'. In *Cloth and Human Experience*, edited by Annette B. Weiner and Jane Schneider, 303–54. Washington DC, London: Smithsonian Institute Press.

Curzon Collection, MSS Eur F 111/323. Minute by His Excellency the Viceroy on Territorial Redistribution in India. Part I, 19 May 1903; Part II, 1 June 1903: 9–10.

Dalmia, Vasudha. 1997. *The Nationalization of Hindu Traditions: Bharatendu Harishchandra and Nineteenth-Century Banaras.* New Delhi: Oxford University Press.

Das Mohapatra, Lalatendu. 2007. *John Beames and Orissa.* Rourkela: Pragati Utkal Sangha.

Dash, G. N. 1978. 'Jagannath and Oriya Nationalism'. In *The Cult of Jagannatha and the Regional Tradition of Orissa*, edited by A. Eschmann, H. Kulke, G. C. Tripathi, 359–74. New Delhi: Manohar.

———. 2007 'Changing One's Own Identity: The Role of Language in the Transformation of a Sub-regional Tradition'. In *Time in India: Concepts and Practices,* edited by A. Malinar, 265–85. New Delhi: Manohar.

Eaton, Richard M. 1993. *The Rise of Islam and the Bengal Frontier, 1204–1760.* Berkeley and Los Angeles: University of California Press.

Freitag, Sandria B. 1990. *Collective Action and Community: Public Arenas and the Emergence of Communalism in North India.* New Delhi: Oxford University Press.

Ghose, Aurobindo. 1907. 'New Thought: The Doctrine of Passive Resistance'. *Bande Mataram.* 9–23 April. (Reprinted as *Doctrine of Passive Resistance.* Calcutta: Arya Publishing House, 1948).

———. 1907. 'Caste and Democracy'. *Bande Mataram* (21 September).

Ghosh, Papiya. 2008. *Community and Nation: Essays on Identity and Politics in Eastern India.* New Delhi: Oxford University Press.

Gordon, Leonard A. 1974. *Bengal: The Nationalist Movement 1876–1940.* New York: Columbia University Press.

Goswami, Manu. 1998. 'From *Swadeshi* to *Swaraj*: Nation, Economy, Territory in Colonial South Asia, 1870 to 1907'. *Comparative Studies in Society and History* 40 (4): 609–36.

Guha, Ranajit. 1997. *Dominance without Hegemony: History and Power in Colonial India.* Cambridge, MA: Harvard University Press.

Guha-Thakurta, Tapati. 1992. *The Making of a New 'Indian' Art: Artists, Aesthetics and Nationalism in Bengal c.1850–1920.* Cambridge: Cambridge University Press.

Hardy, Peter. 1972. *The Muslims of British India.* Cambridge: Cambridge University Press.

Hasan, Mushirul. 1995. 'Muslim Intellectuals, Institutions and the Post-Colonial Predicament'. *Economic and Political Weekly* 30 (47) (25 November): 2995–3000.

———. 1996. 'The Myth of Unity: Colonial and National Narratives'. In *Making India Hindu: Religion, Community, and the Politics of Democracy in India,* edited by David Ludden, 185–210. New Delhi: Oxford University Press.

Heehs, Peter. [1993] 2004. *The Bomb in Bengal: The Rise of Revolutionary Terrorism in India 1900–1910.* New Delhi: Oxford University Press.

———. [1998] 2006. *Nationalism, Terrorism, Communalism: Essays in Modern Indian History.* New Delhi: Oxford University Press.

Huque, Azizul M. 1917. *History and Problems of Moslem Education in Bengal.* Calcutta: University of Calcutta.

Jalal, Ayesha. 2000. *Self and Sovereignty: Individual and Community in South Asian Islam since 1850.* London and New York: Routledge.

Kapoor, Geeta. 2000. *When was Modernism: Essays on Contemporary Cultural Practice in India.* New Delhi: Tulika.

Lahiri, Pradip Kumar. 1991. *Bengali Muslim Thought (1818–1947): Its Liberal and Rational Trends.* Calcutta: K. P. Bagchi & Company.

Lelyveld, David. 1978. *Aligarh's First Generation: Muslim Solidarity in British India.* Princeton, NJ: Princeton University Press.

Low, Sidney. 1907. *A Vision of India.* London: Smith Elder and Company.

Maitra, J. 1984. *Muslim Politics in Bengal, 1855–1906: Collaboration and Confrontation.* Calcutta: K. P. Bagchi & Co.

Masselos, Jim. [1985] 1996. *Indian Nationalism: An History* (Reprint). New Delhi: Sterling Publishers.

McLane, J. R. 1965. 'The Decision to Partition Bengal in 1905'. *The Indian Economic and Social History Review* 2 (3): 221–37.

———, ed. 1970. *The Political Awakening in India*. Englewood Cliffs, NJ: Prentice Hall.

———. 1977. *Indian Nationalism and the Early Congress*. Princeton, NJ: Princeton University Press.

Metcalf, Barbara D. and Thomas R. Metcalf. 2003. *A Concise History of India*. Cambridge: Cambridge University Press.

Minto, Countess of. 1934. *India: Minto and Morley (1905–1910)*. London: Macmillan.

Misra, Sanghamitra. 2005. 'Changing Frontier and Spaces: The Colonial State in Nineteenth Century Goalpara'. *Studies in History* (n.s.) 21(2): 215–246.

Mitra, Sisirkumar. 1954. *The Liberator*. Delhi: Jaico Publishing House.

Mukherjee, Haridas and Uma Mukherjee. 1958a. *Bipin Chandra Pal and India's Struggle for Swaraj*. Calcutta: Firma K. L. Mukhopadhyay.

———. 1958b. *Sri Aurobindo's Political Thought*. Calcutta: Firma K. L. Mukhopadhyay.

Nandy, Ashis. 1994. *The Illegitimacy of Nationalism: Rabindranath Tagore and the Politics of Self*. New Delhi: Oxford University Press.

Nivedita, Sister. 1907. 'The Function of Art in Shaping Nationality. Notes on Bharat-mata'. *The Complete Works of Sister Nivedita*, Vol. 3: 1–18. Calcutta: Sister Nivedita Girls' School.

Pal, Bipin Chandra. 1905. *Bande Mataram*.

———. 1954. *Swadesh and Swaraj, The Rise of New Patriotism*. Calcutta: Yugayatri Prakashak.

———. 1958. *The Soul of India*. Calcutta: Yugayatri Prakashak.

Prabhu, Ramachandra Krishna and Ravindra Kelkar, eds. 1961. *Truth Called Them Differently (Tagore–Gandhi Controversy)*. Ahmedabad: Navajivan Publishing House.

Ray, Rajat Kanta. 1984. *Social Conflict and Political Unrest in Bengal, 1875–1927*. New Delhi: Oxford University Press.

Robb, Peter. 1993. 'The Impact of British Rule on Religious Community: Reflections on the Trial of Maulvi Ahmadullah of Patna in 1865'. In *Society and Ideology: Essays in South Asian History presented to Prof. K. A. Ballhachet*, edited by Peter Robb, 142–176. New Delhi: Oxford University Press.

Robinson, Francis. [1974] 2007. *Separatism Among Indian Muslims: The Politics of the United Provinces' Muslims, 1860–1923*. Cambridge: Cambridge University Press.

Sarkar, Sumit. 1973. *The Swadeshi Movement in Bengal, 1903–1908*. New Delhi: People's Publishing House.

———. [1983] 1995. *Modern India, 1885–1947*. Madras: Macmillan India.

———. 1984. 'The Conditions and Nature of Subaltern Militancy: Bengal from Swadeshi to Non-Co-operation, c. 1905–22'. In *Subaltern Studies III: Writings on South Asian History and Society*, edited by R. Guha, 271–320. New Delhi: Oxford University Press.

Sarkar, Tanika. 1987. 'Nationalist Iconography: Image of Women in Nineteenth-century Bengali Literature'. *Economic and Political Weekly* 22 (47) (21 November): 2011–15.

Sartori, Andrew. 2008. *Bengali in Global Concept History*. Chicago: University of Chicago Press.

Sengupta, Parna. 2011. *Pedagogy for Religion: Missionary Education and the Fashioning of Hindus and Muslims in Bengal*. Berkeley and Los Angeles: University of California Press.

Sinha, Mrinalini. 2011. 'The Strange Death of an Imperial Ideal: The Case of *Civic Britannicus*'. In *Modern Makeovers: Oxford Handbook of Modernity in South Asia*, edited by Saurabh Dube, 29–42. New Delhi: Oxford University Press.

Stein, Burton. 2010. *A History of India*. Revised and edited by David Arnold. Sussex, UK: Wiley-Blackwell. (First published 1998. Oxford: Oxford University Press).

Tagore, Rabindranath. 1917. *Nationalism*. London: Macmillan.

———. 1941. *Rabindra Rachanabali*. Vol. 9. Digital Library of India: www.dli.ernet.in/.../metainfo.cgi?&... Rabindra%20Rachanabali%20%.

———. 1961. *Towards Universal Man*. New York: Asia Publishing House (Original in Bengali 'Swadeshi Samaj'. *Rabindra Rachanaboli* 12: 683–708).

Tripathi, Amales. 1967. *The Extremist Challenge: India Between 1890 and 1910*. Bombay: Orient Longman.

Trivedi, Lisa N. 2003. 'Visually Mapping the "Nation": Swadeshi Politics in Nationalist India, 1920–1930'. *The Journal of Asian Studies* 62 (1): 11–41.

Washbrook, D. A. 1976. *The Emergence of Provincial Politics: The Madras Presidency, 1870–1920*. Cambridge: Cambridge University Press.

Zou, David V. and Satish Kumar. 2011. 'Mapping a Colonial Borderland: Objectifying the Geo-body of India's Northeast'. *The Journal of Asian Studies* 70 (1): 141–70.

The Mahatma Phenomenon 7

M. K. Gandhi visits textile workers in Lancashire, 1931

Chapter outline

'In my opinion it [the *Hind Swaraj*] is a book that can be put into the hands of a child.
It teaches the gospel of love in place of that of hate. It replaces violence with self-sacrifice.
It pits soul force against brute force.'

These 'words of explanation' written by Mohandas Karamchand Gandhi (1869–1948) in his journal *New India* in 1921, about *Hind Swaraj* (1908), a work of his that had drawn considerable attention by the time, bears testimony to the ironies of history. A man who 'taught the gospel of love in place of that of hate' and urged his countrymen to replace 'violence' with 'self-sacrifice' was forced to die a violent death, and his 'greatest aim and achievement'—India's independence from colonial rule—'was marred by the bloody episode of the Partition' (Arnold 2001: 1).

Is Gandhi emblematic of the contradictions of history? How is it that Gandhi, who almost never held any political office, commanded no army, and was not even a compelling orator, made a great mark on his time, and is perhaps the only figure of the twentieth century who has 'stood the test of time'? (Markovits 2003: 1) This chapter explores Gandhi's ideology and strategies of struggle together with the diverse understandings of his message in order to understand his great influence and his continued significance. It also unravels the implications of Gandhi's status as the 'Mahatma', the great soul, and his role as a political leader in an effort to comprehend his polyvalent legacy for colonial and independent India.

Formative Influences

Gandhi was born on 2 October 1869 in Porbandar, a small town in Kathiawad (Saurashtra), a princely state in western Gujarat, in a family of the Modh Bania caste that had a long tradition of service to the rulers of Kathiawad. Politically, Kathiawad was highly fragmented—parts of it belonged to the outer reaches of the Bombay Presidency and parts of it were composed of over 200 semi-independent states ruled by Indian princes. Although the region came under Company's rule between 1802 and 1822 following the defeat of the Marathas, inhabitants of Kathiawad had a strong sense of identity as Kathiawadis, as distinct from the rest of India, and even from the rest of Gujarat (Arnold 2001: 16). Kathiawad was geographically isolated, with extensive creeks and salt marshes of the Rann of Cutch in the north, the desert of Rajasthan in the north-east and the Gulf of Cambay to the south and the east. At the same time, the region had a long tradition of trade with ports in the Arabian Sea and Indian Ocean, the Persian Gulf and Africa, as well as with Rajasthan, Sind and northern India. In other words, the area embodied contradictory trends—isolated yet dynamic, rich in trade but poorer than the fertile parts of eastern Gujarat, except for the merchants.

Gandhi's immediate family lived this idea of isolation and dynamism in significant ways. A middle-class and middle-caste family of Banias, it had intimate ties with local politics. Gandhi's grandfather Uttamchand and father Karamchand served as *diwan*s (prime ministers and advisors) to the rulers of Porbandar, and both, particularly his father, got into trouble on account of their independent spirit. Gandhi admired his grandfather and father as 'models of integrity and courage'. More significantly, his socialization in a 'princely milieu' as the son of a *diwan*, primed Gandhi to think of Indians as leaders of their states, no matter how small they may be, 'not mere subjects of the British, but ministers in their own lands, albeit under the watchful eye of the British political agent' (ibid.: 18).

Notwithstanding their 'backwardness', the states of Kathiawad offered models of an alternative political and moral order that predated British rule. These were states ruled by Muslim princes and their Hindu advisors who were united culturally by a common language, Gujarati, 'a strange mingling of Arabic, Persian, and Hindi words' (Payne 1969: 23). Gandhi's attitude toward the Raj and the Indian interaction with it, argues David Arnold, was crucially shaped by this childhood experience of the presence of Indian rulers and the relative lack of exposure to the British administration. It imbued in him a great sense of power, an inner belief that for all the trials and tribulations of colonial rule 'they [Indians of his status and background] were men fit to rule' or be the power behind the throne (Arnold 2001: 19). This combined in intricate ways with his Bania origins, to which he owed a lot of his social and cultural ideas.

In the *varna* scheme of classification, the Banias belonged to the category of the Vaishyas, although in Gujarat the Vaishyas enjoyed greater prestige than what the 'traditional' classification conferred on them. As traders and moneylenders, Banias were known to be intelligent, but also 'shrewd' and 'wily'. If popular imagination saw them as cold-hearted and grasping, the Banias thought of themselves as being sober, hardworking and thrifty (Hardiman 1996: 88). They had, of necessity, a practical approach to life. The Banias were renowned for their piety, devotion and philanthropy—means by which they protected themselves from 'critical scrutiny and the occasional attack'—concealed their 'wealth behind an unostentatious lifestyle' and purchased 'public respect and approbation through charity and a reputation for good deeds' (Arnold 2001: 25).

Gandhi imbibed traditions of resistance and self-suffering, current among the Bania and other merchant and moneylender castes of Kathiawad. Resistance and self-suffering, employed strategically, served a dual purpose—when directed at tenants and clients they enforced the payment of debts; and against rulers they served as measures of protest against injustice. Some of them could take the form of self-flagellation that morally compelled the debtor, friend or client to meet legitimate demands. Others were relatively more peaceful—they included fasting or sitting on a *dharna*, sitting still at a selected place for hours and days till the time the aggrieved individual's suffering had an impact on the ruler or drew public attention. The techniques, of course, had great effect in the context of face-to-face, personal interaction between the ruler and the subject. Gandhi, as we shall soon see, used them to great advantage to strike deals with the government, first in South Africa, and later in India.

These techniques went well with the eclectic religious beliefs that Gandhi grew up with. His mother Putlibai, his father's fourth wife, belonged to an eighteenth-century sect called Pranami, whose founder had advocated the unity of different faiths and instilled in his followers a belief in the simplicity of living and distaste for formally structured religion. This faith, which 'taught charity, chastity and amity with followers of distinct religions and insisted on the values of a temperate life lived modestly' had a fundamental influence on young Gandhi. Kathiawad, moreover, was the home of Jains, Vaishnavites and Muslims. Many Banias were Jains but the Muslims were mainly poor tenants, although they did have a visible cultural presence in towns such as Ahmedabad. Gandhi absorbed beliefs of the Pranami sect along with the 'non-violence' practised by Jains and Vaishnavas.

Putlibai's regular fasts and austere lifestyle and the 'strong ascetic demands' she made on herself left a lasting impression on Gandhi (Rudolph 1963: 105). As Robert Payne puts it, Putlibai would 'go on fast for the slightest reason or for no reason at all'. She visited the temple every day, said prayers at every meal, and sometimes 'vowed to go without food unless the sun came out' (1969: 29). Decades later in his *Autobiography*, Gandhi defined such practices as 'self-suffering', having incorporated them as a vital part of his strategy for political struggle.

'Self-suffering' also took different forms in the Gandhi household—if a member of the family was angry with another, s/he would punish that member by inflicting suffering on herself/himself (Rudolph 1963: 105). Gandhi, for instance, went without his favourite mangoes for an entire season because the family had refused to invite a friend of his to dinner (Tendulkar 1951: 28). All these distinct influences evolved in discrete ways in the course of Gandhi's life, in tune with the specific needs upon which a lot of his religious and social thinking was contingent.

In September 1888, Gandhi went to London to study law and stayed there till June 1891. In the view of some scholars, these two and a half years were vital in shaping his career (Hunt [1978] 1993). The move, from Rajkot to London, from 'an imperial backwater to the very heart of the British Empire', must have impressed Gandhi, not quite 19 and for the first time on his own. Gandhi was also the first of his caste to go to London, and counted among the very few Indians who resided in England, most of whom were students preparing either for the Civil Services Examination or for the Bar. The conservative Modh Banias imposed a caste ban on Gandhi's crossing of the ocean ('black water', *kalapani*). Gandhi, however, was unperturbed. His *Autobiography* mentions how he, a shy youth, suddenly mustered the courage to appear before the general meeting of the caste and to hold his ground (Gandhi 1960: 40). On his return, he went through a ritual of purification at his elder brother's behest, which worked for some but did not convince the more orthodox sections of his community.

Gandhi's own interest lay in medicine, but his elder brother said a definite no to a career in allopathic medicine. How could a non-violent, vegetarian Vaishnava cut up corpses? (Gandhi 2008: 26). 'Family pressure' obliged him to turn to law, and it was the family's desperate financial circumstances that made his trip to England an imperative. By qualifying as a lawyer, Gandhi was to save the family from ruin. The urge to cure and to possess a healthy body for himself and the nation, however, would remain with Gandhi throughout his life, and find expression in the holistic 'cures' he sought for his countrymen, first in South Africa and then in India (Corzo 2011).

Indeed, Gandhi's notion of health was not limited to the body; it encompassed morality and self-discipline. Morality for him was 'a problem in which truth and biology were equally implicated' (Alter 1996: 301). The several volumes of his *Collected Works* abound in statements that link morals with health. Gandhi firmly believed that only a perfectly moral person can achieve perfect health. Later in his career, he developed this idea to argue that only perfectly moral and perfectly healthy people were fit to attain *swaraj*. Gandhi's *Autobiography*, *My Experiments with Truth*, offers ample evidence of the intricate intermingling of his own experiments with diet, sex, temperance, hygiene and his search for truth.

Unsurprisingly therefore, Gandhi's experiments with truth in England were tied to his experiments with food, diet and morality. Untouched by the social ferment of the turbulent 1880s, a decade marked by economic depression and political unrest, the emergence of the Left and of trade unionism in London, Gandhi turned to the cult of vegetarianism.

Gandhi, we are aware, had grown up in a strictly vegetarian family and had promised his mother to abstain from meat in England. At the same time, as a rebellious teenager he had made a few attempts at eating meat. His friend and advisor had been Sheikh Mehtab, a youth 'hardier, physically stronger, and more daring' who 'dazzled' Gandhi with his immense capacity to put up with corporal punishment (Gandhi 1960: 20; Rudolph 1963: 107). Mehtab embodied all the qualities that Gandhi seems to have lacked, and impressed upon the young Gandhi the innate link between meat-eating and physiological strength. In Kathiawad of those days, writes Susanne Rudolph, the idea that cultural virility and meat-eating were responsible for British imperialism had great hold, and the classical Kshatriyas of the *varna* classification were also meat-eaters.

Gandhi had also been influenced by the widely held belief that meat-eaters were sexually virile; his teenage experiments with meat-eating had been accompanied by a botched attempt to go into a brothel. As we shall see later, 'sexuality' and the control of it would remain a prime concern of Gandhi throughout his life (Kakar 1990). What Rudolph, however, sees in Gandhi's three-year long secret rebellion against caste and family ethic was courage—the courage that Gandhi would draw upon throughout his life (Rudolph 1963: 108).

It bears pointing out here that Gandhi got married to Kasturba as a teenager in 1882, and although later he showed distaste for child marriage, his own marriage was 'one of the happiest on record'. He kept his wife with him when he returned to Kathiawad High School, continued to sleep with her and 'rarely allowed her to return to her own parents' (Payne 1969: 37). Later in life, Gandhi would reflect on his overbearing attitude towards Kasturba and admire her silent but firm ways of resistance and endurance.

Henry Salt's acclaimed work, *A Plea for Vegetarianism*, which spoke of kindness to animals and cogently argued in favour of a vegetarian diet, appealed to Gandhi instantly and made him turn to the vegetarians in England. Apart from solving his problem of 'what to eat', vegetarianism gave him access to 'some of London's most eccentric idealists' (Hay 1989: 81). Through Henry Salt, Gandhi came in contact with Edward Carpenter, whose book *Civilisation: Its Cause and Cure* (1889) provided the groundwork for Gandhi's *Hind Swaraj*.

The association with 'a group of middle-class Britons, members of [the] ruling race, who regarded vegetarianism with un-imperial enthusiasm', impressed Gandhi considerably (Arnold 2001: 28–29). Moreover, Gandhi got to participate in discussions on a wide range of controversial social and economic issues, including vivisection and birth control. All this prompted him to embrace 'vegetarianism by choice, in a spirit that promised a different kind of strength than that which meat promised' (Rudolph 1963: 110). Gandhi came to look upon vegetarianism as an ideal to be cherished and propagated, not a burden of cultural inheritance to be borne under duress. He began his experiments in dietics which, as indicated earlier, was closely tied to his ideals of truth and morality. Two decades later, such ideas would encompass his country and countrymen. 'Non-violence' for Gandhi, affirms Alter, was 'as much an issue of public health, as an issue of politics, morality, and religion' (Alter 1996: 304).

Gandhi's attitude to the law training at the Inner Temple, where he qualified in 1890, was 'fairly matter-of-fact' and did not appear to have aroused much enthusiasm. 'He was mostly interested in the law as a profession through which to earn a living and recoup the family's ailing fortunes rather than a means to achieve social justice and political rights' (Arnold 2001: 16). Neither did Gandhi have much to do with Indians after the first weeks of stay, although he did attend the meetings of the National Indian

Association and heard the speeches given by the nationalist leader Dadabhai Naoroji, who became the first Indian liberal Member of Parliament in 1892. Gandhi moved among the middle-class circles in London and spent the initial part of his stay trying to become an English gentleman, till the time he found it expensive and unfulfilling.

Towards the end of his second year in London, Gandhi was drawn into the circle of theosophists, a middle-class group interested in the esoteric religions of the Orient, namely Hinduism and Buddhism, under the influence of Madam Blavatsky's Theosophical Society in the United States. The theosophists in London were more interested in esoteric Hinduism than Buddhism. Gandhi joined the Blavatsky Lodge of the Society in 1891, but did not participate actively. At the same time, he was invited to help translate the *Bhagavad Gita* from Sanskrit, and to read it alongside Edwin Arnold's *The Song Celestial* (1886), a translation of the *Gita*.

The acquaintance with Edwin Arnold—theosophist, vegetarian, a former principal of Deccan College and 'a leading cross-cultural synthesizer' of Buddhism, Hinduism, Christianity and Victorian Science— possibly made Gandhi aware that religions need not be rigidly compartmentalized (ibid.: 39). Gandhi also got to meet Annie Besant, who had converted to theosophy in 1889 and had become a prominent member of the Theosophical Society of London. Initially fascinated by Besant's 'utter sincerity', Gandhi later came to think of her as a charlatan who represented the occult side of theosophy that Gandhi was uneasy about, and also as a white woman who appropriated Hinduism for her own ends.

In June 1891, Gandhi boarded a ship to return to India. He was a little sad to leave; he had grown fond of London. A harsh reality awaited him in India. Shy and hesitant, he could not establish a law practice either in Rajkot or in Bombay and move into the prestigious rank of the professional middle class, as his family had expected. In addition to the humiliation he suffered in court on account of his inability to speak publicly, he was insulted by the political agent with whom he had become slightly acquainted in London. Gandhi had gone to see him to ask for a favour on behalf of his brother, and when he tried to remind the agent of their acquaintance, he was told sharply that things were different in India and thrown out of the office. When Gandhi sought the advice of veteran leader Pherozeshah Mehta, he was asked to 'pocket the insult'. Neither Gandhi's upbringing nor his stay in London had prepared him for this. He realized to his horror what it meant to be a 'mere colonial subject' without authority, respect and recourse against injustice.

A frustrated and dejected Gandhi was saved by an invitation from a Porbandar-based firm of Dada Abdullah and Co. to represent it in a legal dispute in Durban, Natal. In April 1893, Gandhi left Bombay once more, this time for South Africa. His stay there of 21 years, between 1893 and 1914, formed a decisive phase in his life and fundamentally shaped his career—the 'low point' that would become the 'turning point' (Rudolph 1963: 112). In South Africa, Gandhi learned to 'meld together' aspects of his Indian background with 'maturing understandings' of the West (Arnold 2001: 44).

BEGINNINGS OF A POLITICAL CAREER: SOUTH AFRICA

By the time Gandhi arrived in South Africa in May 1893, it had a large Indian community. Cape Town had been an important port of call for ships sailing between Europe and India from the seventeenth century. However, it was only from the 1860s, with the large-scale extension of the system of indentured labour to the sugar plantations in South Africa, that Indians arrived there in large numbers. This extension of indentured labour was consequent upon the abolition of slavery in 1834; indentured labourers replaced slaves as a mode of cheap labour for the imperialists (Chapter 2). Indians were sent to Mauritius, Guyana and Fiji as well as to the British colony of Natal in south-eastern Africa. By 1891, there were 41,000 Indians in Natal as compared to 45,000 Europeans and 456,000 Africans. By 1904, the number of Indians had crossed 100,000. In addition, there was a significant presence of Indian merchants and traders in the Boer Republic of Transvaal. When the Union of South Africa was carved out of the former Boer republics and British colonies in 1910, Indians constituted a small but a significant minority (about 2 per cent of the population).

The 'community' of Indians in South Africa was diverse. It consisted of indentured labourers—'coolies' who had come on short-term contracts; former 'coolies' who had stayed on in Natal as labourers, hawkers and small-holders; Indians employed in coal mining; Parsis from western India who worked as clerks in commercial enterprises; and 'Arab' traders and merchants, primarily Muslim traders from Gujarat, Porbandar in particular. A majority of the plantation workers were Hindus from lower castes and untouchables who came from the Tamil and Telugu-speaking regions of the Madras Presidency. There was also a prominent presence of Christians from the same region.

By the time Gandhi arrived, the Indian community had earned the wrath of the white population on different grounds—the 'Arab' traders as threatening competitors, and the indentured labourers, the 'coolies,' for being insanitary and dirty, responsible for spreading disease and epidemic such as the plague. For Gandhi, however, white racism became manifest in a distinct way. When he appeared in court for the first time wearing a turban, he was asked to remove it. He left the court in protest (Gandhi 1960: 106). Soon, Gandhi experienced the much-discussed incident of being thrown out of the first-class compartment of a train during his first journey from Durban to Pretoria—although he had a first-class ticket, only whites could travel first class. This incident landed Gandhi in a dilemma—should he ignore the insult, finish the case and return to India, or try and 'root out the deep disease of colour prejudice', suffer hardships in the process, and seek redress for wrongs only to the extent required for 'the removal of the colour prejudice'? Gandhi decided on the second course (ibid.: 112). He took the next train to Pretoria.

These experiences, argues Rudolph, suddenly made Gandhi aware that the skills he had acquired recently—the use of English, an awareness of legal processes and codes and 'a belief that English justice must be enforced'—were desperately needed and lacking among the Indian community' (Rudolph 1963: 112). The awareness that he was the *only* barrister of the Indian community brought about a 'curious change' in Gandhi's outlook—the shy youth who had been unable to speak in court, dared to call a meeting of all Indians in Pretoria within three weeks of his arrival. Gandhi wanted to 'present them a picture of their condition in Transvaal' (Gandhi 1960: 125). 'Skills which had seemed ordinary in India here seemed extraordinary and strengthened Gandhi's self-esteem with apocalyptic abruptness' (Rudolph 1963: 112).

In September 1893, Gandhi sent his first outraged response to an editorial in the *Natal Advertiser* that called the Indian traders 'semi-barbarous' and undesirable elements. He asked if it was 'Christian-like', just and civilized to blame the traders for their simplicity, austerity, frugality and total abstinence from liquor. These were qualities that called for commendation, not damnation (Arnold 2001: 47).

On his return to Durban from India with his wife and children in January 1897, Gandhi faced a white demonstration against a so-called 'Asiatic invasion' as well as against the arrival of ships carrying plague and immigrant labourers. The white attack on Indians' sanitation and lifestyle, and the association of race with disease shook Gandhi to the inner core; it went against his firm belief in the intimate ties between health and morality and his growing pride in Indian civilization.

All this, however, did not turn Gandhi into a mass leader overnight. Although Susanne Rudolph and Judith Brown commend him for his relentless campaign for 20 years 'to stem the tide of racial discrimination which threatened to engulf the Indian community' and argue that this campaign organized 'the previously quiescent Indian community' (Brown 1972: 2–3), others such as Maureen Swan offer a different picture. According to Swan, Gandhi provides a 'romanticized' account of his activities in South Africa in his *Autobiography*. For almost an entire decade of his stay in South Africa, Gandhi remained a representative of the Gujarati merchant elite, which had begun to protest against discrimination under the leadership of Muslim merchants like Haji Ojer Ali and Sheth Haji Habib (Swan 1985). The merchant elite, however, cared very little for the hardships suffered by the 'coolies' till the time new regulations affecting the entire community were introduced.

Gandhi's *Autobiography* does mention that he became identified as a 'coolie barrister' soon after his arrival (Gandhi 1960: 107). 'Coolie' was a pejorative prefix that the whites used against all Indian merchants and clerks who were not 'Arabs' or Parsis. Even though he faced flagrant racism personally soon after his arrival, till 1906 Gandhi used the 'moderate' techniques of prayer and petition in his struggle against racial discrimination (Arnold 2001: 49–50; Sarkar [1983] 1995: 178).

Gandhi was instrumental in establishing the Natal Indian Congress, named after the Indian National Congress, in 1894. The Natal Congress had a high annual membership fee of three pounds, which necessarily limited its membership. The newspaper, *Indian Opinion*, launched in 1903 by Gandhi primarily to air his views and those of the Natal Indian Congress, similarly had very limited circulation. With its English, Gujarati, Tamil and Hindi sections, the *Indian Opinion* could not enlist more than 900 subscribers by 1904. Gandhi also remained a loyal subject of Queen Victoria and expressed the loyalty and devotion of the Indian subjects in Natal to the Queen on the occasion of the Silver Jubilee of her rule (Gandhi 1958 Vol. 2: 317). Moreover, he made no attempt to align with the black population in South Africa in order to organize a concerted struggle against race (Arnold 2001).

A spate of unfair ordinances and regulations starting from 1906 helped forge a community of Indians in South Africa. The Transvaal Ordinance of 1906 made registration and passes compulsory for all Indians. Indian immigrants and former indentured labourers who decided to remain in South Africa were forced to pay a tax of three pounds. All non-Christian Indian marriages were de-recognized when deciding on cases of new entrants; and in 1913 further restrictions were introduced on immigration and it was decided that the tax of three pounds on all former indentured labourers would not be rescinded. The laws and ordinances affected all sections of Indians—a real community came into being that had affluent merchants and lawyers as well as poor mine and plantation workers, and people who belonged to different regions, religions, castes and classes.

Gandhi resorted to 'passive resistance' from 1907, 'when constitutional action failed him'. Prior to that, he had 'contacted high-ranking officials' and travelled to India and England 'to rally support for his cause' against racial discrimination of Indians (Brown 1972: 4). By 1907, Gandhi had also made attempts at communal living and had taken the vow of *brahmacharya*, celibacy, without consulting his wife Kasturba. These measures were indicative of a change in his outlook which was consequent upon dissatisfaction with his 'comfortable and affluent' lifestyle. Gandhi had attended the 1901 session of the Indian National Congress, where he had become familiar with two different styles of leadership—of Gokhale and Tilak, both Maharashtrian Brahmans with very distinct approaches to politics. Gandhi stayed in the same place as Tilak during the Congress session, observed how Tilak sat up in bed and received crowds with 'majestic tolerance'. 'Gandhi was impressed and respectful; but he did not fall under Tilak's spell' (Payne 1969: 132).

Gandhi gave up law practice in 1911, and between 1907 and 1914 he gave leadership to three successive campaigns of passive resistance, soon called satyagraha. The newspaper, *Indian Opinion*, helped Gandhi learn the 'craft of journalism' and served as a means through which 'he endeavoured to educate Indians in matters as diverse as European history and public health' and as an organ that gave practical advice on the tactics of satyagraha to the participants (Brown 1972: 5). *Indian Opinion*, moreover, was addressed to audiences in Africa, Britain and India, and explored ideas of India that were 'not territorially based', but existed among 'the individual sovereignties of its readers and the pathways of circulation that linked them' (Hofmeyr 2013: 4). This meant that Gandhi's notion of self-rule came to be based, not on territory but on the individual and truth (ibid.: 2). Opinions voiced in the columns of the *Indian Opinion* formed the basis of Gandhi's celebrated book *Hind Swaraj or Indian Home Rule*, written in Gujarati in 1908 on a 'return voyage from London to South Africa in answer to the Indian school of violence and its prototype in South Africa' (Gandhi 1938: 16).

At the time he started the first satyagraha, Gandhi was, in Swan's reckoning, still a 'politician of the elite' groping to become 'the leader of a mass movement' (Swan 1985: 144). Natal-born Indian Christians had produced leaders who provided alternative and better leadership to the poorer Indians. It was only in 1913, a year before his departure from the country, that Gandhi led the mine-workers in a 'memorable strike and a cross-country march in October', which made him the leader of a truly mass movement (Sarkar [1983] 1995: 178; Swan 1985). At the same time, it bears pointing out that the Indian community came to stoutly stand by Gandhi by the end of 1907: the *Indian Opinion* came to have 3000 subscribers, more than double of what it was when the passive resistance movement was launched (Guha 2013: 252-53). The success of the spectacular march made Gandhi an all-India figure even before he began his work in India; unlike other political leaders who were often identified with a region, Gandhi came to represent the whole of India and all its communities. Gandhi's experience in South Africa was also crucial in shaping his 'life-long recognition' of the necessity and possibility of Hindu-Muslim unity (Sarkar [1983] 1995: 178).

The methods and techniques of struggle were worked out in South Africa between 1906 and 1913. They depended a lot on the careful training of cadres first in the Phoenix Settlement and then in the Tolstoy Farm set up in Johannesburg in1910. Cadres were trained in self-discipline and subjected to health cures that Gandhi chose for them, in order to make them fit to participate in non-violent satyagraha.

Early indications of Gandhi's search for and ideas on truth and freedom were advanced in the *Hind Swaraj*, written in the form of a dialogue—questions and answers between a nationalist reader and an editor who 'ventriloquized' Gandhi's views. The 'severe condemnation of modern civilization' that the book offers is premised upon careful attention paid to the prefix *swa* (of one's own) of *swaraj*, argues Ajay Skaria. This is because 'a thoughtful consideration of the own' always transforms it into a question of the 'proper' (Skaria 2007: 220).

The *Swaraj* of *Hind Swaraj*, therefore, involved the question of 'proper rule of and for India'. And it was the insistence on the 'proper' that produced Gandhi's attack on civilization, or rather 'modern civilization', since the sovereignty involved in this civilization forgot the *swa* completely. It was anything but proper (ibid.). Gandhi followed Edward Carpenter in calling this civilization 'a disease' under which 'men are enslaved' by 'temptation of money and of the luxuries that money can buy' (Gandhi 1938: 34, 36). It was, in reality, 'irreligion'; and it had taken 'such a hold over the people of Europe that those who are in it appear to be half mad' (ibid.: 37). Modern civilization had to be discarded because it was making India 'irreligious' just as it had made Europe 'irreligious' (Skaria 2011: 155).

Uday Singh Mehta offers yet another suggestive analysis of *Hind Swaraj* and of Gandhi's philosophy. The need for patience, of not being rushed, writes Mehta, runs through *Hind Swaraj* and Gandhi's several other writings with remarkable consistency. In addition to the fact that Gandhi confesses to a certain hesitancy in making the English version of *Hind Swaraj* public because he had 'hurriedly dictated it' to a friend, Gandhi referred to *Hind Swaraj* itself as something that required patience, since his views were to develop in the course of the discourse with the reader (Mehta 2003: 419). The comportment appropriate to *swaraj* in its different forms involved a difficult challenge that drew on 'the complex interiority of the self' (ibid.). And it was precisely because *swaraj* was difficult that Gandhi was hesitant about answering what *swaraj* is. Instead of making declarative statements, he pointed to the difficulties in attaining *swaraj*, difficulties that required patience and a certain lapse of time in order to be properly dealt with (ibid.: 419–20).

In Review: The Meanings of Swaraj

The 'imprecision' in Gandhi's definition of *swaraj* has been commented upon by scholars, and the impact of such imprecision on the varied understandings of Gandhi's message has formed the subject of fascinating studies (Shahid Amin, for instance). Very recent works focus centrally on Gandhi's notion of *swaraj* as the fundamental element of his philosophy and offer incisive insights. A curious shuttling of two senses of *swaraj* course through Gandhi's writings, writes Ajay Skaria (Skaria forthcoming). This is evident in the contrast Gandhi sets up in *Hind Swaraj* between the reader's understanding of *swaraj* as home rule and the editor (Gandhi)'s understanding of it, where *swaraj* often remains untranslated. The title of the book, *Hind Swaraj or Indian Home Rule* conserves this 'recalcitrance' to translation.

The editor's idea of *swaraj* has intimate links with *ahimsa* (non-violence) and *satyagraha* (soul force). The desire and insistence (*agraha*) for truth (*satya*) that is constitutive of being 'foregrounds the active nature of non-violence'. While Gandhi as the leader of the Indian National Congress advocated 'political *swaraj*', he also insisted that the other *swaraj* could be attained only through satyagraha. This *swaraj* was not just different, it was opposed to 'political *swaraj*'. Political *swaraj* only provided the pretext or the point of departure for the other *swaraj*.

Satyagraha, moreover, is conceived as *dharma*, religion, faith and morality. Such religion invoked absolute freedom and equality and allowed Gandhi to move away from the liberal conceptions of equality and freedom. In Gandhi's writings, *dharma* strove for equality of and with the minor, an equality that did not make the minor into a major; an equality arrived at by means of a faithful surrender of the self, an equality premised on love, humility and mutual respect. This wilful surrender made possible a distinctive resistance to domination, where the surrender became a mode of refusing subordination, 'of giving and receiving a freedom and equality that is secreted in the very act of surrender' (ibid.). Satyagrahis, therefore, do not need to take up arms; by enacting 'surrender without subordination' they relinquish the freedom inherent in the everyday exercise of sovereignty and that relinquishment opens onto another freedom. Satyagrahis submit to the other to the extent of giving up their lives, but in this very submission they resist the other and call the other to a similar submission. When they submit, the satyagrahis give to the other only their difference from the other. By so doing, 'they derange both themselves and the other, this derangement is *swaraj*' (ibid.).

Patience, for Gandhi therefore, was 'a psychological adhesive' that embedded values into the self, and was a way of 'crafting of a self', a 'state of inwardness' as the very ground for political and social action (ibid.: 420). Only self-knowledge acquired through patience could guide the self appropriately in the course of everyday life; lives lived vicariously were indifferent to the conditions of self-knowledge and human integrity. Gandhi, therefore, was worried about the inducements of progress, such as modern forms of travel or medicine and the lure of a certain kind of nationalism, because all of them were indifferent to the real needs of the self. They tempted one to lead life as if it was someone else's, freed of its prejudices and arbitrary constraints (ibid.: 421). This stress on patience and actions moulded through time in order to gain maturity marks the basic difference between the editor (Gandhi) and the reader (the nationalist) for whom national self-rule bore 'the imprimatur of moral and political self-evidence' in *Hind Swaraj* (ibid.: 419).

In response to the reader's query as to why England, attacked by the disease of civilization, had been able to take India, the editor answered that the 'English have not taken India; we have given it to them'(Gandhi 1938: 38). The reader's 'constructivist' argument that 'because there are railways today we see the spirit of one people' is countered by the editor's assertion that if there had been no railways, the English would not have had 'such control over Hindustan'. In Skaria's understanding, the editor's 'hostility' to railways is not only because it enables control over the subcontinent, but because in so doing it facilitates the transformation of Hindustan into an object (Skaria 2007: 230). Hindustan, for Gandhi, was not an object but a place (*sthaan*) of the people/nation (*praja*).

For Mehta, on the other hand, Gandhi condemned trains because they reduced the time and eased the effort required in going from one place to another and connected things and places that were naturally segregated from one another and increased, thereby, the likelihood of the spread of disease (Mehta 2003: 423). In response to the reader's remark that railways by connecting India had induced a spirit of nationalism, Gandhi affirmed that a sense of unity had existed prior to the railways and was the result of a long and slow process of sedimentation poised on a shared mode of life. Nationalism, by contrast, was 'spurred by an attitude of political contingency' (ibid.).

In a similar manner, Gandhi's unease with modern doctors stemmed from the fact that they disturbed the natural rhythms of the body by prescribing medicines that sped up cure and tempted one to abuse medicines again. A trip to the doctor on account of indigestion resulting from over-eating started a process where one got cured quickly through medicines and over-ate again. This resulted in a lack of control over mind and body, over self-mastery. Gandhi also targeted lawyers for accentuating 'the evil nature of man'. Together, railways, doctors and lawyers drove men to self-indulgence and vice, which made them weak, immoral and effeminate, and aided India's enslavement (Gandhi 1938: 45–60). The loss of self-control and integrity that produced lack of manliness were all connected with the effects of modern civilization, whose seductions caused internal damage without demonstrating its effects outwardly (Mehta 2003: 423–24). Civilization, in this sense, was a disease one had to be wary of.

The indictment of lack of manliness, which seemed partly to follow the concern of other nationalist leaders with the 'effeminacy' and weakness of Indian men, was distinct in the stress it laid on 'moral failure' (Chatterjee 1984: 157). The subjugation of India was a result of moral failure on the part of Indians—and not of British avarice, deceit or superior power. Indians became a subject people because they were 'seduced by the glitters of modern civilization'; their continued subjection was on account of the acceptance, on the part of 'leading sections of Indians, of the benefits of civilization' (ibid.).

In order to overcome their subjectivity, Indians had to achieve 'true/proper civilization', that mode of conduct 'which points out to man the path of duty'. 'Performance of duty and observance of morality', moreover, 'are convertible terms', since the observance of morality implies the attainment of mastery over mind and passion. The Gujarati equivalent for civilization, stated Gandhi, means 'good conduct' (Gandhi 1938: 61).

Gandhi's search for and examination of the causes of the 'moral failure' of Indians, argues Partha Chatterjee, led him to formulate answers that were almost diametrically opposed to those offered by nationalist leaders, such as Bankimchandra Chattopadhyay (Chatterjee 1986: 86). The meanings of Gandhi's *swaraj* or Indian Home Rule did not, in any way, relate to a simple freedom from colonial government; it evoked a freedom that could only be achieved 'through the ethical government of the self and the rigorous practice of self-discipline in the pursuit of truth' (Pratt and Vernon 2005: 95). Gandhi did not equate self-rule with freedom or with the end of the empire; that is what made him 'strangely accommodating' of the empire (Mehta 2003: 425). At the same time, he also felt that the presence of the empire and of civilization vitiated the possibility of the form of self-knowledge that was to make true self-rule possible.

What lay at the heart of Gandhi's moralized notion of the nation, therefore, was the belief that India could be free only after its individuals had succumbed to the search for truth and non-violence (*ahimsa*), and had reformed themselves and accepted *sarvodaya* (self-less service). Only then would satyagraha (soul force, militant non-violence), Gandhi's 'weapon of strength', be effective as a mode of struggle. A true satyagrahi had to be pure and healthy in body and mind, have complete control over his senses, passion and 'lust' and engage in the pursuit of truth that would open the way for *swaraj*.

This 'theory of India's salvation', affirms Ashis Nandy, involved 'Gandhi's spirited search for the other culture of Britain, and of the West', an anti-thesis of the English that was latent in the English too (1983: 49). It was evident in Gandhi's preference for some Christian hymns and Biblical texts that was much more than a gesture of salute to a 'minority religion'. It contained a firm affirmation that elements of Christianity were perfectly congruent with elements of Hindu and Buddhist world views and that 'the battle he was fighting for the minds of men was actually a universal battle to rediscover the softer side of human nature' (ibid.: 49).

For Brown, the ideology behind 'Gandhian passive resistance' was 'a blend of the Hindu Vaishnava tradition of *ahimsa*, non-violence, and a belief in suffering rather than fighting to overcome an opponent' (1972: 6). In his book titled *Satyagraha* (1951), Gandhi defined it as 'holding on to Truth' or 'Truth-force' and distinguished it from its English translation, passive resistance, associated with the movement of suffragists and non-conformists in England. Passive resistance was 'a weapon of the weak'; it did not exclude the use of physical force or violence in order to achieve its end. Satyagraha, on the other hand, was 'a weapon of the strongest' and did not admit 'the use of violence in any shape or form' (Gandhi 1951: 6).

Gandhi embarked on satyagraha in South Africa as a 'pragmatist' but soon began to think of it as an 'idealist'. For inspiration, he drew on his earlier readings and experiences, defined the sets of circumstances where it was applicable, marked out the type of person who could use it and invested it with his own meaning. This re-definition of passive resistance as satyagraha involved 'a total philosophy of life and action' (Brown 1972: 7). At the heart of his new commitment to satyagraha was the belief that the goal of human life should be the search for truth, but since no one could know the ultimate truth, the methods employed in human action in the search were as important as the goal. The methods, therefore, should never attack another's integrity and his search for truth. 'Only non-violence and suffering willingly accepted could guarantee the integrity of both parties' (Brown 1972: 7; Sarkar [1983] 1995: 179).

Between 1907 and 1914, satyagraha was worked out by means of peaceful violation of specific laws, such as compulsory registration and trade and entry permits, mass courting of arrests, occasional *hartals* (strikes) and spectacular marches. In 1913, 2,037 men, 127 women and 57 children participated in the cross-country march. These satyagrahas, in Sarkar's words, involved a mixture of 'apparently quixotic methods' along with a strict attention to organizational and especially financial details; 'a readiness for negotiations and compromise, at times leading to abrupt unilateral withdrawals which were by no means popular' ([1983] 1995: 179). The 'paucity of evidence' with regard to the satyagrahas testifies to the fact that 'Gandhi rarely delegated responsibility for the organization and preferred to rely on his own influence and actions' (Brown 1972: 8).

Satyagraha, therefore, had a dual impact—it involved the masses but also kept them under strict supervision and control where they were made to act in accordance with the dictates of the leader and to strictly abide by non-violence. The urge to control the masses would often lead to abrupt withdrawal of movements launched under Gandhi's leadership in India. His methods, however, achieved considerable success in South Africa; they 'roused South African Indians' and created 'indignation abroad'. The South African government was compelled to offer a compromise package to the Indians in 1914—the tax of three pounds on former indentured labourers was abolished and Indian marriages were recognized. Understandably, the government showed 'considerable relief' at Gandhi's departure from South Africa (Brown 1972: 3).

India Anew

After Gandhi sailed from South Africa, minister J. C. Smuts is known to have stated sardonically, 'the saint has left our shores I sincerely hope for ever'. This statement testifies to Gandhi's reputation as a 'saint' even in South Africa. At the same time, there was no direct link between his success in South Africa and his 'rise to power' in India. It required time, tactics, struggle and ideology that appealed to the masses before Gandhi became the Mahatma, 'great soul' and the great leader, in India.

The political scene in India in 1915, when Gandhi returned, was confused. The removal of the capital from Calcutta and the construction of a capital in New Delhi, together with the declaration of World War I in 1914, had 'heralded a new though disquieting political and social age for India on top of the residues of the previous decade of turmoil' (Stein 2010: 286). Chapter 6 has briefly indicated that the Home Rule of Annie Besant and the one set up by Tilak on his return from imprisonment had come to command a certain degree of power within the Congress. The demand for Home Rule gained force with the outbreak of World War I and Britain's unilateral decision to involve India in it. Indian support for the war effort, in the view of elite leaders, was consequent upon Britain's granting of Home Rule.

The young revolutionaries in Bengal and the Ghadars in North America, on the other hand, tried to exploit the situation of war by forming alliances with the enemies of the British, the Germans in particular. Armed robberies increased and efforts to obtain arms and ammunition from Germany intensified. Such efforts were thwarted by police infiltration and lack of mass support; the Ghadars' more spectacular attempt to return to India and launch a struggle for liberation, ended in a clash between British Indian police and inmates of the ship *Komagata Maru* on 23 May 1914 in Calcutta in which 22 Ghadars were killed and 8,000 imprisoned. Ironically, Indian participation in the World War surpassed these daring attempts to liberate the country.

The radicalization of Indian politics in 1916–17, reflected in the success of Besant and Tilak's Home Rule movement and the Lucknow Pact of 1916, which brought the Congress and the Muslim League together to press and formulate plans for constitutional reform at a time of war, made the idea of Indian self-rule gain greater legitimacy in British political circles. The new liberal Viceroy, Lord Chelmsford in particular, was acquiescent to the 'progressive realization' of 'Indian self-rule within the Empire' (Robb 1976: 3). Chelmsford is believed to have been influenced by American President Woodrow Wilson's doctrine of 'self-determination' of subject peoples (Gordon 1974: 163; Thompson and Garrat 1958: 540).

Chronology of Minor Political Parties and Organizations, 1912–46

Place/Year	Political Parties and Organizations
1912	Khilafat Movement, significant until 1924. Led by Muhammad Ali and Shaukat Ali. Adopted Gandhian no-cooperation pledge in 1920.
1918	National Liberal Federation (in Bengal, Moderate Party) founded by Tej Bahadur Sapru and M. R. Jayakar.
1919	Jamiat ul Ulama-i-Hind, founded by Maulana Mahmudal Hasan Shaikh-ul-Hind of Deoband School, nationalist Muslim clergy.
1920	Congress Democratic Party, founded by B. G. Tilak to enter elections. Base for Democratic Swaraj Party of 1937.
1921–22	Communist Party organizational work begun by M. N. Roy et al.
1922	Swarajya Party founded as offshoot of Congress to 'wreck' councils from inside, led by C. R. Das, Motilal Nehru, et al.

Place/Year	Political Parties and Organizations
1923	Hindu Mahasabha (founded in 1907 in the Punjab) became active politically after Benares session, led by M. M. Malaviya.
1928	Peasants and Workers Party, established as legal wing of Communists, based on parties in Bengal, Bombay, Madras, U. P., the Punjab.
1929	Majlis-i-Ahrar, founded by Congress-Khilafatist Muslims in Lahore, based in Punjab, also active in Kashmir, U P.
1931	Khaksars, founded by Allama Inayatullah Khan Mashriqi of Lahore; based in Punjab, also active in N.W. Frontier Province, towns of Sind and U. P.
1934	Socialist Party, founded as Congress offshoot by Jayaprakash Narayan et al.
1936	All-India Kisan Sabha, joined by Andhra group founded by N. R. Ranga in 1931 and Bihar Kisan Sabha founded by Swami Sahajananda in 1929; intermittent Congress orientation.
1936	Independent Labour Party, founded by B. R. Ambedkar in Bombay, some influence also in C. P.
1939	Forward Bloc, founded by Subhas Chandra Bose in Calcutta.
1940	Radical Democratic Party, founded by M. N. Roy in Bombay.
1942	Scheduled Caste Federation, founded by B. R. Ambedkar in Nagpur.
1945	Jamiat ul Ulama-i-Islam, founded in Calcutta with Maulana Shabbir Ahmad Usmani as President; pro-League.

Chelmsford's administration allowed a number of 'concessions' to nationalist demands—'lubricants' as the Secretary of State would call them later. War finance demanded a hike in duties on cotton imports, and they were raised from 3.5 to 7.5 per cent without increasing the countervailing excise on Indian textiles; and a ban was imposed on the emigration of indentured labour. A formal declaration of the goals of British rule in India, however, had to await the appointment of Edwin Montagu as the Secretary of State in July 1917 (Bandyopadhyay 2004: 283). On 20 August 1917, Montagu declared in the House of Commons that henceforth British policy in India would be geared towards promoting 'self-governing institutions' that would eventually confer self-rule on India as 'an integral part of the British Empire' (Sarkar [1983] 1995: 165).

This was accompanied by the concrete promise of reforms in 1919, which caused confusion in Indian politics as it generated distinct reactions from Indian leaders. With reforms in the offing, Moderate leaders started having 'second thoughts' about accepting 'a possibly reformed Tilak' in the Congress, and Annie Besant and some of her Indian and European Theosophist colleagues became ready to desert their radical demands (Stein 2010: 289).

The reforms, incorporated in the Government of India Act 1919 and generally referred to as the Montagu-Chelmsford or the 'Montford' Reforms, promoted the cause of 'responsible self-government' by granting provincial autonomy and introducing the device of 'dyarchy'. Certain functions of provincial governments, such as those relating to education, health, agriculture and local bodies were 'transferred' to ministers responsible to legislative assemblies, that is, they were given some executive powers (Sarkar [1983] 1995: 167). Other subjects, of greater importance, such as law and order and finance were kept 'reserved'. The act set up a bicameral system at the centre (Council of State and Imperial Legislature) and granted elected majority to the provincial legislative assemblies.

GOVERNMENTAL ORGANIZATION OF BRITISH INDIA, GOVERNMENT OF INDIA ACT 1919

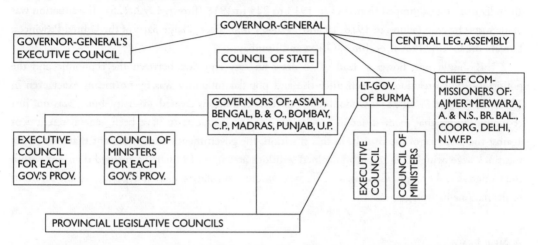

The electorate was enlarged to include 5.5 million for the provinces and 1.5 million for the imperial legislature. At the same time, the elected majority had no control over ministers in charge of the 'transferred' subjects, and the Viceroy was given an enormous power of veto and the authority to push for rejected bills by means of the certificate procedure. Provincial governors also had veto and certificate powers. Revenue resources were divided between the centre and the provinces, with land revenue going to the provinces and income tax remaining with the centre. In effect, the act skillfully incorporated Indian politicians as ministers and induced them to participate in a patronage rat-race, while retaining control over the distribution of financial resources that would actually enable Indian ministers to make improvements in education or health.

'Communal representation', introduced in the Morley-Minto Reforms and opposed by the Congress, was criticized only in theory; it was retained and extended in the Montagu-Chelmsford Reforms. Sikhs were given separate electorate in addition to the Muslims, seats were 'reserved' for non-Brahmans in Madras in compliance with the demands of the Justice Party, and 'depressed classes' were granted 'nominated' seats in legislatures at all levels (Bandyopadhyay 2004: 283; Sarkar [1983] 1995: 167). This is because British administrators, in general, accepted the view of people like Alfred Lyall and Herbert Hope Risley—outstanding figures of the Indian Civil Services—that India was not a nation since it was composed of communities and religious groups, and had no recognizable, unified political society (Kumar 1969: 359; 1983: 50).

The Act of 1919, hailed by some historians as the harbinger of 'parliamentary democracy in India' (Woods 1994: 31), conferred much less than what it promised. It was limited by the basic belief in the continuance of British rule in India, and served the 'twin imperial requirements' of devolution of finances and expansion of the circle of Indian collaborators (Robb 1976; Tomlinson 1976). It did not satisfy Indian politicians, who had started thinking of *swaraj* as their goal, and fell far short of inaugurating political democracy in India.

Massive recruitment for World War I, heavy taxes, war loans and a sharp rise in prices that the War occasioned, adversely affected different sections of Indian society and increased the contradictions between British and Indian interests. The British were caught in 'a spiral of rising prices' in India as the all-India price index jumped from 143 in 1913 to 225 in 1918 (Brown 1972: 125). The situation was made worse by crop failures in 1918–19 and 1920–21 that affected large parts of the United Provinces, Punjab, the Central Provinces, Bihar, Orissa and Bombay.

This should not, however, lead us to draw an easy equation between the economic and the political—'the co-relation between price-rise and popular militancy was by no means exact even in 1919–22' (Sarkar 1984: 287). Undoubtedly, extreme conditions created adversity, but it was not just economic duress that made different groups restive. There appears to have been general resentment against the presence of the British. In this situation, the government's announcement that new police measures were being taken to curb imagined seditious activities of Indians, cemented divisions within the Congress and brought Gandhi, a leader who would soon start a 'mass movement,' to the forefront of the nationalist struggle.

A New Leader

Gandhi's stature as a public celebrity meant that the news of his return to India had generated public interest and speculation about the political role he was to assume. He had great respect for the Moderate Congress leader Gokhale, but it was not certain that he would follow the methods of Moderate politics. Gokhale advised Gandhi not to rush to a decision but to travel in India and see the conditions. Gandhi followed the advice; he travelled extensively in India between 1915 and 1916, 'visiting places as far apart as Sind and Rangoon, and Benares and Madras in order to get to know his homeland' (Brown 1972: 41). At the end of the year, he realized that he had very little in common with the 'constitutionalist views' of Gokhale's followers (Stein 2010: 292).

Drawing upon his South African experience, Gandhi founded the Sabarmati Ashram in Ahmedabad in May 1915, where he hoped to create, among 'a religious community on the traditional Hindu pattern', an environment conducive to the 'spiritual deliverance' of his homeland (Brown 1972: 42–43). The ideals he wished to instill in the inmates of the Ashram were those of 'utter simplicity of life backed by vows of truth, non-violence and celibacy, and the practice of manual labour, hand spinning and use of Indian products' (Gandhi 1958 Vol. 13: 91–98). He also sought to impart 'national education' in the Ashram in the vernacular language, which put stress on religious instruction and practical knowledge of agriculture and weaving, along with the 'customary academic subjects' (Brown 1972: 44).

Reactions to Gandhi's endeavours were varied—while some praised his efforts, the 'Western-educated leaders' came to consider Gandhi as an 'oddity'. In contrast to the 'limited politics' of the classes championed by the Congress (Kumar 1971: 4), Gandhi embarked on campaigns of social justice that involved the 'masses'. He launched three satyagrahas between 1917 and 1918—two of them were in rural areas and one in the town of Ahmedabad. The satyagraha in Champaran, Bihar, was in support of indigo producers; the one in Kheda, Gujarat, upheld the cause of smallholding farmers who often lost their lands on account of debt; the urban one championed the cause of mill-hands in Ahmedabad.

Negotiations were arrived at in all three instances and Gandhi gained a reputation as a man who took up local grievances and arrived at concrete results, unlike the Congress or the Home Rule that rallied around abstract all-India issues, which did not necessarily produce any result (Sarkar [1983] 1995: 183). His methods came to be viewed by the people as being 'bottom-up' rather than top-down, a fact that allowed the spread of rumours about Gandhi 'baba' and 'Gandhi Maharaj' (saint), rumours that would make Gandhi into the Mahatma (Amin 1984; Bhaduri 1973).

In Brown's analysis, *Gandhi's Rise to Power* was made possible by his work among the Muslims, low-caste Hindus and commercial men—'groups who found no place in Congress politics because their interests were not those of the educated few' (Brown 1972: 41). Moreover, the satyagrahas enabled Gandhi to recruit 'subcontractors'—Rajendra Prasad, J. B. Kripalani and Anugraha Narayan Sinha in Champaran, Vallabhbhai Patel (Sardar Patel), Mahadev Desai (later to be his private secretary), and Shankarlal Banker in the two movements in Gujarat—people who played vital roles in peasant and worker mobilization, and people who would serve as Gandhi's life-long lieutenants. These 'subcontractors' represented the emergence of western-educated and vernacular elite of 'backward' areas and small towns in Indian political life, men who would rival and even replace the western-educated elite in presidency towns and enable Gandhi to 'seize power'. The foundations of Gandhi's strength lay in the strong bonds he established with merchant groups and Muslims of Gujarat, Uttar Pradesh and the United Provinces, Bihar and Punjab, groups that were outside the 'political nation as it had existed in relation to Congress politics' (ibid.: 353).

Jacques Pouchepadass's detailed study of Champaran, however, highlights that the region had a long tradition of anti-planter discontent and agitation and the people who played significant roles in peasant mobilization were not Gandhian converts, but rich and middle-ranking peasants as well as local *mahajan*s (moneylenders) and traders who resented planter competition (1974, 1999). Gandhi's participation in the movement was a result of the invitation given to him by the rich and middle peasants. Raj Kumar Shukla, a peasant leader, had travelled to the Lucknow Congress of 1916 to invite Gandhi personally.

Gandhi did not do much more than institute an open enquiry in July 1917 and give all-India publicity to the grievances of Champaran indigo cultivators. But, what he did was totally overshadowed by what he came to stand for—a saint who held out hopes of a millenarian future. His power gave the producers the courage to stand up to the planters; they were no longer afraid. Rumours circulated that Gandhi had been sent to the Viceroy or the King to overrule planters and local officials; they even went to the extent of claiming that the British were to leave Champaran soon (Sarkar [1983] 1995: 184). The compromise reached at the end of the satyagraha came in the form of the Champaran Agricultural Act in November 1918. It did not do away either with planter oppression or peasant protest. Local peasant leaders continued to evoke the name of Gandhi to organize peasants, making this area a strong base for future Gandhian movements (Pouchepadass 1999; Bandyopadhyay 2004: 293).

Gandhi's role in the Kheda satyagraha was also a 'patchy affair', although sustained village work in the district provided Gandhi with a solid core of devoted followers from among the Patidars. As distinct from the impoverished peasant tenants of Champaran, the district of Kheda was a land of relatively affluent Kanbi-Patidar peasant proprietors who grew food grains, cotton and tobacco for the nearby town of Ahmedabad (Sarkar [1983] 1995: 184). At the same time, the 'lesser Patidars' of Kheda were adversely affected by recurrent famine and plague since 1899; revenue payments were seldom reduced while revenue collection became very difficult. In addition, these people were not in a position to make up for their losses through dowry, and they barely managed to enter the civil service of the nearby Baroda state, unlike the more wealthy Patidars who also enjoyed a more privileged position in the caste hierarchy (Hardiman 1981).

In 1917–18 in particular, a poor harvest combined with high prices of kerosene, ironware, cloth and salt, as well as a hike in wages forced upon the lower Patidars by the low-caste Baraiya farm labourers, landed them in a dire situation (Sarkar [1983] 1995: 185). In November 1917, local village leaders gave a call for non-payment of revenue to press for revenue remission. Gandhi took up the cause of no-revenue after a lot of hesitation. By then, a good *rabi* (winter) crop had weakened the 'case for remissions'. Consequently, the Kheda satyagraha, 'the first real Gandhian peasant satyagraha in India' spread only to 70 out of the 559 affected villages, and was called off in June 1918 after only a token concession was granted (Sarkar [1983] 1995: 185). But here too, as in Champaran, peasant and tenant understandings and appropriations of Gandhi's message far surpassed what he actually achieved. A series of burglaries in Patidar houses came in the wake of the Kheda satyagraha—low-caste Baraiyas, confident that British law and order was collapsing under Gandhi's spell, committed such acts, independent of what Gandhi's 'subcontractors' asked them to do.

Indeed, it was the Patidars and not the tenant farmers who provided Gandhi with a core of devoted followers. The Patidars were attracted to Gandhi's non-violence because they were primarily Vaishnavas, and were averse to a 'violent revolution' as property-holders. That Gandhi did not command such devotion among the peasantry is proved by the fact that his campaign for war recruitment evoked very poor response among the villagers, and his disciples who were earlier garlanded were now refused food (Hardiman 1981).

In the middle of the Kheda satyagraha, Gandhi mediated in a conflict between Indian mill-owners and their employees in Ahmedabad. The conflict emerged in February–March 1918 out of the attempt of Amabalal Sarabhai, a mill-owner and a textile magnate, to deprive the workers of a bonus awarded in 1917, on account of the hardship occasioned by plague. The workers, enraged at this prospective 'pay-cut' at a time of rising prices, demanded a 50 per cent hike in wages in lieu of the 'plague bonus'. Sarabhai was willing to concede a 20 per cent hike. Gandhi, who knew Sarabhai personally and had got funds for his Sabarmati Ashram from him, got the workers to agree to a 35 per cent increase in wages and dissuaded them from militant picketing.

The Ahmedabad strike in March 1918 is significant for Gandhi's first use of hunger strike as a political weapon, a mode he would use successively on 15 occasions throughout his later career. In conventional accounts, Gandhi's hunger strike (from 15 March 1918) is presented as an effective attempt to boost the flagging spirit of the workers. The report of the District Magistrate cited by Judith Brown, however, provides a different picture. According to this report, the workers had 'assailed Gandhi bitterly for being a friend of the mill owners, for riding their cars and eating sumptuous meals with them while the weavers starved' and Gandhi, 'stung by these taunts' resorted to the hunger strike (Brown 1972).

The District Magistrate possibly overstated his case, but it is likely that Gandhi's formative influences—his mother's recurrent fasts and family members' practice of going without food to demonstrate their anger against one another—had a major role to play. The inextricable intertwining of the religious and the political, that prompted Gandhi to demand vows and pledges from the people (Skaria 2011), perhaps moved him to return the promise or atone for the moral claims he was making on them. 'So embedded was fasting in Gandhi's everyday life', write Tim Pratt and James Vernon, 'that it is difficult to neatly separate its practice as a regime of the self from its performance as an act of national significance' (2005: 94). This imbrication, moreover, allowed Gandhi to 'inscribe the self upon the nation, and the nation upon the self' and elevated his claims to moral leadership (ibid.: 95).

The hunger strike produced the desired result—the workers won a 35 per cent rise in their wages. The Textile Labour Association set up in 1920 under Gandhi's initiative, consolidated his hold on the Ahmedabad textile workers. The Labour Association was founded on a philosophy of interdependence of capital and labour where the owners were seen as 'trustees' for the workers. Unsurprisingly, the Association believed in the peaceful arbitration of disputes instead of radical measures. Gandhi's influence among the workers, however, did not go much beyond Ahmedabad and he remained 'firmly aloof' from the All India Trade Union Committee even before the Communists became important within it (Sarkar [1983] 1995: 186). His impact was far greater among the peasants since, as Sarkar puts it, exploitation in the countryside put on a 'paternalistic colour' at times, and issues like land revenue or salt tax provided unifying grievances (ibid.:187).

Gandhi's satyagrahas demonstrate a common pattern—in all the three instances Gandhi was asked to give leadership to a 'popular' mobilization that had taken shape under local initiative. In all three, Gandhi advocated compromise, caution and negotiation. Why was Gandhi invited to lead the local movements? Was it because of his South African reputation as a leader of the entire Indian community, or was it on account of his views propounded in the *Hind Swaraj* and other innumerable writings, his insistence on non-violence, his efforts at the Sabarmati Ashram, and his own lifestyle, which possibly made him appear very different from the western-educated elite leaders of the presidency towns? We do not know what ideas of Gandhi circulated among the families and friends of the ex-indentured labourers of South Africa in India. As the satyagrahas and later events revealed, there was wide divergence in the way Gandhi and his message were perceived by the elite and the masses.

From the beginning then, the force of Gandhi's appeal went far beyond what he actually achieved. The three satyagrahas prepared him to suggest and stage an all-India movement in 1919. Till then, Gandhi had barely intervened in all-India politics and had shown scant regard for the reform proposals. Except for protesting against Annie Besant's internment and pleading for the release of the Ali brothers, Mohammad Ali and Shaukat Ali, he had remained an outsider to mainstream politics. The enactment of the stringent Rowlatt Act in February 1919 prompted Gandhi to propose a satyagraha that was to include all of India.

The act, which came to take its name from Justice S. A. T. Rowlatt, the President of the Sedition Committee, sought to tackle 'terrorism' by making war-time restrictions on civil rights permanent. Following the recommendations of the Sedition Committee, the Government of India drafted two bills that were presented to the Imperial Legislative Council on 18 January 1919. The first bill sought to amend the Indian Penal Code in a way so as to enable the government to check activities 'prejudicial' to the security of the state effectively. The second one was designed to invest the government to 'short-circuit' the process of law in dealing with revolutionary crime (Kumar 1983: 189). It permitted detention without trial for up to two years and arbitration in special courts. The bills were rushed through the Imperial Legislative Council on 18 March 1919 and became an act despite unanimous opposition from non-official Indian members.

Arguably, the act was to directly affect active politicians. At the same time, any move to retain arbitrary powers of the government and to grant additional powers to the police was bound to produce alarm and outrage. The government's claim on arbitration negated its promise of a 'democratic' polity; the police, for their part, were notorious as petty oppressors (Bandyopadhyay 2004: 295; Sarkar [1983] 1995: 189). The act was possibly a bid to conciliate conservative 'white' opinion incensed by the promises held out to Indians by the Montford Reforms. The Rowlatt Act was accompanied by assurances on the part of the Viceroy that British commerce and the civil services would not be affected by the forthcoming Reforms.

The Rowlatt Act aroused bitter resentment among all political activists; it was only Gandhi who came forward with the suggestion of an all-India mass protest that was to be non-violent. Gandhi opposed the spirit of the bill because it showed a distrust of common men. His initial programme of protest was modest—he and a few volunteers signed a satyagraha pledge on 24 February 1919 to disobey the bill and similar other unjust laws. They were also to publicly sell prohibited works and court arrest. On 26 February he called upon all Indians to join the satyagraha by means of an 'open letter' and soon put forward the more adventurous idea of an all-India *hartal* (strike) on 30 March which was moved to 6 April later.

The *hartal* was deliberately fixed on a Sunday and Gandhi instructed all employees who were required to work on Sundays to suspend work only if they got permission from their employers. Even with such limitations, the call for *hartal* energized distinct groups of political activists. Members of the Home Rule, dismayed somewhat by Annie Besant's support for the Montford Reforms and by Tilak's departure for England in 1918, decided to accept Gandhi's call, and certain pan-Islamic groups, whose cause Gandhi had supported by demanding the release of the Ali brothers, also joined him. Finally, there were the members of the Satyagraha Sabha he had set up in Bombay in February 1919.

The Delhi session of the Muslim League held in December 1918 witnessed an important change in leadership. The young Moderate group that was in favour of the 1919 Reforms was ousted by more radical politicians like Ansari and the *ulema* of Lucknow (the *ulema* of the *farangi mahal* in Lucknow), among whom was Abdul Bari, the preceptor of the Ali brothers and a close ally of Gandhi. Ansari gave a call to the League to support Gandhi's satyagraha against the Rowlatt Act. Gandhi, in Ansari's opinion, was 'an intrepid leader of India' who had 'endeared himself as much to the Musalmans as to the Hindus' (Sarkar [1983] 1995: 189).

Following this, organization for the satyagraha began in real earnest. Gandhi travelled to Bombay, Delhi, Allahabad, Lucknow and several south Indian cities between March and early April 1919. There was a wide circulation of literature publicizing the satyagraha, and a campaign to collect signatures of people willing to take the satyagraha pledge. And yet, the preparation was grossly disproportionate to the movement that resulted in April 1919—'the biggest and most violent anti-British upsurge which India had seen since 1857' (ibid.).

The British government, without real experience of handling an all-India agitation, arrested Gandhi on 9 April in order to contain the struggle. It backfired—'masses' in Delhi, Amritsar, Lahore, Bombay and Ahmedabad went berserk and openly resorted to violence. This brought about state repression with provincial governments acting on their own judgement of the situation. In Punjab, where there was a significant mobilization of the middle and lower middle-class urban groups and artisans, on account of pronounced anti-British sentiment produced by forced recruitment in the army, war exactions, repression in the wake of the Ghadar outbreaks in 1915 and anti-British propaganda of the Arya Samajists, the administration of Lieutenant Governor Michael O'Dwyer resorted to the most extreme measures.

O'Dwyer was 'an irascible Irishman who possessed the single-eyed vision of a fanatic' (Kumar 1983: 166). He firmly believed that the British government was a powerful and benevolent authority that enforced peace among the warring castes and communities in India. He also felt a special responsibility to 'defend' the simple but sturdy peasants against the oppression of wily moneylenders and rapacious lawyers. Consequently, O'Dwyer had a certain degree of popularity among the peasants but was thoroughly disliked by the urban middle classes. These were the groups that gave full support to Gandhi's satyagraha. Indeed, prominent leaders of Lahore had voiced their opposition to the Rowlatt Bills even before Gandhi proposed the satyagraha and Gandhi's 'open letter' had evoked a very favourable response in Punjab, including among sections of Muslims, among whom featured the poet, Muhammad Iqbal.

Understandably, O'Dwyer's administration took strong exception to public meetings held in support of the Rowlatt satyagraha, in particular the call for *hartal*, which, it felt was a direct challenge to British rule. It tried to quell support for the *hartal* by means of coercion and negotiations with local leaders, which turned out to be utterly inefficacious. The remarkable success of the *hartal* of 6 April revealed 'the extent to which Gandhi's initiative had captured the imagination of the citizens of Lahore' and the 'ability of middle-class leaders to canalize popular discontent creatively in a movement of protest against the British government' (Kumar 1983: 194).

Lahore leaders further articulated their strength in organizing a massive anti-British demonstration on the occasion of Ram Navami (Ramnaumi) on 9 April that involved active participation of Muslims. The united front presented by Hindus, Muslims and Sikhs in Punjab enraged and unnerved O'Dwyer's administration—it decided to make full use of the war-time restrictions that the Rowlatt Act had sanctioned to deal with 'sedition'. Following O'Dwyer's instructions, General Dyer gave the order to fire on a peaceful assembly of men and women—satyagrahis—in Jallianwala Bagh in Amritsar on 13 April; it resulted in the killing of 379 people.

The movement began to lose momentum after this, but there were further instances of violence against the European community in Amritsar and Lahore that came in the wake of Jallianwala Bagh and the wild rumours it generated. The use of violence became too flagrant to be overlooked. Gandhi was forced to call off the satyagraha even though the struggle failed to achieve its object of securing a repeal of the Rowlatt Act. Gandhi admitted to his 'Himalayan blunder' of calling upon people 'insufficiently trained' in the modes and the discipline of non-violent struggle to launch a 'civil disobedience' (Gandhi 1960: 469).

And yet, the Rowlatt satyagraha signalled a significant shift in formal politics—masses participated in it for the first time on a large scale. For the educated community, the Amritsar tragedy 'proved to be more traumatic than the movement itself … Its psychological effects were far-reaching and imponderable' (Ray 1984: 243). The poet, Sir Rabindranath Tagore, broke the spell of stunned silence by his noble gesture of resigning his knighthood by means of a letter to the Viceroy. Gandhi, humbled by his 'blunder' did not lose heart. He became aware that the 'ethics of resistance, if it was to be relevant to a bourgeois political movement, would have to be reconciled with a theory of political obedience' and from this discovery was 'born the political concept of the satyagrahi as a leader' (Chatterjee 1984: 183).

On 9 January 1915, Gandhi had returned to India after almost two decades in South Africa. He had been an outsider to the Indian political scene. On 26 December 1920, he presented a resolution advocating non-cooperation before the delegates of the Indian National Congress in Nagpur, and 'won a sweeping victory over the *prima donnas* of the political stage in India' (Kumar 1969: 361; 1983: 51–52). The news of Gandhi's 'extraordinary influence over the Hindus' was carried to the French humanist, Romain Rolland, by 'a young Bengali Hindu', Dilip Kumar Roy. The entry in Rolland's diary for 23 August 1920 noted that Gandhi, who had given up 'all his property seven or eight years ago to devote himself entirely to the salvation of his people' had a 'magnetic effect' on them (1976: 3). The satyagrahi had successfully emerged as the leader. How do we make sense of this?

As indicated earlier, there have been different analyses of Gandhi's 'rise to power'. Judith Brown's thesis of the early 1970s, which had considerable influence on scholars for a long time, held that Gandhi's success was due to the links he established and the support he commanded from 'vernacular' leaders of regions that were not in the forefront of the nationalist struggle till then. Gandhi's insistence on the use of Hindi and the vernacular of the region in making his speeches, and the language of his political vocabulary, distinct from that of the English-educated leaders, drew the rich and middle peasants and merchants of regions such as Gujarat and Bihar to him.

The unconditional support of these local 'subcontractors' gave Gandhi a base among peasants and artisans in localities and enabled him to displace the elite leaders of Calcutta, Bombay and Madras from their positions of power within the Congress. In a similar vein, the works of Richard Gordon and Francis Robinson analysed the factors that aided Gandhi's 'capture' of national leadership (Gordon 1973; Robinson 1973). These works treat Gandhi's rise as a skillful political game played at the top level of Indian politics. As a result, they fail to adequately explain Gandhi's tremendous success among the peasants, who made him into the 'Mahatma' by ascribing meaning and significance to his message in ways that far surpassed Gandhi's own ideas.

Indeed, it is such perceptions and understandings of peasants that formed the core of insightful analyses of nationalism and the nationalist struggle as well as of subaltern autonomy by the group of subaltern studies scholars, analyses that enabled them to postulate the important idea of a broader notion of the 'political', a political in which the 'peasant' was as much a conscious political agent as nationalist leaders (Guha 1982). This 'political' contained two spheres—one of formal institutional politics and the other of informal and 'autonomous' subaltern politics.

The sphere of the formal political, argued subaltern studies, depended on vertical mobilization and often attempted to co-opt the informal sphere, while in the informal zone, mobilization was largely horizontal and related to ties of caste, community and kinship. This domain often existed independent of the formal sphere although it impinged upon it (Guha 1982, 1983a, 1983b, 1984). Gandhi's leadership provided a brilliant opportunity for the two domains to interact and come together. At the same time, if the 'autonomy' of the informal made Gandhi into a charismatic leader—the 'Mahatma'—it also frustrated Gandhi's attempts to co-opt the 'subalterns' in ways that he wanted to (Amin 1984, 1995, 2004; Chatterjee 1984; Sarkar 1984). We will soon see the implications of this argument for the Non-Cooperation movement.

The preponderance of religious symbols in Gandhi's political vocabulary has been the subject of scrutiny in explorations of his success as a 'saint' and a political leader. A. L. Basham, for instance, argued long ago that the key concepts of Gandhian ideology rested on popular Vaishnavism and popular Jainism; this accounted for his remarkable success among the people of Gujarat (1971). Gandhi's religious ideas, we have seen earlier, were eclectic and 'contingent'; they evolved over time in tune with different situations (Arnold 2001; Nandy 1983). Moreover, as Ravinder Kumar points out, Gandhi's *Autobiography* offers little evidence of this overwhelming influence of Vaishnavism and Jainism. In addition, 'a marriage between popular religion and mass politics' had been anticipated with considerable success by Tilak in Maharashtra and Aurobindo Ghose in Bengal, but the appeal of these leaders was very different from that of Gandhi (Kumar 1969: 360–61; 1983: 51).

For Kumar, Gandhi's success lay in his 'perceptive view of the structure of society in India' along with a deep insight 'into the social loyalties of the individual and how they could be invoked for political action' (Kumar 1969: 361; 1983: 51). Gandhi's predecessors assumed the existence of a homogeneous political society; this seriously constrained their efforts at organizing broad-based political movements. Gandhi, interestingly, shared the view of British administrators such as Risley and Lyall that India was a loose constellation of classes, communities and religious groups; but rather than taking it as a drawback of political society, he effectively appealed to the loyalties of these distinct groups bringing about a mass mobilization unparalleled in the history of India (ibid.).

At the same time, the direct physical form in which the 'masses' appeared in the political arena was always that of a mob (Chatterjee 1984: 185). It had no mind of its own (Gandhi 1958 Vol. 12: 392). In order to involve the 'masses' in political action, it was necessary to create a selfless, enlightened and dedicated group of political workers who would lead the masses and deter them from being misguided. As Markovits puts it, Gandhi's invitation to the people to actively participate in political movements was 'always mediated through his small group of faithful followers who were meant to serve as examples to the masses' (2003: 94). In order to serve as exemplars, this dedicated group of workers needed to gain mastery over the body and overcome fear. And that could only be done through *ahimsa*, non-violence.

Ahimsa both limited satyagraha and made it more than 'purely and simply civil disobedience' (Chatterjee 1984: 185–86). *Ahimsa* was to bridge the disjuncture between morality and politics, between private conscience and public responsibility. This meant that the authority of the political leader derived not so much 'from the reasonableness of his programme' but from 'moral claims of personal courage and sacrifice and a patent adherence to truth', claims that conferred on Gandhi the total allegiance of his people (Chatterjee 1984: 188; Markovits 2003). And, it was on grounds of such moral claims that Gandhi called upon the people repeatedly to make vows, promises and pledges (*vrats* and *yamaniyamas*) during all his campaigns. Such vows and pledges were to 'make the human into a promising animal, into a figure made distinct by repetition and return' (Skaria 2011: 156).

Paradoxically, the more Gandhi tried to discipline and control the people, the more the people drew inspiration from his powers as a saint to fight their own battle for *swaraj* fearlessly. Gandhi's success lay in the spectacular way he reached and drew in the masses as the Mahatma; the limits to his power were also underlined by the 'imperfect' mobilization of the masses who never quite learnt to be non-violent. All this would become evident in the first all-India movement that Gandhi led from the Congress platform.

CONGRESS, KHILAFAT, NON-COOPERATION

The Congress session in Amritsar in December 1919 was presided over by Motilal Nehru, a well-known lawyer from the United Provinces and an early member of the Congress. It adopted a moderate, conciliatory stance towards the British. Gandhi and Jinnah joined in applauding the constitutional reforms that had been announced; condemnation of the actions of Dwyer's troops was withheld in view of an inquiry into the event that was being conducted. The only call for action was given by Jinnah who wanted a Congress campaign in favour of the Khalifa, the Ottoman sultan, who was threatened by a harsh treaty following his defeat in World War I.

The Khilafat movement, which had featured in the agenda of the Muslim League since 1916, gained momentum in India in 1919–20, with rumours about the impending harsh peace treaty. It drew Gandhi's attention after the withdrawal of the Rowlatt satyagraha. The Khilafat movement was so called, because one of its principal aims was to retain the power of the Khalifa, the Turkish sultan, who was also the spiritual head of Islam. Consequently, many Muslims felt that the Khalifa should wield enough temporal power to 'defend the faith and the faithful'; that the Jazirat-ul-Arab—the conglomerate of Arabia, Syria, Iraq and Palestine—'Arabia as defined by Muslim religious authorities, should according to the Prophet's dying injunction remain in Muslim hands', and that the holy places be subject to the Khalifa (Robinson [1974] 2007: 290). The demands were presented by Mohammed Ali before diplomats in Paris in 1920. The Ali brothers also supported the *ulema* of the *farangi mahal* in Lucknow who pressed for 'country-wide hartals' and proposed a Non-Cooperation movement at an All-India Khilafat Conference in Delhi on 22–23 November, a month before the Congress session (Robinson 2001).

This UP group was more radical than the Bombay Khilafat Committee, which had changed its name to the Central Khilafat Committee, and controlled the movement till the end of 1919. Both Minault and Robinson argue that the Khilafat leaders were not particularly concerned with the fate of the Khalifa in the Middle-East; for them, Khilafat was a symbol that united the 'Muslims' in India, a disparate community with wide regional, cultural and class differences (Minault 1982: 10–11; Robinson [1974] 2007: 291). Khilafat, a 'pan-Islamic' symbol, enabled 'pan-Islamic mobilization'. It also allowed the leaders to ask for Hindu cooperation.

Gandhi, the only Hindu leader present at the All-India Khilafat conference, was thanked for his sympathy for the Khilafat cause. More significantly, in Brown's opinion, the conference in November 1919 was remarkable for Gandhi's formal acceptance of withdrawal of cooperation from the British government (Brown 1972: 202). The All-India Conference passed resolutions to boycott the celebrations to mark the end of the War, and eventually to boycott British goods, send deputations to England

and America and resort to non-cooperation with the government if it disregarded their wishes on the Khilafat issue.

Gandhi, who had close links with Abdul Bari and the Ali brothers, 'made himself vital' by playing a mediating role among the 'moderate' and 'radical' Khilafatists, and among leaders of the Khilafat movement and Hindu politicians. With the release of the Ali brothers and Abul Kalam Azad in December 1919, the movement entered its second and more radical phase. Leadership slipped from the hands of the Bombay merchants and went to journalists and preachers of the United Provinces, who made a lot more progress in small towns and villages, in places where there was 'an unsophisticated working or peasant Muslim population, who were susceptible to religious exhortation through local mosques and vernacular papers ...' (Brown 1972: 205).

Gandhi's attitude changed once the harsh terms imposed by the Allied Powers on Turkey in the Treaty of Serves (May 1920) became known. It was hardened by the publication of the Hunter Commission Report on the disturbances in Punjab connected with the Rowlatt satyagraha. This Report protected the officers of the British government by means of an Indemnity Act, acquitted O'Dwyer of blame, and the British House of Lords rejected the censure passed on Dyer. To make matters worse, the *Morning Post* raised a sum of 26,000 pounds for 'the butcher of Jallianwala bagh' (Sarkar [1983] 1995: 196).

Gandhi decided to support the radical group of Khilafatists, who won formal victory at the Allahabad meeting of the Central Khilafat Committee on 19–20 June 1920. The meeting was attended by several other Hindu leaders, and a four-stage programme of non-cooperation was announced— boycott of civil services, police and army, and non-payment of taxes. Gandhi began to press the Congress to adopt a similar programme at its special session in Calcutta between 4 and 9 September 1920 on three issues—the 'Punjab wrong', the 'Khilafat wrong', and Swaraj (self-rule), introduced at the instance of Vijayraghavachari and Motilal Nehru (Gandhi 1960: 499). Termed *asahayog*, the non-cooperation programme involved 'a boycott of the commodities and institutions through which England was able to rule India with the help of Indians' (Amin 1995: 12).

Initially, however, Gandhi was more inclined to a boycott of government institutions than of British commodities (Ray 1984: 249). In Gandhi's programme, the first stage of the campaign consisted of withdrawal from government schools, surrender of government titles, boycott of courts, and reformed legislative councils. This was to be complemented by the boycott of British cloth and the founding of national educational institutions, arbitration courts and the popularization of khadi, home-spun cloth.

Gandhi's proposal found approval only from Congress members from Gujarat and Bihar. Motilal Nehru was hesitant about boycotting the Council elections scheduled for November 1920, which were to be based on the Constitutional Reforms of 1919, and the Extremists—Chittaranjan Das of Bengal, and Tilak and his followers in Maharashtra—who knew that they would do well in Council elections were totally opposed to the programme. Muslim leaders were also not unanimously in favour of non-cooperation. Gandhi and Shaukat Ali toured different parts of India in order to gain support for the movement which was to begin with a *hartal* on 1 August 1920. The *hartal* turned out to be a great success; it also coincided with Tilak's death.

Between August and December 1920, the scene changed dramatically. Motilal Nehru lent his support to Gandhi at the special session of the Congress in Calcutta in September, and Chittaranjan

Das, who had spent a huge sum of money to finance an opposition delegation from Bengal to the regular Congress session in Nagpur in December, moved a resolution accepting 'the entire or any part of the non-violent non co-operation scheme' which entailed a renunciation of voluntary association with the government as well as the refusal to pay taxes (Sarkar [1983] 1995: 197).

The programme was to be implemented at a time decided by the Indian National Congress or the All India Congress Committee (AICC). By then, Council elections were over and Gandhi's promise of 'swaraj within one year' if non-cooperation was accepted, gave him total sway over the Congress for a time. The Congress declared 'the attainment of Swaraj by all legitimate and peaceful means' to be its objective. The non-cooperation programme was to be implemented in stages with civil-disobedience and non-payment of taxes kept for the second stage, only if *swaraj* did not come within a year and the government resorted to repression (Bandyopadhyay 2004: 300–01). *Swaraj*, it is crucial to remember, was left undefined.

The *Hind Swaraj*, we have seen, offered different ideas on *swaraj*, all of which could be deployed diversely. The Congress resolution of 1920 also did not define *swaraj*. Gandhi was not unaware of the lack of precision in some of his key ideas and admitted in one of his innumerable works, 'My language is aphoristic'; 'it lacks precision. It is therefore open to several interpretations' (Gandhi 1958 Vol. 53: 485, cited in Chatterjee 1986: 85).Was this lack of precision deliberate, a way of encouraging self-knowledge, interiority and patience? Mehta is silent on the matter.

Once in control, Gandhi introduced important changes in the Congress organization. He made it a political party of the masses by introducing a *four-anna* (25 paisa) membership; a hierarchy of Congress committees that started at the level of the village and went up, via *taluka*, district, and town to the provincial committees. Provincial Congress committees were reorganized on a linguistic basis in a way as to have representation proportional to the population. Finally, a small 15-member Working Committee was set up as the real executive head. These changes in structure produced a more even distribution in the regional balance of the Congress leadership—Bengal and Maharashtra's dominance was replaced by a greater participation of men from Gujarat and north India (Gordon 1974: 163). In addition, Gandhi and the Congress began to 'tap new sources of support' throughout British India (Krishna 1966).

Several studies of all-India politics have analysed and offered distinct reasons for the change of heart on the part of Congress leaders, as well as for 'Muslim support' in favour of the Non-Cooperation movement. They have also debated whether the Calcutta and the Nagpur sessions marked a victory for Gandhi or for Chittaranjan Das (Bandyopadhyay 1984; Gordon 1973, 1974; Ray 1974). We need not go into those details here. In general, these studies that examine Indian politics from the top and draw heavily upon archival records, seem to argue that a combination of political and economic factors and their successful manipulation by political leaders through 'subcontractors' or 'organization-cum-propaganda' resulted in the generation of a 'mass movement' (Sarkar 1984: 287).

What we should take note of, instead, is the existence of genuine passion and anger not just among leaders but also among the 'common people' in large parts of India generated by the Khilafat and Jallianwala Bagh massacre. The support of the 180 peasant delegates at the Bihar Provincial Conference in Bhagalpur (August 1920) was critical for the passing of the non-cooperation resolution, a support directly linked to the Champaran satyagraha and the enthusiasm for Gandhi it had generated. Similarly, the stout backing of the country-wide network of Marwari businessmen and traders made it possible for Gandhi to have the non-cooperation resolution accepted at the all-India Congress sessions in Calcutta and Nagpur (Sarkar [1983] 1995: 198).

The non-cooperation upsurge, therefore, is best understood if viewed on different registers—as an all-India movement sought to be determined and controlled by Gandhian and Congress leadership and its distinct local and regional variations inflected by participation of different social groups and classes and their diverse deployments of Gandhi's message. The all-India movement launched in January 1921 only called for middle-class participation—it urged students to leave schools and colleges, and lawyers to abandon their legal practice. This was complemented by efforts to establish national schools and arbitration courts, endeavours to spread the use of *charkha* (spinning wheel) and voluntary spinning, and drives to collect funds for the purpose—the Tilak Swaraj Fund, for instance.

Boycott of schools and courts had limited success. The movement began with spectacular student strikes in Lahore and Calcutta and there were serious efforts to establish a large number of national schools and colleges. Chittaranjan Das offered Sir Ashutosh Mukherjee, the Vice-Chancellor of Calcutta University, a million rupees to nationalize the university and suggested the sale of his own house to procure funds for a national laboratory to be set up by Sir Prafullachandra Ray (Bandyopadhyay 1984: 46). Between January and April 1921, an average of 20 headmasters resigned per month from schools, and 11,157 students out of 103,107 left government-aided schools and colleges.

Despite such great enthusiasm, the national educational movement slumped very soon. Only a few important institutions, such as the Jamila Millia Islamia in Aligarh (later moved to Delhi) and the Kashi Vidyapith in Benares and Gujarat survived; a lot of the others perished ingloriously. Rabindranath Tagore, wary of the swadeshi experience, was hostile to educational boycott from the beginning, but his was a lone voice (Bandyopadhyay 1984: 44–45; Gandhi 1997). 'The idea of Non-Cooperation is political asceticism', wrote the poet. 'Our students are bringing offerings of sacrifice to what? Not to a fuller education but to non-education' (Tagore 1921: 612–613). Figures collected by British intelligence officials revealed that the impact of educational boycott at an all-India level was mainly confined to colleges with hardly any boycott of primary schools (Bamford 1925: 103).

The boycott of Council elections was made remarkable by Motilal Nehru and Chittaranjan Das who gave up their practice. Unfortunately, however, only 178 other lawyers followed their example and the total number of titles surrendered remained at 24 out of 5,184. In Madras, the Justice Party, the party of non-Brahmans, participated in Council elections in open defiance of non-cooperation and in support of the Montford Reforms.

Economic boycott—the boycott of foreign cloth in particular—had far greater success. Massive public bonfires of British cloth were organized and the import of British cotton piece goods declined from 1,292 million yards in 1920–21 to 955 yards in 1921–22. The value of total imports of foreign cloth dropped to 570 million in 1921–22 from 1,020 million the previous year (Bandyopadhyay 2004: 302). Support of Gujarati and Marwari merchants and their decision not to import foreign cloth for specific periods were significant here, particularly in view of the fact that the large industrialists remained 'pro-government' (Sarkar [1983] 1995: 174–75). Boycott of foreign cloth went hand in hand with the spread of the *charkha* although it is difficult to track the increase in the use of khadi. All along, there were wide regional variations both in terms of classes and social groups that participated in the movement and in the intensity with which aspects of the non-cooperation programme were taken up.

The radical connotations acquired by the movement were evident within a few months—the arrival, on 17 November 1921, of the Prince of Wales in India on an official visit was marked by a nation-wide strike. The day also witnessed the first outbreak of violence in Bombay—a riot that targeted Europeans, Anglo Indians and Parsis. An incensed Gandhi decided to postpone the second phase of civil disobedience and the no-tax campaign, which was to be conducted only in the *taluka* of Bardoli in Gujarat, an area under Ryotwari Settlement with no large landlords, and hence, no fear of the no-revenue campaign turning into a no-rent one.

Notwithstanding this setback, Khilafat and Non-Cooperation continued with great force for the next few months and 'nearly brought the government to its knees' between November 1921 and February 1922 (Sarkar [1983] 1995: 205). Khilafat leaders, angered by the fresh imprisonment of the Ali brothers in November, began to demand complete independence and threatened to abandon 'non-violence' as a creed. Government repression—large-scale arrests and bans on meetings—alienated the liberals and 'Moderate' leaders, while Gandhi's promise of *swaraj* at a time of distress and excitement brought a large part of the country to the brink of a revolt. In December, senior British officials proposed the release of prisoners and the possibility of holding a Round Table Conference for an early revision of the Reforms of 1919. This did not happen—Gandhi was not willing to compromise at this point and the British Cabinet was not willing to go that far.

Unfortunately, on 11 February 1922, Gandhi abruptly called off the movement when the news of violence committed by angry peasants at Chauri Chaura, in Gorakhpur district in eastern UP, reached him. On 5 February, peasants at Chauri Chaura had set a police station on fire which burnt 22 policemen. Gandhi, shocked and enraged, decided to put an end to non-cooperation. The no-revenue campaign at Bardoli was never launched, *swaraj* was not attained and peasants who firmly believed that 'they also followed Gandhi' became 'murderers' and traitors of the nation overnight (Amin 1995: 48; 2004). Chauri Chaura came to form a sorry footnote in the history and historiography of the nationalist struggle, till the time it was reintegrated with new significance in the history of the nation.

PEOPLE'S GANDHI

Malabar and Moplahs: A Leaflet Issued by the Madras Publicity Bureau in 1921 to explain the Moplah uprising, commented on the intimate link between the uprising and the spread of the message of Khilafat and Non-Cooperation in Malabar. The most important doctrine preached by the Khilafat and Non-Cooperation agitations was that 'the Government of India is Satanic' and 'Hindus and Moslems should unite to paralyse it and establish instead some vaguely conceived "Swaraj"', under whose structure people from all classes were to prosper and be happy (McLane 1970: 120). The 'frugal, industrious and enterprising' Moplahs, the *Leaflet* affirmed, who were far above their 'Hindu competitors in heavy, unskilled manual labour' had long-standing religious and economic grievances; they were fanned to exaggerated proportions in 1921 by vague notions of *swaraj*.

Sumit Sarkar has indicated how distinct interpretations of the word Khilafat by lower-class Muslims encouraged them to take it as a symbol of general revolt against authority. In the United Provinces, for instance, Khilafat was linked to the Urdu word *khilaf* (against); in Malabar the restive Moplahs turned Khilafat into a revolt against the Nambudiri landlords.

There were other factors that aroused 'popular' Muslim sentiments and outraged workers, labourers and peasants, Hindus and Muslims, in different parts of India. The groundswell of 1919–20 found expression in a series of strikes in Bombay, Kanpur, Jamalpur, Madras, Ahmedabad, Jamshedpur and Bengal that involved workers in woollen mills, railways, navigation company, iron and steel factories and jute mills, among others (Das 1923). Peasants in the Mewar region in Rajasthan, Darbhanga region in Bihar and Awadh region in the United Provinces engaged in constant frictions with landlords and their *amla*s (deputies), and in small acts of subterfuge, where the leaders were often influenced by Gandhi's satyagrahas (Henningham 1982; Kumar 1984; Sarkar [1983] 1995: 200–01; Siddiqi 1978).

In this context, Gandhi's promise of *swaraj* within a year proved to be cataclysmic; it fired a wide range of hopes and aspirations. The Non-Cooperation and Khilafat resolution of the Congress spurred a movement on an unprecedented scale; a movement that went far beyond the Congress programme and initiative. For the first time, the Congress succeeded in drawing in regions and groups that had never formed part of earlier Congress initiatives. Peasants were active participants not only in Bihar, but also in Rajasthan, Sind, Gujarat, Assam and Maharashtra, and *adivasi*s organized 'forest satyagrahas' in the Bengal and Andhra delta, while Madras, Bengal and Assam also witnessed labour unrest. More significantly, what Gandhi proposed was superseded by what peasants and workers made of '*swaraj*' which was not always unconnected with the way Congress volunteers made use of Gandhi's reputation as 'Baba' or saint, to draw 'believing people' into the Non-Cooperation struggle.

Indeed, an important aspect of non-cooperation was the way it got conflated with movements for social reform associated with Gandhi. Temperance, or a drive against liquor consumption, never formed a part of the non-cooperation programme, but it became a major rallying point for the 'masses'— *adivasi* and low-caste peasants and agricultural labourers—in large parts of India. Anti-liquor campaigns produced a significant fall in the revenue earned from liquor excise in Bihar, Orissa, south Gujarat, Madras and Punjab, where the targets were often Indian liquor dealers (Hardiman 1984, 1981).

The move to remove untouchability, on the other hand, never acquired great significance even though it was a part of the formal programme. This clause was inserted in the 1920 resolution by Gandhi who made an emotional appeal to 'rid Hinduism of the reproach of untouchability'. Apart from the fact that nationalist leaders did not take up the matter seriously, Gandhi's own approach to and stance on the issue diverged widely from Dalit leaders and caused serious disharmony with the Dalits in the 1930s. The strength and weakness of non-cooperation, therefore, lay in the discrepancy between the actual programme and its diverse apprehensions, appropriations that made Gandhi the 'Mahatma' and foiled his efforts to discipline the people.

Rumours about Gandhi's powers, we have noted earlier, had started circulating much before the Congress formally decided to launch the Khilafat and Non-Cooperation movements. News of 'Ganhi Baba', a great man, with much greater fame and power than the local *gunin* and shaman, who was not married, did not eat meat or fish, and went around stark naked had reached remote tribal areas before 1921–22 (Bhaduri 1973: 26). Gandhi baba had also made miraculous appearances on vegetables to set the seal on his claims to sainthood/divinity (ibid.:28).

Gandhi's simple lifestyle, his use of the vernacular, constant train travels, social reconstruction work and his method of struggle and satyagraha, had all contributed to his image of a saint. In the wave of excitement produced by non-cooperation and *swaraj*, the purity of Gandhi's life intermingled with rumours about his 'thaumaturgic' (magical and miraculous) powers (Amin 1984: 29). This produced fearlessness amongst peasant followers, and heightened Gandhi's charisma as worthy to be worshipped.

C. F. Andrews, a missionary and a close friend of Rabindranath, had shown his clear understanding of Gandhi's charisma in 1920. In a letter to the poet, Andrews had stated that Gandhi had 'the moral power' to 'awaken the lives of the poor who form the bulk of the population'. He said that the poor have no grasp of the Non-Cooperation movement. However, 'they do understand that one tiny man, frail in body and all alone, is challenging the great "Burra Lord Sahib"' (Andrews Papers cited in Ray 1984: 251).

Gandhi baba's appeal and his '*swaraj*' blended with discrete understandings of *kaliyuga*—the last and the most evil of the four epochs in classical Hindu tradition marked by the presence of foreign rule and suffering—to confer on Gandhi the power to bring *kaliyuga* to an end. In apocryphal texts produced by a heterodox religious order in Orissa, Gandhi became identified with the founder of the faith and Kalki, the last incarnation of Lord Vishnu, engaged in an epic battle against the forces of evil, the British, in order to terminate the era of evil and re-establish the era of truth (Banerjee-Dube 2003). Gandhi's brief visit to Gorakhpur, eastern UP in early 1921 generated innumerable rumours about his *pratap* (power/glory) that made him (and his followers) immune to the repressive powers of the colonial state (Amin 1984: 2).

In Amin's succinct formulation, 'Gandhi the person, was in this particular locality [Gorakhpur, eastern UP, where Chauri Chaura eventually came to pass] for less than a day' (8 February 1921) but the 'Mahatma' as an 'idea' was thought out and reworked in popular imagination in subsequent months (Amin 1984: 2). Even in the reckoning of some local Congressmen, this 'deification' assumed 'dangerously distended proportions' (ibid.). At the same time, they admitted that 'no attempt was made by the Congress or the Khilafat to prevent the public from believing in miraculous stories about the Mahatma' (ibid.: 49).

Mahadev Desai, Gandhi's secretary, commented in his diary on 'touching' instances of devotion and childlike manifestations of affection, of homage and offering, that the 'people' of northern India demonstrated during Gandhi's tour in the winter of 1921–22 (Desai 1968). The cries of '*jai*' (victory), raised by peasants who 'invaded' train compartments to have a *darshan* (vision) vividly expressed his deification. Is it surprising then that ideas of Gandhi and his *swaraj* percolated in ways that identified him with Kalki and the end of *kaliyuga*, raising hopes of a better future?

The 'essence' of Gandhi's numerous train tours to propagate the message of non-cooperation, states Amin, was the stops Gandhi made at several stations (2004: 136). The stops, in Gandhi's own words, afforded 'an expectant and believing people' to 'come from all quarters within walking distance and meet me' (Gandhi 1958, Vol. 18: 361). At the same time, Gandhi, the disciplinarian, had formulated elaborate rules to control large crowds and unruly demonstrators, 'mobs' that had to be tamed by trained volunteers. Frequently, however, as Desai's portrayal of 'uncouth' peasants invading train compartments at unearthly hours demanding *darshan* reveal, Gandhi's rules were swept away by the tremendous excitement of the 'mob' (Desai 1968). This was an early indication that attempts at discipline and control were to prove futile.

Trained volunteers were also meant to control the many more 'expectant and believing people' who went to the mammoth meetings that Gandhi addressed and tell them how to strive for *swaraj*. What came to pass, however, was that the peasant volunteers of the Congress recruited through the four-anna membership, the setting up of Congress committees at the lowest levels, as well as through the signing of a 'Pledge form' that started after voluntary organizations were outlawed in November 1921 (Amin 1995: 13), interpreted and deployed Gandhi's message and ideas in ways that diverged widely from the formal, elite programme of non-cooperation.

And so it was that the 'distended proportions' of the idea of the Mahatma led peasant followers in UP to participate in the violent incident of Chauri Chaura on 5 February 1922. In Gorakhpur (and elsewhere), the Mahatma had become associated with a variety of miraculous occurrences; his name also lent itself as a label to all sorts of public meetings, pamphlets and the polysemic word *swaraj*, notions of which took shape independent of the district Congress leadership (Amin 1984: 51). For the local peasantry, 'Swaraj had come to imply a millennium where taxation would be limited to small cash contributions or dues in kind' extracted from fields or threshing floors, and 'where cultivators would hold their lands at little more than nominal rents' (Judgement, Allahabad High Court cited in Amin 1984: 52).

Peasant volunteers who attended a *sabha* (meeting) at Chotki Dumri on 4 February, hours before the clash with the police in the *thana* of Chaura a few miles away, believed (as they claimed during the trial after Chauri Chaura), that they were going to hold a 'Gandhi Mahatma Sabha' that would bring 'Gandhi Swaraj' (Amin 1984: 51). These peasant volunteers, argues Amin, 'were Gandhian as most other peasant volunteers in India in the winter of 1921–2' (Amin 2004: 149).

By late 1921, as local-level volunteer activity had entered a more militant phase, 'the coming of Swaraj was thought of in terms of the direct supplanting of the authority of the police'. This was contrary to the Congress programme and activities of the time (ibid.: 139). Unsurprisingly, therefore, peasant volunteers marched towards the local *thana* after attending the 'Gandhi Mahatma Sabha' where issues had been debated and oaths taken, in order to further the cause of 'Gandhi Swaraj'. A buoyant mood, boosted further by a public feast that had followed the meeting, egged them on to end a perfect day by intimidating the police, a hated symbol of state power. In Gandhi's own words, what the 'mob' tried to do was to retaliate against 'the high-handed tyranny of the police' (Gandhi, editorial in *Aaj* cited in Amin 1995: 48).

When the police tried to deter the crowd by firing in the air and the *daroga* tried to save the situation by apologizing, peasant volunteers took it as a sign of fear on the part of the police. Gandhiji's grace had made 'bullets turn to water' and the *daroga* was 'shit scared'. The fearless and triumphant peasants 'started clapping their hands' and hurtling brickbats at the *thana*; soon the cry was raised to burn the *thana* and kill the policemen in order to make way for Gandhiji's *swaraj* (Amin 2004: 140). It was thus that the *thana* was set on fire and 22 policemen burnt alive.

What followed was not *swaraj*, but repression and punishment not just from the colonial state but also from the Mahatma. The killing of the policemen, in Gandhi's reckoning, was 'murder'. These peasants, declared Gandhi, have killed 'with my name on their lips'. Although a part of him could not even wish them to be arrested, the other part affirmed that 'suffer they must' as 'Gandhi would himself suffer for their breach of the Congress creed' (Amin 1995: 49). Till today, peasant volunteers fail to locate the significance of the riot in the 'grief' it caused to the Mahatma and the brake it put to the nationalist struggle; survivors and the relatives of the 'rioteers' insist on their belief in Gandhiji's power and that their action on the fateful February day was for him.

The 'ambiguous relationship' between Gandhi and his peasant followers finds lucid articulation in a novel Bhojpuri term *otiyar* used by the people of the area to refer to Congress volunteers. To his 'rustic protagonists', 'The Mahatma … was not as he really was'; rather, he was what they had thought him to be. 'Similarly the otiyars were not what the nationalist elite had willed them to be' (Amin 2004: 152). In the absence of a single authorized version of the Mahatma to which the peasants of eastern Bihar and UP could subscribe, their ideas about Gandhi's 'orders' and 'powers' often came to clash with the basic tenets of Gandhism—a paradox that produced Chauri Chaura (Amin 1984: 55). The mutual impingement of the elite and the subaltern produced cracks and left gaps that could never be bridged; and the excess of the subaltern came to haunt formal politics for a long time.

Gandhi remained firm in his stance that the movement had to be called off because of the absence of an environment of non-violence and stressed the need for constructive programme prior to any further political action in the Bardoli resolution. He was perhaps being true to his ideal of patience that helped sediment values over time (Mehta 2003); younger members of the Congress, however, were sorely disappointed. The movement was suspended at its peak without attaining any of its objectives. Studies that explore high politics proffer distinct reasons for the calling off of non-cooperation. The promise of *swaraj* in a short time, they argue, failed to impress most of the leaders; it only enthused students. Similarly, adopting the *charkha* in spreading the use of national products was not taken seriously; it was accepted only out of respect for Gandhi. Finally, the pressure on the part of Marwari traders and businessmen, who had decided to accept boycott of foreign cloth only for a time, also influenced Gandhi's decision for suspension, since the big industrialists were opposed to non-cooperation from the beginning (Bandyopadhyay 1984: 29–31, Bandyopadhyay 2004: 306).

Gandhi was arrested in March 1922 and sentenced to six years in prison. The Khilafat movement died down too, and it became evident to Gandhi that the Khilafat leaders had made strategic use of his appeal without any actual belief in non-violence. Indeed, the overt use of religious symbols and the participation of the *ulema* in the Non-Cooperation Khilafat struggle ended up reinforcing the separate identities of Hindus and Muslims and dividing the communities more than before.

And yet, non-cooperation and *charkha* endured in different parts of India for a long time and came to acquire distinct meanings. Khadi and *charkha* in particular, conjured newer ideas of the nation, which also had significant gender implications. This is what we turn to now.

KHADI, NATION, WOMEN

Gandhi stated that he did not remember ever seeing a handloom or spinning wheel when he described it in *Hind Swaraj* 'as the panacea for the growing pauperism in India'. He assumed 'that anything that helped India to get rid of the grinding poverty of her masses would in the same process also establish Swaraj' (Gandhi 1960: 489). This path to *swaraj*, as Gandhi himself narrates, was not that easy to take. His *Autobiography* recounts the difficulties he and the inmates of the Sabarmati Ashram faced both in finding a spinning wheel and in getting someone willing to train them in the art of spinning.

'At last, after no end of wandering in Gujarat, Gangabehn found the spinning wheel in Vijapur in the Baroda state' (ibid.: 491). Several people there had the *charkha* in their homes, but tucked away in lofts 'as useless lumber'. Those people, however, were willing to resume spinning on condition that they were provided with a regular supply of slivers and that the yarn they spun was bought by someone. Gangabehn communicated the 'joyful news' to Gandhi, and after a halting start, the wheel began to 'hum merrily' in Gandhi's room and in the Ashram in general (ibid.: 493).

Thus began the career of *charkha* and khadi, an innocuous beginning that turned out to be momentous. The meanings and understanding of khadi and *charkha* were distinct and diverse; in a manner similar to *swaraj*, the plurality of understandings made them vibrant and vital symbols of the nation. If we follow Mehta, *charkha* and spinning, as well as other practices that Gandhi endorsed in his later years—celibacy, fasting and silence—all had the effect of 'amplifying the internal domain of the self'. They were practices that did not have any external product; they were practices which accentuated time and strengthened patience (Mehta 2003: 424). Whether or not spinning and *charkha* fortified interiority, they acquired connotations and significance that made them much more than mere 'practices'.

In an early essay, feminist scholar Madhu Kishwar had indicated how the *charkha* enabled Gandhi to raise 'simple, ordinary women' to the status of fellow workers for a common cause. Gangabehn, whose 'discovery' of the *charkha* Gandhi describes with such glee in his *Autobiography*, became 'a pioneer in a new era' from being 'a plain, ignorant Gujarati woman' (Kishwar 1985: 1753). Gangabehn did not only discover the spinning wheel; she also became the first organizer of the khadi movement in India.

The success of the khadi movement owed a lot to Gandhi's insistence not just on the production, but also on the 'exclusive consumption' of hand-spun and hand-woven cloth. Moves to popularize khadi involved exhibitions that demonstrated the process of production and also sold khadi. Such campaigns to popularize khadi, argues Lisa Trivedi, 'privileged a visual discourse of the nation' and turned *charkha* into a visual symbol that spread 'the idea of a national community' (2003: 11). '[S]wadeshi proponents made a map of the Indian nation visible through the figurative displays and literal paths of khadi tours and exhibitions. And in so doing, they 'visually reconfigured the map of India' in order 'both to build a national community and to lay claim to a national land' (Trivedi 2003: 11, 14).

The new visual map of the nation 'was characterized by a geography of community distinct both from the territorial divisions of pre-colonial and colonial India' (ibid.: 15). In addition, by insisting that *every* Indian spend half an hour a day in spinning for the 'benefit' of the nation, the proponents of khadi did not only disavow traditional class, caste and religious boundaries that marked the professions, they also succeeded in 'selecting, adapting, reorganizing and recreating' older representations of the national community (Duara 1995: 55). This visual language had great force and applicability since it appealed to the educated elite and the uneducated masses; it 'legitimized swadeshi by allowing the nationalists to ally with the larger population' (Trivedi 2003: 37). Khadi, in Manu Goswami's terms, provided vital materiality to the discursive discourse of the nation, enabling people to relate concretely to it (Goswami 1998).

For our purposes, it is important to relate the implications of these suggestive arguments to women. Spinning in India was largely associated with women while weavers were mostly men. The moral connotations Gandhi conferred on spinning elevated it to a noble activity undertaken for the cause of the nation, and allowed 'plain, ignorant' women like Ganagbehn to become national leaders. Even as a 'true, economic proposition' that supplied work to 'millions of villagers' (Gandhi 1958 Vol. 63: 77), spinning and weaving of khadi (or *khaddar* cloth) was superior to factory work since it curtailed mechanization that Gandhi was so opposed to (Chatterjee 1986: 89). For Gangabehn and other women who came in close contact with Gandhi, he was the one who followed an ideal and expected 'others to be equal to him in following this ideal' (Kishwar 1985: 1753). It was in this sense that Gandhi strove for 'equality' among men and women workers of the movement.

In addition, Gandhi's insistence on spinning being adopted by all—men and women alike—served, in Kishwar's opinion, to shake up sexual stereotypes. This, together with the fact that Gandhi took great personal care of the inmates of the Ashram that involved nursing them when they were sick, and prescribing a healthy diet which he tried out on himself, made him look more as a mother than as the father, Bapu. Gandhi's keen interest in food, diet and health lay in the close correspondence he saw between a healthy diet and healthy morals, imperative for the subjects of a truly free nation. In addition, he was also concerned about finding a healthy diet that was inexpensive and could be prescribed for the poorest.

The numerous articles that he published in *Young India* and the *Harijan* expressed his ideas on dietary reform and nutrition, as well as his self-assumed role as the physician of the nation. The mix-up of roles between a father who nursed and nurtured like a mother, certainly encouraged women to carve out a space for themselves within Gandhi's social and political programme. Indeed, several works have commented on how Gandhi brought in women, along with the 'masses' on to the public political scene. Women participated in large numbers in pickets, demonstrations and marches, particularly in the spectacular 'salt march' conducted by Gandhi to launch the Civil Disobedience movement in 1932 (Joshi 1988).

Two things need to be taken into consideration here. In the first place, middle-class leaders of the Congress had proposed that women (with property and other qualifications) be given the right to vote in the expanded electorate proposed by the Reforms of 1919. This is in tune with Chatterjee's analysis of the 'resolution of the women's question' by nationalists (Chatterjee 1990, 1993). If nationalist discourse had indeed succeeded in relocating the new, 'educated' and reformed woman within the inner domain of the nation, there was, by implication, no fear of having the truly educated woman participate in the 'public' domain of politics. The Congress leaders' proposal met with scorn from the British; how could Indian women be given the right to vote when most Indian men were not educated enough to vote responsibly? (Menon [1999] 2001: 8). More significant, perhaps, was the fact that women in England did not yet have the right. Could it be conferred on conservative, colonial India?

The second important thing to be borne in mind is that Gandhi's attitude towards women was ambivalent and contradictory. His understanding of the man-woman relationship, as reflected in his *Autobiography*, was highly coloured by his obsession with and revulsion for 'sex and sensuality', which he called 'lust' (Alter 1996; Gandhi 1960; Kishwar 1985: 1756). 'The conquest of lust', he wrote, 'is the highest endeavour of a man and a woman's existence'. Man cannot hope to rule over self without the conquest of lust, and *swaraj* was impossible without the rule over self. This was in consonance with Gandhi's insistence on and practice of *brahmacharya*, which was much more than abstinence or celibacy. *Brahmacharya* was a moral imperative and a philosophy of life that was critical for self-discipline and the health of the mind and body as well as for union with god (Corzo 2011; Gandhi 1921).

Although Gandhi thought of men as being more susceptible to 'lust', he verged on seeing women as temptresses whom men had to avoid in order to curb their lust successfully. His comparison of the British Parliament, which had 'not yet, of its own accord, done a single good thing', with a *veshya* (prostitute) and a *vaanjani* (a sterile woman) in *Hind Swaraj* (Gandhi 1938: 31) was perhaps an inadvertent articulation of this ambiguity. This comparison, comments Skaria, is indicative of the 'sexism' and tension that pervades *Hind Swaraj* (2007: 219). The *vaanjani* and the *veshya* are rejected with such force because they lack the 'proper', the *swa* which has to have a *'sthaan'* and *'thekaana'*—place/destination—to get to (ibid.: 224–25).

We cannot enter in detail into Skaria's intricate arguments; suffice it to say that the choice of words is representative of Gandhi's anxiety with regard to women's sexuality and its effect on men. Recent works have affirmed that in Gandhi's world women could only be mothers, sisters and wives; there was no place for the prostitute and the 'temptress' whom Gandhi attacked virulently (Tambe 2009). This was perhaps in keeping with his early childhood where women were his 'constant companions'—he was very close to his mother, his nurse Rambha, and his elder sister (Payne 1969: 26).

Gandhi valorized women for their powers of endurance and self-suffering, and spiritual and moral courage. This was in contrast to the social reformers of the nineteenth century who saw women as 'victims' to be saved and rescued. For Gandhi, the 'feminine qualities' of endurance, sacrifice and suffering had the strength to combat imperial power. In Nandy's terms, Gandhi upheld the notion that 'the essence of femininity is superior to that of masculinity, which in turn is better than cowardice' (1983: 53). Central to his notion of womanhood was 'the traditional Indian belief in the primacy of maternity over conjugality in feminine identity' (ibid.: 54). By 'rediscovering womanhood as a civilizing force in human society', Gandhi attacked 'the structure of sexual dominance as a homologue of both the colonial situation and the traditional social stratification' and overturned the colonial and patriarchal equation between 'masculinity and aggressive social dominance and between femininity and subjugation' (Nandy 1980: 74).

On the other hand, it is true that the heroines Gandhi chose for women to follow were Sita and Mira, not revered for their maternal instincts. Gandhi idolized these two characters as possessing immense capacity for suffering and self-sacrifice; and not for the power to control their own destiny (Kishwar 1985; Mukta 1994; Patel 1988). Gandhi was not in favour of women who could intervene forcefully to protect their own interests (Menon [1999] 2001: 9); nor did he encourage women to organize as a political force in their own right around their own issues (Kishwar 1985: 1757). It was clear in the role women participants played in the Non-Cooperation and Civil Disobedience movements. They were encouraged to lead pickets, marches and demonstrations since their inclination toward non-violence and self-control was highly valued; but women were hardly ever allowed to take important political decisions.

Gandhi saw the home as the main sphere of activity for women, except the exceptional woman who devoted herself selflessly to the service of humanity, which again was an extension of the domestic role of selfless service (ibid.: 1757). Gandhi's relationship with women in general was that of a leader and his devotees, even though he insisted on absolute personal dignity and autonomy of women in family and society.

When asked by Congress members if the wives should be forced to use khadi or actively participate in his programme to remove untouchability, Gandhi had exclaimed that 'wives were not properties of the husband, and hence should be given the freedom to decide on such matters' (Tendulkar 1960). In real life, however, he took unilateral decisions. He did not consult Kasturba before taking the vow of celibacy in 1906 (an idea he had been toying with since 1901), nor did he show much concern for her feelings when he enjoined her to clean toilets in order to put in practice the dignity of labour (Kishwar 1985: 1755). As stated earlier, his *Autobiography* bears testimony to the fact that over time Gandhi had come to respect Kasturba's stubborn autonomy and her capacity for silent resistance in opposing his initial overbearing attitude towards her. This, however, did not prevent him from coercing or cajoling her to join him in all his major ventures.

In an interesting effort to find reason in Gandhi's unilateral decisions in matrimony, Vinay Lal argues that since Gandhi's notion of *brahmacharya* implied that a married couple could engage in sexual relations only when there was mutual consent (Gandhi 1958 Vol. 30: 143), Gandhi perhaps did not think it necessary to consult Kasturba before taking the decision of desisting from sex (Lal 2000: 111).

Erik Erikson takes this a step further. For him, Gandhi deeply 'minded having to become a householder' and had it not been for the fact that Gandhi was committed to a 'normal course of life by child marriage' he 'might well have been a monastic saint instead of what he became: politician and reformer with an honorary sainthood' (1969: 399). Payne, for his part, feels that Kasturba, the devoted wife, had no problems in falling in line with Gandhi's decision of celibacy (1906). Gandhi's *Autobiography* indicates that Kasturba wanted to lead a celibate life as well, but makes no mention of the fact that he ever sought her opinion.

Kakar and Parekh see in Gandhi's insistence on celibacy a strong desire to acquire control over the body and sexuality (Kakar 1990; Parekh 1989). In Kakar's psychoanalytic approach, Gandhi's concern with celibacy was in harmony with the Hindu psychology of the body and Gandhi's wish to feminize himself. For Parekh, *brahmacharya* was an entirely spiritual project; he sees no connection between diet, health and morality that Gandhi practised and sought to transmit. Kakar too sees in Gandhi's obsession with food a symbolic displacement of sexuality, and disregards its bio-moral implications (Kakar 1990: 91; Corzo 2011).

Returning to the issue of Gandhi and women, scholars have argued that Gandhi's revulsion for sex and sensuality often led him to commit inner violence on people under his charge (Kishwar 1985: 1756). His order to young men and women of the Tolstoy farm to bathe naked in order to prove their sexual control or of his own practice of sharing his bed with younger women—the 18-year-old Manu, his granddaughter, for instance—had come under reproach almost from the beginning.

Nirmal Kumar Bose, who got to know Gandhi personally in 1934 and worked as his secretary during his tour of Noakhali in 1946, discusses the discomfort Gandhi's 'experiment' of self-control that involved sharing the bed with women caused among his close associates (Bose 1953). Distinguished co-workers such as Narahari Parekh and Kishorlal Mashruwala had objected to this 'experiment' on grounds of possible public repercussion and Parasuram, Gandhi's associate and stenographer, left him on account of disagreement over this particular matter (ibid.: 134–36).

Bose did not, in any way, accuse Gandhi of seeking secret sensual gratification; everything about Gandhi was public. Besides, in a letter to Munnalal G. Shah in 1945 Gandhi had openly talked about his practice of sleeping naked with women (Gandhi 1958 Vol. 86). Yet, for Bose, Gandhi's experiment demonstrated a singular 'incapability of understanding the problems of love or sex as they exist in the common human plane' (Bose 1953: 156). Alter finds in Gandhi's 'experiment' an egoism that utilized women as instruments subordinate to his sexual obsession (2000). In an earlier essay, Alter had stated that Gandhi's wish to create a nation free of passion, where every individual would exercise self-control, revealed a world constructed 'entirely from a male perspective, and derived from an unconscious sense of power in himself' (Alter 1994: 54).

In view of all this, one can state that the space women created for themselves within Gandhi's projects was largely the result of their perception and negotiation of Gandhi's message, teachings and activities. It bears pointing out here that a small group of elite Hindu women had begun taking active part in the nationalist struggle from the end of the nineteenth century. Young women students and housewives had distinguished themselves as participants and sympathizers of the Swadeshi movement. From the beginning of the twentieth century, women had also begun to work collectively against 'male supremacy'—a concerted move against 'patriarchal practices and imperialism' (Menon [1999] 2001: 7). This found articulation in the issues discussed by the All India Women's Conference formed in 1927—it focused on female education and the related problems of child-marriage and *purdah*, which in turn were consequent upon India's political subjection. Consequently, the movement for women's liberation got intimately tied to the struggle for independence (Kumar 1993).

Interestingly, while the khadi and *charkha* gave 'ordinary' women a moral right to engage in nationalist political activity, they often caused discomfiture for Gandhi's elite devotees, men and women. Sarala Devi Chaudhurani, a very close associate of Gandhi, whose emotional dependence on him raised quite a few eyebrows, was left pondering on whether a swadeshi (khadi) silk sari or a simple cotton *khaddar* dress would be appropriate for a Conference in May 1920. As she confessed in her letter to Gandhi, 'the point of the dilemma may not be well understood' but for her it was a crucial concern of how to present herself publicly—'to be smart and fashionable as of old or to be simple and common only' (Chaudhurani 1920 cited in Tarlo 2007: 387). Even before non-cooperation that popularized khadi at an all-India level, khadi had become a cause for worry. For Sarala Devi and many others, the dilemma was whether to join the ranks of the 'ordinary' that Gandhi brought into the nationalist struggle or to remain 'fashionable' and distinctive.

In a similar manner, elite women such as Sarojini Naidu were concerned with the aesthetic of the dress; it pained them to adopt the drab cotton khadi as permanent attire. Analogous concerns plagued Congressmen as well; this meant that soon there were distinctions between clothes made of coarse and fine *khaddar* as well as between cotton and silk khadi. It ended up creating hierarchies Gandhi sought to remove.

The dilemma of the elite was caused by Gandhi's avowal that the simplicity of 'dress' was a part of the 'proper' conduct of a true satyagrahi. Emma Tarlo (1996) lucidly portrays the intertwining of dress and identity in constructions of the nation, and argues that the seriousness with which Gandhi addressed the issue brought about a dramatic change not only in his own clothing, but also of others. Here too, as with other parts of his message, Gandhi's adoption of the loincloth, which has attained almost 'folkloric proportions', showed that there were wide discrepancies in the way 'Indians' viewed it (ibid.: 62–64). If the conflation of the loincloth with nudity bestowed divine powers on 'Gandhi Baba', his emphasis on the use of khadi as a moral statement generated awkwardness and confusion among his devoted middle-class followers.

In sum, the force of Gandhi's message lay in its polyvalence and amenability to diverse understandings and appropriations. Such perceptions made him the 'Mahatma'; they also led to his assassination. Gandhi's message revealed the possibilities and limits of a truly national struggle for *swaraj* even as it exposed the many contestations of both *swaraj* and the nation. His violent death perhaps embodies the violence that inheres in nations, making the achievement of a *swa*-raj premised on non-violence an elusive goal.

REFERENCES

Alter, Joseph T. 1994. 'Celibacy, Sexuality and the Transformation of Gender into Nationalism in North India'. *The Journal of Asian Studies* 53 (1): 45–66.

———. 1996. 'Gandhi's Body, Gandhi's Truth: Non-Violence and the Biomoral Imperative of Public Health'. *The Journal of Asian Studies* 55 (2): 301–22.

———. 2000. *Gandhi's Body, Sex, Diet and the Politics of Nationalism*. Pennsylvania, PA: University of Pennsylvania Press.

Amin, Shahid. 1984. 'Gandhi as Mahatma: Gorakhpur District, Eastern UP, 1921–2'. In *Subaltern Studies III: Writings on South Asian History and Society*, edited by R. Guha, 1–61. New Delhi: Oxford University Press.

———. 1995. *Event, Metaphor, Memory: Chauri Chaura 1922–1992*. Princeton, NJ: Princeton University Press.

———. 2004. 'They Also Followed Gandhi'. In *Postcolonial Passages: Contemporary History-writing on India*, edited by Saurabh Dube, 132–158. New Delhi: Oxford University Press.

Arnold, David. 2001. *Gandhi: Profiles in Power*. Edinburgh: Pearson Education.

Arnold, Edwin. 1886. *The Song Celestial or Bhagavad Gita*. London: Trübner and Co.

Bamford, P. C. 1925. *Histories of the Khilafat and Non Co-operation Movements*. Delhi: Government of India (Reprint 1974).

Bandyopadhyay, Gitasree. 1984. *Constraints in Bengal Politics 1921–41: Gandhian Leadership*. Calcutta: Sarat Book House.

Bandyopadhyay, Sekhar. 2004. *From Plassey to Partition: A History of Modern India*. Hyderabad: Orient Longman.

Banerjee-Dube, Ishita. 2003. 'Reading Time: Texts and Pasts in Colonial Eastern India'. *Studies in History* 19 (1): 1–17.

Basham, A. L. 1971. 'Traditional Influences on the Thoughts of Mahatma Gandhi'. In *Essays on Gandhian Politics: The Rowlatt Satyagraha of 1919*, edited by R. Kumar, 17–42. Oxford: Clarendon Press,

Bhaduri, Satinath. 1973. 'Dhorai Charitmanas'. In *Satinath Granthabali*, Vol. 2: 1–296. Calcutta: Signet.

Bose, Nirmal Kumar. 1953. *My Days with Gandhi*. Calcutta: Nishana.

Brown, Judith M. 1972. *Gandhi's Rise to Power: Indian Politics 1915–1922*. Cambridge: Cambridge University Press.

Carpenter, Edward. 1889. *Civilisation: Its Cause and Cure*. London: S. Sonnenschien and Co.

Chatterjee, Partha. 1984. 'Gandhi and the Critique of Civil Society'. In *Subaltern Studies III: Writings on South Asian History and Society*, edited by R. Guha, 153–95. New Delhi: Oxford University Press.

———. 1986. *Nationalist Thought and the Colonial World: A Derivative Discourse?* New Delhi: Oxford University Press.

———. 1990. 'Nationalist Resolution of the Women's Question'. In *Recasting Women*, edited by Kumkum Sangari and Sudesh Vaid, 233–253. New Brunswick: Rutgers University Press.

———. 1993. *The Nation and Its Fragments: Colonial and Postcolonial Histories*. Princeton, NJ: Princeton University Press.

Corzo, Lizzette Maily. 2011. 'Gandhi y su verdad sobre el cuerpo: salud, dieta y sexualidad'. M.A. dissertation. México: El Colegio de México.

Das, R. K. 1923. *Factory Labor in India*. Leipzig: W. de Gruyter & Co.

Desai, Mahadev H. 1968. *Day-to-day with Gandhi: Secretary's Diary*. Varanasi: Sarva Seva Sangh Prakashan.

Duara, Prasenjit. 1995. *Rescuing History from the Nation: Questioning Narratives of Modern China*. Chicago: University of Chicago Press.

Erikson, Eric H. 1969. *Gandhi's Truth: On the Origins of Militant Nonviolence*. New York: W. Norton and Company.

Gandhi, Mohandas Karamchand. 1921. *An Autobiography or The Story of My Experiments with Truth*. Ahmedabad: Navajivan Publishing House.

———. 1938. *Hind Swaraj or Indian Home Rule*. Ahmedabad: Navajivan Publishing House.

———. 1951. *Satyagraha*. Ahmedabad: Navajivan Trust.

———. 1958. *The Collected Works of Mahatma Gandhi*. 87 volumes. New Delhi: Publications Division, Government of India.

———. 1960. *An Autobiography or The Story of My Experiments with Truth*. Trans. Mahadev Desai. Boston: Beacon Press in arrangement with the Navajivan Trust, Bombay. Fourth edition. First published, Bombay: Navajivan Trust, 1940.

———. 1997. *The Mahatma and the Poet: Letters and Debates Between Gandhi and Tagore, 1915–1941*. Edited and compiled by Sabyasachi Bhattacharya. New Delhi: National Book Trust.

———. 2008. *An Autobiography: The Story of My Experiments with Truth*. Kindle edition, Formax Publishing. Online version: http://www.holybooks.com/wp-content/uploads/M.-K.-Gandhi-An-Autobiography-or-The-Story-of-my-Experiments-with-Truth.pdf

Gordon, Leonard A. 1974. *Bengal: The Nationalist Movement 1876–1940*. New York: Columbia University Press.

Gordon, Richard. 1973. 'Non Co-operation and Council Entry, 1919 to 1920'. In *Locality, Province and Nation: Essays on Indian Politics, 1870–1940*, edited by J. Gallagher, Gordon Johnson and Anil Seal, 123–54. Cambridge: Cambridge University Press.

Goswami, Manu. 1998. 'From *Swadeshi* to *Swaraj*: Nation, Economy, Territory in Colonial South Asia, 1870 to 1907'. *Comparative Studies in Society and History* 40 (4): 609–36.

Guha, Ramchandra. 2013. *Gandhi before India*. UK: Penguin books.

Guha, Ranajit ed. 1982. *Subaltern Studies I: Writings on South Asian History and Society*. New Delhi: Oxford University Press.

———. 1983a. *Elementary Aspects of Peasant Insurgency in Colonial India*. New Delhi: Oxford University Press.

———, ed. 1983b. *Subaltern Studies II: Writings on South Asian History and Society*. New Delhi: Oxford University Press.

———, ed. 1984. *Subaltern Studies III: Writings on South Asian History and Society*. New Delhi: Oxford University Press.

Hardiman, David. 1981. *Peasant Nationalists of Gujarat: Kheda District, 1917–1934*. New Delhi: Oxford University Press.

———. 1984. 'Adivasi Assertion in South Gujarat: The Devi Movement of 1922–3.' In *Subaltern Studies III: Writings on South Asian History and Society*, edited by Ranajit Guha, 196–230. New Delhi: Oxford University Press.

———. 1996. *Feeding the Baniya: Peasants and Usurers in Western India*. New Delhi: Oxford University Press.

Hay, Stephen. 1989. 'The Making of a Late-Victorian Hindu: M. K. Gandhi in London, 1888–1891'. *Victorian Studies* 33 (1): 74–98.

Henningham, Stephen. 1982. *Peasant Movements in Colonial India: North Bihar, 1917–1942*. Canberra: Australian National University.

Hofmeyr, Isabel. 2013. *Gandhi's Printing Press: Experiments in Slow Reading*. Cambridge, MA: Harvard University Press.

Hunt, James D. [1978] 1993. *Gandhi in London*. New Delhi: Promilla and Co.

Joshi, Priya. 1988. *Gandhi on Women*. Ahmedabad: Navajivan Trust.

Kakar, Sudhir. 1990. *Intimate Relations: Exploring Indian Sexuality*. Chicago: University of Chicago Press.

Kishwar, Madhu P. 1985. 'Gandhi on Women'. *Economic and Political Weekly* 20 (41) (October 12): 1753–58.

Krishna, Gopal. 1966. 'The Development of the Indian National Congress as a Mass Organization'. *The Journal of Asian Studies* 25 (3): 413–30.

Kumar, Kapil. 1984. *Peasants in Revolt: Tenants, Landlords, Congress and the Raj in Oudh, 1886–1922.* New Delhi: Manohar.

Kumar, Radha. 1993. *The History of Doing: An Illustrated History.* New Delhi: Kali for Women.

Kumar, Ravinder. 1969. 'Class, Community or Nation? Gandhi's Quest for a Popular Consensus in India'. *Modern Asian Studies* 3 (4): 357–76.

———. 1971. Introduction to *Essays on Gandhian Politics: The Rowlatt Satyagraha of 1919*, edited by R. Kumar, 1–16 . Oxford: Clarendon Press.

———. 1983. 'The Rowlatt Satyagraha in Lahore'. In *Essays in the Social History of Modern India*, edited by R. Kumar, 148–212. New Delhi: Oxford University Press.

Lal, Vinay. 2000. 'Nakedness, Non-violence, and *Brahmacharya*: Gandhi's Experiments in Celibate Sexuality'. *Journal of the History of Sexuality* 9 (1–2): 105–36.

Markovits, Claude. 2003. *The Un-Gandhian Gandhi: The Life and Afterlife of the Mahatma.* Delhi: Permanent Black.

McLane, John R, ed. 1970. *The Political Awakening in India.* Englewood Cliffs, NJ: Prentice Hall.

Mehta, Uday S. 2003. 'Patience, Inwardness, and Self-Knowledge in Gandhi's *Hind Swaraj*'. *Public Culture* 23 (2): 417–29.

Menon, Nivedita. [1999] 2001. Introduction to *Gender and Politics in India*, edited by N. Menon, 1–36. New Delhi: Oxford University Press.

Minault, Gail. 1982. *The Khilafat Movement: Religious Symbolism and Political Mobilization in India.* New Delhi: Oxford University Press.

Mukta, Parita. 1994. *Upholding the Common Life: The Community of Mirabai.* New Delhi: Oxford University Press.

Nandy, Ashis. 1980. *At the Edge of Psychology.* New Delhi: Oxford University Press.

———. 1983. *The Intimate Enemy: Loss and Recovery of Self Under Colonialism.* New Delhi: Oxford University Press.

Parekh, Bhikhu. 1989. *Gandhi's Political Philosophy: A Critical Examination.* Notre Dame, IA: University of Notre Dame Press.

Patel, Sujata. 1988. 'The Construction and Reconstruction of Women in Gandhi'. *Economic and Political Weekly* 33 (8): 377–87.

Payne, Robert. 1969. *The Life and Death of Mahatma Gandhi.* London: The Bodley Head.

Pouchepadass, J. 1974. 'Local Leaders and the Intelligentsia in the Champaran Satyagraha (1917): A Study in Peasant Mobilization'. *Contributions to Indian Sociology* (n.s.) 8: 67–87.

———. 1999. *Champaran and Gandhi: Planters, Peasants and Gandhian Politics.* New Delhi: Oxford University Press.

Pratt, Tim and James Vernon. 2005. '"Appeal from This Fiery Bed … ": The Colonial Politics of Gandhi's Fasts and Their Metropolitan Reception'. *Journal of British Studies* 44 (1): 92–114.

Ray, Rajat Kanta. 1974. 'Masses in Politics: The Noncooperation Movement in Bengal 1920–1922'. *The Indian Economic and Social History Review* 11 (4): 343–410.

———. 1984. *Social Conflict and Political Unrest in Bengal, 1875–1927.* New Delhi: Oxford University Press.

Robb, Peter G. 1976. *The Government of India and Reform: Policies Toward Politics and the Constitution, 1916–1921.* Oxford: Oxford University Press.

Robinson, Francis. 1973. 'Municipal Government and Muslim Separatism in the United Provinces, 1883 to 1916'. *Modern Asian Studies* 7 (3): 389–441.

———. [1974] 2007. *Separatism among Indian Muslims: The Politics of the United Provinces' Muslims, 1860–1923*. Cambridge: Cambridge University Press.

———. 2001. *The Ulama of Farangi Mahal and Islamic Culture in South Asia*. London: C. Hurst Publishers.

Rolland, Romain. 1976. *Romain Rolland and Gandhi Correspondence*. New Delhi: Publications Division, Ministry of Information and Broadcasting, Government of India.

Rudolph, Susan H. 1963. 'The New Courage: An Essay on Gandhi's Psychology'. *World Politics* 16 (1): 98–117.

Sarkar, Sumit. [1983] 1995. *Modern India 1885–1947*. Madras: Macmillan India.

———. 1984. 'The Conditions and Nature of Subaltern Militancy: Bengal from Swadeshi to NonCooperation, *c.* 1905–22'. In *Subaltern Studies III: Writings on South Asian History and Society*, edited by R. Guha, 271–320. New Delhi: Oxford University Press.

Siddiqi, Majid. 1978. *Agrarian Unrest in North India: The United Provinces, 1918–1922*. New Delhi: Vikas Publishing House.

Skaria, Ajay. 2007. 'Only One Word, Properly Altered: Gandhi and the Question of the Prostitute'. *Postcolonial Studies* 10 (2): 219–37.

———. 2011. 'Gandhi's Religion'. In *Modern Makeovers: Oxford Handbook of Modernity*, edited by Saurabh Dube, 110–23. New Delhi: Oxford University Press.

———. Forthcoming. 'Introduction: Surrender without Subordination'. In *Immeasurable Equality: Gandhi and the Gift of Religion*. Extracted with permission from the author.

Stein, Burton. 2010. *A History of India*. Revised and edited by David Arnold. Sussex, UK: Wiley-Blackwell. (First published 1998. Oxford: Oxford University Press).

Swan, Maureen. 1985. *Gandhi: The South African Experience*. Johannesburg: Ravan Press.

Tagore, Rabindranath. 1921. '"Letters to a Friend", Rabindranath Tagore to C. F. Andrews'. *Modern Review* xxix (5): 612–15. Included in *The English Writings of Rabindranath Tagore*, Vol. 3, edited by Sisir Kumar Das. New Delhi: Sahitya Akademi, 1996.

Tambe, Ashwini. 2009. *Codes of Misconduct: Regulating Prostitution in Late Colonial Bombay*. Minneapolis: University of Minnesota Press.

Tarlo, Emma. 1996. *Clothing Matters: Dress and Identity in India*. Chicago: University of Chicago Press.

———. 2007. 'Is Khadi the Solution?'. In *Historical Anthropology*, edited by Saurabh Dube, 387–401. New Delhi: Oxford University Press.

Tendulkar, D. G. 1951. *Mahatma: Life of Mohandas Karamchand Gandhi*. Bombay: (n.p.).

———. 1960. *Mahatma*. Vol. 1. New Delhi: Publications Division, Ministry of Information and Broadcasting (First published 1869).

Thompson, Edward and G. T. Garratt. 1958. *Rise and Fulfilment of British Rule in India*. Repr. Allahabad: Central Book Depot.

Tomlinson, B. R. 1976. *The Indian National Congress and the Raj, 1929–1942: The Penultimate Phase*. London: Macmillan.

Trivedi, Lisa N. 2003. 'Visually Mapping the "Nation": Swadeshi Politics in Nationalist India, 1920–1930'. *The Journal of Asian Studies* 62 (1): 11–41.

Woods, P. 1994. 'The Montagu Chelmsford Reforms (1919): A Reassessment'. *South Asia* 17 (1): 25–42.

Difficulties and Initiatives

8

Abdul Ghaffar Khan with 'Red Shirts' in the North West Frontier Province, 1931

Chapter outline

This chapter examines the critical years between 1922 and 1935—the time between the suspension of the Non-Cooperation movement and the passing of the Government of India Act by the colonial state as a step towards self-rule. It is a period in which criss-crossing and contradictory processes and energies, often stimulated by the institutional reforms of the colonial state and moulded by the interface of 'imperialism' and 'nationalism', gave meaning to nation, community and identity and shaped the nationalist struggle in vital ways. It takes a quick look at the activities of peasant organizations prior to, during, and after non-cooperation, examines business attitudes toward nationalism, imperialism, and labour and tracks the evolution of the labour force in the context of both Communist and Congress activities and the effect of world economic processes. Finally, it discusses the Government of India Act of 1935 and its ramifications for colonial and independent India.

The efficacy of the Non-Cooperation movement in involving the 'masses' lay in its ability to draw in a diverse range of local struggles. The active participation of the peasants, in particular, was crucial for the movement. Chapter 7 discussed the critical role played by peasants in the United Provinces (UP), Bihar and several other regions. The annexation of Awadh in 1856 and consequent increase in the power of *taluqdar*s in the region had brought the peasants under extreme strain and made them restive; members of UP's Home Rule League had taken the initiative in organizing the peasants. The UP Kisan Sabha, set up in February 1918, had expanded rapidly to include 450 branches in 173 *tehsil*s of the province (Chandra et al. [1989] 2000: 197; Pandey 1982; Siddiqi 1978).

Baba Ramchandra, a Brahman from Maharashtra who had had a colourful career that included being an indentured labourer in Fiji and a *sadhu* in India, emerged as a leader of the disaffected peasants of Awadh in 1920 (Kumar 1984). In June 1920, he went at the head of a few hundred tenants from Pratapgarh and Jaunpur to Allahabad, where he met Gauri Shankar Misra, leader of Home Rule, and Jawaharlal Nehru of the Indian National Congress, and asked them to visit the villages in order to see the poor condition of the tenants. This established a link between peasant protesters and the Congress, and enabled the Congress to draw in the mobilized peasants within its non-cooperation programme (Dhanagre 1975, 1983; Siddiqi 1978). The Kisan Sabhas, it bears pointing out, had attracted the important cultivating communities of Ahirs, Kurmis and Koeris. Hence, the support of these Sabhas for Congress-led agitations in the 1920s and 1930s considerably enhanced the Congress' strength.

In Bihar and Bengal as well, non-cooperation owed its effectiveness to the participation of peasants. In Bihar they were organized against the planters under the banner of Kisan Sabha and in Midnapore, Bengal, Mahishya peasants rallied against the taxes of the Union Board under the leadership of Birendra Nath Sasmal (Bandyopadhyay 1984: 26–27; Das 1983; Henningham 1982; Ray 1984). There were a series of anti-feudal uprisings in Rajasthan throughout the 1920s—the Bhil movement inspired by Motilal Tejawat in Mewar, the satyagrahas offered by the peasants of Alwar state against a 50 per cent increase in land revenue in 1925 and the insurgencies in Bijonia in 1927 (Sarkar [1983] 1995: 240–41).

Similarly, 'tribal' areas, such as the Kanika region in Orissa, were party to a number of *meli*s, anti-landlord uprisings. The Gudem Rampa Hills in present Andhra Pradesh that had seen insurgency in the nineteenth century (see Chapter 3), together with the Godavari and Krishna deltas and Guntur district in the south became zones of great unrest once again as a direct consequence of the enthusiasm generated by the promise of *swaraj*. Leadership was provided by local chiefs and outsiders who held out the promise of the end of *kaliyuga*. The wide and refracted appeal of Gandhi's message inspired these people; they also regarded 'violence' to be a necessary part of their struggle.

At the same time, peasant struggles that came within the Congress fold were all led by wealthy peasants who kept the poor agricultural labourers in control—the Patidars of Gujarat and the Mahisyas of Midnapore are cases in point (Bandyopadhyay 2004: 307).

In Shahabad, UP, the Ahirs and Kurmis came together in an 'unusual (and perhaps unprecedented) "lower-middle caste" peasant association called the Triveni Sangh' to resist being oppressed and exploited by the upper castes and classes in the area. They remained hostile to Congress-led movements till 1942 (Pandey 1992: 204). The Congress also refused to intervene in any movement in the princely states till 1938, even though the peasants in Alwar adopted Gandhian methods, and the impact of Gandhi led to the emergence of urban middle-class Praja Parishads in the princely states of Baroda and Kathiawad in the second decade of the twentieth century.

The Kisan Sabhas in turn were not united in their programme of action. There were tensions among Kisan Sabhas that totally fell in line with non-cooperation and others that kept a distance from it. In UP, for instance, Kisan Sabhas that owed allegiance to Congress leader Madan Mohan Malaviya, who was critical of non-cooperation, were at odds with the ones that supported non-cooperation wholeheartedly. At the height of the Non-Cooperation movement, when rumours of Gandhi's appearance were circulating, the non-cooperators formed their own Oudh Kisan Sabha, which integrated several others. This Sabha urged peasants not to till *bedakhli* (reclaimed) land, or offer *hari* and *begar* (unpaid labour); it also encouraged them to solve their disputes through panchayats. The Sabha decided to boycott peasants who did not accept these conditions.

The Oudh Kisan Sabha demonstrated its strength in organizing a mammoth public rally on 20 and 21 December 1920; about 100,000 peasants showed up. Soon, however, Kisan Sabha activists were replaced by *sadhus*, holy men, and disinherited proprietors who gave leadership to looting of bazaars, houses, granaries and clashes with the police. This brought forth severe state repression and by April the Kisan Sabha movement had almost died down.

A different movement surfaced in Hardoi, Bahraich and Sitapur districts in UP from the end of 1921. The Eka (unity) movement brought tenants and small zamindars together to protest against forced extraction of rents that were much higher than recorded rent rates; the oppression of *thekadar*s who bought the right of rent collection; and the practice of sharing rents. In the meetings, assembled peasants took a vow to pay only the recorded rent, not leave when evicted, not do forced labour, not help criminals and accept the decisions of the panchayat. Leadership of the movement was provided by Madari Pasi and other lower caste leaders and petty zamindars. Congress and Khilafat leaders gave initial support to the Eka movement but withdrew their support because the lower-caste tenants of the movement did not tow the Congress line of non-violence. This movement was also brought to an end by state repression.

The Akalis (servants of eternal god) in Punjab offered an interesting illustration of the deployment of non-violence. Deriving their name from the small band of martyr warriors formed during the time of Ranjit Singh to defend the faith and inspired by the activities of the Singh Sabha movement in the late-nineteenth century (Oberoi 1994: 235–52; Chapter 3), the Akalis strove to 'purify' Sikhism and demarcate it from other faiths such as Hinduism (Brass 1974; Singh 1966). They established a

Shiromoni Gurdwara Prabandhak Committee in 1920 and tried to reclaim the management of Sikh shrines and gurudwaras from the hands of 'government manipulated loyalist committees' that included non-Sikhs (Bandyopadhyay 2004: 305). The Akalis challenged the appointment of a new manager for the Golden Temple in Amritsar, clashed with the colonial government in 1921, and faced government repression with stolid non-violence.

The Akalis, according to Richard Fox, demonstrated the longest and most efficacious application of Gandhi's programme of satyagraha (1985: 78). However, as is evident from the objectives of the Akalis, except for adopting non-violence as a mode of struggle, they had very little in common with the non-cooperation programme. The Gandhi-led Congress upheld the cause of the Akalis for a while. This enabled the Akalis to coerce the government to return the key of the Golden Temple and leave the management in their hands. Soon, however, the Akalis moved away from the Congress in order to retain their separate religious identity (Bandyopadhyay 2004: 306).

The contingent confluence of forces that gave great significance to non-cooperation meant that once the movement was called off in February 1922, diverse struggles took separate courses, away from the Congress. The popularity of the Congress reached a record low with its membership (in 16 out of 20 provinces) declining to 106,046; far less than the number of members in UP alone in 1920. For British Viceroy Lord Reading, the Congress was almost a spent force: the Bardoli resolution had left it 'without any clearly defined and intelligible objectives', and had produced disorganization, disillusionment and discouragement in the ranks of the party (Chandra et al. [1972] 1975: 139–40).

The Khilafat issue also lost its significance with the rise of Mustafa Kamal Pasha to power in Turkey in 1922. Kamal Pasha stripped the Sultan of all political powers and abolished the Caliphate as a part of his programme of modernizing Turkey and making it secular.

SWARAJ PARTY, HINDU MAHASABHA, COMMUNAL CONFLICT

A spate of riots in the wake of the Khilafat Non-Cooperation struggle violently shook the notion of Hindu-Muslim unity. The report of the committee, set up by the Congress to enquire into the causes of the Kanpur riots in 1931, provided a detailed list of Hindu-Muslim riots that occurred in the 1920s, and stressed the magnitude 'the problem had assumed over the past decade' (Barrier 1976: 228).

Voices that had been drowned in the non-cooperation wave now found expression. The Hindu Mahasabha, formed in 1915 as a part of the Congress but with radical Hindu nationalist objectives, emerged as a strong critic of the Congress in the 1920s. The Mahasabha, it bears pointing out, had emerged out of the spirit of swadeshi and as a reaction to the Muslim League (Mathur 1996). It deployed the idea of swadeshi to 'protect' India's culture and religion, which it took to be Hindu. The Mahasabha had a very limited base in its initial phase; it was composed almost entirely of upper-caste and upper-class Hindu males and had branches only in a few towns and cities of north India—Allahabad, Lucknow, Benares and Lahore (Hansen 2001: 291). Members of the Mahasabha had virulently opposed the Lucknow Pact, in particular the allocation of seats to Muslims in UP which took into account their social standing and not just their numerical strength. Limited both in number and in support base, the Mahasabha did not have much success in 1916.

The emergence of Vinayak Damodar Savarkar, as a leader of the Mahasabha in the 1920s, gave a new boost to the organization. Savarkar had begun his 'political career' at the age of ten in 1893 by throwing stones at a village mosque during the cow-killing riots (McLane 1970: 124). Savarkar, who came to head the Mahasabha in the 1930s, provided the organization with the ideology of Hindutva, which was to have far-reaching consequences (Kent 2011). In his book *Hindutva*, written in Andaman Jail in 1917, Savarkar expounded the idea of a Hindu *rashtra*, state/nation (Pandey 1992: 234; Savarkar 1949). This idea found increasing acceptance in the 1920s. In two sessions held in 1922 and 1923, the Mahasabha declared itself as the defender of the Hindu community against the incursions of Muslims organized under the Muslim League. The limited base of the Mahasabha notwithstanding, its activities further vitiated relations amongst elite Hindus and Muslims in north India and limited the capacity of the Congress to negotiate with the League.

Savarkar's ideology of Hindutva stimulated activities in Maharashtra and indirectly influenced the establishment of the Rashtriya Swayam Sevak Sangh in Nagpur in 1925 by K. B. Hedgewar, an associate of Moonje, Tilak's old follower. Inspired by the idea of a Hindu *rashtra*, Hedgewar argued that since 'Hindu society' had lived in the country 'since times immemorial' and was the 'national society', and since the 'same Hindu people' had built the 'life-values, ideals and culture' of the country, their nationhood was 'self-evident' (Goyal 1979: 40; Hedgewar 1972; Pandey 1992: 235).

The Congress, argues Jaffrelot, came to be haunted by a tussle between two rival notions of nationalism, one that believed in composite culture and held the nation above community, and the other—expounded by the Mahasabha sympathizers in the Congress—that upheld the idea of majority rule by Hindus and the subordination of Muslims (Jaffrelot 1996). Given the fact that the Congress often had to bow down or make compromises with protagonists of the second group, Muslim leaders grew weary and suspicious of the Congress' real intent (Bandyopadhyay 2004: 336).

Within the Congress, the suspension of non-cooperation before the beginning of civil disobedience caused sudden dissipation of enthusiasm. Questions were asked about the efficacy of satyagraha and the possibility of training the 'masses' in the path of non-violence in the near future. Gandhi's constructive programme failed to inspire many. At this stage, Chittaranjan Das and Motilal Nehru suggested that instead of continuing with the boycott of government institutions and, in particular, the councils, it was better to enter the councils and wreck them from within by obstructing all proceedings. The suggestion found ready support among several Congressmen, but stalwart Gandhians, such as Vallabhbhai Patel, Rajendra Prasad and C. Rajagopalachari insisted on continuing with boycott and constructive programme.

The two groups, those who wanted to change or modify the boycott programme in order to enter the councils and those who wanted no change in the Gandhian programme, are referred to in historiography as the 'Pro-changers' and the 'No-changers'. Both groups were opposed to the dyarchy or dual-rule introduced by the 1919 Reforms (Chapter 7). For Das, dyarchy was the British Parliament's attempt to force a foreign system upon the Indian people; the councils therefore, had either to be mended or ended (Bahadur 1983: 79). And that could only be done if Congress entered the councils and boycotted them from within.

The differences between the two groups became evident at the annual session of the Congress in Gaya in December 1922. Chittaranjan Das, the President of the session, made a vigorous attempt to get the decision on entry into the councils accepted by the delegates. He and his supporters, however, failed in front of the stiff opposition put up by the No-changers headed by Rajagopalachari. Following this, Das resigned as President and formed the Congress-Khilafat-Swaraj Party within the Congress on 31 December 1922. He was aided by Motilal Nehru and Malaviya from UP, Lajpat Rai from Punjab, M. R. Jayakar and Vithalbhai Patel from Gujarat, the 'Tilak group' from Bombay and some leaders from south India (Gordon 1974: 188). The party's manifesto was signed in January 1923. It became both a minority faction within the Congress and an independent organization 'running candidates for legislatures outside the purview of the Congress' (ibid.: 190).

The 1923 annual session of the Congress in Coconada adopted a resolution allowing such Congressmen who 'have no religious or other conscientious objections against entering legislature' the liberty to 'stand as candidates and to exercise their right of voting at the forthcoming elections' (Bandyopadhyay 1984: 78).

The plan, programme and constitution of the Swaraj Party (Swarajya Party) were drawn up at its first conference in Allahabad in 1924. Chittaranjan Das became the President of this new party and Motilal Nehru one of its secretaries. Essentially a party of 'upper middle-class intellectuals who had been opposed to mass involvement in politics' (Bandyopadhyay 1984: 82), the Swaraj Party worked out a compromise between socialism and individualism in its programme of action (Bahadur 1983: 106). The programme included mass contact, Hindu–Muslim unity and social work and social reform in addition to the main effort directed at wrecking the constitutional reforms from within.

The attainment of dominion status for India was declared to be the immediate goal of the party, which was to be attained by means of nationalist candidates contesting and securing seats in legislative councils and the assembly in the forthcoming elections (ibid.: 79). Gandhi, released from jail in February 1924 on grounds of health, stoutly opposed the idea of Council-entry even though he maintained good personal relations with Nehru and Das, whom he counted among the 'most valued and respected leaders' who 'have made great sacrifices in the cause of the country' (Chandra et al. [1989] 2000: 239).

The Swaraj Party did not discard the essential principles of non-violent non-cooperation. At the same time, it wanted to participate in the legislative assemblies and councils to try and undo the limited reforms of 1919. The Swarajists wanted to lay claim to the right of framing a constitution for India. If the government refused to grant this right, members of the party intended to resort to 'uniform, consistent and continuous obstruction with a view to make government through the assembly and councils impossible' (Chandra et al. [1972] 1975: 144). The Swaraj Party relied on 'construction through obstruction for the sake of reforms—political, constitutional, social, and economic—all leading to the achievement of swaraj' (Bahadur 1983: x). The party's leaders, it appears, had been considerably influenced by the idea of 'sabotage' outlined in Michael O'Dwyer's book *India as I Knew It*. In this book, O'Dwyer stated that sabotage, or disruption from within, was a strategy of resistance, much more difficult to deal with than open rebellion (ibid.).

The Das–Nehru combine worked well for a time and the Swaraj Party did very well in the Council elections of 1923. It won an absolute majority in the Central Provinces, became the largest party in the Bengal Council and the second largest in UP and Assam, and captured 42 out of 101 seats in the Central Legislative Assembly. It formed a coalition—the Nationalist Party—in the Central Legislative Assembly that included 30 Moderate and Muslim members. Motilal Nehru became the leader of the opposition in the Central Legislative Assembly and N. C. Kelkar and Govind Ballabh Pant played important roles as members of the opposition in the provincial assemblies of the Central Provinces and UP respectively.

In Bengal, B. C. Roy ousted veteran leader Surendranath Banerjea who had become a minister in 1921. 'Deshabandhu' Chittaranjan Das' able and astute leadership allowed the Swarajists to maintain a broad coalition of Calcutta politicians, district leaders, such as Biren Sasmal who had experience of working with the masses, revolutionary cadres, and Muslim leaders. Das, it has been stated, had a 'rare gift' for recruiting and selecting able, intelligent and committed lieutenants and supporters and was 'adept at delegating responsibilities to them' (Gordon 1974: 192). Muslim leaders were won over by the Bengal Pact proposed by Das. It offered 55 per cent of the administrative posts to Muslims in Bengal after the attainment of *swaraj* and suggested the prohibition of music before mosques and non-intervention in cow slaughter during the Bakr-Id festival (Sarkar [1983] 1995: 232).

During its brief period of success in the councils, particularly in the Central Legislative Council, the Swaraj Party demanded the release of all political prisoners, the repeal of repressive laws, provincial autonomy and an immediate Round Table Conference that would discuss a scheme for full control of the government by councils. Vithalbhai Patel, a prominent nationalist from Gujarat, was elected President of the Central Council in March 1925; he demonstrated considerable skills as a parliamentarian.

Elected representatives of the party put pressure on the administration to acquiesce to its demands by threatening to block the voting of (food) supplies and provisions in the Councils. Swarajist members in the Central Council also refused to sanction the salaries of dyarchy ministers in the Central Provinces and in Bengal, which forced them to resign. Members of the Swaraj Party established close links with Indian business groups and were instrumental in pushing the government to grant protection in 1924 to the Tata Industrial Steel Company (TISCO), set up in 1907 at the height of the swadeshi era. Local bodies and municipalities all over the country came to be dominated by Congress members—Jawaharlal Nehru in Allahabad, Vithalbhai Patel in Ahmedabad and Chittaranjan Das and Subhas Bose in Calcutta—who initiated some welfare activities and collected funds.

The Swaraj Party managed to have an impact on the Government of India, the Government at England, and on India as a whole for a brief period. Dyarchy was wrecked in Bengal and in the Central Provinces; salt tax and railway fares were reduced, there was a remission of provincial contributions, a repeal of cotton excise duty, and imposition of duties for the protection of national industries. Swarajist policy forced the governors to use their 'certificate' powers constantly to push through legislations; this exposed the very limited nature of the 1919 Reforms. The House of Commons in the British Parliament became aware of and sympathetic to Indian sentiments (ibid.: 249). In India, remarked Congress leader Rajendra Prasad, the work of the Swaraj Party conducted with tact and firmness, 'was creditable and they achieved whatever could be achieved by their tactics under the constitution' (1927: xxvi).

At the same time, Swarajist activities did not bring about changes in administration as the party had expected. The certificate powers of the Viceroy and governors severely restricted the powers of elected members even if it showed dyarchy to be a sham. For instance, the Swarajists could do nothing when Subhas Bose was detained without trial in 1924 along with several others for suspected terrorist links under an ordinance that became an act in 1925. To make matters worse, the Labour government elected in Britain in 1923 proved to be short lived and the Conservatives returned to power in 1925. The new Secretary of State felt that the 1919 Reforms had gone too far and was totally opposed to the idea of promising further reforms before the ten years, proposed in the 1919 Act, had elapsed. In March 1926, the Swarajists 'contemptuously rejected the collaboration offered', and decided to walk out of the Central Legislative Assembly in search of alternative modes of achieving their object (Nehru cited in Chandra et al. [1972] 1975: 145).

This strategy of 'walk-in' and 'walk-out' was not only ineffective, it also contributed to an erosion of the party's strength, which was badly hit by the sudden death of Chittaranjan Das in 1925. Even before Das' death, Madan Mohan Malaviya, S. B. Tambe, Lajpat Rai and N. C. Kelkar had decided to change strategy and offer 'responsive cooperation' to the government by accepting executive posts (Bahadur 1983). This change of tactics was supposedly meant to safeguard the interest of Hindus against the onslaught of Jinnah and the Muslim League. Even if this were true, there is no denying that access to patronage that executive posts gave had no minor role to play in the decision.

S. B. Tambe was the first to accept a ministerial position in the Central Provinces in October 1925; he was bitterly criticized by Motilal Nehru but supported by Swarajists from Bombay and Maharashtra such as Kelkar, B. S. Moonje and M. R. Jayakar. This fissure at a time when the Hindu Mahasabha and the Muslim League were both becoming active demoralized the party and generated communal tension. Prior to the elections of 1926, Motilal's old rival Malaviya formed the Independent Congress Party with Lajpat Rai and the 'Responsive Cooperators'. It adopted a programme of moderate cooperation and aggressive action against the Muslim League. Motilal Nehru alone could not offer adequate leadership and the election results of 1926 spelled disaster for the Swarajists.

Madan Mohan Malaviya, the Congress-Swarajist leader from UP, increasingly towed the line of the Hindu Mahasabha, and even in Bengal veteran local leader from Midnapur, Birendra Nath Sasmal, was defeated in the elections of 1926 by a fellow Congressman who used the slogan of Hinduism in danger. The Swarajists won 35 out of the 47 Hindu seats in Bengal in the 1926 elections, but only one Muslim seat out of 39; only in Madras could they withstand the joint onslaught of the supporters of the Hindu Mahasabha and partisans of 'responsive cooperation'.

On its part, the Congress staged several small satyagrahas between 1922 and 1926. Two of them were connected to the Akali movement in Punjab. Jawaharlal Nehru participated in the Guru-ke bagh satyagraha of 1922–23 and the Jaito satyagraha of 1924—the first over a minor issue of the cutting of a tree in a disputed land between the ousted *mahant* and the new Shiromoni Gurdwara Prabandhak Committee (SGPC), and the second over the forced abdication of the Maharaja of Nabha, a major patron of the Akali movement. Malcolm Hailey, the 'astute governor of Punjab', deftly dealt with the situation by promulgating the Sikh Gurdwara and Shrines Act in 1925, which accepted SGPC control over Sikh religious centres (Sarkar [1983] 1995: 228). A brief satyagraha was started against a corrupt *mahant* in Tarakeshwar in Bengal by Swami Viswananda; it got Chittaranjan Das' support. Of greater significance were the Barsod satyagraha, led by Vallabhbhai Patel in the Kheda district of Gujarat in 1923–24 and the Vaikom satyagraha in the state of Travancore in 1924–25.

The Barsod satyagraha revolved around the issue of an unjust poll tax (of ₹ 2 and 7 annas) imposed in September 1923 on every adult in Barsod. The tax was to cover police expenses required for the suppression of a wave of dacoities committed by low-caste Baraiyas. The Patidars felt that the tax was an unfair measure designed to punish them for supporting the Congress. Vallabhai Patel took up the cause of the Patidars in rural Gujarat; all the 104 affected villages decided on total non-payment of the new tax in December 1923 and the tax had to be cancelled in January 1924. This success of a Gandhian movement revived the prestige of the Congress, which had been badly bruised by the abrupt retreat of 1922 (Hardiman 1981, 1992).

The Vaikom satyagraha was the first of its kind in two senses—one, it was an extension of the Gandhian satyagraha to a princely state and two, it promoted a cause that had not really been taken up in seriousness by the Congress, that is, the removal of untouchability. Ezhava Congress leader, T. K. Mahadevan, took the initiative in starting this satyagraha; he was supported by Nair Congressmen and, more importantly, by the community of Ezhavas and other untouchable groups. They claimed the right to use the road near a Travancore temple. Termed the 'temple-entry' movement, it was not really a struggle to enter a Hindu temple but to lay claim to the road in front of it. Gandhi visited Vaikom in March 1925 and alienated the Christian community by asking them to stay away from a 'Hindu affair'. Gandhi's idea that 'untouchability' was essentially a problem internal to Hinduism would cause further tension between him and B. R. Ambedkar, a point we will take up in the next chapter. The Vaikom satyagraha petered out after 20 months when the government constructed a different road for use by untouchables (Sarkar [1983] 1995: 229). The 'No-changers' implemented Gandhi's constructive programme in villages by carrying out social work among low castes and untouchables, by popularizing khadi and village industries, and by conducting anti-liquor campaigns. In addition, relief was offered to the flood-affected people in Bengal (1922) and Gujarat (1927). This work did not yield great results—manufacture and use of khadi remained more expensive than imported or Indian mill cloth, and social work among the untouchables did not tackle the basic problem of poverty of the landless or semi-servile agricultural labourers.

Gandhi, moreover, was not opposed to the caste system; he deplored its aberration that had produced untouchability. The disappointment of Ezhava and other low-caste leaders with Gandhi's upholding of *varnasharamadharma*—the hereditary division of labour that marked out the 'ancestral callings' of each group (Gandhi 1920)—had become evident during the Vaikom satyagraha; the rift in understanding widened with the passage of time. Yet, constructive work earned the Congress strong support in rural areas and extended its hold over lower castes and untouchables (Hardiman 1981; Sanyal 1981; Sarkar [1983] 1995: 230).

Constructive work had great impact in Gujarat, in particular in Kheda and Bardoli districts, which came to have a long chain of ashrams and a corps of dedicated *gram sevak*s (village servants). The Congress base extended from the lesser Patidars to poorer sections and came to include the Baraiyas and the *Kaliparaj*, the dark people, who were distinct from the high-caste fair people, the *Ujaliparaj*. In addition, the centres of constructive work also provided the base for civil disobedience in the 1930s.

The year 1926 not only spelled disaster for the Swaraj Party, it was also disastrous for Hindu–Muslim relations. Very violent clashes between Hindus and Muslims in Calcutta between April and July killed 138; Dacca, Patna, Delhi and Rawalpindi witnessed similar clashes and there were 91 outbreaks in UP, the worst-affected province, between 1923 and 1927. Lucknow, Allahabad, Jabalpur and Nagpur were centres of communal tension. The alleged issues were the Muslim demand for stopping music before mosques and the Hindu emphasis on a ban on cow slaughter. As indicated earlier, the Muslim League, the Hindu Mahasabha and a section of the Swarajists all started making political alliances on 'communal' grounds; Motilal Nehru and Maulana Azad failed in their attempts to get the parties to pledge that they would stay out of communal politics.

The genesis of political alliances based on community lay in the very nature of the 1919 Reforms. As discussed in the last chapter, the Montford Reforms retained and extended the principle of separate electorates, first introduced in the Reforms of 1909, even as they widened the franchise. Consequently, for those politicians who were working within the system there was 'a built-in temptation' to make use of 'sectional slogans and gather a following by distributing favours to their own religious, regional or caste groups' (Sarkar [1983] 1995: 234). As Indian nationalism became more militant, the cornered British state tried to take full advantage of the divisions produced by the offering of special privileges to particular groups.

For B. R. Tomlinson (1976: 9–11) and Anil Seal, the 1919 Reforms were significant for the way in which they transformed representative politics. Tomlinson regards the First World War to be a 'landmark' in Indian politics on account of the decisive steps for the devolution of power taken by the British government during and after the War; and Seal considers the expansion of representative politics that brought in its tow a greater need for popular political mobilization to be of great import (Seal 1973). The need to garner 'popular' support often resulted in the use of 'sectional slogans'. Such slogans found ready support among an expanding group of newly educated classes generated by the considerable spread of education in the 1920s, whose rising expectations were not met by an expansion in employment opportunities (Hardy 1972: 204). Consequently, they were ready to cash in on sectarian opportunities offered by the political system.

Lower caste and untouchable leaders too, as we have noted in earlier chapters, rallied around the favours being offered by the colonial state—none of the groups could break out of the framework imposed by institutional reforms. The British strategy of 'devolution of power in stages', therefore, argues R. J. Moore, generated a 'crisis of Indian unity' (Moore 1974). From what we have seen in chapters 5, 6 and 7, it is difficult to accept a facile notion of Indian unity. Yet, it is true that policies of the colonial state channelled the struggle in specific ways where the conflict among different groups and communities became prominent at particular moments, and the idea of independent India as a federation with a strong centre, an idea advocated by the princes, gained ground.

Spurred by the 'imperatives of representative politics' for effective mass mobilization, a series of 'communal' associations came into being; associations that connected the elite and subordinate classes through a common ideology. The Arya Samaj's *shuddhi* and *sangathan* found parallel in the *tabligh* (propaganda) and *tanzim* (organization) of the Muslim League; and the adoption of *shuddhi* and Hindu-defence squads by the newly revitalized Hindu Mahasabha provided a common Hindu front along the Hindi belt. The countervailing trend, apparent in the late-nineteenth and early-twentieth centuries, of working towards establishing national organizations that rose above community mobilizations (Bayly 1975), came to take a back-seat as socio-economic tensions easily took on a 'communal' colour among the lower castes and the rural and the urban poor.

Local conflicts seriously influenced the participation of the urban poor in caste and communal politics, writes Nandini Gooptu (2001: 8). Intensifying class conflicts and 'the experience of exclusion and marginalization' faced by the urban poor in the inter-war years exercised a 'defining influence' on their politics (ibid.: 420). Their participation moreover, was governed by 'past values' and 'traditional' modes of thought since 'religious myths, legends and symbols' enabled workers 'to accommodate and apprehend their social world in a hostile urban milieu' (Joshi 1985).

In the midst of this turmoil, the government announced the appointment of an all-white commission, the Simon Commission, to assess the way the 1919 Reforms had worked and to make suggestions for future reforms. It is difficult to say why the government decided to appoint the commission two years prior to the lapse of the 1919 Reforms, which were valid for ten years. The activity of the Swarajists possibly had something to do with the accelerated speed at which the commission was appointed. The commission, constituted under the Chairmanship of Sir John Allsebrook Simon by a royal warrant in November 1927, consisted of seven other English members in whose knowledge and ability the British Parliament placed great trust. The appointment of an all-white commission offered a great stimulus to the Congress to act together with all other parties on an all-India political basis. It could not, however, overcome Muslim aloofness, a fact that would find reflection in the Congress-led movements in the 1930s.

Capitalists, Workers, Communists

It is in order here to examine the evolution of labour and capital and their intersections with the nationalist struggle. As we have seen in Chapter 4, the second half of the nineteenth century is generally taken to be the period that saw the emergence of a modern Indian capitalist class in consonance with the growth of a large-scale mechanized industry. Western India was the region that saw this development—here Indian traders and financiers 'played a major role in the birth of the modern Indian cotton textile industry in Bombay and Ahmedabad' (Markovits 1985: 8). An exceptional convergence of favourable factors in western India in the 1850s and 1860s enabled the growth of an Indian industry in a colonial situation. This entailed a growing tendency towards import substitution, greater attention to the domestic market and growth in internal trade (Tripathi 1991).

Indeed, as mill operations proved to be successful, the cotton textile industry spread from Bombay and Ahmedabad to Nagpur, Kanpur, Sholapur and Coimbatore to become a well-established industry by the 1880s. Even though China remained the largest market for Indian cotton products (Washbrook 1981: 672), Ahmedabad and Coimbatore mills sold yarn to handlooms in the Indian countryside. This trend became more prominent towards the end of the century when Japanese cloth started competing with Indian goods in the Chinese market. In addition to supplying yarn, Indian mills started weaving cloth for the Indian market, a preserve of Lancashire till the last decade of the century (Markovits 1985: 9). By 1919, Indian cotton had reduced the share of Manchester cloth in the Indian market by 40 per cent (Ray 1979).

'Big business' in India had a distinctive character. It was region specific, primarily urban with no direct links to land but with considerable interest in trade and finance, and composed of a few groups. The stake in trade and finance made possible the existence of capitalists in Calcutta, where the principal industry—jute—was monopolized by the British. Several capitalists came from among the Banias, a middle-ranking caste with some degree of social prestige. The Parsis of Bombay became leading entrepreneurs and complemented the Indian cotton textile industry by investing in iron and steel. The Tata Iron and Steel Company founded (in 1907) as a joint-stock company of Parsi and Hindu investors grew steadily and came to employ a large workforce by the end of the second decade of the century. Big industrialists and capitalists distinguished themselves from the bulk of the commercial classes by the 'size of their financial resources, the range and scale of their activities and their organizational skill' (Markovits 1985: 2).

Initially, Indian capitalists had some control over the economy of the big cities where they predominated, but they did not have much control over the national economy. This is because the 'modern' industrial sector was dominated by foreign, primarily British capital, and Indian businessmen lacked control over land in a largely agricultural economy. Class and caste networks enabled groups, such as the Marwaris, to connect capitalists in Calcutta or Ahmedabad with traders of *mofussil* towns and rural areas, but this flow worked more in terms of men rather than goods, that is, it was not always congruent with trade networks (Timberg 1978). Urban capitalists, however, gave leadership to most regional business associations and sealed their skill of commanding all-India connections by establishing the first all-India indigenous business association, the Federation of Indian Chambers of Commerce and Industry (FICCI), in 1927.

The establishment of FICCI in a way marked the maturity of the Indian capitalists who, since the beginning of the twentieth century, had been showing great enterprise by moving into industries not touched by foreign capital: sugar, paper, cement, and iron and steel, for instance. Indian capital also intruded into finance, insurance, jute, mining and plantation—businesses held by British capital (Bandyopadhyay 2004: 358). The Bengal National Chamber of Commerce, it bears pointing out, had come into existence as early as 1887, and the Indian Merchants Chamber in Bombay had been established in 1907.

What was the attitude of Indian capital to nationalism and imperialism? It is difficult to provide a clear answer. To begin with, there was a wide divergence between the capitalists engaged in trade and finance and those in industries. In trade and finance, Indians seemed to do 'most of the local spadework for the state and British business'; they functioned as 'middlemen who joined the Indian peasant economy to the world market' (Washbrook 1981: 672). In this role, they contributed both to state finance and to British balance of payments, and offered a picture of symbiosis rather than that of direct clash between Indian and British interests (Markovits 1985: 9). Indian industrialists, on the other hand, adopted a stance of simultaneous and sequential cooperation and opposition towards the colonial state, in tune with particular issues and the overall pattern of Indian industrial growth (Ray 1979; Tripathi 1991). This is understandable in view of their pragmatic approach and the course of evolution of the nationalist struggle.

Rajat Ray and Dwijendra Tripathi's work on Indian industries and business warn us against making any 'clear-cut generalization' or speaking of a capitalist 'grand strategy' (Ray 1979: 292; Tripathi 1991: 118). In a similar manner, A. D. D. Gordon's analysis of the political attitude of the Bombay businessmen, and Claude Markovits' study of Indian 'big business', point to a divergence in the composition of the group and a resultant diversity in political attitudes (Gordon 1978; Markovits 1985). Thus, while traders and merchants were largely 'nationalists', big industrialists were 'loyalists'. What all these scholars seem to argue is that it is difficult to identify an Indian capitalist class with a definite strategy and unified interest till the 1930s.

For historians such as Bipan Chandra and Aditya Mukherjee, on the other hand, there was a well-defined Indian capitalist class from the late-nineteenth century, and it developed a 'long-term contradiction with imperialism', even though it demonstrated 'short-term dependence and accommodation' with it. That is, Indian capitalists worked out an astute strategy that wished to do away with imperialism but not capitalism. They were therefore nationalists but Right-wing (Chandra 1979; Mukherjee 1986). From what we have briefly seen in Chapter 6 and the earlier chapter, traders, merchants and 'big business' did not take up the cause of the Swadeshi movement. Gandhi's programme of non-cooperation that included the boycott of foreign cloth was accepted by Marwari traders and businessmen close to him only for the limited period of one year. Ahmedabad and Bombay textile mills reaped huge profits from non-cooperation, since the boycott of foreign cloth gave them a greater hold in the Indian market. Other industrialists desisted from taking a clear stance.

The attitude of Indian business towards nationalism was contingent upon national and international developments. The First World War, for instance, allowed the industrialists to prosper, while merchants and traders were adversely affected by currency fluctuations and high taxes. The collapse of the rupee in December 1920 threatened Indian importers with a possible loss of nearly 30 per cent of their previous contracts; Indian exporters and mill-owners, on the other hand, were faced with the happy prospect of a rise in profit (Bandyopadhyay 2004: 360). New income tax laws affected the joint family businesses of Marwaris and Gujaratis more than those of urban industrialists. The Montagu-Chelmsford Reforms for its part tried to ensure the loyalty of industrialists by providing for their representation (along with that of labour) in the central and provincial legislative councils.

It is not surprising, therefore, that traders and merchants supported Gandhi and the Congress cause more readily than industrialists. Some Gujarati traders, we noted in Chapter 7, were also attracted by Gandhi's ideology of non-violence; they contributed willingly and generously to Gandhi's constructive programme. Big businessmen, such as Jamnalalji Bajaj and G. D. Birla, became Gandhi's close associates and lent continuous support from 1919. Jamnalalji Bajaj in fact, accepted Congress membership and served as the Treasurer of the All India Congress Committee for several years. It has been suggested that these merchants also saw in Gandhi a positive counterbalance to radical socialism and revolutionary activities.

Big industrialists either remained aloof or were directly opposed to mass agitation sanctioned by non-cooperation. If Birla and Bajaj donated huge sums to the Tilak Swaraj Fund (Chapter 7), Purushottamdas Thakurdas and R. D. Tata started an Anti-Non-Cooperation Society in Bombay. Increasing tensions between British imperial and Indian business interests produced a change in attitude after 1922. Tensions also soared between British capitalists in India and their Indian counterparts in cities, such as Bombay and Calcutta. A sense of unease with the concessions granted to Indian business in the 1919 Reforms made British capitalists more vigilant of their racial exclusivity and autonomy; they established an apex body of all European business organizations—the Associated Chambers of

Commerce—in 1922 to protect their interests (Misra 1999). FICCI was in part, an Indian response to this. Purushottamdas Thakurdas gave leadership to FICCI.

Fortunes of Indian capitalists deteriorated as the war-time boom was followed by a slump. Bombay mill-owners had to deal with large unsold stocks and rising labour costs; they were further challenged by competition from Japan. Cheap Japanese products entered Indian markets and pushed down the prices of cotton goods. The abolition of the 3.5 per cent excise duty on cotton in 1925 could not prevent 11 mills in Bombay from going out of business in 1926; it left 13 per cent of the labour force unemployed.

The artificially fixed rupee-sterling exchange rate at 1s 6d prescribed by the Hilton-Young Commission in 1926 and adopted by the government to aid the flow of remittances from India and to maintain India's credit-worthiness added to the woes of Indian importers. Together, all this brought merchants and industrialists closer to the Congress. We have noted earlier how Swarajist support led to the passing of a protective tariffs act in 1924 to help Indian industries. The Great Depression of 1929 would further contribute to an alliance of the Congress and industrialists even though big businessmen would always remain uncertain about the politics of agitation that involved masses. It appeared to be too risky to some while others accepted it as a means to wrest some concessions out of an insensitive government.

Growing labour militancy towards the end of the decade under the revolutionary *Girni Kamgar* unions of the cotton textile mills in Bombay and southern Maharashtra made Bombay mill-owners dependent on government support. The most enterprising Indian capitalists, the Tatas, also remained overwhelmingly loyalist, and decided to throw in their lot with European leaders to stand up against the 'Red leaders of disruption' in 1929.

Arguably, both nationalist and capitalist activities evolved in conjunction with developments in the labour movement, to which we now turn. The history of labour in India is well documented (Chakrabarty 1989; Chandavarkar 1994, Das 1923; Holmstrom 1984; Karnik [1960] 1966; Morris 1965; Newman 1981; Pandey 1970; Sen 1977; for instance). The Indian working class was vast and varied: it consisted of the industrial labour force based in cities and towns, and extensive groups of plantation and mine workers who were employed primarily by Europeans.

In addition, labourers moved between the so-called formal sector, that is, a definite workplace provided by factories and industries, and the unorganized 'informal' one—casual work in construction and transport; manual work in bazaars; and vending, hawking and peddling in the streets, for instance (Breman 1976; Gooptu 2001: 2–3). The permeability of the two sectors made it difficult for the government and nationalists as well as for scholars, to understand working class politics by means of a focus only on the formal, organized sector. Groups of 'informal' workers, argues Gooptu, provided the bulk of the urban labour force in towns with no large industries (2001: 3). The significance of the urban poor in politics increased in the inter-war years in tune with the rapid pace of urbanization, the reconfiguration of institutions and organization of politics, as well as the elaboration of a multiplicity of political 'languages' and ideologies (ibid.: 6–7).

Labour unrest began as early as the 1890s in the white-controlled jute mills of Calcutta (Chakrabarty 1989; Basu 2004). The swadeshi period marked a watershed in the history of labour—it saw the rise of the 'professional agitator' (Sarkar 1973: 183), who succeeded in organizing labour in successful industrial strikes. A few middle-class lawyers took the lead in organizing strikes in the paper and printing mills in and around Calcutta. Strikes in these mills were followed by strikes in tram and railway companies, and efforts were made to involve coolies in addition to lower middle-class clerks, even though the mine and plantation workers remained unaffected (Chapter 6).

Perhaps the most important feature of the labour movement during the swadeshi period, argue Bipan Chandra, Mridula Mukherjee and others, was that there was a shift from agitation and struggles 'on purely economic questions' to 'the involvement of the worker with the wider political issues of the day' (Chandra et al. [1989] 2000: 214). There are serious problems with this understanding of workers' strikes as resulting from 'purely economic questions' (Guha 1982; Sarkar 1984). Yet, the point that the swadeshi era established a vital link between labour and nationalist struggles remains valid. This was evident in the way Tilak's imprisonment and trial in 1908 generated spontaneous political strikes in Bombay.

The period of the First World War was marked by even greater unrest. The direct causes of this were wartime price-rise and the decline of real wages. Among the numerous strikes, particularly in Bombay and western India during this time (Kumar 1971), the Ahmedabad textile strike became famous owing to Gandhi's involvement in it. The question to ask for labour therefore, writes Prathama Banerjee (2010), is not whether there was a working class in India which could produce a radical politics for change, but whether politics itself was able to produce a radical working class in colonial India. The answer clearly is yes.

At the same time, Congress relationship with labour was ambivalent. If, in 1919, the Congress adopted a resolution at its Amritsar meeting to encourage the formation of labour unions throughout India—a resolution that led to the founding of the All India Trade Union Committee (AITUC)—in 1920, it also developed a close relationship with influential Indian capitalists. In a similar manner, if Lajpat Rai and Chittaranjan Das developed intimate links with AITUC, Gandhi and some of his close associates interrogated the politics of conflict between capital and labour, as also between the landlord and the peasant, and talked of class harmony and trusteeship, whereby rich businessmen were exhorted to use their wealth morally and benevolently in the name of the poor.

In 1934, Gandhi made an open declaration in the English daily, *Amrita Bazar Patrika*, that he will 'not be party to dispossessing propertied classes of their property without just cause'. His objective was to reach the heart of propertied classes and convert them so that they may hold all their private property 'in trust for [their] tenants and use it primarily for their welfare'. He was working, he continued, 'for the cooperation and co-ordination of capital and labour, of landlord and tenant' (Gandhi 1934; Sharma 1962: 27–28). On 12 January 1930, Gandhi wrote in the *Navajivan* that although his recent tour of the United Provinces had given him hope because many zamindars and *talukdar*s had simplified their lives, there was still a lot of difference between them and the peasants and they had to realize that the peasants had 'souls similar to theirs and they should hold their wealth as trustees for the benefit of the tenants' (Gandhi 1930a).

The uncertainty of the Congress stance with regard to labour found reflection in the fact that although between 1924 and 1927, AITUC's membership went up with 83 affiliated unions listed in January 1925, the number of strikes per year went down from 376 in 1921 to 130 (Sarkar [1983] 1995:

244). The AITUC leadership remained overwhelmingly moderate during these years and towed the liberal or Congress line in matters of politics.

Labour, however, did not remain docile and submissive to the brakes being imposed by the leadership. Drawing upon a variety of political 'languages' and ideologies, it continued its fight for better working conditions and against racial discrimination and wage cuts. There were four recurrent strikes in the Buckingham Carnatic mills in Madras in 1922–23; the city of Madras also organized the first celebration of May Day in 1923. The Bombay textile mills were struck by massive strikes between January–March 1924 and September–December 1925.

The first round of strikes, which involved 150,000 workers, was over the issue of bonus, and the second was on grounds of a wage cut of 11.5 per cent. On both occasions, the workers held out stubbornly in the face of acute state repression and almost no support from nationalist leaders. They did not get their bonus; but the second wave of strikes forced the government to suspend the cotton excise duty following which mill-owners discarded the wage cut (ibid.: 246). The workers in Bombay, therefore, won for the nationalists a demand they had been making for almost three decades, that is, abolishing excise duty of 3.5 per cent on cotton, imposed in 1894 to help Lancashire. This achievement possibly prompted the government to pass the Trade Union Act in 1926 to restrict workers' involvement in politics.

Congressmen, of course, were not the only ones who tried to organize labour; Communists and revolutionaries also developed close alliances with workers. Often, they formed a conglomerate and gave the lie to British official propaganda that Indian communism was entirely a foreign conspiracy organized by Moscow. For Sumit Sarkar, Indian Communism stemmed from within the national movement—it brought together disillusioned revolutionaries, non-cooperators, Khilafatists, and labour and peasant activists, who sought new roads to social and political emancipation (ibid.: 247).

Communism in India was pioneered by the Bengal revolutionary Narendranath Bhattacharya, alias Manabendra Nath Roy. Member of the undivided Anushilan Samiti (Chapter 6), Roy had played an important role in the so-called Indo-German conspiracy for the import of German arms in 1914–15. When these attempts failed, Roy fled to the US to escape arrest, where he came in contact with American radicals and discovered 'new meanings in the works of Karl Marx' (Bandyopadhyay 1984: 167). He moved to Mexico from the US in 1919, met the Bolshevik Mikhail Borodin and wrote his first socialist essay in Spanish.

Roy's next stop was Berlin and then Moscow, where he went in the summer of 1920 to attend the Second Congress of the Communist International (Adhikari 1971). Here, Roy was engaged in a spirited debate with Lenin over the strategy to be followed by Communists in colonized countries (Ray 1987). Roy, along with Abani Mukherji and Khilafat enthusiasts Mohammad Ali and Mohammad Shafiq, founded the Communist Party of India in Tashkent in October 1920, but it was not until 1922 that this group managed to establish links with embryonic Communist groups in India.

Singaravelu, the Madras Communist who organized the first May Day celebration in 1923, created a stir in the Gaya Congress session in December 1922 by speaking openly in the name of 'the great order of the world communists' and by boldly calling the Bardoli retreat a 'disaster' (Murugesan and Subramanyam 1975). He insisted on the need to combine non-cooperation with national strikes (Sarkar

[1983] 1995: 248). Till 1928, however, the Communists tried to work within mainstream politics even though they criticized the Congress leadership for its many compromises with imperialism.

By 1926–27, Communist activities had produced an important impact—the idea of a broad workers and peasants' front had taken concrete shape. This was reflected in the establishment of organizations, such as the Labour Swaraj Party soon renamed Workers and Peasants Party in Bengal (1925–26), the Kirti Kisan Party in Punjab (1926) and the Workers and Peasants Party in Bombay (1927). It was also evident in a historic act of joint protest by workers and peasants in Bombay in 1927 against the draft Minimum Landholding Act, which would have allowed wealthy farmers to own more land to the detriment of the poorer local peasants. The protest killed the act (Chandra et al. [1972] 1975: 149).

Communists also made their mark in organizing workers of the Khargapur Locomotive Repair and Maintenance Workshop, owned by the British private business-run Bengal Nagpur Railway Company, to go on strike against low wages and arbitrary action by company authorities in February and September 1927. The workers on strike also displayed their antagonism toward the moderate trade union leadership offered by Congress leaders V. V. Giri and Andrews (Bandyopadhyay 1984: 185). The Khargapur strikes were followed by a six-month long bitter struggle between the workers and administrators of the Lilooah Rail Workshop (January–July 1928). The workers showed remarkable resilience during this long battle; they also organized spectacular marches in the industrial suburb of Calcutta.

The enormous workforce in Bombay city, organized under the radical *Girni Kamgar* unions of the cotton textile industry, also came under Communist influence, even though the sheer paucity of numbers prevented the Communists from going into villages. They, however, did speak of the abolition of zamindari and land redistribution right from the start, programmes that the Congress would only hesitantly start debating in the 1930s.

Understandably, Gandhi did not have much sympathy for Communists who, he felt, tried to use union activities for 'political' purposes. He also criticized them for neglecting the peasantry. Gandhi's basic dislike for Communists, of course, stemmed from his apathy and aversion for the path of revolution and violence. The Congress, however, did not remain untouched by Communist ideas. There emerged a young group of socialists, Jawaharlal Nehru and Subhas Bose, for instance, who spoke of achieving emancipation along socialist lines.

Towards the end of 1927, Jawaharlal Nehru joined the renowned Communists—Singaravelu, Joglekar, Spratt, Dange, Dr Bhupendranath Dutta and Dr Kanai Lal Ganguli—in founding the Independence for India League. Subhas Bose decided not to join them. He set up his own Independence League, with the support of the Yugantar revolutionaries (Bandyopadhyay 1984: 183–84). Apart from such rivalries among Congress leaders, there was a greater feud between the Congress and Communists, which was fuelled by labour insurgency.

Congress dealings with labour, on the whole, remained conservative—it encouraged labour unrest in sectors where the capitalists were white, such as in tea plantations and the jute industry, and tried to use co-opted trade unions to play conciliatory roles in sectors where national capital dominated. The Communists and revolutionaries, by questioning the Congress' attitude to labour, also interrogated Congress' claims to unquestioned leadership of the Indian national struggle.

The working class gave proof of its maturity and autonomy once again during the depression years of 1929–30, when the number of strikes in different industries increased phenomenally. Industrial unrest had reached new levels prior to that—26,000 workers of TISCO in Jamshedpur had gone on a momentous strike in 1926, followed by 272,000 workers in the Calcutta jute mills in 1927. The railways were hit by recurrent strikes in 1928 and 1930; 1928 alone recorded 203 strikes involving 505,000 workers (Chandra et al. [1972] 1975: 14). Membership of the *Girni Kamgar* unions had gone up significantly, and unions that pledged to work for revolution had been started by the workers in south India, Madras and southern Maratha railways.

The working classes as a political community came into being through the experience of these militant movements. They did not abide by the dictates of the Congress and got into clashes both with European and Indian owners. That Congress leaders were not totally unaware of the workers' suspicion of the Congress is evident in Jawaharlal Nehru's remark in his *Autobiography*. 'The advanced sections of workers', he wrote, 'fought shy of the National Congress'. They did not trust its leaders and they found 'its ideology bourgeois and reactionary, which indeed it was from the labour point of view' (Nehru 1941: 148). Workers' struggle for better working conditions engaged them in conflict with Indian and English capitalists. Indeed, a remarkably restive working class towards the end of the 1920s led the British administration to believe that the initiative in the anti-Simon agitation was passing to the Left. In order to counter this threat, it appointed another Royal Commission, the Whitley Commission on Labour, to visit India and suggest measures for improving labour relations and promoting labour welfare (Chandra et al. [1972] 1975: 155).

The working classes were not duped—many labour organizations boycotted the Whitley Commission when it arrived in India in 1929. Workers had not forgotten that only a year before, the government had tried to pass, through the Central Legislative Assembly, a Trade Disputes Bill and an amendment to the Public Safety Act that would have severely restricted the workers' freedom of action. The working classes, who continuously straddled formal and informal sectors, came to constitute yet another militant group that the British administration and Indian nationalism had to contend with.

DEPRESSION, SIMON COMMISSION, 'TERRORISM'

'Trade fluctuations were not unknown in India before 1929', wrote Thomas Parakunnel in an early analysis of the impact of the Depression of 1929–34; 'a hundred years ago there was a prolonged economic depression in southern and western India, and there have been some milder slumps since' (Parakunnel 1935: 469). But before 1870, he hastened to add, India's connection with the rest of the world was 'imperfect', which meant that price movements in Europe had no active influence on Indian prices.

The most notable feature of the 1929–31 slump, Parakunnel continues, was the wide disparity between the prices of primary products and finished goods. While rice slumped 52 per cent, oil seeds 55 per cent, raw jute 53 per cent and raw cotton 51 per cent between September 1929 and March 1934, cotton manufactures slumped only 29 per cent, metals 22 per cent and sugar 26 per cent during the same period. Given the fact that by then India's exports consisted chiefly of primary products, this disparity severely affected India's balance of trade. The price-index for exported articles fell by 46 per cent, while that for imported articles fell only by 24–26 per cent, and occasioned a rapid decline in India's balance of trade in merchandise from ₹ 80 crore in 1929 to ₹ 4.5 crore in 1932. The total value of merchandise exports fell from ₹ 330 crore in 1929 to ₹ 132.6 crore in 1932–33 (ibid.: 470).

I have quoted this in detail to offer a general impression of the extreme hardship occasioned by the Depression years. Statisticians H. Sinha and J. C. Sinha divided 'the whole course of world depression' into three broad phases, with the first extending roughly from October 1929 to June 1930, the second from July 1930 to August 1931, and the third from September 1931 to December 1932 (Sinha and Sinha 1938: 202–03). The characteristic feature of the first phase was the sharp fall in the prices of agricultural goods, as well as its heavy incidence in countries producing raw materials and foodstuffs. This was India's case.

The decline in the value of agricultural commodities directly affected the relatively substantial producers, the rural middle classes, who had surpluses to sell and heavy obligations in rent, revenue and interest to pay (Stein 2010: 303). The Congress and peasant organizations drew their following from among this group and all such organizations raised slogans of moratorium on taxes, rents and debts in the early 1930s. Wealthier rural families were also affected by the Depression and they resorted to distress sale of their gold hoardings to tide over the crisis. In fact, this freeing of gold made it possible for Britain to maintain the level of Home Charges—the flow of taxation from India to Britain—during the Depression years.

The worst hit, of course, were the increasing numbers of rural poor, the very poor peasants, artisans whose income had been steadily declining over the entire decade of the 1920s, and small farmers who cultivated with hired labour (Stein 2010: 302). The Depression increased inequalities of distribution between different partners in the agricultural business, comments Parakunnel. The shares of the government, landlords and moneylenders, he stated, 'are fixed', and hence 'the risks have largely fallen on the peasant, who is the least capable of bearing them' (Parakunnel 1935: 472). Bihar and Orissa in the Bengal Presidency were the worst hit by the depression—here the prices of the two principal crops declined by 61 and 58 per cent between 1929 and 1933, as compared to 30 per cent in Bombay and 35 per cent in UP.

Population, we need to keep in mind, had been slowly but steadily growing from the end of the nineteenth century at an annual average of 0.6 per cent, exacerbating competition over scarce resources, particularly food, in rural areas. India's per capita income showed no change between the end of the First World War and the beginning of the Second, but the number of the rural poor masses continued to rise. Popular protests against adverse conditions were met by police and judicial repression.

Workers, who had to accept retrenchment and wage cuts to make up for the losses in Indian industries, also faced severe repression when they showed resistance. In Sinha and Sinha's analysis, the second phase of the depression affected manufactures—the 'catastrophic fall in agricultural prices' tended to bring down manufacturing prices as well and this could no longer be averted in the second phase (Sinha and Sinha 1938: 203). Strikes against wage cuts and for improved working conditions were met with lockouts and repression. The series of trials, staged in Meerut between 1929 and 1933, through which the state succeeded in convicting and imprisoning a number of prominent and 'wholly innocent' trade union leaders for allegedly Bolshevik activities, bear testimony to the highhandedness in controlling labour unrest (Bates 2007: 141). Liberal Britain, of course, had to balance repression with concession, and to this end it appointed a commission to take stock of the working of the 1919 Reforms and suggest future ones for India.

The general Indian reaction to the appointment of the Simon Commission in November 1927 was one of disgust—the commission was to have no Indian member. The appointment radicalized Indian politics and made prospects of unity better. Almost all political groups, except the Justice Party in Madras and the Union Party in Punjab, decided to boycott the Simon Commission. The Congress adopted 'Go back Simon' as its slogan and the arrival of the members of the commission in February 1928 were met with country-wide strikes, *hartals*, black-flag demonstrations and cries of 'Simon Go Back'. Bombay city wore a deserted look on 3 February, the day Simon and his colleagues landed there; the same happened in Calcutta on 19 February.

Strikes and demonstrations did not remain confined to big cities. Cuttack, Balasore, Berhampur, Sambalpur—important towns in Orissa—also observed strikes (Bahadur 1983: 335). There was a renewed movement for the boycott of British goods; great student activity was reflected in numerous youth conferences and associations that demanded complete independence. Students also participated in large numbers in demonstrations. Police efforts to stop the demonstrations resulted in violent clashes and the one in Lahore on 30 October 1928 seriously wounded Lajpat Rai. Rai died on 17 November of cardiac arrest; his death, however, is widely connected to the injuries incurred during the demonstration, a belief that makes him a martyr of the nation (Das 1995). Jawaharlal Nehru and Govind Ballabh Pant got beaten up for leading protest demonstrations in Lucknow on 28–30 November.

The significant rise in the number of students following the transfer of education to elected ministries in the provinces by the 1919 Reforms probably enhanced aspirations and occasioned disillusionment. The number of students rose from 5.04 of the total population in 1922 to 6.91 in 1927 (Sarkar [1983] 1995: 266). The rising aspirations of the educated youth, as indicated earlier, were not matched with greater employment opportunities. This definitely would have caused serious disillusionment although this was not the only reason for student discontent. Communist ideas gained significant hold over lower-middle-class students in urban areas who did not feel attracted to the upper-middle-class Swarajist leaders of the Congress (Chandra et al. [1972] 1975: 154). This was evident in the establishment of a number of youth leagues and the rapidly growing circulation of Communist newspapers, such as *Kirti*, *Mazdur*, *Kisan*, *Spark* and *Kranti* in towns.

The students, however, did not show enough discipline or organization to undertake a socialist struggle on an all-India basis. Industrialists expressed concern at the growing unrest among students in FICCI and the Bombay Chamber of Commerce's meetings and the Congress tried to engage the energies of the youth by organizing the Hindustan Seva Dal. Jawaharlal Nehru and Subhas Bose kept busy throughout 1927 and 1928 addressing student rallies. Subhas Bose also urged Gandhi to launch an all-India campaign. The Mahatma, however, did not see 'light' at this stage (Bose 1935: 38).

'Revolutionary terrorism', a persistent if not a prominent strain since the swadeshi era, became pronounced once more as sections of educated urban youth got tired of verbal radicalism and sought to do something concrete. They did not really have a valid socio-economic programme; very young and impatient, these men were inspired by the 'cult of the heroic self-sacrifice' for the cause of motherland (Sarkar [1983] 1995: 252).

New 'revolt groups' in Bengal decided not to pay heed to the advice of caution and careful preparation given by veteran members of the Yugantar and Anushilan groups, and go out on the offensive against British rule. One such group, the Chittagong Indian Republican Army, founded by Surya Sen, 'Masterda', planned concerted actions with different factions to 'create havoc for the British government in the 1930s' (Roy 1970 cited in Bandyopadhyay 1984: 143). They seized the local armoury in Chittagong, issued a proclamation of independence and fought a fierce pitched battle on Jalalabad Hill on 22 April in which 12 revolutionaries lost their lives. Very far from Gandhi in their methods of struggle, the revolutionaries celebrated the seizure of the armoury with cries of 'Gandhi Raj has come'. This daring raid was followed by an intense wave of 'terrorist' activities in Bengal that included an attack on the government headquarters of Writers Building in Calcutta on 8 December.

The Hindustan Socialist Republican Army (HSRA), on the other hand, showed a strong commitment to socialist and Communist ideas. It was founded by Chandra Sekhar Azad, a well-known revolutionary from UP and a member of the Hindustan Republican Army who had successfully evaded imprisonment and conviction in the Kakori Conspiracy Case in 1925, and the legendary Punjabi revolutionary Bhagat Singh. Azad and Singh were supported by associates and sympathizers from UP and Bihar. They met in the Ferozshah Kotla ground in Delhi in December 1928, and decided to reorganize the Hindustan Republican Army as the HSRA. HSRA's members dreamt of transforming India into an independent socialist republic (Chandra et al. [1972] 1975: 157–58).

In Review: The Martyr Bridegroom

Bhagat Singh's courage and sacrifice for the motherland blended with his youth to give rise to a variety of verses and ballads in Punjab that immortalize him as the martyr bridegroom. The *ghori* (a wedding song that offers tribute to the martyr) of Bhagat Singh, composed and sung in 'the revolutionary ambience of confrontation with British imperialism', portrayed him evocatively as a young bridegroom who weds death to protect his motherland (Gaur 2008:140-41). A region with a long tradition of struggle and heroic history, the motif of marriage-martyrdom has a special place in folk songs and wedding songs that revere virgin martyrs (*shaheeds*) as heroes, saints and protectors. Bhagat Singh joined the ranks of the four sons of Guru Gobind Singh (seventeenth–eighteenth century), and came to share equal honour and veneration with Salar Masud Ghazi (Ghazi Miyan), who received martyrdom on the day of his marriage (in 1033 C.E.) to protect cows. The continued significance of Ghazi Miyan in Punjabi culture was reflected in the annual celebration of a fair (*Chhatri ka Mela*) in Ambala, where the legends of Ghazi Miyan's marriage and martyrdom were sung and performed, at least till the end of the nineteenth century, and the celebration of his marriage in the *dargah* in Bahraich in the month of *Jeth* (May–June) on a grand scale with innumerable guests that included newly-wed couples who sought the saint's blessings (ibid.: 143). The inextricable blending of marriage and martyrdom constitutes a single, 'strong motif in the history of Punjab's literature and culture' (ibid.: 148). If the sons of Guru Gobind Singh are venerated as Babas and Ghazi Miyan as a saint, Bhagat Singh offers comfort and protection as *Shaheed-e-Azam* (the leading martyr, which also became the title of a popular Hindi film released in 2002).

The *ghori* of Bhagat Singh is complemented by *Bhagat Singh di Marhi* (a dirge or funeral hymn or lament). In this, the 'bride of freedom' visits the tomb of Bhagat Singh and laments its deplorable condition, evoking thereby the sad demise of the eager aspirations for freedom of a brave warrior, who wedded death and devalued the death penalty imposed on him by colonial rule. She beseeches the hero to rise from sleep to guide the nation, symbolizing thereby his 'living' presence. Finally, Bhagat Singh's patriotic love finds articulation in the popular genre of *qissa*, where his death is valorized as a sacrifice to awaken India and lay the foundations of a 'revolutionary consciousness' (ibid.: 155). In the *qissa*, his martyrdom does not go waste, it bears fruit (ibid.: 158). Together, the distinctive folk genres keep Bhagat Singh alive as a persona, an 'extraordinarily brave and beautiful' hero (ibid.: 156), lover, saint and martyr who guides, encourages and gives solace.

This group was not wedded to the 'cult of the bomb and pistol' (Bhagat Singh cited in Sarkar [1983] 1995: 268), nor was it stimulated by religious ideals. 'Revolution' for this group meant a total change in society that would see the demise both of foreign and of Indian capital, and the establishing of 'the dictatorship of the proletariat' (ibid.: 268). Remarkable among the several acts of the HSRA are the murder of the British Commissioner Saunders in Lahore in December 1928 to avenge the death of Lajpat Rai, and the throwing of bombs in the Central Legislative Assembly by Bhagat Singh and Batukeswar Dutta in April 1929, when the assembly was discussing an anti-labour Trade Disputes Bill. The HSRA also tried to blow up Viceroy Irwin's train near Delhi in December 1929 and conducted several acts of 'terrorism' in the towns of Punjab and UP in 1930.

The colonial state clamped down heavily on HSRA and arrested or killed most of its members. The 23-year-old Bhagat Singh, arrested for the murder of Saunders, and awaiting execution, embarked on a serious study of Marxism and wrote a moving piece titled *Why I am an Atheist* (Sarkar [1983] 1995: 268). Short-lived but spectacular, the sacrifice of HSRA members made them instant heroes and turned them into martyrs. When Jatin Das died in prison in September 1929, in the wake of a 63-day long hunger strike undertaken to demand better treatment for political prisoners, a two-mile-long procession followed his bier in Calcutta.

In a similar manner, Bhagat Singh's trial electrified the country, and an Intelligence Bureau Report commented that for a time Bhagat Singh displaced Gandhi as the 'foremost political figure of the day' (Intelligence Bureau Report cited in Sarkar [1983] 1995: 269). Bhagat Singh may have displaced Gandhi only temporarily, but the ideals he stood for indicated alternative routes to and visions of independence that these men strove for. The appeal and attraction for such ideals were poignantly invoked in *Rang De Basanti*, a highly successful recent Hindi film that juxtaposed these revolutionaries with current 'terrorists'. Bhagat Singh's life was also the central theme of another acclaimed Bombay film, *The Legend of Bhagat Singh*, released in 2002, which won the National Award and was nominated for several others.

NEHRU REPORT, BARDOLI, PURNA SWARAJ

Mainstream political parties, the Congress and the Muslim League, resentfully rejected the 'all-white' Simon Commission, and decided instead to join forces to devise a constitution for India that was to give her 'dominion status' based on self-rule. The Statute of Westminster of 1926 had granted such status to the white dominions of the British empire (Stein 2010: 305). It is interesting that in the Madras

Congress session in December 1927 where the resolution to boycott the Simon Commission was taken, Jawaharlal Nehru, supported by Subhas Bose, moved a resolution to make *purna swaraj* or complete independence the goal of the Congress struggle.

Congress Position on Self-Rule, 1885–1942

Year	Congress Position
1885	'All that we desire is that the basis of the Government should be widened and that the people should have their proper and legitimate share in it.' (Presidential Address of W. C. Bonnerjee)
1906	'This Congress is of opinion that the system of Government obtaining in the self-governing British Colonies should be extended to India.' (Resolution)
1916	'This Congress demands that a definite step should be taken towards Self-Government by granting the reform contained in the scheme prepared by the All-India Congress Committee in concert with the Reform Committee appointed by the All-India Muslim League.' (Lahore Resolution)
1920	'The object of the Indian National Congress is the attainment of Swarajya by the people of India by all legitimate and peaceful means.' (Nagpur Resolution)
1929	'This Congress ... declares that the word "Swaraj"... shall mean Complete Independence ... and authorizes the All-India Congress Committee ... to launch upon a programme of Civil Disobedience ...'(Resolution)
1942	'The All-India Congress Committee, therefore, repeats with all emphasis the demand for the withdrawal of the British power from India.'

And yet, the Congress decided to embark on the task of drafting a constitution for 'dominion status'. This was, in part, a response to the challenge thrown to the leaders of the Swaraj Party by Secretary of State Lord Birkenhead to 'produce a constitution that carried behind it a fair measure of general agreement among the great peoples of India' (Chandra et al. [1972] 1975: 150), and in part Gandhi's disagreement with Jawaharlal Nehru's snap independence decision passed during his absence. Motilal Nehru, the veteran Swarajist, became the chairman of the Constitution Committee that had Tej Bahadur Sapru as its member. The All India Congress Committee, the Muslim League, the All India Liberal Federation and other organizations met at an All Parties Conference in Lucknow in August 1928 to discuss and adopt the draft constitution drawn up by the Nehru Committee.

The Nehru Report, taken to be the most significant contribution of the Swaraj Party to the constitutional growth of India, and 'a master-piece of work of statesmanship' by Motilal Nehru (Bahadur 1983: 351), provided for responsible government by granting supremacy to a popularly elected legislature, which was to have greater powers than the executive. The Central Legislature, or the Parliament, was to be bicameral, with an upper and a lower house, and was to have autonomous powers similar to the ones enjoyed by the Dominion Parliaments of Canada or Australia. The upper house, the Senate, was to have 200 members elected by the provincial councils on the basis of proportional representation. The lower house or the House of Representatives was to have 500 members elected on the basis of adult suffrage. No special representation in the Central Parliament was allowed except for the Muslims in Bengal and the non-Muslims in the North-West Frontier Province. The provincial councils, on the other hand, would have reserved seats for minority communities.

The issue of separate electorate generated a lot of squabbles among the different parties. Kelkar and the Hindu Mahasabha vehemently opposed the idea of reserved seats for Muslims in Bengal and Punjab and the creation of Sind as a separate Muslim majority province. The Nehru Report took into consideration the opinion of Mahasabha supporters, and provided for reserved seats in the provinces but not in the central legislature. Consequently, Jinnah, who in 1927 had given up separate electorate granted by the Reforms of 1909, and accepted joint electorate with reserved seats in the cause of unity, accused the Congress leaders of going back on their earlier promises.

Jinnah made a last attempt at unity at the All Parties Conference in Calcutta in December 1928. He asked for an immediate separation of Sind, the transfer of residual powers to provinces, reservation of one-third seats in the Central Assembly for Muslims, and reserved seats for Muslims in Punjab and Bengal till the time adult suffrage became operational. Challenged, once again by the Hindu Mahasabha under Jayakar, Jinnah joined hands with the branch of the League that had refused to cooperate with the Congress, and put forward his 14 points, which repeated the demands for new provinces, one-third seats at the centre, and a federal structure with complete autonomy for the provinces (Sarkar [1983] 1995: 263).

The Nehru Report, therefore, failed to resolve the thorny issue of communal representation. The Report, according to Sekhar Bandyopadhyay, represented 'a bunch of uneasy compromises' and 'stood on shaky ground' (2004: 314). The younger generation of Congress members, Jawaharlal Nehru being the most prominent, was disappointed with the 'dominion status' proposed for India. Moreover, the Report's acceptance of an amendment proposed by Malaviya to guarantee all titles to private and personal property enraged members of the UP Kisan Sabha as well as delegates from Bengal.

The Nehru Report, however, remains important as a first effort to draft a constitution for India, with a complete list of central and provincial subjects, fundamental rights and a discussion of the future status of the princely states, an issue the Congress had evaded till then. Significantly, the Nehru Report also proposed universal adult franchise, instead of an electorate limited by property qualifications, a suggestion that could be accepted only in independent India. With regard to the princes, carefully cultivated by the British as a bulwark against Indian nationalism, the Report visualized a complete transfer of power to a unitary but democratic centre of the future, without suggesting any immediate internal change.

Gandhi had remained in relative political seclusion for about five years since his release from jail in 1924. The world of non-cooperation he had left behind in early 1922 had changed quite drastically. Gandhi dedicated his energies to the constructive programme but showed definite reluctance to re-enter politics (Brown 1977: 5). Apart from the fact that this prompted Lord Reading and his successor Lord Irwin to consider him to be a 'spent force' politically, Gandhi also resisted the strong pressure to launch another round of mass struggle. Not only did he refuse Subhas Bose's suggestion for such a struggle, he also managed to push through a compromise formula at the Calcutta session in 1928 that accepted 'dominion status' suggested by the Nehru Report, provided it was granted by 1929. If it wasn't, the Congress would embark on civil disobedience and seek to attain *purna swaraj*.

In Brown's analysis, the Congress session of 1928 and the Bardoli satyagraha in the same year 'thrust Gandhi into political limelight' and 'heralded his return to all-India leadership' (ibid.: 28–29). On both occasions, others resorted to Gandhi because they needed the Mahatma, and Gandhi responded because he felt he could satisfy those needs with his political expertise. The Bardoli satyagraha was a campaign against the enhancement of land revenue led by Vallabhbhai Patel. Bardoli, we have seen, was a *taluka* of Gujarat where the locally dominant Patidar community was well trained to undertake disciplined protests under the Congress banner.

Civil resistance against the increase in land revenue demand went on for several months, from February to August, and forced the Bombay government to enquire into the level of enhancement (Desai [1929] 1957; Bhatt 1970). This success resulted from the able leadership of Vallabhbhai Patel and the tight organization of the community of Patidars. The widely publicized struggle generated a wave of sympathy in Bombay and in other parts of India at a time when the Bombay government was under a lot of strain; it wanted an amicable settlement to the struggle. The constant use of Gandhi's name, the move, by Patel, to seek his consent before launching the struggle, Gandhi's letters to Patel, his press articles on Bardoli, as well as the mediation undertaken by Mahadev Desai, Gandhi's private secretary, made the satyagraha Gandhi's for all practical purposes. Its success enhanced Gandhi's prestige. Bardoli for Gandhi, writes Brown, 'was not just a local satyagraha for the redress of a specific grievance', it 'was a crucial demonstration of the road to swaraj' (1977: 31).

Even after Bardoli and the Congress session of 1928, Gandhi tried to confine Congress activities to constructive work in villages. He toured the countryside to collect funds for khadi, promoted the boycott of British goods and attempted redress of specific issues; he did not speak of an all-India struggle. Incidents of resistance continued unabated—there was an anti-feudal uprising in Rajasthan in 1929 and unrest in remote *adivasi* areas (Baker 1984; Bates 2007: 141).

We can only speculate on the reasons for Gandhi's relative indifference to politics. In Brown's reckoning, these years of rest and forced detachment gave Gandhi the opportunity to reflect. When he re-emerged on the political scene, Gandhi had 'considered afresh his goals and the following he wished to attract' (Brown 1977: 5). Sarkar attributes Gandhi's reluctance to 'bourgeois hesitation and ambiguities', stemming from his lack of control over groups and regions that were the most active politically in 1928–29: students and workers in Bengal, Bombay and Punjab (Sarkar [1983] 1995: 283). Brown affirms this indirectly. She mentions that the increasing signs of violence and terrorism among students made Gandhi uneasy. He found politics to be 'frivolous and disorderly compared with the hard labour for swaraj he recommended' (Brown 1977: 58). Gandhi, moreover, was aware that Congress membership had fallen low, and most provinces did not meet the quotas for members and funds. If, on the other hand, we accept Uday Singh Mehta's argument, Gandhi's indifference was in harmony with his philosophy in which patience and maturity earned through the lapse of time were key elements in the development of the satyagrahi (Mehta 2003). And the *swaraj* he proposed had to be earned by means of slow and careful self-training by the true satyagrahi, in order for it to be *swa* (true/proper) raj (Skaria forthcoming).

Gandhi showed willingness to accept Lord Irwin's offer of compromise made on 29 October 1929. Irwin declared 'dominion status' to be 'the natural issue of India's constitutional progress' and promised to hold a Round Table Conference soon after the Simon Commission's report was published. Gandhi, Motilal Nehru and Malaviya accepted this offer along with the liberals, on condition that the Congress be given majority representation in the Round Table Conference, which had to discuss the concrete details of dominion status. The Congress also asked for amnesty and a policy of general conciliation on the part of the government. Irwin refused to accept the conditions; negotiations fell through.

Gandhi's next move was to have Jawaharlal Nehru accepted as President of the Congress session in Lahore in December 1929 overriding the opposition of most provincial congress committees. Nehru's presidential address declared himself to be a socialist and a republican, and outlined an internationalist and socially radical path for the Indian freedom struggle. He openly criticized Gandhi's 'trusteeship' solution of zamindar–peasant and capital–labour conflicts, calling trusteeship a sham. Gandhi, however, did not lose control of the session; he rejected Subhas Bose's radical proposal that the Congress launch a movement for immediate non-payment of taxes, organize general strikes wherever possible and set up a parallel government. He even passed a resolution condemning HSRA's attack on Irwin's train near Delhi.

This conservative stance notwithstanding, the Lahore session remains memorable in the history of the freedom movement. It saw the final adoption, at midnight of 31 December, of *purna swaraj* to be the goal of the struggle for independence. Dominion status within the Commonwealth was finally rejected. The 'dilly-dallying' with reforms—'always too little, always too late'—was over (Chandra et al. [1972] 1975: 153). Cries of *inquilab zindabad* (long live the revolution), replaced the chanting of *bande mataram* as the Indian flag was unfurled. *Inquilab* had made its incursion into the road to independence as chalked out by the Congress!

This, of course, did not mean that the Moderate leaders as well as Gandhi's followers had lost their hold over the Congress. The independence pledge that the Indian National Congress presented to the world on 26 January 1930 stated that the British government in India had taken away the freedom of Indians and systematically exploited them. It had 'ruined India economically, politically, culturally and spiritually'. Further, the pledge affirmed that as Indians they considered it a sin 'before man and God to submit any longer to a rule that has caused this four-fold disaster to the country' (Pyarelal 1965: 62). The word 'sin' and the term 'four-fold disaster', Erik Erikson rightly points out, 'were obviously Gandhi's' (1969: 265).

These words, according to Erikson, marked a crucial distinction from the American Declaration of Independence, 'which merely marked a separation from England already accomplished on the shores of a vast and as yet empty continent'. 'Teeming India', in contrast, was 'occupied even in 1930 by a foreign nation'. This nation, which claimed to be enlightened and full of 'high ideals', 'had exploited and "drained" the Indian subcontinent, so the nationalists charged, in four areas of national life' (Erikson 1969: 265).

CIVIL DISOBEDIENCE, KHUDAI KHIDMATGARS, WOMEN

The 'sin' and the 'four-fold disaster' prompted Gandhi finally to propose a Civil Disobedience movement in order to achieve *purna swaraj*. Civil disobedience for him was the only way to save the country 'from impending lawlessness and secret crime'. This is because India had a group prone to violence that was not ready to 'listen to speeches, resolutions or conferences', but believed 'only in direct action' (Gandhi: 1930b). 'Disobedience', affirmed Gandhi, 'to be civil has to be open and non-violent. Complete civil disobedience is a state of peaceful rebellion—a refusal to obey every single State-made law'. In Gandhi's estimation, civil disobedience was 'certainly more dangerous than an armed rebellion', because it 'can never be put down if the civil resisters are prepared to face extreme hardships'. Civil disobedience 'is based upon an implicit belief in the absolute efficiency of innocent suffering' (Gandhi [1951] 1958: 173).

Civil disobedience was to begin with immediate boycott of legislatures and foreign cloth. This was to be followed by non-payment of taxes. The call for boycott met with lukewarm response. 'Congress Muslims' such as Dr Ansari were unhappy because there was no discussion of Hindu-Muslim unity, a prime condition for any all-India movement, and the Muslim League and the Muslim Conference dismissed the proposed movement as a ploy to establish Hindu Raj. The Hindu Mahasabha and the Justice Party declared their opposition to civil disobedience and the Sikhs and Indian businessmen showed uncertainty. Even the celebration of Independence Day on 26 January evoked little enthusiasm, although the independence pledge was taken at innumerable meetings all over the country. There were clashes between the police and Congress volunteers in Bihar.

In the face of such discord, Gandhi advanced a compromise formula—he sent an 11-point ultimatum to Irwin on 31 January. If the 11 points were met by 11 March, civil disobedience would not be launched. The 11 points did not envisage any change in the political structure—they included six issues of general interest related to reducing military expenditure and civil salaries, changes in the Arms Act and reform of the Central Investigation Department; three bourgeois demands, such as the lowering of the rupee–sterling exchange rate, protective tariff on foreign cloth and the reservation of coastal traffic for Indian shipping companies; and two claims that directly touched the peasants, the reduction of land revenue by half and its subjection to legislative control, and the abolition of salt tax and government monopoly over salt.

The issue of salt held the widest appeal and was the least divisive. But it was not a major concern for many Congress leaders who felt somewhat bewildered. Jawaharlal Nehru, for instance, had proposed an anti-zamindari rent campaign. Boycotting the salt tax, affirms Crispin Bates, was in fact 'a brilliant choice of target, both tactically and symbolically' (2007: 143). Salt was something abundantly available that anyone could make, and was a prime commodity of everyday use. Besides, salt had great symbolic charge in everyday parlance, in Hindi and other north Indian languages. For someone to have had somebody else's salt (*namak*) means that s/he has been offered food/shelter/help by a person binding her/him to that person with total loyalty. The terms *namak haram*, or *namak halal*, on the other hand, represent a traitor, a man without conscience, someone who lets down the person who has helped him by offering salt.

When Irwin showed no inclination to meet the demands, Gandhi began his historic Salt March, the Dandi March on 12 March 1930, from Sabarmati to the sea-side village of Dandi, about 200 miles from Sabarmati, through the heartland of Gujarat. According to the account offered by D. G. Tendulkar, Gandhi decided to start the march with 78 members drawn from different ashrams in Gujarat. But Vallabhbhai Patel's arrest on 7 March 'roused Gujarat from its temper' (Tendulkar 1969: 30). About 75,000 peasants gathered at Sabarmati to take a solemn pledge not to rest in peace till India was free (Tendulkar 1969: 30). The numbers grew in the course of the journey and the march caught the attention of the entire population of India and got great publicity abroad.

As Gandhi walked, 'leaning on his stick, a frail and peasant-like figure', villagers flocked 'to see

Gandhiji on his way to break a law which by taxes, increased the price of a daily necessity' (Chandra et al. [1972] 1975: 167). Volunteers poured into the ranks of the marchers to make it a 'non-violent column' marching on Dandi (ibid.). British socialist H. N. Brailsford, who was present in India during the march, described the salt satyagraha as the 'Kindergarten stage of revolution' (Brailsford cited in Sharma 1962: 79).

On 6 April, Gandhi and his followers bathed, prayed and picked up dried salt at the beach, symbolically and publicly violating the salt law. His civil disobedience had begun with a bang. It was to last, with minor interruptions, till 1934, and force another major constitutional concession from the British (Stein 2010: 308–09). The Congress Working Committee, in its meeting on 12 May 1930 in Allahabad, resolved to urge all provincial committees to 'take steps to continue and extend the manufacture of contraband salt for sale or consumption wherever possible' and directed that 'technical breaches of the Salt Law shall be continued with redoubled energy…' (Sharma 1962: 97).

A groundswell was evident in the widespread illegal manufacture and sale of salt, boycott of foreign cloth and liquor, and a plea made by the Patidars of Ras in Barsod *taluka* in Kheda district on 19 March, to start non-payment of revenue. Gandhi granted the plea reluctantly, but after his arrest on 7 May, the Congress Working Committee allowed the extension of non-payment of revenue to other ryotwari areas, and gave permission for non-payment of *chowkidari* taxes in the zamindari areas and the violation of forest laws in the Central Provinces. No-rent campaigns, significantly, were not allowed.

The Civil Disobedience movement nevertheless, was radical from the beginning and was not suspended after incidents of violence. Gandhi dismissed such breaches of non-violence as 'minor aberrations, mere details in a general campaign of disciplined satyagraha' (Stein 2010: 313–14). The declared goal of civil disobedience was complete independence, not just the redress of specific grievances and a vague *swaraj*, and it involved deliberate violation of law from the beginning rather than non-cooperation with foreign rule. The number of jail-goers was more than three times higher than during non-cooperation—it was estimated at 92,124 by Nehru, with the largest numbers recorded in Bengal, Bihar, UP, Punjab, the North-West Frontier Province, Bombay city, Delhi, Gujarat, Tamil Nadu, Andhra and Central Provinces (Sarkar [1983] 1995: 289).

When Gandhi was arrested, before he could offer satyagraha and make salt at the government depot in Dharsana, his place was taken by Abbas Tyabji, 'scion of the great Bombay family of nationalist Muslims' (Chandra et al. [1972] 1975: 167–68). He too was arrested and was replaced by Sarojini Naidu, the fiery poet and nationalist. Her attempt to raid Dharsana on 21 May 1930 has been inscribed in the graphic account of American journalist Webb Miller, who had managed to reach the spot with great difficulty. Miller recounts how police rushed on the advancing marchers and 'rained blows on their head with their steel-shod *lathi*s. Not one of the marchers raised an arm to fend off the blows' (Miller quoted in Chandra et al. [1972] 1975: 168).

As the ground was filled with bodies and the police picked up the injured, the first column of marchers was replaced by another and another. Miller was so sickened by 'the spectacle of unresisting men being methodically bashed into bloody pulp' that he had to turn away. 'I felt an indefinable sense of helpless rage and loathing…' (ibid.: 168–69).

The cult of fearlessness, inspired by Gandhi, had reached its moment of glory (Markovits 2003:

97). Prior to the movement, Gandhi had insisted on the necessity of courting imprisonment. 'We must seek arrest and imprisonment', he wrote, 'as a soldier who goes to battle seeks death'. We expect 'to bear down the opposition of the government by courting and not by avoiding imprisonment'. Our triumph consists 'in being imprisoned for no wrong whatsoever'. Indeed, the greater our innocence, 'the greater our strength and the swifter our victory' (Gandhi 1922; [1951] 1958: 173).

Widespread popular support for civil disobedience made several other struggles meld with it. Earlier, we have noted how the Chittagong revolutionaries invoked Gandhi Raj in their celebration of the capture of the armoury. Another remarkable example of Gandhi's appeal was provided by Peshawar, capital of the strategically sensitive North-West Frontier Province. The lead here was taken by Khan Abdul Ghaffar Khan, the son of a prosperous village chief of Utzmanzai near Peshawar.

Inspired by the Deoband nationalist group, the Khilafat movement, and the reforms introduced by the Afghan king Amir Amanullah, Ghaffar Khan had begun educational and social reform work among his Pathan countrymen from 1912. Endearingly called 'Badshah Khan', and later 'Frontier Gandhi', Ghaffar Khan started publishing *Pakhtun*, a political monthly in Pushto in May 1928, and organized *Khudai Khidmatgar* (servants of the god), a volunteer brigade of small and middle-ranking landlords, tenant farmers, poor peasants and agricultural labourers in 1929. By that year, Ghaffar Khan had also become a devoted disciple of Gandhi (Korejo 1993). He attended the Lahore session of the Congress along with several of his followers, and became dedicated to the path of non-violence. The numbers of the brigade increased from 500 to 50,000 in six months following the Lahore Congress, and the creed of non-violence helped reduce internal social tension and conflicts among the Pathans.

The government, unnerved by the mobilization of a strategically sensitive area and suspecting Communist activities by a local branch of the brigade in Peshawar, arrested Badshah Khan on 23 April 1930. An immense popular upsurge followed—large crowds confronted official cars and a big crowd firmly withstood police firing for three hours at Kissakahani Bazaar. The number of persons killed was 30 according to official sources and between 200 and 250 according to non-official ones. Hindu soldiers showed solidarity with their Muslim brethren, a platoon of Garhwal Rifles refused to shoot the unarmed crowd, and the situation remained extremely tense for the next ten days. It required martial law and a reign of terror to bring the situation under control. Such intense outrage against British rule in a province where the Muslim population totalled 92 per cent upset British stereotypes and calculations.

Tribal incursions in other parts of the province towards the end of 1930 clearly demonstrated the wide reach of Ghaffar Khan's appeal. The main area of activity of the *Khudai Khidmatgars* was Peshawar and the settled districts of Kohat, Bantu and Dera Ismail Khan. The tribal areas were far from these settled regions, and the distance made for ingenuity in ways that the messages of Ghaffar Khan, Gandhi and *inquilab* (revolution) travelled. Tribal raiders desisted from looting villages, and raised slogans for the release of Badshah Khan, Malang (naked) Baba (Gandhi), and *inquilab* (Sarkar [1983] 1995: 288). *Inquilab* had not only become personified, it had also become identified with the non-violence of Badshah Khan and Malang Baba.

Mill workers in Sholapur in Maharashtra offered yet another instance of Gandhi's pull. They greeted the news of Gandhi's arrest in May 1930 with a textile strike, assaults on police outposts, law courts, the municipal building and the railway station, all symbols of the hated Raj, and the burning of liquor shops. All this came dangerously close to Chauri Chaura. Indeed, three Muslim policemen were burnt alive just two days before Bakr-Id on 10 May. Surprisingly, there was no communal violence on the day of the festival, and Gandhi did not call off civil disobedience. It appears from the district magistrate's report of 13 May that a parallel government had been set up by Congress volunteers for a few days in Sholapur (Sarkar [1983] 1995: 289).

The participation of urban masses in the Civil Disobedience movement, particularly in UP, was much more extensive than in the 1920s, observes Gooptu. A striking feature of the movement was the 'gathering of large crowds along routes of, and often accompanying Congress processions, as well as at meetings and at sites of pickets outside foreign goods' shops' (Gooptu 2001: 324). This was possibly a consequence of the 'gigantic propaganda campaign' that the Congress had launched from 1929, first to oppose the Simon Commission, and later as a mode to develop a repertoire of powerful oppositional political rituals (Pandey 1978: 81).

Huge gatherings of urban poor went hand in hand with strikes organized by industrial workers. Dock labourers in Karachi went on strike, as did those of the Choolai Mill in Madras. Up-country transport workers in Calcutta and mill workers in neighbouring Budge Budge clashed with the police after Jawaharlal Nehru's arrest in mid-April and Gandhi's in early May. Labourers actively participated in the nationalist struggle even though Gandhi's 11 points did not cover their grievances at all. The Communists, on the other hand, stayed away from civil disobedience and did not have much role to play in labour militancy. They did, however, organize a big but unsuccessful strike of the Great Indian Peninsular Railway in Calcutta in February–March 1930, just before the beginning of civil disobedience (Sarkar [1983] 1995: 273). There were continuous tussles between the Communists and Congress socialists for control of trade unions. Such was the case in the unions of the jute mills in Calcutta, where Subhas Bose intervened actively to counter Communist influence (Bandyopadhyay 1984: 197).

Business groups and peasants showed overwhelming support for civil disobedience. Organizationally, the Congress was stronger than in 1921–22, which accounted for well-prepared movements on select grievances in specific areas, and for discipline and control of popular upsurge.

Unsurprisingly, there were wide regional variations in terms of groups who participated and the way they perceived Gandhian ideas. Gujarat, Bihar, UP and coastal Andhra—strongholds of Gandhi's constructive programme and satyagraha—no longer showed the millenarian hopes Gandhi *baba* had generated in 1921. There were well-organized salt satyagrahas for a time in Bardoli and Kheda in Gujarat; Bankura, Arambagh and Midnapur in Bengal; Bihpur in the Bhagalpur district in Bihar; and Balasore in Orissa, accompanied by picket of liquor shops and of excise license auctions, and followed by the refusal to pay *chowkidari* tax by the peasants in Midnapur and north and central Bihar, once the illegal manufacture of salt became difficult with the onset of monsoon. Bardoli and Kheda also saw successful no-revenue campaigns that forced the Patidars to take refuge in the neigbouring state of Baroda.

The permanently settled areas in Bengal and Bihar were scenes of 'the most acute rural class conflicts' (Stein 2010: 310). In Bihar, the provincial Kisan Sabha founded by Swami Sahajananda Saraswati, a religious leader, led small zamindars and rich peasants in struggles against big landlords. The Kisan Sabha had received Congress support since 1929; it did not, however, have any programme for improving the lot of share-croppers and landless labourers. The ryotwari areas in Madras and Bombay in contrast, demonstrated greater united hostility against the colonial state and greater potency of Congress-led movements.

Central Provinces, Karnataka, Maharashtra and tribal areas of central India—regions that had not come under the strong influence of non-cooperation, still demonstrated 'near millenarian fervour' (Sarkar [1983] 1995: 291). Here the Congress tried to make use of the serious grievances of poor peasants and tribal agriculturists over forest laws to conduct forest satyagrahas by means of satyagraha camps. The camps were set up to select and train forest satyagrahis who were to boycott forest department auctions, peacefully violate grazing and timber restrictions and publicly auction illegally acquired forest produce. The Karnataka Satyagraha Mandal even gave precise instructions on the types of trees to be cut down. The passion for *swaraj*, however, surpassed attempts at control.

In Madras, Gandhian leader C. Rajagopalachari used the onset of civil disobedience to oust his Madras-city based Swarajist rivals, Satyamurti and Srinivas Ayengar, from leadership of the provincial Congress. Rajagopalachari emulated Gandhi in organizing a march from Trichinolpoly to Vedarnniyam on the Tanjore coast where he broke the salt law in April 1930. Picketing of foreign cloth shops followed, and the anti-liquor campaign became powerful in the interior towns of the Madras Presidency. Here too, as elsewhere, popular participation made the movement potent yet violent. Rajaji's careful attempts to stay away from lower castes and poor peasants and labourers such as the Kallars, did not dissuade them from joining. Nor did his efforts to keep his march totally non-violent succeed. In David Arnold's terms, civil disobedience in Tamil Nadu 'thrived upon the violent eruptions of the masses and the violent repression of the police' (Arnold 2005: 265).

Women made themselves conspicuous by participating actively in large numbers in the movement. The last chapter discussed the possibilities and tensions inherent in Gandhi's perception of women and the gendered implications of his *charkha* movement. In *Young India* of 30 April 1930, Gandhi made a direct appeal to women to take up spinning yarn on the *charkha*, and come out of their homes and take part in pickets of shops selling foreign goods or liquor. Spinning (khadi) and salt, the two symbols of struggle, had vital links with women's 'life-sustaining activities' in the 'private' realm. The two together connected the 'private' with the 'public' in a revolutionary manner, and enabled women to carve out a space for themselves (Menon 2001: 10). Women did come out in large numbers, on account both of Gandhi's appeal and of their heightened degree of preparedness.

Colonial rule's impact on women in general had been detrimental. If the codification of land and property rights deprived women of their share of the produce (Oldenburg 2002, for instance); the movement for the betterment of women's condition and their education closed off lines of solidarity across class and caste shared by women (Banerjee 1990; Malhotra 2002, among others), even though some women made use of education and legal institutions of colonial rule to try and improve their lot (Anagol 2005).

The Indian nationalist discourse refashioned the educated Indian woman as the mistress of the family, further separating her from her lower class compatriots and her western other (Chapter 5). The modern woman of anti-colonial nationalist imagination, states Mrinalini Sinha, was 'expected to occupy a precarious position as the symbol of the colonized nation's "betweenness"'. She was to stand on 'a self-conscious middle ground suspended between the poles of "Western" modernity and of an unreformed indigenous "tradition"' (Sinha 2006: 47). Middle class and elite Indian women adopted this male discourse; but they claimed the right of educating women for themselves. They also entered the public sphere either in the field of social reform or in anti-colonial nationalist activities (Chapter 5; Forbes 1998: 75–82). Consequently, the women's movement headed by middle-class urban women that emerged in the 1920s (Chapter 7), gave priority to the nationalist demand of emancipation from imperialism over the redress of gender inequality (Kumar 1993; Menon 2001: 9).

The All India Women's Conference, set up in 1927, realized that the issue of women's education was intimately connected to *purdah* and child marriage, which in turn were related to India's political subjection. This made it stress on national self-government as critical to the realization of women's aspirations. The Congress and other organizations, for their part, supported the cause of women's enfranchisement from 1917, and the Nehru Report fully endorsed universal adult suffrage and sex equality. Several national women's organizations emerged in the 1920s (Forbes 1998), and women who joined Congress committees took part in all forms of civil disobedience and were prominent among revolutionary and Communist groups (Menon 2001: 8).

The arrival of Gandhi changed the scenario because of the way in which he mixed and shook-up role stereotypes. The involvement of women in the Non-cooperation Khilafat movement extended women's roles in the public sphere. At the same time, Gandhi's insistence on women's capacity of endurance and self-sacrifice, and his advocacy of asceticism and celibacy as an alternative to marriage underscored his inability of 'freeing' the sexuality of women in any other way (Menon 2001: 10). His call to women to 'come out of their households' during civil disobedience articulated his faith in the place of women in homes, and also made it clear that he was not thinking of women labourers. Women's participation in the nationalist and gender struggles, therefore, was largely consequent upon their own appropriation of the nationalist discourse and Gandhi's message.

And yet, the narrowness of Gandhi's stated views on women was exceeded by the more radical impact of his influence—the force of his personality, his stress on non-sexual relations between men and women and the novelty of his political strategy that revolved around the 'seemingly trivial but essential details of daily living', all of which enabled women to redefine their role in the political struggle (Kishwar 1985: 1691–1702; Sinha 2006: 48). There emerged a cadre of 'Gandhi's women' that included eminent nationalists, such as Sarala Devi Chaudhurani and Sarojini Naidu, as well as a host of lesser-known women (Morton 1953).

Communist activists, men and women, paid attention to women workers as individuals. Some middle-class women, such as Ushabai Dange, Prabhabati Devi, Anasuya Behn and Parvati Bore, inspired by the struggle of working people, became labour leaders and organized workers in the strikes in the 1920s (Kumar 1993: 66–70; Sen 1994). Nationalist 'Congress' women on the other hand, continued to think of women primarily as nurturers and considered their wages to be subsidiary to that of men, and made almost no effort to ensure a living wage for labouring women. This did not deter women workers from taking the initiative in organizing themselves (Sen 1999). Aided by Communist and trade union activity, they made their presence felt in working class struggle. They assumed prominent roles in the worker's movement, and joined strikes in large numbers. The Bombay textile strike of 1928–29 is a case in point.

In addition, peasant movements, such as the one led by Baba Ramchandra in Awadh and radical anti-caste movements headed by E. V. Ramaswamy Naicker in the south (Chapter 4) and B. R. Ambedkar in western India, addressed issues of exploitation of peasant women and criticized caste and gender hierarchies. At the Mahad Conference on 25 December 1927, marked by a pronounced participation of untouchable women, Ambedkar burnt a copy of the *Manusmriti* as an act of rejecting its implications both for women and for untouchables. All this opened new spaces for women (Sinha 2006: 48).

The general effervescence of civil disobedience therefore attracted women from different backgrounds. If women belonging to families of nationalist leaders and college students in big cities had participated in pickets and demonstrations during non-cooperation, women from ordinary families in big cities, small towns and rural areas, offered civil disobedience and courted arrest in large numbers. Even in a 'socially conservative city like Delhi', the number of women imprisoned for political activity totalled 1,600 (Chandra et al. [1972] 1975).

Women of upwardly mobile peasant castes in rural Bengal, writes Tanika Sarkar, took the movement of the Mahatma as a 'religious mission' and participated with great zeal (Sarkar 1984: 98). Large-scale participation of women led British observers to comment that even if the Civil Disobedience movement had not achieved anything else, it would be remembered for its great contribution to the 'mass social emancipation of Indian women' (Chandra et al. [1972] 1975: 167). Participation in pickets and demonstrations did not, of course, 'emancipate' women; but it did give them political maturity and the confidence to speak for themselves. This would eventually encourage them to raise questions about gender inequality and oppression within families.

The growing strength of the women's movement from the 1920s was reflected in the renewed attention it paid to the law. Even though the 1919 Reforms refused to enfranchise women, the Women's India Association inserted a new clause in its constitution to work for social reform through the newly constituted post-1919 legislative councils (Sinha 2006: 156–57). This prompted nationalists and the colonial state to pay greater attention to 'women's' issues.

The Civil Disobedience movement went beyond non-cooperation in involving intellectuals, industrialists, businessmen, traders and shop assistants, lower-middle class clerks, peasants, workers and women; it, however, fell behind with regard to Muslim participation (Sarkar [1983] 1995; Stein 2010: 309). As discussed earlier, the Hindu–Muslim unity of non-cooperation and Khilafat had given way to a widening rift between the two communities, and except for the North-West Frontier Province and Delhi, different Muslim groups stayed away from the Congress-led movement.

The months between March and August (1930) witnessed the highest enthusiasm for the movement. Overwhelming cooperation of business and capitalists in this early phase made for a sharp fall in British cloth imports from 26 million pounds in 1929 to 13.7 million in 1930 and from 1,248 million yards in 1929–30 to 523 million yards in 1930–31 (Sarkar [1983] 1995: 293). The world economic depression did lead to contraction in trade, but boycott and civil disobedience had a greater role to play. G. D. Birla donated between one and five hundred thousand rupees to the movement according to British Intelligence estimates, and did his best to convince Marwari traders in Calcutta who imported foreign piece goods to establish links with the cotton mills in Ahmedabad and Bombay instead. FICCI, under the aegis of Walchand Hirachand, decided to support the Congress and boycott the Round Table Conference till the time Gandhi agreed to join it.

Merchants and petty traders were even more forthcoming—they took pledges not to indent foreign goods. Imports of all British products suffered and between May and August 1930, the British Trade Commissioner's office was flooded with panic-stricken letters and complaints sent by white firms. This concrete support of merchants and traders made boycott more effective than the picketing organized by Congress volunteers. Bombay remained the principal citadel of civil disobedience, and the overwhelming presence of Congress volunteers, picketers, huge marches and demonstrations caused considerable concern to the authorities.

Bolstered by the success of the movement in its initial phase, Gandhi turned down the first attempts at negotiation, the Yeravda jail negotiation, that the government attempted through the mediation of Tej Bahadur Sapru and M. R. Jayakar in July-August 1930. Gandhi left the final decision to Nehru, and on 15 August, Gandhi and Nehru sent a letter demanding the right of secession from the Commonwealth, a national government with total control over defence and finance and an independent tribunal to settle British financial claims. The negotiations broke down. The Legislative Assembly elections of September 1930 showed considerable decline in the participation of voters. Only 8 per cent voted in the urban Hindu constituencies in Bombay, and the overall average participation declined to 26.1 per cent as compared to 48.07 in 1926.

The Congress boycotted the First Round Table Conference; it was attended by various Muslim groups, members of the Hindu Mahasabha, Sikhs, 'a set of secular politicians calling themselves Liberals', and a large contingent of Indian princes (Stein 2010: 315). The discussions did not amount to much—the representatives failed to come to an agreement over the allocation of seats in provincial legislatures.

From September 1930, enthusiasm for civil disobedience dwindled. Urban merchants and dealers broke the seals put by the Congress on imported goods in Benares, Bombay and Amritsar and started selling foreign cloth on the sly. Business groups started raising cries of alarm; resistance in the countryside started fraying under severe repression. Gandhi's idea of boycott of foreign cloth, it bears pointing out, was to replace it with khadi and not cloth produced by the mills. He was willing to accept 'some amount of profiteering by Indian mill-owners, but this had to be contained within limits' (Bandyopadhyay 2004: 364). Pledges of boycott had come after lengthy negotiations with Bombay and Ahmedabad textile mill-owners, and even then eight mills had refused to take the pledge. Traders and mill-owners, faced with large unsold stocks by September 1930, lost their enthusiasm for civil disobedience. Merchants and traders complained against the harassment occasioned by repeated *hartals*, and big industrialists were alarmed by the growing civil unrest and lack of respect for authority; they read in them signs of a social revolution.

It is true that there were indications of a second wave of less controlled and potentially more dangerous popular no-rent campaigns and tribal insurgency. By February 1931, Gandhi and other Congress members were ready to revert to negotiation. The liberals who returned from London in early 1931 also urged the Congress to attend the second session of the Round Table Conference. Lord Irwin agreed to come and meet Gandhi and his associates.

The Gandhi–Irwin Pact of March 1931 offered the Congress very little in return for Gandhi's decision to suspend an all out fight against British rule. The Civil Disobedience movement was called off with some assurance by the government that indemnities would be paid to those who had suffered in it. But Irwin did not accept any of Gandhi's important demands including the withdrawal of special ordinances, reparations for those whose lands had been confiscated and the revocation of the death sentence for Bhagat Singh, Sukhdev and Rajguru. All three were executed on 23 March.

The reasons behind Gandhi's decision once again are a matter of contention. While Aditya Mukherjee claims that Gandhi's decision to call off civil disobedience and attend the Second Round Table Conference as the sole representative of the Congress was determined by a host of factors (1986: 281), others insist that business pressure was the primary reason (Bandyopadhyay 1984: 200; Bandyopadhyay 2004: 365; Stein 2010: 315). The Congress Working Committee could not unanimously uphold the pact as a victory for Gandhiji. He had to face hostile demonstrations when he arrived in Karachi to attend a Congress session on 29 March, soon after the executions. The Workers and Peasants Party and the All India Youth League held parallel sessions in Karachi; they condemned the Gandhi–Irwin Pact and adopted resolutions on labour and peasant questions that went much further than the Congress' resolutions on fundamental rights and economic policy of the Karachi session (Chandra et al. [1972] 1975: 180–82).

Gandhi went to the Second Round Table Conference and returned from London empty-handed. Although he had agreed to open discussions on the basis of agreements reached in the First Round Table Conference, he could not accept the idea of separate communal electorates proposed by the British and favoured by representatives of the Muslims and depressed classes—'untouchables', Anglo-Indians, Indian Christians and Europeans.

In April 1931, Lord Irwin had been replaced by Lord Willingdon, who was less ready to take a liberal position and accept Gandhi's terms. In December 1931, after the delegates of the Second Round Table Conference failed to come to an agreement, British Prime Minister Ramsay Macdonald decided to outline the main points of the proposed Government of India Act. This was in accordance with the concord of the First Round Table Conference and Willingdon's policy. It provided for a strong federal centre and provincial autonomy with limited powers of self-government for the provinces. The most important federal areas of defence, foreign relations and finance were left to the Parliament in Westminster and to the Viceroy. Gandhi returned to India in disgust.

Civil disobedience was resumed in January 1932 under pressure from an impoverished countryside. Agrarian radicalism was present everywhere, from Kashmir and UP in the north to Andhra and Travancore in the south (Stein 2010: 316). Business support, however, was clearly absent, and the business community got split into three or four warring fronts with attitudes ranging from support for civil disobedience (Ahmedabad mill-owners) to vacillation (FICCI under Birla and Thakurdas), to opposition (Bombay, Calcutta and the south) to open condemnation (Tata and Homi Mody). Gandhi suggested individual civil disobedience through special action rather than collective civil disobedience. He was perhaps worried about violence resulting from mass action.

The situation in the country was very tense. State repression increased, all important political leaders were put in jail and the Congress was declared to be illegal. Jail beatings of political prisoners and their treatment as common criminals became rampant; there were also incidents of firing on prisoners, including in the notorious Hijli prison near Khargapur in 1932. As a corollary, revolutionary reprisals against official terror spiralled. At this stage, Ramsay Macdonald announced the 'Communal Award', that granted separate electorates to Hindus, Muslims and 'untouchables' for the new federal legislatures. Gandhi began a fast unto death in Yervada jail, demanding the substitution of separate electorate for 'untouchables' by joint electorate with reserved seats. Dr Ambedkar, the leader of the depressed classes, was forced to compromise. The result was the Poona Pact of September 1932. We will discuss this in greater detail in the following chapter. It is time to turn our attention to the Government of India Act of 1935 that finally concretized the reforms that the government and nationalists had been negotiating for so long.

THE ACT OF 1935: CENTRE, STATES, PRINCES

The Act, with a long period of gestation and almost no Indian contribution, replaced dyarchy of the 1919 Reforms with responsible self-government in all the departments in the provinces. At the same time, it gave provincial governors enormous 'discretionary power' to call the legislature, to not give consent to bills passed in legislatures and, most important and undemocratic of all, to take over the control of a province from its elected majority ministry on grounds of public order (Stein 2010: 326). The governors were also to command special powers to safeguard minority rights, privileges of civil servants and British business interests.

Dyarchy was introduced at the centre under condition of several safeguards and the Viceroy retained full control over foreign affairs, defence and internal security. The centre was to have a federal structure, but the federal state could become effective only after half the princes in India agreed to join it by signing the Instrument of Accession. This instrument was to override all previous treaties of the princes with the British Crown.

GOVERNMENTAL ORGANIZATION OF BRITISH INDIA, GOVERNMENT OF INDIA ACT 1935

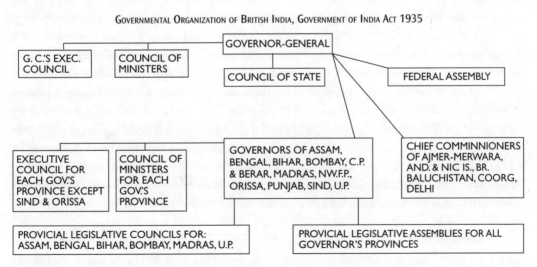

The Act conceded the long-standing demand of the Government of India for fiscal autonomy by transferring financial control from London to New Delhi. It also expanded the size of the electorate to 30 million, but retained high property qualifications. This meant that only 10 per cent of the Indian population got the right to vote. Rich and middle peasants, considered to be the Congress' main support base in rural areas, were enfranchised as a ploy to win away their loyalty from the Congress to the colonial government. In addition, the princes were given the right to nominate 30 to 40 per cent of the members to the bicameral central legislature, thereby ruling out the possibility of a Congress majority.

The Act, in D. A. Low's opinion, reflected the desire of the government to compete with the Congress for the allegiance of the dominant peasant communities ([1977] 2005: 24). The Act, moreover, granted separate electorate to the Muslims and reserved seats to the Scheduled Castes (a new term coined for the 'untouchables' or 'depressed classes') in the provincial and central legislatures. In sum, it sought to protect British interests in India by means of devolution and sharing of power with loyalist elements, a fact the Labour Opposition in London did not fail to point out.

Interestingly, the Act expanded women's franchise through preferential or special franchise qualifications; it also reserved seats for women in legislatures in accordance with the allocation of seats for different communities. This was a direct result of the attention paid to women by the colonial state, and the bold declaration, made in the Simon Commission Report of 1930 on proposed constitutional reforms for India that 'the women's movement in India, holds the key to progress' (Sinha 2006: 200). The Act of 1935, by granting political powers to women, paradoxically limited their scope for collective agency (ibid.).

The Act made no mention of dominion status granted during the Civil Disobedience movement. Conceived in parliamentary debates in Britain in which 'a small band of members sympathetic to the Indian cause pitted themselves against a vindictive majority led by Winston Churchill' (Stein 2010: 326), the Act was devised 'primarily to protect British interests rather than hand over control in vital areas' (Bridge 1986: ix). In effect, it diverted the attention of the Congress to the provinces and left a strong centre under imperial control. The Viceroy got many of the powers exercised by the Secretary of State, and the apex of the system of imperial control moved from London to Delhi (Tomlinson 1976: 130). This gave a new orientation to the Indo–British relationship, without harming imperial interest in any way.

For David Washbrook, the Act of 1935 was the most amazing of a series of strategies the British Raj devised 'to extend representation and promote economic growth without, apparently, changing any of the basic relations of power and wealth' constructed under its long period of rule (Washbrook 1997: 37).

No group in India had anything good to say about the act; the centralization of power by means of strengthening the executive was denounced by most. And yet, the fact that the act did not actually introduce a federal system suited many in India as it did the British political establishment. The Muslims had no desire for a strong, democratic central government, which they feared would be dominated by a large Hindu majority. The princes, for their part, were content to leave their relationship with the British unchanged (Stein 2010: 326). The act addressed the main problems that would come to haunt independent India—the structure of the state, centre–state relations and the interface of the executive and the legislature.

Interestingly, the Act of 1935 did not totally fade away with the rule of the King-Emperor—at the time 'India wrote "her own" Constitution in 1950, she took more than 250 of its clauses straight out of the relevant Parliamentary publication' (Washbrook 1997: 37). Surprisingly, the Indian Constitution took the discretionary power granted to governors to dissolve an elected ministry for reasons of public safety, a clause Indira Gandhi later used 'constitutionally' to suspend the Constitution and to revive a form of President/Viceroy's rule first seen in 1939.

REFERENCES

Adhikari, G, ed. 1971. *Documents of the History of the Communist Party of India, I, 1917–22*. New Delhi: People's Publishing House.

Anagol, Padma. 2005. *The Emergence of Feminism in India, 1850–1920*. Aldershot, Hampshire: Ashgate Publishing.

Arnold, David. 2005. 'The Politics of Coalescence: The Congress in Tamilnadu'. In *Congress and the Raj: Facets of the Indian Struggle, 1917–47*, edited by D. A. Low, 259–288. London: Heinemann; New Delhi: Oxford University Press (First published 1977).

Bahadur, Lal. 1983. *Indian Freedom Movement and Thought: Politics of "Pro-Change" versus "No-Change", 1919–1929*. New Delhi: Sterling Publishers.

Baker, David. 1984. '"A Serious Time": Forest Satyagraha in Madhya Pradesh, 1930'. *The Indian Economic and Social History Review* 21 (1): 71–90.

Bandyopadhyay, Gitasree. 1984. *Constraints in Bengal Politics 1921–41: Gandhian Leadership*. Calcutta: Sarat Book House.

Bandyopadhyay, Sekhar. 2004. *From Plassey to Partition: A History of Modern India*. Hyderabad: Orient Longman.

Banerjee, Prathama. 2010. 'Nationalism and Social Groups: Interfaces'. Delhi University E-lessons (http://www.illldu.edu.in/course/category.php?id=430). Accessed on: 15 May 2012.

Banerjee, Sumanta. 1990. 'Marginalisation of Women's Popular Culture in Nineteenth Century Bengal'. In *Recasting Women: Essays in Indian Colonial History*, edited by Kumkum Sangari and Sudesh Vaid, 127–79. New Brunswick: Rutgers University Press.

Barrier, N. G, ed. 1976. *Cawnpore Riots Enquiry Committee Report*. New Delhi: Oxford University Press. Reprinted in *Roots of Communal Politics: The Cawnpur Riot Commission Report*. Columbia, Mo.: South Asia Books.

Basu, Subho. 2004. *Does Class Matter? Colonial Capital and Workers' Resistance in Bengal, 1890–1937*. New Delhi: Oxford University Press.

Bates, Crispin. 2007. *Subalterns and the Raj: South Asia Since 1600*. London and New York: Routledge.

Bayly, C. A. 1975. *The Local Roots of Indian Politics: Allahabad, 1880–1920*. Oxford: Clarendon Press.

Bhatt, A. 1970. 'Caste and Political Mobilization in a Gujarat District'. In *Caste in Indian Politics*, edited by Rajni Kothari, 299–339. New Delhi: Oxford University Press.

Bose, Subhas Chandra. 1935. *The Indian Struggle, 1920–1934*. London: Wishart and Company Ltd.

Brass, Paul. 1974. *Language/Religion and Politics in Northern India*. London: Cambridge University Press.

Breman, Jan. 1976. 'A Dualistic Labour System: A Critique of the "Informal Sector" Concept'. *Economic and Political Weekly* Part 1, 11 (48) (27 November): 1870–1876; Part 2, 11 (49) (4 December): 1905–1908; Part 3, 11(50): 1939–44.

Bridge, Carl. 1986. *Holding India to the Empire: The British Conservative Party and the 1935 Constitution*. New Delhi: Sterling Publishers.

Brown, Judith M. 1977. *Gandhi and Civil Disobedience: The Mahatma in Indian Politics 1928–34*. Cambridge: Cambridge University Press.

Chakrabarty, Dipesh. 1989. *Rethinking Working-Class History: Bengal, 1890–1940*. Princeton, NJ: Princeton University Press.

Chandavarkar, Rajnarayan 1994. *The Origins of Industrial Capitalism in India: Business Strategies and Working Classes in Bombay, 1900–1940*. Cambridge: Cambridge University Press.

Chandra, Bipan. 1979. *Nationalism and Colonialism in Modern India*. New Delhi: Orient Longman.

Chandra, Bipan, Amales Tripathi and Barun De. [1972] 1975. *Freedom Struggle*. New Delhi: National Book Trust.

Chandra, Bipan, Mridula Mukherjee, Aditya Mukherjee, K. N. Panikkar, Sucheta Mahajan. [1989] 2000. *India's Struggle for Independence*. New Delhi: Penguin Books.

Das, Arvind Narayan. 1983. *Agrarian Unrest and Socio-Economic Change in North Bihar, 1900–80*. New Delhi: Oxford University Press.

Das, Rajani Kanta. 1923. *Factory Labour in India*. Berlin: De Gruyter.

Das, Veena. 1995. *Critical Events: An Anthropological Perspective on Contemporary India*. New Delhi: Oxford University Press.

Desai, M. [1929] 1957. *The Story of Bardoli*. Ahmedabad: Navajivan Trust.

Dhanagre, D. N. 1975. *Agrarian Movements and Gandhian Politics*. Agra: Institute of Social Sciences, Agra University.

———. 1983. *Peasant Movements in India, 1920–1950*. New Delhi: Oxford University Press.

Erikson, Eric H. 1969. *Gandhi's Truth: On the Origins of Militant Nonviolence*. New York: W. Norton and Company.

Forbes, Geraldine H. 1998. *Women in Modern India*. New Delhi: Foundation Books (South Asia edition). (First published by Cambridge University Press, 1997).

Fox, Richard G. 1985. *Lions of the Punjab: Culture in the Making*. Berkeley and Los Angeles: University of California Press.

Gandhi, M. K. 1922. 'Young India'. *Young India*, 5 January.

———. 1930a. 'Zamindars and Talukdars'. *Navajivan*, 12 January.

———. 1930b. 'To the Indian Critics'. *Young India*, 23 January.

———. 1934. 'Feature'. *Amrita Bazar Patrika*, 2 August.

———. [1951] 1958. *Satyagraha, Non Violent Resistance*. Ahmedabad: Navajivan Publishing House.

Gaur, Ishwar Dayal. 2008. *Martyr as Bridegroom: A Folk Representation of Bhagat Singh*. Delhi: Anthem Press India.

Gooptu, Nandini. 2001. *The Politics of the Urban Poor in Early Twentieth Century India*. Cambridge: Cambridge University Press.

Gordon, A. D. D. 1978. *Businessmen and Politics: Rising Nationalism and a Modernising Economy in Bombay, 1918–1933*. New Delhi: Manohar.

Gordon, L. A. 1974. *Bengal: The Nationalist Movement 1876–1940*. New York: Columbia University Press.

Goyal, D. R. 1979. *Rashtriya Swayamsevak Sangh*. New Delhi: Radha Krishna.

Guha, Ranajit. 1983. *Elementary Aspects of Peasant Insurgency in Colonial India*. New Delhi: Oxford University Press.

Hansen, Thomas Blom. 2001. 'The Ethics of Hindutva and the Spirit of Capitalism'. In *The BJP and the Compulsions of Politics in India*, edited by Thomas Blom Hansen and Christophe Jaffrelot, 291–314. New Delhi: Oxford University Press.

Hardiman, David. 1981. *Peasant Nationalists of Gujarat: Kheda District, 1917–1934*. New Delhi: Oxford University Press.

———. 1992. *Peasant Resistance in India*. New Delhi: Oxford University Press (Paperback edition 1994).

Hardy, Peter. 1972. *The Muslims of British India*. Cambridge: Cambridge University Press.

Hedgewar, Keshav Baliram. 1972. *Rashtriya Swayamsevak Sangh* (n.p).

Henningham, S. 1982. *Peasant Movements in Colonial India: North Bihar 1917–42*. Canberra: Australian National University.

Holmstrom, M. 1984. *Industry and Inequality: The Social Anthropology of Indian Labour*. Cambridge: Cambridge University Press.

Jaffrelot, Christophe. 1996. *The Hindu Nationalist Movement and Indian Politics, 1925 to the 1990s*. New Delhi: Penguin Books.

Joshi, Chitra. 1985. 'Bonds of Community, Ties of Religion: Kanpur Textile Workers in the Early Twentieth Century'. *The Indian Economic and Social History Review* 22 (3): 251–80.

Karnik, V. B. [1960] 1966. *Indian Trade Unions: A Survey*. Bombay: Manaktalas.

Kent Carrasco, Daniel. 2011. `V.D. Savarkar y la Hindú Mahasabha: hindutva y la Contingencia Política en la Década de 1940'. Unpublished Master's Thesis. Center of Asian and African Studies. México: El Colegio de Mexico.

Kishwar, Madhu. 1985. 'Gandhi on Women'. *Economic and Political Weekly* 20 (41) (12 October): 1753–1758.

Korejo, M. S. 1993. *The Frontier Gandhi, His Place in History.* Karachi: Oxford University Press.

Kumar, Kapil. 1984. *Peasants in Revolt: Tenants, Landlords, Congress and the Raj in Oudh, 1886–1922*. New Delhi: Manohar.

Kumar, Radha. 1993. *A History of Doing: An Illustrated Account of Movements for Women's Rights and Feminism in India*. New Delhi: Kali for Women.

Kumar, Ravinder. 1971. 'Bombay Textile Strikes 1919'. *The Indian Economic and Social History Review* 8 (1): 1–12.

Low, D. A. [1977] 2005. 'Introduction: The Climatic Years'. In *Congress and the Raj: Facets of the Indian Struggle, 1917–47*, edited by D. A. Low, 1–46. New Delhi: Oxford University Press.

Malhotra, Anshu. 2002. *Gender, Caste, and Religious Identities: Restructuring Class in Colonial Punjab*. New Delhi: Oxford University Press.

Markovits, Claude. 1985. *Indian Business and Nationalist Politics 1931–39: The Indigenous Capitalist Class and the Rise of the Congress Party*. Cambridge: Cambridge University Press.

———. 2003. *The Un-Gandhian Gandhi: The Life and Afterlife of the Mahatma*. Delhi: Permanent Black.

Mathur, Sobhag. 1996. *Hindu Revivalism and the Indian National Movement: A Documentary Study of the Ideals and Policies of the Hindu Mahasabha, 1939–1945*. Jodhpur: Kusumanjali Prakashan.

McLane, John R, ed. 1970. *The Political Awakening in India*. Englewood Cliffs, NJ: Prentice Hall.

Mehta, Uday S. 2003. 'Patience, Inwardness, and Self-Knowledge in Gandhi's *Hind Swaraj*'. *Public Culture* 23 (2): 417–29.

Menon, Nivedita, ed. 2001. *Gender and Politics in India*. New Delhi: Oxford University Press.

Misra, Maria. 1999. *Business, Race and Politics in British India, c.1850–1960*. Oxford: Clarendon Press.

Moore, R. J. 1974. *The Crisis of Indian Unity, 1917–1940*. New Delhi: Oxford University Press.

Morris, M. D. 1965. *The Emergence of an Industrial Labor Force in India: A Study of the Bombay Cotton Mills*. Berkeley and Los Angeles: University of California Press.

Morton, Eleanor. 1953. *The Women in Gandhi's Life*. New York: Dodd, Mead.

Mukherjee, Aditya. 1986. 'The Indian Capitalist Class: Aspects of its Economic, Political and Ideological Development in the Colonial Period, 1927–47'. In *Situating Indian History for Sarvepalli Gopal*, edited by S. Bhattacharya and R. Thapar, 239–287. New Delhi: Oxford University Press.

Murugesan, K. and C. S. Subramanyam. 1975. *Singaravelu—First Communist of South India*. New Delhi: People's Publishing House.

Nehru, Jawaharlal. 1941. *Toward Freedom: The Autobiography of Jawaharlal Nehru*. New York: The John Day Company.

Newman, R. 1981. *Workers and Unions in Bombay, 1918–29: A Study of the Organisation in Cotton Mills*. Canberra: Australian National University.

Oberoi, Harjot. 1994. *The Construction of Religious Boundaries: Culture, Identity, and Diversity in the Sikh Tradition*. Chicago: University of Chicago Press.

Oldenburg, Veena Talwar. 2002. *Dowry Murder: The Imperial Origins of a Cultural Crime*. New York: Oxford University Press.

Pandey, Gyanendra. 1978. *The Ascendancy of the Congress in Uttar Pradesh, 1926–34: A Study in Imperfect Mobilization*. New Delhi: Oxford University Press.

———. 1982. 'Peasant Revolt and Indian Nationalism: The Peasant Movement in Awadh, 1919–22'. In *Subaltern Studies I: Writings on South Asian History and Society*, edited by Ranajit Guha, 143–197. New Delhi: Oxford University Press.

———. 1992. *The Construction of Communalism in Colonial India*. New York: Oxford University Press.

Pandey, S. M. 1970. *As Labour Organises: A Study of Unionism in the Kanpur Cotton Textile Industry*. New Delhi: Shri Ram Centre for Industrial Relations.

Parakunnel, Thomas J. 1935. 'India in the World Depression'. *The Economic Journal* 45 (179): 469–83.

Prasad, Rajendra. 1927. Introduction to *Young India 1924–26*, by M. K. Gandhi. Triplicane, Madras: S. Ganesa.

Pyarelal. 1965. *Mahatma Gandhi, Volume 1, The Early Phase*. Ahmedabad: Navajivan Trust; also see Gandhi at: http://www.gandhiserve.org/cwmg/VOL048.PDF:212. Accessed on: January 2012.

Ray, R. K. 1979. *Industrialization in India: Growth and Conflict in the Private Corporate Sector, 1914–47*. New York: Oxford University Press.

———. 1984. *Social Conflict and Political Unrest in Bengal, 1857–1927*. New Delhi: Oxford University Press.

Ray, Sibnarayan, ed. 1987. *Selected Works of Manabendra Nath Roy*. New Delhi: Oxford University Press.

Roy, Bhupendra Kishore Rakshit. 1970. *Bharate Sasastra Biplab*. Kolkata, (n.p).

Sanyal, Hitesh Ranjan. 1981. *Social Mobility in Bengal*. Calcutta: Papyrus.

Sarkar, Sumit. 1973. *The Swadeshi Movement in Bengal, 1903–8*. Delhi: People's Publishing House.

———. [1983] 1995. *Modern India, 1885–1947*. Madras: Macmillan India.

———. 1984. 'The Conditions and Nature of Subaltern Militancy: Bengal from Swadeshi to Non Cooperation, c.1905–22'. In *Subaltern Studies III: Writings on South Asian History and Society*, edited by Ranajit Guha, 271–320. New Delhi: Oxford University Press.

Sarkar, Tanika. 1984. 'Politics and Women in Bengal: The Conditions and Meaning of Participation'. *The Indian Economic and Social History Review* 21 (1): 91–101.

Savarkar, V. D. 1949. *Hindu Rashtra Darshan: A Collection of the Presidential Speeches Delivered from the Hindu Mahasabha Platform*. Bombay: L. G. Kharo.

Seal, Anil. 1973. 'Imperialism and Nationalism in India'. In *Locality, Province and Nation: Essays on Indian Politics, 1870–1940*, edited by J. Gallagher, G. Johnson and A. Seal, 1–28. Cambridge: Cambridge University Press.

Sen, Samita. 1999. *Women and Labour in Late Colonial India: The Bengal Jute Industry*. Cambridge: Cambridge University Press.

Sen, Sukomal. 1977. *Working Class of India: History of Emergence and Movement, 1830–1970*. Calcutta: K. P. Bagchi & Co.

Sen, Sunil Kumar. 1994. *Working Class Movements in India, 1885–1975*. New Delhi: Oxford University Press.

Sharma, J. S., ed. 1962. *India's Struggle for Freedom: Select Documents and Sources*. Vol. 1. Delhi: S. Chand and Co.

Siddiqi, Majid Hayat. 1978. *Agrarian Unrest in North India: The United Provinces*. New Delhi: Vikas Publishing House.

Singh, Khuswant. 1966. *A History of the Sikhs, Vol. 2, 1839–1964*. Princeton, NJ: Princeton University Press.

Sinha, H. and J. C. Sinha. 1938. 'India Through the Depression'. *Sankhya: The Indian Journal of Statistics* 4 (2): 193–220.

Sinha, Mrinalini. 2006. *Specters of Mother India. The Global Restructuring of an Empire*. Durham, NC: Duke University Press.

Skaria, Ajay. (Forthcoming). *Immeasurable Equality: Gandhi and the Gift of Religion*. Extracted with permission from the author.

Stein, Burton. 1969. *Mahatma: Life of Mohandas Karamchand Gandhi*. New Delhi: Government of India, Ministry of Information and Broadcasting.

———. 2010. *A History of India*. Revised and edited by David Arnold. Sussex, UK: Wiley-Blackwell. (First published 1998. Oxford: Oxford University Press).

Timberg, Thomas A. 1978. *The Marwaris: From Traders to Industrialists*. New Delhi: Vikas Publishing House.

Tomlinson, B. R. 1976. *The Indian National Congress and the Raj, 1929–1942: The Penultimate Phase*. London: Macmillan.

Tripathi, D., ed. 1991. *Business and Politics in India: A Historical Perspective*. New Delhi: Manohar.

Washbrook, David A. 1981. 'Law, State, and Agrarian Society in Colonial India'. *Modern Asian Studies* 15 (3): 649–721.

———. 1997. 'Rhetoric of Democracy and Development in Late Colonial India'. In *Nationalism, Democracy and Development: State and Politics in India*, edited by Sugata Bose and Ayesha Jalal, 36–49. New Delhi: Oxford University Press.

Many Pathways of a Nation

9

Pencil sketch of B. R. Ambedkar

Chapter outline

The story of nationalism and nationalist struggle that we have tracked so far is riddled with contention and negotiation. This is because, on the one hand, there were distinct ways of imagining the nation, and on the other, there were diverse understandings of Indian society that generated an array of visions with regard to individuals, groups and communities who peopled the society and were to inhabit the independent nation.

The Indian National Congress, established consciously as a 'national' organization, constantly accommodated contending groups and ideas in order to provide shelter to all factions and project itself as an all-encompassing consolidated entity representing Indian interests. Over time, fissures within the Congress became pronounced, and its claim as the political representative of all India came to be challenged and interrogated by a variety of associations and groups. The reforms introduced periodically by the British Raj from the second half of the nineteenth century, exacerbated this tension and competition.

The reforms, intended to give educated Indians some share in the governance of their own country, assured the Indians that they would eventually be given the responsibility of a representative self-government. The notion of representation, in conjunction with measures that categorized different groups and communities of Indians numerically and socially, came to engage the attention of different social groups, and a lot of energy was invested in trying to secure equal representation for all communities. Different political parties vied with each other over claims of representation; competition grew intense as the institutional reforms of the twentieth century marked out different groups as 'minority', 'backward' or 'depressed' and gave them special privileges. As social categories got transformed into political ones, the nationalist struggle came to revolve around the offers being made by the reforms and got confined almost exclusively to the sphere of institutional politics; it never managed to interrogate the basic premises on which the reforms were based.

The 'Muslims', delineated by census and other operations of the colonial state as the largest 'minority', were not very enthusiastic about the Congress from the beginning. This lack of enthusiasm got transformed into competition and hostility as the promise of representative government produced the threat of political domination by a majority, the Hindus, who predominated in the Congress.

Sir Sayyid Ahmad Khan was among the first Muslim aristocrats who voiced this concern of being dominated by a majority. As discussed in Chapter 4, the Revolt of 1857 and a prior trip to England prompted Sayyid Ahmad to reflect critically on the condition of Muslims in India and their relation with the colonial state. As members of the Muslim aristocracy and the former ruling class, Sayyid Ahmad and many others of his milieu were shocked by the status of minority, as well as the label of 'backward' ascribed to Muslims in influential works of British administrators-cum-ethnographers. Sayyid Ahmad strongly believed that the political rights of communities needed to be decided on the basis of their entitlement and position in society, and Muslims, being members of the former ruling class, had a special place within the cosmopolitan British empire. He also urged the colonial state to redress the lack of Muslim representation in education and government employment. Sayyid Ahmad's ideas were opposed both by the ulema and by Muslim scholars attached to their 'societal moors' and the idea of a universal Muslim *ummah* (nation/community) in the late nineteenth century. Such scholars called for Hindu–Muslim unity as the first step to dislodge colonialism (Jalal 1997: 79). In the changed context of the twentieth century, however, Sayyid Ahmad's policy came to hold sway.

Curzon's open affirmation of the benefits of a Muslim-majority province of eastern Bengal and Assam for Muslims had inspired some Muslim elite in eastern Bengal to found the Muslim League in 1906. The granting of a separate electorate to Muslims in the Morley–Minto Reforms of 1909 transformed the Muslims into an all-India political category; it also made them a 'perpetual minority' (Jalal [1985] 1994). Henceforth, relations between the Congress and the Muslim League came to be governed by the 'structural imperatives' of representative government. Brief periods of amity and cooperation—for instance, the Lucknow Pact of 1916 and the Non-Cooperation Khilafat campaign of 1921–22—were to be countered by fierce competition and conflicts among the Congress and the League, as well as between 'Hindus' and 'Muslims', often a direct result of efforts at mobilization.

Added to these were tensions generated by class, caste, regional, socio-cultural, economic and religious differences among a vast and diverse population; differences that acquired significance at different moments depending on the contingent forging of identities prompted by the imperatives of representative politics. This chapter studies some articulations of these distinctions in vision, imaginings and understandings of the nation. The paradox of a struggle that emerged out of the colonial situation and was simultaneously governed and constrained by it resulted in contradictions and fissures that could not be contained by the idea of an imagined, united community. Efforts to produce a national community raised serious issues about whose nation and what kind of nation that did not find adequate answers, and attempts to fashion an economically, culturally and territorially bound independent community succeeded in acquiring independence through division, a story we will track in the following chapter.

Chronology of Events Leading to Independence, 1861–1947

Year		Leading Events
1861		Indian Councils Act enlarges membership of Legislative Council by 6 to 12 new members, half to be non-official; re-establishes powers of Presidency Councils and enables establishment of other Provincial Councils. Three Indians appointed to Central Legislature in 1862.
1883		Ilbert Bill, giving equal rights to Indian judges, provokes agitation among Europeans; amendation provokes nationalist response from Indians.
1885	December	First session of Indian National Congress at Bombay.
1892		Indian Councils Act enhances size and powers of Legislative Councils at centre and in provinces by 15 to 20 new members.
1905	May	Announcement of partition of Bengal.
1906	October	Muslim deputation, led by Agha Khan, petitions Viceroy at Simla for separate Muslim electorate, weightage in representation.
	December	Muslim League established by Mohammedan Educational Conference meeting at Dacca, then capital of newly created Muslim majority province.
	December	Congress President Naoroji declares for *swaraj* (self-government).
1909		Punjab Hindu Sabha holds conference at Lahore. Political aspects of this Sabha culminate in formation of All-India Mahasabha party in 1923.
		Morley–Minto legislative reforms provide for Indian member of Executive Council, separate electorates for Muslims.

Year		Leading Events
1911		Coronation Durbar of George V held at Delhi. Announcement of reunification of Bengal and change of seat of Government from Calcutta to Delhi, effective 1912.
1913	March	Muslim League adopts self-government as goal.
1915	January	Mohandas K. Gandhi returns to India from South Africa.
1916		Indian National Congress and Muslim League announce the Lucknow Pact, a joint constitutional scheme for India on the basis of dominion status.
1917	August	Secretary of State, E. S. Montagu, announces 'responsible government' is goal of British policy in India.
1918		National Liberal Federation (Liberal Party) formed by T. B. Sapru and M. R. Jayakar.
1919	February	Rowlatt Bills passed, empowering Government to try political cases without juries.
	April 6	All India *hartal* (work stoppage) to protest Rowlatt Bills.
	April 13	Amritsar firing during martial law enforcement following *hartal* disturbances in Punjab.
	December	Parliament passes Government of India Bill, based on Montagu-Chelmsford reforms.
1920	May	Khilafat Committee accepts Gandhi's non-cooperation program.
	December	Congress resolution on non-cooperation program. Congress goal now attainment of *swaraj*. Twenty-one provincial committees based on language areas created by Indian National Congress, now under Gandhi's leadership.
1921		First elected Legislative Councils under Montagu-Chelmsford reforms.
		Trial of Shaukat and Mohammad Ali, leaders of Khilafat movement.
1922		Creation of Swaraj Party by C. R. Das and Motilal Nehru to wreck legislative councils from within.
1925		Muddiman Committee report on working of Montagu-Chelmsford reforms. Revisions include enfranchisement of women, increased nominated representation of Depressed Classes.
1928		Motilal Nehru report on constitutional matters adopted by All-Parties Conference. Jinnah branch of Muslim League dissenting.
		Simon Commission tour to examine working of Montagu-Chelmsford reforms, boycotted by Congress and Muslim League.
1930		January 26 declared 'Independence Day' by Congress. Mohammad Iqbal presents idea for Muslim State within Indian Federation to Muslim League meeting.
1930–32		Three Indian Round Table Conferences held in London to discuss questions of forthcoming Indian Constitution.
1931	March	Gandhi–Irwin Pact, ends Civil Disobedience campaign and enables Gandhi to participate in Second Round Table Conference as Congress representative. Failure on Round Table agreement resulted in 1932–35 individual Civil Disobedience campaign inaugurated by Gandhi.
1932		Communal award grants separate electorates to Muslims, Sikhs and Depressed Classes. Gandhi fasts in Yervada jail over latter award, resultant Poona Pact cancels separate electorates for Depressed Classes, includes reserved seats.
1934		Socialist Party founded as Congress offshoot.

Year		Leading Events
1935		Government of India Act.
1937		Elections for Provincial Legislatures under 1935 Government of India Act. Congress wins in 9 of 11 provinces.
1939		Resignation of Congress ministries over Government of India war declaration without consultation with Indians.
1940		Muslim League declaration for Pakistan.
1942	March– April	First Cabinet Mission. Cripps offer of Dominion Status after the end of the war refused by Congress.
1945		Simla Conference of all political groups called by Lord Wavell fails over issue of strength and composition of Legislative Council
1945–46		General elections in India.
1946		Second Cabinet Mission fails in attempt to win support for Federal Government in India
1947	February	Britain announces intention to quit India by June 1948; sends Lord Mountbattan as Viceroy to arrange transfer of power.
	August 15	Independence granted to India, Pakistan.

CRITIQUES OF CASTE: NON-BRAHMAN AND 'UNTOUCHABLE' MOVEMENTS

The other groups that took note of the lack of representation and social privilege were the 'untouchables' and lower castes. Marked out in censuses and surveys as the 'depressed classes' roughly from the 1850s, these groups also came to be defined as backward and worthy of colonial concern.

Colonial intervention, it bears pointing out, set in motion two contradictory processes. On the one hand, there was a secularization of caste because the government 'abdicated direct responsibility of adjudicating issues of ritual status, religious rights, and community standing'. This produced 'new openings for challenging caste discipline and Brahmanical norms' (Rao 2009: 43). The promulgation of uniform law and certain other administrative measures along with the spread of education removed legal inequality in the treatment of castes, except for the 'depressed castes' that were not given the right to enter temples (Ghurye [1950] 1958 in Banerjee-Dube 2008: 42).

On the other hand, there was a 'novel association of caste with Hindu religion'. Even though a caste could not administer justice, the government respected the customs of a caste in matters of civil law unless they went against public policy (Ghurye 2008: 42). The policy of 'non-interference in religious and social customs of the people', argue Bharat Patankar and Gail Omvedt, made legal equality almost meaningless (1979: 411). Courts enforced religious and ritual restrictions, and treated defilement of religious norms as a 'criminal offence' in punishing the wrongdoer. On another plane, construction of colonial knowledge depended crucially on the mediation of Brahmanical knowledge and the secularization of the Brahman's power as a state functionary. Power now came to be exercised through the binary registers of the 'religious' and the 'political' that respected neither social experience nor popular categorization (Rao 2009: 43).

Caste-wise enumeration in the census and the outlining of the 'depressed' castes, working in tandem with the activities of Christian missionaries from the early-nineteenth century, who, we have seen, made caste a principal target of attack and condemnation, produced 'new investments in history and caste identity'. Alongside, a new range of modern institutions—schools and colleges, law courts and hospitals—opened new spaces which could be used by the 'downtrodden' to try and attain social mobility (ibid.: 44). New experiences of the self emerged out of the multiple and dispersed effects of colonial rule, and allowed a radical egalitarian ideology to permeate caste discourse.

Chapter 4 traced the growth of lower caste and non-Brahman movements in the second half of the nineteenth century. Made aware by the census and other surveys of their numerical strength in the population, these groups clamoured for a certain degree of equality in public employment and demanded representation equivalent to their numbers in local legislative councils, which started to include 'native' members from the 1880s. We have also seen how rulers of the princely states of Mysore and Kolhapur introduced caste-based reservation in public employment for members of the 'depressed classes' in order to redress the huge gap in numerical strength and lack of access to privileges.

Demand and competition for education, public employment and representation was only one part of the story; a new and distinctive critique of caste evolved over the late-nineteenth and early-twentieth centuries as ideas of self-respect and equality among inmates expanded to include a critical reflection on the structured socio-political-economic inequities inherent in Brahmanism. Western and southern India saw the emergence of powerful movements that asserted 'untouchable', lower caste and Dravidian identity, and held the caste system and Brahmans responsible for the plight of untouchables and Shudras (non-Brahmans).

The south and the west, it bears pointing out, had also been strong centres of the *bhakti* movement. Many of the *bhakti* saints, Tukaram and Chokhamela of Maharashtra for instance, had interrogated social discrimination sanctioned by caste, decried rituals and priests and professed the equality of all before the divine. The new movements drew on these ideas in discrete ways to question social and political inequality and claim equity in the public sphere and in institutional politics. A combination of *bhakti* and protestant religiosity resulted in the resurgence of sects, such as the Sri Narayana Dharma Paripalana Yogam among the Ezhavas in Kerala and the Matua sect among the Namasudars in eastern Bengal, which propagated the message of simple devotion and social equality, and questioned Hindu social hierarchy (Bandyopadhyay 2004: 352).

At the same time, *bhakti*, argues Omvedt, induced a trend towards re-absorption into Hinduism. Many of the movements attempted to appropriate certain visible symbols of high ritual status, such as wearing of the sacred thread and participating in rituals and ceremonies that they were barred from, and demanding the right to enter Hindu temples, a movement that became pronounced in the second and third decades of the twentieth century. Movements of lower castes and 'untouchables' in Omvedt's analysis, took two different paths—one of radical assertion of autonomy from Hinduism and from Hindu social and political organizations, and the other of integration with them (Omvedt 1994: 133–34). These two trends are variously referred to as radical and conservative in historiography.

The non-Brahman movement in western India demonstrated these two trends in the early-twentieth century. The first one, led by Shahu Chhatrapati, a descendant of Shivaji and the ruler of Kolhapur, and by relatively wealthy non-Brahmans, placed full trust in the colonial government. It demanded special privileges, such as reservation of seats in education and government institutions as well as in legislative councils. Sympathetic to the aspirations of untouchables, Shahu's main objective was creating a non-Brahman elite class among the peasant castes. He helped non-Brahman students to get scholarships, encouraged educated non-Brahmans to settle in higher professions and participate in the politics of Bombay Presidency and extended help to non-Brahman journalists (Pandit 1979: 431).

The non-Brahman elite defied the supremacy of Brahmans in social and religious fields and showed scant regard for the demands being made by the Congress for constitutional reforms. In their reckoning, only Brahmans stood to gain from political rights and political reforms. This group remained openly loyal to the British government, particularly after their demand for special privileges was granted by the 1919 Reforms. A non-Brahman political party, the Non-Brahman Association, set up after the Montagu-Chelmsford Reforms, disregarded the Congress call for non-cooperation, contested elections to provincial legislative councils and secured a few seats. Political power made the elite abandon the struggle for social reform. Phule's dream of a united front of Shudras and Ati-Shudras turned out to be ephemeral, and the non-Brahman Association slowly dissociated itself from the powerful 'untouchable' movement taking shape under B. R. Ambedkar (Pandit 1979: 431; Rao 2009).

The radical trend, represented by Phule's Satyashodhak Samaj, took inspiration from the militant movements of workers and peasants in the 1920s to develop 'class content'. It spoke of the inherent contradictions between the *bahujan samaj* or majority community of the masses, and that of '*shetji-bhatji*', the elite community of merchants and Brahmans (Bandyopadhyay 2004: 347; Omvedt 1976). Members of the Satyashodhak Samaj toured villages in the 1920s and urged peasants to resist Brahman domination. At the same time, they were impressed by Gandhi's constructive programme, his championing of the dignity of labour and open criticism of untouchability and constant reference to the welfare of the downtrodden as the only justification for *swaraj*. Under the leadership of Keshavrao Jedhe in Poona, they responded to the Congress call and participated in the Civil Disobedience movement (Pandit 1979: 431). Jedhe's alliance with Congress leader N.V. Gadgil strengthened the Congress base in Maharashtra and the non-Brahman movement of the Bombay Presidency formally decided to merge with the Congress at its Vidarbha session in 1938.

Jotirao Phule, we are aware, had innovatively inversed the Orientalist myth of an Aryan invasion (O'Hanlon 1985), reconstructed history as one of caste conflict and reclaimed a non-Aryan Kshatriya past for subordinate groups in Maharashtra (Chapter 4). He had also asserted that the Mahars and the Mangs, the original inhabitants of Maharashtra (Ethnoven 1922; Russell and Hira Lal 1916: 1938), had made themselves exemplary by offering the strongest resistance to Aryan invaders with the result that the Mahars—the largest group of untouchables in Maharashtra, whose spread is said to have defined the territorial contours of Maharashtra (Pandit 1979: 409)—had to pay the price of their resistance once the Aryans established themselves.

The movement in the south closely resembled the one in the west. Here the loyal, conservative trend was represented by the Justice Party in the Madras Presidency and the *Prajamitramandali* in the princely state of Mysore. These parties participated in the 'rat race to join the ranks of government clericaldom' (Nagaraj 1993: 5), and once this need was satisfied, abandoned the larger and more important issue of social change. The Reforms of 1919 granted 28 reserved seats to non-Brahmans in the Madras Legislative Council, and the Justice Party, as we have seen in Chapter 7, participated in the elections in 1920 in total violation of the Congress programme of non-cooperation. The high point in the achievements of the Justice Party was the formation of a ministry in 1920, which also marked the beginning of its decline. The elite non-Brahmans began using and abusing their newly gained power and started neglecting the 'untouchables' who left the party in disgust. This led to an erosion of support for the party; it performed disastrously in the 1926 elections. The Justice Party was almost completely ousted by the Swaraj Party. The Congress regained its influence in the region and the Civil Disobedience movement attained great success.

The more radical trend, represented by 'Periyar' E. V. Ramaswamy Naicker and his 'Self-Respect' Movement (Chapter 4), showed great enthusiasm for non-cooperation. By 1925, however, Naicker was sorely disappointed with Gandhi and the Congress because they were not willing to offer 'substantive' citizenship to non-Brahmans (Pandian 1993). Gandhi's continued support of *varnasharamadharma* also upset Naicker. Following Gandhi's 1927 tour of Madras, Naicker came up with a cogent critique of Aryanism, Brahmanism and Hinduism, all of which contained multiple structures of subjection for Shudras, Ati-Dravidas (untouchables) and women (Bandyopadhyay 2004: 349).

The Reforms of 1919, undoubtedly, provided the 'untouchables' with a 'spark' to organize, but even more significant were the subsequent 'massive economic and political upheavals of the post-war period' (Patankar and Omvedt 1979: 415). All over India, the depressed classes came forward to assert their identity— Ad-Dharm in Punjab, Ati-Dravida in Tamil Nadu, Namasudras in Bengal, Adi-Andhra in Andhra, Adi-Hindu in UP with its centre at Kanpur, Mahars in Maharashtra, and Pulayas and Chenumars in Kerala. Notwithstanding the regional and linguistic base of the movements that made for important variations, there was considerable exchange of ideas among the different groups and a sharing of core ideology.

In Review: Divine Tamil and Demanding Dalit

The socio-political milieu that nurtured the growth of Dravidian ideology in the late-nineteenth and early-twentieth centuries had three important features: (1) a near monopoly exercised by English educated Brahmans over the public administration of Madras Presidency accompanied by, (2) a privileging of Sanskrit as a cultural marker and a simultaneous debasement of Tamil culture/identity, and (3) the efflorescence of a kind of Orientalist scholarship that spoke of a glorious Tamil/Dravidian past as distinct from a Sanskrit/Aryan past (Pandian 1994: 85). In the existing political and cultural configuration of power, the construction of a hoary history of Tamil conferred on the language a distinct, superior identity and allowed the relatively disempowered non-Brahman Vellala elite—who viewed the Congress as a party of the Brahmans—a certain degree of power and prestige (ibid.: 88).

The separation and gradation of Sanskrit and Tamil emerged out of the colonial categorization of linguistic families into Indo-Aryan and Dravidian. Such classification did not only inspire competition between Sanskrit and Tamil; it crucially contributed to the shaping of a regional identity in the South. Almost all important political movements of twentieth-century southern India, argues Lisa Mitchell, 'have appealed to the commonality of shared language defined in relation to origins' as a partial or complete foundation for their claims (Mitchell 2009: 103). In the case of Tamil, however, veneration and valorization reached new heights with the proclamation of Tamil as a goddess, who was the breath, the consciousness, and the life of its speakers (Ramaswamy 1997: 4). Such complete identification prompted many to sacrifice themselves at the altar of Tamil (ibid.: 1–2). This attachment to Tamil was by no means singular: over the late-nineteenth and twentieth century, Tamil attracted multiple, even contrary imaginings, and became the repository of diverse sentiments (ibid.: 22). One such imagining linked Tamil with neo-Shaivism to give Dravidian identity an enhanced significance. Shiva was hailed as a Dravidian god whose worship was stated to have prevailed all over India prior to the advent of the Aryans, and Shaivism was said to form the basis of an egalitarian society untainted by the oppressive, hierarchical Aryan institution of caste (ibid.: 29). These initial assertions got transformed into 'overt antagonism' towards Sanskritic-Brahmanical-Aryan Hindusim by the 1920s and calls for a complete break with Sanskritic-Aryan Hindusim. Several factors and processes accounted for this shift; crucial among them were changes in the curriculum of Madras University followed by bitter debates (from 1906) over the compulsory study of Sanskrit and the elimination of the 'vernaculars'; the British promise of self-government in stages (from 1917) and subsequent colonial efforts to play off the non-Brahmans against the Brahmans in electoral politics; and the 'iconoclastic atheism' of E. V. Ramaswamy and his followers (ibid.: 30). Together, these forces created a community of Dravidians held together by love and passion for Tamil; a community that offered serious competition to the sentiments being claimed for the imagined community of the nation.

If the Tamil-Dravidian South interrogated the nationalist imaginings of the Aryan-North, Ambedkar and his followers demonstrated a different kind of political antagonism by transposing the caste ordering of social space onto historical time (Rao 2011: 97). In his dual efforts to represent Dalits as an alternative ethical community and a political constituency, Ambedkar accepted the transformation of community into constituency brought about by colonial rule and its promise of eventual representative self-rule by Indians. At the same time, he tried to harness the logic of this transformation to a different political purpose as he offered 'strategic responses' to the political conjunctures in which he found himself (ibid.). This explains why, in a series of representations between 1918 and 1928 on the issue of franchise before the Southborough Committee and the Simon Commission, Ambedkar argued that the Depressed Classes required special representation because they constituted a 'third community' alongside Hindus and Muslims (ibid.: 99).

This representation was distinct from the communal electorate of Muslims since, unlike the Muslims, the entire community of Depressed Classes suffered civic and economic disabilities. Ambedkar's demands on behalf of an 'emergent political community' were premised on a generic theory of representative government constituted by adult franchise (ibid.: 100). The positing of a third community produced by the practice of power and inequality within Hinduism questioned the 'colonial obsession' with Hindu and Muslim communities as 'primordial political actors' and subverted the discourse of 'community as constituency'.

The 'political' in Ambedkar's thought that generated the grounding principles for a new conception of minority was complemented by the 'socio-legal', reflected in a theorization of caste as a double structure of symbolic and material dispossession (ibid.: 97). Contrary to the dominant ethno-historical characterizations of the caste order that gave precedence to the Brahman as the fulcrum of the system, Ambedkar gave centrality to untouchability as the key element, the 'glue' that gave coherence to the caste order by providing the single point of unification for the fragmented touchable castes (ibid.: 103). The principle of *bahiskar*, or caste boycott, or withholding of sociality, acquired immense significance in Ambedkar's arguments as the lone coercive force that held the caste order together. An understanding of Hindu ideology as justifying a complex form of inequality characterized by secular and religio-ritual exclusion enabled Ambedkar to question Gandhi's (and Congress nationalists') perception of untouchability as a problem of religious inclusion (ibid.: 105). Ambedkar politicized the split between the secular and the religio-ritual, probed the terms of religious and political inclusion, and argued that the 'horizon of emancipation' could not be contained within the existing social relations (ibid.). The option of separate electorate, therefore, suggested itself as a mechanism of 'historical redress': it conferred on the Depressed Classes 'political value' by positioning them as an exceptional community at par with both Hindus and Muslims (ibid.: 106).

The theme of *adi*, original, framed most definitions of untouchables as the original inhabitants of the land, while a claim that their own ideology and traditions upheld equality and unity pervaded the untouchable assault on the caste system. There were organized struggles against all forms of feudal bondage imposed on untouchables. Resistance often got articulated in the refusal to perform customary caste duties, such as carrying away dead animals and performing forced labour for village headmen and government officials. This was accompanied by a related fight for rights to education and employment as a way out of the social and economic injunctions imposed on untouchables (ibid.: 415–16). By the end of the 1920s, the untouchables had definitely opted for the path of radical autonomy from Hinduism rather than absorption in it.

An important marker of their belligerence was the coining of the new term, Dalit (broken/oppressed), by the untouchables in the 1930s. Dalit—a direct translation of the colonial category of 'depressed classes'—was taken over as an evocative metaphor of the low socio-economic status and continued exploitation of untouchables in Hindu India, a term that defined their condition much better than Gandhi's *Harijan* (people of Hari/Vishnu, generally translated as 'children of god'). The sustained and vehement attack on Dalits in the *varna-jati* classification of caste and its concomitant socio-ritual stigmatization made the issue of untouchability a 'politically salient one' (Omvedt 1994: 107). Indeed, in M. S. S. Pandian's reckoning, men like Ambedkar and Periyar unsettled the boundary between the material and the cultural (spiritual) spheres of Indian nationalism, where the culture of the upper-caste Hindu elite masqueraded as sovereign, uncolonized 'national culture' and reclaimed a space for caste in the colonial public sphere (2002: 1737).

At the same time, the path of radical autonomy (from Hinduism) that the Dalit struggle adopted opened up difficult questions and choices—what was to be its stand on imperialism and nationalism? Who were to be its allies—which parties and which social groups—and who its enemies? There was considerable ambiguity on the part of Dalits with regard to their stance on nationalism. While they recognized the lack of British commitment to the cause of untouchable liberation, they were also aware that colonial rule had opened up opportunities for them that they did not enjoy before. The Congress was dominated by high-caste Hindus, some of whom were hostile to untouchables. Gandhi was committed to the cause of untouchables, but his prescriptions 'were hortatory rather than confrontational' and always made subordinate to the cause of national unity in the 1920s' (Mendelsohn and Vicziany 2000: 103–04). In sum, Dalit action had to be based on 'some theoretical understanding of the total situation in which they found themselves, some *ideology*' (Omvedt 1994: 134–35). This was provided by Bhimrao Ramji—Babasaheb—Ambedkar, who provided skilful leadership to the emerging autonomous Dalit movement.

Babasaheb: A New Leader in the Making

Bhimrao Ramji Ambedkar was born on 14 April 1891 in the garrison town of Mhow (Military Headquarters of War), in a Mahar family in service of the army. Ambedkar's ancestral village was Ambavade in Mandangad *taluka* in Ratnagiri district of the Bombay Presidency, a region that underwent serious socio-political and economic upheaval in the wake of European mercantile and political expansion. A direct consequence was the recruitment of Mahars, in large numbers, in the British army (Rodrigues 2002: 7). Ambedkar's father, Ramji Sakpal, had become a *subedar* and was appointed head of the Army Normal school. Ambedkar's mother, Bhimabai, came from a Mahar family with a distinguished record in military service—her father and six uncles were *subedars* (majors) (Jaffrelot 2005: 26). Since education was compulsory for army children, both men and women of Ambedkar's family were literate.

Members of Bhimabai's family were followers of the Kabirpanth, and Ramji Sakpal, an admirer of Phule with deep attachment to the mystical Varkari sect, also became a Kabirpanthi. Ambedkar grew up in a family that had regular sessions of devotional singing and recitation of holy texts (Rodrigues 2002: 7). His father, moreover, made himself conspicuous by campaigning in favour of continued recruitment of Mahars in the army and their proper treatment in the 1890s.

Ambedkar, a promising student, graduated with a B. A. in English and Persian from Elphinstone College Bombay in 1912 and joined the army of the princely state of Baroda in 1913 as a lieutenant. His father's death a fortnight later brought about a change of plans. He left the army in order to resume his studies with the financial aid provided by the Maharaja of Baroda, a Maratha leader, who was sympathetic to the cause of non-Brahmans and had taken an initiative in establishing schools for the untouchables (Jaffrelot 2005: 27).

The Maharaja made a uniquely generous offer—he would sponsor Ambedkar's study in the United States provided he agreed to serve the Baroda state for ten years upon his return. Arguably, Ambedkar's intelligence as a student had attracted the attention of his teacher at Elphinstone College who took him to the Maharaja. It is equally true that 'his good fortune' owed much to the Maratha princely elite: non-Brahman solidarity would be 'a decisive plank in his career' (ibid.).

Ambedkar went to Columbia University in New York in 1913, did a master's in economics in 1915, and went to England in 1916 to continue his studies at the London School of Economics. Influenced by inspiring professors at Columbia—John Dewey, Edwin Seligman and A. A. Goldenweiser—and possibly impelled by his earlier experience in India where he had not been allowed to study Sanskrit on account of his caste status, Ambedkar wrote his first essay on caste in 1916. Titled 'Castes in India, their Mechanism, Genesis and Development' and presented at an anthropology seminar, this essay applied concepts of western sociology to the study of India. The essay, published the following year in

Indian Antiquary, advanced 'a theory of caste' that challenged the idea of Aryan invasion propounded by prominent British ethnographers such as Risley, and claimed that caste was a 'social phenomenon' and not a 'racial one' (Ambedkar 1917; Jaffrelot 2005: 32).

In England, Ambedkar imbibed a great deal of Fabianism and British idealism that privileged the role of the state, and joined the Grey's Inn for Bar-at-Law, which he had to cut short on account of his bond to the Maharaja of Baroda. He returned to India in July 1917, and started working as Military Secretary to the Maharaja in the Baroda state administration. The unpleasant experience of not being able to find a place to stay in the city of Baroda, of having to pose as a Parsi to rent a room, and then of being thrown out once his caste was disclosed, had a decisive influence on him. It marked the beginning of his career as a political fighter.

Ambedkar returned to England in 1920 to continue his studies, this time with the help of the Maharaja of Kolhapur. He obtained an M.Sc. in economics from the London School of Economics in June 1921, and went on to write a D.Sc. dissertation under the guidance of Edwin Canon, one of the renowned professors of economics of the time. The dissertation was published by King and Co. in 1923 with the title, *The Problem of the Rupee, Its Origin and Solution*. Ambedkar also did a Ph.D. at Columbia University and became the first 'untouchable' to formally obtain a doctorate in 1927. His Ph.D. dissertation was published by King and Co. as *The Evolution of Provincial Finance in British India* (1925).

On his return from England, Ambedkar registered at the Bombay bar in 1923, and started legal practice in the Bombay High Court the following year. Once again, his low ritual status stood in the way of his practice and he was forced to complement his income by teaching. Even if he did not succeed in the legal profession, his training in law was to prove extremely valuable for his later career. It helped him argue forcefully and persuasively for untouchables in courts, at negotiating tables and in the political arena. It was 'not by chance' therefore, writes Jaffrelot, 'that Ambedkar became the first pan-Indian untouchable leader' (Jaffrelot 2005: 29).

The only 'untouchable' with a graduate degree in the Bombay Presidency in 1919, Ambedkar was consulted by the Southborough Committee entrusted to look into the issue of electoral franchise to be included in the constitutional reforms of 1919. Backed by his knowledge of sociology, Ambedkar stated before the committee that the real cleavage in Hindu society was not between the Brahmans and non-Brahmans, but between the 'touchables' and 'untouchables', an argument that set him apart from Phule and members of the Satyasodhak Samaj. He rejected an electoral system based on territorial constituencies because that would keep the 'untouchables' as a minority, and advanced 'personal representation' as the only mode to achieve popular government, since it would represent the interests and opinions of the majority and minority communities (Ambedkar 1919 in Thorat and Kumar 2009: 68–69). He also asked for the lowering of the taxable rating level applied to untouchables in order to make a greater number of them eligible to vote (Jaffrelot 2005: 53).

In 1920, Ambedkar started publishing *Mooknayak*, a fortnightly that spoke of the necessity of a forum to 'deliberate on the injustices let loose or likely to be let loose on the depressed people'. In collaboration with Shahu Chhatrapati, the Maharaja of Kolhapur, he formed the first forum for depressed classes, which, in turn, organized the first All India Conference of the Depressed Classes in Nagpur in May 1920 (Rodrigues 2002: 9). In 1924, he founded the *Bahiskrit Hitakarni Sabha* (Society for the Uplift of Outcastes), started a hostel in Sholapur for members of the depressed classes, and gave leadership to the famous Mahad satyagraha in 1927 that asserted the right of untouchables to have access to wells and tanks used by all. A resultant confrontation with caste Hindus led to the public burning of the *Manusmriti* by Ambedkar and his followers in December 1927. This sent a clear message that the 'untouchables' were no longer prepared to abide by the religious and ritual exclusion sanctioned by caste Hindus (ibid.: 10). The struggle of the Mahars to enter Parvati temple in Poona in 1929 also used the Gandhian method of non-violence, but it was not approved by Gandhi or the Congress. The satyagraha failed, and Ambedkar and Mahar distrust of Gandhi and the Congress increased.

In the early 1920s, after Gandhi had included the clause for the removal of untouchability in the non-cooperation programme, Ambedkar had attempted to radicalize the initiatives taken by Gandhi. Undoubtedly, Gandhi's emphasis on the removal of untouchability as a precondition for attaining *swaraj* had made untouchability an issue of public concern. But Gandhi's belief in *varnasharamadharma* and his reluctance to directly criticize caste had disappointed Ambedkar. Ambedkar's struggle, both as a member of the Legislative Assembly of the Bombay Province (to which he was nominated in 1927 for five years to represent the 'untouchables' which was renewed for another five in 1932), as well as for social justice outside the administrative arena, drove home certain lessons. He realized that the British administration was not sympathetic to the pleas of the untouchables, and that upper castes were not willing to concede social and religious changes that would advance the cause of equality. He slowly became hostile to Gandhi for being 'too soft on orthodoxy and its proponents', a hostility that would come to include Brahmanism (Rodrigues 2002: 11).

This strong anti-Congress and mildly anti-British stance would become manifest in the presidential address he gave to his own organization, the All India Depressed Classes Congress, founded in 1930 (Bandyopadhyay 2004: 354). It also signalled a parting of ways between Ambedkar and the All India Depressed Classes Association headed by M. C. Rajah of Madras. This association had come into being in the wake of the All India Depressed Classes Leaders' Conference held in Nagpur in 1926. Ambedkar had not attended the conference; but he was elected one of the vice presidents of the association.

In 1928, in his evidence before the Simon Commission—the statutory commission appointed to enquire into the system of government and propose reforms—Ambedkar made a strong case for separate political representation of the depressed classes through elections and for adopting a different system of franchise. The depressed classes, he stated, would not insist on communal representation if reserved seats were granted in general constituencies, and election was based on universal suffrage. In the absence of that, the depressed classes needed separate electorates, that is, separate constituencies for untouchables where they would elect candidates from among their castes to the legislatures (Ambedkar 1928 in Thorat and Kumar 2009: 109–10). This is because if only individuals with property and tax-paying capacity were allowed to vote, most 'untouchables', poor and without property and tax-paying ability, were to remain excluded. The only way to get a voice in the legislatures was for them to have separate electorates. In addition, Ambedkar sought safeguards for the depressed classes in education and employment in the public services of the state and the army, and insisted on the necessity of protecting their civil rights.

The Depressed Classes Education Society, set up in June 1928 under Ambedkar's initiative, established high schools and hostels for untouchable students in different towns in Maharashtra. In his 'Statement on Education' submitted to the Simon Commission, Ambedkar stressed the social discrimination faced by 'untouchables' in their everyday lives and reiterated the need for a new education system for the depressed classes. 'Untouchability', he asserted, has been 'an insuperable bar' in the way of untouchables' acquiring literacy. 'Even the government has bowed before it and sacrificed the rights of the Depressed Classes to admission in public schools to the exigencies of the social system in India' (Ambedkar 1929 in Rodrigues 2002: 68; *BAWS* 1982, Vol. 2: 418–20).

That the Simon Commission paid due attention to Ambedkar's testimony and written statements is borne out by the policy it proposed—multi-member joint electorates with seats reserved for members of the depressed classes in provincial legislatures. By 1930, write Mendelsohn and Vicziany, activities of regional and all-India untouchable groups and associations had produced an important change—all 'political protagonists, Gandhi included' were prepared to agree 'that untouchables were both a distinctive and an oppressed segment of the Indian population'. This agreement provided the basis for a 'huge machinery of institutional privilege' erected 'to right the historic wrongs' (Mendelsohn and Vicziany 2000: 14), a process fraught with tension and conflicts, as we shall soon see.

On the strength of his submissions before the Simon Commission, Ambedkar was invited to the First Round Table Conference to be held in London in December 1930, to discuss the proposals of the Simon Commission. The Congress, we saw in the last chapter, did not attend this First Conference. As one of the two representatives of the depressed classes, Ambedkar emphasized that untouchables needed political power and that it could only be gained within the framework of an India that was independent (Omvedt 1994: 168). In such a scenario, he wanted the 'problem' of the depressed classes to be solved immediately and 'not left to time' as a 'social problem' whose solution lies elsewhere. He insisted that the problem of depressed classes could never be solved unless they got political power in their own hands (Ambedkar 1930 in Ahir 2007: 46–47).

Ambedkar spoke of a unitary state and adult suffrage with reserved seats and safeguards for untouchables at a time when the assembled delegates representing princely states and various minority interests pushed for separate electorates. Subsequently, however, Ambedkar accepted separate electorate once it became clear that universal adult suffrage would not be granted, and the All India Depressed Classes Leaders' Conference held at Bombay in May 1931 resolved to demand separate electorates for untouchables as a 'minority community' (Galanter 1984: 31). Gandhi, we are aware, called off the Civil Disobedience movement after the First Round Table Conference, signed the Gandhi–Irwin Pact, and appeared at the Second Round Table Conference with 'all the prestige of the national movement behind him and claiming to be the sole real representative of the Indian people' (Omvedt 1994: 169).

CONTENDING VISIONS: BAPUJI AND BABASAHEB

Gandhi and Ambedkar came to a direct clash at the Second Round Table Conference in December 1931. Ambedkar's demand for separate electorate for the depressed classes went completely against Gandhi's idea of the unity of Hindus, and of untouchability as a social problem that needed to be solved with the change of heart on the part of upper-caste Hindus who had to 'atone' for this 'greatest blot on Hinduism'. This 'blot' had led to a corruption of the 'purity' of the faith and an erasure of community (Alter 2000: 47; Gandhi 1970: 298, 295; Zelliot 1972: 198). Moreover, the prospect of separate electorate for untouchables threatened to legally entrench them as a distinct caste, rather than eradicate such a distinction.

It is worth mentioning in this connection that although the first time Ambedkar had made public statements about Gandhian methods was during the Vaikom Satyagraha in 1924–25, the first meeting between the two leaders had to wait till 1931. Speaking of the Vaikom Satyagraha and its upper-caste participants at the first public meeting of the *Bahiskrit Hitakarni Sabha*, Ambedkar had underlined the political importance of the untouchable, and not accorded much attention to caste-Hindu sympathies (Zelliot 1972: 199). When Gandhi and Ambedkar met in Bombay a few months before the Round Table Conference, Gandhi, who apparently did not know that Ambedkar was a Dalit (Desai 1953: 52), and thought that he was a Brahman feigning to be a friend of the untouchables, treated him with lack of even normal politeness. Ambedkar stormed out of the meeting after a scathing speech condemning the Congress and the famous statement 'Mahatmaji, I have no country' (Mendelsohn and Vicziany 2000: 104; Omvedt 1994: 170). That unfortunate meeting probably set the tone for the clash at the Second Round Table Conference.

Both Gandhi and Ambedkar spoke with emotion and eloquence at the conference, demonstrating the self-assurance of leaders who could gather masses behind them. There was a wide divergence in their points of view—while Ambedkar stressed the need for political power for the Dalits, Gandhi insisted on reform and protection from above, since the problem of untouchability was, for him, a problem of the self, the 'collective Hindu self' (Nagaraj 1993: 10). 'I can understand the claims advanced by other minorities', he stated, 'but the claims advanced on behalf of the untouchables' is the 'unkindest cut of all' (Speech at the Minorities Committee Meeting, 13 November 1931; Gandhi 1958, Vol. 54: 159).

The fault, in Gandhi's view, lay in the politicization of a 'social problem', that is, 'untouchability' (ibid.). He saw in it a colonial ploy to divide India, and was very critical of Ambedkar, who was willing to take the state's help to fight for the political power of untouchables, as autonomous from Hindus. 'Those who speak of political rights of untouchables do not know their India ...' Gandhi retorted. He made mention of 'the body of reformers' who wanted to eradicate this 'blot' and asserted that 'I would far rather that Hinduism die than untouchability live' (ibid.).

Gandhi also had no doubt as to who should be the true leader of untouchables—'I claim myself in my own person to represent the vast mass of untouchables ...' (ibid.: 158). This right, he stated, he had earned by virtue of his experience of living among the untouchables and his public identification with their plight. Ambedkar, in his opinion, was not fit to lead them, since his experiences 'had warped his judgement' (*BAWS* 1982, Vol. 2: 661–62). What the untouchables needed, he argued further, 'more than election to legislatures is protection from social and religious persecution' (Gandhi 1958, Vol. 54: 159; *BAWS* 1982, Vol. 2: 661).

Ambedkar, on the other hand, claimed that 'Gandhism' could offer no hope to the untouchables. This is because it did not represent any radical departure from the very institution of Hinduism, which was responsible for the oppression of the untouchables. Hinduism, he declared, had created a 'veritable chamber of horrors' for the untouchables (Ambedkar 1945: 296; Dobbin 1970: 112). The conference ended abruptly on a note of bitter disagreement.

As a way out of the impasse, Ambedkar signed a pact with representatives of minority communities, the Minorities Pact, even though he lost the support of the All India Depressed Classes Association. M. C. Rajah, the second representative of untouchables at the Round Table Conference, had supported Ambedkar during the conference. Soon afterwards, however, Rajah became anxious to avoid what he felt would be a 'damaging conflict' for the untouchables, and entered in a pact with Moonje, the President of the Hindu Mahasabha—the Rajah-Moonje Pact—that advocated joint electorate on the basis of reserved seats for untouchables. For a time, therefore, the issue of electorate split Dalit leadership 'down the middle'. Ambedkar got the support of most Mahar leaders and a number of other organizations, such as the Ad-Dharm Mandal and an organ of the Namasudras, while Rajah was supported by important Chamar leaders of Maharashtra, including P. N. Rajbhog. The succeeding months saw bitter and violent exchanges between the two rival groups (Mendelsohn and Vicziany 2000: 105).

The British government announced the Communal Award, which granted separate electorates to Muslims, Sikhs and several other minorities, including the few thousand European expatriates and the depressed classes, at this critical juncture. The depressed classes were to have a fixed, separate quota of seats to be filled only by members belonging to untouchable castes. They were also to have the right to vote for candidates via general electorate, that is, they were to have a 'double vote' (Ambedkar 1945: 90).

Gandhi, in consonance with his threat at the Second Round Table Conference, resorted to his 'epic' fast unto death in the Yeravda prison (where he was on account of resuming civil disobedience), against the award on 20 September 1932 (Pyarelal 1932: 101). Gandhi, it needs to be remembered, had assured British Prime Minister Ramsay Macdonald that he and the Congress would accept separate electorates for Muslims and Sikhs, but resist if separate electorates or statutory reservation of seats in legislatures were granted to any other minority (Gandhi 1958, Vol. 58: 302). After the Communal Award was announced, he directed his fast only against separate electorate for depressed classes, not the several other minorities mentioned in the award. Threatened by the prospect of the Mahatma's martyrdom, Ambedkar had to agree to a compromise. The Poona Pact on 24 September 1932 between Gandhi and Ambedkar replaced separate electorate by a joint electorate with a substantial increase in the number of reserved seats in legislative councils for candidates from untouchable castes. The number accorded was 148, more than double the number granted by the Communal Award, and was nearly equivalent to the proportion of untouchables in the population.

At the same time, the depressed classes lost their right to vote separately in the 148 constituencies where they predominated; in these constituencies, they could now nominate four candidates for whom all voters of the constituency, irrespective of caste, had to vote (Jaffrelot 2005: 66–67; Kumar 1987). In Ambedkar's terms, the Dalits lost their 'double vote', a 'priceless privilege' and 'a political weapon beyond reckoning' (Ambedkar 1945: 90).

The Communal Award, Gandhi's fast and the subsequent Poona Pact, produced varied reactions; they have also generated distinct understandings by scholars (Jaffrelot 2005; Kumar 1987; Nagaraj 1993; Omvedt 1994; Zelliot 1972, for instance). For Gandhi, the fast was not a 'political gesture' but a 'divine act of penance' resolved in the name of god and 'upon his call' directed not so much at British rule but at the Hindu community, to cleanse it of the stigma of untouchability (Gandhi to the Government of Bombay in Pyarelal 1932: 113). Pyarelal, Gandhi's devotee and for a time his secretary, presented it as a 'supreme gesture' of 'stupendous self-sacrifice', a 'resplendent self-sacrifice' that demonstrated the power of satyagraha (1932: 117). The decision perhaps arose from Gandhi's very close personal identification with the problem of untouchability and his belief that he had the sole right to champion the cause of untouchables (Hubel 1996: 151–52).

Most upper-caste nationalist leaders accepted Gandhi's position, while Hindu nationalists and revivalists condemned the pact as a sell-out of the interests of Hindus. The leftists, for their part, criticized the fast as a distraction from real anti-imperialist work. Nationalist historians such as Bipan Chandra have taken this notion of detracting from 'real anti-imperialist work' in a different direction. They argue that the British government deliberately 'hand-picked' the delegates of the Round Table Conferences from among 'loyalists, communalists, careerists, and place-hunters, big landlords and representatives of princes'. These delegates were sure to challenge the Congress claim to represent the interests of all Indians vis-à-vis imperialism and 'neutralize Gandhiji and all his efforts to confront the imperialist rulers with the basic question of freedom' (Chandra et al. 2000: 285).

Such an understanding of the nationalist struggle that prioritizes political freedom from imperial rule as the 'basic' issue for every Indian, fails to take into account contending visions about the nature of 'freedom' that was being sought. For Ambedkar and many others, freedom from Hindu and elite dominance was a far more basic need than gaining freedom from imperialism (Hubel 1996: 150).

Recent scholars have seen the fast as one of the most crucial in Gandhi's intertwined project of national and self (re)formation (Alter 2000: 28; Arnold 2001: 181). Also considered to be among the most 'dramatic' of the 15 fasts undertaken by Gandhi during his political career (Pratt and Vernon 2005: 94–95), this 11-day fast found wide coverage in British newspapers. The fast, moreover, was very troubling for the British press, possibly because the 'lines of cleavage were unclear' and because the press had to explain the politics of Gandhi's fasts for the first time to the British public (ibid.: 97). And, for all their attempts to 'locate and explain Gandhi's fast historically, there remained widespread confusion as to whether the fast was an act of opposition against the colonial government or to the leader of the depressed classes' (ibid.: 100).

For Ravinder Kumar, the outcome of the fast, that is, the Poona Pact, was a victory for Gandhi. He managed to stall an institutional arrangement premised on the position that the untouchables were as distinct from Hindus as Muslims, and upheld the principle that the untouchables were Hindus. This vindicated his position that untouchability was a religious issue internal to Hinduism. Gandhi, moreover, had 'achieved what as a true Satyagrahi he always strove for—he had won his opponents heart!' (Kumar 1987: 98–99). This is because Ambedkar is said to have praised Gandhi for 'his generosity' and expressed his 'gratitude to him at the final meeting after the Poona Pact' (*Bombay Chronicle*, 26 September 1932).

This 'Gandhian' interpretation of Ambedkar's praise and gratitude for the Mahatma, argues Omvedt, 'is built on sand' (1994: 175). Ambedkar was trying to build an independent political identity for Dalits in the structures of social, economic and political powers (Nagaraj 1993: 10). What he tried to emphasize at the Round Table Conferences was that it was not enough for untouchables to have the right to be represented in the legislatures; they had to have the right to be represented in the Cabinet to have a real voice (Ambedkar 1945: 95). Gandhi's fast against the award upset Ambedkar: he considered it to be directed against the untouchables, and saw in it an attempt to keep the untouchables within the Hindu fold. He also thought of it as 'moral blackmail' since Gandhi's death would have brought about tremendous retribution upon Dalits throughout the villages. For Patankar and Omvedt therefore, the Yeravda fast, Gandhi's first ever on the issue of untouchability, was 'a fast against the Dalits themselves to force them to give up their demands' rather than a fast against the oppressive caste system (Patankar and Omvedt 1979: 419).

Gandhi's double stance of empathy and control towards the 'untouchables' has puzzled many scholars. Gandhi's real concern for untouchables was unquestionable; but his insistence that the amelioration of their condition lay only in the hands of caste Hindus, or rather in his hands, the true satyagrahi, made the untouchables passive agents in his campaign. They were to be educated, taught personal hygiene and dissuaded from eating carrion. But they were 'not expected to break caste taboos, go on strike, fast or participate in any other form of protest against untouchability'. In other words, they were asked to 'remain nonresistant at the very moment when their resistance might have effected profound change within Hindu society' (Hubel 1996: 153). For scholars such as Trilok Nath, Gandhi's demand that 'Depressed Classes should rely on the Congress' and not seek to uplift their conditions through their own efforts is 'beyond comprehension'—it went against his own doctrine that 'progress could come only through personal efforts' (Nath 1987: 134).

In D. R. Nagaraj's understanding, Gandhi, the satyagrahi, was well aware that his victory (in the conflict with Ambedkar) stood on very shaky ground; he had to know the 'truth'. After 1932, he made 'untouchability work' a major programme of the Congress, and for many the crucial moral part of the 'Indian national movement'. He set up the All India Anti-Untouchability League at a meeting in Bombay in September 1932 presided by Madan Mohan Malaviya of the Hindu Mahasabha. Industrialist G. D. Birla was made the President of the Anti-Untouchability League and Amritlal V. Thakkar, a social worker, its secretary. Gandhi started using the term Harijan for untouchables, and strove to establish dignity of labour by performing the tasks Harijan were traditionally assigned.

Ambedkar was made a member of the central board, but his association with the League did not last long. On his way to the Third Round Table Conference in 1932, Ambedkar wrote a long letter to Thakkar in which he clarified that he wanted the League to be concerned primarily with civic rights and equal opportunities in economic matters and social intercourse, concerns that were very different from those of its founders (Zelliot 1972: 205). Ambedkar resigned and other untouchable members 'disappeared quietly'. When the League changed its name to the Harijan Sevak Sangh, 'harijan' were debarred from becoming leaders (ibid.). This was in tune with Gandhi's stance—the Sangh was an organization of penitents, 'for the expiation of the guilt of the caste Hindus' (Ambedkar 1945: 142; Pyarelal 1958: 667).

From September 1932, Gandhi embarked on a massive drive to uplift the condition of untouchables. He launched an 'Untouchability Abolition Week' in September–October 1932, started publishing the weekly *Harijan* in February 1933 and went on a tour of India between November 1933 and August 1934 in order to promote the interests of the untouchables (Jaffrelot 2005: 67). Earlier, he had started a campaign to allow harijans entry into temples, a campaign he led from inside the prison, with the support of the British Raj. Gandhi had also started soliciting the help of the Viceroy and other British officials to pass the Temple Entry bill. During his tour of 1932–33, he faced opposition from orthodox Hindus of the Sanatan Dharma Sabha and the Hindu Mahasabha, who were campaigning against the Temple Entry Bill, and was met with black flags and 'Go back Gandhi slogans' in South Kanara and Bellary by Dalits, gestures of hostility no one would have dreamt of two or three years ago (Ray 1996: 117).

At a different level, Gandhi's attitude of cooperation with the British aroused the ire of young Congress members, Subhas Bose in particular. Bose referred to the several resolutions that were being passed on many platforms at the instance of Congress leaders at the end of 1932, resolutions that requested the Viceroy 'to accord sanction to the Temple Entry bills in the Madras Legislative Council and the Indian Legislative Assembly' and remarked, 'Civil Disobedience indeed!' (Bose 1935: 258).

The Poona (Yeravda) Pact did not satisfy either group—Hindu or Dalit politicians. Bengal, in particular, was enraged by the large number of reserved seats accorded to members of depressed classes, since it unduly reduced the number of seats available to caste Hindus in a province that had a large Muslim population. It is significant that neither the Congress High Command nor Bengal politicians complained against the 'incredibly high' representation granted to Europeans in Bengal and Assam. In Bengal, the Benthalls, who constituted less than 0.01 per cent of the population, were awarded 10 per cent of the reserved seats in the Assembly (Ghosh 1992: 1080).

Dalit politicians, for their part, found the primary system expensive and unwieldy and some felt that the Congress did not nominate 'able and truly representative' depressed class leaders for the reserved seats (Zelliot 1972: 204). 'Disliked by the Hindus and disfavoured by the untouchables, the Poona Pact was given recognition by both parties and was embodied in the Government of India Act' (Ambedkar 1945: 91).

Toward Self-Rule: Business, Congress and the Provincial Government

The implementation of the Government of India Act of 1935, with limited autonomy to Indians to form ministries in the 11 provinces of British India, got Congress and other parties interested in the forthcoming elections. Rather than working towards removing untouchability, Congress leaders got involved in creating a political front to mobilize Dalits in order to win reserved seats in the forthcoming elections. The All-India Depressed Classes League was formed in 1935 with Jagjivan Ram, a Dalit leader from Bihar with Congress sympathies, as the President.

Different sections of big business, Marwari businessmen of Calcutta under G. D. Birla who were very close to Gandhi and the Congress, and Bombay, Ahmedabad and Kanpur industrialists who often had conflicts with Congress policies, all got attracted to the prospect of responsible government in the provinces and wanted the Congress back in the legislatures as an 'effective pressure group' (Sarkar [1983] 1995: 330). All these groups, as we have seen in the last chapter, had pressed for a withdrawal of the Civil Disobedience movement after 1932. The Bombay group, in fact, had concluded the Lees–Mody Pact in 1933 in an effort to present a united front of Lancashire and Bombay cotton-mill interests against Japanese competition. Differences among business groups persisted even after the abandonment of civil disobedience, but became less and less marked as differences between the Lancashire and Bombay groups became pronounced, and Bombay industrialists became aware of the new moderation in Congress leadership (Markovits 1981: 489).

The provision of elections under the 1935 Act made the Congress, until then 'a broadly-based movement with a general commitment to fight foreign rule', evolve into 'a more organized party with aspirations to political dominance' (ibid.: 487). The years of peace following the abandonment of the Civil Disobedience movement, argues Markovits, greatly helped the Congress make this changeover.

The abandonment of civil disobedience and the increasing power of the Right, as indicated earlier, had made many young Congress leaders really upset. Jawaharlal Nehru, who represented the Congress Socialists along with Subhas Bose and had been instrumental in having a resolution that sketched socialist objectives adopted by the Congress session in Karachi in 1931, was frustrated by the recurrent talk of 'peace' between the Congress and the Raj. When the Civil Disobedience movement had been suspended for six weeks in June 1933, he had written in his prison diary—'Civil disobedience again suspended'. Among 'the mighty ones so deciding was G. D. Birla. *Heigh-ho!*' And once mass civil disobedience was withdrawn completely, he exclaimed, in frustration and disappointment, 'there can be no further cooperation between Bapu and me ... we had better go our different ways!' (Nehru 1984: 484, 489).

Such disappointment notwithstanding, the Congress demonstrated a marked tendency to follow the line of institutional politics from 1933. Satyamurty, the Congress leader from Madras, floated a plan to return to electoral politics by means of a revived Swaraj Party in October 1933. It was taken up seriously by Bhulabhai Desai, Asaf Ali Ansari, K. S. Nariman, K. M. Munshi and B. C. Roy in 1934. Gandhi, it seems, had been counselling the earlier supporters of 'Council-entry' to form a party and execute the Council-entry programme. He gave a formal nod to the revival of the Swaraj Party when he acknowledged, in his letter to Birla in 1934, that 'there will always be a party within the Congress wedded to the idea of Council-entry'. And that group should hold the 'reins of the Congress' (Birla 1953: 138).

Satyamurty approached the Madras Governor in 1934 and was assured that the government will not interfere with the formation of a Swaraj Party. Satyamurty, it appears, appraised the Governor of the expediency of a 'soft line' towards the Congress since civil disobedience had ceased to exist and was unlikely to be revived (Low 1977: 187; Misra 1976: 302–03).

C. Rajagopalachari, the staunch 'No-Changer' of the 1920s, also supported Satyamurty's proposal of Council-entry. Orthodox Gandhian constructive workers and advocates of Council-entry came together in the mid-1930s to form a common front against the Left; and business advice and pressure played an important role in the formation of 'a definite Congress right' (Markovits 1981: 488; Sarkar [1983] 1995: 331). Birla was clear that funds should be given to the Swaraj Party to fight the elections only if 'the right type of men' were being sent. In August 1934, he remarked to Purushottamdas Thakurdas that while 'Vallabhbhai, Rajaji and Rajendra Babu' are 'fighting Communism and Socialism', it was necessary 'for some of us who represent the healthy Capitalism' to help Gandhiji 'as far as possible and work with a common object' (Thakurdas Papers cited in Sarkar [1983] 1995: 331).

Some scholars have stressed the crucial role played by Birla in the transformation of the Congress into a 'parliamentary' party. The earlier Swarajist objective, they point out, was to enter the councils in order to make the 1919 constitution unworkable. The Congress decision to participate in the elections and form ministries in 1936–37, on the other hand, was to work 'the new British-imposed constitution' and to collaborate with the Raj as an 'adjunct to the colonial state machinery'—a drastic change from the attitude of non-cooperation and civil disobedience (Ghosh 1992: 1079).

Interestingly, the years 1935 and 1936 were marked by significant socialist and Communist activity, worker and peasant struggles, the formation of several Left-led all-India mass organizations and presidential addresses by Jawaharlal Nehru at Congress sessions that seemed to represent leftist aspirations. The Congress' election manifesto and its agrarian programme, ratified by the Congress session in Faizpur in 1936, demonstrated a change in its conservative posture and generated expectations of socio-economic change.

The agrarian programme was based on recommendations submitted by Congress provincial committees with regard to issues of 'freedom of organization of agricultural labourers and peasants', safeguarding of peasants' interests against intermediaries and 'just relief from agricultural indebtedness including arrears in rent and revenue' among others (Sharma 1962: 28–29). With regard to industrial workers, the election manifesto stated that the Congress would try to secure for them 'a decent standard of living, hours of work, and conditions of labour' congruent with international standards to the extent permitted by the economic condition of the country. It also recognized the right of workers to form trade unions and to strive to protect their interests (Krishna 1992: 1497).

Leaders and volunteers achieved great success in making use of the pre-eminent status of the Congress under Mahatma Gandhi in persuading the electorate. An electorate composed of 30 million adults, one-sixth of the total adult population that included some women (Chapter 8), accorded the Congress a stunning victory. It captured 758 out of 1,585 seats in the provincial legislatures and formed governments in seven (and soon in eight) of the 11 provinces. The Congress won absolute majority in five provinces—Madras, Bihar, Orissa, the Central Provinces and the United Provinces—a near majority in Bombay (86 seats out of 175), and emerged as the single largest party in Assam, Bengal and the North-West Frontier Province (Bandyopadhyay 1984: 315). Only in the Muslim majority provinces of Punjab and Sind did it fare badly, and it did not get absolute majority in Bengal, even though it won a majority of general seats in these provinces (Markovits 1981: 490–91). The Justice Party of Madras and the National Agriculturist Party in UP were routed completely despite official backing (Sarkar [1983] 1995: 349).

The Muslim League, it is worth remembering, performed miserably in Sind, Punjab and the North-West Frontier Province, and not too well in Bengal, a fact that negated its claim of being the sole representative of Muslims. The League, till 1937, claims Ayesha Jalal, was a little more than 'a debating forum for a few articulate Muslims in the minority provinces'; it barely had any presence in the 'majority provinces' ([1985] 1994: 19–20). Her statement appears to be true in view of the fact that the League did not win a single seat in the North-West Frontier Province, and got only two of the 84 in Punjab and three out of 33 reserved seats in Sind. In total, it won 108 of 485 Muslim seats.

The regional parties in Muslim majority provinces—the Unionist Party in Punjab and the Krishak

Praja (farmer and subject) Party in Bengal—on the other hand, performed well. The Unionist Party, led by Fazl-i-Husain, Sikander Hayat Khan and Jat leader Chhotu Ram, represented the interests of wealthy Muslim, Hindu and Sikh landlords and peasant producers who had benefitted from the Punjab Land Alienation Act of 1900. The party dominated rural politics (Talbot 1988).

In Bengal, on the other hand, Fazlul Huq's Krishak Praja Party, appealed to Muslim and lower-caste Hindu peasants on class-based demands, and successfully competed with the Muslim League for Muslim votes (Chatterjee 1984). Fazlul Huq's election speech at Dacca attracted the people by a clear declaration that 'the grim fight between zamindars and capitalists on one side and the poor people on the other' was about to begin. The fight was 'not at all a civil war in the Muslim community', but 'a fight in which the people of Bengal are divided on a purely economic issue' (Begum 1994: 33; Biswas 1966: 27–28).

The pattern of voting in the Muslim majority provinces demonstrated that the Muslim electorate was moved more by local and regional issues and considerations than by national ones (D. Pandey 1978: 629). It also underscored the validity of arguments that claim that community identities can and do cross-cut in all possible ways (Kooiman 1995: 2123), and that an individual can belong to several communities at the same time and be mobilized along different, mutually exclusive lines of community identity (Alavi and Harriss 1989: 223; Shah 1994: 1133).

Arguably, the Muslim electorate showed scant regard for the Congress. The Congress contested 58 Muslim seats and won 26 (Menon 1957: 55). Dalit distrust of the Congress got reflected in the great success of Ambedkar's Independent Labour Party in Bombay—it won 13 out of 15 reserved seats, and demonstrated the strength of Babasaheb's leadership.

Electoral success bolstered the 'Right' pressure on the Congress to take office. The All India Congress Committee session of March 1937 accepted a resolution, moved by Rajendra Prasad and Vallabhbhai Patel, of conditional acceptance of forming ministries. The only 'condition' was that the leader of the Congress assembly of a province needed to be satisfied that the Governor will not use his special powers. The amendment proposed by Jayaprakash Narayan of the Congress Socialist Party that rejected the acceptance of office was defeated. This happened at a time when the prominence of the socialists within the Congress had been reflected in the election of Jawaharlal Nehru as the Congress President in 1936 for two successive sessions. In his presidential address at the Lucknow Congress of 1936, Nehru had pleaded openly for the acceptance of socialism as the Congress goal, as a way, both of coming closer to the peasants and the urban working class, and of 'weaning them away from communalism' (Chandra et al. [1972] 1975: 194).

Understandably, Birla, in his letter to Linlithgow's secretary, hailed the resolution to accept office as a 'triumph' for the Right-wing of the Congress (Birla 1953: 214). The Congress Working Committee decided to form ministries in July 1937 (in Bihar, Bombay, the Central Provinces, Madras, Orissa, the United Provinces, and in North-West Frontier Province and Assam a few months later), with no assurance from the Viceroy that 'special powers' will not be used by governors. By the summer of 1937, Congress ministries were being formed in different provinces to work 'a significant part of the Constitution which everyone had denounced for years' (Sarkar [1983] 1995: 338).

Business attitude towards Congress, as discussed in the previous chapter, was neither uniform nor consistent. Of the 23 seats reserved for business, commercial and industrial interests under the new regime, the Congress only contested six and won three. Eight other seats went to businessmen with pro-Congress leanings and seven to those hostile to the Congress (three of whom won against Congress candidates), while the rest were won by capitalists without overt political leanings (Markovits 1981: 491). In Madras, in particular, where industry was still dominated by the British, the Indian business community showed complete disregard for the Congress—it did not win a single reserved seat. Business groups here had closer relations with non-Congress forces such as the Justice Party (Arnold 1977a: 158).

The Congress found greater support in Bombay, Ahmedabad and Bengal, although its primacy was not uncontested. The business community in the United Provinces was divided in its loyalty to the Congress and the Hindu Mahasabha and, as indicated by Pandey, local traders and petty merchants were closer to the Congress than big businessmen (G. Pandey 1978: 57).

The Congress came out stronger in relation to non-commercial seats: very few businessmen could draw upon a rural clientele without the support of an organized political party, in particular after the great extension of franchise provided by the Act of 1935 (Markovits 1981: 494). This was also true for Muslim merchants who won in rural constituencies on Muslim League tickets. An open alliance with the League did not bring British opprobrium as an alliance with the Congress did, and given the fact that most businessmen and merchants still depended considerably on government support, open business participation in politics remained limited.

What businessmen did instead was to work behind the scenes and make use of their financial powers to influence the Congress (Markovits 1981: 494). The huge cost of participating in elections on a much wider scale had made the Congress dependent on funds and support from industrialists and businessmen in towns, and landlords and dominant peasant groups in rural areas. Moreover, donations did not cover the cost of the elections and most candidates were expected to cover their own expenses. This induced a bias in favour of propertied men, most evident in Bihar where Kisan Sabha militants were denied nomination as candidates. In Bombay again, business pressure made prominent trade union leaders lose their opportunity of being candidates (Tomlinson 1976: 85, 83).

And yet, Congress triumph meant that over the major part of the country, 'the persecuted of yesterday had become ministers, and new assemblies met to the strain of *Bande Mataram*' and the national flag 'flew proudly' over public buildings (Sarkar [1983] 1995: 350–51). Congress membership increased phenomenally and the provincial ministries gave a boost to all forms of anti-imperialist and anti-feudal struggles in princely states.

Soon, however, the enthusiasm faded. Once in power, the Congress kept only a few of its promises. This was in consonance with the dominance of the 'Right' within the Congress. In a situation where Congress ministries were constrained by limited financial resources, which were firmly controlled by the British at the centre (Tomlinson 1979: 131), Congress governments tended to fall in line with the 'Right'. Provincial ministries functioned in accordance with the dictates of industrial and professional elite and wealthy peasants, and failed to do much for poor peasants and agricultural labourers, except adopting measures to relieve indebtedness.

The Congress, with its claim of being a *kisan* party, had to take certain measures for agrarian reform. Tenancy legislations passed by Congress ministries in different provinces reduced debt burden by fixing the rates of interest on debt, and elevated the statutory tenants in Agra and Awadh to the status of ryots (*raiyats*) with hereditary occupancy rights. Rents of occupancy tenants were not allowed to be changed before the expiry of ten years, enhancing rents was restricted and tenants could no longer be arrested and imprisoned for non-payment of rent. Some occupancy ryots, evicted during the depression years, were restored to their lands in Bihar, *khoti* sub-tenants of ryotwari (*raiyatwari*) landholders in Bombay were given some rights, and in Orissa free transfer of tenancy holdings was allowed, interest on arrears was reduced and illegal levies on tenants abolished. In recognition of the demands made during forest satyagrahas, grazing fees were abolished in Bombay and reduced in Madras (Chandra et al. 2000: 329–30; Sarkar [1983] 1995: 362–63).

The reforms fell far short of the major changes promised in the Faizpur resolution, and the resolutions of the provincial Congress committees in Bihar and UP to abolish zamindari were forgotten after the Congress came to power. Congress ministries had to deal, on the one hand, with a very militant and widespread peasant movement, and, on the other, with the threat of 'civil disobedience' by zamindars in Bihar and landholders in other areas. It tried to balance contending pressures by offering limited reform.

The Congress was also beset by factional squabbles and growing tensions between the central High Command and local leaders with influence and power in the provinces. In the Central Provinces, for instance, N. B. Khare was ousted from premiership by Ravi Shankar Shukla, and even though this was presented as a result of regional tension between Marathi-speaking and the Hindi-speaking districts of Jabalpur-Raipur, the real problem was the difficulty of balancing opposing interests. It became impossible for the Congress as a ruling party to please Hindus and Muslims, landlords and peasants, and industrialists and workers at the same time (Sarkar [1983] 1995: 351). Under such pressure, the Congress High Command and the provincial governments inclined more and more towards the Right between 1937–39, although they did not give up the Left rhetoric entirely.

Provincial Congress ministries kept amicable relations with British provincial governors and worked for the enforcement of law and order in line with its colonial predecessors. This entailed adopting an increasingly hostile attitude towards the Kisan Sabha and labour militancy. It appeared, therefore, that Congress ministries were 'playing fair', in the precise sense the 'arch imperialist' Winston Churchill had told Birla the Congress should do (during their meeting in London in July 1937), in the hope of getting 'fair play' in return from the British (Ghosh 1992: 1087).

THE GREAT DIVIDE: CONGRESS AND THE MUSLIM LEAGUE

Congress ministries failed miserably in winning over their Muslim compatriots. The failure resulted in part from 'unintended slights' and in part from the inability to comprehend deeply felt anxieties (Metcalf and Metcalf 2003: 194). Bolstered by success, the Congress disdainfully turned down the Muslim League's offer to form a coalition government in UP, and told the League's leader that its members could join the government only by dissolving the League in UP and by becoming members of the Congress Party, sharing the same privileges and obligations as other members of the Congress

(D. Pandey 1978: 631). Nehru declared arrogantly that there were just two parties in India, the Congress and the Raj.

The Congress was happy that it had won an absolute majority of the general legislative seats; it overlooked the very important fact that it had not won a single reserved seat and the Muslim League had won 29 of them. It was clear even to Congress leaders that the terms proposed by the Congress were harsh and that 'the Muslim League would not accept any place in the Cabinet on those terms' (G. B. Pant to Nehru, 12 April 1937, Nehru Papers cited in D. Pandey 1978: 632). Mohammad Ali Jinnah and other leaders of the League considered maintaining the solidarity of 'Muslims' in this period of crisis to be of utmost importance, and declared that the Congress and Nehru's policy was aimed at disrupting that solidarity (*The Times of India*, 6 May 1937).

The Congress stood firm in its stand that it was not ready to accept the League as the sole representative organization of the Muslims. Apart from the fact that the Congress had numerous Muslim members, there were other Muslim parties and organizations, such as the Jamait-ul-Ulemai-Hind, which also represented Muslim interests. Moreover, agreeing to form a coalition with the League 'on equal terms' as demanded by Jinnah, would label the Congress as a 'Hindu' Party and severely compromise its position as the leading national party, not attached to any particular community. While one can understand the Congress' refusal to be marked as a 'Hindu' party, as well as Nehru's fear that a coalition with the League, which had no radical programme of land reform, would hamper the implementation of any radical socio-economic reform, the accusation that the League was a 'communal' party and could not be made a partner of the Congress, disregarded the deeply felt anxieties of the aristocratic Muslims.

In princely states, the tension of aristocratic Muslims stemmed from their desire to have a share in power and maintain a separate identity as a 'minority' community (Kooiman1995). The Congress and the League did not intervene in the politics of the princely states at this stage, and the two parties maintained friendly relations during the elections. The Muslim League's election manifesto displayed a critical attitude similar to that of the Congress towards the Act of 1935.

Jinnah, who had taken up the reins of the Muslim League in 1934, after a brief period of self-imposed exile in London, had supported the Congress in its opposition to the British proposal of a loose federal structure (Jalal [1985] 1994: 13). Jinnah's talks with Congress President Rajendra Prasad in January and February 1935 had resulted in an accord. Jinnah accepted the idea of a joint electorate in return for the Congress' acceptance of Muslim control in the Muslim majority provinces of Punjab and Bengal. Jinnah's consent to a joint electorate, Rajendra Prasad informed Vallabhbhai Patel, offered 'great possibilities for the future' because it opened the way for 'joint action' by the Congress and the League (Rajendra Prasad to Vallabhbhai Patel, 14 February 1935, cited in Gallagher 1973: 630). Both the Congress and the League, moreover, had tried to fight the reactionary National Agriculturist Party of the Raja of Chhatari. It was not a matter of surprise therefore that the League expected to cooperate with the Congress after the elections in accordance with terms laid down in the Lucknow Pact (1916, Chapter 6).

Arguably, the League had very little all-India standing till 1937. At the same time, it is true that the 'Muslims' as a political community had come to be firmly established. Separate electorate for them had become an integral part of the Constitution, and Muslim parties had acquired political power in

ELECTION SYMBOLS OF NATIONAL AND
MAJOR REGIONAL PARTIES, 1952

Communist Party
of India–Marxist

Communist Party
of India

Samyukta Socialist Party

Praja Socialist Party

Indian National Congress

Bharatiya Jana Sangh

Swatantra Party

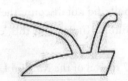

All Party Hill Leaders
Conference-Assam

J & K National Conference
Jammu & Kashmir

Muslim League-
Kerala

Dravida Munnetra
Kazhagam Madras

Akali Dal (–Sant Group)

Maharashtrawadi Gomantak-
Goa, Daman & Diu

United Goans
(Sequeira Gp.) GD & D

Muslim majority provinces (Moore 1988). The League's demand that the Muslim majority provinces of Sind and the North-West Frontier Province be made full provinces had also been met. In this situation, the Congress' arrogant stance after the elections in which the League had suffered a debacle, humiliated the League.

The Muslim mass contact campaign launched by Jawaharlal Nehru in the United Provinces heightened the sense of betrayal. The mass campaign programme was sabotaged by the Hindu Mahasabha (Hasan 1988); but the Congress effort to bypass the League generated fears of Hindu domination. Jinnah gave vivid political articulation to this collective sense of fear and disaffection. The League, he stated, was willing to work with 'any group or party for the good of the country, but on equal terms', not as camp followers or a subject race of a Hindu Raj (*Indian Annual Register, 1937*, Vol. 1).

As later events would reveal, the Congress' failure to come to terms with the League would prove fatal for the nationalist struggle. This bitter engagement would make the League turn completely against the Congress; henceforth, it would not lose a single opportunity to make public the wrongs suffered by Muslims under Congress rule (Ehrmann 1947: 671; D. Pandey 1978: 635). Soon—in the Patna Session of the League in December 1938—Jinnah started speaking of 'Congress Fascism' and projecting its mass contact movement as a knife at the throat of every Muslim politician (Jalal [1985] 1994: 43). League spokesmen were not the only ones to attribute Muslim alienation to this bitter disagreement of 1937; 'nationalist' Muslims, such as Maulana Abul Kalam Azad, also regarded the Congress attitude between 1937 and 1939 as crucial to a rift between the Congress and Muslims (Azad in Kabir 1959).

Jinnah, the astute politician, realized that both the Congress High Command, 'anxious to storm the centre' and the British, 'anxious to ward them off', needed someone to speak for Muslims at the all-India level. The division of Muslims at the polls did not discount their importance as a 'formidable' political category in discussions about the future of India. And this 'enabled Jinnah to live to fight another day' (Jalal [1985] 1994: 34).

It is significant that most of the post-1937 revival of the Muslim League happened in the United Provinces. After the election debacle and its humiliating encounter with the Congress, the League devoted full attention to the building of a 'populist' image by making use of 'religion as community'. The Shariat Implementation Act, which was passed by the Central Legislative Assembly in 1937 after a spirited advocacy by Jinnah, vindicated his efforts to garner support for 'Muslim solidarity' on a national scale. It also proved, according to David Gilmartin, that internal dissensions and divisions can be overcome in the interest of a 'cause' (Gilmartin 1988).

Encouraged by this success, Jinnah embarked on a mass contact campaign that involved the services of the *ulema*, and was shored by the stolid support given by the emotionally charged students of Aligarh (Bandyopadhyay 2004: 340). By the time the Congress High Command realized that it had underestimated the League's capacity for survival and its ability to play on the 'fears' of Muslims, and made tentative attempts to negotiate with Jinnah, the latter had become determined not to parley with the Congress unless it accepted the League as the 'authoritative and representative organization of the Indian Muslims' (Jalal [1985] 1994: 44). When the Congress ministries resigned in November

1939, in protest against the unilateral decision of the Raj to draw India into the Second World War, Jinnah decided to celebrate it as 'Deliverance Day'. By December 1939, the membership of the Muslim League had touched 3 million, and Jinnah had emerged as 'the sole spokesman' of the Muslims (ibid.).

On the other hand, the term in office helped Congress politicians, trained so far in agitational and oppositional politics, to gain valuable experience in running governments. By the time the ministries resigned in 1939, 28 months of rule had prepared Congress leaders to take over the reins of governing India.

THE LEFT AND LABOUR

The huge and diverse groups of working classes became organized in the decade of the 1920s, through the formation of several trade unions. A convergence of various 'socio-economic' and 'ideological-cultural forces' led to the formation of the All India Trade Union Conference (AITUC) in 1920: it intended to coordinate the activities of the existing trade unions and the ones that were to emerge subsequently (Bose 1979a: 31). A section of the Congress had supported the establishing of AITUC although Gandhi had remained opposed to the idea of introducing 'politics' among the working class. He also felt that all trade unions had to first orient themselves to the model of 'trusteeship' represented by the Ahmedabad union, before coming together in a central body (ibid.: 32).

The Congress, of course, was not homogeneous in its political thinking; nor were its leaders the only organizers of trade unions. The workers showed great initiative, and they were aided by different groups of Communists and revolutionaries in different parts of the country. The early phase of trade unionism (1919–23), writes Sanat Bose, was characterized by 'Gandhian, nationalist, and moderate' trends. By the middle of the 1920s, the trade union movement had gathered force and momentum, and all-India bodies, such as the Indian National Trade Union Congress (INTUC), Centre of Indian Trade Unions (CITU) and the National Federation of Trade Unions (NFTU) had come into being to coordinate the activities of the numerous trade unions (Bose 1979b: 3). As we have seen in Chapter 8, workers' struggle had intimate links with the nationalist movement, but workers did not necessarily abide by the dictates of the Congress or of moderate trade union leaders.

The Communists had a clear sense of divergence of interest between the struggle of labourers and the nationalists. At the second Congress of the Communist International (Comintern), M. N. Roy had separated the 'nationalist anti-imperialist' movement of the bourgeoisie from the 'real revolutionary movement' of the class-conscious (Indian) proletariat and landless peasantry (Roy 1964: 499). 'The bourgeois national democrats in the colonies strive for the establishment of a free national state', he had argued, 'whereas the masses of workers and poor peasants are revolting, even though in many cases unconsciously, against the system which permits such brutal exploitation' (Bose 1979a: 26). Most of Roy's famous debates with Lenin had centred on the interface of anti-imperialist struggles in the colonies and proletarian revolutions in the metropolis, as well as the attitude of the Comintern towards nationalist struggles in the colonies (Bose 1979a: 26; Ray 1987; Roy 1964: 499–500).

The Communists or the Left, however, were not united in their appraisal of the nationalist struggle or on the strategy to be adopted by workers in colonies. Their attitude to the Congress and the workers varied, as did the workers' own understanding of the nationalist struggle. Small groups of Communists, who did not form a part of the Communist Party of India, had become very active in the trade unions from the mid-1920s. They were instrumental in bringing a definite concept of class and class-struggle into trade unions and labour-capital relations (Bose 1979b: 6). The Congress, in turn, made a consistent and concerted attempt to rally the workers, in spite of fissures among the Right, the Moderate and the Left within the Congress. All this made for periods of convergence and divergence of distinct trends, as noted in the last chapter.

The withdrawal of the Civil Disobedience movement in 1933–34 saw a resurgence of Communist activities. In the summer of 1935, the Communist International decided to adopt the strategy of a 'united front' and the Congress Socialists and Communists worked together for a time (Bandyopadhyay 2004: 380). In 1930, the Comintern had directed the Indian Communists to start activities among Indian workers, and the Communist Party of Great Britain had urged its Indian members to return to India in order to help Indian Communists (Mitra 1981: 1843).

The Communist Party of India and the Red Flag Trade Union Federation were banned by the British government in 1934. Consequently, the Communists who were released from prison after the end of the Meerut trials were left with no choice but to renew their membership of AITUC in order to continue with their work (Chandra et a. [1972] 1975: 195). Increased enthusiasm and militancy on the part of the working classes were bolstered by the formation of popular ministries in the provinces. AITUC and moderate NFTU also came together and held a joint meeting in Nagpur in April 1938.

All this led to a 50 per cent increase in the membership of trade unions between 1937 and 1938. These years were marked by strikes all over the country—a general strike in the Bengal Jute Mills (March–May 1937), recurrent *hartals* in Kanpur cotton mills, textile strikes in Amritsar, Ahmedabad and Madras, strike in Martin Burn's Iron and Steel Works located at Kulti and Hirapur in 1938 and a prolonged and bitter struggle in the Digboi oil works in Assam (April–October 1939).

Prior to the provincial elections in 1937, leaders of the Congress Left had made serious efforts to enlist the support of workers. Jawaharlal Nehru toured Tamil Nadu in November 1936, where the Congress Socialist Party had been established in 1934 by Jayaprakash Narayan and Acharya Narendra Dev. Nehru, the Congress President at the time, had aroused great expectations by declaring in rallies that if people voted for the Congress, independence would be achieved, and after independence the problems of poverty and unemployment would be solved through the introduction of socialism (Krishna 1992: 1497). Pandit Nehru's appeal and the thorough work of Satyamurty, Rajagopalachari and others created an accord between the AITUC and the Indian National Congress. AITUC did not even contest all the labour seats in order to make way for the Congress.

The Congress tried to retain labour support for a short while after taking office. Jawaharlal Nehru and Subhas Bose organized a big labour rally in Calcutta in 1937 where they urged the workers to unite, organize and join hands with the Congress. Conservative Vallabhbhai Patel, Rajendra Prasad and J. B. Kripalani founded a Hindustan Majdur Sabha in 1938. It was relatively easy for the Congress Working Committee to empathize with the Bengal jute workers and criticize the harsh measures adopted by the rival coalition ministry of Fazlul Huq and his Krishak Praja Party when it passed the Bengal Jute

Ordinance of 1939 that reduced hours of work and adversely affected jute mill workers and jute growers (Mitra 1981: 1840). The Congress also expressed sympathy towards workers in Punjab, where the Unionist Party was in power.

In its own provinces, however, the Congress had to change what Bipan Chandra and others have called its 'pro-labour stance' (Chandra et al. 2000: 331) very quickly as the capitalists, headed by Birla, complained of rampant 'indiscipline' in Congress provinces (Birla 1953: 227). Birla and his compatriots also threatened to move capital from Bombay and UP to the neighbouring princely states which hardly had any labour laws. In the provinces with elected ministries, on the other hand, liberal and/or leftist and Communist leaders predominated, and the Ahmedabad textile strike in 1937 pointed to the fact that Communists were penetrating a Gandhian stronghold (Sarkar [1983] 1995: 361).

The capitalist threat of moving capital from Bombay made the Congress ministry there act with alacrity—it rushed through an act in two months, without discussions in the Select Committee. The Trade Disputes Act, implemented in November 1938, included severe provisions to control strikes and curb labour unrest. It imposed compulsory arbitration, imprisonment of six months for illegal strikes without corresponding provisions for arbitrary lockouts and strict rules for registering new trade unions that made it virtually impossible for such unions to be registered without the sanction of the management (Sarkar [1983] 1995: 362). If Communists were invading Gandhian strongholds, the Congress was aiming to control labour militancy in the strongest base of the Communists. The Bombay ministry went back on the promise, made in the election manifesto, that Congress would recognize the right of workers to form trade unions and strive to protect their interests. Congress ministries showed no inclination to ask for a removal of the ban on the Communist Party of India, on grounds that the decision lay with the Raj.

Understandably, the entire trade union movement, with the exception of the Ahmedabad union under Gandhian leaders Gurzarilal Nanda and Khandubhai Desai, opposed the act, and nearly all non-Congress parties, the Muslim League and Ambedkar's party among them, collaborated with the trade unions. A rally addressed by Communist leaders S. A. Dange and Indulal Yagnik and Ambedkar on 6 November was attended by 80,000 people, and the following day, a strike rocked the entire province. Interestingly, Nehru only had some objections to the clause of registration of new unions, but had no problems with the act as a whole. Subhas Bose, the Socialist President of the Congress, protested in private to Sardar Patel, but did not make any public statement against the act.

Even in Madras, where the Congress had got full cooperation from AITUC and veteran union leader V. V. Giri had become the industrial and labour minister, the Congress ministry fell far short of taking a 'pro-labour stance' during strikes by the Coimbatore textile mill workers between 1937 and 1939. The history of Coimbatore labour during the 1930s, remarks Murphy Eamon, was 'one of bitter struggle—militant workers opposed to intransigent, ruthless employers', both Indian and European (Eamon 1981: 29). During the struggle, the Congress government tended to put brakes more on the workers than on the employers.

Addressing the workers during a general strike in 1937, V. V. Giri made it clear that the Congress ministry did not approve of strikes when other methods of representation had not been exhausted, and that the government preferred internal methods of settlement to external ones (Krishna 1992: 1503). The

Congress ministry, argues C. S. Krishna, did not 'advance the class interests of workers' and the Congress union took a 'reformist' rather than a 'revolutionary' approach towards the proletariat (ibid.: 1504).

In David Arnold's view, Congressmen in office often found themselves torn between the workers, many of whom had voted for or identified with the Congress, and the industrialists. More significantly, British capitalists managed to manipulate the 'ambiguities and conflicting ambitions of Congress' effectively to 'espouse their interests during industrial disputes', a fact that became evident in the industrial conflict in the Nellikuppam sugar factory in South Arcot between 1937 and 1939 (Arnold 1977b: 17). The European-controlled management successfully made the Congress ministry take its side. Even though ministerial support for European industrialists was 'neither automatic nor inevitable', in the end the 'pull of capital' turned out to be stronger than 'the appeal of labour' (Arnold 1977b:17–18).

It is true that the Communists and the workers were united, to a certain degree, by a commonality of interests—both were opposed to capitalists and the state. At the same time, 'shared antagonisms' did not automatically result in an alliance (Chandavarkar 1994: 411–12). There were other factors at work. Communists were outsiders in factories and had no base in the workplace. Their endeavours to present themselves as an alternative source of patronage, therefore, had to take into account existing social relations among workers in their neigbourhoods. At the same time, the development of new institutional structures and a legal framework made the services offered by Communists very valuable for the workers. Mutual interest and constraint enabled an alliance in which Communists gained a strong foothold in trade unions, but made frequent use of ties of caste and religion in organizing the workers in general and strikes in particular (Joshi 1985).

On the whole, Communist participation lent a radical edge to the workers' struggle, best demonstrated in recurrent strikes all over India from the decade of the 1920s. The brief period of cooperation between Congress Socialists and Communists in the mid-1930s produced another wave of strikes in 1937–38. This cooperation came to an end as Congress governments began to adopt severe measures to curb labour militancy. The Congress Left failed to persuade the Congress leadership to take a more sympathetic attitude towards trade unions and Kisan Sabhas.

The Communists, it has been argued with reference to Bengal, failed to understand the close links between jute mill workers and jute growers. Migration to the jute mills of Calcutta was largely cyclical; most mill workers retained their connection with villages and went back during times of harvest (Chakrabarty 1989), since lack of land was not the only factor for migration (De Haan 1995). This lack of understanding on the part of Communists meant that they could not encourage the growth of united workers' and peasant movements (Mitra 1981: 1846–47).

The crisis of the Congress Left became clear in the Tripuri session of the Congress in 1939. Subhas Bose, elected President of the Congress in the Haripura session in 1938, decided to stand for re-election. In his first year as president, Bose had tried to push for *swaraj* as a 'National Demand', opposed the idea of a federation and sent an ultimatum to the British government. Bose's candidacy for the 1939 session was rivalled by Sitaramayya, whom Gandhi declared to be his nominee. Subhas Bose won by 1,580 votes against Sitaramayya's 1,377, and got massive leads in Bengal and Punjab and substantial ones in Kerala, Karnataka, Tamil Nadu, UP and Assam.

And yet, Gandhi and the Congress Right managed to turn things around very quickly. Fifteen out of thirteen members of the Congress Working Committee, including Jawaharlal Nehru, resigned and Subhas Bose was directed to nominate his new executive 'in accordance with the wishes of Gandhiji' by means of a resolution moved by Govind Ballav Pant. The resolution won in the Subjects Committee on account of disunity within the Left. Subhas Bose tried in vain for two months to set up a working committee that was acceptable to all. He was forced to resign (Bandyopadhyay 1984: 323–35; Gordon 1974: 274–75). He started the Forward Bloc within the Congress in an effort to bring the Left together, but did not achieve much success. Rajendra Prasad, a staunch Right-winger, replaced Bose as the Congress President.

In 1942, when the ban on the Communist Party was lifted because it backed British War efforts, the tug of war between the Congress and Communists over the leadership of workers got a distinct twist. Soviet Russia was Britain's ally in the Second World War, and Indian Communists were directed to support the War. This pro-state stance of the Communists made workers move away from them and turn towards the Congress. Once more, the workers demonstrated autonomy in their dealings with capitalists, Communists and the state; they did not render unconditional support either to the Congress or to the Communists. Different meanings of freedom and distinct modes of achieving it continued to lend dynamism and diversity to the nationalist struggle (Bandyopadhyay 2004: 381).

THE FEDERATION AND THE PRINCES

The provincial part of the 1935 Act became effective with the elections in 1937. The federal part, however, remained a 'non-starter' since no one seemed interested in it (Bandyopadhyay 2004: 326; Sarkar [1983] 1995: 338). As discussed in the last chapter, Muslim leaders felt that the federal structure was still too unitary and would result in the domination by the Congress and Hindu majority at the centre. The princes, who had initially suggested that princely states and British India should form a federation, became unenthusiastic once the prospect of Congress takeover of the central government receded with the waning of the Civil Disobedience movement. In the perception of a contemporary observer, the division between British India and the native states 'greatly complicated and retarded' the 'political progress of India' (Farley 1942: 96).

The 562 princely states, comprising almost two-fifths of India's territory, had remained 'walled off' and relatively autonomous internally since they were under the loose supervision of British residents posted at their courts, although their external relations remained under British control (Fisher 1991; Kooiman 1995: 2125, 2002: 15; Lee-Warner 1894). The outbreak of the First World War brought the larger princes close to the Raj. They donated generously to War funds, provided military service and welcomed army recruitment in their states. Consequently, they wanted some recognition of their services from the British government at the end of the War. They asked to be spared from the increasing vigilance of the British political department and from the political turmoil in British India, and demanded greater participation in the consultations carried out by the British with Indians (Copland 1997: 33–34). They made use of the enquiries initiated by the government with regard to constitutional reforms to ask for a Chamber of Princes, an advisory body with direct access to the Government of India.

The desire for an association that could bring the opinion of princes on topics of mutual concern directly to the Government of India, and not through the mediation of the political department and its agents, had been expressed by some of the more 'progressive' princes since 1908 (Richter and Ramusack 1975: 757). This was a corollary to Lord Minto's policy of entering into a 'partnership' with the princes, a policy strongly supported by the new political secretary, Sir Harcourt Butler. 'Partnership' involved less and less interference in the internal affairs of the princely states in an effort to ensure greater cooperation. In his declaration in Udaipur (1909), Minto had praised loyal Rajputana for remaining free of 'the poison of sedition' scattered elsewhere (Kooiman 2002: 71).

In 1914, the Maharaja of Bikaner had made a direct appeal to Viceroy Lord Hardinge for establishing a federal chamber that represented all states. Hardinge had expressed sympathy but had put off the decision. The 'fear of the impact of constitutional changes' consequent upon the Montagu declaration in 1917 that promised 'progressive realization of responsible self-government' by Indians, induced ruling princes and chiefs to constitute themselves as a 'pressure group'. They wanted to express their concerns more forcefully in the Conference of Princes and Chiefs convened by Lord Chelmsford (Richter and Ramusack 1975: 757).

The princes accepted the idea of a federation at the centre suggested in the Nehru Report. Made aware of their vulnerability by the growing strength of the nationalist struggle, they proposed that princely states should form part of an autonomous all-India federation with British India. By 1935, however, the princes had become fearful of the loss of autonomy implied by a federation and wanted to sit and watch which way the wind blew in order to gain better bargaining power.

It is evident from what has been stated so far that the princely states were not as insulated as one would like to believe. Economically, most princely states formed part of the internal trade networks of British India and the international market, and politically most of them were aware of what was happening in British India. Indeed, the situation of princely states under British Raj has been compared to 'client states' in international systems, autonomous and yet subject to external influences within an 'asymmetrical power relationship' (Rudolph, Rudolph and Singh 1975: 720).

The state of Baroda, it bears pointing out, had a system of local administration based on the elective principle from the end of the nineteenth century even though the ruler of Baroda was considered to be 'the fountainhead of all power, authority and justice' (Kooiman 1995: 2126). In a similar manner, the princely government of Travancore was up to date with the political reforms in British India, and its subjects were well-informed about what people were demanding beyond their frontiers (Kooiman 2002: 73). This was also true of Hyderabad, where the sixth Nizam, 'probably stimulated by the promulgation of a Councils Act in British India', issued a *firman* 'announcing the establishment of a Legislative Council' (Kooiman 2002: 78).The Council was empowered to make laws and to call for public opinion on any matter under consideration. The setting up of the Council came in the wake of a modernization of administration underway since the 1870s.

The Wadiyar Rajas of Mysore, placed in power by the British after the fall of Tipu Sultan in 1799, carefully cultivated a public image as 'model administrators' who ruled over the 'most progressive' princely state (Manor 1975: 32). From the end of the nineteenth century, Mysore had a representative assembly with delegates from every *taluka* that met as a 'petitioning body' in audience with the princely authorities at the time of Dasera Durbar in October, and in 1907, Mysore established a legislative assembly on the model of the provinces of British India (ibid.: 36–37).

Non-Brahman movements, we have seen, had a base in states in the south and the west, and the ruler of Kolhapur led the elite non-Brahman movement of Maharashtra. Mysore and Kolhapur were among the first to introduce caste-based reservations in their administrations. The maharajas and *diwans* of Mysore were held in high esteem by nationalists as 'model' Indian rulers, and the Mysore administration adopted elements of Gandhi's constructive programme after 1920, which included uplift of 'untouchables', the teaching of Hindi and the propagation of khadi. Rulers of Alwar and Bharatpur, for their part, extended support to Arya Samaj and Hindu nationalist activities in the early twentieth century. They upheld the cause of Hindi against Urdu, patronized cow protection and consciously Hinduized their states (Bandyopadhyay 2004: 327).

The introduction of elections in Baroda at the end of the nineteenth century had inspired the forming of a Baroda *prajamandal* (State People's Conference) in 1917 (Handa 1968: 89). This conference worked for the improvement of the condition of the state's subjects. *Prajamandals* soon emerged in almost all the princely states, leading to the foundation of the All-India States' People's Conference in 1927 with its headquarters in Bombay. Headed by middle-class leaders, the All-India States' People's Conference demanded moderate democratic rights and constitutional changes. Its greater significance lay in the fact that it coordinated the activities of different *prajamandals* and brought together isolated struggles of peoples of different states. This made 'local incidents' acquire 'an all-India identity' (Chandra et al. [1972] 1975: 201).

The 1920 Nagpur session of the Congress had called on the princes to introduce full responsible government in their states. At the same time, Congress resolutions had made it clear that while subjects in princely states (called state's people), could become members of the Congress in their individual capacity, they could not use their Congress membership to interfere in the affairs of the states (Chandra et al. [1972] 1975: 199–200). Political activities of the princely states, in Congress' perception, were best left to their *prajamandals*.

Chapter 7 looked at how Gandhi's message and influence spilled into princely states and 'tribal' areas, occasioning anti-feudal uprisings against *jagirdari* oppression and land taxes by the governments in Rajasthan and Gujarat in the 1920s. The Congress did not intervene; but local leaders established links with the nationalist struggle and were dubbed 'local Gandhi'. The rapid spread of the states' peoples' movement moreover had encouraged Jawaharlal Nehru to declare in his presidential address at the historic Lahore Congress (1929) that 'Indian states cannot live apart from the rest of India ... the only people who have the right to determine the future of the states must be the people of these states' (cited in Chandra et al. [1972] 1975: 201). Along with the resolution of *purna swaraj*, this session of the Congress also passed a resolution endorsing the demands of the All-India States' People's Conference.

The formation of Congress ministries in the provinces in 1937 gave a boost to the states' people's movements. The Congress, however, desisted from intervening in the politics of the princely states till 1938. The Haripura session of the Congress, under Subhas Bose's leadership, expressed 'moral support and sympathy' for the states' people's movements (Kooiman 2002: 117), even though it did not amount to much more than 'an elaborate restatement' of existing policy without committing the Congress to active help (Copland 1987: 123–24; Jeffrey 1978: 13–15). It was only in 1939 that Gandhi finally decided to try out his technique of controlled mass struggle in the princely state of Jaipur. He also intervened in the Praja Parishad movement in Rajkot, but had to accept defeat (Sarkar [1983] 1995: 366–67).

Some princes responded sharply and tried to repress the people's movements in their states; they also actively opposed Congress activities. The Congress nevertheless, had a certain degree of control over the politics of Mysore and Travancore (Jeffrey 1978; Manor 1977), and the princes of Mysore, Travancore, Baroda and Cochin granted constitutional reforms (Ramusack 1978). These inconsistencies notwithstanding, powerful popular movements developed in many parts of princely India, with demands that ranged from the legitimization of the Congress and responsible government to the abolition of forced labour and feudal extortions and to demands for communal representation and separate electorates.

Given the fact that the reactions of princes, the Congress and Communists to the states' peoples' movements were diverse, the movements won small victories for the subjects at times and were ruthlessly suppressed at other instances. In sum, politics in the princely states showed wide variations, and there was no clear decision on the issue of a federation. A recurring problem in deliberations on the federation related to the system of government to be adopted by the states that acceded to the Indian union. Congress spokesmen, brimming with confidence after the electoral victories in 1937, insisted that the princely states were to send their representatives to the federal assembly by means of elections, a claim that was strongly resisted by Hyderabad and other states (Kooiman 2002: 187). In the end, Hyderabad and Travancore would make use of the War in 1939 to turn down the offer of a federation.

Hence, it was not just the political map of India that represented 'a crazy quilt' in which the 11 provinces of British India mingled in an intricate pattern with the 562 native states and a few commissioner's provinces (Farley 1942: 96); the politics of the distinct divisions also resembled a jigsaw puzzle.

The British government for its part was not unhappy with a deadlock that allowed the 1919 system of official control at the centre to continue indefinitely. The Act of 1935, which came six years after Lord Irwin's offer of dominion status, made no mention of it. Viceroy Linlithgow's assessment that the Act of 1935 would preserve British influence in India turned out to be true. The British were in no hurry to hand over control to Indian hands.

REFERENCES

Ahir, D. C. 2007. *Dr. Babasaheb Ambedkar Writings and Speeches (A Ready Reference Manual of 17 Volumes)*. Delhi: B. R. Publishing Corporation.

Alavi, Hamza and J. Harriss. 1989. 'Politics of Ethnicity in India and Pakistan'. In *Sociology of 'Developing Societies'*, edited by Hamza Alavi and J. Harriss, 222–46. Hampshire: Macmillan.

Alter, Joseph S. 2000. *Gandhi's Body: Sex, Diet, and the Politics of Nationhood*. Philadelphia, PA: The University of Pennsylvania Press.

Ambedkar, B. R. 1917. 'Castes in India, Their Mechanism, Genesis and Development'. *Indian Antiquary* XLI (May). *Babasaheb Ambedkar Writings and Speeches (BAWS)*, ed. Vasant Moon. Vol. 1 (1990): 3–22. Bombay: Education Department, Government of Maharashtra. Electronic edition: http://drambedkarbooks.files. wordpress.com/2009/03/selected-work-of-dr-b-r-ambedkar.pdf.

———.1919. 'Evidence Before the Southborough Committee on Franchise'. In *Dr. Babasaheb Ambedkar: Writings and Speeches (BAWS)*, ed. Vasant Moon. Vol. 1 (1979): 245–277. Bombay: Education Department, Government of Maharashtra.

———.1925. *The Evolution of Provincial Finance in British India*. London: P. S. King and Son.

———. 1928. 'Evidence of Dr. Ambedkar before the Indian Statutory Commission'. In *Dr. Babasaheb Ambedkar: Writings and Speeches (BAWS)*, ed. Vasant Moon. Vol. 2 (1982): 459–490. Bombay, Education Department, Government of Maharashtra.

———.1929. 'Statement on Education of the Depressed Classes in the Bombay Presidency: 29 May 1928'. In *Perspectives on Social Exclusion and Inclusive Policies* (2009), edited by Sukhdeo Thorat and Narendra Kumar, 105–108. First Published 2008. New Delhi: Oxford University Press.

———. 1945. *What Congress and Gandhi Have Done to the Untouchables*. London: Thacker & Co. (Reprinted in 1990). *Dr. Babasaheb Ambedkar Writings and Speeches (BAWS)*, ed. Vasant Moon. Bombay: Education Department, Government of Maharashtra.

Arnold, David. 1977a. *The Congress in Tamil Nadu, Nationalist Politics in South India 1919–1937*. London: Curzon Press.

———.1977b. 'Labour Relations in a South Indian Sugar Factory 1937–39'. *Social Scientist* 6 (5): 16–33.

———. 2001. *Gandhi: Profiles in Power*. London: Pearson Education.

Bandyopadhyay, Gitasree. 1984. *Constraints in Bengal Politics 1921–41: Gandhian Leadership*. Calcutta: Sarat Book House.

Bandyopadhyay, Sekhar. 2004. *From Plassey to Partition: A History of Modern India*. Hyderabad: Orient Longman.

Banerjee-Dube, Ishita, ed. 2008. *Caste in History*. New Delhi: Oxford University Press.

Begum, Jahanara. 1994. *The Last Decades of Undivided Bengal: Parties, Politics [and] Personalities*. Calcutta: Minerva.

Birla, G. D. 1953. *In the Shadow of the Mahatma*. Bombay: Orient Longman.

Biswas, K. P. 1966. *Yukta Banglar Sesh Adhyay*. Calcutta, (n.p).

Bose, Sanat. 1979a. 'Communist International and Indian Trade Union Movement (1919–1923)'. *Social Scientist* 8 (4): 23–36.

———. 1979b. 'Parties and Politics in Indian Trade Union Movement: Early Phase (1917–1924)'. *Social Scientist* 7 (12): 3–12.

Bose, Subhas Chandra. 1935. *The Indian Struggle, 1920 -1934*. London: Wishart and Company Ltd.

Chakrabarty, Dipesh 1989. *Rethinking Working Class History: Bengal, 1890-1940*. Princeton, NJ: Princeton University Press.

Chandavarkar, Rajnarayan. 1994. *The Origins of Industrial Capitalism in India: Business Strategies and the Working Classes in Bombay, 1900–1940*. Cambridge: Cambridge University Press.

Chandra, Bipan, Amales Tripathi, Barun De. [1972] 1975. *Freedom Struggle*. New Delhi: National Book Trust.

Chandra, Bipan, Mridula Mukherjee, Aditya Mukherjee, K. N. Panikkar, Sucheta Mahajan. 2000. *India's Struggle for Independence*. New Delhi: Penguin Books.

Chatterjee, Partha. 1984. *Bengal, 1920–1940: The Land Question*. Calcutta: K. P. Bagchi and Co.

Copland, Ian. 1987. 'Congress Paternalism: The "High Command" and the Struggle for Freedom in Princely India'. *South Asia* 8 (1–2): 121–41.

———. 1997. *The Princes of India in the Endgame of Empire 1917–47*. Cambridge: Cambridge University Press.

De Haan, Arjan. 1995. 'Migration in Eastern India: A Segmented Labour Market'. *The Indian Economic and Social History Review* 31 (1): 51–93.

Desai, Mahadev. 1953. 'Yeravda-Pact Eve'. *The Diary of Mahadev Desai*. Vol. 1. Ahmedabad: Navajivan Publishing House.

Dobbin, Christine E. 1970. *Basic Documents in the Development of Modern India and Pakistan*. London: Van Nostrand Reinhold.

Eamon, Murphy. 1981. *Unions in Conflict: A Comparative Study of Four South Indian Textile Centres, 1918–1939*. New Delhi: Manohar.

Ehrmann, Winston W. 1947. 'Post-War Government and Politics in India'. *The Journal of Politics* 9 (4): 653–91.

Ethnoven, R. E. 1922. *The Tribes and Castes of Bombay*. Vol. 2. Bombay: Government Central Press.

Farley, Miriam S. 1942. 'India: A Political Primer'. *Far Eastern Survey* 11 (8): 94–101.

Fisher, Michael H. 1991. *Indirect Rule in India: Residents and the Residency System 1764–1858*. New Delhi: Oxford University Press.

Galanter, Marc. 1984. *Competing Equalities: Law and the Backward Classes in India*. Berkeley and Los Angeles: University of California Press.

Gallagher, J. 1973. 'Congress in Decline: Bengal, 1930 to 1939'. *Modern Asian Studies* 7 (3): 589–645.

Gandhi, M. K. 1920. *Young India*. 'Caste Must Go and the Sin of Untouchability'. Ahmedabad (8 December).

———. 1958–1994. *The Collected Works of Mahatma Gandhi*. Vols. 1–100. New Delhi: Publications Division, Government of India. Electronic version 1999: http://www.gandhiserve.org/cwmg/cwmg.html.

———. 1970. *M. K. Gandhi Select Writings*. New Delhi: Sagor Publications.

Ghosh, Suniti Kumar. 1992. '"Play Fair and We Will Play Fair": Pages from Congress History'. *Economic and Political Weekly* 27 (20/21) (16–23 May): 1079–1088.

Ghurye, G. S. [1950] 1958. *Caste and Class in India*. Bombay: Popular Book Depot.

———. 2008. 'Caste and British Rule'. In *Caste in History*, edited by Ishita Banerjee-Dube, 40–45. New Delhi: Oxford University Press.

Gilmartin, D. 1988. *Empire and Islam: Punjab and the Making of Pakistan*. Berkeley and Los Angeles: University of California Press.

Gordon, Leonard A. 1974. *Bengal: The Nationalist Movement 1876–1940*. New York: Columbia University Press.

Handa, R. L. 1968. *History of Freedom Struggle in Princely States*. Delhi: Central News Agency.

Hasan, Mushirul. 1988. 'The Muslim Mass Contact Campaign: Analysis of a Strategy of Political Mobilization'. In *Congress and Indian Nationalism: The Pre-Independence Phase*, edited by R. Sisson and S. Wolpert, 198–222. Berkeley and Los Angeles: University of California Press.

Hubel, Teresa. 1996. *Whose India? The Independence Struggle in British and Indian Fiction and History*. Durham and London: Duke University Press.

Jaffrelot, Christophe. 2005. *Analysing and Fighting Caste: Dr Ambedkar and Untouchability*. Delhi: Permanent Black.

Jalal, Ayesha. [1985] 1994. *The Sole Spokesman: Jinnah, the Muslim League and the Demand for Pakistan*. New Delhi: Foundation Books (Cambridge University Press).

———. 1997. 'Exploding Communalism: The Politics of Muslim Identity in South Asia'. In *Nationalism, Democracy and Development: State and Politics in India*, edited by Sugata Bose and Ayesha Jalal, 76–103. New Delhi: Oxford University Press.

Jeffrey, R, ed. 1978. *People, Princes and Paramount Power: Society and Politics in the Indian Princely States*. New Delhi: Oxford University Press.

Joshi, Chitra. 1985. 'Bonds of Community, Ties of Religion: Kanpur Textile Workers in the Early Twentieth Century'. *The Indian Economic and Social History Review* 22 (3): 251–80.

Kabir, Humayun. 1959. *Maulana Abul Kalam Azad: A Memorial Volume*. New York: Asia Publishing House.

Kooiman, Dick. 1995. 'Communalism and Indian Princely States: A Comparison with British India'. *Economic and Political Weekly* 30 (34) (26 August): 2123–2133.

———. 2002. *Communalism and Indian Princely States: Travancore, Baroda and Hyderabad in the 1930s*. New Delhi: Manohar.

Krishna, C. S. 1992. 'First Congress Ministry and Labour Struggles of Textile Mill Workers in Coimbatore, 1937–39'. *Economic and Political Weekly* 47 (28) (11 July): 1497–1506.

Kumar, Ravinder. 1987. 'Gandhi, Ambedkar and the Poona Pact, 1932'. In *Struggling and Ruling: The Indian National Congress, 1885–1985*, edited by J. Masselos, 87–101. New Delhi: Sterling Publishers.

Lee-Warner, William. 1894. *Protected Princes of India*. London: Macmillan.

Low, D. A. 1977. 'Civil Martial Law: The Government of India and the Civil Disobedience Movement, 1930–34'. In *Congress and the Raj*, edited by D. A. Low, 165–198. London: Heinemann.

Manor, James. 1975. 'Princely Mysore before the Storm: The State-Level Political System of India's Model State 1920–1936'. *Modern Asian Studies* 9 (1): 31–58.

———. 1977. *Political Change in an Indian State: Mysore, 1917–1955*. New Delhi: Oxford University Press.

Markovits, Claude. 1981. 'Indian Business and the Congress Provincial Governments, 1937–1939'. *Modern Asian Studies* 15 (3): 487–526.

Mendelsohn, Oliver and Marika Vicziany. 2000. *The Untouchables: Subordination, Poverty and the State in Modern India*. New Delhi: Foundation Books. First published, Cambridge University Press.

Menon, V. P. 1957. *The Transfer of Power in India*. Princeton, NJ: Princeton University Press.

Metcalf, Barbara D. and Thomas R. Metcalf. 2003. *A Concise History of India*. Cambridge: Cambridge University Press.

Misra, B. B. 1976. *The Indian Political Parties*. New Delhi: Oxford University Press.

Mitchell, Lisa. 2009. *Language, Emotion, and Politics in South India: The Making of a Mother Tongue*. Bloomington, IA: Indiana University Press.

Mitra, Ira. 1981. 'Growth of Trade Union Consciousness among Jute Mill Workers, 1920–40'. *Economic and Political Weekly* 16 (44/46) (Special number): 1839–1847.

Moore, R. J. 1988. *Endgames of Empire: Studies of Britain's Indian Problem*. New Delhi: Oxford University Press.

Nagaraj, D. R. 1993. *The Flaming Feet: A Study of the Dalit Movement*. Bangalore: South Forum Press and Institute for Cultural Research and Action.

Nath, Trilok. 1987. *Politics of the Depressed Classes*. Delhi: Deputy Publications.

Nehru, Jawaharlal. 1984. *Selected Works of Jawaharlal Nehru*. Vol. V. Delhi: Nehru Memorial Fund.

O'Hanlon, Rosalind. 1985. *Caste, Conflict and Ideology: Mahatma Jotirao Phule and Low Caste Protest in Nineteenth-Century Western India*. Cambridge: Cambridge University Press.

Omvedt, Gail. 1976. *Cultural Revolt in a Colonial Society: The Non-Brahman Movement in Western India, 1873–1930*. Bombay: Scientific Socialist Education Trust.

———. 1994. *Dalits and the Democratic Revolution: Dr. Ambedkar and the Dalit Movement in Colonial India*. New Delhi: Sage Publications India.

Pandey, Deepak. 1978. 'Congress Muslim League Relations, 1937–39: "The Parting of Ways"'. *Modern Asian Studies* 12 (4): 629–54.

Pandey, Gyanendra. 1978. *The Ascendancy of the Congress in Uttar Pradesh, 1926–1934: A Study in Imperfect Mobilization*. New Delhi: Oxford University Press.

Pandian, M. S. S. 1993. '"Denationalising" the Past: "Nation" in E.V. Ramaswamy's Political Discourse'. *Economic and Political Weekly* 28 (42) (16 October): 2282–2287.

———. 1994. 'Notes on the Transformation of "Dravidian" Ideology: Tamilnadu, c. 1900–1940'. *Social Scientist* 22 (5/6): 84–104.

———. 2002. 'One Step Outside Modernity: Caste, Identity Politics and Public Sphere'. *Economic and Political Weekly* 37 (18) (4 May): 1735–1741.

Pandit, Nalini. 1979. 'Class and Caste in Maharashtra'. *Economic and Political Weekly* 14 (7/8) (Annual number): 425–36.

Patankar, Bharat and Gail Omvedt. 1979. 'The Dalit Liberation Movement in Colonial Period'. *Economic and Political Weekly* 14 (7/8) (Annual number): 409–24.

Pratt, Tim and James Vernon. 2005. '"Appeal from this Fiery Bed…": The Colonial Politics of Gandhi's Fasts and Their Metropolitan Reception'. *Journal of British Studies* 44 (1): 92–114.

Pyarelal. [1932] 1958. *The Epic Fast*. Ahmedabad: M. M. Bhatt (First published 1932).

Ramaswamy, Sumathi. 1997. *Passions of the Tongue: Language Devotion in Tamil India, 1891–1970*. Berkeley and Los Angeles: University of California Press.

Ramusack, Barbara N. 1978. *The Princes of India in the Twilight of Empire: Dissolution of a Patron-Client System, 1914–1939*. Columbus, OH: Ohio State University Press.

Rao, Anupama. 2009. *The Caste Question: Dalits and the Politics of Modern India*. Berkeley and Los Angeles: University of California Press.

———. 2011. 'Minority and Modernity: B. R. Ambedkar and Dalit Politics'. In *Modern Makeovers: Oxford Handbook of Modernity in South Asia*, edited by Saurabh Dube, 93–109. New Delhi: Oxford University Press.

Ray, B, ed. 1996. *Gandhi's Campaign against Untouchability, 1933–34: An Account from the Raj's Secret Official Reports*. New Delhi: Gandhi Peace Foundation.

Ray, S., ed. 1987. *Selected Works of Manabendra Nath Roy*. New Delhi: Oxford University Press.

Richter, William and Barbara Ramusack. 1975. 'The Chamber and the Consultation: Changing Forms of Princely Association in India'. *The Journal of Asian Studies* 34 (3): 755–776.

Rodrigues, Valerian, ed. 2002. *The Essential Writings of B. R. Ambedkar*. New Delhi: Oxford University Press.

Roy, M. N. 1964. *Memoirs*. Bombay: Allied Publishers.

Rudolph, Susanne H., Lloyd I. Rudolph and Mohan Singh. 1975. 'A Bureaucratic Lineage in Princely India: Elite Formation and Conflict in a Patrimonial System'. *The Journal of Asian Studies* 34 (3): 717–753.

Russell, R. V. and Rai Bahadur Hira Lal. 1916. *The Tribes and Castes of the Central Provinces*. Vol. 4. London: Macmillan.

Sarkar, Sumit. [1983] 1995. *Modern India, 1885–1947*. Madras: Macmillan India.

Shah, Ghanshyam. 1994. 'Identity, Communal Consciousness and Politics'. *Economic and Political Weekly* 29 (19) (7 May): 1133–1140.

Sharma, J. S., ed. 1962. *India's Struggle for Freedom: Select Documents and Sources*. Vol. 1. Delhi: S. Chand and Co.

Talbot, Ian. 1988. *Provincial Politics and the Pakistan Movement*. Karachi: Oxford University Press.

Thorat, S. and N. Kumar, eds. 2009. *B. R. Ambedkar: Perspectives on Social Exclusion and Inclusive Policies*. New Delhi: Oxford University Press (Paperback edition. First published 2008).

Tomlinson, B. R. 1976. *The Indian National Congress and the Raj: The Penultimate Phase*. London: Macmillan.

———. 1979. *The Political Economy of the Raj: The Economics of Decolonization in India, 1914–1947*. London: Macmillan.

Zelliot, Eleanor. 1972. 'Gandhi and Ambedkar: A Study in Leadership'. In *Untouchables in Contemporary India*, edited by J. Michael Mahar, 69–95. Tucson: University of Arizona Press. Also in *Caste in History*, 2008, edited by Ishita Banerjee-Dube, 197–209. New Delhi: Oxford University Press.

The Tumultuous Forties

10

Women demonstrators during the Quit India movement, 1942

Chapter outline

BRITISH MOVES: THE CRIPPS MISSION

THE CALL TO 'QUIT INDIA'

NETAJI AND THE AZAD HIND FAUJ

NEGOTIATION AND CONFRONTATION: THE ROUGH ROAD TO FREEDOM

FINAL MOVES: ELECTIONS AND CABINET MISSION

PARTITIONED FREEDOM

The theme of battles, wars and struggles dominates this chapter: the Second World War and India's reaction to being involved in it; the all out 'do or die' Quit India movement against the British, the effort of Netaji Subhas and his Indian National Army to liberate India by means of an armed struggle, the final battle to win freedom without territorial division. Alongside, there is an examination of British overtures at conciliation and the hurried decision to transfer power that occasioned frenetic negotiation, contestation and turbulence and eventually culminated in the enormous tragedy of the partition.

In September 1939, India was declared a 'belligerent' against Germany in the Second World War along with Britain (Farley 1942: 99). India's automatic and arbitrary involvement, without consultation with the provincial ministries or nationalist leaders, was bitterly resented by the Congress and Indian nationalists, even though the Congress had been much more consistent in its hostility towards fascist aggression than Britain. It is worth remembering in this connection that Jawaharlal Nehru had attended the Congress of Oppressed Nationalities at Brussels in 1927, where revolutionaries and political exiles from Asian, African and Latin American countries had come together to develop a strategy for united struggle against imperialism. The founding of the League against Imperialism had been a result of this Congress and Nehru had been elected its member (Chandra et al. [1972] 1975: 203–04).

Through the 1930s, the Congress openly supported nationalist movements in several countries in Asia and Africa, demonstrating thereby its stand against imperialism. It also expressed unease with the growth of fascism and supported the suffering people of Spain, Ethiopia and Czechoslovakia. After Britain involved India in the Second World War, the Congress Working Committee in its meeting in September 1939 condemned German, Italian and Japanese fascism and insisted that 'if Great Britain fights for the maintenance and extension of democracy then she must necessarily end imperialism in her own possessions' (Farley 1942: 99). The Indian people had to have the right to self-determination to frame their own constitution through a Constituent Assembly without external interference. 'A free democratic India' will then 'gladly associate with other free nations for mutual defense against aggression and for economic cooperation', but cooperation had to be between equals and on mutual consent (Chandra et al. [1972] 1975: 212; Farley 1942: 99). The concessions demanded by Congress in exchange for its support to British war efforts were an immediate national government at the centre and a promise of independence after the War.

The Muslim League offered to cooperate with Britain only if rights of Muslims in India were guaranteed. Jinnah insisted on the League's status as the sole spokesperson for Indian Muslims and demanded that the League be given the right to veto future constitutional changes (Sarkar [1983] 1995: 378). Viceroy Linlithgow's government rejected the Congress' proposal on the ground that transfer of substantial power to Indians was impracticable during the War. It issued a White Paper on 14 October 1939 that merely repeated the promise of eventual dominion status for Indians, with an increase in the number of Indian members in the Executive Council and the formation of an advisory committee with representatives of all important political parties. In direct consonance with the League's demand, the White Paper made it clear that the British were not willing to transfer responsibilities to any system of government whose authority was challenged by large and powerful elements in India's national life.

Linlithgow's terms were not acceptable to the Congress; Congress ministries in the provinces resigned at the end of October in protest. As stated in the previous chapter, Jinnah and his Muslim League celebrated the resignation of Congress governments as a 'Day of Deliverance'; they were supported by B. R. Ambedkar. The British Government became alert to the possibility of drawing benefits from this rift between the Congress, and the League and Ambedkar.

Linlithgow's attitude, it has been pointed out, was in tune with the general British policy that wanted to take advantage of the War and reclaim, for the white-dominated central government and bureaucracy, the ground lost to the Congress from 1937 and earlier (Sarkar [1983] 1995: 376). Labour and liberal circles in Britain, however, expressed their dissatisfaction with the government's stance towards India.

Disagreements surfaced within the Congress over the issue of launching civil disobedience. Gandhi discouraged the idea, because he did not want to take advantage of Britain's difficulties, while several other leaders urged action. The Ramgarh Congress Session in March 1940 resolved to demand complete independence and a Constituent Assembly; it also authorized the Working Committee to launch civil disobedience at its discretion (Farley 1942: 99). The timing and the form of the movement was left entirely to Gandhi's jurisdiction.

In August 1940, Linlithgow made another declaration that reiterated the terms set in the 1939 White Paper. Once again, it was rejected by the Congress and other groups. Gandhi resumed leadership of the Congress and launched 'limited civil disobedience' that consisted of speeches and 'other mild demonstrations against Indian participation in the war' (ibid.). This limited, individual satyagraha was intended to disprove the British claim that India was helping the War effort wholeheartedly. Gandhi selected Vinoba Bhabe to become the first leader to offer satyagraha, which was to be followed by Jawaharlal Nehru. The British government resorted to large-scale arrests of Congress leaders.

In July 1941, the government proceeded to expand the Viceroy's (executive) Council by including five Indian members. An Advisory National Defence Council, with Indian members, was also set up. The Indians included were prominent Moderates but none from among the Congress or the Muslim League. The concessions came in the wake of another pressing need, namely, the use of Indian troops in the service of the empire.

Slowly but steadily since the 1920s, in the aftermath of the First World War, the Indian army had slipped out of the total grasp of the home government. As early as 1923, the British Cabinet had to concede to the argument of the Committee of Imperial Defence that 'the Indian Army cannot be treated as if it were absolutely at the disposal of His Majesty's government for service outside India'. In addition, it was emphasized that except in situations of 'gravest emergency' the Indian army could not be employed in service outside India without consulting the Viceroy (Report of the subcommittee on India military requirements, 22 June 1922, amended and approved by His Majesty's Government 26 January 1923; cited in Gallagher and Seal 1981: 402). The Cabinet also agreed that the cost of the Indian army had to be reduced because it meant a heavy burden on Indian tax payers. Indian politicians and the Government of India were both averse to spending extensively on the army.

These decisions notwithstanding, the triple threat of Germany, Italy and Japan during the Second World War made Britain's imperial commitment stronger. By 1939, she needed Indian troops to go to Egypt, Singapore and Burma, and Indian artillery to Kenya. In other words, Indian troops had to be 'moved around the world in British interests' (ibid.: 412). However, the conditions under which troops were to be provided had changed drastically. The Indian army, which had been used sparingly in the course of the last ten years, had to be 'modernized and mechanized' but for the first time since the eighteenth century, the British tax payer had to pay for the revival of the empire (Gallagher and Seal 1981).

India in World Affairs, 1914–1948

Year	Leading Events
Aug. 4, '14	Britain declares war on Germany
Nov. 5, '14	Britain declares war on Turkey.
Oct. 30, '18	Armistice with Turkey signed.
Nov. 11, '18	Armistice with Germany signed.
Jan.–June 1919	Versailles Peace Conference. Indian representatives sign Peace Treaty whereby India becomes original member of League of Nations.
Dec. '19	Congress protests British attitude on Khilafat question; demands settlement consonant with sentiments of India's Muslims.
Sept. '20	Indian delegates attend Congress of the Orient in Baku, U.S.S.R. convened by Third International.
Mar. '21	Agha Khan leads delegation of Indian Muslims to England, meets PM Lloyd George to present views on Khilafat.
Nov. '21	Congress passes first formal resolution on foreign policy; challenges Britain's right to make treaties on India's behalf.
Dec. '21	Britain recognizes Afghan independence in external, as well as internal, affairs.
Dec. '23	Britain formally recognizes Nepal's complete independence in a treaty of peace and friendship.
June '24	M. N. Roy, of India, is elected full member of Executive Committee of Communist International and candidate member of its Presidium at Fifth Comintern Congress in Moscow.
Feb. '27	Jawaharlal Nehru attends International Congress against Imperialism at Brussels as official I.N.C. delegate.
Dec. '27	Congress calls for withdrawal of all Indian troops abroad.
July–Sept. '28	First Indian delegation in history of Communist International attends Sixth World Congress in Moscow.
Dec. '28	Communist Party of India, meeting in Calcutta, decides to affiliate to Communist International.
May '34	Indian and Ceylonese delegates attend Pan-Asiatic Labor Conference in Colombo. Afghanistan joins League of Nations.
Apr. '36	Congress resolution condemns great powers and League of Nations for their policy on Italo-Abyssinian War.
Sept. '36	V. K. Krishna Menon attends World Congress for Peace in Brussels as I.N.C. delegate.
Dec. '36	Congress expresses solidarity with Republican Spain.
1937	Agha Khan elected President of 18th Assembly of the League of Nations.
Oct. '37	AICC expresses concern at Japanese aggression in China; calls for Indian boycott of Japanese goods.

Year	Leading Events
Feb. '38	Congress condemns British decision to partition Palestine; expresses sympathy for Arabs in their struggle for freedom.
Feb. '38	Congress warns against attempt to involve India in war, without express consent of Indian people.
Sept. '38	Ambulance unit sent by Congress to China.
Sept. '38	Congress resolution of sympathy to people of Czechoslovakia.
Mar. '39	Congress denounces British foreign policy culminating in Munich Pact, Anglo-Italian Agreement and recognition of Franco's Spain; declares necessity of India's directing its own foreign policy.
Sept. 3 '39	Germany and Britain in state of war.
Sept. '39	Congress declares interest of free India in building world order based on democracy, but states that 'India cannot associate herself in a war said to be for democratic freedom when that very freedom is denied to her…'
June 10 '40	Italy declares war on UK.
Dec. 7 '41	Japan declares war on UK.
Jan.–Feb. '41	First branches of the 'Indian Independence League' established in Japanese East Asia, with headquarters in Tokyo.
Oct. '43	Rash Behari Bose forms Provisional Government of Free India with headquarters in Singapore; Subhas Chandra Bose becomes Head of State; war declared on Britain and the US.
May 7 '45	Germany surrenders.
June '45	India participates in San Francisco Conference and signs UN Charter as original member.
July '45	Congress resolution criticizes UN domination by Great Powers; notes that Indian delegates to San Francisco Conference represent the alien government and not the people of India.
Aug. 15 '45	Japan surrenders.
Sept. '45	AICC opposes continued imperialist domination over any part of S.E. or West Asia.
Apr. '46	Muslim League declares support for Indonesian independence.
Nov. '46	UN General Assembly approves entry of Afghanistan.
Mar–Apr '47	India convenes Asian Relations Conference in New Delhi.
Aug. '47	India and Pakistan gain independence.
Jan. '48	Burma becomes independent.
Feb. '48	Ceylon becomes independent.

Japan's rapid and unexpected advance towards Indian borders gave a new urgency to the situation and forced the government and Indian leaders to reconsider their position. In December 1941, Japan joined the War with a surprise attack on Pearl Harbour. India supported China against Japanese aggression. Between December 1941 and March 1942, Japan captured Hong Kong, Borneo, Manila,

Singapore, Java, Rangoon, Sumatra and the Andaman and Nicobar Islands. Colombo in Ceylon and the Indian coastal towns of Vishakhapatnam and Coconada were bombed in April 1942.

Indian support for the War became imperative, and along with it a discussion of India's constitutional future (Bandyopadhyay 2004: 412). President Roosevelt of the United States of America and Chiang Kai Shek of China urged Churchill, who had taken over as Premier of a coalition War Cabinet, to settle differences with Indian leaders in view of the 'critical military situation of the United Nations' (Farley 1942: 99).

After protracted conferences in London, the British Cabinet announced on 11 March 1942 that His Majesty's Government, having considered the concerns expressed in Britain and in India regarding 'the fulfilment of promises made in regard to the future of India' had decided to indicate in precise terms, 'the steps which they propose shall be taken for the earliest possible realization of self-government in India' (*Declaration of the British Government 11 March 1942*, in Sharma 1962: 590). In his speech in the House of Commons, the British Prime Minister made it clear that this 'offer' was essential in order to ensure Indian support. The 'crisis in Indian affairs arising out of the Japanese advance' had made the British 'wish to rally all the forces of Indian life, to guard their land from the menace of the invader' (Sharma 1962: 589). To make the proposal serve its purpose, the Cabinet decided to send Sir Stafford Cripps, a member of the War Cabinet, to India. Sir Stafford could 'satisfy himself upon the spot by personal consultation' that the offer being made would lead to a 'just and final solution' (ibid.: 589–90).

BRITISH MOVES: THE CRIPPS MISSION

The British government's draft declaration provided for dominion status for India immediately after the War, and left India to decide on remaining within or seceding from the British Commonwealth. To implement the proposal, a constitution of India was to be drafted by a Constituent Assembly, as soon as hostilities ceased. The assembly was to have members from British India and native (princely) states, in accordance with their population. Unless Indian leaders decided on a different method, members of the Constituent Assembly of the provinces were to be elected by the lower house of provincial legislatures by means of popular vote, and the Indian princes were to appoint their own representatives. Great Britain agreed to accept the constitution framed by the assembly and negotiate a treaty with India in order to transfer power to Indian hands and protect the rights of minorities. It, however, allowed the provinces the right to be a part of or remain outside the Indian union. Provinces desiring to remain outside could draft their own constitution and be granted the status of union government directly by Britain.

Current treaty arrangements with the native states were to be revised if they decided to join the Indian union. No constitutional changes were proposed for the duration of the War but Britain expressed the hope that Indian parties and leaders would agree to cooperate in the formation and functioning of a 'National Government'. Britain also retained the responsibility for India's defence for the time being, even though it invited Indians to participate in the 'counsels of their country, of the Commonwealth, and of the United Nations' (Chandra et al. [1972] 1975: 215; Farley 1942: 100).

On his arrival in India on 22 March, Cripps entered into immediate consultation with the

Viceroy and other important British officials, General Wavell and representatives of Indian groups—the Congress, the Muslim League, the Hindu Mahasabha and the Indian princes. He declared that the British plan had to be accepted or rejected as a whole, with room for little negotiation with regard to Indian representation in the present government.

The declaration was rejected by almost all parties although for different and sometimes opposed reasons. The Congress was unhappy about the clause of non-accession granted to the provinces, even though it accepted the democratic principle of self-determination. The right of the provinces to remain outside the Indian union was, in the perception of the Congress, a 'severe blow' to the conception of Indian unity and 'an apple of discord' that was likely to generate severe trouble in the provinces (Farley 1942: 100). It also did not like the idea of the presence of nominated members from the princely states in the Constituent Assembly, since it denied the people of the native states the right to democratic self-expression. Finally and most importantly, the Congress wanted an immediate and significant share of power; it did not want to rely on future promises (Chandra et al. [1972] 1975: 216). Britain's retention of responsibility for defence virtually eliminated Indians from a share in power since defence covered almost every aspect of life and administration in the wartime situation.

The Muslim League found the idea of non-accession welcoming, since it left the way open for Muslim-majority provinces not to accede to the Indian union. At the same time, it found the procedure of exercising self-determination by the provinces inadequate. The Hindu Mahasabha totally opposed non-accession and the prospect of 'partition' it entailed, while Punjabi Sikhs were alarmed by the possibility of non-accession because it would make them a minority in a Muslim-majority province. Ambedkar and sections of Dalits feared that the proposal did not confer enough rights on them and left the Dalits at the mercy of caste Hindus. All groups found the proposals for the interim period imprecise and hence unacceptable because the measure of Indian share in the government was not spelled out.

The proposal was rejected once Stafford Cripps, who had spoken of a 'national government' and a 'cabinet' in the initial phase of the talks, clarified that Congress demands for an immediate change of the constitution and a national government responsible neither to the Viceroy nor to the legislature were 'impracticable'. Nehru, who wanted a settlement in order to mobilize 'genuine and effective Indian support in the anti-fascist war' was disgruntled. He expressed his sentiments in a curt cable he sent to Krishna Menon apprising him of the situation. Nehru referred to the 'entirely different picture' Cripps provided in the final stages from what he had suggested initially (Moore 1979: 129–30).

Cripps failed in his 'mission' of resolving the deadlock. In his final statements, he defended the British plan, expressed concern for India's future and 'deplored' the absence of a spirit of compromise, which was essential for 'a free and strong India' (Farley 1942: 100). There was, no doubt, an element of 'bluff and double-dealing' on the part of the British; but it is also true that Gandhi and the Congress leadership were cynical and unenthusiastic from the beginning (Sarkar [1983] 1995: 388). For Churchill too, what mattered more was not what was done, but the show that an attempt had been made (Tomlinson 1976: 156). He congratulated Cripps warmly for demonstrating the strong British desire to reach a settlement.

THE CALL TO 'QUIT INDIA'

The failure of the Cripps Mission combined with the socio-economic effects of the War produced widespread frustration in India. The immediate impact of the war had been a rise in commodity prices that had benefitted industrialists, merchants and rich peasants who produced for the market. War demand and reduction in imports forced greater reliance on indigenous products and gave a great boost to Indian industries, a fact reflected in the huge increase in the number of industrial workers between 1939 and 1942. The War also reduced the pressure of rent on tenant cultivators.

At the same time, a shortfall in the supply of rice made the price index of food grains jump by 60 points in north India between April and August 1942 (Bandyopadhyay 2004: 413). A combination of bad harvest, the cessation of supply of Burmese rice and the stringent procurement policy of the British produced this shortage. A precautionary 'defence in depth' measure of the British, that caused the destruction of thousands of small river boats in Bengal—to prevent them from falling into enemy hands in the instance of an invasion from the eastern frontier —added to the crisis by creating havoc with the distribution of food supplies (Chandra et al. [1972] 1975: 271). This was to have a direct effect on the Bengal famine of 1943–44. While the poor suffered on account of the rise in the price of food grains, the rich were hit by excess profit tax, forcible collection for war funds and coercive sale of war bonds.

All this generated panic and belligerence—British power seemed to be faced with imminent collapse at the hands of the Japanese. A Bengali doggerel of the time exuberantly mentioned the presence of a cobra in the bomb dropped by the *Japani* (Japanese) and how that was making the British pant in terror.

Streams of refugees flowing into India from Malay and Burma carried stories of the collapse of British power in South East Asia and the heartless abandonment of Indian refugees by the British. There was widespread fear that the British would do the same in India, a fear that grew as a Japanese invasion became a distinct possibility. American and Australian soldiers started coming to India from May 1942 and soon became villains in stories of rape and racial harassment of the civilian population (Bandyopadhyay 2004: 414). By the middle of the year, there was a general perception that Britain will be defeated by Japan and this was accompanied by a mixed feeling of alarm and enthusiasm—alarm about the uncertainties of military aggression and enthusiasm for a struggle to liberate India from British rule.

Gandhi, the astute politician, understood this belligerence of the people much better than the Communists. The summer of 1942 found him in 'a strange and uniquely militant mood' (Sarkar [1983] 1995: 388). He repeatedly urged the British to leave India to god or to anarchy, stating that he was willing to risk 'complete lawlessness' in place of the 'orderly disciplined anarchy' of the British (Gandhi, Press Interview, 16 May 1942 in Gandhi 1958, Vol. 82: 289). He felt that the only way the people of India could be made to shed all fear and fight the aggressor was to make them feel that they were their own masters and that the defence of the country was their duty and responsibility. He therefore decided to launch a movement calling for 'an orderly withdrawal' of the British from India after they had handed over power to Indians (Chopra 1976).

Not all Congress leaders felt that the moment was opportune to make such a demand, and there were long and bitter arguments and discussions. But Gandhi remained firm and was 'overwhelmingly persuasive' (Chandra et al. [1972] 1975: 218). The Congress Working Committee at its meeting in Wardha on 14 July passed the historic 'Quit India' resolution and formulated a 'national demand'—that the British transfer power immediately to Indians and quit India. The term 'Quit India', writes Paul Greenough, was coined by an American journalist to suit the purpose of compact news headlines. Gandhi had initially used the phrase 'orderly withdrawal' but soon changed over to Quit India (Greenough 1983: 354). It is, however, highly likely that the American journalist drew upon the Hindi expression— *Bharat chodo*—in his concise formulation in English. Whatever the origin, this catchy slogan generated a 'legendary struggle' that became famous as the 'August revolution' (Chandra et al. 2000: 457) in nationalist parlance.

The 'Quit India' resolution affirmed that if the proposal was rejected by the government, Congress would be 'reluctantly compelled' to utilize all its non-violent strength for the vindication of the political rights and liberty of India under the leadership of Mahatma Gandhi (Diwaker 1948: 84). The resolution also showed an unusual note of social radicalism in stating that power and authority must 'eventually belong' to the workers in the fields and factories and elsewhere, from whom the princes, zamindars, *jagirdars* and propertied classes derived their wealth (Mansergh Vol. 2: 388, cited in Sarkar [1983] 1995: 389).

The resolution was endorsed by the All India Congress Committee on 8 August 1942 in Bombay. It sanctioned the starting of a mass struggle on the widest possible scale, for the vindication of India's inalienable right to freedom and independence and to utilize 'all the non-violent strength' India has gathered 'during the last 22 years of peaceful struggle' (Diwaker 1948: 84). No distinction was made between the people of British India and the princely states; every Indian was to participate (Chandra et al. 2000: 369). The struggle had to be 'inevitably' under the leadership of Mahatma Gandhi.

Addressing the assembled delegates after the resolution was passed, Gandhi made it clear that the 'actual struggle does not commence at this very moment' (Gandhi 1958, Vol. 83: 196). First, he had to wait upon the Viceroy and plead with him to accept the Congress demand, and that might take two or three weeks. During that time, Congress volunteers and 'every Indian who desires freedom and strives for it' had to consider themselves 'free' and 'be his own guide' (ibid.: 366). The same was to apply if the 'Congress leadership is removed by arrest'.

In a passionate 'Do or Die' speech delivered on the occasion, Gandhi stated that since this was going to be the final battle—a 'fight to the finish'—'mere jail going' was not enough. 'We shall either free India or die in the attempt; we shall not leave to see the perpetuation of our slavery' (ibid.: 197). He went to the extent of stating that he was not going to flinch even if a general strike became a dire necessity. For the first time, remarks Sumit Sarkar, Gandhi was prepared to 'countenance political strikes, precisely at a moment when the Communists were bound to keep aloof from them' (Sarkar [1983] 1995: 389).

The British government gave no chance to Gandhi to 'wait upon the Viceroy'. He and all other leaders of the Congress Working Committee were arrested and 'hustled away from Bombay in a special train' before the next day commenced. Gandhi was detained in the Agha Khan Palace in Poona and the others were sent to Ahmednagar fort (Chandra et al. [1972] 1975: 220). The government also sequestered AICC's files and funds and although the Congress as a whole was not outlawed, its national and provincial committees were banned and most of the members arrested (Bhuyan 1975: 64–66; Hutchins 1971: 67–70).

As news of the Quit India resolution and the arrest of Congress leaders reached the people simultaneously on the morning of 9 August, reaction was immediate and spontaneous. In large parts of the country—Bombay, Gujarat, United Provinces, Central Provinces, Delhi, Bihar, Orissa, Bengal, Madras and Punjab—public life almost came to a standstill and businesses were suspended. Cities and towns all over the country observed *hartals*, and processions and demonstrations pervaded the streets. National songs were accompanied by slogans demanding the release of the leaders. The large crowds remained overwhelmingly peaceful; but their massive size made the government nervous. Consequently, when demonstrators refused to pay heed to orders that asked them to disperse, the police opened fire. In Delhi alone, the police fired on demonstrators on 27 occasions over just two days—11 and 12 August. It killed 76 people and injured well over a 100.

Very soon, the situation went out of control. There was a massive groundswell, the leaders were in jail, and the people had been asked to 'be their own guide'. Gandhi's call upon 'men and women' to behave 'like free individuals' if leaders were put in jail, writes Gyanendra Pandey, had provided 'a tremendous psychological break' (1988: 131). The situation was made worse inadvertently by Leopold Amery, the Secretary of State for India. In trying to explain why the government had resorted to pre-emptive arrests of all Congress leaders, he accused the Congress of trying to foment strikes in commerce and industry, administration and law courts, schools and colleges, of interrupting traffic and public utility services, of disconnecting telephone and telegraph lines and for picketing troops and recruiting stations.

Amery's speech was widely reported in Indian newspapers on 10 August; it lent credibility to all kinds of activities that had not been authorized by the Congress leadership (Greenough 1983: 359). Amery, therefore, became 'the chief instrument in broadcasting the supposed Congress programme; what he said was avidly believed by the people' (Bhuyan 1975: 90). 'What Amery said was the Congress plan, was accepted as the Congress plan by indignant demonstrators groping for direction' (Hutchins 1971: 272). The 'chief irony of 1942 in India', in Paul Greenough's terms, was that the supreme power of the printed word 'to inspire united action' was 'unleashed by the British government; the radicalizing text was the composition of Leopold Amery, not Mahatma Gandhi' (Greenough 1983: 360). Such confusions and provocations in a charged situation gave rise to the 'August revolt', whose intensity and immeasurable fury took everyone by surprise.

Students, workers and peasants came to head the 'Revolt'. There were strikes in factories, colleges and schools. Police stations, post offices and railway stations, the hated symbols of colonial authority, were attacked, set on fire or wrecked. Charged with passion, the movement was violent from the beginning. The British were shocked by the extent of its fierceness. In a private telegram to Winston Churchill, Viceroy Linlithgow characterized it as 'by far the most serious rebellion since that of 1857'. He said that the seriousness of this event and the extent of it had been 'so far concealed from the world for reasons of military security' (Mansergh and Lumby 1971–1983, 2: 953).

British documents of the time, Tottenham's *Congress Responsibility for the Disturbances* (1943) for instance, held the 'pro-Axis sympathies' of the Congress responsible both for its change of stance and for the disturbances that this change produced. The August upsurge was described as a 'fifth-columnist' conspiracy. Evidently, the allegation was 'hollow'. It was made to 'win world anti-fascist opinion for brutal repression of an undoubtedly massive popular rebellion' (Sarkar [1983] 1995: 389).

Historians such as F. G. Hutchins have characterized the Quit India movement as a 'spontaneous revolution' that emerged out of the Congress' call on the people to 'fight to the finish'. The 'revolution' assumed massive proportions at a time when all top Congress leaders were in jail and the Congress organization had almost ceased to function. Hutchins draws attention to the varying pattern of mobilization in different regions and argues that in the absence of Congress directives to the revolutionaries at the grassroots level, participants carried on the struggle in accordance with the exigencies of the local situation. Moreover, such 'instantaneous and uniform results' could only come out of spontaneous action and not from any preconceived plan (Hutchins 1973: 217, 240).

For Nirad C. Chaudhuri, on the other hand, the Quit India movement 'was a freak and an impulsive outburst of anger at what the Indian people took as an exhibition of outrageous impudence of the British administration in India in arresting the Congress leaders' (1988: 704). It did not amount to much more than 'mere disturbances' that intended to give notice to British rule in India to quit, a 'face-saving' gesture on the part of the Congress, an effort to counteract the impression generated by the failure of the Cripps Mission that the Congress was 'powerless to do anything against British intransigence' (ibid.).

Such views notwithstanding, recent studies of the movement insist on the degree of preparedness on the part of the people. This was largely due to the militancy displayed by workers and peasants in their own organizations as well as the sustained work of Communists, Congress Socialists and Gandhian constructive workers. The long-term processes of organization under the banner of the All India Trade Union Congress, the Congress Socialist Party, the All India Kisan Sabha and the Forward Bloc, to name only the ones associated with the Congress, combined in intricate ways with the new mood of anti-white fury and exuberance about the impending collapse of British rule in India to result in a movement on an unprecedented scale.

The Congress' Quit India resolution, it bears pointing out, was remarkably vague about the details of the forthcoming movement. Gandhi, moreover, had made it clear that the movement would be launched only after his pleas to the Viceroy were rejected. The six-point programme of the movement, mentioned in a circular of the Andhra Provincial Congress Committee in July 1942, did not go beyond 'traditional' Gandhian weapons of producing salt, boycotting courts, schools and government services, picketing foreign cloth and liquor and a no-tax campaign at the last stage. It did mention the organization of labour strikes and the stopping of trains by pulling chains as measures that were 'not encouraged' but neither prohibited. The same applied to travelling without tickets and the cutting of telephone and telegraph wires. More or less the same was repeated in the 12-point programme hurriedly drawn up by the few AICC members still free on 9 August. This programme prominently featured Gandhi's instruction of 'Do or Die' and a co-relative slogan of 'Victory or Death' (Greenough 1983: 360–61). Both the six and the 12-point programmes were a far cry from the severe assault on communications and all symbols of state authority that the August revolution produced.

As top leaders were put behind bars, internal communication within the Congress hierarchy was suspended and the flow of directives from the leaders to the mass of followers was done through the national press halted by severe censorship, leadership passed on to the hands of younger and more militant local Congress cadres. They were more amenable to pressures from below. While some believed that attacks on communications had been sanctioned by AICC, some others gave 'instructions' in the name of AICC members, most of whom were in jail, once again demonstrating the 'autonomy' of grassroots politics.

As indicated earlier, the first round of the movement, characterized by massive fury on an all-India scale, was primarily urban. Headed by students and workers, it found expression in strikes and *hartals* and marches and demonstrations that led to clashes with the police and the army. If Delhi suffered heavy casualties on 11 and 12 August, Bombay was rocked by strikes and demonstrations between 9 and 14 August and Calcutta between 10 and 17 August. The British government lost virtual control of Patna for two days following a major confrontation in front of the secretariat building on 11 August that resulted when Congress workers, at the head of a mammoth rally, tried to enter the secretariat and hoist the Indian flag atop the building. There were strikes in Lucknow, Kanpur, Bombay, Nagpur and Ahmedabad, and the Tata Steel plant remained closed between 13 and 20 August because the workers declared that they would resume work only after a national government had been formed (Mansergh and Lumby 1971–1983, 2: 669, 683, 777).

If the British were surprised by the immense fury, they were also quick to unleash unparalleled repression. The wartime presence of the army was put to full use and the police and army opened fire indiscriminately to 'control' the crowds. This led to a rapid suppression of the first phase of the movement. By the middle of August, urban strikes and demonstrations had almost disappeared. The movement, however, lingered on till the end of 1943 passing through two more phases. In some parts of India, the movement was intense but short-lived, while in others it was less forceful but more enduring.

By the end of 1943, 91,836 people were arrested, with the maximum number coming from Bombay Presidency (21,416), followed by UP (16,796) and Bihar (16,202); 218 police outposts, 332 railway stations and 943 post offices were wrecked or damaged, and 664 bomb explosions had taken place. The Home Political files (cited in Chakrabarty 1992a: 797) state that 1,060 people had died in police and army firing, 63 policemen in trying to control the upsurge and 216 policemen had 'defected' to the rebels' side.

The rapid spread and sudden collapse of an uprising that had the potential of surpassing the Non-Cooperation and Civil Disobedience movements prompted Judith Brown to depict the confrontation between the people moved by 'immense fury' and the British state as 'a flotilla of rafts colliding with a battleship' (Brown 1985: 311–12). State measures of repression literally assumed battleship proportions, particularly in view of the extensive use of the army (57 battalions), not let loose on crowds during earlier agitations.

The 'battle' was undoubtedly mismatched since unarmed Congress volunteers and Congress supporters fought against fully armed British police and army. But the battle shook the colonial administration; Linlithgow's order of 'machine gunning from air' on crowds disrupting communication around Patna, and the employment of airplanes to 'fire on Congress rebels in Bhagalpur and Monghyr in Bihar, Nadia and Tamluk in Bengal, and Talcher in Orissa' demonstrate the extent of British fear (Home Political cited in Chakrabarty 1992a: 797). The Quit India upsurge, therefore, amounted to much more than 'a flotilla of rafts' even though its strength varied widely across regions.

From the middle of August 1942, the movement entered what can roughly be called its second phase, and the focus shifted to the countryside. Students moved into rural areas from towns and cities like Benares, Patna and Cuttack, caused havoc to communication and led a 'veritable peasant rebellion against white authority strongly reminiscent in some ways of 1857' (Sarkar [1983] 1995: 395). Northern and western Bihar and eastern UP, Midnapur in Bengal, and certain parts of Gujarat, Maharashtra, Orissa and Karnataka emerged as powerful centres in this phase.

Peasant insurgency was the strongest in Bihar, where the Kisan Sabha had been organizing peasants for a long time. Following the clash in Patna on 11 August, peasants in almost every district in Bihar, prompted by students, attacked and looted treasury buildings and railway stations, stormed police stations and killed unarmed European officials in public in an effort to physically do away with European presence. Such use of violence was a clear deviation from the Congress path outlined by Gandhi; but the intensity deriving from the 'Do or Die' spirit of the people, surpassed and sabotaged the lead given by local Congressmen. The movement also got the support of zamindars and merchants, police and civil officers. Landlords and merchants covertly supplied funds, and local policemen and administrators indirectly aided the takeover and destruction of isolated police outposts by offering no resistance and also vacating their posts in certain cases.

While 218 police stations were attacked in Bihar, the highest in all of India, the number of bomb incidents here was only eight in comparison to 447 in Bombay. According to Sumit Sarkar, this demonstrates that there was greater popular participation in Bihar and more organized terrorist activity in Bombay. Such militancy, however, brought forth brutal state repression. Entire districts such as Saran were identified as 'criminal' in official reports, where over 16,000 people were imprisoned, and many lost their lives.

The hallmark of the second phase was the widespread underground 'terrorist activities' carried out by different groups of revolutionaries all over India. Such activities involved attempts to sabotage War efforts by dislocating communication, disseminating messages inspiring 'subversive' acts through slogans, pamphlets, leaflets, handbills and other 'incendiary' underground publications and a clandestine radio station run by one Usha Mehta from 'somewhere in India' (Bandyopadhyay 2004: 416). Acts of sabotage were carried out not just by students and revolutionaries, ordinary peasants too participated willingly. Practiced and popularized in Karnataka, where part-time peasant squads engaged in farming by day and sabotage activities by night, this tactic came to be known as the 'Karnataka method'. The 'underground' of official parlance therefore came to include the 'entire nation' since no Indian could any longer be trusted by the authorities (ibid.).

In Hutchins' analysis, 'terrorist activities' took three different paths—guerilla warfare along the India–Nepal border carried on by a radical group under Jayaprakash Narayan; acts of sabotage organized by volunteers mobilized by the moderate group of Aruna Asaf Ali; and the Gandhian path of constructive programme and non-violent action carried on under the aegis of Sucheta Kripalani and others (Hutchins 1973: 250–51).

The second phase also saw the establishment of provisional 'national governments' in a number of places which, although temporary, further consolidated anti-British sentiment and demonstrated the capacity of the subjects of British India to conduct their own affairs by 'evolving a parallel administration' (Chakrabarty 1992a: 800). Ahmedabad, for instance, saw the establishment of an *Azad* (independent) government. In a manner similar to the workers of the Tata Steel Plant in Jamshedpur, factory workers in Ahmedabad went on a strike on political demands. And industrialists, believing that the Congress would come to power soon, did nothing to end the strike, which went on for three and a half months (Bandyopadhyay 2004: 421). This happened at a time when the Communists decided to support the British and stayed away from the Quit India movement.

Acts of sabotage marked the Gujarat countryside between September and December 1942, but unlike earlier Congress-led satyagrahas, no-revenue campaigns campaigns were not launched. Leadership remained in the hands of rich Patidar peasants, and even though tribal peasants participated in the movement, Dalit peasants and agricultural labourers in Kheda and Mehsana districts kept away from it and even opposed it on account of their disaffection with the provincial Congress ministry (Hardiman 1988). B. R. Ambedkar, who had become the labour member in the Viceroy's Executive Council, did not offer support to Quit India. This, did not, however, prevent all Dalit groups from joining the movement. In Broach, Kheda and Surat districts in Gujarat, for instance, there was remarkable unity across caste and class lines that made for a virtual 'disappearance' of British authority from the region. It was only re-established by recourse to ruthless repression (Bandyopadhyay 2004: 421).

People of the princely state of Baroda, where Congress had considerable influence, participated enthusiastically in the movement. Traders' unions and caste enclaves came forward in organizing strikes, *hartals* and rioting. In comparison, the movement was relatively mild in the Madras Presidency except for small pockets in Guntur and Coimbatore and coastal Andhra. Leaders such as Rajagopalachari were not in favour of it and constitutionalism had had a strong base in the region. The Communists of Kerala and the strong non-Brahman group of the south also remained indifferent, and the Muslims consciously kept away (Arnold 1988). Karnataka, we have seen, was a strong centre for Quit India, and the princely state of Mysore was seriously rocked by it. The movement in Mysore followed the all-India pattern—demonstrations and strikes in Bangalore in the first phase followed by village movements, particularly in Shimoga and Hasan districts, and acts of sabotage by secret students' groups (Sarkar [1983] 1995: 399).

In the third phase, that began roughly from the end of September 1942 and lasted over a year, the movement came to be centred in Satara in Maharashtra, Midnapur in Bengal and Talcher in Orissa, all of which had parallel 'national governments'. The Prati Sarkar (parallel government) in Satara, closely allied with non-Brahman *bahujan samaj* activism, started off following the usual Congress/Gandhian method of satyagraha entailing boycott, strikes, marches and underground activities expressed primarily in attacks on government property (Omvedt 1988). Several local groups operated separately under the loose overall leadership of Y. V. Chavan, and carried out different acts of sabotage.

Around the beginning of 1943, underground activists in Karad and Walva *talukas* of Maharashtra took two major decisions. The first was to disregard repression and carry on with the movement, and reinforce it by means of a new ethic of struggle that was to boost 'people's power' in the village (Chakrabarty 1992a: 801). The ideal freedom fighter was no longer the *moral satyagrahi* who willingly courted arrest; instead, the satyagrahi now had to successfully evade imprisonment and carry on fighting. The second decision was a corollary of the first; the Prati Sarkar involved the peasantry directly in its campaign against dacoity that was seriously undermining the underground organization of civil disobedience. Peasant participation helped a great deal in subduing the dacoits by the end of 1943, and this left the Prati Sarkar free to devote full energy to the settlement of peasant problems (Omvedt 1988).

The Prati Sarkar carried on its activities on three fronts—against the British as a part of Quit India movement; against dacoity; and towards the settlement of peasant issues of indebtedness and land disputes (Chakrabarty 1992a: 801). In order to do it efficiently, the Prati Sarkar set up three different village-based institutions—the *nyandan mandals* or people's courts that settled disputes; the *gram samitis* that looked after constructive work and village welfare; and *toofan senas* or youth militia drawn from village wrestling groups that protected the peasants against moneylender harassment. The *toofan sena* acted in conjunction with the *nyandan mandals* and often punished offenders. In brief, the Prati Sarkar demonstrated all the qualities of a well-organized, effective government.

A similar successful experiment was carried out in Midnapur in Bengal, a solid base of Congress mobilization since the days of non-cooperation, with a long history of peasant militancy under the leadership of Birendra Nath Sasmal. The leadership of the peasants, as is true of most Congress leadership, came from among the rich peasant and the Jotedar class. However, the share-croppers, aware of their importance in contributing to the success of non-cooperation in the region, had begun organizing themselves under ordinary village-level Congress workers (Sanyal 1979). As early as 1922, they had asserted themselves by demanding a reduction in illegal taxation. Their belligerence had intensified during the Civil Disobedience movement, and the Congress cry of fighting the final battle in 1942 had a magical effect in rousing them and the masses.

This accounted for the unimaginable momentum that the Quit India movement gained in the region. Between August 1942 and March 1943, it passed through three phases—the preparatory, the retaliatory and the consolidated phase of the 'national government' (Chakrabarty 1992b: 79–80). Women participated in large numbers and this added a new vitality to the movement (Chakrabarty 1992a: 805). The 'jatiya sarkar' or national government established in Tamluk *taluka* in Midnapur in September 1942 resisted 'relentless repression' and lasted till late August 1944. The 'national government' was composed of members drawn from the Congress sub-divisional committee and had 'fewer than 1,000 full-time adherents'. It, however, enjoyed tacit middle-class and peasant support and managed to carry on several disruptive actions (Greenough 1983: 368).

Interestingly, the 'sarkar' took propaganda activity very seriously. Its mouthpiece, the weekly *Biplabi* (revolutionary), deployed distinct modes of persuasion and instigation in order to increase the level of political involvement of the people (Chakrabarty 1992a, 1992b; Greenough 1983: 369). The editor of *Biplabi* recorded the long series of disasters—natural and man-made—in the region and severely condemned the criminal conduct of security forces as well as the 'beastliness' of the British, the proof of which lay in the man-made nature of the Bengal famine (1943–44).

Biplabi achieved great success initially; crowds of 5 to 10,000 participated in raids on government offices, police stations and landlords' courts in September 1942. But as repression drove the revolutionaries into hiding, and as a cyclone and the onset of famine made the initiative move away from the Congress, the editor devoted greater attention to police and army atrocities and man-made causes of disasters in an attempt to turn suffering into political support. The reason behind this intriguing tactic, argues Greenough, was the tremendous significance of Gandhi's message of endurance, sacrifice and suffering for the cause of *swaraj*. '[M]ortality from starvation, disease or disaster, while not so estimable as martyrdom, was nonetheless understood and valued as a politically meaningful kind of sacrifice' (Greenough 1983: 380).

Indeed, in Greenough's engaging analysis, even though the movement was violent from the beginning, the terms of the debate on violence had been set by Gandhi and Gandhians. This meant that successful aggressive action of the kind led by Jayaprakash Narayan that carried 'death to the enemies' was 'disesteemed'. 'Doing by dying' as the fulfilment of a vow came to be held as the ideal of martyrdom rather than causing death, even by publications such as *Biplabi* (ibid.: 379–80). On the other hand, mass mortality on account of the famine was seen as the onset of the great deluge, *pralaya*, that was to bring the evil era (*kaliyuga*) and British rule to an end. Together, these diverse ideas 'made peasant death meaningful' (Greenough 1983: 380).

The 'jatiya sarkar', feels Greenough, kept true to the faith of Gandhism in its tactics, even though it employed different terms, idioms and understandings. This argument counters Bidyut Chakrabarty's statement that the movement was 'not Gadhian *per se*, for the Congress volunteers resorted to open violence in a number of cases' (Chakrabarty 1992a: 796). Gandhi, argues Chakrabarty, possibly would not have allowed the movement to continue. Chakrabarty's statement is partly borne out by the fact that on his release from jail in May 1944, Gandhi severely condemned the underground movement and urged the rebels to give themselves up to the police. This is because 'imprisonment voluntarily undergone actually helped the freedom movement' (Gandhi 1958, Vol. 77: 265–68). The rebels answered Gandhi's call and dismantled the national government. The last issue of *Biplabi* announced the end of the 'jatiya sarkar' and stated, 'the Mahatma is our one and only leader—there is no question of working beyond the limits of his directives' (*Biplabi*, August 27 1944 cited in Greenough 1983: 382).

A similar blending of share-cropper militancy and stoicism shored up by understandings of *kaliyuga* characterized the Quit India movement in Orissa. Its distinguishing feature was the coming together of the Praja Mandal and the Congress-led movement. The Congress resolution, we have seen, had made no distinction between the people of British India and the princely states in urging them to participate in the mass struggle. The people of Orissa answered this call. Koraput and the coastal districts of British India as well as several tributary states (*garhjat*s) were marked by popular upsurge.

The Praja Mandal of the small princely state of Talcher, under the leadership of Pabitra Mohan Pradhan, took a very prominent part in the Quit India movement (Rath 1993; Pradhan 1979). On 7 September 1942, writes Jagannath Patnaik, 'the Direct Action Day', about 40,000 people from every nook and corner of Talcher shouting slogans like 'Do or Die', 'Strike before we die', 'Strike the Raja', 'Drive the British Government from Talcher' proceeded towards the palace of the Raja after burning the Government House, dak bungalows, police stations and forest offices. Railway tracks of the Talcher–Puri rail line were removed for some miles, bridges and roads in the state were destroyed and telegraph and telephone lines were cut. This was followed by the formation of a Praja Mandal government, the government of farmers and labourers (Patnaik 2006: 433).

The action of the people made the raja, his coteries and the state police panic. They requested the British government to send a military force from Choudwar. The army and the police together created a 'smoke wall', dropped bombs and fired from the air. This killed six protesters. Talcher came to provide one of the five instances where the intensity of popular militancy drove the government to launch an aerial attack on the satyagrahis (ibid.: 433; Mishra 1998).

The Praja Mandal government in Talcher did not last beyond the middle of 1943; but its double-pronged action against the Oriya prince and the British state made it remarkable. The tributary states of Dhenkanal and Nilgiri also witnessed considerable Praja Mandal activities during the Quit India movement. Even if it is true that 'very few traces of the Quit India movement were left in Orissa' by the beginning of 1943 and the movement was retained in popular memory as a period of 'doom and repression' (Pati 1992: 353, 1999: 76), notions of *kaliyuga* as an era of disaster, made more potent by a cyclone in coastal Orissa and the famine, offered solace by conjuring visions of the impending collapse of the world, British rule and the evil era.

The famine and its attendant misery strengthened peasant militancy spearheaded by the Kisan Sangha. Twenty-three delegates from Orissa attended the All India Kisan Sabha session in Vijaywada in 1944, where Sahajananda Saraswati, elected President, paid critical attention to famine and famine relief, the problem of landlessness and the release of political prisoners (Pati 1992: 354, 1999: 77). The final success of the Talcher Praja Mandal lay in its power to force the prince to sign the Document of Merger with India in 1947 (Mishra 1998).

The 1942 Quit India movement therefore was a mixture of opposites. Unusual both on account of the magnitude of popular participation and the lack of clear directives from the Congress High Command, as well as for the articulation of anger and 'hatred' against British rule, the movement brought the subjects of British India and the states' peoples in a joint action against the Raj. At the same time, it failed to ensure the participation of Muslims and certain groups of Dalits and non-Brahmans. The Muslims remained aloof; they did not actively oppose it. Leaders of the Hindu Mahasabha condemned the Quit India movement as 'sterile, unmanly and injurious to the Hindu cause' (Anderson and Damle 1987: 44). V. D. Savarkar, B. S. Moonje and Shyama Prasad Mukherjee stoutly stood behind the British government, which was harassed by the War and the Congress campaign. Punjab too, saw little anti-British activity between 1942 and 1945 since the 'lines of tripartite communal conflict among Muslims, Sikhs and Hindus had so hardened as to make resistance to the Raj secondary' (Stein 2010: 345).

The Quit India movement did, however, make 'the ruling elite aware of the possible strength of any future Congress movement' that could shake the empire's foundation particularly after the War when imperial authority had 'neither the legitimacy nor was well-equipped psychologically or materially to assure the continuity of the British Raj' (Chakrabarty 1992a: 798–99). Archibald Wavell, the Commander-in-Chief of the British–Indian army who became the Viceroy in late 1943, told Churchill that the repressive force necessary to hold India after the War would exceed British means, 'even if world opinion permitted such an effort' (Stein 2010: 345). The 'defeatism and demoralization' among British leaders was partly the result of clear signs of strain and disaffection amongst the Indian components of the bureaucracy and police, two vital institutions of the Raj, parts of which supported Quit India. In this sense, the movement marks an important 'signpost' in the disintegration of the Raj.

NETAJI AND THE AZAD HIND FAUJ

Let us now briefly examine another heroic but unsuccessful attempt to free India by means of a relentless struggle against imperialism in post-1942 India. The attempt was made by 'Netaji' Subhas Chandra Bose and the Azad Hind Fauj (Indian National Army), initially formed by the Japanese with Indian troops surrendered by a British commander at Singapore in early 1942. Subhas Bose, who had formed an Indian legion with Indians recruited from European prison camps during his stay in Germany, reorganized and revitalized the Indian National Army (INA) established by the Japanese first under Mohan Singh and then under Major-General Shah Nawaz Khan, after his arrival in Singapore in May 1943 (Cohen 1963–64: 412).

After the 'Tripuri crisis' of 1938–39, Subhas Bose, as we have seen in the preceding chapter, formed the Forward Bloc within the Congress to foment leftist and Socialist activities. He travelled alone across India to stir an anti-British movement but did not get much support. Bose, however, managed to forge a link with the Muslim League in Bengal and decided to start a civil disobedience movement to destroy the Holwell monument in Calcutta that stood as a reminder of the 'Black hole tragedy', an incident of June 1756 recorded by John Z. Holwell in which several Europeans were believed to have been killed on account of being crammed in a small room by Nawab Sirajuddaula during his attack on Calcutta, that Bose and many others felt had never happened. Bose was arrested under the 'Defence of India Act' in July 1940 before he could launch the campaign. He was released from jail in December when he began a fast unto death and was put under house arrest. Subhas Bose undertook a 'daring escape' from Calcutta (Bose 2005: 251), and travelled by 'road, rail, air, pack animal and on foot if necessary' in different disguises to traverse India from the east to the north-west and through Kabul into Soviet Union, and finally, Berlin (ibid.).

Subhas Bose's dramatic escape, wrote Maulana Azad in his memoirs, 'had made a great impression on Gandhiji'. Gandhi, who had not approved of many of Bose's actions earlier, 'came to admire the courage and resourcefulness Subhas Bose had displayed in making his escape from India' (Azad 1959: 41). Bose's war-time alliance with Nazi Germany, we are aware, has become 'the subject of permanent controversy' (Bose 2005: 250). While his critics have denounced him as a fascist sympathizer, more sympathetic assessments have affirmed that Subhas Bose's decision was a pragmatic one, made in the cause of India's freedom.

Sarmila Bose, who has closely followed Bose's private papers, argues that the journey to Berlin was as much 'political' as 'physical', prompted equally by Subhas Bose's personal desire of being with his love, Emilie Schenkel, as by the need of finding friends among Britain's enemies (Bose 2005). Why else, writes Bose, would a 'highly intelligent, well-educated Indian socialist, proudly nationalist and familiar with European politics' make such a bid to rush physically to a regime about whose 'prejudices about Indians he protested to Hitler himself' (ibid.: 253).

Of greater significance is Bose's statement that Subhas Bose possibly persuaded himself that he was serving the nationalist cause more by going to Germany which also enabled him to pursue his personal happiness. Subhas Bose certainly seemed more comfortable with the 'public bravado of fighting the British by all means possible than acknowledging the reality of his private life' (ibid.). Whether or not we accept this argument, Sarmila Bose makes a persuasive case for the play of the intimate and the personal, of affect and emotion in public actions of political leaders.

Subhas Bose did not get much support in Germany. He was allowed to start his Azad Hind (Free India) Radio. The Indian prisoners of war captured in North Africa by Germany were given to him, and with them he formed the Indian legion as mentioned earlier. Subhas could not get the Axis powers to declare in favour of Indian independence; and this became more difficult after the German reverses in Stalingrad (Bandyopadhyay 2004: 425). Bose turned his attention to South East Asia where the Japanese had begun to show increasing interest in Indian independence. In June 1942, a united Indian Independence League was formed as a civilian political body that had control over the army. Mohan Singh headed the army composed of Indian prisoners of war. Rash Behari Bose, a veteran Bengali revolutionary then living in Japan, went to Singapore to preside over the civilian body. By September 1942, the Indian National Army (INA) had become a formal body even though it required Subhas Bose's arrival in South East Asia in the following year to become an energized force.

In order to reach South East Asia through a war-torn Europe, Bose had to make another daring and dangerous 90-day journey with his close aide Abid Hasan in a German submarine from Kiel in North Germany, past northern Scotland, down the Atlantic, past Africa and the Cape of Good Hope into the Indian Ocean, past Madagascar, where he and Hasan transferred into a rubber dingy provided by the Japanese. This took them to Sumatra from where they flew to Tokyo. In this instance, *Bharat Mata* came to prevail over Bose's personal love, as he made this dangerous journey at a time when he learnt about his 'impending fatherhood' (Bose 2005: 255).

After Subhas Bose became INA's supreme commander, it managed to recruit about 40,000 men by 1945. Civilians, such as Indian plantation labourers in Malaya, petty traders in Burma and shopkeepers in Thailand, swelled its ranks. And 'Punjabi, Muslim, Sikh and Pathan professional soldiers mingled with Tamil and Malayali workers in a national army led by a Bengali' (Bose and Jalal 1998: 161). The Azad Hind Fauj also had a women's regiment named after Rani Lakshmibai of Jhansi, the legendary rebel of 1857.

Several reasons are adduced for the change of heart on the part of Indian army personnel of British India who joined and fought in the INA. These include discriminatory treatment of Indian officers as well as the lure of personal gain. The most significant by all accounts, however, appears to be Subhas Bose's charismatic leadership—'without him it is doubtful that a force could have been deployed at all' (Cohen 1963–64: 415). Bose's impact upon officers and men of the INA was both 'instantaneous and electric' (Ayer 1951 cited in Cohen 1963–64: 416). Bose's personal leadership, it is stated, was responsible for 'turning the INA affair from a footnote in history' into enough of 'a threat to create serious concern among the British' (Cohen 1963–64: 416).

In October 1943, Subhas Bose set up a provisional government of Free India which was recognized by Japan and later by eight other countries. Subhas gave his famous call '*chalo* Delhi' (march to Delhi) and the provisional government declared war on Great Britain. INA launched an organized armed struggle against the British from the north-eastern frontier of India. The idea was to march, along with the Japanese army, through Burma to Imphal (Manipur) and then to Assam, where the Indians were expected to join them in an open struggle to free India. But the Imphal campaign, launched by Japan's Southern Army and two INA regiments, ended in disaster. Lack of air power, breakdown in the chain of command, disruption in the line of supply and the strength of the Allied offensive were important factors; but most important was the withdrawal of Japanese support at a crucial moment (Lebra 1971). The dropping of atomic bombs on Hiroshima and Nagasaki (in August 1945) by the US forced Japan to surrender, and the INA was left to beat a retreat under extreme conditions.

The dream of liberating India by means of an armed campaign ended rudely. Subhas Bose, writes Bandyopadhyay (2004), held his spirits high and thought of regrouping and seeking Soviet support after Japan's surrender. The Japanese offered to provide him transport till Manchuria from where he could travel to Russia. Bose is believed to have died in an air crash on 18 August 1945 in Taiwan, a crash that many Indians still feel never happened (ibid.: 427).

In Sarmila Bose's sympathetic assessment, the 'mystery' surrounding Subhas Bose's death is less mysterious than the issue of why Subhas Bose thought of going to Soviet Russia. The safer option, suggested by Bose's German and Japanese advisors, was for him to remain in hiding in the jungles of South East Asia, where he had local support, and try to reach India at a later stage. 'Bose's longstanding interest in the Soviet Union seemed never to have been reciprocated by Moscow'. And even if he managed to reach Russia, he would have 'arrived at an unknown and hostile environment', an Axis ally seeking assistance from an Allied power, 'which had never shown the slightest support for his cause' (Bose 2005: 254). This last journey, once again, was governed by Subhas Bose's personal longing to be united with his wife and daughter, a journey he could not complete, but a journey that ended in a way that 'eluded his enemy as well' (ibid.: 255).

The political impact of Subhas Bose's effort was felt in India after his journey was over. The 20,000 INA soldiers who surrendered were interrogated and sent back to India. Of them, the ones that appeared to have been 'misled' by the Japanese and INA propaganda, were classified as 'Greys' and 'Whites' and were either set free or reincorporated in the army. The others, the most committed to the cause, were listed as 'Blacks' and put through court martial. There were ten trials in total; the most celebrated one was that of the three INA commanders—P. K. Sehgal, G. S. Dhillon and Shah Nawaz Khan—in the Red Fort in Delhi. Sehgal, Dhillon and Khan were charged with treason, murder and abatement of murder.

The government's idea behind the public trial was to appraise the public of the 'horrors' committed by INA and ruthlessly penalize the army officers for treason. The exact opposite came to pass. With the withdrawal of press censorship at the end of the War, details of the INA campaign were circulated by the media on a daily basis and INA officers came to be regarded as great patriots rather than traitors by Indians. The strange coincidence of the three defendants belonging to the Hindu, the Sikh and the Muslim communities added to the nationalist fervour—together they embodied the spirit of united India and its emphatic bid for freedom. Moreover, INA had been led by a Bengali, the least 'martial' of Indian 'races' in traditional British stereotype (Sarkar [1983] 1995: 411; Chapter 6). This added further to the patriotic imagination of an actual army fighting for the country's liberation.

The 'British', states Cohen, 'could not have deliberately created a better stimulus to nationalist public opinion, and the nationalists were given a golden opportunity to rail against the British' (Cohen 1963–64: 418). Congress leaders, sensitive to public opinion, decided to defend the accused of the INA trial and the AICC announced the formation of a Defence Committee for these 'misguided patriots'.

A 'mass upheaval' occurred during the days of the INA trials which began on 5 November 1945. 'Never before in Indian history', Nehru remarked later, 'had such unified sentiments been manifested by various divergent sections of the population'. The trials were held at Red Fort, the symbol of Mughal glory that bore sad memories of Mughal humiliation and India's subjection; Bahadur Shah II had been tried there after the Revolt of 1857. Detailed media coverage of the trial as well as reports of INA activities evoked nostalgia and wistfulness as well as pride in the sacrifices made by INA members. An INA week was observed between 5 and 11 November and 12 November was celebrated as INA Day.

Political parties of distinct hues and colours, including the Congress, the Muslim League, the Hindu Mahasabha, the Unionist Party, the Justice Party, the Congress Socialists and the Communists participated in protests against the trial. Rioting against British and American military establishments began in Calcutta on 21 November; soon riots broke out in all major Indian cities including Bombay, Karachi, Patna, Allahabad, Benares and Rawalpindi.

The spectacular anti-British spirit and remarkable communal harmony demonstrated in the riots unnerved the colonial administration, and despite serious opposition by hardcore British army officers, the three INA commanders, found guilty of treason, had their sentences remitted by the Commander-in-Chief and were set free on 3 January 1946. They walked out of the Red Fort 'to a hero's welcome at public meetings' (Bandyopadhyay 2004: 429). Demonstrations accompanied other INA trials in Calcutta. The seven years' rigorous imprisonment meted out to Abdul Rashid in February 1946 saw a fresh round of protests in Calcutta. A general strike led by the Communists paralysed the city on 12 February, while a massive rally demonstrated a unique unity of the Muslim League, the Communists and the Congress.

What disturbed the British the most was the impact of the INA trials on the loyalty of the army. Even though a majority of Indian army personnel remained loyal (Cohen 1963–64), there was great empathy and admiration for INA commanders. Many donated money openly to the INA relief fund and some even attended rallies in uniform. All this indirectly obliged the British Commander-in-Chief to remit Sehgal, Dhillon and Khan's sentences. In January 1946, members of the Royal Indian Air Force went on strike to articulate their serious grievances, and in February 1946 the Royal Indian Navy rebelled against the Raj.

The mutiny began in Bombay where the naval ratings in HMIS Talwar went on hunger strike against bad food and racial discrimination. It spread to other naval bases in different parts of India as well as to some ships on sea, where strikes were observed. At the height of the mutiny, 78 ships, 20 shore establishments and 20,000 ratings were involved. Common people showed great solidarity with the rebellious navy personnel, evident in roadblocks and rioting as well as industrial strikes in Bombay and Calcutta. The mutiny was quickly put down, but its psychological effect far outlived its duration. Two army battalions were needed to restore order in Bombay, and the official casualty figures of 226 civilians killed and 1,046 injured demonstrated the extent of popular participation (Mansergh and Lumby 1976, 6: 1082–83). The colonial administration became increasingly aware of the growing political consciousness of the army personnel, made worse by their fraternity with civilians who raised the prospect of an open revolt.

The Congress, however, was not in a mood to take advantage of this revolutionary potential in 1945–46. Sardar Patel, supported, surprisingly, by Jinnah, persuaded the naval ratings to surrender on 23 February by assuring them that national parties would prevent 'any victimization'. This promise was quickly forgotten. Patel mentioned in a letter to the Andhra Congress leader Viswanathan in March

1946 that the discipline of the army 'cannot be tampered with' since '[w]e will want an army even in free India' (*Sardar's Letters* 6: 165 cited in Sarkar [1983] 1995: 425).

Gandhi was as hostile to the rebel naval ratings as Patel and Nehru, who initially accepted the Socialist leader Aruna Asaf Ali's invitation to come to Bombay, but soon became aware of 'the necessity of curbing the wild outburst of violence' (Mansergh and Lumby 1976, 6: 1117). Leaders such as Nehru began to think of a smooth 'transfer of power' from British to Indian hands, to be worked out in the course of two to five years, and showed far greater inclination to come to negotiations on the constitutional front than offer support to disaffected army men and workers.

The Communists, on the other hand, gave wholehearted support to the rebels and workers. They participated actively in the riots in Bombay and Calcutta where they had a solid base among industrial workers; they also extended their activities among poor peasants and share-croppers. The Bengal Provincial Kisan Sabha (BPKS) had come under virtual control of the Communists by 1940, and the Sabha mobilized the peasantry in northern, eastern and central Bengal around radical issues, such as the collection of tolls by union boards at village marts and the extraction of illegal *abwab*s (taxes) by zamindars. The devastating Bengal famine, that took a toll of between 2.1 million and 3.8 million lives according to the estimates given by Dyson and Maharatna (1991: 296), Sen (1980: 202) and Greenough (1982: 309), enabled the Communists to ally closely with the poorer peasantry. They carried out sustained relief work through provincial Kisan Sabhas and Mahila Samitis (women committees) and criticized the government's food policy in several meetings. The Communists tried to avoid direct confrontation with the government at this stage; but the participation of poor peasants meant that BPKS often got embroiled in clashes with zamindars and grain dealers.

The most significant outcome was the Tebhaga movement of share-croppers, who belonged primarily to tribal and Dalit groups of Rajbansis and Namasudras (Bandyopadhyay 2004: 433). The movement got its name from the fact that the share-croppers demanded two-thirds (*tebhag*) of the produce instead of the customary half (Bandyopadhyay 2001; Bhowmik 1986; Cooper 1988). Even though there was the organization of the BPKS, the Tebhaga movement, according to Sugata Bose, demonstrated class consciousness and concern about individual rights to such an extent that Rajbansi and Muslim share-croppers did not have any qualms in attacking Rajbansi and Muslim *jotedars* (Bose 1986, 1993).

Peasant unions of north Malabar also came under complete control of the Communists in the early 1940s, when the region suffered acute food shortage and near famine conditions. Recent studies have argued that the close alliance of the Communists with the nationalist struggle gave them greater strength in the region than in Bengal (Desai 2001). Parts of Andhra and the princely states of Travancore and Hyderabad became solid strongholds of Communist operations that continued into independent India (Dhanagare 1991; Elliott 1974). Noteworthy among these is the prolonged Telengana movement in Hyderabad that at one stage came to cover 3,000 villages with a population of 3 million and a geographical spread of 16,000 square miles (Gray 1971; Pavier 1974; Ram 1973; Sundarayya 1979: 532–34).

In brief, there were diverse and wide-ranging activities at different levels of society that aimed both at freedom and at a better future for India. The Congress undoubtedly had wide social support; but from the time of Quit India it had become evident that the 'masses' did not necessarily require constant Congress guidance and supervision. Indeed, the Congress Right's stand on the mutiny of the naval ratings, as reflected in Sardar Patel's letters and Gandhi's comment mentioned in Patel's letters, showed a lack of understanding of the pulse of the nation. Gandhi felt that the naval ratings were setting 'a bad and unbecoming example for India' and affirmed that 'a combination between Hindus and Muslims and others for the purpose of violent action is unholy ...' (Gandhi's comment mentioned in *Sardar's Letters*, 6, Ahmedabad 1977: 162–3, cited in Sarkar [1983] 1995: 425).

Congress Socialist Aruna Asaf Ali's indignant response to this comment, that it would be a lot easier to 'unite the Hindus and Muslims at the barricade than on the constitutional front' demonstrated a far better understanding; her prophecy turned out to be 'tragically true' (Sarkar [1983] 1995: 425). Congress leaders perhaps would have done better if they had valued the commonality of interests demonstrated by 'the unholy alliance of Hindus and Muslims' for violent action and the coming together of men in the services and on the streets. The naval ratings' strike was a 'historic event' in the assessment of the Naval Central Strike Committee since it witnessed the first ever flowing of blood of men in the services and on the streets for a common cause (*The RIN Strike*: 175, cited in Sarkar [1983] 1995: 425). This statement unfortunately was not taken up seriously and efforts at uniting Hindus and Muslims on the constitutional front turned out to be elusive and impossible, as we shall soon see.

NEGOTIATION AND CONFRONTATION: THE ROUGH ROAD TO FREEDOM

Two themes dominate in discussions of the years immediately prior to independence—whether partition was inevitable and whether Indian independence was a voluntary transfer of power by the British, or whether freedom was won by Indians by means of a prolonged and bitter struggle. The first theme requires a thorough discussion of the Indian political scene in the 1940s with special attention to the Muslim-majority provinces, and the second, an exploration of the forces at work in Britain and India that combined to result in Indian independence in 1947. An important dimension that has only recently been taken into consideration is the play of passion and emotion in the frenetic processes that eventually ended up in independence with partition, and the enormous human tragedy that it embodied.

The parting of ways between the Congress and the Muslim League in the wake of the 1937 elections (Chapter 9) turned out to be a major obstacle in the way of a constitutional settlement. It is noteworthy that Congress leaders and the first President of independent India, Rajendra Prasad, almost echoed the opinion of the Governor of UP in his memoirs that if Congress had agreed to establish a coalition government with the 'Independent Muslims', the 'communal animosity', which the Muslim League whipped up later, would never have come to pass (Prasad 1957: 446). The UP Governor had written to Viceroy Linlithgow in June 1939 that 'Muslim solidarity would have been undermined' had the Congress 'agreed to a coalition with the League' (Haig to Linlithgow cited in Hasan [1993] 1994: 15).

In the ambience of distrust and estrangement of 1937–38, an idea floated by poet Muhammad Iqbal in 1930 as President of the Muslim League—of a centralized territory for Islam within the body-politic of India—began to find much wider acceptance than it had in 1930. Iqbal's proposal had been to unite Punjab, North-West Frontier Province, Sind and Baluchistan as a 'domain of Islam'. This idea was given greater flourish by Cambridge student Rehmat Ali, who spoke of a 'Pakistan' that was to include Kashmir in addition to the four provinces mentioned by Iqbal.

In the early 1930s these were mere ideas; there was 'no blueprint of a future Pakistan': 'no Islamic flag, no visible symbol, no common platform, no shared goals and objectives' (ibid.: 6). Iqbal, whose 'vibrant patriotic poems continued to be sung in schools and colleges all over India' referred to autonomous states being formed on the basis of unity of languages, history, religion, and identity of common interests in 'India where we are destined to live' (ibid.: 6–7). Rehmat Ali's scheme, on the other hand, caused political embarrassment in India and was dismissed as 'chimerical' and 'impracticable' (Ahmad 1967: 189). At the same time, if we pay heed to Faisal Devji's suggestive argument, Pakistan as a nation was brought into being by 'national will': here was 'the force of the idea' that converted the people into nationhood (Devji 2013: 47–48). It was, therefore, not the result, either of the intention of its scheming leaders, or of its reworking at a popular level. Rather at work stood a combination of ideas and interests that defies a causal relation between the two, and equally inhibits 'cutting and pasting' by scholars of 'historical content to fill it out' (Devi 2013: 7–8).

The issue of Pakistan was taken up seriously at the Karachi Session of the Sind branch of the Muslim League in 1939, presided over by Jinnah. The session passed a resolution, affirming the need for 'political self-determination of the two nations, known as Hindus and Muslims, and urged the League to undertake appropriate measures to realize it (Moore 1988: 113). The first proclamation of the 'two nation theory' proposed two federations to be united by means of a common centre, not a division of territory. Public discussions on the practicality of a constitutional arrangement that could concretize this abstract notion followed. Inputs came from a variety of Muslim leaders—from Sind and Lahore—as well as from prominent Aligarh scholars. The Lahore session of the Muslim League formally proclaimed the Muslims as a nation in March 1940 (Bandyopadhyay 2004: 341). Once more, the 'Pakistan' demand insisted that 'Muslim India's right to national self-determination must not be transgressed'; it did not speak of 'separate statehood' to be 'embodied in a constitutional settlement. Jinnah drew the distinction explicitly in his speeches' (Moore 1983: 551). Was it because Jinnah's 'ambiguously religious' way of imagining nationality represented 'a tradition of collective belonging' that required no necessary reference to 'shared bold and a rootedness in the soil'? (Devji 2013: 2).

The Lahore Resolution was a compromise with different groups of Muslims in the Muslim-majority and minority provinces. It included the extant schemes current in 1940 embodying 'Pakistan' (ibid.). This had to be so since at no stage did the talk of 'autonomy' and 'self-determination' include the Muslim-minority provinces, particularly UP, the League and Jinnah's primary support base at this stage, and the League's claim to represent all Muslims was seriously rivalled in the Muslim-majority provinces. Jinnah treaded carefully and cautiously; he 'balanced, trimmed and obfuscated' in order to ensure support. Consequently, the Resolution made a vague mention of the grouping of Muslim-majority provinces in order to constitute 'Independent states in which the constituent units shall be autonomous and sovereign' but sovereignty was deferred to an indefinite future (Jalal 1994: 58).

Initial reactions to the 'Pakistan Resolution' did not bring much 'comfort' to League diehards. Sikander Hyat Khan of the Unionist Party was 'disturbed' by Jinnah's intrusion into his political territory and by the Resolution's insistence of maintaining definite links with the centre (Hasan [1993] 1994: 27). Muslim leaders in Bombay found little in Jinnah's scheme to bolster their self-confidence, and the Socialists, Congress Muslims, Khudai Khidmatgars and the Momins, repudiated the two-nation theory and 'doggedly adhered to their vision of a united India' (ibid.: 28–29).

At the same time, the Resolution made the Muslims a 'nation' rather than a 'minority'; henceforth, Jinnah insisted on the participation and consent of Muslims on an equal basis in any constitutional arrangement. It was this insistence perhaps that made the 'communal issue' a 'stumbling block' in the eyes of the British masters.

The Cripps Mission had failed to satisfy any political group or party; Jinnah and the League, as seen earlier, had found the idea of non-accession welcome but inadequate since it did not recognize the Muslims' right as a 'nation' to self-determination. The Cripps Mission, stated Jinnah, had overlooked the question of 'the integrity of the Muslim community' and had 'failed to recognize' that India's problem was primarily 'international in character' (Jinnah, Presidential address cited in Shaikh 1986: 451, 1994: 95). The issue was not whether a province wished to accede or not to the Union, but whether a 'nation' could assert its right to self-determination and equality with another.

The Quit India movement, the exigencies of the War and the INA's attempt had stalled further British overtures for three years. Attempts were renewed in 1945, when General Wavell, the Commander-in-Chief of the British–Indian Army, succeeded Linlithgow as Viceroy. Even before assuming office as Viceroy, Wavell had spoken of the necessity to set up a provisional political government at the centre, a coalition of the Congress and the Muslim League, in order to divert Indian energies from agitation and to ensure greater cooperation in the War effort (Sarkar [1983] 1995: 415).

Wavell corresponded with Gandhi as soon as he was released from jail on 5 May 1944 on grounds of ill health. The Viceroy's offer fell far short of the Congress demand for a genuine national government responsible to the assembly with temporary British control over War operations, and a definite and clear promise of independence after the War. Gandhi nevertheless, decided to enter into negotiations with the Muslim League in July 1944, a fact that aroused the ire of the Hindu Mahasabha. The talks between Gandhi and Jinnah, based on the 'C. R. formula' or the 'Rajagopalachari formula', fell through.

In April 1944 C. Rajagopalachari, veteran Congress leader, had advocated establishing a post-War commission to demarcate the adjacent districts of north-west and north-east India with Muslim majority, hold a plebiscite among the adult inhabitants of these areas to decide if they wanted a separate Pakistan, and finally implement a scheme of cooperation needed to run essential services in case a separate Pakistan was created after the full transfer of power. Partition, affirms Ayesha Jalal, was, for Rajagopalachari, 'by far the lesser evil than forcing Muslim provinces to stay in' (1994: 82). That way, the Congress could be assured of a strong centre and the League would probably fade 'into oblivion' once the two Muslim majority provinces were separated.

When Gandhi approached Jinnah for a settlement in accordance with the C. R. formula, Jinnah reiterated the demand for a full separation of all the six Muslim provinces, and asserted that the separation could not be deferred till the full transfer of power. Some scholars hold a vital difference in perspective among the two leaders responsible for the breakdown of the talks. For Gandhi, the separation was 'within the family' and required the retention of some elements of partnership while for Jinnah 'sovereignty' was essential and that could come only with total separation (Singh 1987: 109–11).

It is difficult to gauge whether Gandhi really thought of separation with collaboration or Jinnah wanted total sovereignty. If we follow Jalal, Jinnah and the Muslim League did not 'expand, revise, or make more specific' the 'imprecise', incomplete and contradictory proposals included in the Lahore Resolution till the arrival of the Cabinet Mission in 1946 (Jalal 1994: 5, 59). Moore, on the other hand, argues that there was a gradual definition of the Pakistan demand between 1941 and 1944. In his presidential address to the Madras Session of the League in April 1941, Jinnah emphasized the goal of 'completely Independent States in the North-Western and Eastern Zones of India, with full control of Defence, Foreign Affairs, Communications, Customs, Currency, Exchange etc.' and, in February 1944, he urged Britain to 'frame a new constitution dividing India into two sovereign nations', Pakistan and Hindustan, with 'a transitional period for settlement and adjustment', the length of which 'would depend upon the speed with which the two peoples and Britain adjusted to the new constitution' (Moore 1983: 552–53).

At the same time, Moore also states that throughout the War, Jinnah contemplated the post-War emergence of one or two Pakistan 'dominions' co-existing with one or two Hindustan 'dominions' and princely states, and with Britain retaining power over defence and foreign affairs (Moore 1983: 554). It seems likely that Jinnah was fighting for the parity of Muslims with Hindus as two equal nations, where Muslims would belong collectively without being grounded in a separate, sovereign territorial state.

As elections in Britain approached, Churchill finally allowed Wavell to start negotiations with Indian leaders. Wavell ordered the release of all Congress Working Committee members and lifted the ban on the Congress. His broadcast on 14 June 1945 declared the 'communal issue' to be 'the main stumbling block' and stated that, 'His Majesty's Government had hoped' that the leaders of the Indian political parties 'would agree amongst themselves on a settlement of the issue'. The hope, however, 'has not been fulfilled' (Sharma 1962: 617). This is because Gandhi and Jinnah's failure to agree on 'Pakistan' had made a 'direct solution' of the 'communal problem impossible' (ibid.).

The Viceroy invited 'Indian leaders of Central and Provincial politics' to 'take counsel' with him with a view to the formation of 'a new Executive Council more representative of organized political opinion' (ibid.: 618). Wavell convened a conference in the summer capital of Simla, in the exuberant setting of the Viceregal Lodge on Summer Hill (that now houses the Indian Institute of Advanced Study), in late June 1945, to discuss the formation and composition of the Executive Council.

The Executive Council was to be entirely Indian except for the Viceroy and the Commander-in-Chief. It was to work independent of the Central Assembly, and was to give equal representation to 'caste Hindus' and Muslims, and separate representation to scheduled castes. The option was left open for discussions on a new constitution once the War had been fully won (Sarkar [1983] 1995: 416).

Understandably, the Congress objected to being reduced to the status of a 'caste Hindu' party and affirmed that it was to include members of all communities among its representatives to the Executive Council; the Congress claim was reinforced by the fact that its delegation was led by Maulana Abul Kalam Azad. What really occasioned a breakdown of the talks at the Simla Conference was Jinnah's 'intransigent' line. He demanded parity inside the Executive Council with 'all other parties combined', the right to choose all Muslim members of the Council, and the right of a 'communal' veto that would require decisions opposed by the Muslims in the executive to be passed only by two-thirds majority (Jalal 1994: 131; Sarkar [1983] 1995: 417). Jinnah also dismissed the proposal for interim government as a device to shelve the Pakistan issue, and establish a unitary government in India with the Congress at the helm.

Jinnah's claims made the Viceroy conclude that he had never any 'intention of accepting the offer' and that it was 'difficult to see why he came to Simla at all' (Moon 1973: 155). Jinnah, argues Jalal, had to take such a hard stand because he was aware that the Punjabi Muslim of the Unionist Party and the two Congress Muslims on the Executive Council would have cut 'at the very root and very existence of the Muslim League' (*Indian Annual Register* 1945 cited in Jalal 1994: 132).

FINAL MOVES: ELECTIONS AND CABINET MISSION

The failure of the Simla Conference (24 June–14 July 1945) and Jinnah's strong stance made Labour leaders in London aware of the fact that an interim government was not the answer; the time had come for final solutions. The massive Labour victory in the elections in July 1945 brought politicians associated with the Cripps offer into power. Labour took office on 26 July 1945 and Clement Atlee, the new Prime Minister, and Pethick Lawrence, the new Secretary of State, called for an immediate review of the Indian situation. All provincial governors in India, except for the one in Punjab, favoured fresh elections.

Perhaps too much has been made of the impact of the Labour victory on Indian independence. Variously described as 'Labour's parting gift to India' (Brasted and Bridge 1990), and 'the main factor responsible for the early transfer of power' (Menon 1957: 436), the 'long commitment of Stafford Cripps, Clement Atlee and Pethick Lawrence to the cause of Indian independence' has found commendable mention (Pandey 1969). Cripps' offer, we are aware, mentioned 'dominion status' to be granted to India after the War; it did not speak of total independence. Constitutional arrangements till 1935 demonstrated the British intention of retaining their hold over India rather than letting go. The Labour Party, it is true, had mentioned Indian independence in its election manifesto of 1935, but the war had brought about a serious change of attitude on the part of Pethick Lawrence and Stafford Cripps. India's significance for Britain's economic and defence interests made an early withdrawal from India an unfavourable proposition.

Consequently, the Labour stance on 'foreign, defence and imperial policy' turned out to be much less radical than their election manifesto (Darwin 1988: 71–72), and cleared Wavell and his associates' apprehensions. Indeed, as Anita Inder Singh points out, there was a clear British desire to 'acquire a strategic foothold in independent India' that governed British negotiations on transfer of power, even though this was never mentioned. Discussion on this 'Top Secret' matter 'was confined to the cabinet, the Viceroy, the British Chiefs of Staff, and the Commander-in-Chief India, and India Office officials at the highest levels' (Singh 1982: 568–69).

At the same time, there were several other factors that impressed upon Labour leaders the need to grant freedom to India. To begin with, there had been a drastic transformation in India–Britain relations in the course of the Second World War. Earlier in the chapter, we have seen how the army had slowly slipped out of Britain's control and how the huge expenses on the army during the War were no longer covered by Indian tax payers. India, which had been both 'a training ground for British officers' and 'a financial reserve for imperial defence' (ibid.: 569), was no longer under complete British control. During the War, the Indian economy changed over from being 'a debtor, whose service charges augmented the Home Charges, into a major holder of British debt as a result of forced loans and deferred-payment purchase of war goods' (Stein 2010: 346).

India, in Tomlinson's assessment, had become 'a potential or actual source of weakness' instead of being an asset (1985: 158). The momentum given to technical development by the War had enabled Indian producers to add a new range of goods, such as aircraft, to their industrial output, and leading industrialists and capitalists J. R. D. Tata and G. D. Birla had initiated technical agreements and collaboration with UK and US firms.

Worldwide opinion had turned overwhelmingly anti-imperialist. Nazi Germany had been destroyed, Japan had surrendered, socially-radical regimes led or aided by Communists were emerging in Eastern Europe, and the Chinese revolution was making headway. Different countries in South East Asia, Vietnam and Indonesia in particular, were vehemently resisting the restoration of French and Dutch colonial rule. Britain had to think of moving out of India, because India as a colony was no longer a reasonable proposition; it was better controlled informally rather than formally.

In India, anti-British feeling among the population in general had reached momentous proportions since the days of Quit India. When Congress leaders were released from jail in mid-June 1945, they found 'tumultuous crowds waiting for them, impatient to do something, restless and determinedly anti-British' instead of 'a demoralized people, benumbed by the repression of 1942, bewildered by the absence of leadership and battered by the privations that the War brought' (Chandra et al. 2000: 474). British officials feared another Congress revolt in the autumn-winter of 1945, in a situation made turbulent by INA trials and the British use of Indian army to restore French and Dutch colonial rule in Vietnam and Indonesia.

The Congress High Command decided to avoid mass movements in order to focus full attention on fighting the elections. Jawaharlal Nehru, once again, was the 'star' speaker in the election campaign while Sardar Patel controlled operations, virtually taking Gandhi's position in Birla's 'hot line' with the Congress High Command (Birla 1953: 328). Birla assured Wavell that there would be less and less fiery speeches by Congress leaders, and Congress leaders sought to distance themselves from the periodic popular explosions in Calcutta and elsewhere in November 1945 and February 1946, in connection with the INA trials (Sarkar [1983] 1995: 425–26).

The results of the elections demonstrated the success of both the Congress and the Muslim League. In this 'endgame' of the Raj, election results swept 'the board of minor players, reduced the political scene to the Congress and the Muslim League, now as never before pitted directly against each other' (Metcalf and Metcalf 2003: 209). The Congress emerged as the most important representative of India that voted in 'general' constituencies and the Muslim League, the sole representative of 'Muslim' opinion. The Congress captured 57 of the 102 seats in the Central Assembly as opposed to 34 in 1937, and won 91.3 per cent of the non-Muslim votes. It also got the majority in all the provinces except Bengal, Sind and Punjab.

Congress' success came at the cost of the Hindu Mahasabha and the Communists. The Hindu Mahasabha was routed almost completely—it won only three seats—and the Communists won eight seats on the whole, a few seats in the provinces and some from labour constituencies. Ambedkar's All India Scheduled Castes Federation won just two of the 151 seats reserved for Scheduled Castes. The Dalit and non-Brahman movements were fractured at this stage, and, as discussed in Chapter 8, sections of Dalits and non-Brahmans merged with the Congress-led nationalist struggle. This was in part a result of the patriotic fervour occasioned by Quit India and the INA trials.

It is, however, important to keep in mind that E. V. Ramaswamy Naicker, who had joined the Justice Party in 1937, had raised the demand for a separate 'Dravidian state' in his presidential address in 1938. This was a direct reaction to the Gopalachari-led Congress government's move to introduce

Hindi in Madras. The demand did not gather momentum till the time it was taken up by Naicker's close associate C. N. Annadurai in independent India (McLane 1970: 166–67).

What plagued the Dalit movement in the years prior to independence was a '*crisis* of *representation* or *legitimacy*'. The process of transfer of power defined for India 'her political mainstream, that is, the Congress, and identified the minorities, primarily on the basis of religion' and 'marginalized all other streams of politics or political identities' (Bandyopadhyay 2000: 895). This allowed the Congress to 'appropriate' Dalit politics during the last phase of colonial rule (1994: 34). Eleanor Zelliot, however, sees the Ambedkar–Congress alliance as an expression of political generosity by the Congress, an act that brought together the different strains of the 'Gandhi-Congress-Untouchable' situation (Zelliot 1988: 193–94, 1992: 172–73).

The Congress, it bears pointing out, had compelled all its Communist members to resign in December 1945, and this separation had possibly assuaged the fears of the Right. At the same time, the Communists emerged as Congress contenders in several provinces, marking the emergence of the Left as a significant 'opposition' at the centre, a trend that has endured.

The Muslim League rivalled the Congress in its success with regard to 'reserved' constituencies. It won all the 30 reserved constituencies and 86.6 per cent of Muslim votes at the centre and bagged 442 out of 509 Muslim votes in the provinces. The League's success, in comparison with its miserable performance in 1937, was more spectacular than that of the Congress and requires greater examination.

We have indicated earlier that the 'resurgence' of the League occurred in UP, which was not a Muslim-majority province but a province with a significant Muslim aristocracy. The success of the demand for Pakistan lay in its very vagueness; it provided the League with 'an excellent instrument for a Muslim mass mobilization campaign in the 1940s'. The main intention of this was 'to construct a Muslim national identity transcending class and regional barriers' (Bandyopadhyay 2004: 445). By espousing the cause of a Muslim 'national identity', the League managed to overcome the limited patronage provided by the landed elite, and win the support of a cross-section of Muslim professional and business groups who liked the idea of the absence of Hindu competition in a separate state of Pakistan (Hasan 1997: 70–77). *Ulemas*, *pirs* and *maulavis* offered additional and vital sustenance to the notion of Pakistan.

'Pakistan', for the average Muslim voter, came to denote two things simultaneously. As a 'modern nation-state for India's Muslim peoples', it was 'the logical culmination' of the long process of colonial Muslim politics. As a symbol of Muslim identity, on the other hand, Pakistan 'transcended the ordinary structures of the state' and evoked 'an ideal Islamic political order, in which the realization of an Islamic life would be fused with the state's ritual authority' (Metcalf and Metcalf 2003: 211).

Pakistan enabled Jinnah to institutionalize Muslim politics at the national level and establish control over the provincial branches of the League. In a manner somewhat similar to Gandhi, Jinnah emerged as the Muslims' 'national' leader particularly because he did not have strong 'local' support. The Muslim-majority provinces of Punjab and Bengal, we are aware, had their own provincial leaders and parties—the Unionist Party under Sikander Hyat Khan in Punjab and the Krishak Praja Party of Fazlul Huq in Bengal, parties that catered to 'local' interests of their supporters and had an ambiguous and contentious relationship with the League. Pakistan in the 1940s provided an ideological rallying symbol that brought together a heterogeneous and fissured 'community' of Muslims, and the growing legitimacy of Pakistan allowed Jinnah to root out rivalries.

It is in order here to make a slight detour and offer a glimpse of the contradictory perceptions of Jinnah's claims and the incomprehensibility of his demands among sections of the Hindu elite, in particular of a prominent member of the Congress. Sarala Ghosal (Devi Chaudhurani), an eminent writer and the founder of the first women's organization in 1910 (*Bharat Stree Mahamandala* in Allahabad), and a very close associate of Gandhi, had this to say about Jinnah in her memoirs.

Writing possibly at the beginning of the 1940s, after the Pakistan Resolution was adopted by the League, Sarala Devi lamented how Jina, a Gujarati word signifying tiny or little or small, a son of Hindustan, was making determined attempts to slash his mother's breast and make her bleed. Just as in Bengal terms such as 'khokon' are used by the mother as terms of endearment for her small baby boy, and the word sticks to the boy even after he has grown up, the term Jina had become the title of the family, a family that had converted to Islam but had been adopted by the mother country. Jina, the dear little boy, had retained his title even after reaching adulthood. Why then had he become determined to sacrifice Hindustan, his own mother? Did he not realize the acute self-deception this entailed? What was driving him? The need for leadership or the desire to build a political party and command it? (Chaudhurani 1975: 171).

Sarala Devi's personal intimacy with Gandhi and her parents' and husband's long and close ties with the Congress possibly made her identify completely with the Congress position. Her perception of Jinnah as the adopted and accepted (*desastha*) loved son of Hindustan is remarkable for materially grounding notions of nurture and care. And yet, Sarala Devi, as the representative of the mother, could only articulate helplessness and incomprehension in the face of a son's selfish, unjust demands, and not an openness to try and understand the anxieties that moved 'adopted' sons.

Fazlul Huq and Sikander Hyat Khan were censored by Jinnah because they joined the Viceroy's National Defence Council in 1941; a Council that did not recognize Jinnah's claim of 'parity' of Muslims in its membership. The League, it is true, did not win majorities in Punjab and Bengal, but it did ring the death knell of the Krishak Praja Party in Bengal and substantially subdued the Unionist Party of Punjab in the 1946 elections.

Fazlul Huq, we need to remember, had come to an agreement with the League soon after the 1937 elections and had formed a coalition government with the League in Bengal. Huq, who had been supported by Communists and Socialists on account of his party's radical programme (Gordon 1974: 280), had begun to lose support after assuming power because he turned more and towards zamindars and rich peasants and went back on many of the promises made during the election campaign.

Huq's relationship with League leaders in Bengal and with Jinnah remained strained all along (Gopal 1959; Pirzada 1966: 57–60; Sayeed 1968: 213–14). While Huq introduced the Lahore Resolution in Bengal, he also resigned from the League and the Viceroy's National Defence Council in 1941 on being reprimanded by Jinnah. Towards the end of the same year, Huq joined hands with the Hindu Mahasabha and formed another coalition ministry with Mahasabha leader Shyama Prasad Mukherjee as the co-leader. This ministry received the support of Congress leaders, such as Sarat Bose, Subash Bose's elder brother. John Herbert, the Bengal Governor, indirectly aided the fall of this 'Progressive Coalition Ministry' in March 1943: it had come under severe pressure on account of the Japanese advance towards the eastern frontier and the onset of the Bengal famine. A new government under the leadership of Khwaza Nazimuddin of the Muslim League was installed in April 1943 (Begum 1994: 117–139).

The Muslim League gained in prestige in Bengal, opened branches all over the province, and launched mass mobilization campaigns (Sen 1976). League leaders toured all of eastern Bengal spreading the idea of Pakistan and the moral, economic and political objectives of the movement. 'Pakistan' came to be presented as the ideal state where peasants would be free from the harassment of Hindu landlords and moneylenders. Consequently, Pakistan as an ideological symbol of Muslim solidarity earned almost universal acceptance among Muslim peasants in Bengal by the mid-1940s (Hashmi 1992: 248). If this ensured the League's success at the centre, it did not eliminate fierce competition for Muslim seats in the provincial assembly (Jalal 1994: 160). As many as 433 candidates contested the elections for the 117 rural and urban seats. In the end, the League won 115 of the Muslim seats, although not always with ease, and lost six. Fazlul Huq alone managed to beat a League candidate. The League's victory was overwhelming; it got 93 per cent of the total Muslim urban vote and 84.6 per cent of the Muslim rural vote, and bagged 119 of the 250 seats in the assembly.

The situation in Punjab, described as the 'cornerstone of Pakistan' by Jinnah, and strategically more important than Bengal for its geographical location, its large Muslim majority and its agricultural wealth, was more intricate than in Bengal. Politically and structurally, there were divisions between west Punjab, where large estates predominated and local factions were led by large landlords and 'rural religious elite, the Sufi *pirs*', and east Punjab, with fewer large estates, where politics was controlled by leaders of *biradari*s (kinship groups). In a situation dominated by rural-urban factionalism, which also marked a division between the *sajjada nashin*s (Sufi *pir*s) and the reformist *ulema* (Gilmartin 1979: 504, 1994: 219), the Unionist Party operated 'more as a grand coalition of the leading factions than as a modern political party' (Talbot 1994: 237).

The *biradari*s, Sufi religious networks, and the patron–client relationship between landlords and tenants were vital in mobilizing political support in the countryside; the Unionist Party had a clear understanding of this. It was careful to select its candidates from among the leaders of *biradari*s in east Punjab and the Canal Colony districts that had a significant presence of peasant proprietors during the 1937 elections. This enabled the party to capture both rural Muslim and Hindu seats in the eastern Rohtak district (ibid.: 239). In western Punjab, the Unionist Party enrolled the support of leading landlords and *pir*s, which again aided its triumph. The Muslim League had barely any support among the rural population and could not match the Unionist Party.

Less than a year after the 1937 elections, however, Sikander Hyat Khan came to an agreement with Jinnah and formed a coalition government with the League. The Jinnah–Sikander Pact recognized the authority of the Unionists in Punjab politics, but gave Jinnah 'much additional authority in the Punjab itself' by establishing the League as 'a representative Muslim body' to which both urban and rural Muslim leaders could turn for the 'expression of Muslim political aspirations at the all-India level' (Gilmartin 1979: 505, 1994: 220). The relationship between the two parties remained uneasy. Sikander Hyat helped in the organization of the Lahore Session of the League as also in the drafting of the Pakistan Resolution. At the same time, he did not think of Pakistan as bringing in 'unalloyed Muslim Raj in the Punjab' (ibid.).

Sikander's sudden death in December 1942 gave Jinnah greater leeway. Leadership of the Unionist

Party passed to Malik Khir Hyat Khan Tiwana, a relatively inexperienced urban politician who was opposed by a group of young leaders from rural areas. They turned to Jinnah and the League. Jinnah found an opportunity to free himself of the dependence on the Unionist Party and exerted greater pressure on Tiwana. When Tiwana refused to comply with the League's demands and rename his ministry the Muslim League Coalition Ministry in 1944, Jinnah abrogated the Sikander–Jinnah Pact and expelled Tiwana from the League (Gilmartin 1979: 507, 1994: 221–22).

The War-time economic dislocation greatly aided Jinnah's efforts to supersede the Unionist Party. Jinnah's strategy to undermine the Unionists was two-pronged (Metcalf and Metcalf 2003). He sought to take advantage of factional rivalries among the loosely knit groups of landlords; and tried to appeal directly to the peasant voter over the heads of clan leaders (ibid.: 210). The first strategy paid off after Sikander Hyat's death. The second started bearing fruit once Jinnah realized, after trial and error, that the League's effort to appeal directly to the 'religious sentiments' of the peasants by means of propaganda in the mosques, was not enough; he had to enlist the support of the rural aristocracy and religious leaders. Paradoxically, states Gilmartin, Jinnah's isolation from any organized group of religious leaders, allowed him to win religious support against the Unionists in rural areas, the *sajjada nashin*s in particular, whom he had alienated by initially allying with the reformist urban *ulema* (Gilmartin 1979: 508, 1994: 222).

According to Ian Talbot, 'a multiplicity of social, economic, and religious reasons' underlay the decision of landlords and *pir*s to quit the Unionist Party. The growing realization that the British would soon leave India as the War drew to a close, made many Punjabi Muslims feel that the Unionists' 'non-communal approach to politics' and their 'loyalist stance' had outlived their usefulness (Talbot 1994: 253–54). *Pir*s used *fatwa*s on behalf of the League and landlords used their economic influence and social prestige in kinship networks to transform support for the Unionist Party into support for the League during the 1946 elections. The Unionists were beaten at their 'own electioneering game' and the League secured a 'resounding victory' in the cornerstone of Pakistan (ibid.: 256).

The Congress, in turn, managed to undercut the Unionist Party in east Punjab; the Akalis also fared pretty well. The Unionist Party won just 18 of the 175 seats in the Punjab Assembly, the Congress 51, the Akalis 22 and the Muslim League 75 (Bandyopadhyay 2004: 448). The Unionist Party managed to hang on to power for a short while by entering into an alliance with the Congress and the Akalis to set up a coalition; but the acceptance of Pakistan by Punjabi Muslims was too evident to be ignored.

At this stage, the Labour Ministry sent a three-member mission, the Cabinet Mission, to India in March 1946 to negotiate the terms of transfer of power. The Cabinet Mission was headed by Sir Pethick Lawrence, the Secretary of State for India, and included Sir Stafford Cripps, now the President of the Board of Trade, and First Lord Admiralty A. V. Alexander. The mission had two main tasks—to discuss the principles and procedures of framing a new constitution in order to grant independence to India and to form an interim government on the widest possible agreement among political parties to facilitate the transfer of power.

'Agreement' proved to be a chimera in a situation where the two major political players, the Congress and the Muslim League, had become more assertive and increasingly intolerant of each other. The Muslim League Legislator's Convention, held in Delhi on 7–9 April, proclaimed that Muslims were certain that in order to 'save Muslim India from the domination of the Hindus and in order to afford them full scope to develop themselves', it was necessary 'to constitute a sovereign independent state' comprising Bengal and Assam in the north-east zone and Punjab, the North-West Frontier Province, Sind and Baluchistan in the north-west zone (Resolution passed by the Muslim League Legislator's Convention, 9 April 1946 published in *Indian Annual Register*, (1946, Vol. 1): 194–95, included in Sharma 1962: 639–41). The Congress, on the other hand, declared on 15 April that complete independence of a 'united India' was its primary objective.

The Cabinet Mission rejected the idea of a sovereign Pakistan composed of six provinces. It offered instead on 15 May—after extensive consultation with parties and politicians of different shades and opinions—a loose three-tiered federal structure for the Union of India that was to include the provinces and princely states.

The Union Government at the top was to control defence, foreign affairs, communication, and have the necessary power to raise revenue to conduct such affairs; all other residual powers were to be vested in the provincial governments that were given the right to form groups. Each group again could have its own executive and legislature and the freedom to decide on what provincial subjects to handle. A Constituent Assembly was to be elected by the newly formed provincial assemblies in order to draft the constitution for the whole of India. It was to meet first at the Union level and then split into three sections—Section A with Hindu-majority provinces; Section B with Muslim-majority provinces of the north-west; and Section C with Bengal and Assam (Bandyopadhyay 2004: 450).

Princely states were ensured sufficient representation in the central Constituent Assembly. After the constitution was drafted for all the three levels— Union, group and province—a province would have the right to move out of one group and into another; it could not, however, opt out of the Indian Union. There was a provision for the review of the constitution after ten years. While all this was being put in place, an interim government would carry on the work of everyday administration. India, declared Sir Pethick Lawrence, was to be independent soon, and the Indians were to decide whether they wanted to stay within or move out of the British Commonwealth (Mansergh and Lumby, Vol. 7: 285).

On 22 May, Jinnah made a statement that indicated his general acceptance of the Cabinet Mission's plan with a few comments and reservations that reiterated the demand for parity between the 'Pakistan Group' and the 'Hindustan Group' in the Union executive and legislature and the right of the Pakistan group to secede from the Indian Union after the initial period of ten years (Gwyer and Appadorai 1957, Vol. 2: 587–88). On 6 June, the Muslim League formally accepted the Cabinet plan that had rejected its demand for a sovereign Pakistan. Scholars attribute different reasons for this.

R. J. Moore points to the fact that Cripps had asked Jinnah in April 1946 to choose between a truncated but independent and sovereign Pakistan limited only to the Muslim-majority areas, and a grouping of all the six provinces the League demanded within an Indian Union. The final proposal of the Cabinet Mission, with the offer of 'a powerful subnational Pakistan' with its own flag, internal autonomy and parity with Hindustan in an all-India government, had emerged after Jinnah's refusal to accept the earlier options. For Moore, therefore, 'it is hardly surprising that Jinnah and the League were drawn into negotiations' on the basis of the Cabinet Mission scheme (Moore 1983: 555, 1994: 190).

Ayesha Jalal makes a similar point in a different manner. In her opinion, the Cabinet Mission offered Jinnah 'the substance of what he was really after'—a Pakistan that did not throw away the advantages of an undivided Punjab and Bengal and ensure the security of the Muslims in Hindustan (Jalal 1994: 186–87). The scheme also satisfied Jinnah's need of restraining 'the regionalism of Muslim-majority provinces so as to bring their combined weight to bear at the all-India level' (Jalal 1995: 15). Asim Roy concurs with this. In his words, the Cabinet Mission recompensed Jinnah 'for much of what was denied to him by Cripps'. It 'offered him the effective contents of a Muslim federation on a platter, and brought the Muslim provinces under the control of the League at the centre' (Roy 1990: 404, 1994: 121).

The Congress, on the other hand, had several problems with the scheme. In the first place, its top priority was immediate Indian independence, which the Cabinet Mission made conditional upon the drafting of the constitution. Secondly, it was not happy with the grouping of Assam and the North-West Frontier Province, where the Congress had won majorities, with the Muslim-majority provinces. Finally, the Congress wanted a stronger centre with the power to intervene if there was a breakdown of law and order. A strong centre was also favoured by the Indian business community—a group of industrialists had formulated a plan in 1944, the Bombay Plan, which envisioned the rapid development of basic industries under the guidance of the state, a plan totally in tune with Nehru's vision of independent India. The All India Congress Committee offered only conditional support to the long-term plan of the Cabinet Mission on 6 July.

Chronology of India in World Affairs, 1914-1948

Year		Leading Events
1885		The first meeting of the Indian National Congress, Bombay.
1905		The first partition of Bengal.
1906		Formation of the Muslim League.
1920		Mahatma Gandhi leads the Congress; Non-cooperation Movement.
1922		Civil Disobedience Movement.
1925		Reforms Enquiry Committee Report.
1928		Simon Commission comes to India; boycott by all parties.
1929		Lord Irwin promises Dominion Status for India.
1930		Civil Disobedience Movement continues; Salt Satyagraha; Gandhi's Dandi March; First Round Table Conference.
1931		Second Round Table Conference; Irwin–Gandhi Pact; Census of India.
1932		Suppression of the Congress movement; Third Round Table Conference.
1934		Civil Disobedience Movement called off.
1935		The Government of India Act receives Royal Assent.
1937		Elections held for provincial assemblies.
1938		
	July	Gandhi–Jinnah negotiations for the settlement of the communal problem, which began in February, fail.
	Dec	The Muslim League forms a committee of enquiry into alleged Congress persecution of Muslims.

Year		Leading Events
1939		
3	Sep	Viceroy Linlithgow announces that India is at war with Germany.
18	Oct	Viceroy's Statement on War Aims and the War Effort: reiterates that goal of British policy is Dominion status for India, but that the 1935 Act is open to modification at the end of the war, in the light of Indian opinion. Offers association of Indian opinion in war effort through consultative group representing the major political parties in British India and the princes.
	Oct	Resignation of Congress Ministries.
22	Dec	Observed as 'Deliverance Day' from Congress rule by the Muslim League.
1940		
23	Mar	Lahore Resolution of the Muslim League demands for a separate state for the Muslims of India.
	May	Churchill becomes Prime Minister in Britain.
7	Aug	Viceroy makes a statement on India's constitutional development, the August Offer, and announces that more places would be open to representative Indians in an expanded Executive Council and on a new War Advisory Council.
	Sep	Congress and League reject the August Offer.
17	Oct	Congress launches civil disobedience.
1941		
	Dec	Congress civil disobedience prisoners set free.
1942		Subhas Chandra Bose forms the Indian National Army.
11	Mar	British Government announces its decision to send Sir Stafford Cripps to India.
30	Mar	Cripps proposals published.
2	Apr	Congress and League reject the Cripps proposals.
8–9	Aug	Congress launches 'Quit India movement' and is declared an unlawful organization; Gandhi and all members of the Congress Working Committee are arrested.
1943		
	Oct	Wavell succeeds Linlithgow as Viceroy.
1944		
9–27	Sep	Gandhi–Jinnah talks end in failure.
1945		First trial of the Indian National Army men opened.
7	May	Germany surrenders.
15	Jun	Imprisoned Congress leaders released.
26	Jul	Labour Government comes into power in Britain.
14	Aug	Japan surrenders.
	Dec-Jan	General Elections in India.
1946		
23 Mar–29 Jun		Cabinet Mission visits India.

Year		Leading Events
16	May	Cabinet Mission announces its constitutional scheme.
6	Jun	Muslim League accepts Cabinet Mission's constitutional scheme.
16	Jun	Cabinet Mission presents scheme for the formation of an interim government at the centre.
25	Jun	Congress rejects 16 June proposals for an interim government but accepts 16 May scheme, agreeing thereby to join the proposed Constituent Assembly. Muslim League accepts the 16 June scheme and agrees to join the interim government.
29	Jul	Muslim League passes resolutions retracting its acceptance of the Cabinet Mission plan and calling upon Muslims to observe 16 August as 'Direct Action Day'.
16	Aug	'Direct Action Day'.
16–18	Aug	The 'Great Calcutta Killing'.
2	Sept	Congress forms the interim government with Nehru as the Vice-President.
13	Oct	Muslim League decides to join the interim government.
25	Oct	Interim Government reconstituted.
3–6	Dec	Aborted London conference of major Indian leaders.
9	Dec	Constituent Assembly meets without Muslim League members.
1947		
29	Jan	Muslim League demands dissolution of Constituent Assembly.
	Feb	Communal rioting in Punjab.
20	Feb	Prime Minister Attlee announces the British intention of leaving India by June 1948, and Mountbatten to succeed as Viceroy.
23	Feb	Jinnah declares that the Muslim League will not yield an inch in their demand for Pakistan.
4–5	March	Outbreak of communal disturbances in Lahore, Multan and other Punjabi towns.
12	March	Gandhi begins a tour of the riot-affected areas of Bihar.
18	March	Prime Minister's letter sent to Viceroy-designate on the policy and principles in accordance with which power should be transferred.
24	March	Mountbatten sworn in as Viceroy and Governor-General.
31	March	Viceroy holds the first of five interviews with Gandhi.
5	April	Viceroy holds the first of six interviews with Jinnah.
15–16	April	Conference of Governors; approval for draft proposals for the transfer of power.
15	April	Issue of joint Gandhi–Jinnah appeal for abstention from acts of violence and disorder.
1	May	Nehru acquaints Mountbatten with Congress Working Committee's reactions to recent developments.
18	May	Mountbatten leaves for London for talks with Cabinet.
28	May	Cabinet India and Burma Committee; concluding meeting with Mountbatten.
30	May	Mountbatten arrives back in Delhi.
2	June	Mountbatten meets Indian leaders and gives them Partition Plan.
3	June	Mountbatten, Nehru, Jinnah and Baldev Singh give a broadcast on the Plan over All India Radio.

Year		Leading Events
4	June	Mountbatten gives a Press Conference on the Plan.
5–7	June	Mountbatten discusses partition machinery with Indian leaders and Indian Cabinet.
12	June	First meeting of Partition Committee.
20	June	Votes in Bengal Legislative Assembly result in decision that Province should be partitioned.
25	June	Indian Cabinet agrees to establish States Department.
4	July	Indian Independence Bill is published.
9	July	Mountbatten advises Attlee of his decision to accept the Governor-Generalship of India.
16	July	Last meeting of the Interim Government.
18	July	Indian Independence Bill receives Royal Assent.
19	July	The Executive Council (Transitional Provisions) Order, reconstituting the Interim Government into two separate groups representing the two successor governments of India and Pakistan, published.
11	August	Jinnah elected President of the Constituent Assembly of Pakistan.
14	August	Pakistan Independence Celebrations in Karachi; Viceroy addresses Pakistan Consituent Assembly.
14–15	August midnight	Power transferred.
15	August	Jinnah sworn in as Governor-General of Pakistan; Mountbatten sworn in as Governor-General of India; Independence Day celebrations in Delhi

Four days later, Jawaharlal Nehru, the newly elected President, declared in a 'provocative speech' that the Congress would only participate in the Constituent Assembly, that is, in the drafting of the constitution. Nehru repudiated the notion of the 'grouping' of provinces, the 'key to Jinnah's Pakistan' because he was fairly certain that it would collapse. He believed that Assam and the North-West Frontier Province would not agree to join Sections B and C—the Muslim provinces (Bandyopadhyay 2004: 451; Metcalf and Metcalf 2003: 213). The 'short-term' plan of forming an interim government floundered on the issue of parity—the Congress, much to Jinnah's chagrin, insisted on including Muslim and Dalit candidates among its nominees. Jinnah had wanted the government to be composed of five Congress and five Muslim League representatives, along with one Sikh and one member of the Scheduled Caste. Unable to resolve the impasse and threatened by the prospect of mass action centring on an all-India strike in the railways and a postal walk-out, Wavell set up a caretaker government consisting of British officials on 4 July.

For *Quaid-i-Azam* Jinnah, this was the last straw—the final instance of Congress' betrayal. On 27 July, the Council of the League met and declared that in view of the Congress' attitude, the League was withdrawing its acceptance of the long-term plan of the Cabinet Mission. The Council further announced that the League would use 'Direct Action' to 'achieve Pakistan' and assert the Muslims' 'just right' as well as 'vindicate their honour and get rid of the present slavery' (McLane 1970: 171). The days of constitutional manoeuvring were over for Jinnah, the confirmed constitutionalist (Wolpert 2000: 344). The time had come for 'agitational politics'.

PARTITIONED FREEDOM

16 August 1946 had been set as the day for 'Direct Action' by the League, a day that was to mark the formal commencement of the fight for Pakistan by means of a nation-wide *hartal*, protests and demonstrations. In the poignant portrayal of Margaret Bourke-White, an American photographer, presented as the eye-witness account of Nanda Lal, the proprietor of 'East Bengal Cabin' a modest snack-store on Harrison Road in Calcutta, the morning began with the streets looking 'reassuringly quiet'. The sight of a nearly empty tramcar at a time when it 'bulges with people' confirmed Nanda Lal's fears that 'this day was to be unlike all other days' (Bourke-White included in McLane 1970: 172). And indeed it was.

The 'Direct Action' day witnessed the 'Great Calcutta Killing'. The day had been declared a holiday by the Muslim League ministry headed by H. S. Suhrawardy. It had also organized a huge public rally at the Ochterlony monument in central Calcutta. Suhrawardy had promised the crowd immunity from police interference. On its way back from the rally, the 'crowd' went berserk; it attacked Hindus, looted their homes and property. The Hindu counter attack was not slow to come. The carnage continued for four days; 4,000 people were killed and 10,000 injured.

The intensity of the riots and the killings, it has been argued, was a direct result of the Muslim League and Hindu Mahasabha activities that had sharply polarized Muslims and Hindus in their support for Pakistan and a Hindu *rashtra* (Das 1991: 161–88). The 'communal' riots of the 1940s were, in Suranjan Das' reckoning, qualitatively different from the earlier ones in terms both of the magnitude of violence and passion and a clear identification of the target. While this is partly true, it cannot be denied that the 1946 riots in Calcutta and the subsequent riots in other parts of the country showed 'significant variation' insofar as their form, extent or immediate responsibility was concerned (Sarkar [1983] 1995: 432).

Riots began in Bombay on 1 September, in Noakhali in Bengal on 10 October, in Bihar on 25 October, in Garmukteswar in UP in November and engulfed the whole of Punjab from March 1947. Deaths in Bombay resulted more from 'stray stabbing' than large-scale rioting and the numbers remained confined to 162 Hindus and 158 Muslims. In Noakhali, in eastern Bengal, with a tradition of agrarian unrest of Muslim tenants against Hindu landlords and traders, attacks on property and rape were much more common than murder, the main feature of the Calcutta killings. In Bihar, on the other hand, where riots came in the wake of the observance of Noakhali day, Hindu peasants rose against Muslims killing them indiscriminately, a massacre that left 7,000 dead (ibid.: 433).

News of this Hindu offensive in Bihar and UP travelled to the far-off North-West Frontier Province where a Congress government was in power; local Muslims observed civil disobedience and Pathan tribesmen, respecting their code of honour and prompted by local *pir*s, began to attack Hindus and Sikhs from December 1946 in Dehra Ismail Khan and Tonk.

The province that bore the brunt of the violence was Punjab, where Hindu, Muslims and Sikhs attacked and killed each other for several months starting from March 1947. Tensions soared when the Unionist ministry, on the advice of the British Governor, banned the Muslim National Guard and the Rashtriya Swayamsevak Sangh (RSS) in January. This sparked a civil disobedience movement organized by the Muslim League that gained momentum with the participation of Muslim men and women in processions and demonstrations, leading eventually to the resignation of the Khizir ministry on 3 March. A powerful protest demonstration of Sikhs in front of the Assembly Chamber on 4 March was followed by riots in Lahore, Amritsar, Multan, Attock and Rawalpindi. Rural areas of the Muslim-majority districts of Multan, Attock and Rawalpindi also became party to the riots, and Sikh and Hindu traders and moneylenders were the main victims. By August 1947, 5,000 people had been killed in Punjab, a bare minimum compared to the colossal holocaust that was to follow the partition.

Wavell and British officials in general did precious little to contain the violence (Moon 1973: 374), and the Congress interim government under Nehru, sworn in on 2 September 1946, presided 'helplessly over this growing communal inferno' (Sarkar [1983] 1995: 435). The interim government, for all practical purposes, was a continuation of the earlier Executive Council. Wavell still wielded great power, which he demonstrated in his last Cabinet meeting in March 1947, when he overruled the decision of the ministers to release INA prisoners. In October 1946, Wavell had persuaded the Muslim League to join the interim government; this made the functioning of the government even more difficult. The Constituent Assembly started meeting from 9 December, but the League withdrew because the Congress refused to accede to its demand of sectional meetings to draft group constitutions (Bandyopadhyay 2004: 453).

A deadlock prevailed in high politics while the country was rocked by violence. Gandhiji, a man of 77, and by now a lonely figure, travelled alone from Noakhali to Calcutta to Bihar to Delhi trying to assuage hurt sentiments and ruffled passions, and vindicate his life-long principles of 'change of heart and non-violence' (Sarkar [1983] 1995: 437). His presence had a great calming effect, but it was temporary. In Sarvepalli Gopal's succinct surmise, Gandhi by now had become like a retired Oxbridge professor, highly respected but with no influence in the 'governing body' (Gopal 1975: 343).

Hence, Gandhi's advice both to 'the people of India' and to his Congress colleagues 'not to submit to the tyranny of Mr Jinnah' did not have much effect (Bose 1953: 15). To Gandhi, the idea of a high-level bargain for attaining quick power by the Congress at the cost of the partition along religious lines seemed shocking and unimaginable. His Congress colleagues, including Patel and Nehru, disillusioned and exhausted by the continued bloodshed and the non-viability of a Congress-League ministry at the centre, began to think of partition in early 1947, something unthinkable so far. On 3 June 1947, Nehru announced that the Congress Working Committee had come to a decision favourable to the division of India; the Working Committee wanted the resolution to be ratified by the representative assemblies of the people.

British officials, on their part, had also thought of a 'Breakdown Plan' that would allow them to retreat to the six Pakistan provinces leaving the Congress to handle the rest of India. This proposal of Wavell had been rejected by the Home Government in 1946 on grounds that it was 'dishonourable' for Britain to withdraw without a universally agreed arrangement for the transfer of power. Wavell, however, continued to affirm that it would be virtually impossible for British rule to last beyond the spring of 1948. Incensed by his 'defeatist' attitude, the British Prime Minister replaced Wavell with Lord Mountbatten in December. By January 1947, however, Clement Atlee had to admit that British withdrawal could hardly be postponed any longer since 'the whole of the politically minded population' of India was actively opposed to British rule (Bandyopadhyay 2004: 454).

In February, the Prime Minister declared that power would be transferred to Indian hands by June

1948 in a way that would best suit the interests of the Indian people. On 22 March, Lord Mountbatten arrived in India with clear directives for a fast withdrawal and powers to decide things on the spot. By mid-April, Mountbatten was ready with 'plan Balkan'—it advocated the division of Punjab and Bengal and the handover of power to provinces and sub-provinces, free to join one or more of the group constituent assemblies on the basis of self-determination. The interim government was to remain in force till June 1948 to oversee the arrangements. Nehru and the Congress rejected plan Balkan because, in their view, a weak centre and autonomous provinces would indeed lead to a 'Balkanisation' of India, promoting 'disruptive tendencies' and chaos and disorder everywhere (Moore 1983; Philips 1970). Jinnah, for his part, was not satisfied with just two Muslim-majority provinces that would constitute a 'truncated or mutilated, a moth-eaten Pakistan' (Jinnah quoted in Moore 1983: 260).

Mountbatten's alternative, innovative plan was to confer 'dominion status' on successor governments of India and Pakistan instead of waiting for agreement in the Constituent Assembly. Nehru accepted the offer of partition; according to his biographer, he thought of dominion status as a temporary measure. On 3 June, Mountbatten proposed a new plan and moved forward the date of transfer of power by six months—to 15 August 1947. Punjab and Bengal were to be partitioned; the Muslim-majority provinces of Punjab, Sind, Baluchistan, NWFP and Bengal were to be given the right to choose between joining the existing Constituent Assembly or opt for a new one for Pakistan to be decided by their provincial assemblies; the Hindu majority provinces were to remain within the existing Constituent Assembly. Nehru, Jinnah and Sardar Baldev Singh on behalf of the Sikhs endorsed the plan on 4 June. The forced swift slog to freedom began.

This sudden change of date of the transfer of power blocked some other alternative plans. League leaders from Bengal—Suhrawardy and Abdul Hashem—not very happy at the prospect of being ruled from distant Punjab, proposed a plan for a 'United Sovereign Bengal' that got the support of Congress leader Sarat Bose. The plan, however, found little support among Bengali Hindus who saw in it a ploy to incorporate western Bengal, and particularly Calcutta, into an enlarged Pakistan (Chakrabarty 1993). The North-West Frontier Province raised the call for an independent Pathan state. The riots in NWFP had weakened the Pathans' long identification with Congress nationalism, and they did not want to be united with the League-led Pakistan. A plebiscite was forced on the people; it was boycotted by the Congress ministry in power. Consequently, NWFP had to join Pakistan on the basis of 50.99 per cent votes obtained from a very limited electorate. In anger and frustration, 'Frontier Gandhi' remarked that the Congress leadership had thrown his movement to the wolves.

In Punjab, the Akali Dal had been speaking of a separate land for the Sikhs since the 1930s, a demand that was reiterated after the Lahore Resolution of the League. Although the Shiromoni Akali Dal opposed the radical demand for 'Khalistan' advanced in the 1940s by a section of Sikhs— of a separate territory for the Sikhs consisting of regions between Jammu and Jamrud, as a buffer state between Pakistan and India—it became anxious to protect the territorial integrity of the Sikhs, once Pakistan began to get serious consideration (Bandyopadhyay 2004: 456). Different proposals for an Azad Punjab or a Sikh homeland surfaced again. Such anxieties were a direct result of a major flaw in the Pakistan demand—neither Jinnah nor the League ever discussed the issue of the rights of minority communities in Pakistan (Jalal 2000: 403).

The third major problem was the future of the princely states, which, as we have seen, had been left to their own resources so far. While powerful and ambitious princes, such as that of Bhopal, Hyderabad and Travancore dreamt of continuing to retain their autonomy, powerful states' people's movements in almost all the princely states, urged for political rights and elective representatives in the Constituent Assembly. The Congress criticized the Cabinet Mission scheme of overlooking the need of the princely states to have elected representatives in the Constituent Assembly. Nehru presided over the Gwalior Session of the All India States Peoples Conference in April 1947 and classified the states not willing to join the Indian Union as 'hostile'. In addition to such verbal threats, Sardar Patel, who became the head of the new States Department that replaced the Political Department, and V. P. Menon, who became the Secretary, made use of popular movements in the princely states to restrain prices and coerce them to accede to India.

Kashmir offers an illustrative example. In May–June 1946, Nehru had offered support to Sheikh Abdullah, leader of the National Conference, in his 'Quit Kashmir' struggle against the unpopular Hindu Maharaja of a Muslim-majority state. An incensed Patel informed Wavell that Nehru had gone to Kashmir against his advice. He also began negotiations with Kak, Kashmir's Prime Minister, which eventually led to the accession of the Maharaja into India, when raiders from Pakistan invaded Kashmir in October 1947 (Sarkar [1983] 1995: 450).

Patel was candid about his position with regard to the princely states. In response to anxieties voiced by the Nawab of Bhopal over the appointment of Patel and Menon as heads of the new States Department, Patel asserted that while the Congress was not 'an enemy' of the princes, it wished them and their people, 'prosperity, contentment and happiness' under the aegis of the Congress (Menon 1957: 96).

By June 1947, Pakistan had become a settled fact—the Bengal Assembly on 20 June and the Punjab Assembly on 23 June voted in favour of partition. West Punjab and East Bengal were to go to Pakistan; the rest was to remain in India. The princes were asked to opt for India or Pakistan, with very limited power of 'option'. The 'integration' of princely states into the Indian Union took place in two phases, 'with a skilful combination of baits and threats of mass pressure in both' (Sarkar [1983] 1995: 451). By 15 August, all princes except Kashmir, Junagadh and Hyderabad had agreed to sign the Instrument of Accession with India, while Bhawalpur had opted for Pakistan. NWFP, Sind and Baluchistan went to Pakistan, and Kashmir to India, both against the will of a considerable part of their population.

Mountbatten appointed two boundary commissions, for Bengal and Punjab, under Sir Cyril Radcliffe to mark out international frontiers in a very limited period of time. Lines were arbitrarily drawn on a map, lines that divided homes, families and property, and caused anguish to millions of people. The Mountbatten Plan was put into effect with remarkable speed. Political leaders of Bengali and Punjabi Hindus as well as those of Sikhs espoused the cause of partition with greater fervour than the Muslim League. With 'unprecedented unanimity' they set forth together 'on a path leading straight to man slaughter' (Moon 1973: 70). The Indian Independence Act was ratified by the British Crown on 18 July and implemented on 14/15 August 1947.

Pakistan came into being on 14 August. A simple ceremony was held in Karachi where Mountbatten read out the King's message and conferred power on Jinnah as the first Governor-General of the Dominion of Pakistan. More elaborate and pompous rituals and ceremonies, painstakingly planned, marked the transfer of power from Britain to India. The Constituent Assembly met at the stroke of midnight on 14/15 August, and free India's 'tryst with destiny' began.

Nehru was sworn in as the Prime Minister of a new, free India on 15 August. Millions rejoiced throughout the subcontinent making 15 August an unforgettable experience. Arguably, if there was cause to rejoice there was also a lot to grieve for. Freedom, for many in India and Pakistan meant uncertainty, confusion and displacement; the sudden assault of being told that their home was now in a different country, uncertainty and fear carried to horrific proportions by the worst violence in the history of the subcontinent, of trains moving between the two free countries carrying nothing but dead bodies. Literature and films tried to evoke such moments of acute pain and trauma—the shock of losing everything, of being uprooted and forced to join the endless stream of refugees (Hasan 1995, vols. 1 and 2; Fraser 2006, for instance). Scholars took much longer to come to grips with and place themselves at a distance from the tragedy. It was not until the late 1990s that nuanced accounts of the 'gravity, uncertainty and jagged edges of the violence that was Partition' came to be recounted (Butalia 1998; Menon and Bhasin 1998; Pandey 2001: 5).

Gandhi, totally opposed to the partition, did not participate in the celebrations; he spent the day fasting and in prayer. Hindu militants in the Mahasabha and the RSS, who wanted an undivided India, campaigned against the 15 August celebrations (Tan and Kudaisya 2000). If Hindu militants were incensed by freedom with partition, for Muslim ideologues of Pakistan partition was freedom.

How do we make sense of this immensely significant but acutely contradictory event that marked the founding moment of two independent nation states? Can we really grasp it in terms of whether partition was inevitable or who was to blame for it? These questions as well as the related one of whether it was a mere 'transfer of power' or freedom won by Indians by means of struggle and sacrifice demonstrate a near exclusive focus on 'high politics'. 'Never before in South Asian history', remarks Mushirul Hasan, did so few decide the fate of so many. And rarely did so few 'ignore the sentiments of so many in the continent' (Hasan [1993] 1994: 42).

The validity of these emotional statements become evident if we bear in mind the extremely limited nature of the electorate, even in the 1946 elections. In the final decision of partition, the choice of the restricted franchise was treated as the 'verdict of the people' (ibid.: 41). Partha Chatterjee reiterates the same with regard to Bengal—it is 'historically inaccurate to suggest that the decision to partition the province of Bengal along religious-demographic lines actually involved the participation of masses of people' ([1997] 1998: 37).

There is no clear answer to the questions of who was to blame and whether the 'partition' was inevitable. In Percival Spear's opinion, 'all parties must share the blame for the Partition'—there were 'cardinal errors' in policy. And 'errors' there were. Whether it was Mountbatten's unseemly haste to withdraw from India, or Nehru's hurry for freedom at any cost (a fact regretted by Maulana Azad in the much awaited 30 pages of his autobiography finally published in 1988), or Jinnah's swift change of position in 1946–47 between a demand for Pakistan composed of six provinces, an acceptance of 'dominionhood' within the Union of India, the provision of a 'Free State of Bengal' and the final acceptance of a 'moth-eaten Pakistan' (Moore 1983: 561), mistakes there were a plenty. And yet, continues Spear, in these directions 'neither wisdom nor justice lies'. The lesson from this tragedy can only be learnt 'if each party asks itself the question: in what way did our actions and policy contribute to the result?' (Spear 1958: 179).

Earlier chapters have discussed the multiple and contradictory ways in which separate communities came to be demarcated over the nineteenth and twentieth centuries and their interaction with political mobilization. Important works have also traced the origin and development of the ideas and sentiments of 'two nations'. Farzana Shaikh's sophisticated analysis of the significance of notions of 'consensus' in modernist Indo-Islamic thought and its role in the linking of political action to Islamically derived political discourse (Shaikh 1989), has been complemented by Joya Chatterji's thorough analysis of activities of several Hindu organizations in Bengal that actively aroused Hindu nationalist passions among the Bengali *bhadralok* (Chatterji 1995), Christophe Jaffrelot's study of Hindu organizations in the Hindi belt (Jaffrelot 1996), and Papiya Ghosh's innovative analysis of the negative stereotyping of the 'Congress Muslim' in Bihar (Ghosh 1991). The construction of distinct identities, regional and religious, of Hindus and Muslims and Sikhs, and of the growing hostility and antagonism between the communities has been subjected to scholarly scrutiny. But did this carving of 'communal' blocs necessarily make the partition inevitable or is there 'a lack of wisdom and justice' in our posing of the question? (Spear 1958).

In Review: The 'In-Between' People

The Meos of Rajasthan—who maintained a prolonged 'dual identity', provide an evocative example of the 'making, unmaking and remaking of lifeworlds' occasioned by the processes of state and nation formation in the twentieth century (Mayaram 1997: 1). The Meos, who lived in the Mewat region located within the triangle of Delhi, Agra and Jaipur for almost a millennium, were recorded as Muslims in the nineteenth century censuses, but their beliefs and practices were drawn from both Hinduism and Islam. As 'in-between' people, the Meos had aroused the ire of central authority for a long time; if the Mughals termed them 'rebels', Victoria's rule catalogued them under 'criminal tribes'. The Meos, who had come to reside primarily in the princely states of Alwar and Bharatpur in the twentieth century, became prime targets during the partition riots. Mayaram's emotive study tracks how the imagined community of Pakistan, projected as the homeland of the 'Muslims' by the Muslim League, entered popular discourse to deterritorialize the Meos of their 'homeland', and how a totalization of 'Muslims' served to obliterate the sense of a shared regional culture and collective memory (ibid.: 188). Meos, identified completely as Muslims, were subjected to *shuddhi*, as condition for protection by Jats and other Hindu inhabitants of the region.

Meo peasant protest, moreover, was turned into 'Muslim mob' action in official discourse. Meos were slaughtered mercilessly in the riots of 1947; a result not just of spurts of violence but of a well-articulated state policy of 'cleansing' that comprised conversion, capture of women who had 'no religion', and mass killing. About 82,000 Meos lost their lives, and the hapless survivors who had fled or left for Pakistan could only recover a small part of their lands on their return, now taken over by Hindu and Sikh local cultivators and refugees, despite the Congress promise of restoration of property (ibid.: 205). The combined onslaught of extraordinary violence and marginalization brought about a rupture in Meo language: traditional forms of heroic mythic history through which the community transmitted collective identity suffered a breakdown. Violence in its 'annihilatory form performed a rite of expulsion' (ibid.: 208). For the survivors, it has meant a renegotiation of individual lifeworlds and the dissolution and re-making of community identity along the lines of the postcolonial state's tidy categories that has no room for a liminal people like the Meos, a people in-between Hindusim and Islam.

In an insightful analysis of the 'Second Partition of Bengal', Chatterjee cautions us against disentangling the many different roots of an 'event' such as the partition—roots that run along different levels of determination and with different temporalities—in order to provide all of them with a single closure, that is, the partition. A construction of such a singular narrative confers uniformity upon histories that are very different, histories in which categories such as 'religion' and 'nationalism' have 'entirely different signification' (Chatterjee [1997] 1998: 33). To make his point, Chatterjee raises the question, did the growth of Hindu communalism in Bengal provincial politics in the 1930s and 1940s make organized opinion among Hindus less anti-British? (ibid.: 35).

In a similar vein, Gyanendra Pandey has interrogated the writing of histories of partition as histories of 'communalism'—as accounts of 'origins' or 'causes', investigations of the chances, of political mistakes, and the 'less amenable social and economic developments that brought about this tragic event' (1997: 4). In other words, he questions the very basis of histories that project the nationalist struggle as a 'noble endeavour' pertaining to 'secular, democratic, non-violent and tolerant nationalism' which won for India her freedom (Chandra et al. 2000, for instance). This remarkable dominance of the nationalist paradigm in the writing of partition and independence underscores, in Pandey's view, how 'history writing is part of a larger nationalist discourse' (1997: 6).

Recent works, interestingly, have explored popular aspects of the partition to argue that it was not just the decision of a few (Hashmi 1999; Talbot 1996) and, at the same time, to question its inevitability (Hasan [1993] 1994, 1997; Mahajan 2000; Singh 1987). They have, however, not managed to overcome the 'nationalist paradigm' of history writing in that they do not question the idea of the 'natural flow' of Indian history as 'peaceful' or 'non-violent' in which events such as the partition break forth as exceptional and as an aberration. In a later work, Pandey offers a history of the partition in which 'violence and community constitute one another' and narratives of particular experiences of violence go towards making the 'community' and the subject of history (Pandey 2001: 4). This has been extended by Vazira Zamindar, who argues that the killings of 1947 marked the beginning of violence, where the rioters and victims were only 'co-actors' of the partition. The states of India and Pakistan and the bureaucracy were the principal perpetrators of prolonged violence on different fronts, the architects of a 'long partition' (Zamindar 2007), a point we explore in the next chapter.

We will draw our history of the making of a nation to a close at this precise juncture to try and rethink the history of partition, of nationhood, of nationalism and nationalist politics, and look with new eyes at the story that unfolded after 15 August 1947.

ORGANIZATION OF PAKISTAN, CONSTITUTION OF 1962*

*This constitution was in force from March 1962 until the declaration of Marital Law in March 1970. Previously Pakistan was governed under the Government of India Act of 1935; the Constitution of March 1956, suspended in October 1958; and the Marital Law regime of General Ayub Khan from 1958–62. A Third Constitution was promulgated in August 1973.

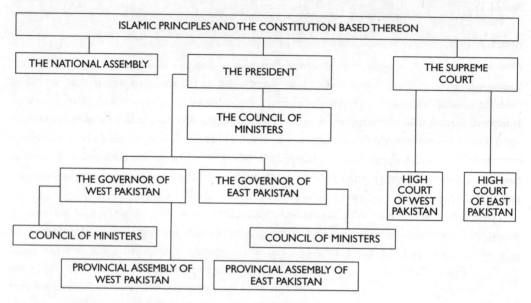

REFERENCES

Ahmad, Aziz. 1967. *Islamic Modernism in India and Pakistan*. London: Oxford University Press.

Anderson, W. K. and S. D. Damle. 1987. *The Brotherhood in Saffron: The Rashtriya Swayamsevak Sangh and Hindu Revivalism*. New Delhi: Vistaar Publications.

Arnold, David A. 1988. 'Quit India in Madras: Hiatus of Climacteric'. In *The Indian Nation in 1942*, edited by G. Pandey, 207–22. Calcutta: K. P. Bagchi & Co.

Ayer, S. A. 1951. *Unto Him a Witness*. Bombay: Thacker, Spink and Co.

Azad, Maulana Abul Kalam. 1959. *India Wins Freedom*. Bombay: Orient Longman.

Bandyopadhyay, D. 2001. 'Tebhaga Movement in Bengal: A Retrospect'. *Economic and Political Weekly* 36 (41) (13 October): 3901–3907.

Bandyopadhyay, Sekhar. 2000. 'Transfer of Power and the Crisis of Dalit Politics in India, 1945–47'. *Modern Asian Studies* 34 (4): 893–944.

———. 2004. *From Plassey to Partition: A History of Modern India*. Hyderabad: Orient Longman.

Begum, Jahanara. 1994. *The Last Decades of Undivided Bengal: Parties, Politics [and] Personalities*. Calcutta: Minerva.

Bhowmik, Sharit K. 1986. 'Tebhaga Movement in Dooars: Some Issues Regarding Ethnicity and Class Formation'. *Economic and Political Weekly* 21 (22) (31 May): 977–80.

Bhuyan, A. C. 1975. *The Quit India Movement, the Second World War and Indian Nationalism*. New Delhi: Manas.

Birla, G. D. 1953. *In the Shadow of the Mahatma*. Bombay: Orient Longman.

Bose, Nirmal Kumar. 1953. *My Days with Gandhi*. Calcutta: Nishana.

Bose, Sarmila. 2005. 'Love in the Time of War: Subhas Chandra Bose's Journeys to Nazi Germany (1941) and Towards the Soviet Union (1945)'. *Economic and Political Weekly* 40 (3) (15 January): 249–56.

Bose, Sugata. 1986. *Agrarian Bengal: Economy, Social Structure and Politics, 1909–1947*. Cambridge: Cambridge University Press.

———. 1993. 'Peasant Labour and Colonial Capital: Rural Bengal Since 1770'. *New Cambridge History of India* (Vol. 3.2). Cambridge: Cambridge University Press.

Bose, Sugata and Ayesha Jalal. 1998. *Modern South Asia: History, Culture, Political Economy*. Paperback edition, 2000. London: Routledge.

Brasted, Howard V. and Carl Bridge. 1990. '"15 August 1947": Labour's Parting Gift to India'. In *India: Creating a Modern Nation*, edited by J. Masselos, 1–35. New Delhi: Sterling Publishers.

Brown, Judith. 1985. *Modern India*. New Delhi: Oxford University Press.

Butalia, Urvashi. 1998. *The Other Side of Silence: Voices from the Partition of India*. New Delhi: Viking.

Chakrabarty, Bidyut. 1992a. 'Political Mobilization in the Localities: The 1942 Quit India Movement in Midnapur'. *Modern Asian Studies* 26 (4): 791–814.

———. 1992b. 'Defiance and Confrontation: The 1942 Quit India Movement in Midnapur'. *Social Scientist* 20 (7/8): 75–93.

———. 1993. 'The 1947 United Bengal Movement: A Thesis Without Synthesis'. *The Indian Economic and Social History Review* 30 (4): 467–88.

Chandra, Bipan, Mridula Mukherjee, Aditya Mukherjee, K. N. Panikkar and Sucheta Mahajan. 2000. *India's Struggle for Independence*. New Delhi: Penguin Books.

Chandra, Bipan, Amales Tripathi, Barun De. [1972] 1975. *Freedom Struggle*. New Delhi: National Book Trust.

Chatterjee, Partha. [1997] 1998. 'The Second Partition of Bengal'. In *The Present History of West Bengal: Essays in Political Criticism*, P. Chatterjee, 27–46. New Delhi: Oxford University Press.

Chatterji, Joya. 1995. *Bengal Divided: Hindu Communalism and Partition 1932–1947*. Cambridge: Cambridge University Press.

Chaudhurani, Sarala Devi. 1975. *Jibanaer Jharapata* (The Fallen Leaves of Life). Calcutta: Rupa and Co.

Chaudhuri, Nirad C. 1988. *Thy Hand Great Anarch: India 1921–52*. London: Chatto and Windus.

Chopra, P. N., ed. 1976. *Quit India Movement: British Secret Report* [Wickenden Report 1943]. Faridabad: Thomson Press.

Cohen, Stephen P. 1963–1964. 'Subhas Chandra Bose and the Indian National Army'. *Pacific Affairs* 36 (4): 411–29.

Cooper, Adrienne. 1988. *Sharecropping and Sharecroppers' Struggles in Bengal, 1930–1950*. Delhi: K. P. Bagchi.

Darwin, J. 1988. *Britain and Decolonisation: The Retreat from Empire in the Post-war World*. Basingstoke: Macmillan.

Das, Suranjan. 1991. *Communal Riots in Bengal, 1905–1947*. New Delhi: Oxford University Press.

Desai, Manali. 2001. 'Party Formation, Political Power, and the Capacity for Reform: Comparing Left Parties in Kerala and West Bengal, India'. *Social Forces* 80 (1): 37–60.

Devji, Faisal. 2013. *Muslim Zion: Pakistan as a Political Idea*. London: Hurst and Co.

Dhanagare, D. N. 1991. *Peasant Movements in India, 1920–1950*. New Delhi: Oxford University Press.

Diwaker, R. R. 1948. *Satyagraha: The Power of Truth*. Hinsdale, IL: Henry Regnery Co.

Dyson, T. and A. Maharatna. 1991. 'Excess Mortality During the Bengal Famine: A Re-evaluation'. *The Indian Economic and Social History Review* 28 (3): 281–97.

Elliott, Carolyn M. 1974. 'Decline of a Patrimonial Regime: The Telengana Rebellion in India, 1946–51'. *The Journal of Asian Studies* 34 (1): 27–47.

Farley, Miriam S. 1942. 'India: A Political Primer'. *Far Eastern Survey* 11 (8): 94–101.

Fraser, Bashabi ed. 2006. *Bengal Partition Stories: An Unclosed Chapter*. London: Anthem Press.

Gallagher, John and Anil Seal. 1981. 'Britain and India Between the Wars'. *Modern Asian Studies* 15 (3): 387–414.

Gandhi, M. K. 1958. *Collected Works of Mahatma Gandhi*. Vols. 1–90. New Delhi, Publications Division, Government of India (Vol. 77, 83, 1981). Electronic version, 1999: http://www.gandhiserve.org/cwmg/cwmg.htmlk

Ghosh, Papiya. 1991. 'The Making of the Congress Muslim Stereotype: Bihar, 1937–39'. *The Indian Economic and Social History Review* 28 (4): 417–34.

Gilmartin, David. 1979/1994. 'Religious Leadership and the Pakistan Movement in the Panjab'. *Modern Asian Studies* 13 (3): 485–517. Included in M. Hasan ed. 1994. *India's Partition: Process, Strategy and Mobilization*. New Delhi: Oxford University Press.

Gopal, Ram. 1959. *The Indian Muslims: A Political History*. Bombay: Asia Publishing House.

Gopal, S. 1975. *Jawaharlal Nehru: A Biography, 1889–1947*. Vol. 1. London: Jonathan Cape.

Gordon, Leonard A. 1974. *Bengal: The Nationalist Movement 1876–1940*. New York: Columbia University Press.

Gray, Hugh. 1971. 'The Demand for a Separate Telengana State in India'. *Asian Survey* 11 (5): 463–74.

Greenough, Paul R. 1982. *Prosperity and Misery in Modern Bengal: The Famine of 1943–44*. New York: Oxford University Press.

———. 1983. 'Political Mobilization and the Underground Literature of the Quit India Movement, 1942–44'. *Modern Asian Studies* 17 (3): 353–86.

Gwyer, M. and A. Appadorai. 1957. *Speeches and Documents on the Indian Constitution*. Vol. 2. Bombay: Oxford University Press.

Hardiman, David. 1988. 'The Quit India Movement in Gujarat'. In *The Indian Nation in 1942*, edited by G. Pandey, 77–121. Calcutta: K. P. Bagchi and Co.

Hasan, Mushirul, ed. [1993] 1994. Introduction to *India's Partition: Process, Strategy and Mobilization*, edited by Mushirul Hasan, 1–43. New Delhi: Oxford University Press.

———, ed. 1995. *India Partitioned: The Other Face of Freedom*. Vols. 1 and 2. New Delhi: Roli Books.

———. 1997. *Legacy of a Divided Nation: India's Muslims Since Independence*. Boulder, Colorado: Westview Press.

Hashmi, T. I. 1992. *Pakistan as a Peasant Utopia: The Communalization of Class Politics in East Bengal, 1920–1947*. Boulder, Colorado: Westview Press.

———. 1999. 'Peasant Nationalism and the Politics of Partition: The Class-Communal Symbiosis in East Bengal, 1940–47'. In *Region and Partitions: Bengal, Panjab and the Partition of the Subcontinent*, edited by I. Talbot and G. Singh, 6–41. Karachi: Oxford University Press.

Hutchins, F. G. 1971. *Spontaneous Revolution: The Quit India Movement*. New Delhi: Manohar.

———. 1973. *India's Revolution: Gandhi and the Quit India Movement*. Cambridge, MA: Harvard University Press.

Jaffrelot, Christophe. 1996. *The Hindu Nationalist Movement and Indian Politics 1925 to the 1990s*. London: Hurst & Co.

Jalal, Ayesha. 1994. *The Sole Spokesman: Jinnah, the Muslim League and the Demand for Pakistan*. New Delhi: Cambridge University Press.

———. 1995. *Democracy and Authoritarianism in South Asia: A Comparative and Historical Perspective*. New York: Cambridge University Press.

———. 2000. *Self and Sovereignty: Individual and Community in South Asian Islam Since 1850*. London: Routledge.

Lebra, Joyce C. 1971. *Jungle Alliance*. Singapore: Donald Moore for Asia Pacific Press.

Mahajan, Sucheta. 2000. *Independence and Partition: The Erosion of Colonial Power in India*. New Delhi: Sage Publications.

Mansergh, N. and E. W. R. Lumby, eds. 1971–1983. *The Transfer of Power in India* (Vol. 2, 1971; Vol. 6, 1976; Vol. 7, 1977). London: HMSO.

Mayaram, Shail. 1997. *Resisting Regimes: Myth, Memory and the Shaping of a Muslim Identity*. New Delhi: Oxford University Press.

McLane, John R. 1970. *The Political Awakening in India*. Engelwood Cliffs, NJ: Prentice Hall.

Menon, Ritu and Kamla Bhasin. 1998. *Borders and Boundaries: Women in India's Partition*. New Brunswick, NJ: Rutgers University Press.

Menon, V. P. 1957. *The Transfer of Power in India*. Calcutta: Orient Longman.

Metcalf, Barbara D. and Thomas R. Metcalf. 2003. *A Concise History of India*. Cambridge: Cambridge University Press.

Mishra, Debi P. 1998. *People's Revolt in Orissa: A Study of Talcher*. New Delhi: Atlantic Publishers and Distributors.

Moon, Penderel, ed. 1973. *Wavell: The Viceroy's Journal*. London: Oxford University Press.

Moore, R. J. 1979. *Churchill, Cripps and India, 1939–45*. Oxford: Clarendon Press.

———. 1983. 'Jinnah and the Pakistan Demand'. *Modern Asian Studies* 17 (4): 529–61. Also included in M. Hasan ed. 1994. *India's Partition: Process, Strategy and Mobilization*, 160–197. New Delhi: Oxford University Press.

———. 1988. *Endgames of Empire: Studies of Britain's Indian Problem*. New Delhi: Oxford University Press.

Omvedt, Gail. 1988. 'The Satara Prati Sarkar'. In *The Indian Nation in 1942*, edited by G. Pandey, 223–62. Calcutta: K. P. Bagchi & Co.

Pandey, B. N. 1969. *The Break-up of British India*. London: Macmillan.

Pandey, Gyanendra. 1988. 'The Revolt of August 1942 in Eastern UP and Bihar'. In *The Indian Nation in 1942*, edited by G. Pandey, 123–164. Calcutta: K. P. Bagchi & Co.

———. 1997. 'In Defense of the Fragment: Writing about Hindu-Muslim Riots in India Today'. In *A Subaltern Studies Reader 1986–1995*, edited by Ranajit Guha, 1–33. Minneapolis: University of Minnesota Press.

———. 2001. *Remembering Partition: Violence, Nationalism and History in India*. Cambridge: Cambridge University Press.

Pati, Biswamoy. 1992/1999. 'Dialectics of Transition: Orissa, 1943–50.' *Economic and Political Weekly* 27 (7): 353–64. A slightly modified version: 'Dialectics of Retreat: Odisha, 1943–50'. *Social Scientist* 27 (7/8): 75–112.

Patnaik, Jagannath. 2006. *Quit India Movement*. (Freedom Struggle in Orissa, Vol. 2). Bhubaneswar: Department of Culture, Government of Orissa.

Pavier, Barry. 1974. 'The Telengana Armed Struggle'. *Economic and Political Weekly* 9 (32/34) (Sp. number August): 1413, 1417–20.

Philips, C. H. 1970. *The Partition of India: Policies and Perspectives, 1935–1947*. London: Allen & Unwin Ltd.

Pirzada, S. S. 1966. *Quaid-e-Azam Jinnah's Correspondence*. Karachi: National Publishing House.

Pradhan, Pabitra M. 1979. *Mukti Pathe Sainika*. Cuttack: n.e.

Prasad, Rajendra. 1957. *Autobiography*. Bombay: Asia Publishing House.

Ram, Mohan. 1973. 'The Telengana Peasant Armed Struggle, 1946–51'. *Economic and Political Weekly* 8 (23) (9 June): 1025–32.

Rath, Bijay Chandra. 1993. *Unrest in the Princely States of Dhenkanal and Talcher*. Cuttack: Arya Prakashan.

Roy, Asim. 1990/1994. 'The High-Politics of India's Partition: The Revisionist Perspective' (Review Article). *Modern Asian Studies* 24 (2): 385–415. Included in M. Mushirul Hasan ed. 1994. *India's Partition: Process, Strategy and Mobilization*, 102–132. New Delhi: Oxford University Press.

Sanyal, Hitesranjan. 1979. 'Congress Movement in the Villages of Eastern Midnapore, 1921–1931'. In *Asia Du Sud, Traditions et Changements,* edited by Marc Gaborieau and Alice Thorner, 169–178 . Paris: Centre National de la Recherche Scientifique.

Sarkar, Sumit. [1983] 1995. *Modern India: 1885–1947*. Madras: Macmillan India.

Sayeed, Khalid B. 1968. *Pakistan, The Formative Phase*. London: Oxford University Press (Second edition).

Sen, A. K. 1980. 'Famine Mortality: A Study of the Bengal Famine of 1943'. In *Peasants in History: Essays in Honour of Daniel Thorner*, edited by E. J. Hobsbawm, W. Kula, A. Mitra, K. N. Raj and I. Sachs, 194–220. Calcutta: Oxford University Press.

Sen, Shila. 1976. *Muslim Politics in Bengal, 1937–47*. New Delhi: Impex India.

Shaikh, Farzana. 1986. 'Muslims and Political Representation in Colonial India: The Making of Pakistan'. *Modern Asian Studies* 20 (3): 539–57. Also included in Mushirul Hasan ed. 1994. *India's Partition: Process, Strategy and Mobilization*, 81–101. New Delhi: Oxford University Press.

———. 1989. *Community and Consensus in Islam: Muslim Representation in Colonial India*. Cambridge: Cambridge University Press.

Sharma, Jagdish S, ed. 1962. *India's Struggle for Freedom, Select Documents and Sources*. Vol. 1. Delhi: S. Chand & Co.

Singh, Anita Inder. 1982. 'Imperial Defence and the Transfer of Power in India, 1946–1947'. *The International History Review* 4 (4): 568–88.

———. 1987. *The Origins of the Partition of India, 1936–1947*. New Delhi: Oxford University Press.

Spear, Percival. 1958. 'Britain's Transfer of Power in India'. *Pacific Affairs* 31 (2): 173–80.

Stein, Burton. 2010. *A History of India*. Revised and edited by David Arnold. Sussex, UK: Wiley-Blackwell. (First published 1998. Oxford: Oxford University Press).

Sundarayya, P. 1979. 'Hyderabad State—Its Socio-Political Background; The Communist Movement in Andhra: Terror Regime, 1948–1951; Entry of Indian Army and Immediately After'. In *Peasant Struggles in India*, edited by A. R. Desai, 537–568. New Delhi: Oxford University Press.

Talbot, Ian A. 1994. 'The Growth of the Muslim League in the Punjab, 1937–46'. In *India's Partition: Process, Strategy and Mobilization*, edited by M. Hasan, 230–253. New Delhi: Oxford University Press.

———. 1996. *Freedom's Cry: Popular Dimension in the Pakistan Movement and Partition Experience*. Karachi: Oxford University Press.

Tan, Tai Yong and Gyanesh Kudaisya. 2000. *The Aftermath of Partition in South Asia*. London and New York: Routledge.

Tomlinson, B. R. 1976. *The Indian National Congress and the Raj, 1929–1942: The Penultimate Phase*. London: Macmillan.

———. 1985. 'Indo-British Relations in the Post Colonial Era: The Sterling Balances Negotiations, 1947–49'. *The Journal of Imperial and Commonwealth History* 13 (3): 142–62.

Tottenham, Sir Richard, ed. 1943. *Congress Responsibility for the Disturbances, 1942–1943*. Delhi: Manager for Publications.

Wolpert, Stanley. 2000. *A New History of India*. New York: Oxford University Press.

Zamindar, Vazira Fazila-Yacoobali. 2007. *The Long Partition and the Making of Modern South Asia: Refugees, Boundaries, Histories*. New York: Columbia University Press.

Zelliot, Eleanor. 1988. 'Congress and the Untouchables, 1917–1959'. In *Congress and Indian Nationalism*, edited by Richard Sisson and Stanley Wolpert, 182–197. Berkeley and Los Angeles: University of California Press.

———. 1992. *From Untouchable to Dalit: Essays on the Ambedkar Movement*. New Delhi: Manohar.

1947 and After

11

Jawaharlal Nehru at Bhangi Sweepers Colony, Delhi, October 1946

Chapter outline

THE IMPONDERABLES OF PARTITION

THE CONSTITUTION: DEMOCRACY, MAJORITY AND 'MINORITIES'

CASTE AND EQUALITY

SECULARISM IN CRISIS

CENTRE–STATE RELATIONS

POLITICAL ECONOMY

India's 'tryst with destiny' began at the stroke of midnight of 14 August. While the world slept, India awoke to 'life and freedom'; the 'soul of a nation, long suppressed' found utterance. A 'period of ill fortune' ended and India discovered herself again (Nehru 1950: 3). Nehru's speech, delivered at the Constituent Assembly in New Delhi on the midnight of 14 August 1947, articulated the first Prime Minister's enthusiasm and exuberance at the birth of free India.

Nehru possibly could not have used a better phrase for his speech. Tryst it was indeed, with parts of the country barely recovering from the effects of a devastating famine and some others reeling from the magnitude of the violence occasioned by the partition. Nehru, too conscious of the calamity to ignore it, referred to 'all the pains of labour' Indians had to endure to give birth to 'free, sovereign India' and stated that 'some of the pains continue even now'. Nevertheless, he hastened to add, 'the past is over and it is the future that beckons us now' (Nehru 1947).

What was this future that beckoned, and what were the pangs of the past that still continued? To understand this, we need to track the ideologies, policies, elements and processes that have crucially shaped India's democratic career for over 65 years of its existence.

The political partition of the country was a central fact of this birth—it critically marked the 'present' of the two nations and shaped the future in crucial ways. The other pains that continued into the future, albeit with distinct emphases, lay in the political system and the legal structure. A lot of it was foreshadowed in the negotiations that went on prior to the transfer of power—the actual structure of the state, relations between the centre and the states of British India and states under princes and the modes of sharing of power among them. What beckoned was the framing of a new constitution, work on which had begun earlier, but which held out the promise and the possibility of shaping independent India in accordance with the visions of its leaders, and, of course, of giving shape to independent India by means of policy, planning and implementation. The framing of the constitution embodied fundamental issues relating to the form of the nation-state, implicit notions of the citizen and citizenship and the position of 'minorities' that in turn involved issues of justice and legality. We examine these issues one by one in order to unearth their impact on the socio-political and cultural processes of independent India.

THE IMPONDERABLES OF PARTITION

The partition, 'one of the great human convulsions of history' (Butalia 1998: 3), has left a permanent imprint on policies and political processes in India and Pakistan. 'Communal violence' that has been described as the 'birthmark' of the new nations, has been enduring and has left significant traces. Violence in Punjab, it has been argued, had a lot to do with the arbitrary and secret way in which the frontiers of India and Pakistan were fixed by Mountbatten's officials (Stein 2010: 357). The Boundary Award announced on 16 August 1947 sliced the Sikh community, with their lands and shrines, into two, and the cession of western Punjab to Pakistan truncated tracts inhabited by the Sikhs for a very long time.

This abrupt and arbitrary dismemberment brought a new frenzy to the violence in Punjab which had started in March, with initial attacks on Hindus and Sikhs in Muslim west Punjab. Enraged Sikhs, a large number of them consisting of demobilized soldiers who had served in the British–Indian Army, utilized their training and knowledge of modern weaponry to organize and direct systematic attacks on villages, trains and refugee columns (Metcalf and Metcalf 2003: 217). Immediate and mutual hatred on both sides of the frontier resulted in carnage; the loss of life was immense with estimates ranging from several hundred thousand up to a million. Official reports in India and Pakistan indicate that neither the Congress nor the Muslim League had anticipated the partition's genocidal chain of violence (Brass 2003: 71). In this context, the 'unthinkability' of the violence during partition conveys, not 'the willful or unwitting failure to see violent consequences', but 'the more systematic disconnect in the final years of colonial rule between elite and popular constructions of territory, nationalism and nationality' (Naqvi 2007: 45).

Survivors of the partition violence were moved by fear; they felt safe only among members of their own community. This fear helped to consolidate loyalties towards the state, and loyalty of Punjabi Muslims offered Pakistan a visible territorial reality for the first time (Metcalf and Metcalf 2003: 218). The tension was aggravated by the fight between India and Pakistan over the Kashmir issue, which also turned critically on Punjab (Stein 2010: 357).

In Review: Peoples, Refugees, Citizens

'Moving between memory and record', writes Vazira Zamindar, I recover here 'a remarkable history of how, in the midst of incomprehensible violence, two postcolonial states comprehended, intervened, *and shaped* the colossal displacements of Partition'. The making of refugees as a governmental category, and refugee rehabilitation as a tool of planning, shored up the creation of the new nations and their borders, and 'people, including families, were divided' (Zamindar 2007: 3). Zamindar views the partition as a dialogic process between states where genocidal violence, mass displacement, refugee rehabilitation, and control over the movement of people contributed to the definition of political and regional boundaries, and definitions of citizenship.

Focussing on the 'Muslim community' in north India, not as a religious and/or linguistic community, but as a constructed 'political community' that came into existence under colonial rule and was mobilized by political institutions, such as the Muslim League, Zamindar argues that once the partition was agreed upon in the political high spheres, new issues came to confront India and Pakistan, since 'nation as community' was transformed into 'nations as citizens' of two states.

'Transfer of power took place from colonial rule to national rule in what was a crisis, a state of emergency'. The post-colonial states, formed from a divided yet unchanged colonial structure of governance, had to restage 'the modern state on behalf of the nation'. Their response to the crisis, therefore, became crucial for legitimacy. Both states responded almost immediately by setting up parallel Emergency Committees of the cabinet to bring law and order in 'murder-cleaved-Punjab and Delhi' as well as Ministries of Relief and Rehabilitation to 'manage' the well-being of the millions displaced. The figure of the 'refugee' emerged to carry 'the scripted and rescripted labor of postcolonial governmentality' (ibid.: 6).

The concept/category of 'migration' offered the two governments a handy tool to control and fix the *displacement* of people, despite the fact that many of the 'migrants' had fled their homes and were hoping to return to their homeland. 'Migration' acquired bureaucratic and juridical meaning as it was used to confine people in one country or another. The refugees were tied to a country because the two states also affixed a certain nationality to a certain religious community. Thus, Muslims were—or should have been—Pakistanis, and Hindus Indians (ibid.: 8).

Consequently, the 'problem' of 'returning Muslim refugees', people who had gone to 'visit' relatives on the other side of the border, prompted the Indian government to introduce a permit system in 1948 (ibid.: 81–82). The influx of returning Muslim refugees acquired 'threatening significance' in bureaucratic record as it folded into the discourse of housing and rehabilitation of Hindu and Sikh refugees (ibid.: 83). While this permit evoked the tragedy of a Partition which now divided 'hearts' for the returning refugees, the control of movement of a specific people at a time of massive displacement set in motion a political process with immense institutional significance. 'Doubtful' and 'disloyal' came to serve as critical categories in the transformation of markers of religious community into citizens of new nation states (ibid.: 119).

Kashmir, it bears pointing out, was neither as large nor as old and independent as Hyderabad where the Nizam opted for autonomy and a powerful Islamic Party stoutly resisted accession with the Indian union. The Nizam sought to maintain his independence with the help of an irregular army recruited from among the Muslim aristocracy of the state (Metcalf and Metcalf 2003: 220). But his effort turned out to be futile. His territories were surrounded by India on all sides and a majority of his subjects were Hindus. His irregular force could not even bring the Telengana rebels under control and proved no match for the troops sent by the Indian government in September 1948. The army engaged in 'police action' that disarmed the opposition and brought two centuries of Nizam rule in Hyderabad, and with it, 'the only site for patronage of Islamic culture and learning in the Deccan', to an end. Hyderabad merged with the Indian union in 1950 and came to form part of the new state of Andhra Pradesh (Metcalf and Metcalf 2003: 220; Stein 2010: 357–58).

Kashmir, created 'rather off-handedly' (Stein 2010: 357) by the British after the first defeat of the Sikhs in 1846 to reward a formal official who had supported the British, became a bone of contention between India and Pakistan, not on account of its wealth or mineral resources, but because it bolstered the claims of 'self-determination' of the two nations. The original home of the Nehru family, this Himalayan kingdom was connected to India through a district in Punjab but it shared a boundary with Pakistan. Kashmir's population was predominantly Muslim, about 77 per cent, but it was under the rule of a Hindu Maharaja. Pakistan had assumed that Kashmir would decide to join it at the end of British rule. When the Maharaja hesitated, Pakistan sponsored guerilla warfare in order to frighten the ruler into submission. The Maharaja appealed to Mountbatten for help, and the Viceroy agreed on condition that Kashmir join India. Indian soldiers marched into Kashmir and drove out the guerrilla force from all but a little part of Kashmir. The United Nations was invited to mediate in the quarrel; it proposed a plebiscite to ascertain the opinion of Kashmiris.

India and Pakistan agreed upon a ceasefire towards the end of 1948 under the aegis of the UN Mission, even though India refused to conduct the plebiscite till the time Kashmir had been cleared of 'irregulars'. The plebiscite, we are aware, has not yet taken place and the part occupied by the guerrilla warriors has come to be designated as 'Pakistan occupied Kashmir' by India and as 'independent Kashmir' by Pakistan. Frictions and tensions continue and the two nations have come to blows on several occasions over Kashmir, a 'constant reminder of the difficulties that marked the births of the new states' (Stein 2010: 358).

The quarrel over Kashmir, unfortunately, has meant that a lot of the official discourse in India and Pakistan has centred on making an enemy out of the other. This in turn has governed discussions on national security and generated a race for nuclear self-sufficiency and compatibility. It has also coloured ideas of the 'majority' about minorities, and impeded effective collaboration between the two states, much required for 'a better South Asia based on mutual understanding and cooperation' (Bose and Jalal 1998: 244).

The immediate problem that faced the two states after independence was an exchange of population. In the course of just four months, 12 million people crossed borders. The movement of refugees was more dramatic in the case of Punjab; there was also a clearer policy and agreement with regard to the 'refugees' and the people crossing over. Re-settling of the people who had crossed over became a major problem that the new governments had to pay immediate attention to, and the situation was made tense and complicated by the issue of 'abducted women' which was turned into a question of national honour by both the states. Consequently, their recovery by the 'rightful' state became an honourable duty (Das 1995a).

The figures mentioned by a civil servant, who had access to the files of the 'Fact Finding Organization' on communal violence set up by the Indian state, referred to 12,000 Hindu or Sikh women 'recovered' from Punjab and the frontier regions of Pakistan and 8,000 Muslim women from the districts of eastern Punjab, between 1947 and 1949 (Khosla cited in Das 1995a: 59). Sexual and reproductive violence to which these women had been subjected was transposed from the family on to the nation and came to be 'doubly articulated' in the domains of kinship and politics. As a result, 'the political programme of creating the two nations of India and Pakistan was inscribed upon the bodies of women' (Das 1995a: 56). In many cases, years lapsed between the abduction and the 'recovery'; in that time, some women had converted to a different religion, had married their abductors and had had children with them. The 'recovery', therefore, ravaged the fragile security that these women had somehow managed to find in their anguished lives and forced them to go back to their natal families where they were not welcome.

India never formulated a definite policy with regard to the status and rights of the peoples who moved from eastern Bengal, and it was not until October 1952 that India and Pakistan required the cross-border travellers to have proper documents to prove their citizenship (Rahman and Schendel 2003: 557). Indeed, for both India and East Pakistan, establishing the border on the ground was as much of a challenge as regulating movement of people across it. The movement of people on the eastern border has been continuous; some starting well before the partition, with certain periods of greater flows. Moreover, not all were refugees in the strict sense of the term; there were cross-border settlers—brides joining their husbands in villages on the other side of the border—cross-border labour migrants and border-refugees (ibid.: 556–57).

Literature on the reverse flow of refugees from West Bengal to East Bengal and later Bangladesh is almost non-existent. This is partly the result of the exclusive focus of the Pakistan state on refugees to West Pakistan and partly because of 'a disinterest in the refugee problematic in post-1971 Bangladesh' (ibid.: 555). Moreover, studies on the partition take into account only the movement of population in the two partitioned provinces of Punjab and Bengal; very few scholars have looked at provinces such as Sind, Bihar, Assam or Rajasthan, which witnessed considerable migration (Ansari 1994; Baruah 1997; Copland 1998; Ghosh 1997).

Prior to the partition, some groups and families in eastern Bengal had been given the option of choosing their country. After independence, however, the harassed Indian state attempted to discourage the migration of non-Muslims from East to West Bengal (Tan and Kudaisya 2000: 144). They were forced to pledge their allegiance to Pakistan and offered 'temporary and limited relief rather than permanent rehabilitation'. This, of course, has 'not deterred migration from Eastern Bengal' and the presence of over 8 million refugees has 'irrevocably shaped' West Bengal's political economy and popular imagination and 'is seen to be symptomatic of Bengali decline' (Chatterjee, 'Interrogating Victimhood'). The partition, therefore, affirms Nilanjana Chatterjee, is much more than an association 'with national and personal trauma' for many Bengalis.

Evidently, the partition and its accompanying violence need to be understood not just in terms of 'neutral' facts and figures of 'victims' and refugees. Moreover, the 'systematic disconnect' between elite nationalist discourse and popular constructions, and the 'unthinkability' of the violence of partition within the elite discourse ended up conferring on the post-independence states 'the sovereign power of deciding on life and death'. Practices of knowledge and power produced the 'refugee' ambivalently, 'as a figure of right and an object of governmentality' (Naqvi 2007: 45). Equally, the event marked lives and families and moulded memories in modes that can barely be recovered by history.

The physical slaughter and the feeling of being torn asunder, the disease, malnutrition and death, and often callous and cruel treatment meted out to 'refugees' in their 'new countries', for long confined to the domain of art—of films and literature—is only recently being sought to be recovered by historians and anthropologists. They focus 'on the woes of divided families, the deepening nostalgia for places people lived in for generations forcibly abandoned, and the agony of parting with friends and neighbours' (Butalia 1998; Chakrabarty 2002; Das 1995a; Hasan 1997: 29; Menon and Bhasin 1998; Pandey 2001).

Chronology of India In World Affairs, 1947–1971

Year	Leading Events
Oct '48	The three new dominions, India, Pakistan and Ceylon, are first represented at a Commonwealth Prime Ministers' Conference in London.
Jan '49	New Delhi conference on Indonesia.
Apr '49	Commonwealth Prime Ministers' Conference evolves formula accepting republican form of government as compatible with membership. India affirms desire to maintain Commonwealth membership after adopting republican constitution.
Jan '50	Commonwealth Foreign Ministers' meeting in Colombo, the first of 3 conferences in 1950 which prepare the Colombo Plan for Cooperative Economic Development in South and South-East Asia; the Plan comes into force in July' 51.
Apr '50	Liaquat–Nehru Pact concluded to protect minorities in India and Pakistan.

Year	Leading Events
May '50	At Baguio Conference, India, Pakistan and Ceylon join Australia, Indonesia, the Philippines and Thailand in framing general recommendations on economic and cultural cooperation.
Jun '51	First major shipment of US aid to India as part of $190 million loan for purchase of American grain requested by India during food crisis.
Sept '51	Japanese Peace Treaty.
1953	Vijaya Lakshmi Pandit, of India, elected President of the Eighth Session of the UN General Assembly, the first South Asian and the first woman so to serve.
Apr–May '54	First Conference of South East Asian Prime Ministers (representing Burma, Ceylon, India, Indonesia, Pakistan) convened in Colombo to discuss problems of common interest including peace in Indo–China, recognition of Peoples' Republic of China by UN, and ending of colonialism in Tunisia and Morocco.
Apr '54	Sino–Indian Agreement on Tibet.
May '54	Pakistan signs 'Mutual Defense Assistance Agreement' with the US.
1954–70	Indian involvement in Indo–China.
Sept '54	Pakistan signs South East Asia Collective Defense Treaty at Manila, joining US, UK, France, Australia, New Zealand, Thailand, and the Philippines in establishing South East Asia Treaty Organization (SEATO).
Dec. '54	Bogor Conference of South East Asian Prime Ministers makes arrangements for convening of Afro-Asian Conference, first proposed at Colombo Powers Conference, April–May '54.
Apr '55	First Afro-Asian Conference held at Bandung, Indonesia, with Afghanistan, Ceylon, India, Nepal and Pakistan among the 29 nations attending.
May '55	Simla Conference called by India at US suggestion to discuss use of proposed $200 million US fund for Asian regional development. Colombo Plan members, except for Burma and Ceylon, attend. Conference rejects plan for permanent Colombo Plan secretariat and demands that aid programs remain bilateral.
Sept '55	Bagdad Pact.
Mar '59	India, Pakistan, Nepal and Ceylon among 14 nations attending Asian Productivity Conference in Tokyo.
Mar '59	Pakistan signs Bilateral Agreement of Cooperation with the US.
Mar '59	Dalai Lama flees Tibet and is given asylum in India.
Apr '60	World Court decides in favour of India in blocking passage of Portuguese troops across Indian territory to reach Portuguese enclaves occupied by Indian dissidents.
Sept '60	India and Pakistan sign Indus Waters Treaty.
1961–62	India one of 14 nations taking part in the International Conference on the Settlement of the Laotian Question, which opened at Geneva, 12 May, '61. India a signatory to the Declaration on Neutrality of Laos issued at the conclusion of the Conference, 23 July '62.
Sept' 61	Afghanistan breaks off diplomatic relations with Pakistan, following intensification of dispute over 'Pakhtunistan'. Diplomatic relations resumed May '63.

Year	Leading Events
Sept '61	Belgrade Conference of Non-Aligned States attended by 25 countries, including Afghanistan, Ceylon, India and Nepal.
Nov '61	India occupies Goa; UN Security Council fails to censure India because of Soviet veto.
1962	Sir Muhammad Zafrulla Khan, of Pakistan, elected President of the Seventeenth Session of the UN General Assembly.
Sept–Nov '62	Sino–Indian border war.
Oct '62	US grants Indian request for military aid.
Mar '63	Sino–Pakistani boundary treaty.
Jul '64	Establishment of R.C.D.
Oct '64	Second Conference of Non-Aligned Nations held in Cairo; Afghanistan, Ceylon, India, and Nepal among 47 nations represented.
Jan–June '65	Armed clash between India and Pakistan in the Rann of Kutch.
Aug–Sept '65	Indo–Pakistan conflict. UN Security Council resolution demanding ceasefire is accepted by both parties.
Jan '66	Tashkent Agreement.
Apri '67	US State Department announces it will not resume military assistance to either India or Pakistan (excepting spare parts for equipment already acquired).
Apr '68	Pakistan informs US of intention not to renew 10-year lease on communications base near Peshawar, established in 1959.
Jun '68	USSR begins arms aid to Pakistan.
Sept '69	Rabat Islamic Summit Conference. India denied a seat after Pakistani objections.
1970	Sir Muhammad Zafrulla Khan elected President, International Court of Justice. First South Asian so to serve.
Mar '70	First Islamic Conference of Foreign Ministers held in Jidda. 22 Islamic countries represented, including Afghanistan and Pakistan.
Sept '70	Third Summit Conference of Non-Aligned Nations held at Lusaka (Zambia); attended by representatives of 54 countries including Afghanistan, Ceylon, India and Nepal.
Oct '70	US announces intention to sell replacements of certain military equipment to Pakistan, as an exception to general policy.
Dec. '70	Second Islamic Conference of Foreign Ministers held in Karachi. Afghanistan and Pakistan among the 23 nations represented.
Mar. '71	Civil war erupts in East Pakistan. Bangladesh secedes and forms government in exile in India. Nearly 10 million refugees flee to India by December.
Dec. '71	US suspends all future licenses for arms shipments to India and cancels licenses for arms already approved. Indo–Pakistani war resulting in Indian victory, freedom for Bangladesh and overthrow of Yahya Khan. Soviet Union and China give firm support to Indian and Pakistani positions respectively. US officially neutral, but leans toward Pakistani position.

If 'implicit logics of official commensuration with the violence of the mass' informed the potential and actual movement of populations (Naqvi 2007: 45), physical violence was contained by the new governments with 'surprising speed'. This fact, for some scholars, 'testifies to the resilience of the structures of the colonial state on which the two successor states had established themselves' (Metcalf and Metcalf 2003: 219).

A different kind of violence struck India at the beginning of 1948—the assassination of Mahatma Gandhi, the 'father of the nation' on 30 January by Nathuram Godse, a member of the Rashtriya Swayam Sevak Sangh (RSS). Gandhi was shot while he was leading a prayer meeting in Delhi. 'The light has gone out of our lives and there is darkness everywhere', stated Nehru in a radio broadcast as he announced the death of Gandhiji to the nation (Nehru 1950: 17–19). The news was met with grief and a deep sense of loss all over India. Gandhi, however, had become increasingly marginal to India's political life since the end of the Second World War.

The assassination made visible the presence of Hindu nationalist politics that had its roots in the cow protection movement of the late nineteenth century and had assumed institutional form with the founding of the Hindu Mahasabha in 1915. Subdued and often co-opted by the Congress-led nationalist struggle, Hindu nationalism bounced back with a vengeance in the 1980s and 90s as we shall soon see.

THE CONSTITUTION: DEMOCRACY, MAJORITY AND 'MINORITIES'

'WE, THE PEOPLE OF INDIA' proclaimed the preamble to the Constitution, have solemnly resolved to constitute India into 'a SOVEREIGN, DEMOCRATIC, REPUBLIC' and to secure to all her citizens 'JUSTICE, social, economic and political; LIBERTY, of thought, expression, belief, faith and worship; EQUALITY, of status and opportunity'. The new Constitution came into force on 26 January 1950, a day that commemorated the Lahore declaration of 'Purna Swaraj' 20 years earlier. 'For the first time in their history', writes Rajeev Bhargava, a large number of distinct individuals and groups 'became the people of a single book, one that reflects their commitment to protect their mutual rights and which articulates a collective identity' (Bhargava [2008] 2010: 1). Following Bhargava, we will examine the Constitution as a 'moral document' in order to understand the possible meanings and implications of its conceptual structure regarding 'rights', 'citizenship', 'democracy' and 'minority' (ibid.: 4–5).

India inherited the unitary central apparatus and the 'international personality' of British India as well as the civil bureaucracy, the military and the police (Bose and Jalal 1998: 203–04). The 'trinity of a charismatic national leadership, a mass party, and effective civil services, plus the already functioning legislatures, executive and courts, gave representative democracy a head start' in India (Austin 1999: 17). The military had traditions of obedience to civilian rule; the judiciary was 'advanced', there were flourishing universities and scientific establishments, and a partly industrialized economy, all of which would enable a completion of the 'modernization' of India (Stein 2010: 358). The earlier federal structure continued, with power to be shared between the centre and the provinces, now designated states. About 200 articles of the Government of India Act of 1935 were incorporated in the new Constitution (Metcalf and Metcalf 2003: 227–28).

The Congress government, under the aegis of Nehru—'the English-educated Brahmin patrician

ORGANIZATION OF INDIA, CONSTITUTION OF 1950

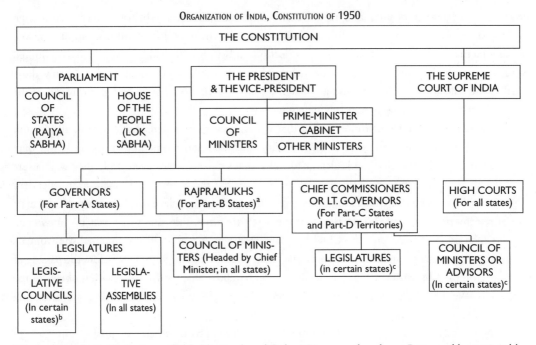

Notes: a) Jammu & Kashmir was headed by an elected Sadar-i-Riyasat, rather than a Rajpramukh appointed by the president, b) These included Bihar, Bombay, Madras, Mysore, Punjab, Uttar Pradesh and West Bengal in 1950; subsequently Councils were added in Andhra (Later Andhra Pradesh) and Jammu & Kashmir. c) Creation of Councils/legislatures to be at the discretion of Parliament.

Major constitutional changes since 1950: With the States Reorganization Amendment of 1956, the distinctions between Part-A and Part-B States were eliminated; these became simply 'States', while Part-C States and Part-D Territories were thereafter constituted as Union Territories.

from Allahabad', an 'impatient democrat' and 'national nanny' (Austin 1999: 17), decided on a system of parliamentary democracy, a 'Westminster style of government' for the new, 'modern' India. The Central Legislative Council got transformed into a bicameral Parliament with an upper house (Rajya Sabha) and a lower house (Lok Sabha). The Lok Sabha was to be composed of representatives elected on the basis of universal adult franchise. The leader of the majority party in the Lok Sabha was to become the Prime Minister and head the new government at the centre for a period of five years. The same pattern was replicated in the federal states, where the bicameral legislative assemblies were to have elected representatives in the lower house, to be headed by chief ministers, leaders of the respective parties that had won majorities in the states.

Elements of the presidential system were retained, perhaps in deference to the 'Right' within the Congress, Vallabhbhai Patel and the first President, Rajendra Prasad. The President was made the titular head of state with governors as his representatives in each of the federal states. The President was to be elected by members of an electoral college composed of the elected members of both houses of Parliament and elected members of the legislative assemblies in the states. As indicated in Chapter 8, a clause in the 1935 Act that gave the President the power to dissolve the elected government at the centre and in the states in special cases of crisis and 'emergency' was incorporated in the Constitution of free India.

The proclamation of India as a 'republic' ended her allegiance to the British Crown even though she continued to form a part of the British Commonwealth. The provision of universal adult franchise made for a major break with the colonial past. Elections in British India had been conducted on limited franchise, on the 'contingent principle of inclusion' (Dahl 1989); these were confined to only those qualified to rule and to claim citizenship (Bhargava [2008] 2010: 16). The elected governments of the colonial period, therefore, were not truly representative.

The framers of the Constitution agreed that if India was to be a democratic nation, all its adult citizens had to have the right to vote. This decision was bold and momentous in more senses than one—apart from the fact that the leaders made all Indians equal citizens even while they were aware that not all were ready to exercise the right to vote responsibly, the women's movement in independent India never had to fight for women's right to vote (After women's franchise had been proposed by male social reformers and Congress leaders before the 1919 Reforms, the issue was taken up by women leaders such as Sarojini Naidu. The Child Marriage Restraint Act of 1929 invigourated the women's struggle and women's organisations all over India pressed for women's right to vote before the passing of the Governmet of India Act, 1935. For details, see Sinha 2007, chapter 4). The opening phrase of the Preamble, 'We the people', underscores this stress on the 'people' as collectively owning and belonging to the nation-state of India.

The Preamble to the Constitution commits India to certain basic principles—justice comes first in the list, followed by liberty, equality, fraternity and dignity of the individual. The Constitution of India, 'a monumental tome of 315 articles' was crafted in the course of 'intense debates' in the Constituent Assembly that met between 1947 and 1949 (Jaffrelot 2005: 110). It established a set of principles and institutions that have governed India's political life till the present. A brief look into these debates will offer a better understanding of the values as well as the contesting visions that undergird the Constitution.

What are the fundamental concepts that were debated and what was finally included in the Constitution? India's 'original contribution' to Constitution-making, it has been stated, lies in its immense capacity of 'accommodation, the ability to reconcile, to harmonize and to make work without changing their content apparently incompatible concepts' (Austin 1966). The apparently 'incompatible concepts' are those of legal plurality that relates directly to individual and collective rights, and of 'compensatory discrimination' that puts: the notion of liberal equality under severe strain. For some scholars, this simultaneous commitment to 'incompatible concepts' makes India's stance on equality and secularism contradictory.

The Indian Constitution grants equal rights to all its citizens and 'collective' rights to communities. It also recognizes no distinction of caste, class, religion, gender and so on, in the rights it accords to all its citizens but has special provisions of 'positive discrimination' for members of 'backward castes and classes'. The Constitution provides for a Uniform Code of Civil Procedure (Uniform Civil Code) and a Uniform Code of Criminal Procedure (Uniform Criminal Code) that apply to all citizens irrespective of their religion. At the same time, it also accepts personal laws—laws pertaining to inheritance, marriage, divorce, maintenance and adoption—for minority communities, communities demarcated on the basis of religion. These provisions have been at the root of severe debates and bitter fights and have provided the ground for mobilization and friction. Let us unpack their underlying principles and implications.

CONSTITUENT ASSEMBLIES OF INDIA AND PAKISTAN
NUMBER OF SEATS AS OF 31 DECEMBER, 1947

INDIA	Total Seats	Seats Reserved for Muslims	PAKISTAN	Total Seats	Seats Reserved for Non-Muslims
United Provinces	55	7	East Bengal	44	13
Madras	49	4	West Punjab	22	5[c]
Bihar	36	5	Sind	5	-
Bombay	21	2	N.W.Frontier Province	3	-
West Bengal	19	4	Baluchistan	1	-
C.P. & Berar	17	1			
East Punjab	12[a]	4	PROVINCIAL TOTAL	75	18
Orissa	9	-	TOTAL FOR		
Assam	8	2	PRINCELY STATES	4	-
Delhi	1	-			
Ajmer-Merwara	1	-	GRAND TOTAL	79	18
Coorg	1	-			
PROVINCIAL TOTAL	229	29			
TOTAL FOR PRINCELY STATES[b]	70	-			
GRAND TOTAL	299	29			

Notes: a) Includes 2 seats reserved for Sikhs,

b) Excludes Hyderabad, Jammu & Kashmir and lesser states which had not yet acceded to India, or for which accession was regarded as provisional.

c) Includes 3 seats reserved for Hindus and 2 seats reserved for Sikhs.

The genesis of 'personal laws' can be traced back to the time of the first Governor-General Warren Hastings who, in his intent to let the natives be governed by the 'customs of their own land', made a clear division between the civil, criminal and 'family' law and left family law beyond the jurisdiction of the English courts of justice. The 'natives' were classified into 'Gentoos' (Hindus) and 'Mahometans' and their separate law codes drawn up and codified accordingly (Chapter 2). Over time, family law became a crucial marker of 'community' identity and, in the charged context of the partition, an essential element for the protection of the rights of minority communities and for the respect of religious difference.

The issue of retention and reform of personal law generated intense debates in the Constituent Assembly. In the end, the assembly recognized four communities that could have their separate personal law—Muslims, Christians, Parsis and Hindus. These communities have their family law codified separately from the main body of civil law. The four codes again, are a 'mixture of scriptural sanctions, heterogeneous customs and practices' and 'precepts advanced and established through the political manoeuvrings of powerful spokespersons belonging to dominant groups within these communities' (Sen 2002: 485–86).

Needless to say, personal laws are both ambiguous and anomalous—their operation has involved the state and the judiciary in innumerable controversies. Family laws are called personal laws in India, because they relate to the sphere of 'personal relations' and they are 'person-specific' (ibid.: 485). In matters that come under the jurisdiction of personal laws, members of the four communities as Indian citizens have the right to abide by the Uniform Civil Code or their personal law. The Constitution does not treat personal laws as 'religion' even though the collective 'community' to which they are granted is identified by religion.

The Indian Constitution gives protection to different religions and religious groups by means of religious rights within the 'Fundamental Rights' it grants to all its citizens. At the same time, the Constitution does not equate religion with freedom of conscience; neither does it treat the freedom of religion as an absolute one. It is subject to regulation by the state (Pal 2001: 25). In effect, a powerful and autonomous judiciary scrutinizes the practice and propagation of religion and maintains the formal separation of religion and politics. In addition, the state distances itself from all religions; it professes to 'protect' all religions and maintain neutrality and equal distance from them. This is the cornerstone of the Indian state's practice of 'secularism'. Viewed thus, personal laws ratify rather than nullify the constitutional commitment to secularism. It bears pointing out in this connection that the word 'secular' was added to the Preamble of the Indian Constitution only in 1976; over 25 years after the Constitution had been in force.

Article 44 of the Indian Constitution mandates the state to 'endeavour to secure for the citizens a uniform civil code throughout the territory of India'. The underlying assumption is that a uniform code will create a sense of 'Indianness' and strengthen national unity (ibid.: 27). Article 44, however, is a part of the Directive Principles of State Policy, not of Fundamental Rights. This effectively means that it is not enforceable by law, even though it is considered to be 'fundamental' in the governance of the country.

Personal laws are a colonial heritage and are immensely problematic on account of the fact that they demarcate communities on the basis of 'religion'. At the same time, the 'moral' principle that underlies their retention is that of responsiveness to the needs of 'many varying communities of faith' in India (Pal 2001: 25). Personal laws challenge the Indian legal system to treat all citizens fairly and to handle 'difference' in a responsible and responsive manner. Apart from the muddles this 'legal plurality' generates, 'personal laws' often contravene the full exercise of their rights by women as citizens. This became clear in one of the most publicized and hotly debated cases surrounding personal law, that of Shah Bano in the late 1970s and early 1980s.

Given the fact that personal laws have become critical markers of the political identity of the community, no government has dared to 'reform' the personal laws of 'minority communities'. The matter had been debated in the Constituent Assembly and discussed by Prime Minister Jawaharlal Nehru and Law Minister B. R. Ambedkar, both of whom considered the uniform code to be an instrument of modernization, secularization and national unity. But in the fraught political situation of post-partition independent India, they decided to reform Hindu personal law first and proposed a comprehensive Hindu Civil Code.

The purpose behind this code, we need to remember, was to unify and homogenize an extremely heterogeneous community in order to consolidate the power of the state and not bring about gender equality. Introducing a discussion on the Bill in the Select Committee of the Constituent Assembly, B. R. Ambedkar stated categorically that, this bill, which wanted 'to codify the rules of Hindu Law' that were 'scattered in innumerable decisions of the High Courts and of the Privy Council' constituted a 'bewildering motley to the common man and [gave] constant rise to litigation ...' (Constituent Assembly Legislative Debates included in Ambedkar 1995, 14: 5).

With a similar objective, leaders of the Muslim community had also introduced important changes in the application of the *sharia*, and the legislations of 1937 and 1939 had granted Muslim women the right to divorce under certain conditions and protect them from the arbitrary use of the power to divorce by husbands (Agnes 1999: 77). However, since marriage in Islam is taken to be a 'contract' and hence dissoluble, unlike the Hindu or Christian notion of marriage as indissoluble, these legislations did not take up the matter of whether a divorced wife had a right to alimony.

The comprehensive Hindu Code was discussed and debated over several years (1941–55) before the Hindu Code Bill was passed. The Uniform Civil Code was invoked both by those in favour and those opposed to the Hindu Civil Code (Everett 1981; Parashar 1992). The opponents of the Hindu Civil Code, in particular, pointed to the unfairness of targeting one community for reform and let the minorities, especially the Muslims, have the 'special privilege' of personal laws.

Unfortunately, the controversy that surrounded the Shah Bano case also came to revolve around the 'special privilege' of a minority community. Certain sections of the Muslim community, on the other hand, used the negative statements about Islamic law made in the verdict by 'Hindu' judges of the Supreme Court to try and forge a 'community in danger'. Shah Bano, a 76-year-old Muslim woman's recourse to the Uniform Code of Criminal Procedure in order to seek alimony from her lawyer husband who had divorced her after over 50 years of matrimony, got transformed into a battle between certain sections of the 'majority' and the 'minority' communities, and provided the ground for strong political mobilization along 'communal' lines.

The concept of secular rights allowed sections of the majority community to pose as progressive and nationalist and urge for the implementation of the Uniform Code. Sections of the 'minority community' drew upon the 'cultural capital' embodied in personal rights to subordinate the right of an individual female member of the community. 'Minority privilege', aptly remarks Samita Sen, implies 'minority male privilege'. Clearly, men were the spokespersons of the community, just as in British India, and the 'interest of the community' continued to be identified with male interests (Sen 2002: 489).

In a succinct analysis of 'cultural rights' and the controversy around the Shah Bano case, Veena Das poses a potent question. She asks that when a community's 'right to its own culture' includes 'the right to legally govern its members in the sphere of the family', what recourse is left for the vulnerable women or children, 'who may be oppressed by the pathologies of the family', for redress? (1995b: 105). Without the alternative of opting out of the community or of rejecting or criticizing some of its norms, such women and children are coerced to fall in line with the 'community'.

How then should we react to the presence of personal laws? This was an extremely difficult question that the women's movement faced during the Shah Bano affair, and emerged more mature out of it. Pressing for a uniform code rejects legal plurality, an ideologically commendable even if practically uncomfortable way of dealing with 'difference' and allows for forcible standardization; accepting personal laws permits the 'community' excessive power over matters of family that often puts women's rights in jeopardy—a paradox.

What is required is a sensitive manoeuvring of 'personal laws' in order to ensure 'justice' to the highest degree possible. And the very valuable work of Flavia Agnes demonstrates that Muslim women and 'a concerned and sensitive judiciary' have carved out a space for the protection of women's rights from what appeared to be 'an erroneously conceived, badly formulated, and blatantly discriminatory statute'—the Muslim Women (Protection of Rights on Divorce) Act, 1986. What has enabled judges to carve out this space is a clause in the act that stipulated that a divorced woman is entitled to 'a reasonable and fair provision to be made and paid to her within the *iddat* period by her former husband'. This clause, of personal rights, has offered better protection to divorced Muslim women than Article 25 of the Uniform Criminal Code that allows destitute women the right to alimony (Agnes 2007: 308–09). And, this silent yet significant change has come about without any backlash.

Caste and Equality

For Nehru, one of the principal architects of modern India, caste was 'the symbol and embodiment of exclusiveness among the Hindus'. It had 'no place left' in 'the social organization of today'. 'If merit is the only criterion and opportunity is thrown open to everybody', he wrote in *The Discovery of India*, 'then caste loses its present day distinguishing feature, and, in fact, ends' (Nehru 1997: 520). Nehru was convinced that caste was an 'archaic' and 'parochial' institution that pertained entirely to the domain of the traditional-cultural. It was to die out with the spread of education and the growth of science and technology—in other words, with the blossoming of India as a modern nation.

For B. R. Ambedkar, head of the drafting committee of the Constitution, on the other hand, caste belonged to the domain of the social and the political, the root cause of the socio-economic backwardness of members of untouchable communities. Ambedkar and Nehru shared their vision of liberal democracy posited on individual rights. They also believed that education and employment would eventually do away with the hierarchy represented by caste. Both believed in the necessity of a strong centre—that went against the Gandhian vision of decentralized power moving up from the village level—for the uniform application of the Constitution and for implementing measures of 'modernization'. At the same time, the two liberal democrats differed on their assessment of caste.

Ambedkar tried to seek a political solution to the problem of caste. In this he diverged from Nehru who, like Gandhi, felt that caste was a matter internal to Hinduism and had to be kept out of the political arena. Ambedkar turned the colonial legacy of 'reservation' for Dalits and members of backward classes in public employment into an instrument to fight 'social injustice' and advance of the 'weak' (Bayly 1999: 270). It is interesting that the advocates of liberal democracy understood that 'equal opportunities' could be granted to all citizens only when 'conditions were equal'. They coincided on concerns of offering 'substantive' socio-political equality to all Indian citizens.

The Constitution declared the practice of 'untouchability' to be illegal. At the same time, recognition of the fact that 'conditions were not equal' prompted the framers of the Constitution to include a clause that offered particular privileges to disadvantaged groups in educational institutions run by the state, in public employment and in electoral constituencies. This was the genesis of the much-debated 'reservation' or compensatory discrimination, adopted as a temporary measure for ten years. The idea was that special privileges for a specific period of time will enable 'backward' sections of society to be at par with others and compete with them on an equal basis.

The reverse, however, has happened. More and more groups have come forward to stake claims on grounds of 'reservation' and 'backwardness' and the provision of reservation has been extended continually for subsequent periods of ten years. These groups have turned fond ideas of progress and modernity as well as anthropological notions of Sanskritization on their head. Their claims, moreover, have produced a paradoxical situation. The acceptance of the logic of caste as the primary (though not the only) ground for positive discrimination has made this specific stipulation qualify the provision of bourgeois freedom and equality granted by the Constitution (Chatterjee [1989] 1992: 207).

In addition, disharmony between a legal order committed to total equality which, at the same time, admits of the existence of a social order marked by stratification and makes provisions for the gradual erasure of social discrimination, has produced a 'legal muddle' (Galanter 1984). The clause of 'reservation' has actually enabled certain sections of Dalits and backward classes to press for greater privileges; it has also allowed members of the privileged upper classes and castes to speak in terms of bourgeois equality and merit and question 'compensatory discrimination' (Banerjee-Dube 2008: xxvii). In their view, positive discrimination is a negative force that reinforces inequality.

The fiercest battles around reservation have turned not on reservation for Dalits but for 'other backward classes', a vague category that has flared passions and produced bitter conflicts. As the category indicates, caste is taken to be a principal criterion of 'backwardness' but not the only one, which has allowed several groups to claim a 'backward' status. This 'investment in backwardness' has, in turn, occasioned an upper-caste backlash, and given leeway to parties of the Hindu Right.

The dominant notion of caste as being tied almost exclusively to ritual and religion has engendered another kind of debate with regard to the 'secular' credentials of Indian democracy. The effect of caste on Indian democracy was debated seriously in the 1960s and 1970s (Kothari 1970: 4–5, for instance), after the appointment of the first Backward Classes Commission in 1953 radicalized lower caste politics in the north (Banerjee-Dube 2008: xxvii). The commission was given the responsibility of identifying the 'backward classes' and framing a scheme for the 'reservation' of seats in legislatures and public employment for members of backward classes in north India. The commission took 'caste' to be the 'most prominent criterion' for backwardness, although not the only one; its report presented to the Constituent Assembly in 1955 produced passionate debates and was never implemented.

The appointment of the commission, however, 'constituted a milestone for the lower caste movement in north India' in that it bolstered lower caste mobilization on an 'unprecedented scale' resulting in a 'silent revolution' (Jaffrelot 2002: 227–29). The revolution has been primarily political— lower caste representation in politics has increased significantly, with a larger number of Members of Parliament and, in particular, members of the legislative assemblies in the states. The mobilization of lower castes in northern India was accompanied by economic processes, such as the 'Green Revolution' in Punjab during Indira Gandhi's rule, which produced a class of relatively wealthy middle peasants who wanted a higher social status. Indeed, a combination of the leaders of peasant and 'quota' (reservation) politics brought forth the first national alternative to the Congress in the 1977 elections. Although it did not remain in power for the full five years, this coalition demonstrated the significance of the rise of lower castes in politics.

This joint articulation of caste and politics underlined the impossibility of treating caste only as a religious institution, and produced 'a scholarly shift in emphasis from caste the system to caste the component' (Conlon 1977: 7). At the same time, the idea that caste was traditional and pertained to the domain of the 'religious-cultural' was not abandoned. The terms of the debate therefore hinged on whether caste was good or bad for Indian democracy, which in turn was posited on the belief that caste and politics belonged to two totally distinct realms. Consequently, the presence of caste in politics is tainted by illegitimacy; it causes 'deep embarrassment' since it sits uncomfortably with the 'modernist-universalist desire' to transcend narrow sectional identities (Nigam 2006: 226).

The second round of serious debates with regard to the future of the secular Indian democracy occurred in the late 1980s and early 1990s, in the wake of increased assertion in politics on the part of Dalits and members of lower castes, and the resurgence of the Hindu Right. The immediate occasion was provided by the Report of the Second Backward Classes Commission, widely known as the Mandal Commission, appointed by the Janata Government in 1978.

The commission, constituted entirely of lower caste members, regarded caste to be the 'root cause of structural inequality' and the principal factor behind the 'backwardness' of Other Backward Classes (OBCs). At the same time, it deployed educational and economic indicators along with the social one of caste to provide 'a statistical straight-point which could be used for affirmative action' (Jaffrelot 2002: 322). The objective of affirmative action was, of course, to give the OBCs access to power and not just to jobs. The commission's report suggested a 27 per cent reservation of seats for OBC students in all scientific, technical and professional institutions run by the central and state governments. The report, presented in 1980, induced the state government of Gujarat to adopt new schemes of reservation and produced the first serious riots on the issue of reservation (Baxi 1990, for instance); the central government, however, desisted from acting upon it for almost ten years.

The Janata Dal government at the centre under the premiership of V. P. Singh announced the adoption of appropriate steps for the implementation of the recommendations of the Mandal Commission towards the end of 1989. The commission had proposed quotas for 'backward castes' for recruitment in central and state governments, for private undertakings receiving financial aid from the government and for all government universities and affiliated colleges. It supplemented constitutional reservations for Scheduled Castes and Tribes set at 22.5 per cent, by introducing proportionate representation for backward castes for another 27 per cent, not included in the earlier provision. This was to bring 'quota' to the limit of 50 per cent permitted by the Constitution.

V. P. Singh did not consider his decision as being governed by the imperatives of a 'mass employment scheme', since 27 per cent represented relatively few jobs. The decision, however, aroused severe protest—on 27 September 1990 Rajeev Goswami, a student of Delhi University, set himself on fire by dousing his body with kerosene. The impassioned protest from upper and middle castes and classes against the government decision was induced by what they thought was a real threat to their long-held privileges (Banerjee-Dube 2008: xxx); the future prospect of all 'respectable employment' going away from young people with upper caste background. Rajeev Goswami's fiery protest caused horror not only because of the 'unfairness' of the government's decision, but also because with this spectacle caste 'leaked simultaneously out of the traditional world of the subaltern and the village and into the middle-class enclaves of new India' (Dirks 2001: 275).

An implicit interrogation of the consensual nature of Indian democracy and the idea of the 'majority' underlay the assertive demand for representation more in conjunction with their numbers on the part of lower castes. This 'threat' was taken seriously by parties of the Hindu Right and their campaign for a strong Hindu nation gave succour to upper caste fears. The controversy over Mandal generated a political consensus that made Hindu fundamentalism more acceptable (Dirks 2001: 276).

SECULARISM IN CRISIS

Parties of the Hindu Right, disgraced after the assassination of Gandhi by an RSS member, had been working silently from the late 1950s. The turbulent political situation of the 1980s allowed them to come to the forefront of the national political stage (Basu et al. 1993). In an attempt to gloss over severe tensions among members of the 'majority' community, they argued that the problems had stemmed from the 'pseudo-secular' stance of the Congress governments that had constantly appeased 'minority' communities, especially Muslims, and that India's problems would be solved if her citizens went back to their cultural roots, that is, Hinduism. This appeal to the 'Hindu' identity of most of its citizens transferred the animosity of the privileged groups who thought of themselves as the 'majority', from the internal other, Dalits and members of OBCs, to the external other, the 'Muslim' (Menon 2006). The internal 'Other', it bears pointing out, had been the Sikhs only a few years earlier. The assassination of Indira Gandhi by her Sikh bodyguards in 1984 had produced severe anti-Sikh riots in Delhi and other parts of India.

In a situation where the upper and middle-class urban citizens were under tremendous pressure, accentuated by problems resulting from the liberalization of the economy, the Hindu Right acquired remarkable success. Moving away completely from issues of poverty and education, it focused attention on the town of Ayodhya, where a mosque was supposed to have been constructed by the first Mughal Emperor Babur, on a temple of god Ram, whose birthplace, it is believed, is Ayodhya. This Ramjanmabhoomi-Babri Masjid controversy allowed the Vishwa Hindu Parishad (VHP) and the RSS and a conglomerate of other Right groups to gain remarkable political prominence, and through the Bharatiya Janta Party (BJP), their political wing which was a revived version of the earlier Jana Sangh, these 'cultural' Hindu nationalist organizations formed a government at the centre in 1999 and remained in power for five years.

The dual development of lower-caste affirmation and the rise of the Hindu Right to power produced rich debates on the 'crisis of secularism' in the 1990s. Intellectuals and policy planners, who were complacent that India's secular credentials were totally secure, were forced to pause and reflect on what had generated this 'crisis'. How had the working of a multi-party democracy created conditions for the rise of the Hindu Right? (Hansen 1999).

Academics and scholars dwelt insightfully on the different meanings, understandings and deployment of secularism in different democracies crisscrossed by multiple identities and difference, and pointed to the prevalence of the flawed idea that all western democracies are marked by a unique, uncomplicated separation of religion from the state (Bhargava 1998, for instance). As indicated earlier, the secular stance of the state in India implies neutrality and equal distance from all religions, not total indifference to them.

Secularism, it is important to remember, implies much more than the separation of religion from the secular institutions of government. Taking a cue from the brilliant insights of Talal Asad, we need to make a distinction between the secular as an episteme and secularism as an ideology (Asad 2003). Secularism as a doctrine posits particular understandings of religion, ethics and politics and introduces a moral hierarchy. This normative element of secularism has generated a variety of responses, ranging from a total negation of it through a critique of it as something western and hence alien, to an insistence that its context-specific genealogy does not disqualify its global relevance. The rich debates in India reflected serious engagement with all these distinct stances (see Bhargava 1998).

The desirability of caste for democracy became a focus of the debate once again. While some saw in lower-caste affirmation and 'reservation' a positive use of caste identity in a struggle against oppression (Betéille 1992; Galanter [1989] 1992; Kothari 1990, 1994), others were alarmed by the divisive impact of articulated caste consciousness threatening the integrity of the nation (Kumar 1994; Srinivas et al. 1990).

The debate, of course, did not remain confined to the academic arena in the charged political situation marked by bitter contests over the Shah Bano case, the passing of the Muslim Women (Protection of Rights on Divorce) Act, 1986, the opening of the lock of the Ram temple in the disputed site of the Babri Masjid in Ayodhya, flared passions over the proposed implementation of the recommendations of the Mandal Commission, the destruction of the Babri Masjid on 6 December 1992, and finally, the capture of power at the centre by parties of the Hindu Right in 1999. These political developments eventually fuelled the massacre of Godhra in Gujarat in 2002.

On 27 February 2002, some Muslims, it was alleged, had attacked the Sabarmati Express that was carrying Hindu pilgrims returning from Ayodhya, at the Godhra railway station in Gujarat. This incident provoked widespread attacks on Muslims in Ahmedabad and other places in Gujarat, and brought back 'secularism' as a critical theme of discussion (Dingwaney Needham and Sunder Rajan 2007, for instance).

Although the success of the Congress and its allies (the United Progressive Alliance) in the general elections in April 2004 against the BJP-led National Democratic Alliance caused relief to many and was viewed as providing 'the crucial breathing space' within which a different secular politics could be articulated (ibid.: Preface), Indian secularism remains a hotly debated and highly controversial issue. The questions that challenge scholars and policymakers are whether the programme of Indian secularism has offered the solution it was envisioned to offer to a multi-religious Indian polity, and whether and how far secularism, instead of being the solution, is itself the problem (Nandy 1990, for instance).

CENTRE–STATE RELATIONS

'India's need for a federal system', argues Jalal, 'was more an imperative than a political choice' (Jalal 1995: 161). This is on account of the existence of a 'multitude of languages and dialects' in addition to a wide range of cultural diversities. Yet, in Jalal's understanding, India's 'early state managers' were more concerned about making 'central powers commensurate with the goal of an integrated and united India' than with adopting a 'genuinely federal system' (ibid.). This is partly true.

Chronology of Major Events and Enactments Relating to Official Languages and Organization of Linguistic States and Provinces

Year	Leading Events
INDIA	
1920	Cong. Party sets up 'Congress Provinces' based mainly on language; demands parallel reconstitution of British India.
1950	Constitution establishes Hindi in Devanagari script as the official language, while allowing continuing use of English for official purposes for 15 years. The 8th Schedule recognizes 14 major Indian languages: Assamese, Bengali, Gujarati, Hindi, Kannada, Kashmiri, Malayalam, Marathi, Oriya, Punjabi, Sanskrit, Tamil, Telugu, and Urdu.
1953	Creation of Telugu-speaking Andhra state.
1953	States Reorganization Commission established to consider creation of linguistic states; report (1955) recommends major changes.
1956	Linguistic reorganization of states reduces number of states from 27 to 14, plus 6 territories.
1957	Official Language Commission recommends increasing use of Hindi for official purposes, but fails to endorse changeover from English by 1965.
1960	Bombay State divided into linguistic states of Gujarat and Maharashtra.
1961	Chief Ministers' Conference approves '3-Language Formula' providing for study of Hindi, another Indian language, and English in secondary schools; the plan endorsed by National Integration Conference.
1963	Official Languages Act provides for continuation of English for official purposes beyond 15 year period originally prescribed.
1966	Punjab Reorganization Bill sets up new state of Haryana, leaving truncated Punjab with Punjabi-speaking majority.
1967	Constitutional Amendment adds Sindhi to list of major recognized Indian languages.
1967	Union Education Minister states Government in principle accepts that regional languages should be used for education in all stages and subjects.
1967	Official Languages (Amendment) Bill and accompanying Resolution provides for English for communication between Union and states not having adopted Hindi as state language and also between such states; regulates interim use of Hindi and English for intra-government purposes at Union level; provides for continuing use of both languages for official documents.
PAKISTAN AND BANGLADESH	
1955	Essentially linguistic provinces of West Pakistan amalgamated into a single unit.
1956	Constitution establishes both Urdu and Bengali as official languages, while providing for official use of English for 20 years.
1962	New Constitution establishes Bengali and Urdu as national languages; limits official use of English to 10 years.

Year	Leading Events
1969	Government proposes to require teaching of both Urdu and Bengali in East and West Pakistan; to require government officials to achieve proficiency in both by 1973; and to abolish English as official language by 1975.
1970	Linguistic provinces restored in West Pakistan.
1971	Linguistic differences between East and West Pakistan are among reasons for breakaway of Bangladesh.

AFGHANISTAN

1936	Pushtu declared official language; Persian remains, in fact, language of administration, higher education, and literature.

CEYLON-SRI LANKA

1951	Official Languages Commission created to consider means of adopting Sinhalese and Tamil as official languages.
1952	Ministry of Education initiates policy of replacing English by Sinhalese and Tamil in Jr. and Sr. Secondary Schools.
1956	Official Language Act makes Sinhalese sole official language.
1957	Bandaranaike-Chlevanayakam Pact to allow Tamil as administrative language of N. and E. Provinces. Later repudiated by Prime Minister Bandaranaike under pressure of 'Sinhalese only' advocates.
1958	Tamil Language (Special Provisions) Act provides for use of Tamil in education, public service entrance exams, and administration in the N. and E. Provinces.
1966	First regulations to put into effect 1958 legislation for use of Tamil.

In the context of the partition, Nehru and the Congress were afraid of total fragmentation in the political system that would prevent a powerful centre from 'determining India's profile in the world at large' (Stein 2010: 361). Moreover, Nehru and Ambedkar were both in favour of a strong centre that could ensure proper formulation and implementation of policies on education, economy and development at a national level. This led them to abandon the Gandhian scheme of a decentralized federal structure where the exercise of power moved up starting from the village level. Other options for a federal structure with greater autonomy for the states were also ignored.

For political theorists, such as Atul Kohli, political arrangements in the early phase of independent India directed largely by an educated nationalist elite, enabled the state to 'govern (that is, the capacity to promote development and to accommodate diverse interests)' (Kohli 1990: 5). From the mid-1960s, widespread political activism outside established political channels has not only led to violence, but has increased the state's incapacity to deal with the pressing problems of law and order, corruption and poverty. A strong centre, in such a view, is crucial and desirable for the proper governance of the country.

The Constitution called India 'Bharat' and described it as a 'Union of States' consisting of different kinds of territories derived from the colonial past—British Indian provinces, now designated states, princely states that were often coerced to accede and old and new centrally administered regions, such as Delhi. There was a growing demand that states be reorganized in accordance with language and cultural affinities, a demand that had a lot to do with Gandhi's reforms in the Congress organization along linguistic lines in 1920, and had encouraged Telugu speakers of the Madras province to form an Andhra Pradesh Committee. Earlier, a strong movement among Oriya (Odia) speakers divided between

Bengal and Madras presidencies and the Central Provinces in the British administrative structure, for unification, had led to the formation of Orissa in 1936 (Chapters 5 and 6).

Nehru accepted the legitimacy of the demands, but was worried that it would lead to the 'Balkanisation' of India, signifying thereby that the demands had the potency of allowing the division of India into fragments, often hostile to each other, as was the case of the Balkan Peninsula that was formerly under Ottoman rule, but split into different states over the nineteenth and twentieth centuries. Nehru stalled the reorganization of states on a linguistic basis, until the death by fast of the Andhra leader Potti Sriramalu in December 1952 made the reorganization necessary. Four states came into being in the south: Andhra Pradesh (Telugu speakers); Tamil Nadu (Tamil speakers); Karnataka out of earlier Mysore with primarily Kannada speakers and Kerala that united Malayalam speakers of Travancore and Cochin with parts of the former Madras Presidency.

This was the beginning of a full-fledged reorganization—a States Reorganization Commission was set up, and the implementation of its report produced a re-ordered India with 14 states divided on the basis of language in 1956. In addition to the 14 states, there were six small union territories governed directly from Delhi. The Nehru government did not touch the Bombay Presidency and Punjab. Bombay Presidency had Gujarati and Marathi speakers spread roughly over the north and the south; but the city of Bombay had a mixed population with Gujaratis forming the dominant group of traders, merchants and industrialists and the Marathi speakers composing the working class. A powerful movement soon began for a separate state of Maharashtra with two newly established political parties backing the claim. A series of deadly riots in Bombay city compelled the centre to separate Gujarat and Maharashtra in 1960.

Punjab posed a trickier problem to handle. Here, the language Punjabi was also closely tied to the identity of a 'religious' community, the Sikhs. The issue therefore was not just of separating the Hindi-speaking part of Punjab from its Punjabi-speaking part since the Sikhs prevailed in the Punjabi-speaking part. The Akali Dal of the Sikhs demanded a Punjabi-speaking state, which came dangerously close to the demand for a separate Sikh homeland. Understandably, Nehru was totally opposed to the creation of a state based on religious identity. After his death, a separation did take place, apparently on linguistic lines in 1966. The Punjabi-speaking part became Punjab, and the Hindi-speaking areas were divided into Haryana and Himachal Pradesh. This, however, did not resolve the problem of the Sikh homeland; the demand assumed a virulent form during Indira Gandhi's rule, largely on account of an inflexibility and highhandedness on the part of the centre.

The tussle between a strong centre and states that want greater autonomy has been a constant feature of Indian democracy. It is probably inevitable, given the magnitude of the population and the immense diversity of culture. The functioning of a multi-party democracy has meant that governments in the states have often been formed by parties different from the one at the centre, which has induced a further scramble for the sharing of power and resources and have brought the states in competition with one another. The North-East of the country, virtually neglected by the centre, has seen forceful struggles for self-determination as well as for greater support from the centre. These problems bring us back to another paradox—a strong centre, viewed by many to be essential for the proper governance of the country, often fails to deal with diverse interests with sensitivity.

In the case of both India and Pakistan, writes Jalal, 'inclusionary nationalisms in conjunction with state power sought to bundle the rich mosaic of sensibilities and aspirations among South Asia's peoples into unified wholes'. Consequently, federalism as a principle was handed down from above and was not the result of 'freely negotiated political and economic unions from below'. The states' structures therefore have remained virtually 'unitary in substance and only nominally federal in form' (Jalal 1995: 160). While Jalal's point is well taken, there has been a crucial difference between India and Pakistan in the role played by the army in deciding the politics of the two countries. India, which inherited most of the civil, bureaucratic and judicial structures of the colonial regime, has fared much better in curbing the role of the army in politics than Pakistan.

POLITICAL ECONOMY

India's first general elections under universal suffrage took place in the winter of 1951/52. For the first time in the world, free elections were held on such a massive scale—with an electorate of 200 million. The successful completion of the elections demonstrated India's political training (Metcalf and Metcalf 2003: 230), and proudly proclaimed India's suitability as a 'sovereign, democratic republic' which the Constitution declared it to be. The Congress Party won the elections both at the national and state levels.

With Jawaharlal Nehru as the Prime Minister (1947–64), state planning and 'development' became the key words of national policy. The British had left India poor and underdeveloped in terms of industry; this had to be remedied through the advancement of science and technology. The national executive endorsed the Socialist principles of state ownership; it also pursued liberal economic policies and gave incentives to private investment. As an effective mode of planned development, sequential Five Year Plans were drawn up by a council of experts who belonged to the national 'Planning Commission'.

The first 'Five Year Plan' published in 1952 indicated 'a new approach to economic development that incorporated a strategy for peaceful social change' (Frankel 2005: 94). Although this Plan laid great emphasis on the development of the industrial sector, particularly heavy electrical, mineral and iron and steel industries, it made agriculture its primary target. The First Plan was striking in its approach to agricultural development. Rather than recommend measures to increase productivity, which could only be carried out by rich farmers, it tried to reconcile the goals of growth and equity. The Plan tried to increase output by eliminating exploitative social and economic relations that impeded efficient use of labour-intensive production practices. These measures resulted in a 25 per cent increase in agricultural production.

At the same time, these efforts were constrained by the existing pattern of landholding, which was characterized by shortage and extremely unequal distribution of land. The agrarian reforms and efforts of the Congress government—land ceiling and abolition of zamindari—did not go very far since the bulk of the Congress support came from wealthy peasants and landlords. Moreover, according to the Constitution, land reforms as a subject is allocated to the states, which enabled the affluent local leaders of the Congress to make sure that the limit on land ownership was set high. The abolition of zamindari brought no relief to poor agricultural labourers and cultivating tenants had to make payments to the government over several years in order to gain full title to their land (Metcalf and Metcalf 2003: 239). This gap, between intent and practice, would become a constant feature of government policy and come to represent one of the major problems of Indian democracy.

The Second Five Year Plan focused on industry, particularly state-run heavy industry. The goal was to substitute import by means of creating a large industrial base, a policy that would give India greater economic self-sufficiency. The public sector was given priority over the private, and India's nascent industries were given protection by means of heavy tariff imposed on imported goods. The private sector was brought under close state supervision and was not allowed to make significant changes or expand without a 'license' from the central government, a qualification that subsequently produced favouritism and corruption and earned for the Congress Raj the pseudonym of being 'license Raj'.

Nevertheless, planned 'development' over the first ten years enabled India to break out of the economic stagnation of the last decades of the colonial regime; agricultural production grew by 25 per cent during the First Plan and another 20 per cent during the Second, and industrial output increased by about 7 per cent. India's national income grew 4 per cent. Although a 2 per cent increase in population offset the good effects somewhat, there was still a growth of about 2 per cent.

State-directed planning was balanced by Nehru's championing of non-alignment in foreign policy. In a world polarized between two blocs (the US and Soviet), non-alignment offered a 'third space' to many countries as it helped Nehru carry out his plan for India's rapid development. In a speech delivered before the Constituent Assembly in December 1947 Nehru made his purpose clear. He said that foreign policy was 'the outcome of economic policy' and 'until India has properly evolved her economic policy' her foreign policy will be 'rather vague, rather inchoate, and will be groping' (Nehru 1950: 201). Investment in industries and agriculture was matched by the emphasis on higher education, and all this required limited spending on defence. Non-alignment gave India the much-needed respite from defence spending.

A new India took shape under the commanding presence and guidance of Nehru; an India that believed in the modernist notion of 'progress' and development. Nehru's vision found ample articulation in the construction of the modern city of Chandigarh, the capital of Punjab and Haryana, by renowned French architect Le Corbusier; in the founding of institutes of higher learning in science and technology that produced skilled engineers and technicians; the significance assumed by the Atomic Research Centre, and in state-controlled planning that helped India break out of the economic stagnation of the last years of colonial rule. The mood of enthusiasm found eloquent expression in the films produced in Bombay (Mumbai). At the same time, all this was done by means of centralization, both of power and of the Congress Party, which impeded general democratization.

The centralization of power in the person of the Prime minister, leader of the executive branch of the government, and the head of Congress Party, reached new heights under Indira Gandhi (1966–77, 1980–84). Faced with a variety of challenges—to her power within the Congress Party, radical challenges in the states of West Bengal and Kerala, and Maoist Naxalite movement involving poor peasants and students in West Bengal that spread to neighbouring states, Indira Gandhi set about trying to link the top and bottom layers of agrarian society through renewed efforts to woo high caste and old landed elites, along with an advocacy of the interests of subordinate castes and classes of Hindus and Muslims that cut across regions.

A 'masterful politician', Indira Gandhi was fully aware that her popular image was that of a leader of the Left. She built up on those credentials, 'not by careful implementation of Socialist policies but by undertaking highly visible measures'. These included the 'nationalization of banks, pursuit of antimonopoly legislation, and espousal of poverty alleviation as the central plank of her party and government' (Kohli 1990: 314). She also took measures to abolish the privy purses of former princes.

Plagued by the prospect of an acute shortage of food grain and a possible famine, Indira Gandhi abandoned the ideal of the First Plan and turned to new methods of agriculture. Such measures were championed by the American Ford Foundation and aimed at increasing agricultural productivity at any cost. In order to get US aid, Indira Gandhi devalued the rupee and turned to a new agricultural technology. The new methods produced the so-called 'Green Revolution' in Punjab and significantly increased the production of wheat. At the same time, it aggravated social disparity by helping rich peasants become richer without alleviating the condition of poor peasants. The new methods could not help rice cultivation very much since it was much more labour-intensive and paddy fields were smaller in size and scattered. A much larger area under wheat cultivation was brought under irrigation by 1980 than for rice. All this produced a different kind of tension between the wheat-growing and rice-growing regions.

The Five Year Plans during Indira Gandhi's rule focused on 'results' instead of ideology. All along, however, her socio-economic programme was captured by the ringing populist slogan *garibi hatao* (eliminate poverty). This meant that her attempts to liberalize the economy did not produce sharp reaction; the scale of the change was not drastic and there was a deliberate attempt to maintain an image of continuity. Indira Gandhi's astuteness prompted her to act with remarkable speed, change tactic, and strike before her opponents could strike (Kaviraj 1986). Although this bore fruit initially, her high-handed behaviour generated serious tension. India's political attention turned increasingly towards turbulence in states, such as Assam and Punjab, and away from economic policies. Indira and her Congress scored a resounding victory in the elections of 1971 and 1972 at the centre and in the states.

This victory also coincided with the success of the 'war of liberation' in East Pakistan and the creation of Bangladesh. Indira followed this success with another spectacular demonstration of her and India's power. In September 1972, she gave verbal authorization to scientists at the Bhabha Atomic Research Centre to manufacture and prepare for testing a nuclear device that they had designed. Called 'the peaceful nuclear explosive' and dubbed 'the smiling Buddha', this device was tested in Pokhran (Rajasthan) on 18 May 1974, a day when India celebrated the birth anniversary of Gautam Buddha. The tests announced India's nuclear ability to the world and also the slow abandonment of non-alignment in foreign policy.

The extraordinary personalization of power complemented by Indira Gandhi's efforts to manage divisions within the party by playing off one leader against another, and by claiming personal loyalty from local leaders, caused havoc in the structure of the Congress Party. A variety of socio-economic and political problems—food shortage and energy crisis, and strong opposition from veteran leaders such as Jayaprakash Narayan, and finally the verdict of the Allahabad High Court that she had rigged the elections, led her to urge the President of India to declare an extraordinary state of emergency in June 1975. By imposing the emergency between 1975–77, Indira Gandhi tried to combat regional challenges by making the centre the sole repository of supra-local and supra-regional populist programmes. A workable strategy in the short run, it lacked legitimacy and could not withstand concerted opposition from an array of political forces. She lost the general elections in 1977.

The Janata Party, a loose conglomeration of regional, Left and Right-wing parties, united only in their opposition to Indira Gandhi, came to power in 1977. It soon disintegrated on account of its internal contradictions. Indira Gandhi returned to power in 1980, determined to fight regional dissidence to the bitter end. The problems in Punjab, Assam and to a certain extent Kashmir were all creations of the high-handed policies pursued by a Congress-dominated centre. In the end, Indira Gandhi's attempt to intervene strongly in the internal affairs of the federal states resulted in the powerful Khalistan movement in Punjab which culminated in her assassination in 1984, followed by a series of anti-Sikh riots in Delhi and in other parts of India.

Riding a sympathy wave, Indira Gandhi's son, Rajiv Gandhi (Prime Minister 1984–89), swept the elections with the help of the Hindu card. Imbued with colonial ideas of viewing Indian society as composed of majority and minority communities, the young pilot tried to placate both Hindus and Muslims with a couple of momentous decisions that gave a new meaning to the dialectic of communalism and regionalism. On the economic front, the liberalization of the country's economy was carried out in a manner that made India accumulate a huge national debt—India came to be ruled by the dictates of the World Bank and the International Monetary Fund. Finally, to reinforce the notion of a strong nation, and distract attention from serious internal disaffection, Rajiv Gandhi sent troops to Sri Lanka, ostensibly to enforce peace between the Liberation Tigers of Tamil Elam fighting for Tamil autonomy and the Sri Lankan state. He was killed by a suicide bomber belonging to a group of Tamil rebels of Sri Lanka in 1989.

As indicated earlier, India's politics in the 1990s was dominated by the Hindu Right, although till 1999, the Congress, in alliance with other parties, remained in power at the centre. Under the Congress Prime Minister, Narasimha Rao, liberalization of the economy was taken up as a principal project in the early and mid-1990s. This was spearheaded by Dr Manmohan Singh, a Cambridge-trained economist who was the Finance Minister under Rao and is India's current Prime Minister. Liberalization brought a range of consumer goods to India—it pandered to the needs of an ever-increasing middle class—but totally neglected the requirements of a vast majority of the poor who were struggling to stay alive.

Interestingly, the Hindu Right, which sought to build a strong 'Hindu' nation by returning to India's 'true' cultural roots, did nothing to offset liberalization. It encouraged foreign investment and investment by non-resident Indians (NRIs), while it advanced a programme of swadeshi (literally of one's own country)—of being and buying Indian—as an electoral campaign within India. The Hindu Right took full credit for the growth of the economy produced by liberalization, and the success of the information technology (IT) industry that was consequent upon India's preparedness in terms of infrastructure and trained professionals to take full advantage of 'out-sourcing'. Finally, to articulate its vision of a strong Hindu nation ready to face the challenge of Islamic Pakistan, the Hindu Right authorized the conducting of a second round of underground nuclear detonations in 1998. These tests earned for the Hindu Right world opprobrium. Within India, however, the nuclear tests found great favour both from large sections of the middle classes and from the media, a support that encouraged the BJP to adopt the 'India shining' slogan.

Interestingly, the image of 'India shining' has remained not only among the ever-increasing urban middle and upper classes, but also in large parts of the world, even though the expensive campaign did not help the National Democratic Alliance to remain in power. Intended initially to promote India internationally, this 20 million dollar advertising campaign has borne fruit, not for the political party but for the image it has projected of India.

Why is there a lack of fit between what the large majority of the Indian electorate thinks and what the world thinks of India? India's democratic experience has been mixed. Positive discrimination has allowed numerous social groups to make their presence felt and allowed for 'democratization' of politics with regard to representation. At the same time, corruption has become rampant and a large part of the bureaucracy has lost its integrity. Atul Kohli takes this to be the 'politically corrosive impact' of social mobilization, which is mitigated somewhat by the state's remarkable capacity to 'accommodate diverse interests' (Kohli 1988: 15). Poverty alleviation schemes, we are aware, have been limited in scope and not properly implemented. India, 'shining' on account of her brilliant scientists, engineers and technicians, portrays herself in a very poor light when it comes to primary education. 'While more than 60 million Indians own a television, nearly a third of the adult population' (and more than half of all adult women) 'remain illiterate' (Stein 2010: 416).

The liberalization of the economy has brought in new consumer goods and new values; it has also witnessed the growth of an extremely diverse and teeming middle class with a new lifestyle made increasingly visible by the ever-expanding television and satellite networks. Sadly, it has also increased class and regional deprivation, and pushed basic commodities like food grains and medicines out of the reach of a vast multitude. Economic liberalization has increased India's national debt, aggravated class, caste and ethnic tensions, made the poor poorer and the rich richer. Through ups and downs, success and failure, India has sustained freedom and democracy, even if it has failed to offer to its very poor and its marginalized and minority communities, the promising future it had promised.

REFERENCES

Agnes, Flavia. 1999. *Law and Gender Inequality: The Politics of Women's Rights in India*. New Delhi: Oxford University Press.

———. 2007. 'The Supreme Court, the Media, and the Uniform Civil Code Debate'. In *The Crisis of Secularism in India*, edited by Anuradha Dingwaney Needham and Rajeswari Sunder Rajan, 294–315 . Durham, NC: Duke University Press.

Ambedkar, B. R. 1995. *Dr. Babasaheb Ambedkar Writings and Speeches*. Vol. 14, Part 1. Mumbai: Government of Maharashtra, Education Department.

Ansari, Sarah. 1994. 'The Movement of Indian Muslims to West Pakistan after 1947: Partition Related Migration and Its Consequences for the Pakistani Province of Sind'. In *Migration: The Asian Experience*, edited by Judith M. Brown and Rosemary Foots, 149–168. Oxford: St. Martin's Press.

Asad, Talal. 2003. *Formations of the Secular: Christianity, Islam, Modernity*. Stanford: Stanford University Press.

Austin, Granville. 1966. *The Indian Constitution: Cornerstone of a Nation*. Oxford: Clarendon Press.

———. 1999. *Working a Democratic Constitution: The Indian Experience*. New Delhi: Oxford University Press.

Banerjee-Dube, Ishita. 2008. 'Introduction: Questions of Caste'. In *Caste in History*, edited by I. Banerjee-Dube, i–lxiv. New Delhi: Oxford University Press.

Baruah, Sanjib. 1997. *India Against Itself: Assam and the Politics of Nationality*. New Delhi: Oxford University Press.

Basu, Tapan, Pradip Datta, Sumit Sarkar, Tanika Sarkar and Sambuddha Sen. 1993. *Khaki Shorts, Saffron Flags*. Hyderabad: Orient Longman.

Baxi, Upendra. 1990. 'Reflections on the Reservations Crisis in Gujarat'. In *Mirrors of Violence: Communities, Riots and Survivors In South Asia*, edited by Veena Das, 215–39 . New Delhi: Oxford University Press.

Bayly, Susan. 1999. *Caste, Society and Politics in India: From the Eighteenth Century to the Modern Age*. Cambridge: Cambridge University Press.

Betéille, Andre. 1992. *The Backward Classes in Contemporary India*. New Delhi: Oxford University Press.

Bhargava, Rajeev, ed. 1998. *Secularism and Its Critics*. New Delhi: Oxford University Press.

———. [2008] 2010. *Politics and Ethics of the Indian Constitution*. New Delhi: Oxford University Press.

Bose, Sugata and Ayesha Jalal. 1998. *Modern South Asia: History, Culture, Political Economy*. London and New York: Routledge. Paperback edition 2000.

Brass, Paul. 2003. 'The Partition of India and Retributive Genocide in the Panjab, 1946–47: Means, Methods and Purposes'. *Journal of Genocide Research* 5 (1): 71–101.

Butalia, Urvashi. 1998. *The Other Side of Silence: Voices from Partition of India*. New Delhi: Penguin Books.

Chakrabarty, Dipesh. 2002. 'Memories of Displacement: The Poetry and Prejudice of Dwelling'. In *Habitations of Modernity: Essays in the Wake of Subaltern Studies*, Dipesh Chakrabarty, 115–137. Chicago: Chicago University Press.

Chatterjee, Nilanjana. 'Interrogating Victimhood: East Bengali Refugee Narratives of Communal Violence', Department of Anthropology, University of North Carolina-Chapel Hill, n.d. Available at http://www.swadhinata.org.uk/document/chatterjeeEastBengal%20Refugee.pdf

Chatterjee, Partha. [1989] 1992. 'Caste and Subaltern Consciousness'. In *Subaltern Studies VI: Writings on South Asian History and Society*, edited by R. Guha, 169–209. New Delhi: Oxford University Press.

Conlon, Frank F. 1977. *A Caste in a Changing World: The Chitrapur Saraswat Brahmans, 1700–1935.* Berkeley and Los Angeles: University of California Press.

Copland, Ian. 1998. 'The Further Shores of Partition: Ethnic Cleansing in Rajasthan'. *Past and Present* 160: 203–39.

Dahl, Robert. 1989. *Democracy and its Critics.* New Haven, NJ: Yale University Press.

Das, Veena. 1995a. 'National Honour and Practical Kinship: Of Unwanted Women and Children'. In *Critical Events: An Anthropological Perspective on Contemporary India*, edited by Veena Das, 55–83. New Delhi: Oxford University Press.

———. 1995b. 'Communities as Political Actors: The Question of Cultural Rights'. In *Critical Events: An Anthropological Perspective on Contemporary India*, edited by Veena Das, 84–117. New Delhi: Oxford University Press.

Dingwaney Needham, Anuradha and Rajeshwari Sunder Rajan, eds. 2007. *The Crisis of Secularism in India.* Durham, NC: Duke University Press.

Dirks, Nicholas B. 2001. *Castes of Mind: Colonialism and the Making of Modern India.* Princeton, NJ: Princeton University Press.

Everett, J. M. 1981. *Women and Social Change in India.* Delhi: Heritage Publishers.

Frankel, Françine R. 2005. *India's Political Economy, 1947–2004.* New Delhi: Oxford University Press.

Galanter, Marc. 1984. *Competing Equalities: Law and the Backward Classes in India.* Berkeley and Los Angeles: University of California Press.

———. [1989] 1992. *Law and Society in Modern India.* New Delhi: Oxford University Press.

Ghosh, Papiya. 1997. 'Partition's Biharis'. *Comparative Studies of South Asia, Africa, and the Middle East* 17 (2): 21–34. Included in Papiya Ghosh. 2008. *Community and Nation: Essays on Identity and Politics in Eastern India.* New Delhi: Oxford University Press.

Hansen, Thomas Blom. 1999. *The Saffron Wave: Democracy and Hindu Nationalism in Modern India.* Princeton, NJ: Princeton University Press.

Hasan, Mushirul. 1997. *Legacy of a Divided Nation: India's Muslims Since Independence.* New Delhi: Thomson Press Ltd.

Jaffrelot, Christophe. 2002. *India's Silent Revolution: The Rise of Low Castes in North Indian Politics.* Delhi: Permanent Black.

———. 2005. *Analysing and Fighting Caste: Dr Ambedkar and Untouchability.* Delhi: Permanent Black.

Jalal, Ayesha. 1995. *Democracy and Authoritarianism in South Asia: A Comparative and Historical Perspective.* New York: Cambridge University Press.

Kaviraj, Sudipta. 1986. 'Indira Gandhi and Indian Politics'. *Economic and Political Weekly* 21 (38/39) (20 Sept.): 1697–1708.

Kohli, Atul. 1988. 'Introduction: Interpreting India's Democracy, A State Society Framework'. In *India's Democracy: An Analysis of Changing State-Society Relations*, edited by A. Kohli, 3–17 . Princeton, NJ: Princeton University Press.

———. 1990. *Democracy and Discontent: India's Growing Crisis of Governability.* Cambridge: Cambridge University Press.

Kothari, Rajni. 1970. *Caste and Politics in India.* Delhi: Orient Longman.

———. 1990. 'Caste and Politics: The Great Secular Upsurge'. *The Times of India.* 28 September.

———. 1994. 'The Rise of Dalits and the Renewed Debate on Caste'. *Economic and Political Weekly* 22 (26) (25 June): 1589–1594.

Kumar, Dharma. 1994. 'Indian Secularism: A Note'. *Modern Asian Studies* 28 (1): 223–24.

Menon, Dilip. 2006. *The Blindness of Insight: Essays on Caste in Modern India*. Pondicherry: Navayana Publishing.

Menon, Ritu and Kamla Bhasin. 1998. *Borders and Boundaries: Women in India's Partition*. New Brunswick, NJ: Rutgers University Press.

Metcalf, Barbara D. and Thomas R. Metcalf. 2003. *A Concise History of India*. Cambridge: Cambridge University Press.

Nandy, Ashis. 1990. 'The Politics of Secularism and the Recovery of Religious Tolerance'. In *Mirrors of Violence: Communities, Riots and Survivors In South Asia*, edited by Veena Das, 69–93. New Delhi: Oxford University Press.

Naqvi, Tahir Hasnain. 2007. 'The Politics of Commensuration: The Violence of Partition and the Making of the Pakistani State'. *Journal of Historical Sociology* 20 (1): 44–71.

Nehru, Jawaharlal. 14 August 1947. 'Tryst with Destiny: Speech on the Granting of Indian Independence'. In Jawaharlal Nehru. 1950. *Independence and After: A Collection of Speeches 1946–1949*. New York: The John Day Co.

———. 1950. *Independence and After: A Collection of Speeches 1946–1949*. New York: The John Day Co.

———. 1997. *The Discovery of India*. New Delhi: Oxford University Press (First published 1946).

Nigam, Aditya. 2006. *The Insurrection of Little Selves: The Crisis of Secular-Nationalism in India*. New Delhi: Oxford University Press.

Pal, Ruma. 2001. 'Religious Minorities and the Law'. In *Religion and Personal Law in Secular India: A Call to Judgement*, edited by Gerlad Larson, 24–35. Bloomington, IA: Indiana University Press.

Pandey, Gyanendra. 2001. *Remembering Partition: Violence, Nationalism and History in India*. Cambridge: Cambridge University Press.

Parashar, Archana. 1992. *Women and Family Law Reform in India: Uniform Civil Code and Gender Equality*. New Delhi: Sage Publications.

Rahman, Mahbubar and Willem van Schendel. 2003. '"I'm *Not* a Refugee": Rethinking Partition Migration'. *Modern Asian Studies* 34 (3): 551–84.

Sen, Samita. 2002. 'Towards a Feminist Politics? The Indian Women's Movement in Historical Perspective'. In *The Violence of Development: The Politics of Identity, Gender & Social Inequalities in India*, edited by Karin Kapadia, 459–524. London: Zed Books.

Sinha, Mrinalini. 2007. *Specters of Mother India: The Global Restructuring of an Empire*. Durham and London: Duke University Press.

Srininivas, M. N., G. Shah and B. R. Baviskar. 1990. 'Kothari's Illusion of a Secular Upsurge'. *The Times of India*. 17 October.

Stein, Burton. 2010. *A History of India*. Revised and edited by David Arnold. Sussex, UK: Wiley-Blackwell. (First published 1998. Oxford: Oxford University Press).

Tan, Tai Yong and Gyanesh Kudaisya. 2000. *The Aftermath of Partition in South Asia*. London and New York: Routledge.

Zamindar, Vazira Fazila-Yacoobali. 2007. *The Long Partition and the Making of Modern South Asia: Refugees, Boundaries, Histories*. New York: Columbia University Press.

Index

M. K. Gandhi and Muhammed Ali Jinnah in Mumbai, September 1944